DATE DUE

APR 0 8 1996	
OCT 2 5 1996	
FEB 0 5 1997	
SEP 2 5 1997	
DEC 1 4 2000	
JAN 0 4 2001	
MAR 1 6 2004	
OCT 0 6 2006	
APR 0 7 2011	
JUL 3 1 2012	

DEMCO, INC. 38-2931

TALES OF THE
DARK KNIGHT

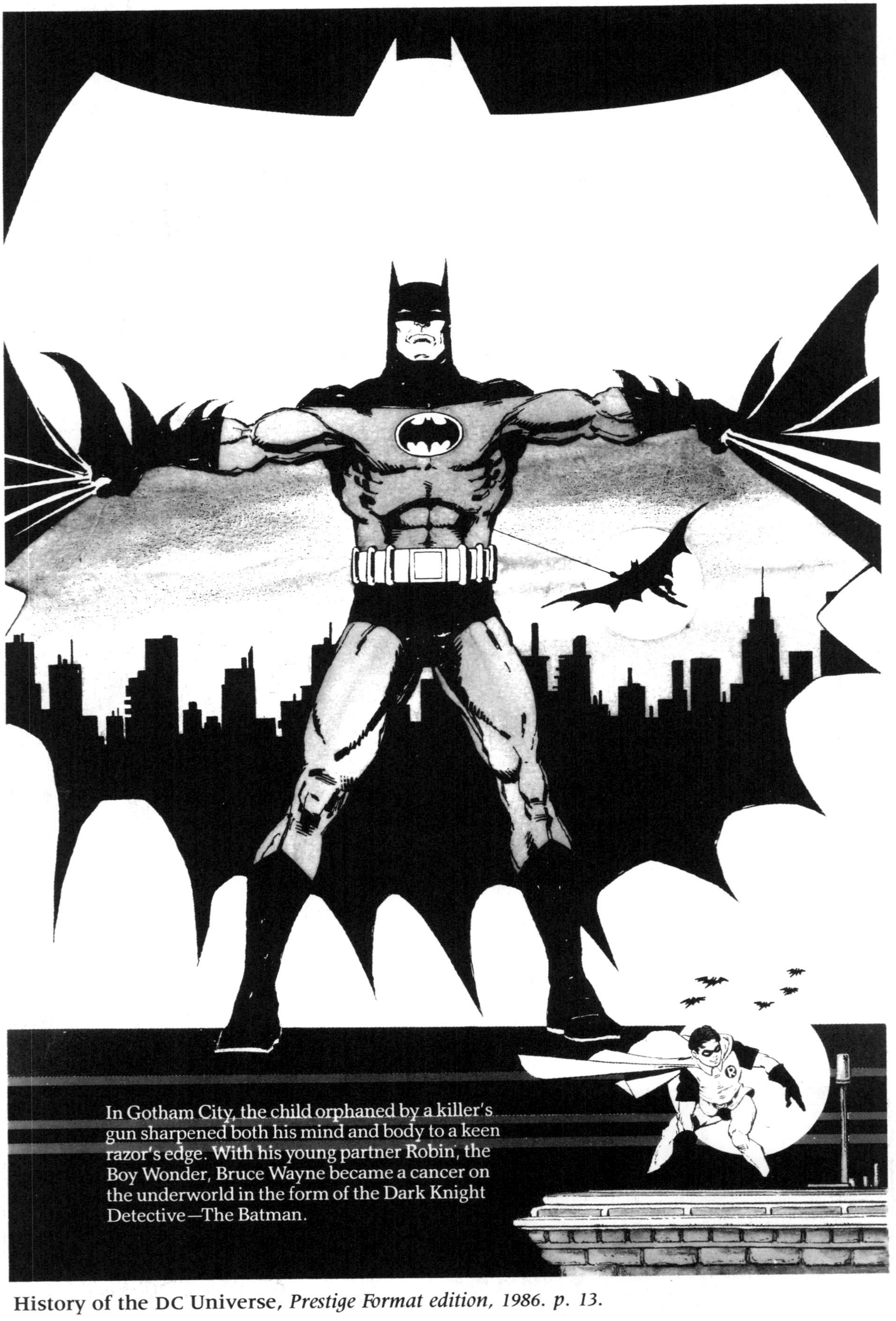
In Gotham City, the child orphaned by a killer's gun sharpened both his mind and body to a keen razor's edge. With his young partner Robin, the Boy Wonder, Bruce Wayne became a cancer on the underworld in the form of the Dark Knight Detective—The Batman.

History of the DC Universe, *Prestige Format edition, 1986. p. 13.*

TALES OF THE DARK KNIGHT

BATMAN'S FIRST FIFTY YEARS: 1939–1989
MARK COTTA VAZ

BALLANTINE BOOKS · NEW YORK

Published in the United States
by Ballantine Books, a division
of Random House, Inc., New
York, and simultaneously
in Canada by Random House
of Canada Limited, Toronto.

Library of Congress Catalog Card
Number: 88-92872
ISBN: 0-345-36013-3

Cover painting by Sigmond Pifko
Cover and text design
by Alex Jay/Studio J

Manufactured in
the United States of America
First Edition: November 1989
10 9 8 7 6 5 4 3 2 1

To Bob Kane; Bill Finger,
Jerry Robinson, Dick Sprang,
and the other Golden Age greats;
and to five decades of fans and
creators who have dreamed
of the Dark Knight.

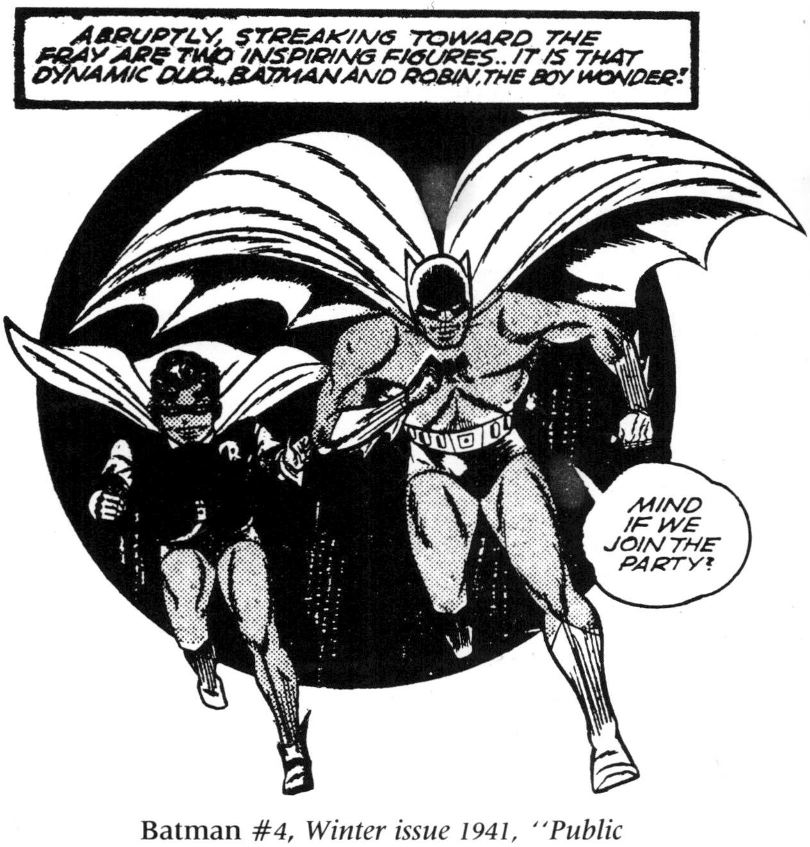
ABRUPTLY, STREAKING TOWARD THE FRAY ARE TWO INSPIRING FIGURES.. IT IS THAT DYNAMIC DUO.. BATMAN AND ROBIN, THE BOY WONDER!
MIND IF WE JOIN THE PARTY?

Batman #4, *Winter issue 1941, "Public Enemy No. 1," p. 9 [panel].*

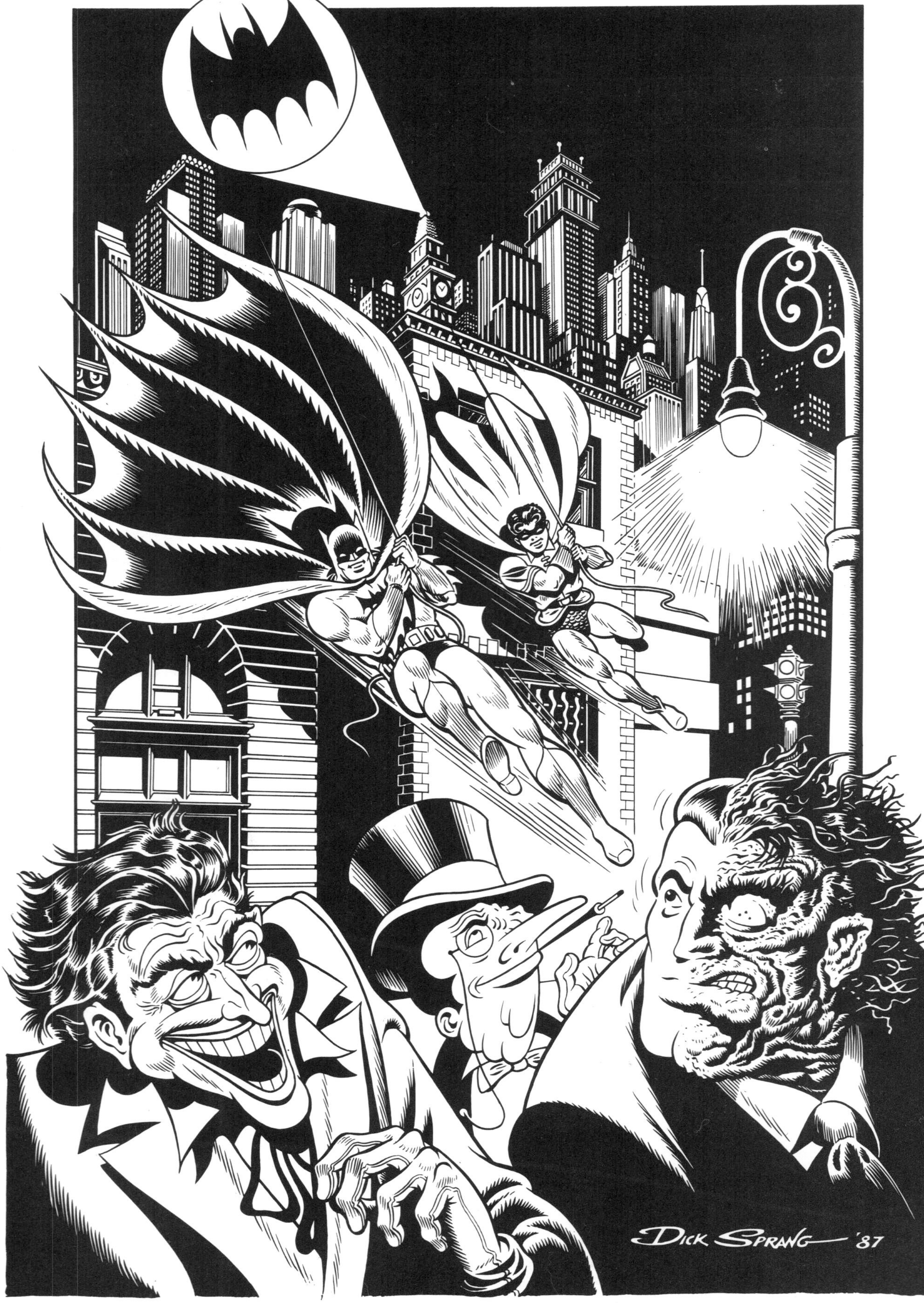
DICK SPRANG '87

ACKNOWLEDGMENTS

There are a number of people who have helped clear a path for this writer's journey into Batman's world.

Thanks to Joe Orlando, Angelina Genduso and Joey Cavalieri for coordinating logistics at DC. Special thanks to the keepers of DC's archives for making available the dozens of bound volumes that hold the Batman chronicles. A special appreciation to: Jenette Kahn, Dick Giordano, Paul Levitz, Denny O'Neil, Mary Moebus, and Cheryl Rubin for all their help and hospitality.

My thanks to the legends of Batman, including Bob Kane, Jerry Robinson, and Dick Sprang, who shined the Bat-Light on matters of history.

Bill Blackbeard of the San Francisco Academy of Comic Art also provided important research material on Batman, as well as the pulp and comic strip crime fighters who influenced the Dark Knight's creation. And may the Bat-Signal shine in the sky to honor Ron Schwartz of the Cartoon Art Museum in California—as a lifelong collector of Batman comics and memorabilia, he was a superb reference on Batman lore.

My special thanks to those who helped me prepare the manuscript by computer. May the spirit of Batman watch over and protect: August Vaz, my father, whose mastery of high-tech matters makes me feel positively aboriginal; David Modjeska, software king of Silicon Valley, for various Dark Knight meditations and computer assists; and Derek Duarte, another high-tech superhero, who spent many hours helping format the material.

And when all of the above are honored at a ticker tape parade through Gotham City, add Jack Boulware and Bryan W. Martin to the list of honored dignitaries—as desktop publishing aces at Speedway Copy System in San Francisco, they saw to the printing of the manuscript.

Thanks also to my mother and father, and my brothers and sisters: Katherine, Maria, Patrick, Peter, and Teresa, for their love and support. And a big hug for Daniel, my little nephew.

Thanks to Pam, Robert, and Mike at Image Makers Plus in San Francisco for shooting some of the visual material.

And thanks to Batman and the people of Gotham City, of course.

—Mark Cotta Vaz
San Francisco, 1989

Opposite: History of the DC Universe, *hardcover edition, ''The Dark Knight Detective: The Legacy of Batman,'' 1988. Dick Sprang page.*

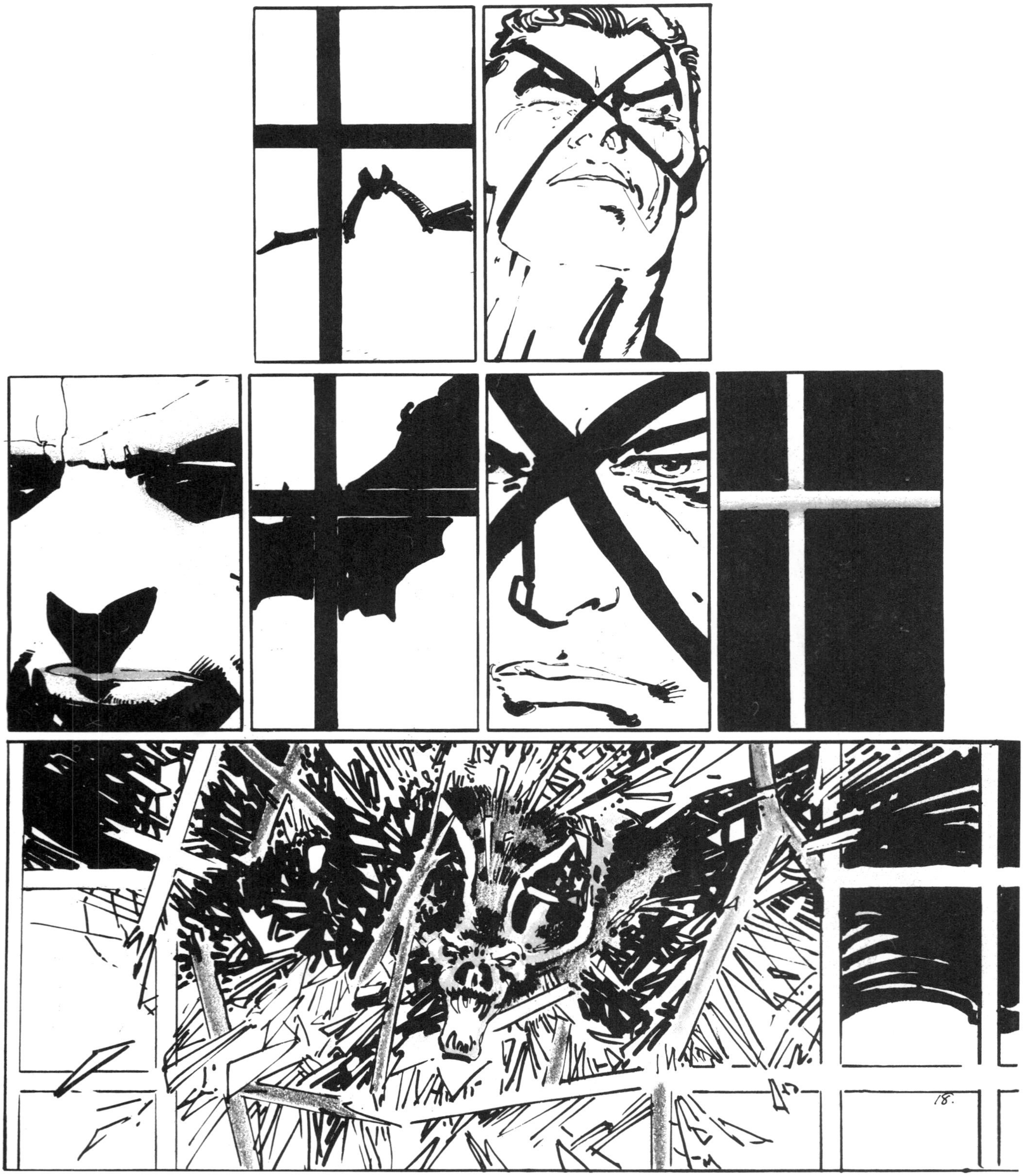
18.

The Dark Knight Returns, *Book One, 1986, p. 18 (select panels).*

CONTENTS

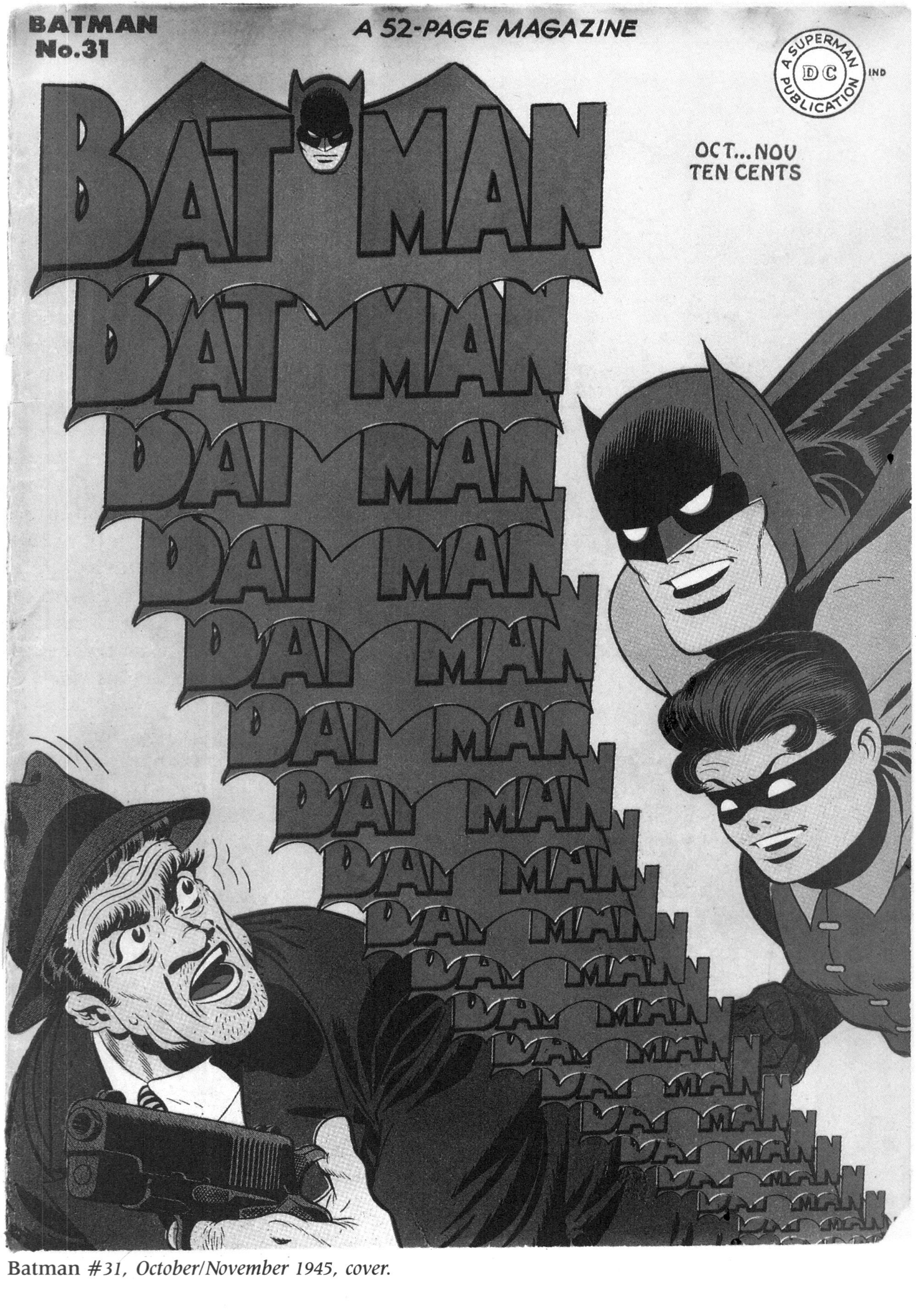
BATMAN
No.31
A 52-PAGE MAGAZINE
A SUPERMAN DC PUBLICATION
IND
BATMAN
OCT...NOV
TEN CENTS

Batman *#31, October/November 1945, cover.*

AMERICA'S COMIC BOOK SUPERHEROES, ushered into national folklore with Superman's arrival in 1938, represented an evolutionary leap over the beat cops and vigilantes who had previously been the standard-bearers for justice in the pulp magazines and comic strips.

The new superpowered crime fighters were usually endowed by fate with superhuman strength, speed, vision, invisibility, and even elasticity. And these heroes, with the exception of Superman, Wonder Woman, and a few others, were usually ordinary Joes and Janes with no heroic pretensions—until a chance splash of chemicals or a miraculous burst of radiation gave them the gift of superpowers.

Invariably the novice superhero immediately turned his or her new abilities to crime fighting (armed with a secret identity and outfitted in lurid regalia, of course).

The Batman is, and has always been, different from such superbeings. He was never blessed with instant superpowers—it took him fifteen years to hone himself into a physical marvel and scientific and deductive genius. Given his mortality, a secret identity was not a luxury, but a necessity. His costume wasn't designed to make a fashion statement but to strike fear into the hearts of the criminals infesting his home turf of Gotham City.

The reasons for the Batman's decades-long crime-fighting career have never been revealed to the people of Gotham City. Only a handful of trusted intimates (and comics fans throughout the years) know his millionaire Bruce "playboy" Wayne cover and understand the reasons for his obsessive, intensely personal, all-out war against crime.

Batman has never forgotten that nighttime walk with his parents so many years before when "the man with frightened, hollow eyes and a voice like glass being crushed"[1] appeared out of the darkness with a gun drawn, demanded his mother's necklace, and then fired two shots as his father moved to defend his wife. In the next shattering seconds Thomas and Martha Wayne lay dead on the deserted sidewalk. Bruce Wayne's childhood died that moment as well— but a legend was born with his teary bedside vow days later to avenge their deaths by devoting his life to a war against the criminal element.

Bruce Wayne bided his time before picking up the crime-fighting gauntlet fate had thrown down to him. With the millions he inherited from his father, a prominent Gotham physician, he could afford the time and resources needed to prepare. And while he trained his mind and body to a super level, he controlled the secret, vengeful rage that burned within him.

And when he was finally ready to go to war, it took an omen—the sight of a black bat flying in through the open window of his mansion—to finally manifest his Batman identity.

This hero called the Dark Knight would probably have a very different place in comics history if not for that brutal origin, the memories of which are always lurking in the shadows of his mind and in the background of the mythos. The crime-fighting passion born of that tragedy has fascinated fans through the decades.

But Batman's obsession goes far beyond a personal vendetta against the underworld. Over the years the Dark Knight has fashioned his crime-fighting efforts into a crusade on behalf of the oppressed innocents of society. He developed a personal code which includes his vow

---

1. "Batman Year One, Part One," *Batman* 404 (February 1987), p. 21.

never to take a life. His professional concerns do not end with the capture of a wanted criminal, either—Batman believes in rehabilitating evil-doers and making them useful members of society. Given the menace and evil he deals with daily, it's a code of honor that ennobles the Dark Knight. He is a true figure of justice, not a vigilante who has stepped across the often indistinct line between good and evil in this shadowy domain of urban crime fighting.

The Batman's world is not the sunny place most superheroes are accustomed to. Few superpowered beings would forsake the warmth of day for the Dark Knight's midnight patrols. Fewer still could stand to be out of sight of their adoring public, moving through the shadows of deserted city streets in the Batman style.

Batman's world is a place where capricious fate can deal out sudden death to innocents. It's a harsh landscape that includes the psychodramas engineered by insane criminals. It's a place where the sullen sight of an omnipresent full moon seems to look down on Gotham's mean streets with cosmic indifference.

It's a place where the dark, taciturn Batman—he with the visage of Adonis and the build of Hercules—tries to cut through the darkness with a sword of justice.

But despite the risks and the air of menace (perhaps because of them), fans for fifty years have been plunging into the darkness with the Batman.

Detective writer Raymond Chandler, a master at creating mystery tales played out against similarly dark, urban landscapes, once provided a definition for the quintessential hero that is certainly descriptive of Batman.

Chandler's hero is a man who must walk mean streets but "who is not himself mean." He is everyman, but at the same time "an unusual man...a man of honor...a man fit for adventure." Chandler likens the tales of such a hero to a dream that provides the readers some escape from "the deadly rhythm of their private thoughts."[2]

Our escape it may be—but it is also Batman's escape. In the heat of action, in the thrill of a case, he comes to terms with his dread origin. By overcoming his tragic beginnings, he faces the mortality that haunts us all.

In these tales we can glory in adventure—and redemption.

2. Raymond Chandler, "The Simple Art of Murder," in *The Simple Art of Murder* (New York: Ballantine Books, 1977), pp. 13, 20–21.

Following pages: *With brutal swiftness, young Bruce Wayne becomes an orphan. In the classic origin sequence we see the boy's resulting transformation beginning with the bedside vow, the years of preparation, the acceptance of the mantle of millionaire, one final meditation on the blight of criminality, a path for the crusade brought in on the wings of a bat, and the haunting image of a "weird figure of the dark—" all in the space of one page. (Batman #1, Spring Issue 1940, "The Legend of the Batman," pp. 1–2.)*

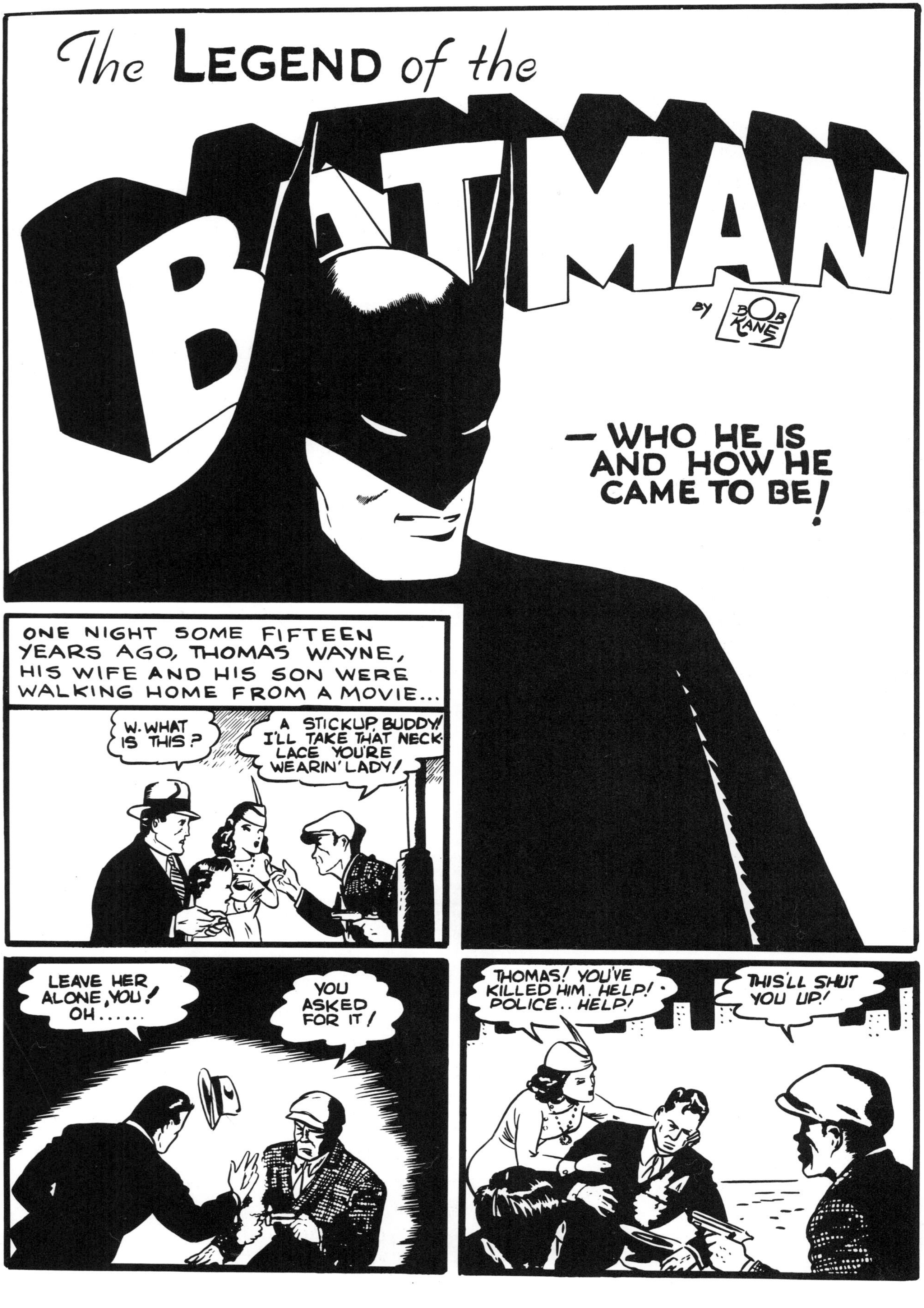
The LEGEND of the
BATMAN
BY BOB KANE
— WHO HE IS AND HOW HE CAME TO BE!
ONE NIGHT SOME FIFTEEN YEARS AGO, THOMAS WAYNE, HIS WIFE AND HIS SON WERE WALKING HOME FROM A MOVIE...
W. WHAT IS THIS?
A STICKUP, BUDDY! I'LL TAKE THAT NECKLACE YOU'RE WEARIN' LADY!
LEAVE HER ALONE, YOU! OH......
YOU ASKED FOR IT!
THOMAS! YOU'VE KILLED HIM. HELP! POLICE.. HELP!
THIS'LL SHUT YOU UP!

THE BOY'S EYES ARE WIDE WITH TERROR AND SHOCK AS THE HORRIBLE SCENE IS SPREAD BEFORE HIM.  FATHER.. MOTHER!	 ...DEAD! THEY'RE D..DEAD	DAYS LATER, A CURIOUS AND STRANGE SCENE TAKES PLACE.  AND I SWEAR BY THE SPIRITS OF MY PARENTS TO AVENGE THEIR DEATHS BY SPENDING THE REST OF MY LIFE WARRING ON ALL CRIMINALS
AS THE YEARS PASS BRUCE WAYNE PREPARES HIMSELF FOR HIS CAREER. HE BECOMES A MASTER SCIENTIST. 	TRAINS HIS BODY TO PHYSICAL PERFECTION UNTIL HE IS ABLE TO PERFORM AMAZING ATHLETIC FEATS. 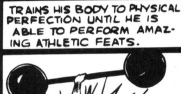 	 DAD'S ESTATE LEFT ME WEALTHY. I AM READY.. BUT FIRST I MUST HAVE A DISGUISE.
CRIMINALS ARE A SUPERSTITIOUS COWARDLY LOT, SO MY DISGUISE MUST BE ABLE TO STRIKE TERROR INTO THEIR HEARTS. I MUST BE A CREATURE OF THE NIGHT, BLACK, TERRIBLE..A A.. 	-AS IF IN ANSWER, A HUGE BAT FLIES IN THE OPEN WINDOW!  A BAT! THAT'S IT! IT'S AN OMEN.. I SHALL BECOME A BAT!	AND THUS IS BORN THIS WEIRD FIGURE OF THE DARK.. THIS AVENGER OF EVIL..THE BATMAN 

TALES OF THE
DARK KNIGHT

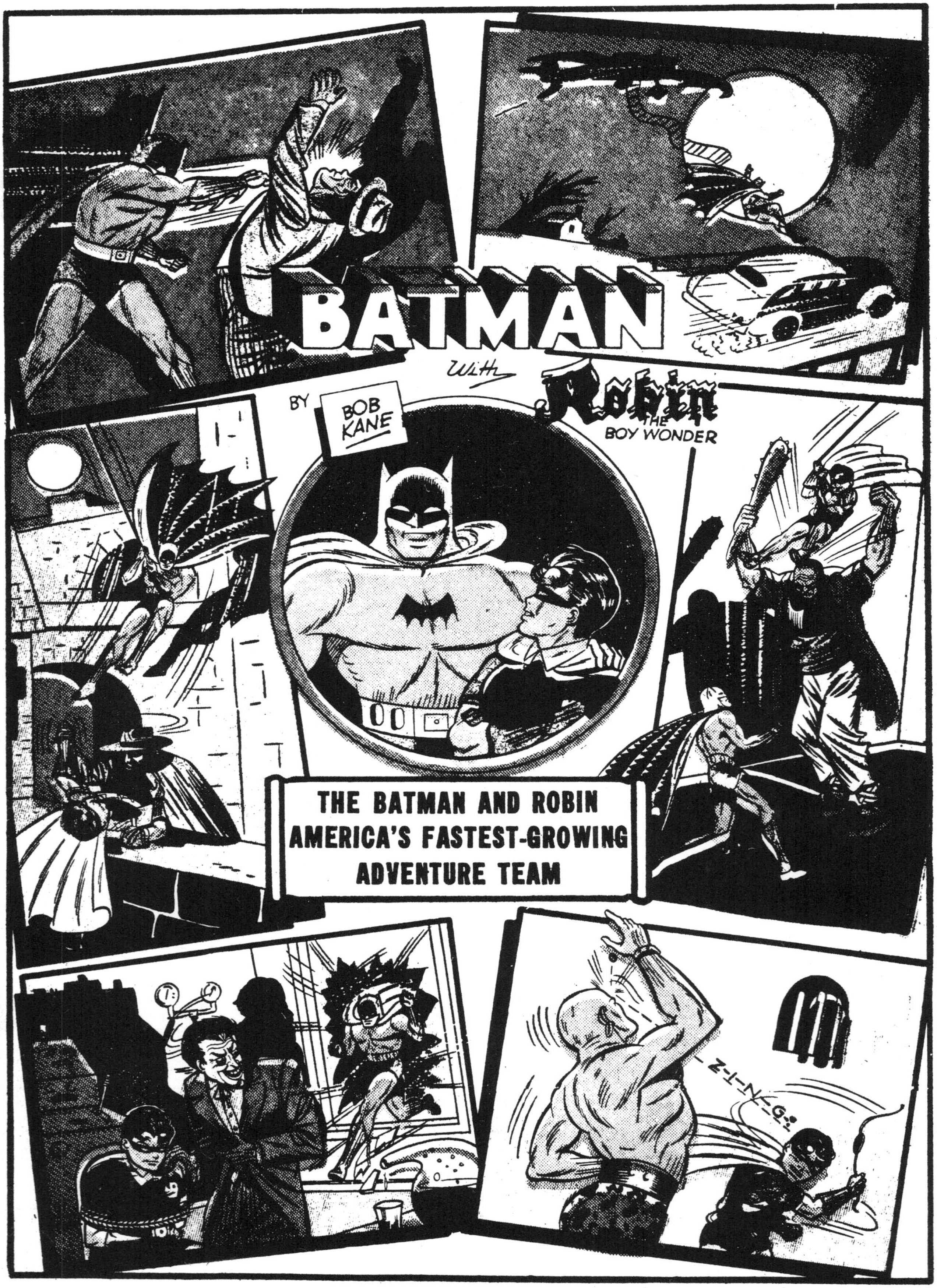
BATMAN
with Robin THE BOY WONDER
BY BOB KANE
THE BATMAN AND ROBIN
AMERICA'S FASTEST-GROWING
ADVENTURE TEAM
Z-I-N-G!

Batman #4, *Winter 1941. Frontispiece.*

INTRODUCTION

N 1846 EDGAR ALLAN POE TOOK UP RESI-
dence in a simple white frame farmhouse in
Fordham, just north of New York City. The
famed writer of the macabre held the desperate hope that the country air would cure his
precious wife, Virginia, of her tuberculosis.
But the pastoral region would deliver no angel of
mercy. Poe could only watch helplessly as his
wife coughed blood during the terrible hemor-
rhages that marked her road to a burial vault in
the Fordham Dutch Reformed Church.

Within the next century the little village of
Fordham became part of the Bronx. Poe's cottage
would be preserved in a little patch of green
among the surrounding apartments and com-
mercial buildings of the Grand Concourse area.

It was to Poe Park that a young cartoonist
named Bob Kane and a writer named Bill Finger
often came to sit on a bench in front of Poe's cottage and discuss story ideas for the Batman,
Kane's new comic book character. The mysterious crime fighter had made his debut on the
cover and in the pages of *Detective Comics* 27, in
May, 1939.

At the time no one at Detective Comics, Inc.
(later known as DC), knew how big a hit Batman
would become. In the DC pantheon of superheroes the Dark Knight would ultimately stand
second only to Superman.

Batman is the only comic book superhero
(other than Superman and, for a brief hiatus,
Wonder Woman) who has been continuously
published since that dawning era of comic books
now known as the Golden Age of Comics.

Time—a more formidable adversary than the
Joker, the Penguin, Two-Face, the Riddler, and
the other evil characters who have plagued
Gotham City over the years—has still not bested
the Dark Knight.

Batman has spanned virtually the entire history of the comic book medium: from those glory
days of the 1940s, to the resulting crackdown of
the 1950s, when critics charged that the comics
were undermining American youth, through the
period of slumping sales that lasted into the
1960s, and on into the revival of the 1970s and
the comic book renaissance of the 1980s.

The Batman himself has gone through some
dramatic changes these past five decades. In the
1950's the Dark Knight of the Golden Age became "this sort of benign scoutmaster who
would walk down the streets of Gotham City in
broad daylight," according to current Batman
editor Denny O'Neil. Then there was the science
fiction Batman who battled aliens and traveled to
other dimensions in the late 1950s and early
1960s, the campy Batman of the television show
era, and the return to the character's Dark Knight
roots in the 1970s and 1980s.

The creative teams have also changed over
the years. Kane couldn't pencil and ink all the
action needed for the growing list of Batman stories, so the likes of Jerry Robinson and Dick
Sprang were enlisted. When Kane stopped regular work on the character in the 1960s, it opened
the door to other creative influences, from Denny
O'Neil and Neal Adams to Frank Miller, David
Mazzucchelli, Brian Bolland, and Berni
Wrightson.

But there were other factors that helped make
Batman an instant, and enduring, hit.

He has always been a figure of mystery. Even
in his debut in *Detective* 27, it was not until the
final panel (and just after a Batman left cross had
knocked the lead villain into an acid tank) that
the crime fighter's identity was revealed as that
of a rich idler named Bruce Wayne.

And, of course, his very vulnerability made

him a hero we all could identify with.

"Batman is an ordinary mortal who made himself a superhero," observes Jenette Kahn, current president and editor-in-chief of DC Comics, and a Batman fan since her youth. "Through discipline and determination and commitment, he made himself into the best. I always thought that meant that I could be anything I wanted to be."

The Batman saga has generated its own lore and sense of place. The famed East Coast metropolis of Gotham City, for example, is a fully realized locale. Over the years Batman fans have toured the town from Chinatown to the Bowery, from Fifth Avenue to Central Park. We've dined and danced at high-society functions and listened in on criminal plots hatched in seedy hotel rooms. We've met the town's eccentrics, politicians, shopkeepers, and giants of commerce.

We've also walked the stately halls of Wayne Manor and descended into the mysterious Bat Cave, marveled at the Bat Signal flashing in the night sky over Gotham, and listened for the answering roar of the Batmobile as the Caped Crusader answers the call to action.

And the characters who form the inner circle of Batman's world are like old friends.

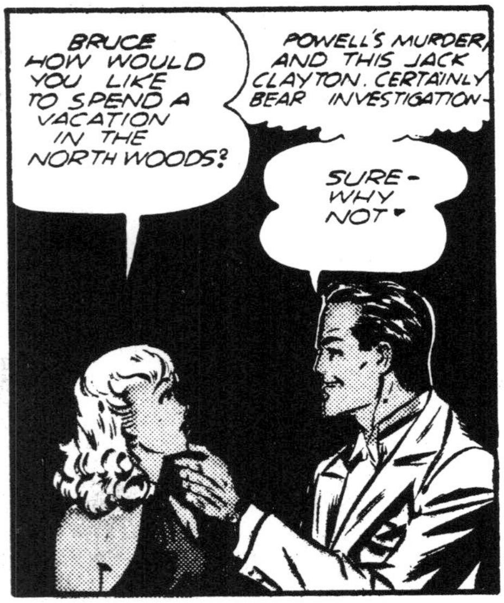
BRUCE HOW WOULD YOU LIKE TO SPEND A VACATION IN THE NORTH WOODS?
POWELL'S MURDER, AND THIS JACK CLAYTON. CERTAINLY BEAR INVESTIGATION-
SURE - WHY NOT

Even in his guise as millionaire Bruce Wayne, our hero has always managed to combine pleasure with crime-fighting. (Batman *#7, October/November 1941, "The North Woods Mystery!" p. 3 [panel].*)

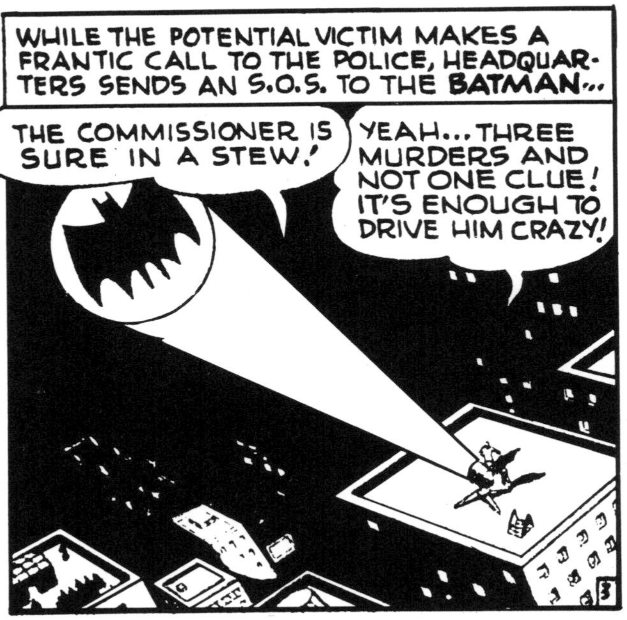
WHILE THE POTENTIAL VICTIM MAKES A FRANTIC CALL TO THE POLICE, HEADQUARTERS SENDS AN S.O.S. TO THE BATMAN...
THE COMMISSIONER IS SURE IN A STEW!
YEAH... THREE MURDERS AND NOT ONE CLUE! IT'S ENOUGH TO DRIVE HIM CRAZY!
3

For decades the Bat Signal has been Gotham's S.O.S. *summons for the Dynamic Duo. The famous logo, emblazoned across the night sky, has not only been a call to action for Batman and Robin but a sign of relief to the good citizens of the crime-ridden Big Town.* (Batman *#38, December/January 1947, "The Carbon Copy Crimes," p. 3 [panel].*)

There's Police Commissioner Gordon, the only other continuing character to have debuted with Batman in *Detective* 27. In that issue Gordon, initially distrustful of the mysterious crime fighter, had ordered his men to apprehend the Batman.[1]

It had all come to a head when Batman and Gordon were both present in a crowded courtroom and an indignant district attorney had called Batman a meddler in the course of justice and ordered his arrest.

It was then that Commissioner Gordon came to Batman's defense.

"I speak for the Batman—the friend of the people!" Gordon proclaimed in *Batman* 7. "Yes—he works 'outside the law,' as you call it, but the legal devices that hamper us are hurdled by this crimefighter so he may bring these men of evil to justice.... The eminent district attorney calls him a meddler with a theory—Washington, the Wright brothers, Lincoln, Edison and others, they were 'meddlers,' too—who proved their

theories. They made sacrifices so that we might enjoy the security and comfort we do. The Batman has done that, too!"

And then the commissioner sealed his pact, putting one hand on Batman's shoulder, exchanging a strong handshake with the other.

"Perhaps this comes a little late," Gordon said to Batman, "but I, the Police Commissioner of Gotham City, appoint you an honorary member of the police department! From now on, you work hand in hand with the police!"[2]

The support of the police department not only eased the public apprehension about the Batman, but provided the Caped Crusader with the intelligence pipeline he needed for his war on crime.

Gordon, however, has never learned the Batman's true identity. That secret has belonged over the years to Alfred Pennyworth, the butler of Wayne Manor, and Bruce Wayne's ward and crime-fighting sidekick, Dick Grayson (Robin, the Boy Wonder!).

For decades Alfred, who would be every inch a gentleman even without his butler's uniform of tie and tailcoat, has been serving tea and advice

1. "The Case of the Chemical Syndicate," *Detective Comics* 27 (May 1939), p. 3.

2. Michael L. Fleisher, *The Encyclopedia of Comic Book Heroes* (New York: Collier Books, 1976), vol. 1, *Batman*, p. 112.

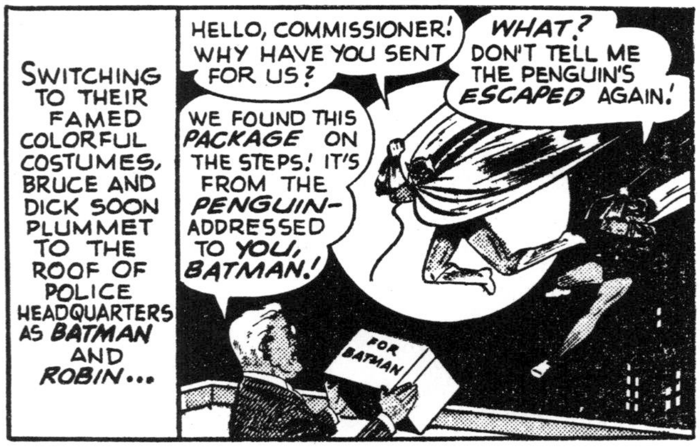
SWITCHING TO THEIR FAMED COLORFUL COSTUMES, BRUCE AND DICK SOON PLUMMET TO THE ROOF OF POLICE HEADQUARTERS AS BATMAN AND ROBIN...
HELLO, COMMISSIONER! WHY HAVE YOU SENT FOR US?
WHAT? DON'T TELL ME THE PENGUIN'S ESCAPED AGAIN!
WE FOUND THIS PACKAGE ON THE STEPS! IT'S FROM THE PENGUIN-ADDRESSED TO YOU, BATMAN!
FOR BATMAN

You're Police Commissioner Gordon, your harried officers are hard-pressed to keep up with the pickpockets and purse snatchers and then you hear that another maniacal super villain is back in town—so who ya gonna call? (Batman *#61, October/November 1950, "The Mystery of The Winged People!" p. 3 [panel].*)

Commissioner James Gordon

Gordon began his law enforcement career as a detective. Despite the corruption within the department and the influence of mobsters such as "Boss" Zucco, Gordon was always above reproach. His detective years would become legendary even as he rose through the ranks to the commissioner's office.

Known as a by-the-book cop, his unusual alliance with Batman has periodically drawn criticism.

Gordon had the Bat Signal installed on the roof of police headquarters and has been using it for decades to call Batman to action.

The commissioner counts both millionaire Bruce Wayne and Batman as close friends. Batman has never revealed his secret identity to him.

In the early days Gordon was suspicious of Batman's motives: "He's making the police department look ridiculous," Gordon once complained of the costumed crime buster.

In 1953 Gordon established the little-known Secret Star organization—a group of five handpicked men who would be trained and ready to carry on the Batman legend in case of the Caped Crusader's disability or death.

Gordon's daughter, Barbara, is Batgirl.

In the 1980s Gordon became a target of corrupt Mayor Hamilton Hill. During the scandal, when the mayor tried to get Gordon drummed off the force, the commissioner suffered a near fatal heart attack. Batman helped bring about Hill's downfall, and Gordon recovered to continue his duties.

He often thinks of a life of retirement with his wife.

to Masters Bruce and Dick. The scene of Alfred descending into the Bat Cave from the spiral staircase hidden behind the grandfather clock in Bruce Wayne's study, carrying a tray laden with tea and nourishment for Batman and Robin, is one of the little rituals fans have enjoyed over the years.

But no one has known Batman as well as Robin, the other half of the proclaimed "Dynamic Duo." Dick Grayson, also orphaned by criminals, was a quick study when he asked Batman to teach him the crime fighter's art.

There has been a legion of minor and major supporting characters over the years, from police veteran Harvey Hainer, who has operated the Bat-Signal from the roof of police headquarters, to the mysterious Professor Carter Nichols, who has sent the Dynamic Duo on many time-traveling adventures. There have been love interests, from Vicki Vale and the Catwoman to Batwoman and Talia.

And there are the villains, the deadliest in the business. The menacing roster of mentally, and sometimes physically, twisted foes includes the Joker, Two-Face, Penguin, Riddler, and Killer Croc.

But ultimately it is Batman we come to see. We've thrilled to the Dark Knight swinging from the mightiest skyscraper on the slender thread of his Bat-Rope, cheered as he's waded into a pack of criminals with both fists flying, and marveled at a career that has taken him from the darkest

BATMAN'S ORIGIN — REVISITED

The murder of Thomas and Martha Wayne by an unknown hold-up man (as originally recorded in *Detective* #33, November 1939), was the kind of brutal business rarely seen in the comics. Bruce Wayne would make countless criminal collars as The Batman—but his thirst for vengeance could never slacken since his parent's killer had escaped justice and disappeared into the city shadows.

Subsequent retellings of Batman's origin would soften the impact of the saga's seminal criminal act. In 1948 Thomas and Martha Wayne's killer was revealed as Joe Chill, a small-time gunman (*Batman* #47, June/July 1948, "The Origin of Batman!"). Batman revealed himself to Chill as "the son of the man you murdered! I'm Bruce Wayne." A shaken Chill sought refuge in the Underworld—but this time there was no escaping justice. He was killed by his own criminal fellows after revealing he was responsible for Batman's existence.

Later revisionism further revealed that Chill "only pretended to be a hold-up man," and had actually been hired to kill Thomas Wayne by one Lew Moxon, a vengeful mobster Thomas Wayne had helped send to jail (*Dectective* #235, September 1956, "The First Batman!"). When Chill killed Thomas Wayne, Martha died from shock due to her "weak heart." This watered-down recounting also claimed Bruce Wayne's "Batman" inspiration was due to an unconscious childhood memory of seeing his father costumed as a batman for a masquerade party.

Recent retellings of the origin have returned to the haunting injustice of the original version, notably Frank Miller's *The Dark Knight Returns* in 1986, and Miller and David Mazzucchelli's "Batman Year One," chapter one (*Batman* 404, February 1987).

The impact of the original origin, with its swiftly executed (and ultimately unresolved) murders and Bruce Wayne's ensuing emotional catharsis as Batman, sets the perfect tone of menace and mystery for the mythos.

Right: *The fateful moment when Batman encounters his parents' killer.* (Batman #47, *June/July 1948, "The Origin of Batman," p. 10 [select panels]*).

Gotham City alley to the farthest reaches of time and space.

From decade to decade Batman has been something special. Stop a stranger on the street and just mention "Batman" and they'll know who you're talking about. In such a poll you're likely to meet fans who can give chapter and verse of the Caped Crusader's greatest adventures, while others will hum the theme from the 1960s "Batman" TV show, which made the character famous even to people who had never read the comic book.

This book is a fiftieth birthday celebration for one of the greatest characters in the comics. Batman's longevity is significant, given the mercurial attention the public often gives its icons of popular culture.

In these pages we will appreciate the elements that have made Batman such an enduring, haunting character. We will also consider the influences that have shaped the Dark Knight's mythos over the decades, and thrill again to the action imagery of the Dark Knight's tales.

Over the years Batman's crime-fighting mood has run the gamut from grim to grinning. It was in the early stages of his career, before Robin entered the picture, that the Dark Knight dispensed justice with a maniacal determination.

As we shall see, the Dark Knight of the early Golden Age was not loath to deal death to an evildoer.

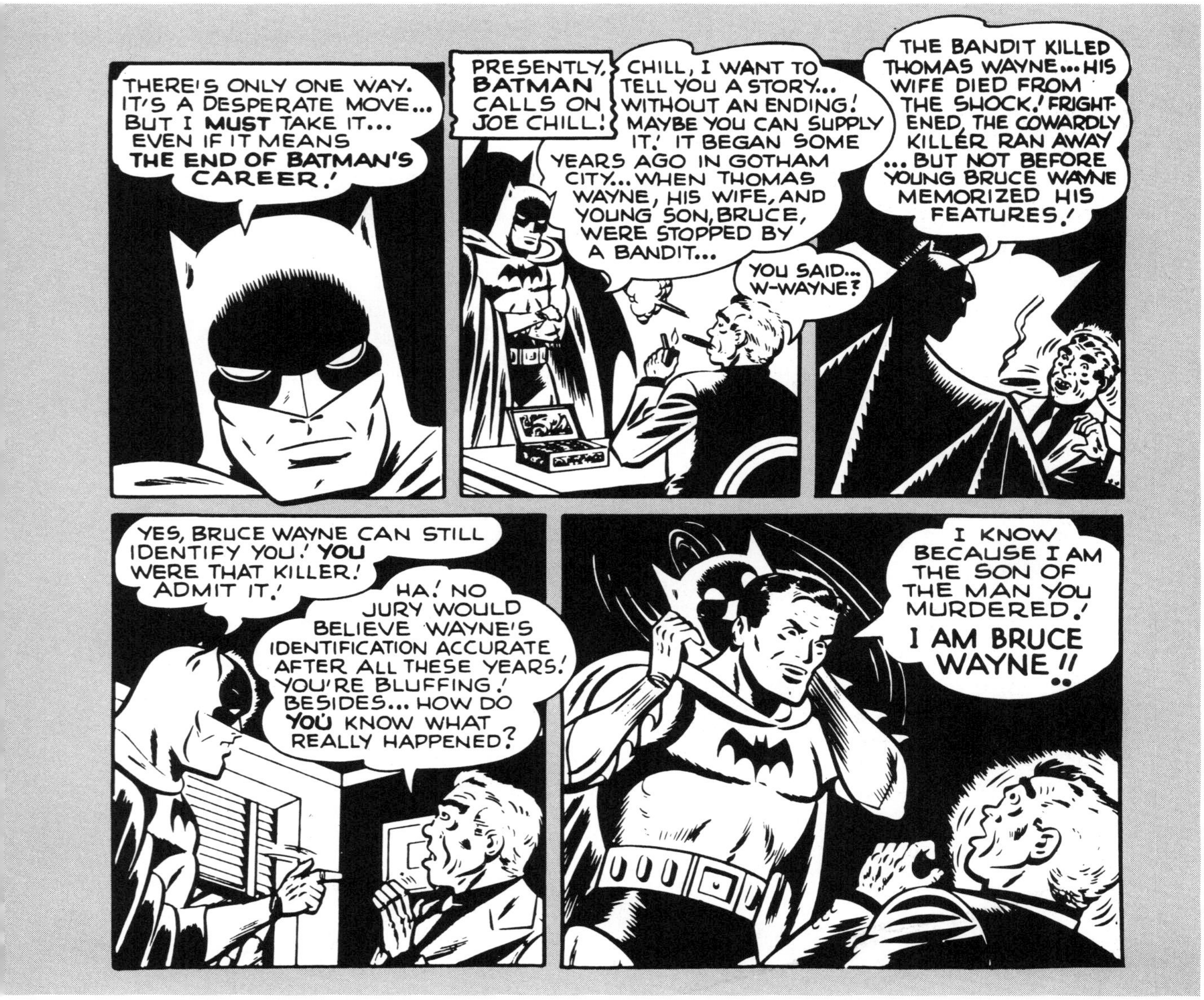
THERE'S ONLY ONE WAY. IT'S A DESPERATE MOVE... BUT I MUST TAKE IT... EVEN IF IT MEANS THE END OF BATMAN'S CAREER!
PRESENTLY, BATMAN CALLS ON JOE CHILL!
CHILL, I WANT TO TELL YOU A STORY... WITHOUT AN ENDING! MAYBE YOU CAN SUPPLY IT! IT BEGAN SOME YEARS AGO IN GOTHAM CITY... WHEN THOMAS WAYNE, HIS WIFE, AND YOUNG SON, BRUCE, WERE STOPPED BY A BANDIT...
YOU SAID... W-WAYNE?
THE BANDIT KILLED THOMAS WAYNE... HIS WIFE DIED FROM THE SHOCK! FRIGHTENED, THE COWARDLY KILLER RAN AWAY ... BUT NOT BEFORE YOUNG BRUCE WAYNE MEMORIZED HIS FEATURES!
YES, BRUCE WAYNE CAN STILL IDENTIFY YOU! YOU WERE THAT KILLER! ADMIT IT!
HA! NO JURY WOULD BELIEVE WAYNE'S IDENTIFICATION ACCURATE AFTER ALL THESE YEARS! YOU'RE BLUFFING! BESIDES... HOW DO YOU KNOW WHAT REALLY HAPPENED?
I KNOW BECAUSE I AM THE SON OF THE MAN YOU MURDERED! I AM BRUCE WAYNE!!

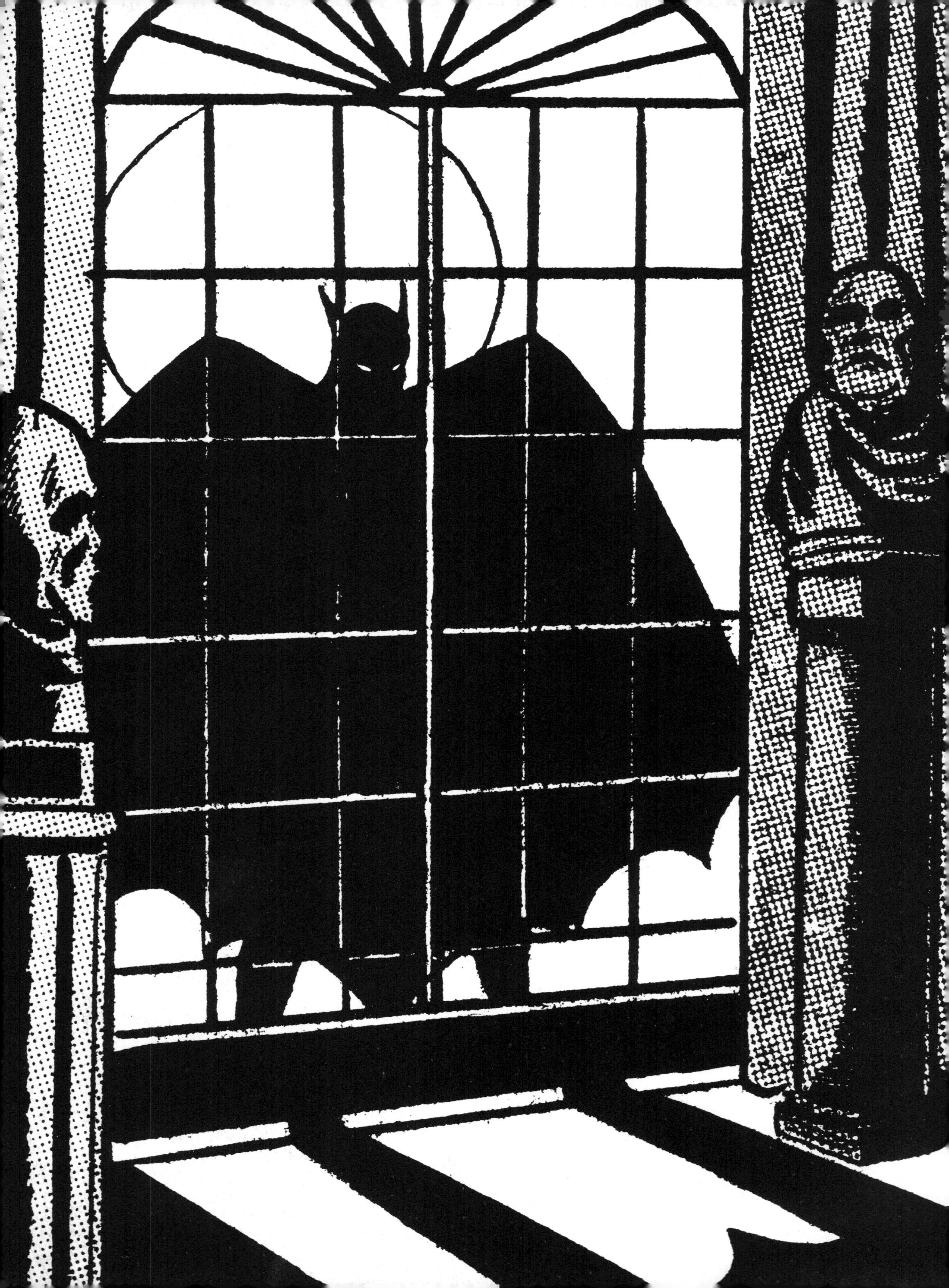

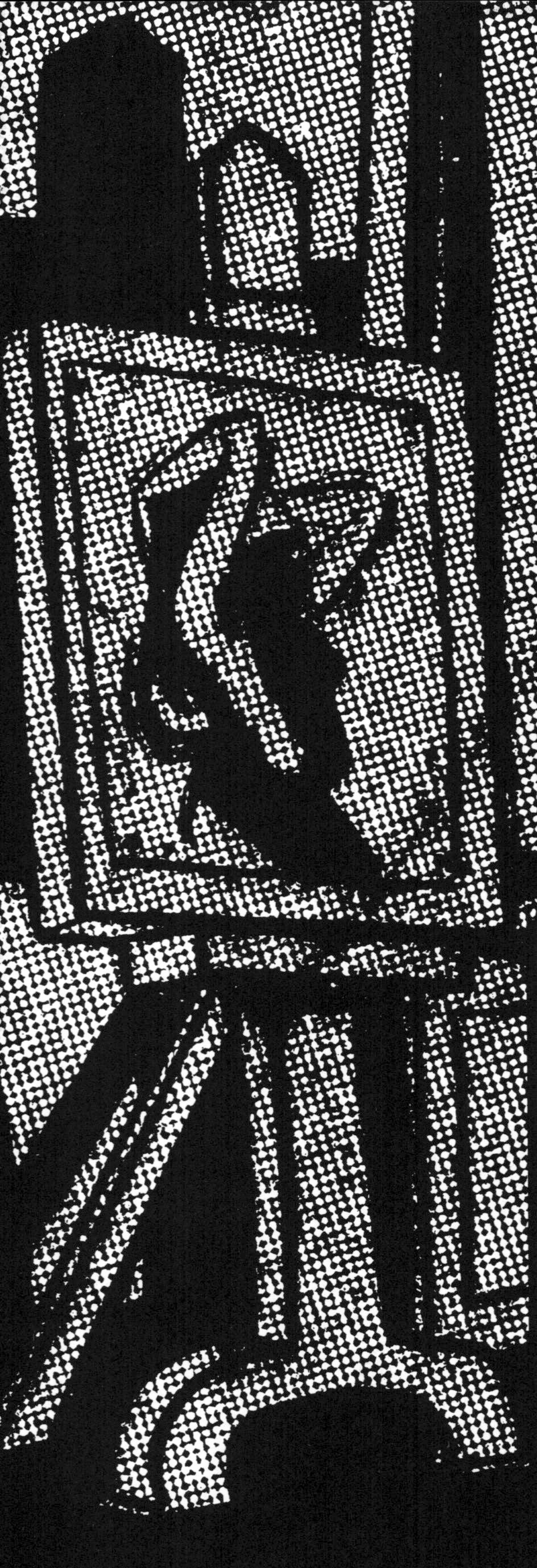

CHAPTER 1

SHADOW OF THE BATMAN

BATMAN WAS BORN INTO AN AMERICA IN the grip of prewar jitters. The newspaper, radio, and weekly movie newsreel reports seemed to bring the tumultuous events looming across both great oceans ever closer.

When Orson Welles's 1938 Halloween "War of the Worlds" radio drama simulated an imaginary Martian invasion, millions of listeners, their nerves already stretched taut by war fears, were driven into a frenzy.

Despite the impending conflagration (the war had already broken out in Europe in 1939), the country produced not one, but two 1939 world's fairs—the New York Fair, showcasing "The World of Tomorrow," and San Francisco's Golden Gate Exposition. But everyone knew this was a momentary escape before the ultimate loss of innocence.

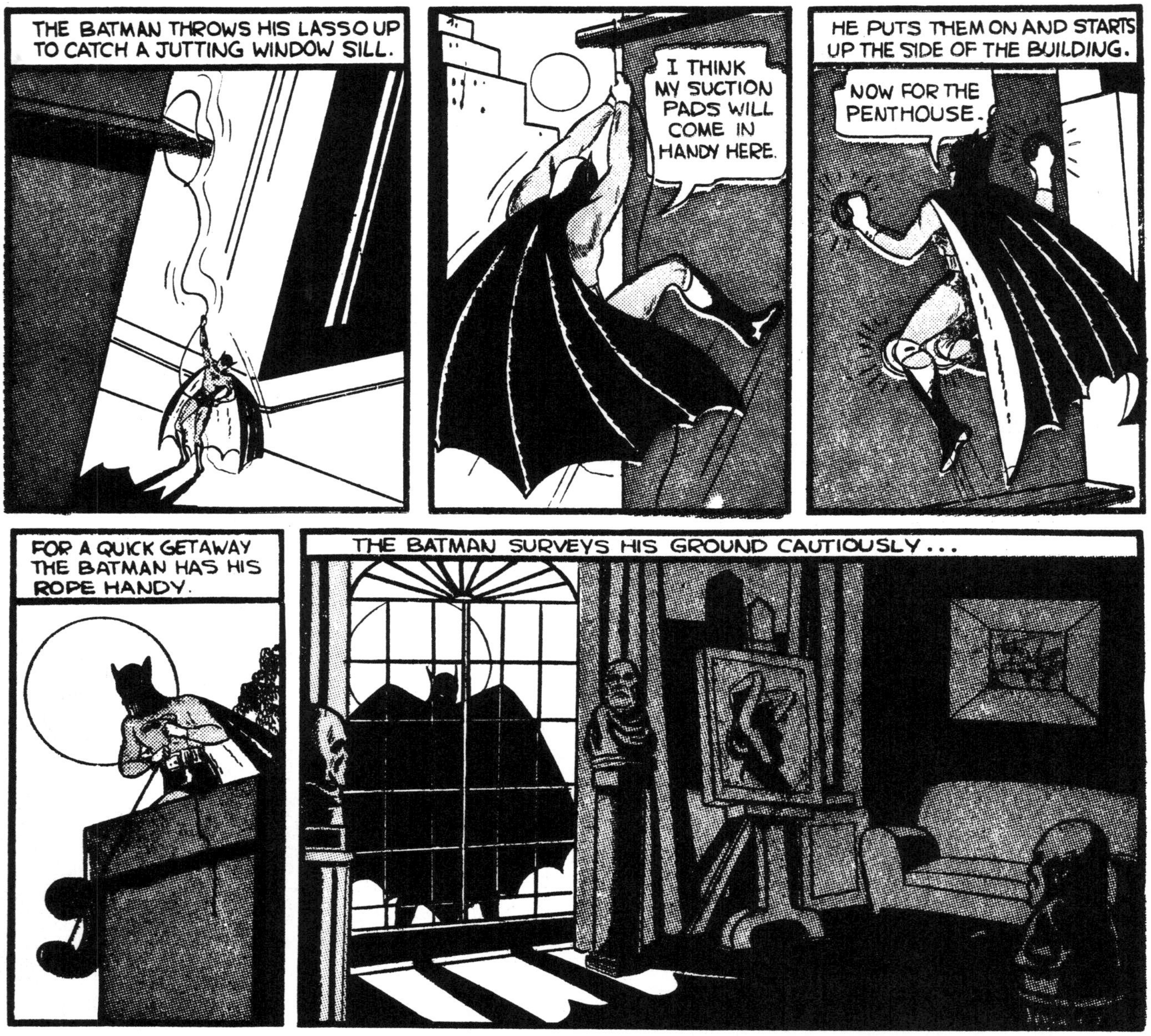
THE BATMAN THROWS HIS LASSO UP TO CATCH A JUTTING WINDOW SILL.
I THINK MY SUCTION PADS WILL COME IN HANDY HERE.
HE PUTS THEM ON AND STARTS UP THE SIDE OF THE BUILDING.
NOW FOR THE PENTHOUSE.
FOR A QUICK GETAWAY THE BATMAN HAS HIS ROPE HANDY.
THE BATMAN SURVEYS HIS GROUND CAUTIOUSLY...

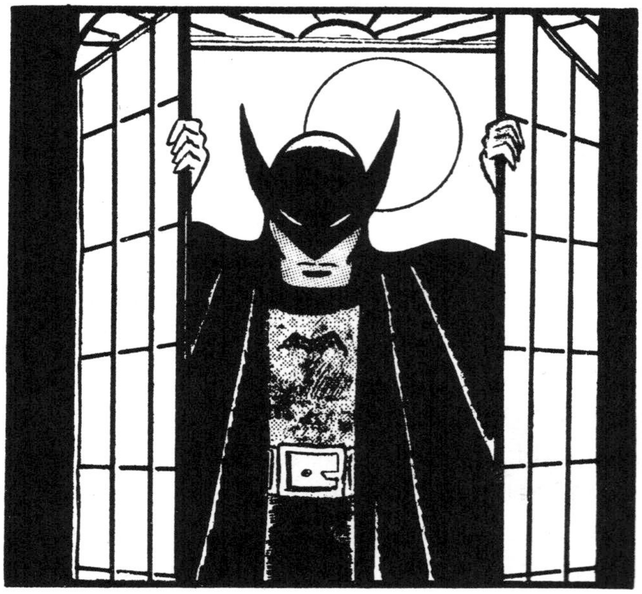

In his early days as a lone crimefighter the Dark Knight polished his pose as a "weird figure of the dark." Here we see the mechanics (lassos and suction pads), that go into making those dramatic midnight entrances. (Detective #29, July 1939, *"The Batman Meets Doctor Death." pp. 3–4 [select panels].*)

"As a harbinger of style, the (San Francisco) Exposition had totally failed," author Richard Reinhardt recalls. "It left no permanent monuments.... It set no artistic or architectural trends. The times were against it; nobody was building or designing anything but military camps.... The world was too distracted to support a bright new bubble of creative energy. If this generation was to make a mark on history, it would have to do so in another way, by fighting a war we had been hoping to avoid."[1]

When Batman began punching and kicking his way through the scum of the underworld in 1939, it was the perfect reaction to a dangerous, complex world that was closing in.

To survive, the times demanded a righteous sense of Us versus Them. In Batman's world as well, the demarcation line between good and evil was clearly drawn. (Only until the 1970s would Batman's own inner conflicts, and his tightrope walk between the light and dark, be fully developed into the mythos.)

Just as propaganda cartoons depicted the Axis enemy as subhuman monsters—characterizations faithfully accepted by the public—so, too, were the criminals of Gotham City clearly venal rats worthy of extermination. And the avenging Dark Knight was happy to oblige.

During his first ever tussle with hoodlums, a rooftop battle recorded in *Detective* 27, the Dark Knight grabbed one burly foe in a headlock and, with "a mighty heave," hurled the crook off the roof, presumably to his death. In the next issue of *Detective* another crook, this time a member of the Frenchy Blake gang, was also given a rooftop dive, courtesy of the Batman.

Lest such rooftop scenes prove too tedious, Batman found other ways of dealing death. In subsequent issues he dispatched evildoers by strangling them with his lasso, delivering neck-breaking kicks to the head, and by berserk punches that sent many a foe to a fatal fall.

Sometimes Batman was depicted with a smoking automatic pistol. Once he used a gun, with silver bullets, to kill vampires at point-blank range as they lay in their open coffins (*Detective* 32). And in the Spring 1940 issue of *Batman* 1, a grim Dark Knight killed henchman of the evil Professor Hugo Strange behind the blazing machine gun he had mounted on the fuselage of the swooping Batplane.

"Much as I hate to take human life, I'm afraid *this time* it's necessary!" Batman sneered over the staccato *rat-tat-tat* of his machine gun.

When Robin appeared in April 1940, Batman's moral code prohibited killing. In *The Steranko History of Comics* artist/author James Steranko credits much of Batman's longevity to the arrival of Robin.[2] The Boy Wonder brought a

1. Richard Reinhardt, *Treasure Island 1939–1940: San Francisco's Exposition Years* (Mill Valley, California: Squarebooks, Inc., 1978), p. 159.
2. James Steranko, *The Steranko History of Comics* (Reading, Pennysl-vania: A Supergraphics Publication, 1970), p. 47.

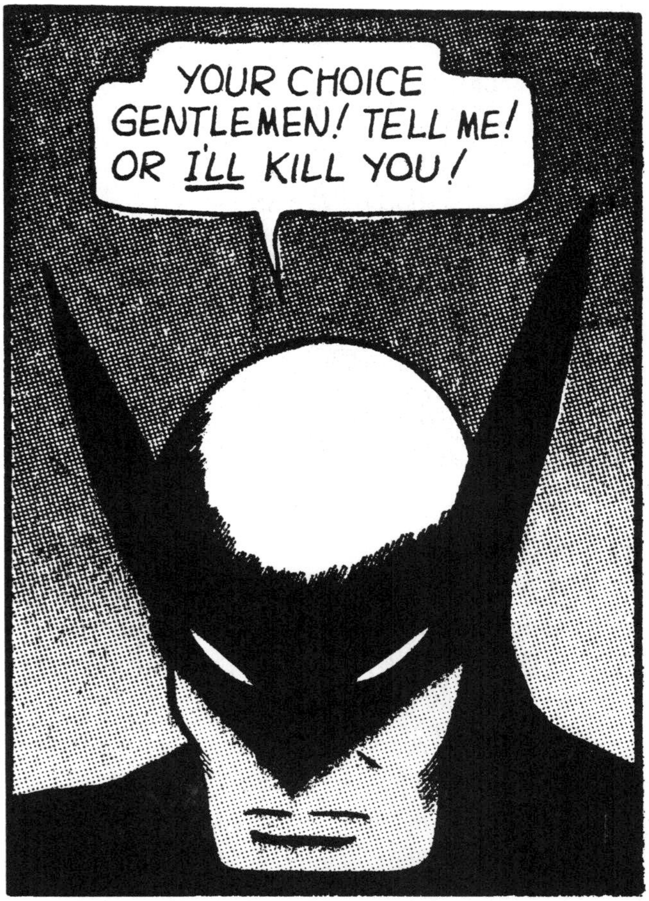
YOUR CHOICE GENTLEMEN! TELL ME! OR I'LL KILL YOU!

In the early days the Dark Knight went to war against crime—and didn't plan on taking prisoners. (Detective *#29, July 1939, "The Batman Meets Doctor Death." p. 5 [panel].*)

sense of adventure and compassion to the saga.

The United States entered the global conflict with the bombing of Pearl Harbor on December 7, 1941. The times demanded a special discipline. It might have been unseemly to have a rabid Batman running loose on the midnight streets of Gotham serving as judge, jury, and executioner while the rest of America was coping with rationing and air raid drills.

The editors at DC had also decided that it was a mistake to have a gun-toting Batman, since Batman's parents were killed by a criminal with a handgun. One of the last times Batman used a gun during the Golden Age, it was almost as an afterthought. He had scooped up a pistol dropped by a gangster and fired a shot at a fleeing crook wielding a submachine gun.

"Just want to wing him!" Batman said. As if that weren't enough to underline the Dark Knight's newfound revulsion against guns, the

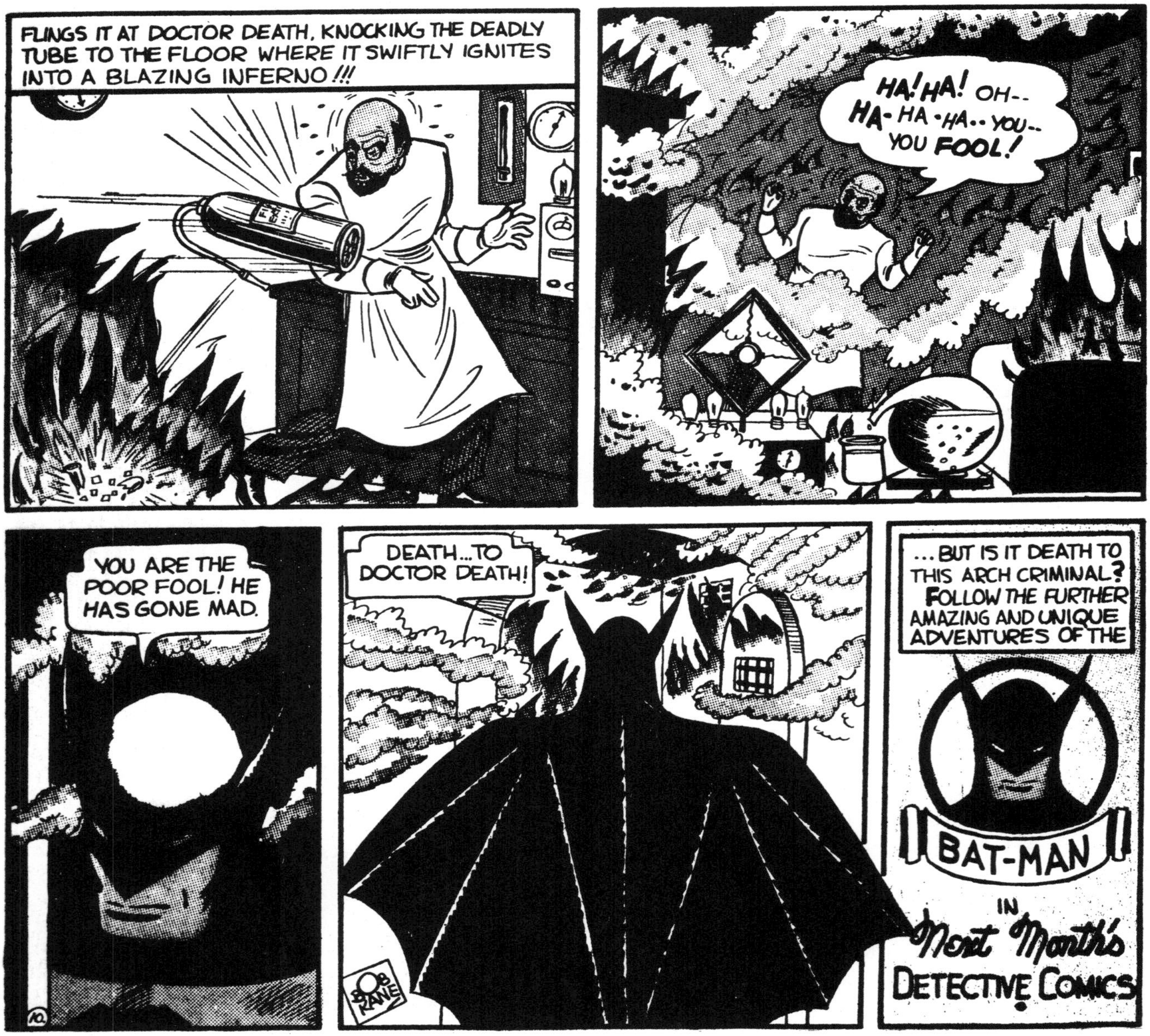
FLINGS IT AT DOCTOR DEATH, KNOCKING THE DEADLY TUBE TO THE FLOOR WHERE IT SWIFTLY IGNITES INTO A BLAZING INFERNO !!!
HA! HA! OH-- HA-HA-HA-- YOU-- YOU FOOL!
YOU ARE THE POOR FOOL! HE HAS GONE MAD.
DEATH...TO DOCTOR DEATH!
... BUT IS IT DEATH TO THIS ARCH CRIMINAL? FOLLOW THE FURTHER AMAZING AND UNIQUE ADVENTURES OF THE
BAT-MAN
IN
Next Month's
DETECTIVE COMICS
BOB KANE

At the beginning of his career the taciturn Dark Knight wasn't concerned with rehabilitating criminals—why bother when you can just watch them burn? (Detective *#29, July 1939, ''The Batman Meets Doctor Death.'' p. 10 [select panels].*)

narrative text served to remind: "The Batman never carries or kills with a gun!" (*Batman* 4/4, Winter 1941)

Earlier in that same issue Batman and Robin, each armed with a cutlass, found themselves battling the swashbuckling Blackbeard and his pirate horde.

"Use only the *flat* of your sword, Robin!" Batman cried. "Remember, we never kill with weapons of any kind!" (*Batman* 4/2)

Of course, such adversaries as Dr. Death, Hugo Strange, the Joker, Two-Face, Catwoman, and the Penguin had no compunction against killing. But many of Batman's foes were victims of fate, rather than calculating killers and thieves.

There was the strange case of Adam Lamb (*Batman* 2/2), a mild-mannered museum custodian who suffered an accidental blow to his head, causing him to enter into a murderous delirium

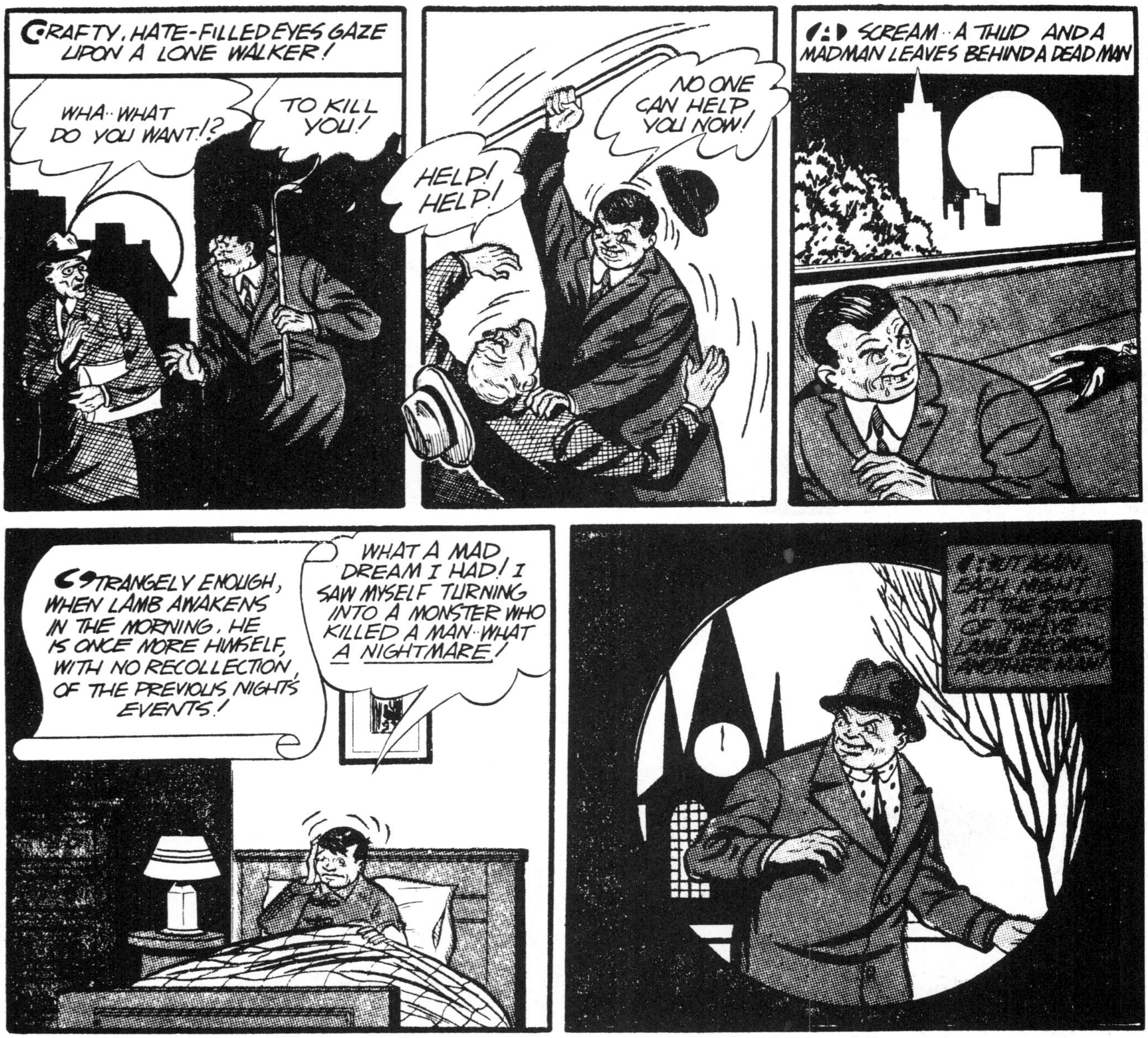

CRAFTY, HATE-FILLED EYES GAZE UPON A LONE WALKER!
WHA-- WHAT DO YOU WANT!?
TO KILL YOU!
NO ONE CAN HELP YOU NOW!
HELP! HELP!
A SCREAM -- A THUD AND A MADMAN LEAVES BEHIND A DEAD MAN
STRANGELY ENOUGH, WHEN LAMB AWAKENS IN THE MORNING, HE IS ONCE MORE HIMSELF, WITH NO RECOLLECTION OF THE PREVIOUS NIGHT'S EVENTS!
WHAT A MAD DREAM I HAD! I SAW MYSELF TURNING INTO A MONSTER WHO KILLED A MAN-- WHAT A NIGHTMARE!

Injustice and insanity didn't begin and end with the tragic murder of Bruce Wayne's parents. Batman's world has always been full of macabre twists of fate. Consider the strange case of Adam Lamb, a gentle museum custodian, who is transformed each night into a murdering maniac after an accidental bump on the head. (Batman *#2, Summer 1940, "The Crime Master." p. 4 [select panels].*)

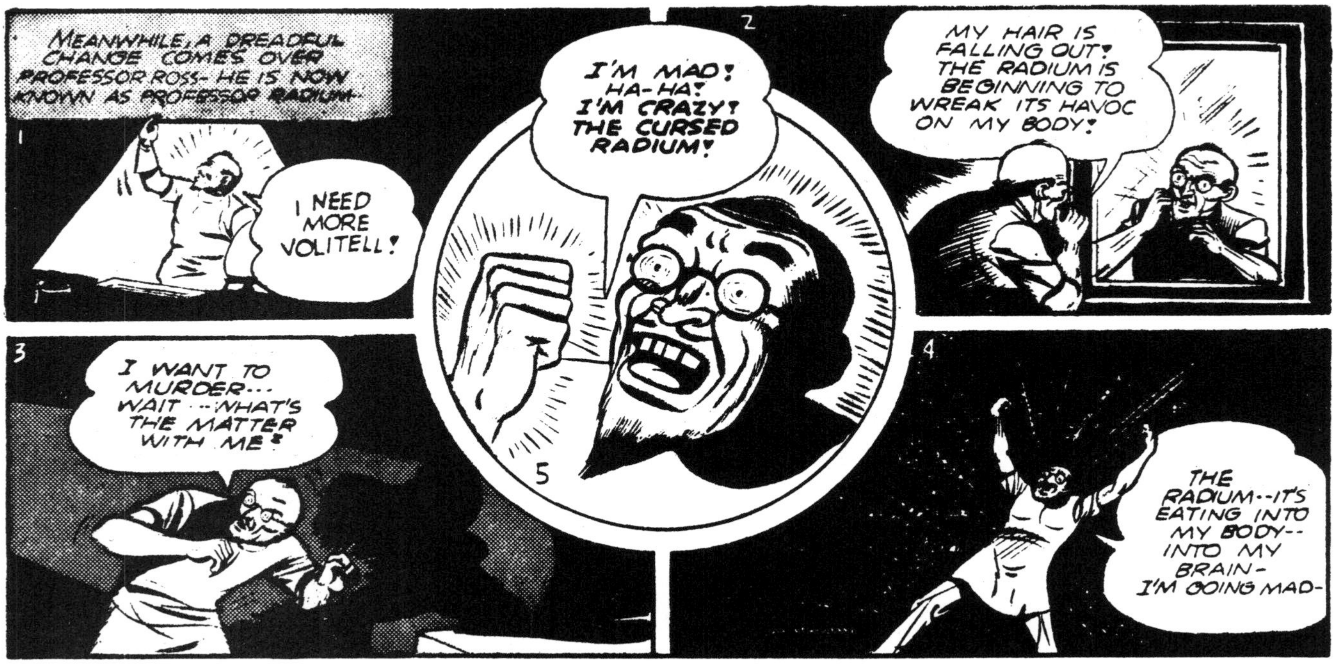
MEANWHILE, A DREADFUL CHANGE COMES OVER PROFESSOR ROSS- HE IS NOW KNOWN AS PROFESSOR RADIUM-
I NEED MORE VOLITELL!
I'M MAD! HA-HA! I'M CRAZY! THE CURSED RADIUM!
MY HAIR IS FALLING OUT! THE RADIUM IS BEGINNING TO WREAK ITS HAVOC ON MY BODY!
I WANT TO MURDER--- WAIT --WHAT'S THE MATTER WITH ME?
THE RADIUM--IT'S EATING INTO MY BODY-- INTO MY BRAIN- I'M GOING MAD-

Pity Professor Henry Ross—he only wanted to help humanity when he swallowed an experimental dose of Radium serum. (Batman *#8 January 1942 ''The Strange Case of Professor Radium,'' p.10 [select panels].*)

ALFRED PENNYWORTH

The English butler has been serving as Bruce Wayne's servant and Batman's friend and confidant since 1943.

When he first appeared, he was a slightly bumbling, rotund fellow who considered himself "an amateur criminologist of little experience but much talent." In later issues he would shape up as the lean, mustached character most familiar to generations of fans.

The Pennyworth lineage has excelled in domestic service for generations. Alfred carried on the tradition as a final promise to his dying father. The elder Pennyworth had once served a Gotham physician named Thomas Wayne. When Alfred came to the United States, he took up service at Wayne Manor—despite the gentle protestations of Bruce Wayne and Dick Grayson.

Soon after settling into his duties, Alfred discovered the Bat Cave and the alter egos of his employers.

During World War II Alfred risked his life to help refugees escape Nazi tyranny.

In 1959 a freak accident gave Alfred superstrength and leaping ability. Before losing his powers, Alfred gave himself the moniker "The Eagle," outfitted himself in a golden eagle costume, and attempted to be a crime-fighting partner with the Dynamic Duo.

Alfred is an amateur novelist, having written many imaginary tales about the Dynamic Duo. Because he openly writes about Batman's secret identity, this body of work will never be published.

Periodically Alfred has worn a Batman costume and appeared with Bruce Wayne to refute allegations that Wayne is the Caped Crusader. The well-padded costume has never aroused further suspicions.

Alfred has one daughter, Julie Remarque, a writer. For a time Alfred was troubled that his loving daughter never used her Pennyworth name in a byline.

Before the promise to his father that led to his career as a butler, Alfred was an acclaimed Shakespearean actor on the London stage.

every night at the stroke of midnight. Lamb's Jekyll/Hyde rampage was finally ended when he died from a broken neck caused by a mighty Batman blow.

"The only time I was ever sorry to see a criminal die," the Dark Knight would say with genuine regret. "Medical attention might have cured him."

Another tortured soul was Basil Karlo (*Detective* 40, June 1940), a great character actor from the movies who wore a horrible mask and assumed the role of Clayface for a killing spree on the set of the film *Dread Castle.*

"He had played so many horror roles in pictures that they had taken possession of his mind and soul!" Batman grimly concluded after his successful capture of Clayface. "He made up as Clayface, one of his old roles, and then followed the plot of 'Dread Castle' and killed off each one as they 'died' in the picture."

But whether a cold-blooded killer like the Joker, or a misguided tool of fate like Adam Lamb, Batman's code of justice mandated that if you broke the law, you faced the penalty.

"I think Robin and I make it pretty clear that WE HATE CRIME AND CRIMINALS!" Batman said to the readers in an early issue. "There's nothing we like better than to crack down on the distasteful denizens of the underworld.

"Why? Because we're proud of being AMERICANS—and we know there's no place in this great country of ours for lawbreakers!

"That phrase, 'CRIME DOESN'T PAY,' has been used over and over again to the point where I hesitate to repeat it. But remember this: IT'S JUST AS TRUE NOW AS IT EVER WAS—AND THAT'S PLENTY TRUE!

"Sure, it may seem that lawbreakers DO get away with breaking the law. Some may get away with it longer than others. But in the end, every crook gets what's coming to him—and that means plenty of trouble with the law!

"Robin and I hope that our adventures may help to 'put over' that fact. We'd like to feel that our efforts may help every youngster to grow up into an honest, useful citizen.... You've got to govern your own lives so that they can be worthwhile, fruitful lives—not lives wasted in prison, or even thrown away altogether before the ready guns of the law enforcement agents whose duty it is to guard those of us who are honest and those who are not. And not only must you guide your OWN life in the proper channels—you must also strive to be a good influence on the lives of others.

"If you do this, if you are definitely on the side of Law and Order, then Robin and I salute you and are glad to number you among our friends!"[3]

To understand the urgency of Batman's crusade we have to consider the tradition that influenced his own crime-fighting vow. There were others that came before, paving the way for the Caped Crusader of Gotham City.

Many of these heroes of old were wealthy social gadabouts by day who slipped on masks and battled crime at night. Others, with special powers, were harbingers of the cult of the Golden Age superhero.

It's time to visit Dark Knights of the past....

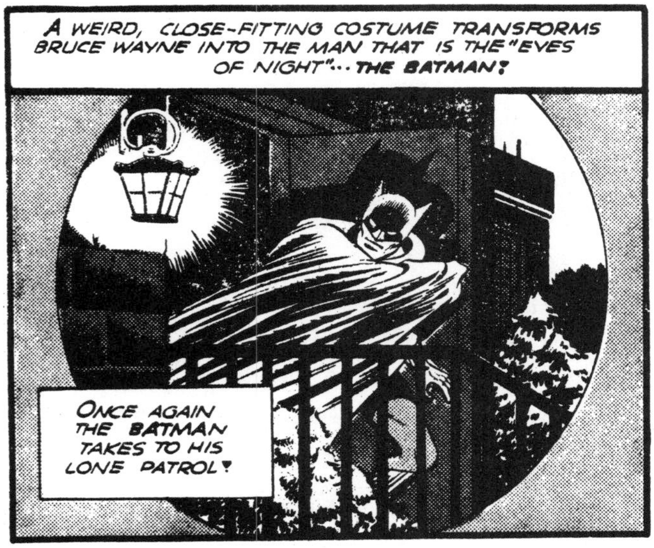
A WEIRD, CLOSE-FITTING COSTUME TRANSFORMS BRUCE WAYNE INTO THE MAN THAT IS THE "EYES OF NIGHT"... THE BATMAN!
ONCE AGAIN THE BATMAN TAKES TO HIS LONE PATROL!

Detective #52, *June 1941, "The Secret of the Jade Box," p. 3 (panel).*

3. "The Batman Says:" *Batman* 3 (1940). Note: All Batman and Robin dialogue in this chapter taken from the chronicles.

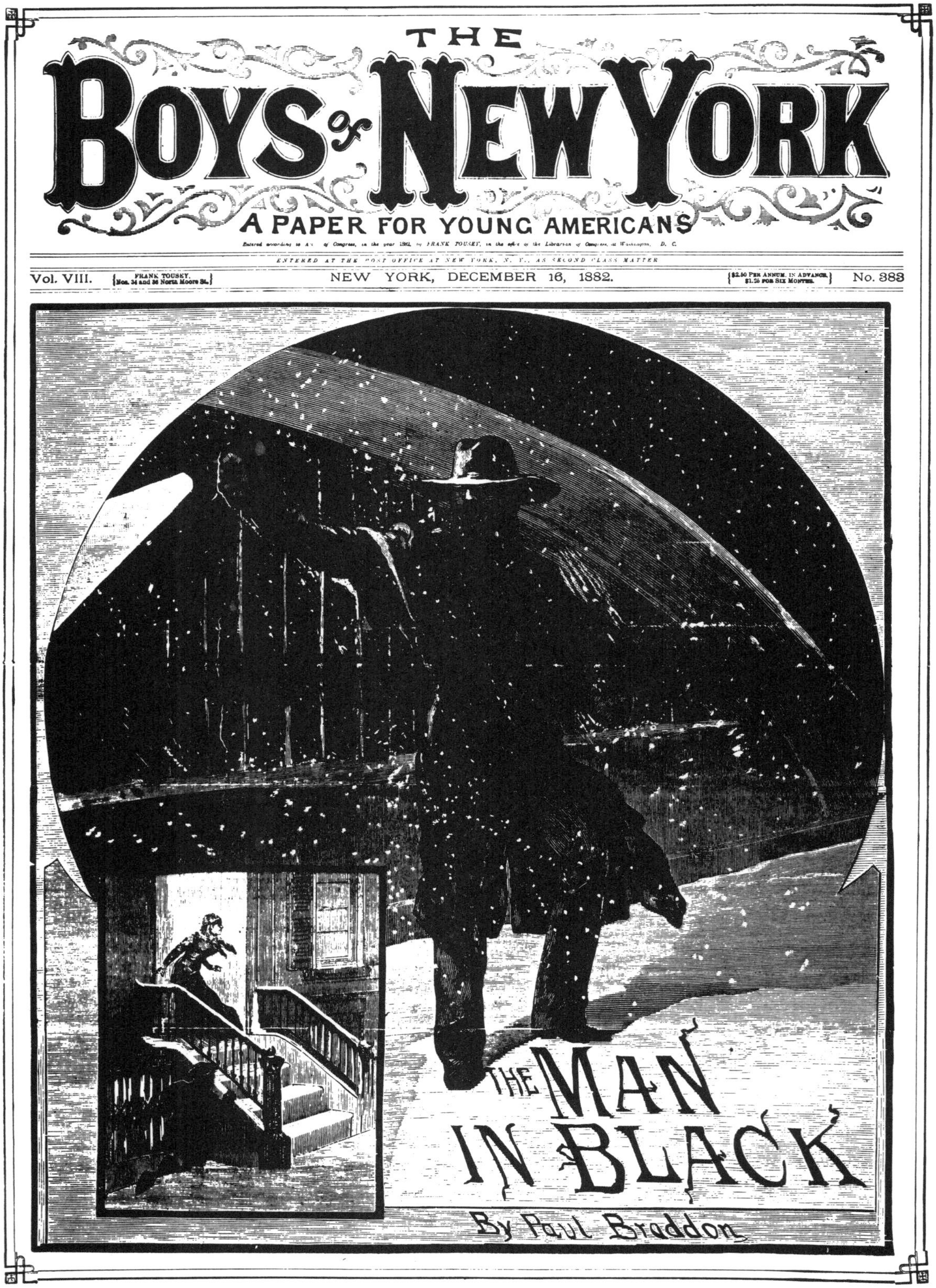

THE
BOYS of NEW YORK
A PAPER FOR YOUNG AMERICANS

Entered according to Act of Congress, in the year 1882, by FRANK TOUSEY, in the office of the Librarian of Congress, at Washington, D. C.

ENTERED AT THE POST OFFICE AT NEW YORK, N. Y., AS SECOND CLASS MATTER

Vol. VIII. {FRANK TOUSEY, Nos. 34 and 36 North Moore St.} NEW YORK, DECEMBER 16, 1882. {$2.50 Per Annum, in Advance, $1.25 for Six Months.} No. 383

THE MAN IN BLACK

By Paul Braddon

Before the dark avengers of the comic books, even before the crimebusters of the pulp magazines, there were mysterious strangers like "The Man In Black," who haunted the pages of papers like The Boys of New York. *With his slouch hat, prominent nose, and swirling cloak, the Man in Black could pass for The Shadow—who wouldn't even be born until the 1930s.* (The Boys of New York, *New York. Reproduction provided by the San Francisco Academy of Comic Art.*)

CHAPTER 2

THE DARK KNIGHTS OF THE PAST

I F WE WISHED TO DOCUMENT ALL THE MYTH-ologies dealing with heroism and the battle between good and evil, it would lead us on an odyssey through time and space as momentous as the greatest epics experienced by the warriors of old.

We could start with the clay tablets deciphered in the last century that tell *The Epic of Gilgamesh*, a tale estimated to be fifteen hundred years older than Homer, in which the hero Gilgamesh searches for immortality. From there we could journey on and meet the superpowered warriors of *The Mahabharata*, a Sanskrit work that first saw written form in the fifth or sixth century B.C.

We might yearn to experience the magic myths of Homer, or journey to the icy Nordic climes to hear how Thor wielded his mighty hammer to slay the foes of the gods, or we could join a campfire for the song of how Beowulf won a kingdom and died protecting it from a great dragon. We could even sail along the Polynesian islands, stopping at seaport villages to take in their local legends with our daily bread.

"It would not be too much to say that myth is the secret opening through which the inexhaustible energies of the cosmos pour into human cultural manifestation," writes Joseph Campbell. "Religions, philosophies, arts, the social forms of primitive and historic man, prime discoveries in science and technology, the very dreams that blister sleep, boil up from the basic, magic ring of myth."[1]

Our modern epics spring from this same rich tradition. But, like every culture throughout time and place, we take the elements of myth and mold them to fit the reality we live in and the dreams we aspire to.

Today the crime fighter is our knight-errant.

Unlike the heroes of old who set out on long voyages to find wrongs and right them, the modern crime fighter does not need to journey to unknown places to discover evil—just going across town will do.

The heroes created in the modern day, no matter the time period of their chronicles, are essentially loners. The status quo not only rarely supports them, but is likely to be a hindrance at best, an enemy at worst.

One only has to see the trouble Clint Eastwood's San Francisco cop "Dirty" Harry Callahan gets into with the top brass whenever he dispatches a criminal with a blast from his .44 Magnum to understand why crime fighters compelled to protect society often wear masks and keep their identities secret.

And while Batman soon disdained the use of guns and the role of judge, jury, and executioner, he would not be displaying the mythic qualities of the modern crime fighter if he had to fill out police reports and sweat for his pension.

One early tabloid feature that cloaked its characters in an aura of mystery was the serial adventure "The Man in Black," which debuted in *The Boys of New York: A Paper for Young Americans* on December 16, 1882.

In the tale of the intrigues of a secret society, the Man in Black wears a loose black overcoat, a cape, and a black slouch hat that covers his face. When similarly dressed members of the secret society denounce the Man in Black as a traitor and stab him a dozen times and toss his body over a bridge into an icy river, he is left for dead.

The Man in Black, however, returns to confront the secret society and a masked man named Number Ten, who had ordered his death. At a

---

1. Joseph Campbell, *The Hero with a Thousand Faces* (Princeton, New Jersey: University Press, 1973), p. 3.

secret meeting where Number Ten is enjoying a vote in favor of his leadership, the Man in Black makes an appearance that anticipates the coming of the famed pulp and radio crime fighter, the Shadow.

"No dissenting voice was raised, and through his mask the eyes of Ten flashed with triumph.

"'Then I am the chief.... We are men, and we look and long and strive and search for liberty!'

"He paused; a mocking laugh, an old-witch laugh that seemed to be repeated time and again, answered him.

"Then as the echoes died away a low, calm voice broke the silence.

"'The liberty of the guillotine.'

"For a moment or two no voice was raised; then Number Ten spoke.

"'It is but a trick of ventriloquism. We are men. Whatever happens—'.

"He stopped suddenly, a gasp of fear choking his utterance; the rest also started to their feet.

"Then, coming from none of them knew where, a black-robed figure stood before them....

"He stood attired as the twelve had seen him the previous night, only now his attire was covered with blood; from a dozen wounds in his breast the crimson life-tide was flowing.

"Only a mocking, sarcastic smile curled the corners of his lips as he regarded them."[2]

In addition to an atmosphere of mystery, the use of a secret identity was considered useful for the lone avenger of injustice.

In *The Scarlet Pimpernel*, the heroic action, set in Paris in the seventeenth century, involves the Pimpernel's rescuing French aristocrats from the guillotine and spiriting them to the safety of England's shores. The Pimpernel bedeviled his adversaries by leaving a note of triumph signed with the star-shaped pimpernel flower. (Batman would also use a calling card in his early cases, marked with the silhouette of a black bat.)

The guise of the Scarlet Pimpernel, in reality the wealthy Sir Percy Blakeney, was "chosen to hide the identity of the best and bravest man in all the world so that he may better succeed in accomplishing the noble task he has set himself to do."[3]

Another wealthy sort who used a secret identity to right wrongs was Don Diego Vega, who, as the legendary Zorro, wore a black mask and cape and battled the Spaniards who occupied the territories of Old California.

When he is captured and unmasked, the wealthy Vega explains why he adopted the Zorro persona.

"It began ten years ago, when I was but a lad of fifteen," he reveals. "I heard tales of persecution. I saw my friends and *frailes*, annoyed and robbed. I saw soldiers beat an old native who was my friend. And then I determined to play this game.

"It would be a difficult game to play, I knew. So I pretended to have small interest in life, so that men never would connect my name with that of the highwayman I expected to become. In secret, I practiced horsemanship and learned how to handle a blade....

"One half of me was the languid Don Diego you all know, and the other half was the Curse of Capistrano I hoped one day to be. And then the time came and my work began.

It is a peculiar thing to explain.... The moment I donned cloak and mask, the Don Diego part of me fell away. My body straightened, new blood seemed to course through my veins, my voice grew strong and firm, fire came to me! And the moment I removed cloak and mask I was the languid Don Diego again. Is it not a peculiar thing?"[4]

But the concept of the modern loner operating outside of the social niceties took a strange turn in the post-Depression years of the 1930s as the criminal element that Batman would dedicate his life to fighting enjoyed folk-hero status. Even a real-life bank robber like John Dillinger was held as a self-made man who was simply beating a corrupt system. All this wasn't lost on Hollywood, which, intentionally or not, glorified gangsters in films.

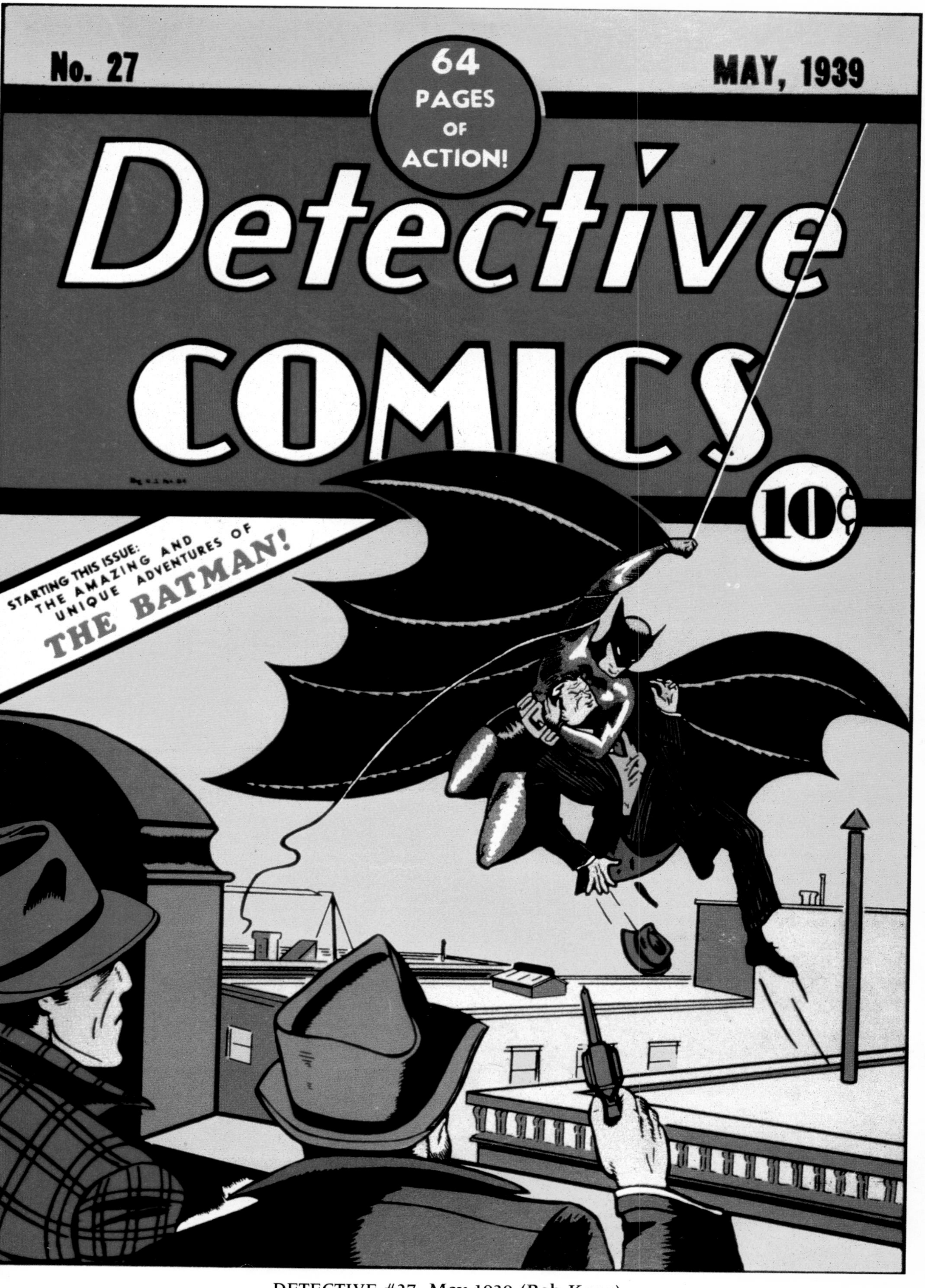
No. 27
64 PAGES OF ACTION!
MAY, 1939
Detective COMICS
10¢
STARTING THIS ISSUE: THE AMAZING AND UNIQUE ADVENTURES OF THE BATMAN!

DETECTIVE #27, May 1939 (Bob Kane)

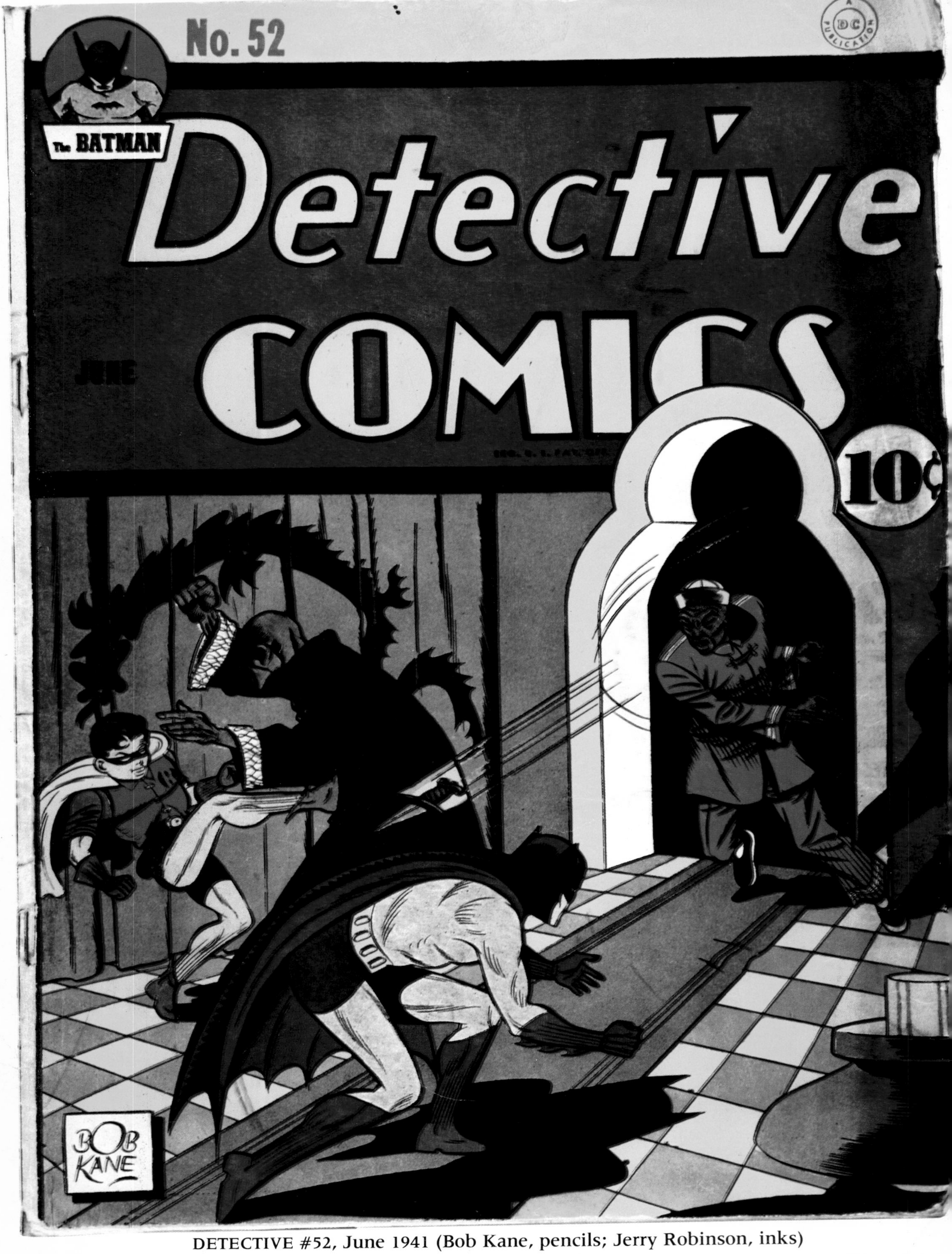
No. 52
A DC PUBLICATION
The BATMAN
Detective
COMICS
JUNE
10¢
BOB KANE

DETECTIVE #52, June 1941 (Bob Kane, pencils; Jerry Robinson, inks)

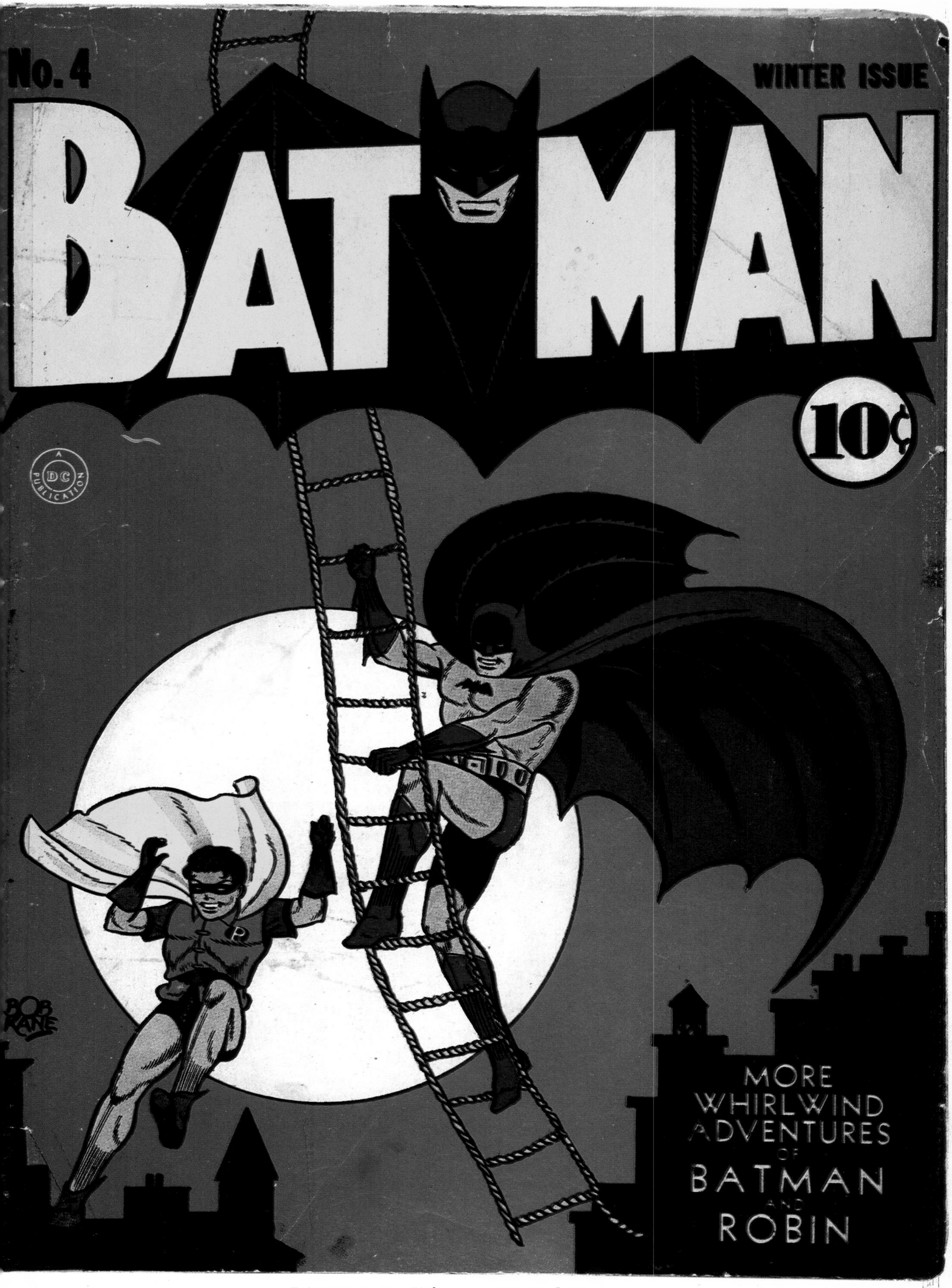
No. 4
WINTER ISSUE
BATMAN
10¢
A DC PUBLICATION
BOB KANE
MORE WHIRLWIND ADVENTURES OF BATMAN AND ROBIN

BATMAN #4, Winter 1941 (Bob Kane)

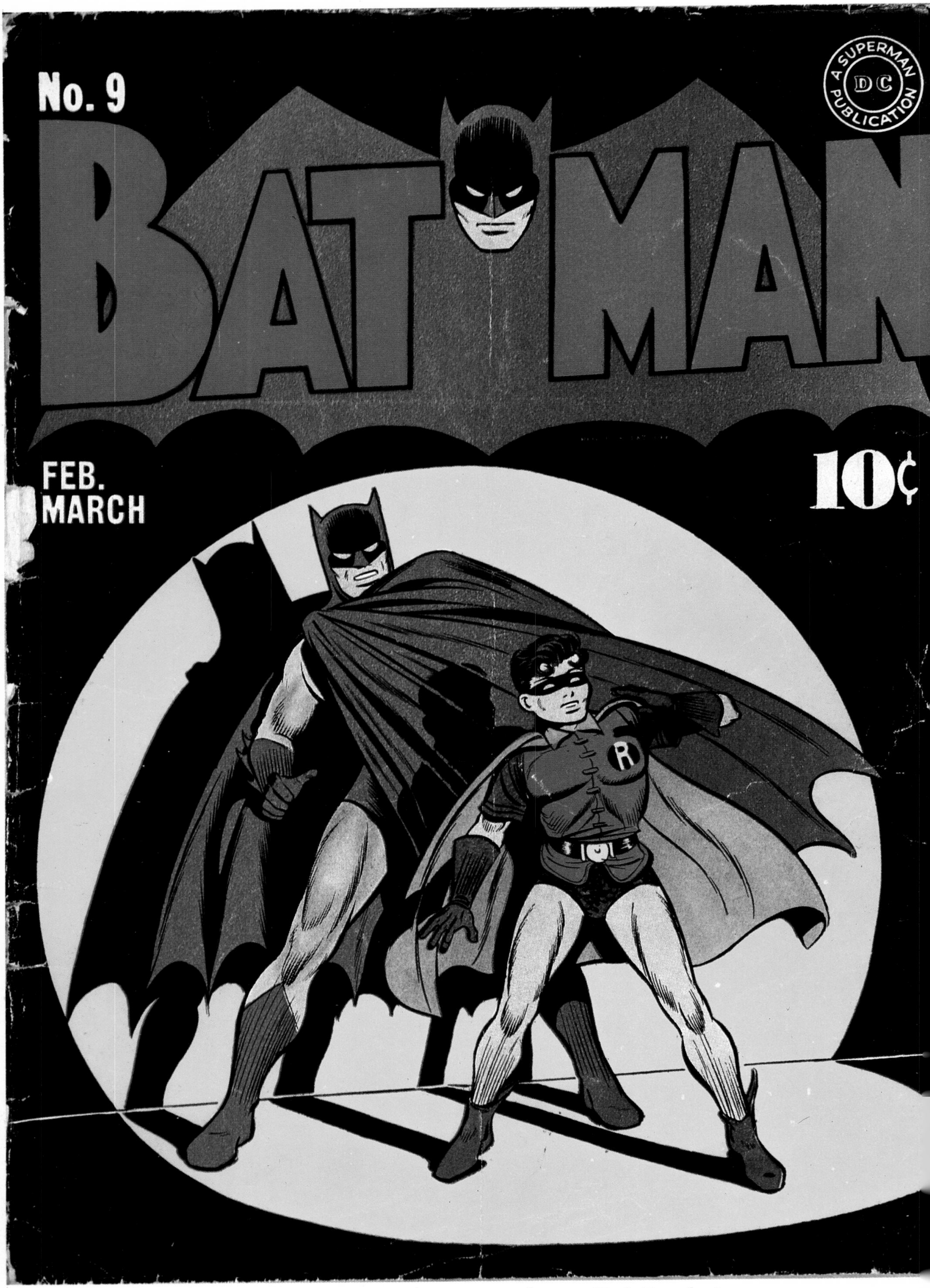
No. 9
BATMAN
A SUPERMAN DC PUBLICATION
FEB. MARCH
10¢

BATMAN #9, February/March 1942 (Jack Burnley)

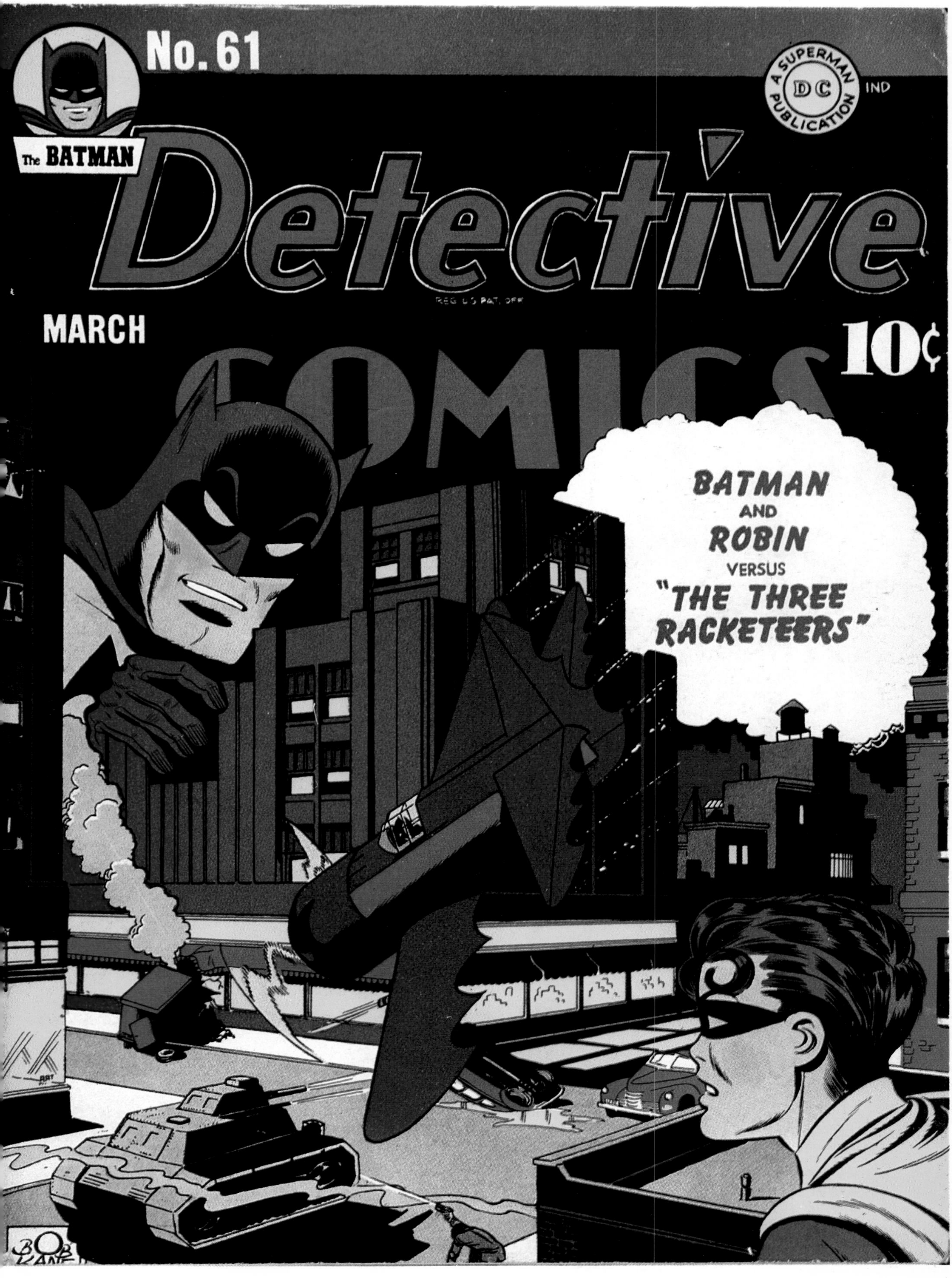
No. 61
The BATMAN
A SUPERMAN DC PUBLICATION
IND
Detective
REG. U.S. PAT. OFF.
MARCH
10¢
COMICS
BATMAN
AND
ROBIN
VERSUS
"THE THREE
RACKETEERS"
BOB KANE

DETECTIVE #61, March 1942 (Bob Kane)

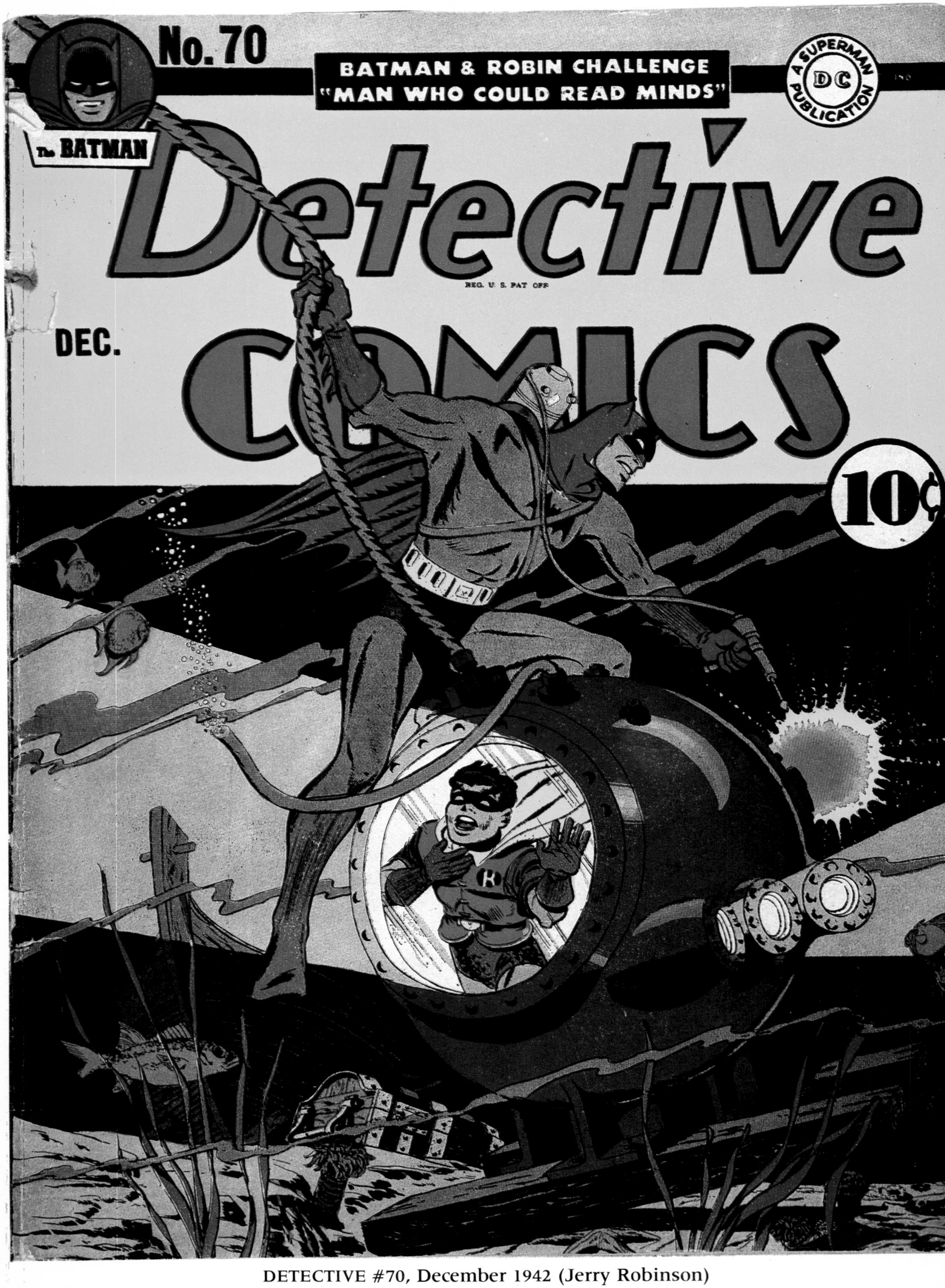

No. 70
The BATMAN
BATMAN & ROBIN CHALLENGE
"MAN WHO COULD READ MINDS"
A SUPERMAN DC PUBLICATION
Detective
REG. U. S. PAT OFF
DEC.
COMICS
10¢

DETECTIVE #70, December 1942 (Jerry Robinson)

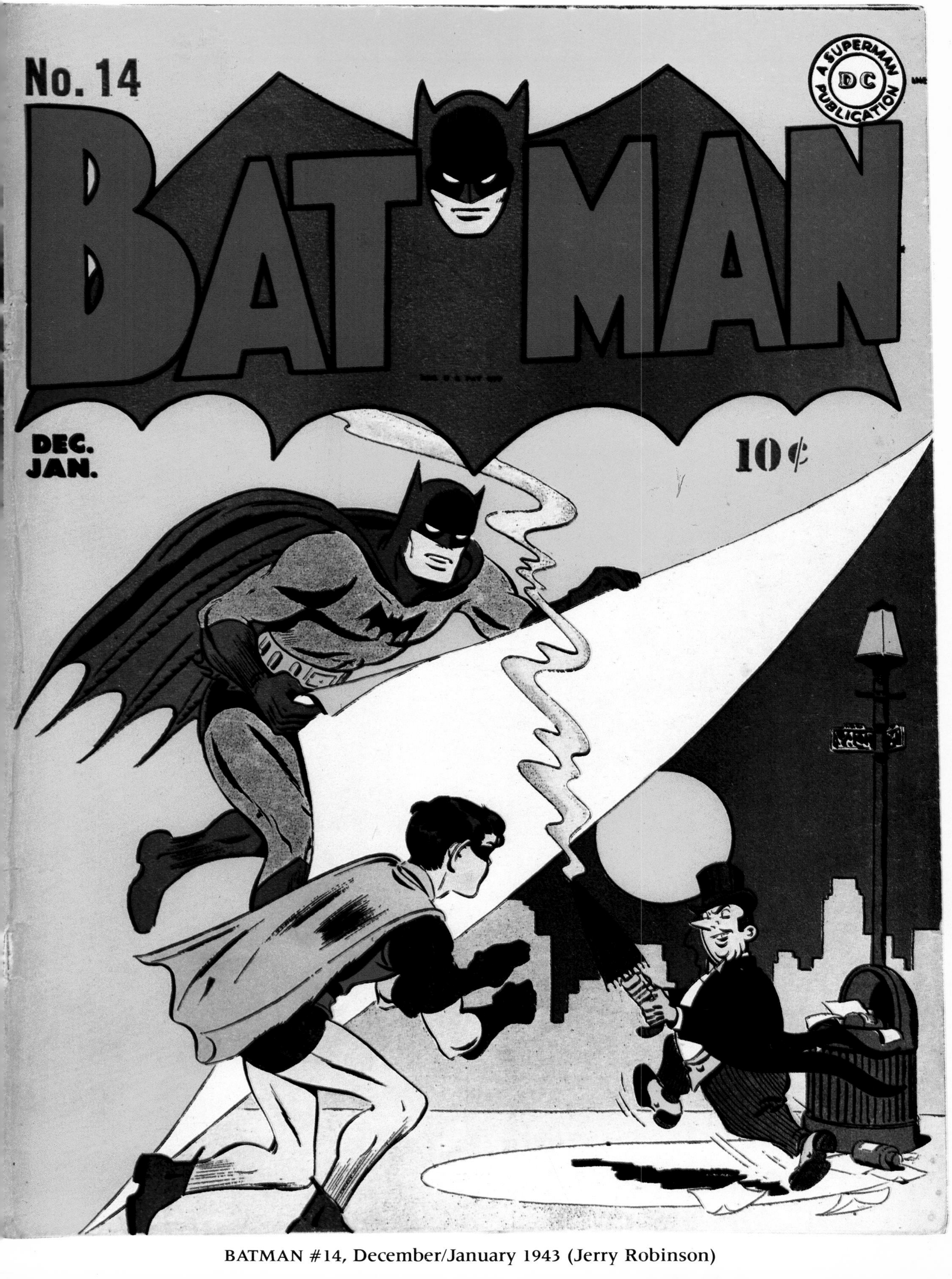
No. 14
BATMAN
A SUPERMAN DC PUBLICATION
DEC. JAN.
10¢

BATMAN #14, December/January 1943 (Jerry Robinson)

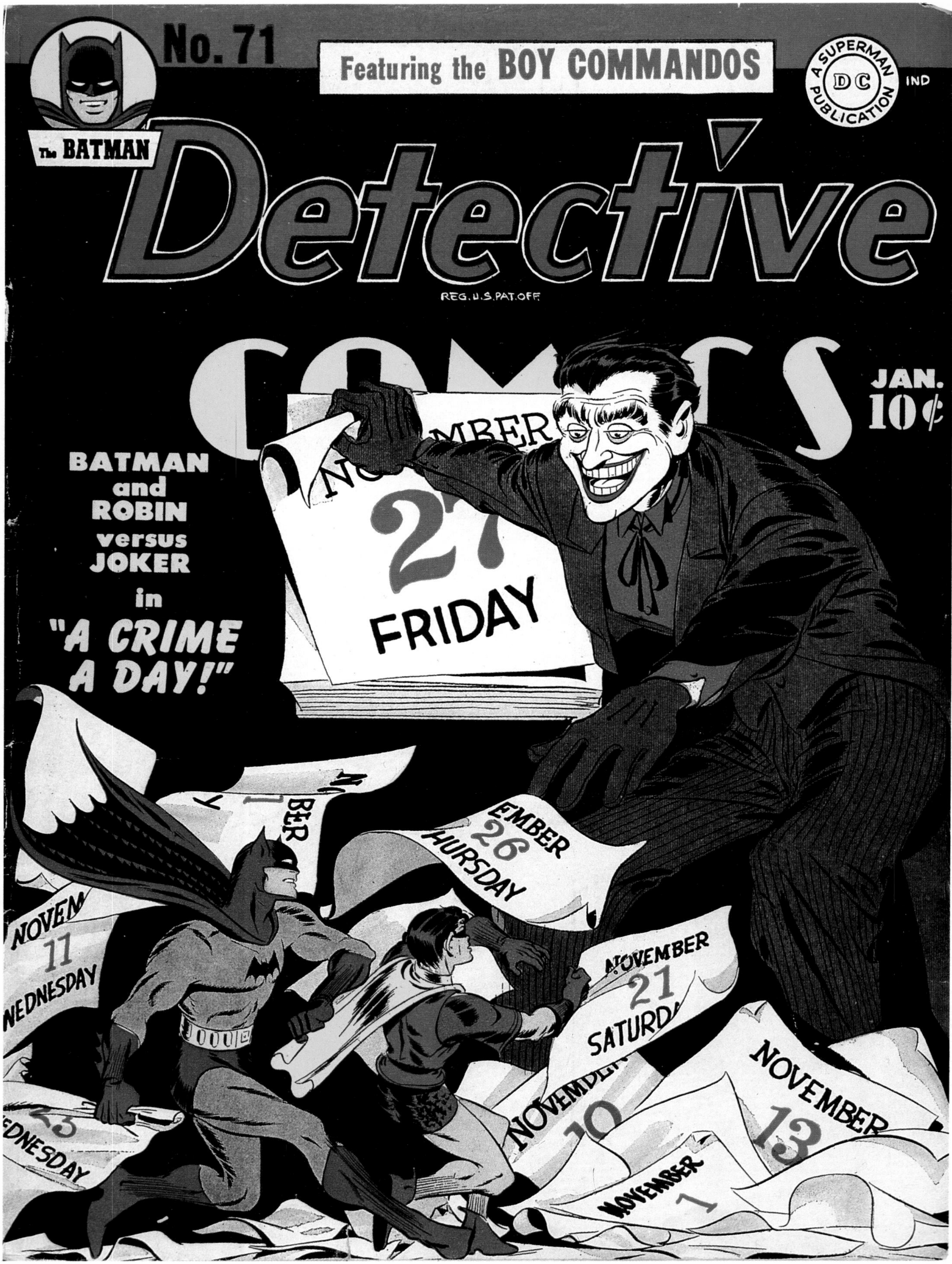

No. 71
Featuring the BOY COMMANDOS
A SUPERMAN DC PUBLICATION
IND
The BATMAN
Detective
REG. U.S. PAT. OFF.
COMICS
JAN.
10¢
BATMAN
and
ROBIN
versus
JOKER
in
"A CRIME
A DAY!"
27
FRIDAY
26
HURSDAY
NOVEMBER
21
SATURD
NOVEMBER
13
NOVEMBER
1
WEDNESDAY

DETECTIVE #71, January 1943 (Jerry Robinson)

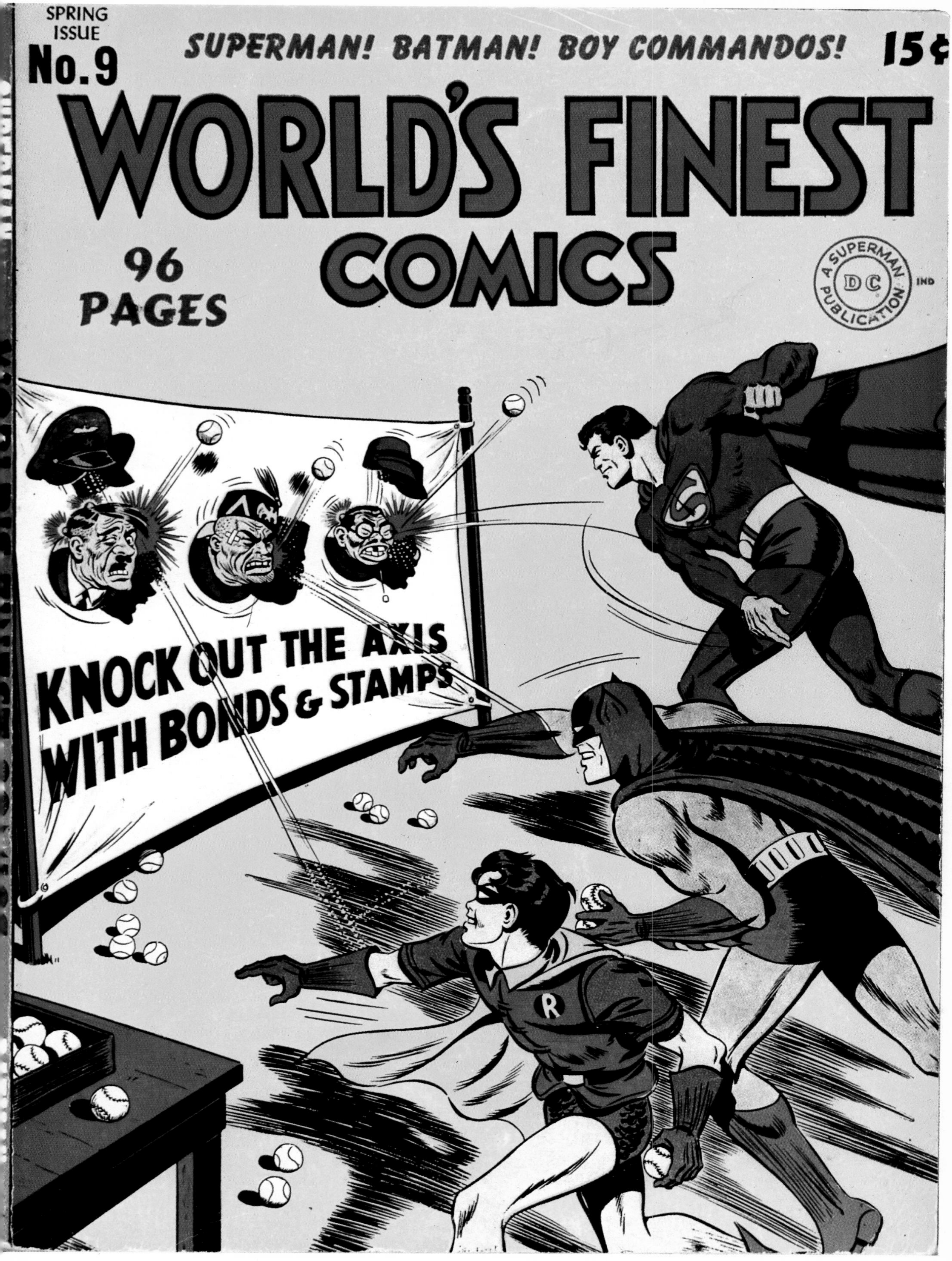
SPRING ISSUE
No. 9
SUPERMAN! BATMAN! BOY COMMANDOS!
15¢
WORLD'S FINEST COMICS
96 PAGES
A SUPERMAN DC PUBLICATION
KNOCK OUT THE AXIS WITH BONDS & STAMPS

WORLD'S FINEST #9, Spring 1943 (Jack Burnley)

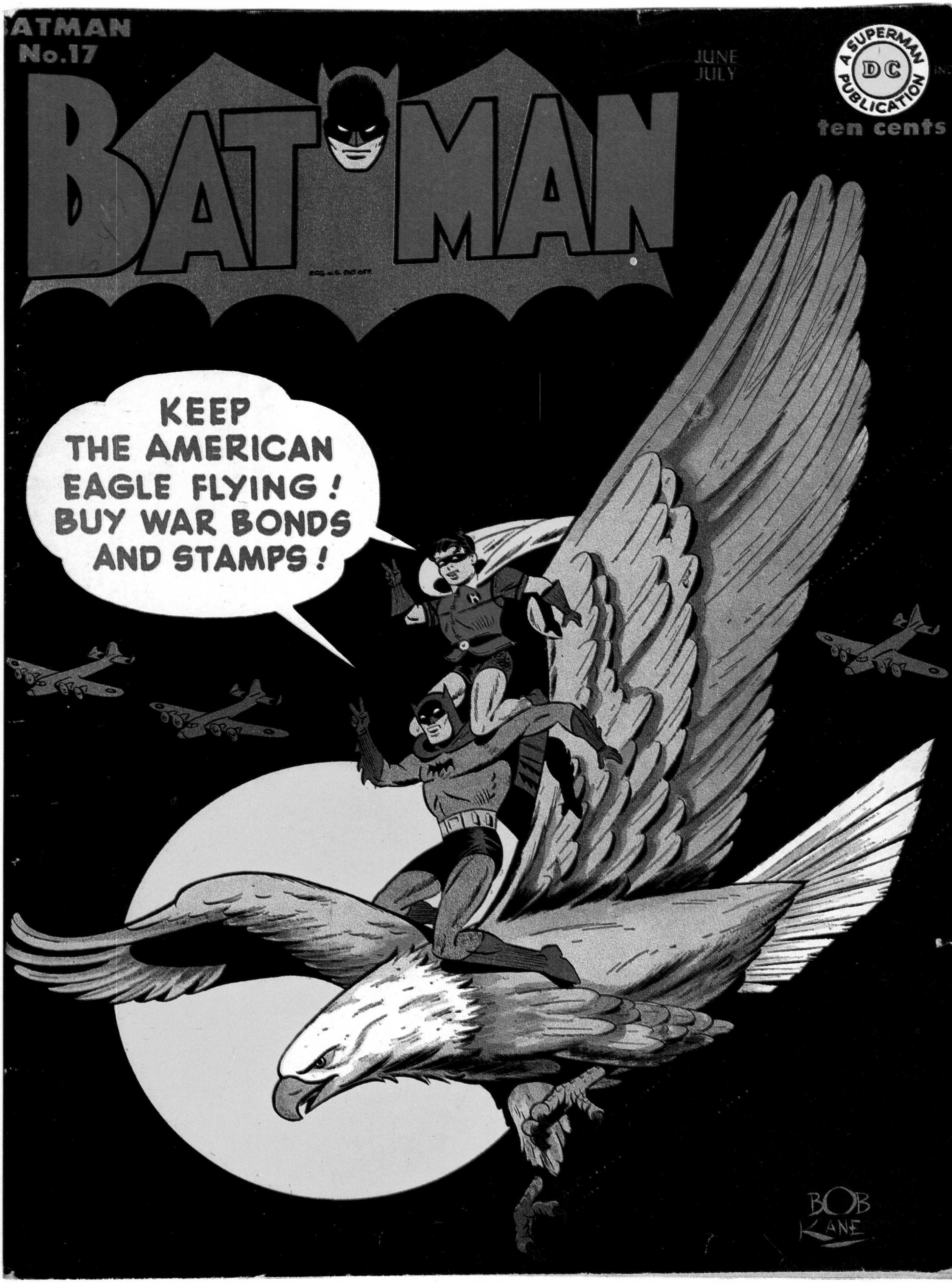
BATMAN
No.17
JUNE
JULY
A SUPERMAN DC PUBLICATION
ten cents
BATMAN
KEEP THE AMERICAN EAGLE FLYING! BUY WAR BONDS AND STAMPS!
BOB KANE

BATMAN #17, June/July 1943 (Bob Kane)

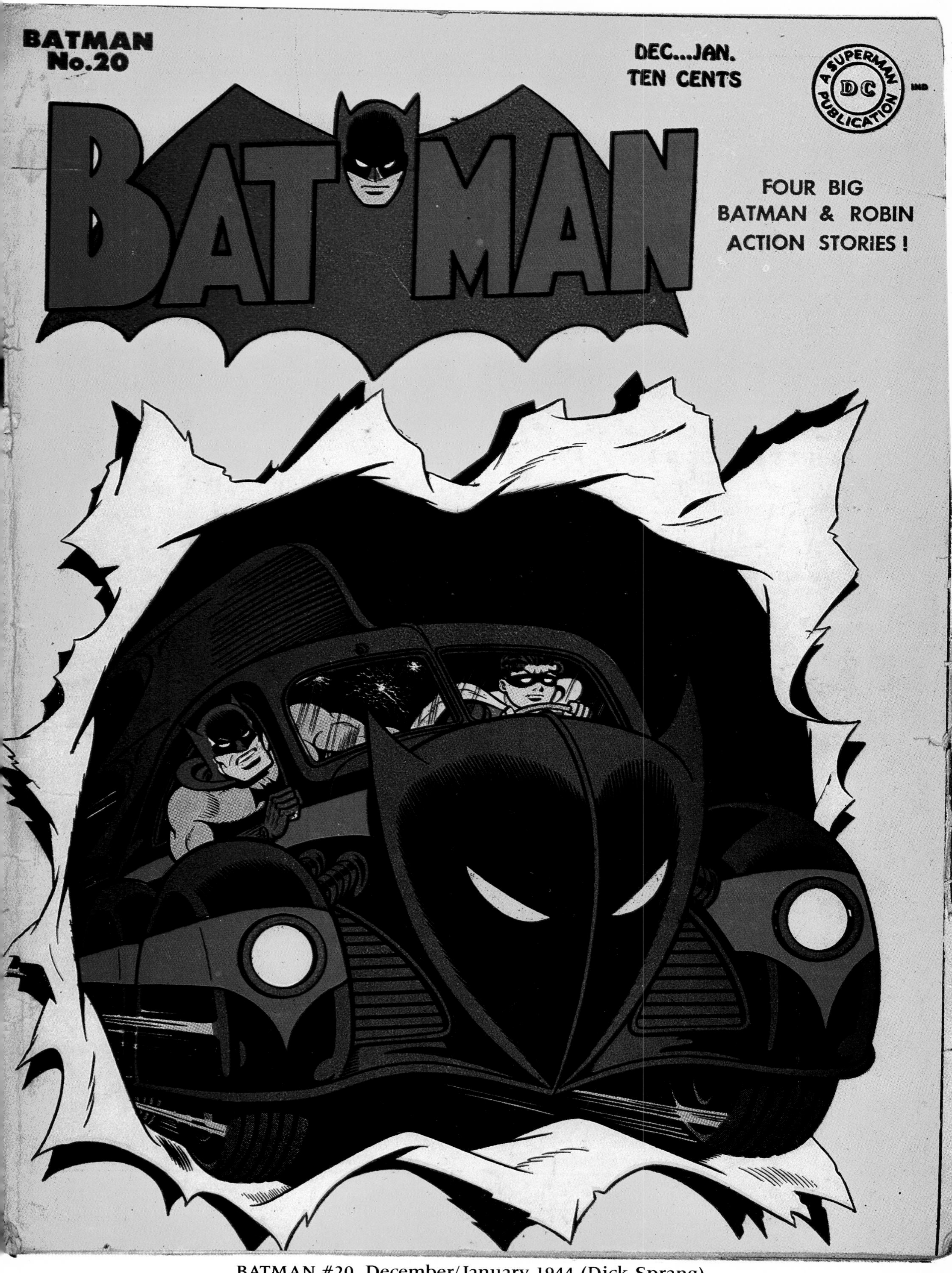
BATMAN
No.20
DEC...JAN.
TEN CENTS
A SUPERMAN DC PUBLICATION
BATMAN
FOUR BIG
BATMAN & ROBIN
ACTION STORIES!

BATMAN #20, December/January 1944 (Dick Sprang)

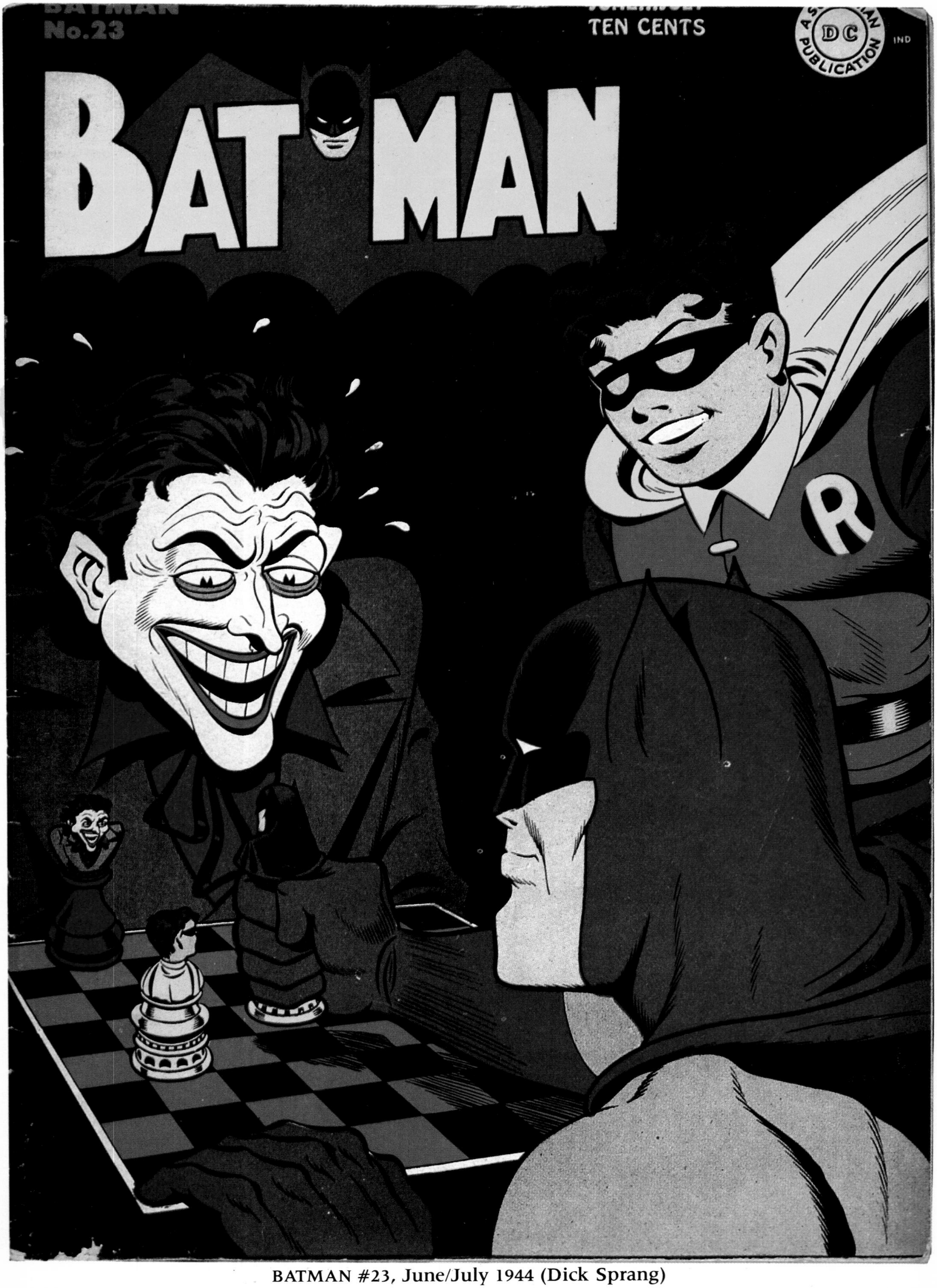
No.23
TEN CENTS
DC
PUBLICATION
IND
BATMAN
R

BATMAN #23, June/July 1944 (Dick Sprang)

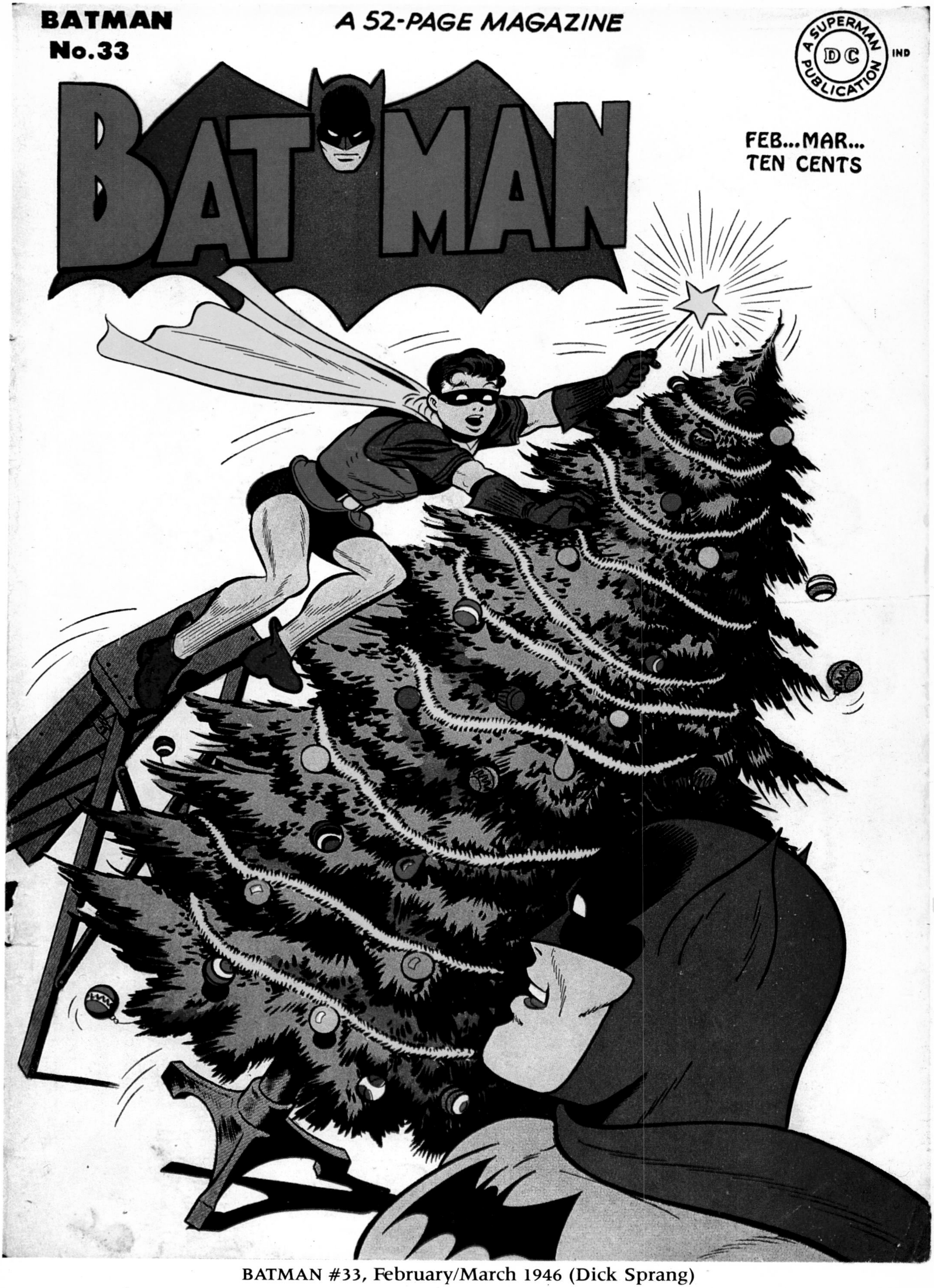
BATMAN
No.33
A 52-PAGE MAGAZINE
A SUPERMAN DC PUBLICATION
IND
BATMAN
FEB...MAR...
TEN CENTS

BATMAN #33, February/March 1946 (Dick Sprang)

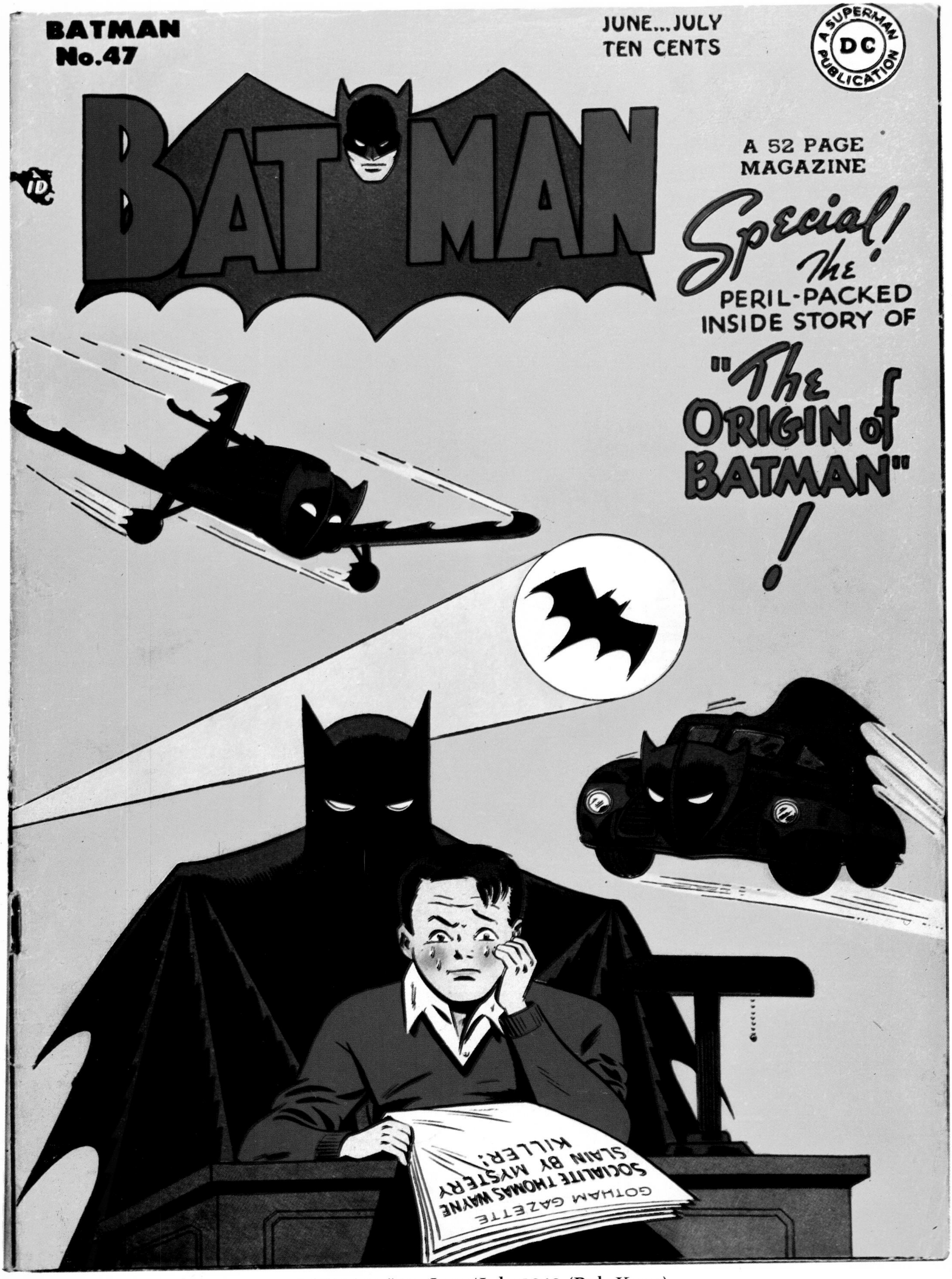
BATMAN
No.47
JUNE...JULY
TEN CENTS
A SUPERMAN DC PUBLICATION
BATMAN
A 52 PAGE
MAGAZINE
Special! The
PERIL-PACKED
INSIDE STORY OF
"The ORIGIN of BATMAN"!
GOTHAM GAZETTE
SOCIALITE THOMAS WAYNE
SLAIN BY MYSTERY
KILLER!

BATMAN #47, June/July 1948 (Bob Kane)

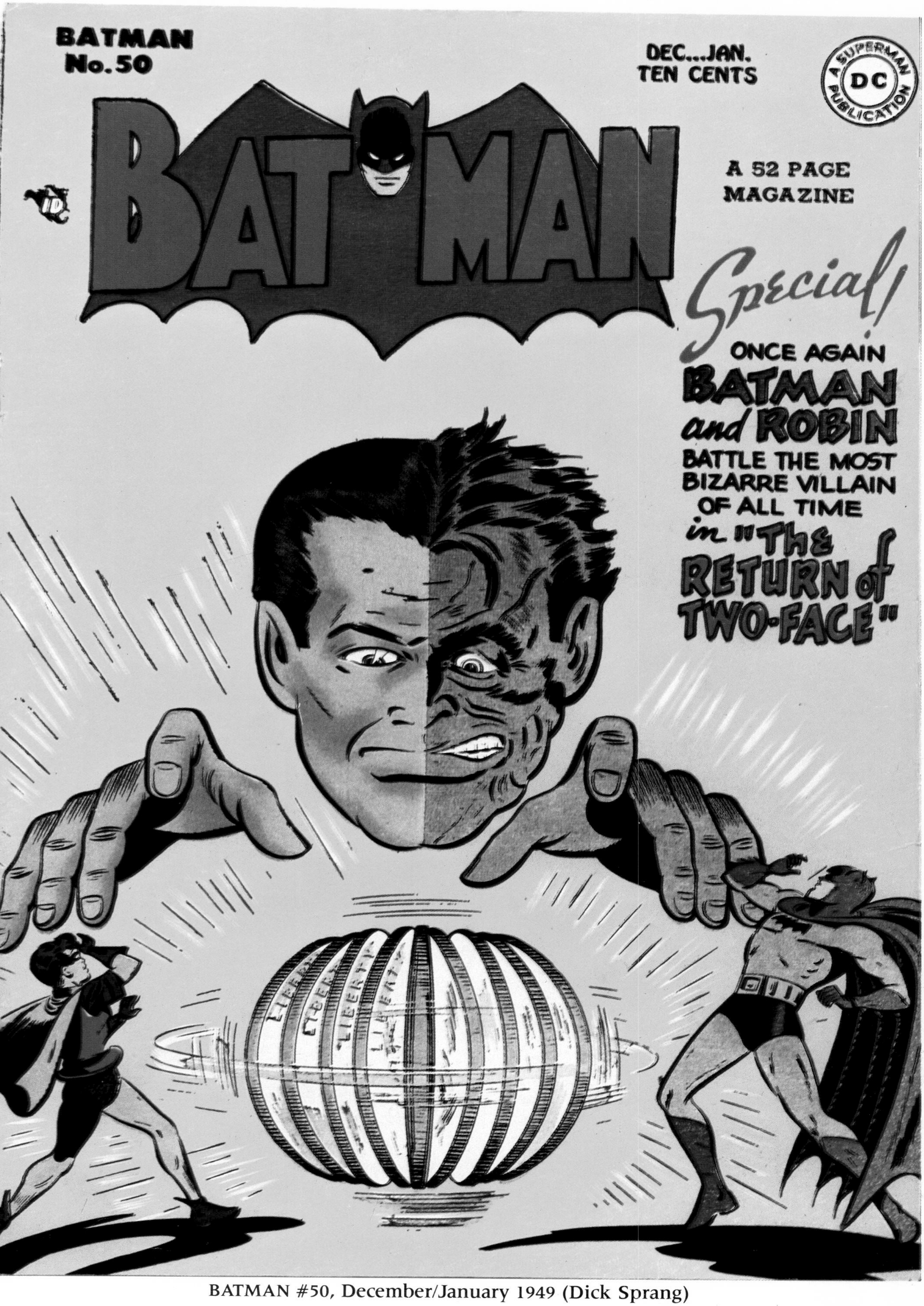
BATMAN
No.50
DEC...JAN.
TEN CENTS
A SUPERMAN
DC
PUBLICATION
BATMAN
A 52 PAGE
MAGAZINE
Special!
ONCE AGAIN
BATMAN
and ROBIN
BATTLE THE MOST
BIZARRE VILLAIN
OF ALL TIME
in "The
RETURN of
TWO-FACE"

BATMAN #50, December/January 1949 (Dick Sprang)

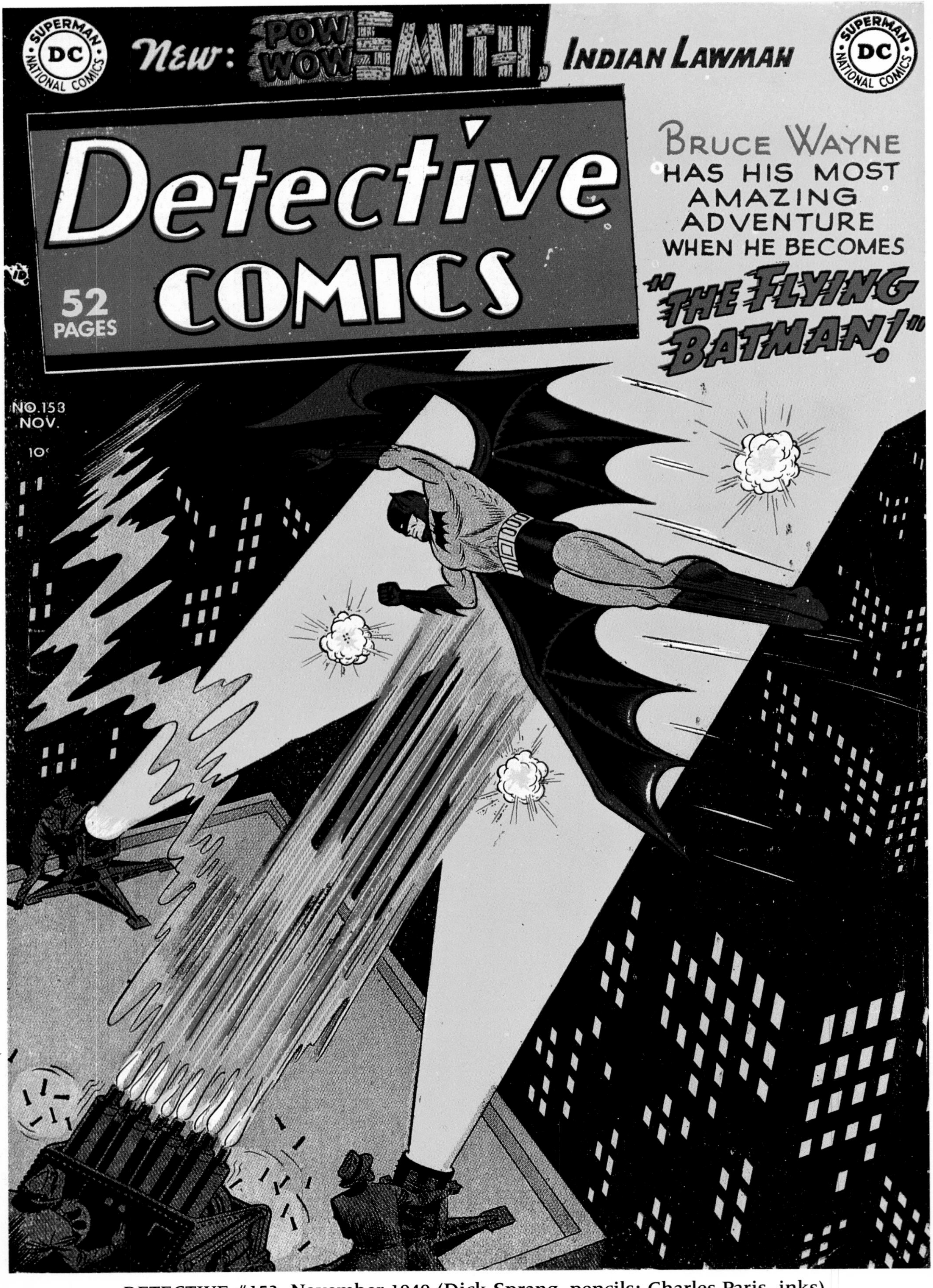
New: POW WOW SMITH, INDIAN LAWMAN
SUPERMAN DC NATIONAL COMICS
Detective COMICS
52 PAGES
NO.153 NOV.
BRUCE WAYNE HAS HIS MOST AMAZING ADVENTURE WHEN HE BECOMES "THE FLYING BATMAN!"

DETECTIVE #153, November 1949 (Dick Sprang, pencils; Charles Paris, inks)

"Gangster movies, more than any other genre, crystallized the flavour of the 'thirties, with its portent for chaos and social disaster," Terence Pettigrew writes in his book *Raising Hell: The Rebel in the Movies*. " . . . The gangster figure was an energetic, resourceful go-getter, hungry for success, taking what he wanted from a society too timid or dim-witted to obstruct him . . . .

"For a while, the law's apparent powerlessness had the effect of turning public enemies such as John Dillinger and Machine Gun Kelly into folk-heroes. The early 'thirties crime movies often showed the law out-manoeuvred at every turn or in some smart gangboss's pocket—which in many cases was no exaggeration of the truth."[5]

But the national mood would quickly sour on the notion of folk-hero criminals. Rather than a frontier romance, the American gangster would become a symbol of the corruption of an entire nation.

A 1931 poll listed the "paramount problems of the United States" as, in order of severity: prohibition, administration of justice, and lawlessness.

The opening salvo against the crime lords came not from law enforcement agencies, but from a manifestation of the crime-fighter mythos. Although the character was a cop, he did not have to worry about the red tape that sometimes frustrated real-life police agencies. In his comic strip world there were no cops or judges on the take, no blurring of the borders between right and wrong. The cop's name was Dick Tracy, the creation of cartoonist Chester Gould.

"Chester Gould produced a contemporary knight in shining armor who was ready, willing, and able to fight the criminal with, if necessary, the criminal's own weapons, to fight the toughs with equal or even greater toughness," detective fiction writer Ellery Queen wrote. "Chester Gould created Dick Tracy to meet the desperate need of the times. Dick Tracy's job was to regain the almost vanished respect for the law and to be the instrument of his enforcement. As Gould once said in an interview: 'I decided that if the police couldn't catch the gangsters, I'd create a fellow who would.'"[6]

In 1931 the first Dick Tracy promotion in the Chicago Tribune Newspapers Syndicate noted:

"Dick Tracy is a plainclothes man, a member of the police department. He is the prototype of the present hero—but on the *positive* side. An antidote to maudlin sympathy with society's enemies, he creates no glamour for the underworld."[7]

Dick Tracy's war on crime, just like Batman's crusade to come, was a personal one. During a holdup Tracy watched gunmen rob and kill the father of his fiancée, Tess Trueheart, kidnap Tess, and knock him unconscious. When the police arrived and Tracy regained consciousness, he looked heavenward and made an oath to Tess over the body of her fallen father that he would avenge the outrage. That day he joined the police force as a plainclothes detective. (Tess was rescued, but Tracy's war against crime would continue.)

Although Gould himself loved to weave sticky, inextricable webs around his villains, his square-jawed detective was no sadist. Tracy would, however, use force whenever he had to.

"If you just go along and don't raise a big stink every so often with Dick Tracy, it means you're starting to go flat," Gould once wrote. "My last real stink was when Tracy vaporized

2. Paul Braddon, "The Man in Black," in *The Boys of New York*, December 16 and 23, 1882. Material used with the permission of the San Francisco Academy of Comic Art; Bill Blackbeard, director.

3. Baroness Emmuska Orczy, *The Scarlet Pimpernel* (Laurel, New York: Lightyear Press, 1981), p. 31.

4. Johnston McCulley, *The Mark of Zorro* (New York: The American Reprint Company, 1976), pp. 297–98.

5. Terence Pettigrew, *Raising Hell: The Rebel in the Movies* (New York: St. Martin's Press, 1986), pp. 8–9, 20–21.

6. Ellery Queen, "Introduction: The Importance of Being Ernest; or, The Survival of the Finest," in *The Celebrated Cases of Dick Tracy*, ed. Herb Galewitz (New York: Bonanza Books, 1970), p. xxi.

7. "Dick Tracy: Detective," advertisement reproduction in *Dick Tracy: America's Most Famous Detective*, ed. Bill Crouch, Jr. (Secaucus, New Jersey: Citadel Press, 1987), p. 48.

the villain Intro with a laser cannon. Somebody asks Tracy where Intro is and the response is, 'You're breathing him.' "[8]

Real-life crime fighting began to catch up with the emerging mythos when new laws passed in 1933 strengthened the Federal Bureau of Investigation, including giving the agency jurisdiction over crimes previously handled by local police forces.

In a provocative article for *True Detective Mysteries* entitled "Roosevelt Puts Crime on the Spot," Joseph B. Keenan, assistant attorney general of the United States, challenged the "super-criminals" who had "roamed the length and breadth of the land, leaving bloodshed and terror in their wake.

"Uncle Sam is definitely aroused," Keenan wrote in his 1934 article. "The underworld has overstepped itself, and its challenge is being heeded....

"We are going to give no quarter and ask none... For this is war—war to the finish."

Keenan reserved special scorn for the killer John Dillinger, who had escaped from an Indiana prison and was still at large. In his article Keenan penned a vitriolic message to Dillinger—and to the youth of the country—about the bitter fruit you could expect from a life of crime.

"Although Dillinger is a murderer, and like a cornered rat has shot his way out on two occasions, it is to be hoped that the youth of our country will not be disillusioned as to his frame of mind.... He realizes that the law is on his trail and that sooner or later he will be brought to justice.... He is like a desperate, frightened animal, and has forfeited his right to remain alive on this earth among civilized people, and at this very hour realizes that he is not assured of a peaceful hour's rest, and that any moment is apt to be his last one. If he is the super-criminal, what an unenviable ambition he has realized! What a loathsome, pitiful creature he has become!"[9]

With the red tape cut, the Bureau went after the underworld with a vengeance. The publicity highlight of their early campaign was when FBI agents finally caught up with Dillinger and shot him dead as he left a Chicago movie theater. The picture playing there was *Manhattan Melodrama,* wherein a gangster dies in the electric chair.

With the Bureau crossing off the names on its Most Wanted list with bullet holes, Hollywood began seeing the box office potential of gangbusters over gangsters. FBI Director J. Edgar Hoover, initially angered about filmdom's previous glorification of crime, eventually allowed Warner Brothers to produce *G-Men* (1935), which featured James Cagney as a former New York slum delinquent who joins the FBI when a close friend is murdered by hoodlums.

But it was in the pulps, named for the cheap, wood-fiber-flecked paper on which they were printed, that the crime-fighting mythos was truly joined by some of the greatest crime fighters ever to spring from the imagination.

There was Doc Savage, a bronzed-skinned

TRUE DETECTIVE
AUGUST 25¢
MACFADDEN PUBLICATION
Mysteries
ROOSEVELT
Puts
CRIME
on the SPOT

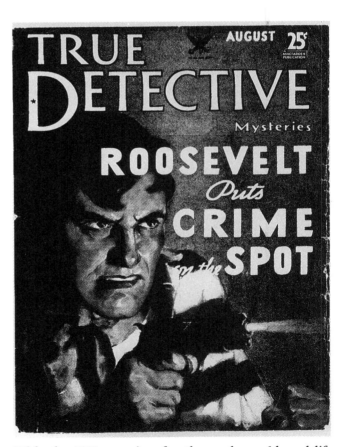

With the FBI gunning for the underworld real-life crimebusting was almost as exciting as the movie crime pictures. (True Detective Mysteries, *August 1934, cover.*)

giant who was a super athlete and scientist. With five coadventurers he traveled the world, battling evil masterminds.

There was the Shadow, a crime fighter with the "power to cloud men's minds" and the grim wherewithal to execute evildoers on the spot with hot bursts of explosive justice from his twin .45 automatics.

The Shadow's public identity was that of the urbane Lamont Cranston. But like Don Diego Vega, Bruce Wayne, and others of their ilk, they truly came alive the moment they dropped their positions of wealth and social breeding and adopted their mysterious guises and plunged into their deadly missions. For Cranston, this meant wearing a concealing slouch hat and a swirling black cloak, and dropping into the shadowy depths of the criminal underworld, his chilling laughter heralding his presence in the darkness.

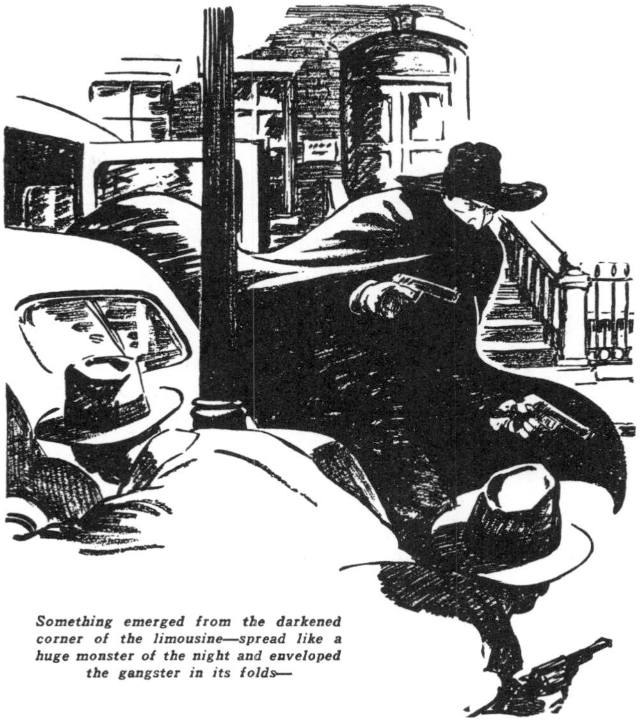
Something emerged from the darkened corner of the limousine—spread like a huge monster of the night and enveloped the gangster in its folds—

The Shadow Annual, *1942 edition, "The Living Shadow," by Maxwell Grant, (art and text), p. 5.*

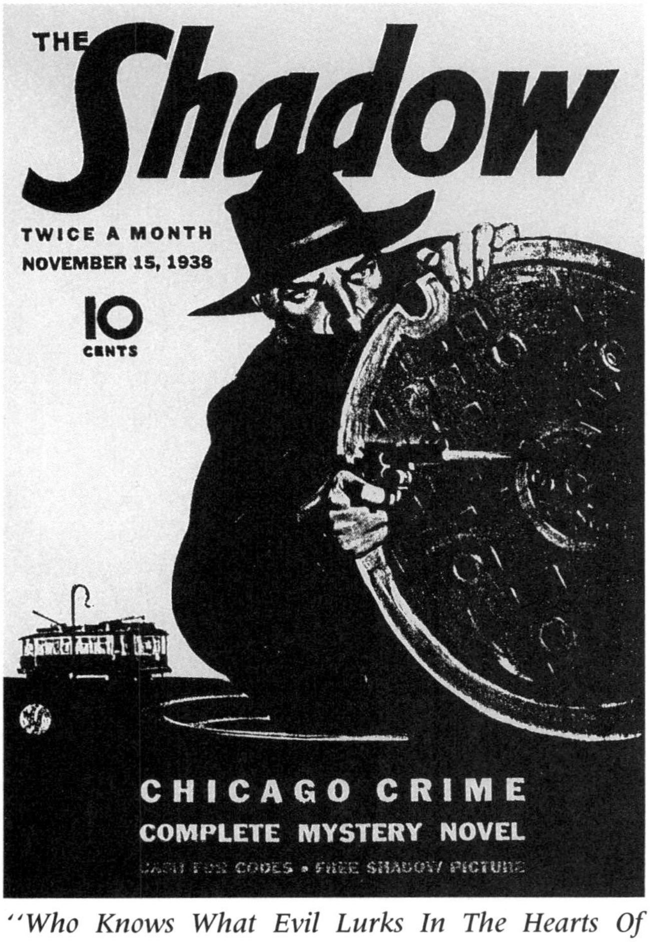
THE Shadow
TWICE A MONTH
NOVEMBER 15, 1938
10 CENTS
CHICAGO CRIME
COMPLETE MYSTERY NOVEL

"Who Knows What Evil Lurks In The Hearts Of Men?" Why, The Shadow, of course. (The Shadow, *November 15, 1938, cover. [Street & Smith Publications, Inc.]*)

"The Shadow epitomized the pulp heroes and the style of writing used to tell their exploits," Jim Steranko writes in his *History of Comics*. "Stories were all plot. Characterization was almost nonexistent. It would have slowed down the juggernaut velocity of the script. . . . Dialogue was always to the point. Every single word kept the story moving."[10]

Detective crime stories were a stable of the pulps. The tradition of the modern detective story had begun with Edgar Allan Poe's "The Murders in the Rue Morgue." Sir Arthur Conan Doyle's famed master of deduction, Sherlock Holmes (along with Dr. Watson, his assistant) helped personalize the genre. In 1929 Dashiell Hammett (an alumnus of the pulp *Black Mask*) introduced the world-weary private eye Sam Spade in *The Maltese Falcon*.

---

8. Ibid., p. 41.
9. Joseph B. Keenan, "Roosevelt Puts Crime on the Spot," *True Detective Mysteries*, August 1934, pp. 7, 10, 69.
10. Steranko, *History of Comics*, p. 15.

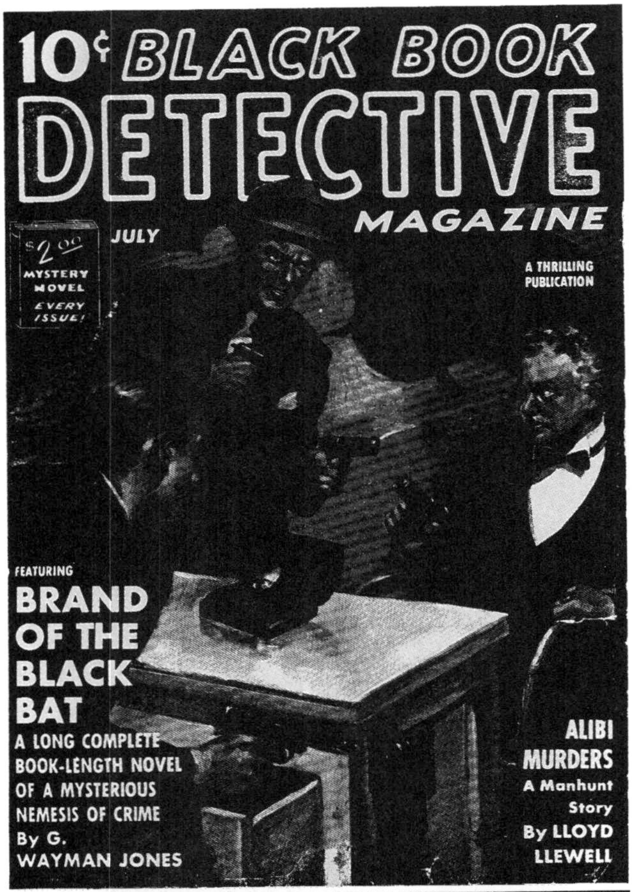
10¢ BLACK BOOK
DETECTIVE
MAGAZINE
JULY
$2.00 MYSTERY NOVEL EVERY ISSUE!
A THRILLING PUBLICATION
FEATURING
BRAND OF THE BLACK BAT
A LONG COMPLETE BOOK-LENGTH NOVEL OF A MYSTERIOUS NEMESIS OF CRIME
By G. WAYMAN JONES
ALIBI MURDERS
A Manhunt Story
By LLOYD LLEWELL

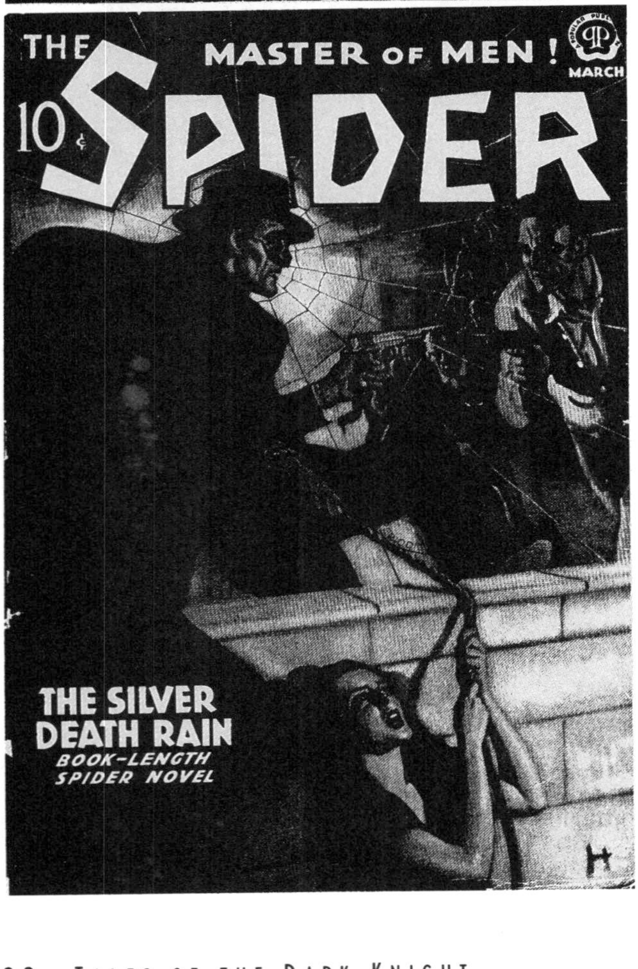
THE
MASTER OF MEN!
MARCH
10¢
SPIDER
THE SILVER DEATH RAIN
BOOK-LENGTH SPIDER NOVEL

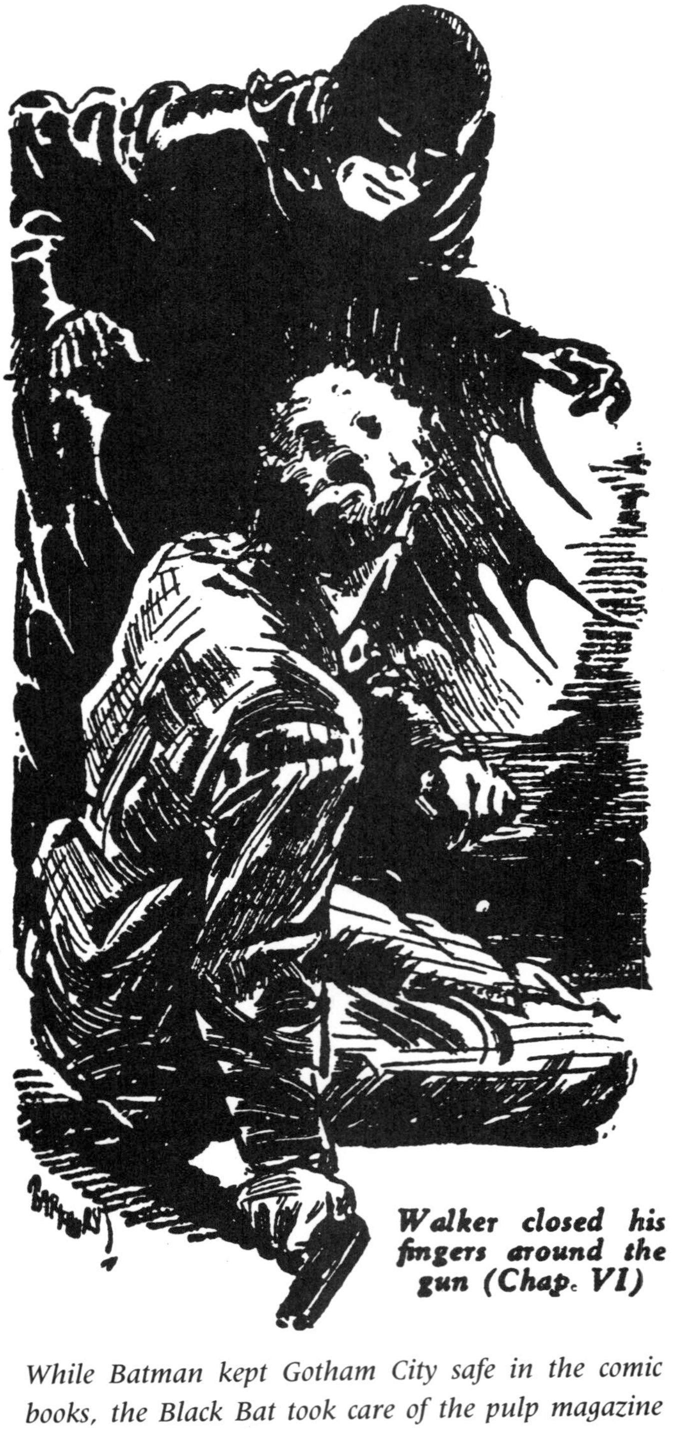
Walker closed his fingers around the gun (Chap. VI)

While Batman kept Gotham City safe in the comic books, the Black Bat took care of the pulp magazine underworld. (Top left: Black Book Detective, *July 1939, cover [New York: Better Publications, Inc.].*) Top right: *The Black Bat makes his first appearance. (Black Book Detective, July 1939.)* Bottom left: *The pantheon of pulp crimebusters, including such legendary names as The Shadow, Doc Savage, the Black Bat, and The Spider, helped set the moody tone of the comic book crimefighters to come.* (The Spider: Master of Men!, *March 1939, cover [New York: Popular Publications].)*

In 1939 a new crime fighter joined the pulp ranks in the pages of *Black Book Detective.* In one of the great coincidences in the whole of the crime-fighting mythos, the Black Bat, a character almost identical to Batman, appeared in the July 1939 issue of *Black Book Detective.* (Bob Kane reports he had no knowledge of the Black Bat when he created his Caped Crusader. At the time there was talk of a lawsuit against Batman, which was never pursued. The Black Bat's career lasted until the winter of 1953.)

Like the Batman, the Black Bat wore black clothing with a black hood concealing his face and a black coat that was fashioned to resemble bat's wings. The guise was designed to strike terror into the hearts of criminals. But he differed in one major respect from the crime-fighting code of The Batman:

"The police sought him also, in his Black Bat role, for he cared nothing for the red tape of the law," went the explanation in *Black Book Detective.* "He shot when necessary, burglarized if by so doing he could outwit crooks. He battled them hard, and when it had to be, killers died at his hands."[11]

The bat imagery was a natural part of the mythic mix of shadows and fears that fueled the melodramas of the pulps and tabloids. Even as far back as 1909–1910 a London tabloid, *Jack's Paper: The New Adventure Story Weekly,* featured "The Human Bat," a man actually outfitted in a hang-gliding ensemble that resembled gigantic wings when he stretched his arms out.[12]

By the end of the 1930s the pulp tradition was waning. The new medium of comic books was emerging as a livelier alternative to the plodding pace of the pulps.

A Golden Age for the mythos of the crime fighter was just over the horizon. All the legendary fictional crime fighters who had gone before would help Bob Kane, a young cartoonist from the Bronx, to create his famous, dark avenger of evil.

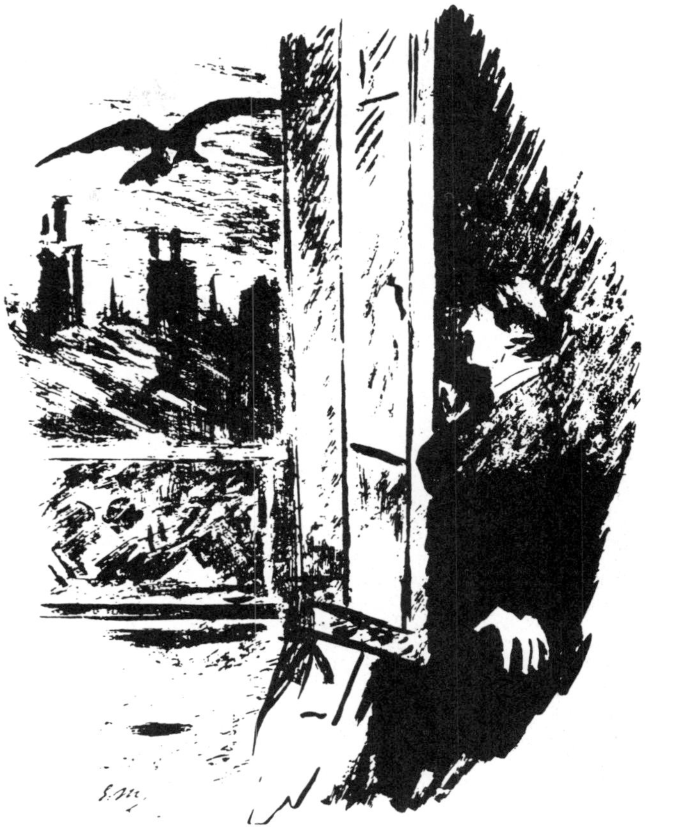

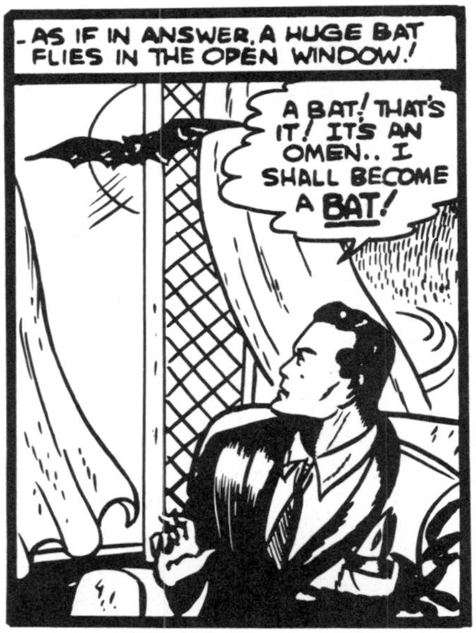

AS IF IN ANSWER, A HUGE BAT FLIES IN THE OPEN WINDOW!
A BAT! THAT'S IT! IT'S AN OMEN.. I SHALL BECOME A BAT!

The dark world of the Batman has always been plugged into a moody mythos. This lithograph that illustrated the original New York Mirror *publication of Edgar Allan Poe's* The Raven (top) *bears an uncanny resemblance to a certain pivotal moment in the life of Bruce Wayne.* (Batman *#1, Spring 1940, "The Legend of the Batman," p. 2 [panel].) Lithograph taken from: Wolf Mankowitz,* The Extraordinary Mr. Poe *(New York: Summit Books, 1978), p. 183.*

11. Ibid., p. 23.
12. Reference: The San Francisco Academy of Cartoon Art.

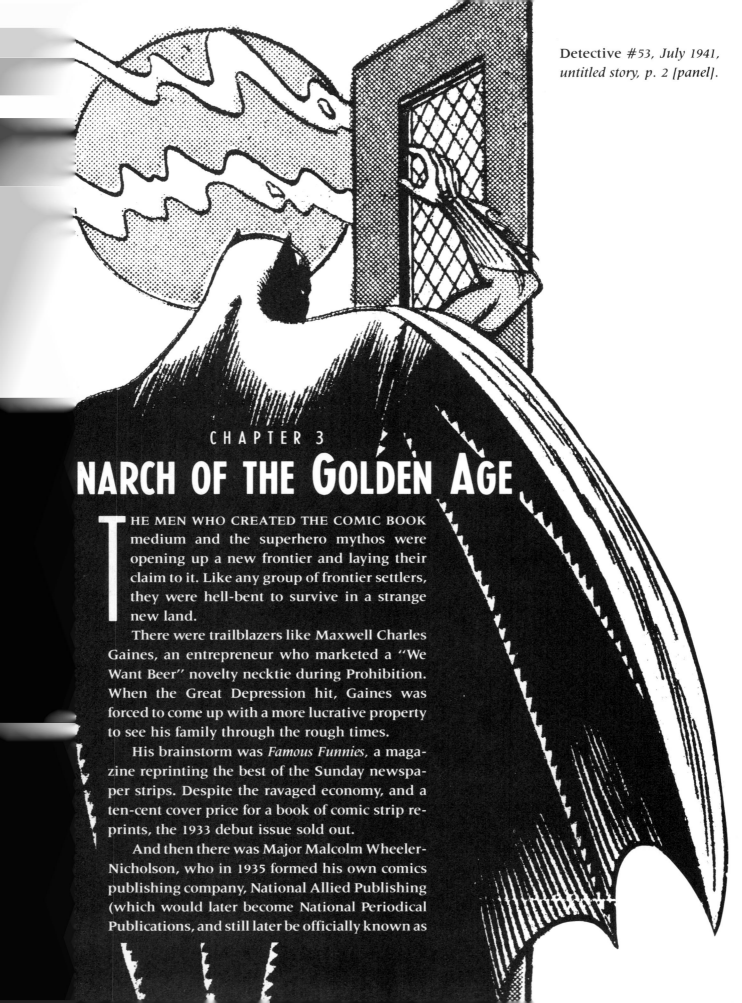

*Detective #53, July 1941,
untitled story, p. 2 [panel].*

CHAPTER 3
NARCH OF THE GOLDEN AGE

THE MEN WHO CREATED THE COMIC BOOK medium and the superhero mythos were opening up a new frontier and laying their claim to it. Like any group of frontier settlers, they were hell-bent to survive in a strange new land.

There were trailblazers like Maxwell Charles Gaines, an entrepreneur who marketed a "We Want Beer" novelty necktie during Prohibition. When the Great Depression hit, Gaines was forced to come up with a more lucrative property to see his family through the rough times.

His brainstorm was *Famous Funnies*, a magazine reprinting the best of the Sunday newspaper strips. Despite the ravaged economy, and a ten-cent cover price for a book of comic strip reprints, the 1933 debut issue sold out.

And then there was Major Malcolm Wheeler-Nicholson, who in 1935 formed his own comics publishing company, National Allied Publishing (which would later become National Periodical Publications, and still later be officially known as

DC). The major went Gaines's comic book efforts one better and in 1935 released the first issue of *New Fun Comics,* the first title to feature original comic strips.

Major Nicholson was a true adventurer, someone whose life story seemed straight out of the pulps. Let him tell you in his own words:

"I was born in the South, raised on a western ranch, worked for a while as a cub newspaper reporter, became a second lieutenant of cavalry in the regular army, chased bandits on the Mexican border, fought fevers and played polo in the Philippines, led a battalion of infantry against the Bolsheviki in Siberia, helped straighten out the affairs of the army in France, commanded the headquarters cavalry of the American force in the Rhine, and left the army as a major equipped with a select assortment of racing and polo cups, a sabre, and a battered typewriter."[1]

Nicholson sold out his interests in his comic book company to Harry Donenfeld in 1937. That same year Donenfeld produced a crime-busting action title called *Detective Comics.*

Early issues of the title showcased the seminal works of youthful creators who would soon become legends in the field: Jerry Siegel and Joe Shuster, who had been developing the idea for Superman since 1933, produced "Spy" and "Slam Bradley" for the magazine; Will Eisner, who was in the process of cofounding a comics studio with Jerry Iger (and who, in 1940, would create his great crime fighter "the Spirit"), did the no-nonsense thriller "Mess 'Em Up"; and Bob Kane was turning out detective stories as well as the pratfalls of "Cleo and Clancy," a pair of slapstick flatfoots who resembled Laurel and Hardy.

And then the comic book industry was changed for all time when Donenfeld and his new business partner, Jack Liebowitz, released the first issue of *Action Comics* in 1938.

On the cover was Superman, lifting a car over his head and ramming the front end into the side of a mountain. This was no mere gun-toting, two-fisted crime buster, but a god made human.

The two-hundred-thousand-copy print run of *Action* 1 quickly sold out. Suddenly the creation of a truly "super" hero revealed a verdant path in the comic book frontier. To be good, a hero now had to be super.

DC editor Vincent Sullivan asked then twenty-two-year-old Bob Kane to come up with a superhero to complement the Man of Steel.

So many different elements were plugged into the creation of Batman, it's amazing the character did not emerge as an amorphous oddity.

The heroic form of Superman and even Flash Gordon provided inspiration, as did the quixotic quality of the Long Ranger, Zorro, the Phantom, and other masked heroes. The dark menace of the Shadow provided a piece of the puzzle, as did the grim purpose (and weird villains) of detective Dick Tracy. The swashbuckling adventure of such films as *The Mark of Zorro* and *Robin Hood* was

Bob Kane, creator of Batman.

1. Ron Goulart, *Great History of Comic Books* (Chicago: Contemporary Books, Inc., 1986), p. 55.

also present at the creation, as was *The Bat Whispers,* where the villain wore a bat costume. Even Kane's childhood memory of a book reprinting Leonardo da Vinci's original sketches for a glider contraption was important—they reminded him of bat wings.

Soon the first sketches of Batman were completed.

"I called in my friend Bill Finger who was a pulp writer just starting out to write for the comic books," Kane wrote. "He made several suggestions which enhanced my crude Batman sketch. He told me to remove the eye-balls from the slits in the mask to make it appear more sinister looking, and also to bring the eye-mask that I had originally drawn over his face into a Bat-cowl. After awhile the first innovative Batman sketch was completed.

"However, I soon refined his early look by elongating the short ears on the Bat-cowl, scalloping the side of the long gloves and changing the stiff bat wings into a scalloped Bat-cape which would billow out behind him in action to make him appear like a large bat."[2]

And most important of all, Kane gave Batman a reason for crime fighting.

"Vengeance is a great reason," says Kane. "It would take all the violence, the rage, he felt inside over his parents' murder to fight injustice. It motivated him to take his vengeance on all the

I'M SKETCHING A NEW CHARACTER—A CREATURE OF THE NIGHT—BATMAN! HE'LL BE A DARING, ACROBATIC HERO—A SUPER-SLEUTH WHO, IN A SECRET IDENTITY, WILL FIGHT CRIME.'

WEEKS LATER; AT THE EDITORIAL OFFICES OF SUPERMAN DC MAGAZINES..
YOU'VE CREATED AN EXCITING CHARACTER, SON. I THINK WE CAN DO SOMETHING WITH HIM.
UNDER EXPERT EDITORIAL GUIDANCE, KANE BEGAN TO MOLD HIS CARTOON CREATION INTO A DYNAMIC PERSONALITY..
THE STAGE FOR MY STORIES WILL BE GOTHAM CITY—AND THIS MODEL REPLICA SHOULD HELP ME VISUALIZE IT.' I WANT EVERYTHING TO BE AUTHENTIC, BASED ON SCIENTIFIC FACTS.
3

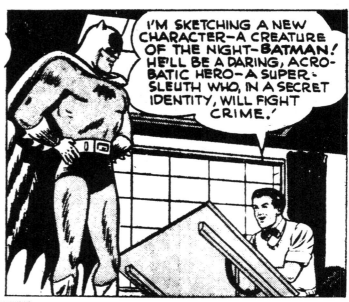

Idealized comic book account of Bob Kane's creation of Batman. (Real Fact Comics #5, *November/December 1946, "The true story of Batman and Robin!" pp. 3–4 [select panels].)*

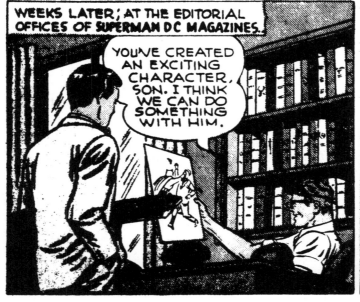

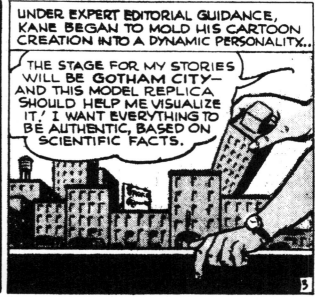

criminal element. Wouldn't you try to hunt the criminal if it happened to you?"

What had emerged from Kane's long creative process was a new breed of crime fighter. Batman was a detective, but he was also a costumed hero. And unlike his fellow superheroes, Batman was a mortal, albeit impressive, figure. Recognizing their unique property, DC accepted Batman. Kane was recognized as the creator and hired to produce the character.

"I was at his house in the Bronx the day he went down with his father to sign the first contract for Batman," recalls Will Eisner, who has known Kane since high school. "We both dreamed of careers. Bob dreamed of theatrical-type success. I wasn't so sure comics wasn't a stopover. It was very surprising when Bob did Batman. We had talked about doing this mysterious thing. My judgment was he was responding to a market, a need, and he turned his hand to it—we had both grown up with the Saturday adventure serials.

"But it's unfair to second-guess him. We were kind of swimming together in the same pond."

Batman became such a hit that a lone adventure in *Detective* only cramped his style. In 1940

2. Bob Kane, "The Dark Detective: The Legacy of Batman," in *History of the DC Universe*, eds. Marv Wolfman and George Perez (New York: DC Comics, 1988), p. 15.

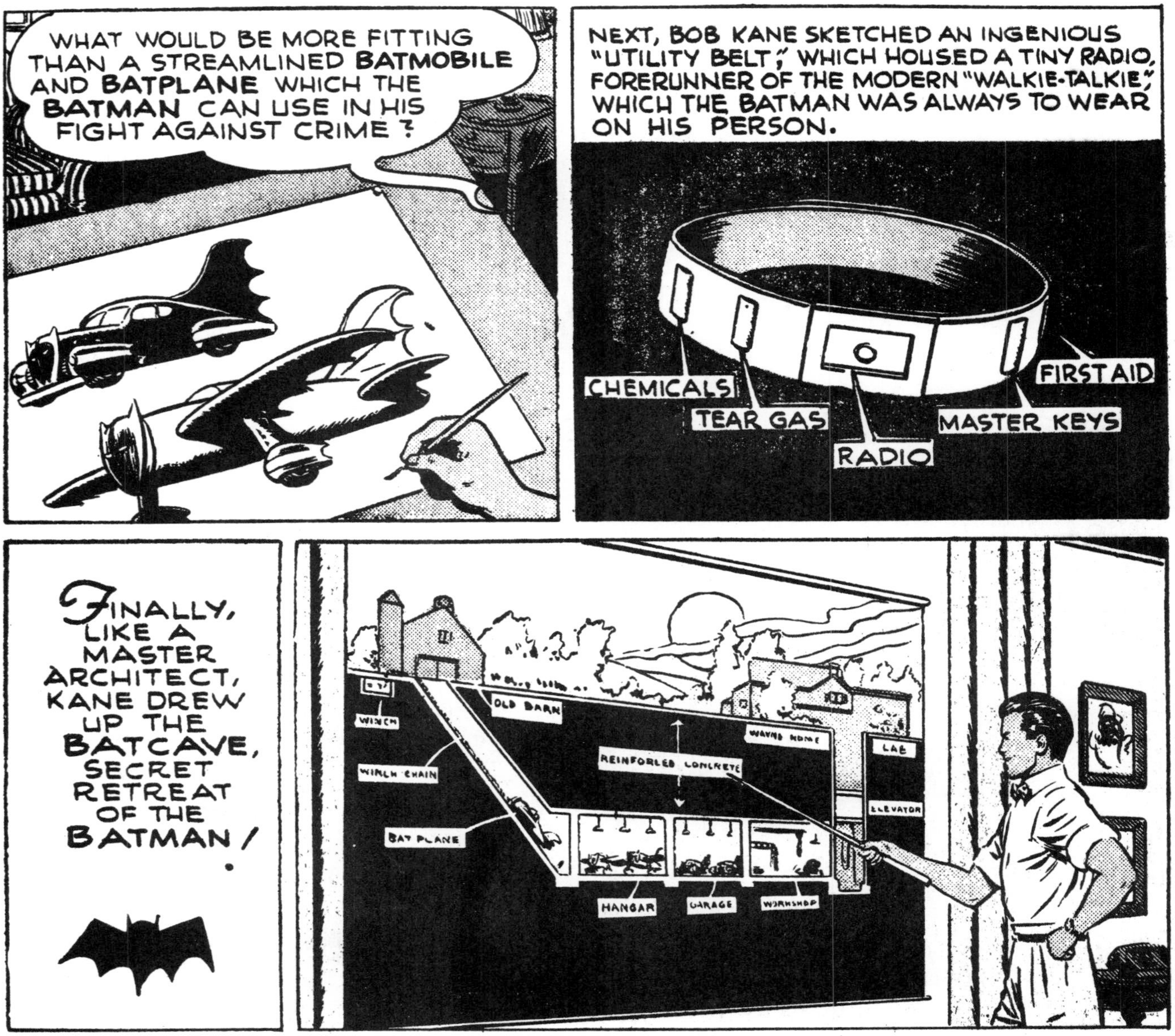

WHAT WOULD BE MORE FITTING THAN A STREAMLINED BATMOBILE AND BATPLANE WHICH THE BATMAN CAN USE IN HIS FIGHT AGAINST CRIME ?
NEXT, BOB KANE SKETCHED AN INGENIOUS "UTILITY BELT," WHICH HOUSED A TINY RADIO, FORERUNNER OF THE MODERN "WALKIE-TALKIE," WHICH THE BATMAN WAS ALWAYS TO WEAR ON HIS PERSON.
CHEMICALS
TEAR GAS
RADIO
MASTER KEYS
FIRST AID
FINALLY, LIKE A MASTER ARCHITECT, KANE DREW UP THE BATCAVE, SECRET RETREAT OF THE BATMAN!
OLD BARN
WINCH
WINCH CHAIN
REINFORCED CONCRETE
WAYNE HOME
LAB
ELEVATOR
BAT PLANE
HANGAR
GARAGE
WORKSHOP

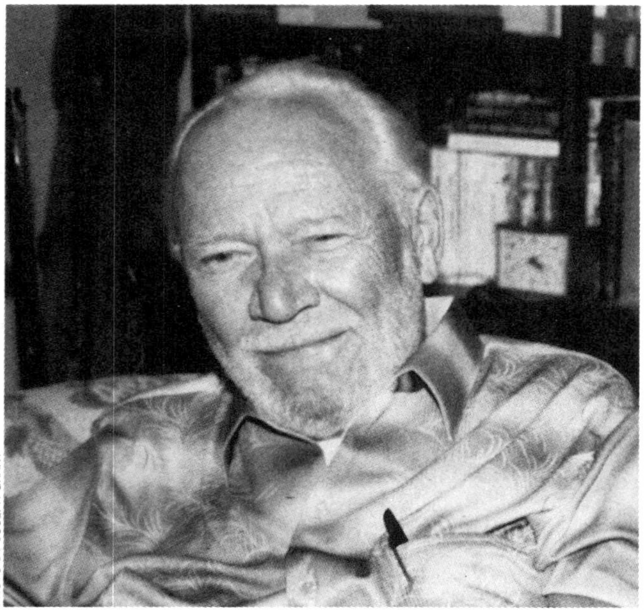

PHOTO BY JOSEPH GRANT

Above: *Dick Sprang drew Batman as a ''wary and resourceful avenger looming in the night.''* Opposite: *''We were always striving for mood,'' recalls Golden Age Batman artist Jerry Robinson.*

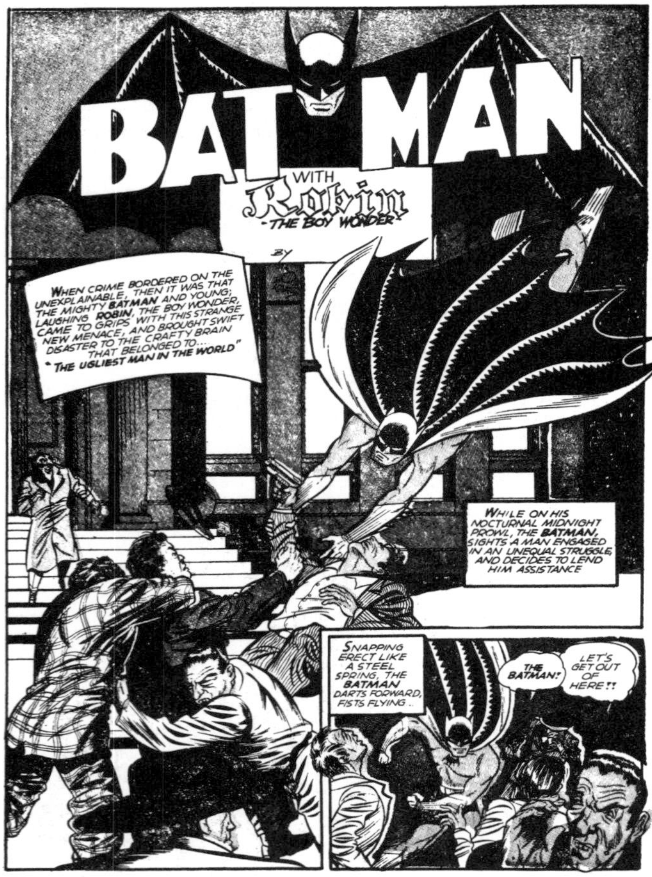

BATMAN
WITH
Robin
-THE BOY WONDER
BY
WHEN CRIME BORDERED ON THE UNEXPLAINABLE, THEN IT WAS THAT THE MIGHTY BATMAN AND YOUNG; LAUGHING ROBIN, THE BOY WONDER, CAME TO GRIPS WITH THIS STRANGE NEW MENACE, AND BROUGHT SWIFT DISASTER TO THE CRAFTY BRAIN THAT BELONGED TO... "THE UGLIEST MAN IN THE WORLD"
WHILE ON HIS NOCTURNAL MIDNIGHT PROWL, THE BATMAN, SIGHTS A MAN ENGAGED IN AN UNEQUAL STRUGGLE, AND DECIDES TO LEND HIM ASSISTANCE
SNAPPING ERECT LIKE A STEEL SPRING, THE BATMAN DARTS FORWARD, FISTS FLYING..
THE BATMAN!
LET'S GET OUT OF HERE!!

It's no contest when a gang of hapless hoods meet the Monarch of The Golden Age. (Batman #3, *Fall 1940, ''The Ugliest Man In The World,'' p. 1 [splash page].*)

Batman 1 hit the stands. With Bill Finger as the main writer, Kane hired other artists who would ghost Batman stories.

Two of the most famous early Batman pencillers were Jerry Robinson, who, with Kane and Finger, formed the original inner circle for Batman creativity, and Dick Sprang.

Sprang, whose impeccable draftsmanship and kinetic imagery contributed to the character for over two decades, remembers the special qualities that made Batman a success.

"For one, he was vulnerable," Sprang says. "He could be overpowered, wounded, and thus identified with. The guy was human. His personality was benign, intelligent, and, as Bruce Wayne, somewhat laid-back. His goals were simple, his method of fighting crime was cerebral as well as physical....

"His billowing cape provided movement in a static medium.... With his ward, Robin, also neatly costumed, he functioned as a father, or pal, figure, guiding the kid to maturity.

"To the artist he wasn't just a dumb macho hero battling his way through a mob of dumb crooks. His superpowers resided in the thrust of his intellect and athletic ability. He commanded respect as a wary and resourceful avenger looming out of the night. I enjoyed projecting his image in an age more innocent than the one we now live in."

Despite the dozens of different creators who would handle the character over the years, there was always a strong editorial vision that kept Batman on track.

"If you think of Batman as a property that's been around for fifty years, it's been predominately edited during that time by Jack Schiff and Julie Schwartz," Says Paul Levitz, DC executive vice president and publisher. "Between them, the two account for thirty-five years or so of his fifty-year history. The people who followed Julie on the series—myself, Dick Giordano, Len Wein, Denny O'Neil—with the exception of myself, all those people had worked for Julie doing Batman, so they represent some form of linear continuity. And although I hadn't been working for

Julie, I had been working as the editorial co-ordinator in those days, so I was fairly closely associated with everything that was going on in the editorial process. It's a pretty straight continuity."

It took sure hands and a strong direction to make Batman a monarch of the Golden Age. The entire era was exciting, but for many creators it was a struggle as well.

"I worked in my apartment, cold and shivering, because my family could not afford coal to heat the rooms," Joe Shuster wrote of the pre-Superman days when he illustrated stories for *Detective Comics*. "I could barely draw because my hands were so frozen. So I wore cotton gloves and several layers of sweaters. I used my mother's breadboard as a drawing board and on Friday nights, the night my mother baked the bread for the weekend meals, she would say, 'Joe, I need the breadboard now.' My artwork went into limbo until she had finished baking."[3]

Most of the comic book creators lived in or around New York City, where all the major publishing houses were. For the comic book creators the dream was an uptown move to the news-paper syndicates. As Will Eisner recalls, "The so-called Golden Age didn't seem so golden at the time.

"A lot of strange and seedy characters were starting comics. I remember one guy who had no teeth, and he'd chew little bits of newspaper while he talked to you.

"It's hard to convey the gritty look of those days—it was a dangerous time. Publishers could start a comic easy if they could get a distributor who would then sell to the newsstands. Starting a comic was dependent on getting a distributor.

"Distributing has always been a rough game. It was real gangster stuff. I remember once when I was selling newspapers on Wall Street during the mid-1930s.... At three in the afternoon a truck would roll by, and packages of papers would be kicked off to all of us who were waiting for our quota. Out of the truck would also come a route man. On his finger was a ring that had a half-moon-shaped claw or hook on it so you could cut the rope that tied the papers together. Occasionally two distributors would show up at

3. Joe Shuster, correspondence, 45th Anniversary letters page, *Detective Comics* 512 (March 1982).

the same corner at the same time, and there'd be a fight. I once saw one guy cut another pretty good with this hook."

But Eisner recalls that in the early years, an artist producing five pages a week could make thirty-five to forty dollars. It wasn't exactly uptown, but it was nothing to walk away from, either. With the pulps drying up, and the comics industry expanding to fill the entertainment void, there was money to be made.

To break into the big publishing houses, the aspiring creator often had to wade through what Jules Feiffer has called "the countless schlock houses" that sprouted up all over town in the rush to make a buck. Struggling cartoonists would work out of their parents' house, or join forces and board together, creating makeshift studios. To meet impossible deadlines required working around the clock, fueled on pots of coffee, deli sandwiches, and dreams.

"We were always on deadline with Batman," Jerry Robinson recalls. "I remember having to do a thirteen-page story over a weekend. So we worked around the clock in shifts. You can only do that when you're very young.

"We invested a lot of our emotions and our creative abilities into Batman. We were constantly trying to think of things to improve, new ways of telling a story, like the first time we did a splash panel. Usually the page was crammed full of panels—the publishers thought they were getting more drawings for the money.

"Actually, the format came from the Sunday papers, because the first comic books were reprints of the newspapers. So they already had that format of all these panels on the standard comics page.

"I remember fighting over making a splash panel on Batman, because we'd have to eliminate a couple of panels on the page. So each of these steps is kind of an innovation. The first time we strung a panel across a page for an effect, or broke up a panel into different shapes to tell the story—every little thing we would do was like a first.... We didn't think of it in historical terms at the time, but it was very exciting."

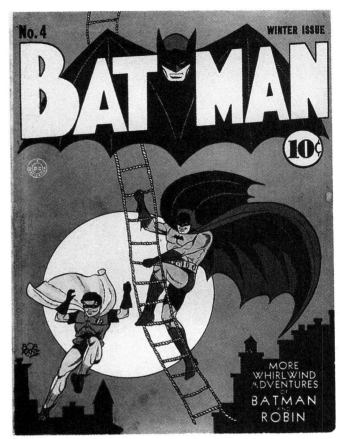

No. 4
WINTER ISSUE
BATMAN
10¢
BOB KANE
MORE WHIRLWIND ADVENTURES OF BATMAN AND ROBIN
Batman *#4, Winter 1941, cover.*

Kane, Finger, and Robinson often met to discuss ideas. The effort was always made to make everything authentic. It was an exacting process that stood out from most of the competition's hastily conceived and executed work, which usually resulted in lackluster stories and crude drawings.

While Kane produced the moody visuals, Finger worked to give the scripts a polished, authentic feel.

"Bill Finger wrote complete scripts, scene by scene, caption by caption, dialogue, and so forth," Robinson says. "And he would attach his research to the script when it was delivered to the artist. He was a very good visual writer; he knew what could translate visually. Bill wasn't a cartoonist himself, but he knew the limitations and the potential of the art form. He was very painstaking. He was always behind in his deadlines because he was so exacting and so hard on himself. He was a perfectionist."

"If Bill Finger had written the script, usual-

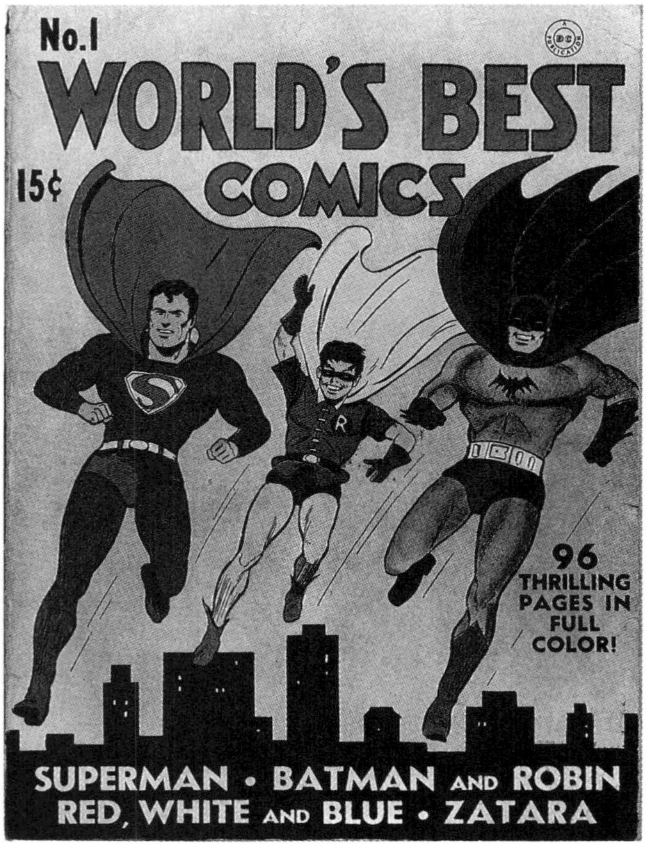
No.1
WORLD'S BEST
COMICS
15¢
96
THRILLING
PAGES IN
FULL
COLOR!
SUPERMAN • BATMAN AND ROBIN
RED, WHITE AND BLUE • ZATARA

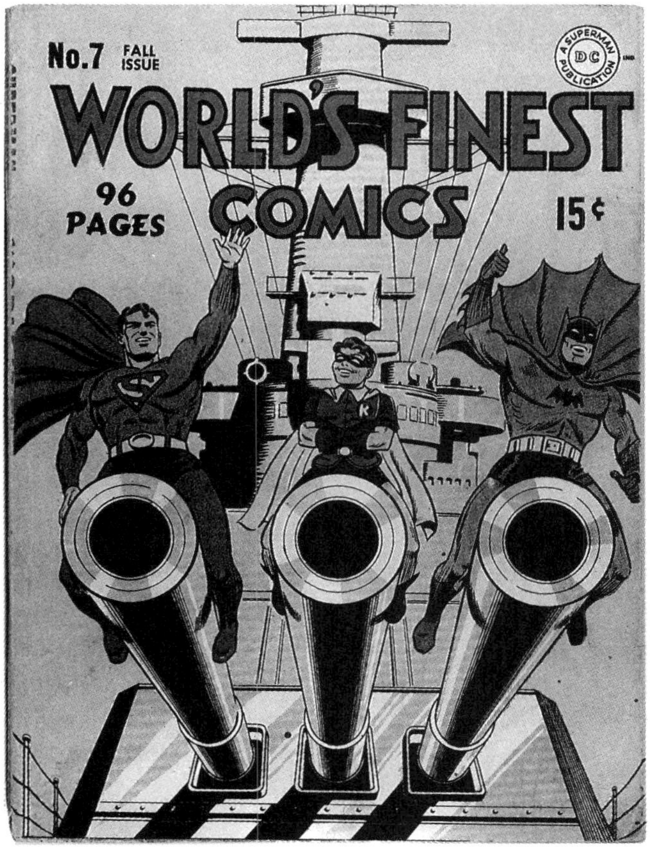
No.7 FALL ISSUE
WORLD'S FINEST
COMICS
96
PAGES
15¢

Left: *The Dynamic Duo and the Man of Steel together for the first time! (The magazine would be changed to* World's Finest Comics *with the next issue.) Although they wouldn't team up until* World's Finest Comics *#71, Golden Age fans had the thrill of seeing this formidable trio star on each cover of that title.* (World's Best Comics *#1, Spring 1941, cover.*) Right: World's Finest Comics *#7, Fall issue 1942, cover.*

ly one of his back-in-time stories, he would generously supply a few clippings that illustrated portions of the physical setting," agrees Dick Sprang, who had left New York early in his career and would work out of his home in Arizona. "These were always welcome supplements to my own extensive files of historical architecture, costumes, ship rigging, weaponry, horse gear, and the like."

The hard work paid off in a large following for Batman. Comic book fans often defined themselves by their allegiance to either Superman or Batman. In his book, *The Great Comic Book Heroes,* Jules Feiffer fancied Superman's invulnerability, but admired Batman's mortal pluck. And then there was the matter of the Dark Knight's world....

"Batman, as a feature, was infinitely better plotted, better villained, and better looking than Superman," Feiffer wrote. "Batman inhabited a world where no one, no matter the time of day, cast anything but long shadows—seen from weird perspectives. Batman's world was scary; Superman's, never."[4]

The debut of the superheroes came at a scary time for the real world as well. Adolf Hitler's Nazi forces were moving in waves of conquest across the globe. With the Japanese bombing of Pearl Harbor, America was called to arms. In addition to his regular Gotham crime-busting duties, Batman would have to drum up support for the Allied cause as well as protect the home front from any Nazi intrusion.

It was to be World War fought on all fronts—including the pages of comic books.

4. Jules Feiffer, *The Great Comic Book Heroes* (New York: Dial Press, 1965), pp. 27–28.

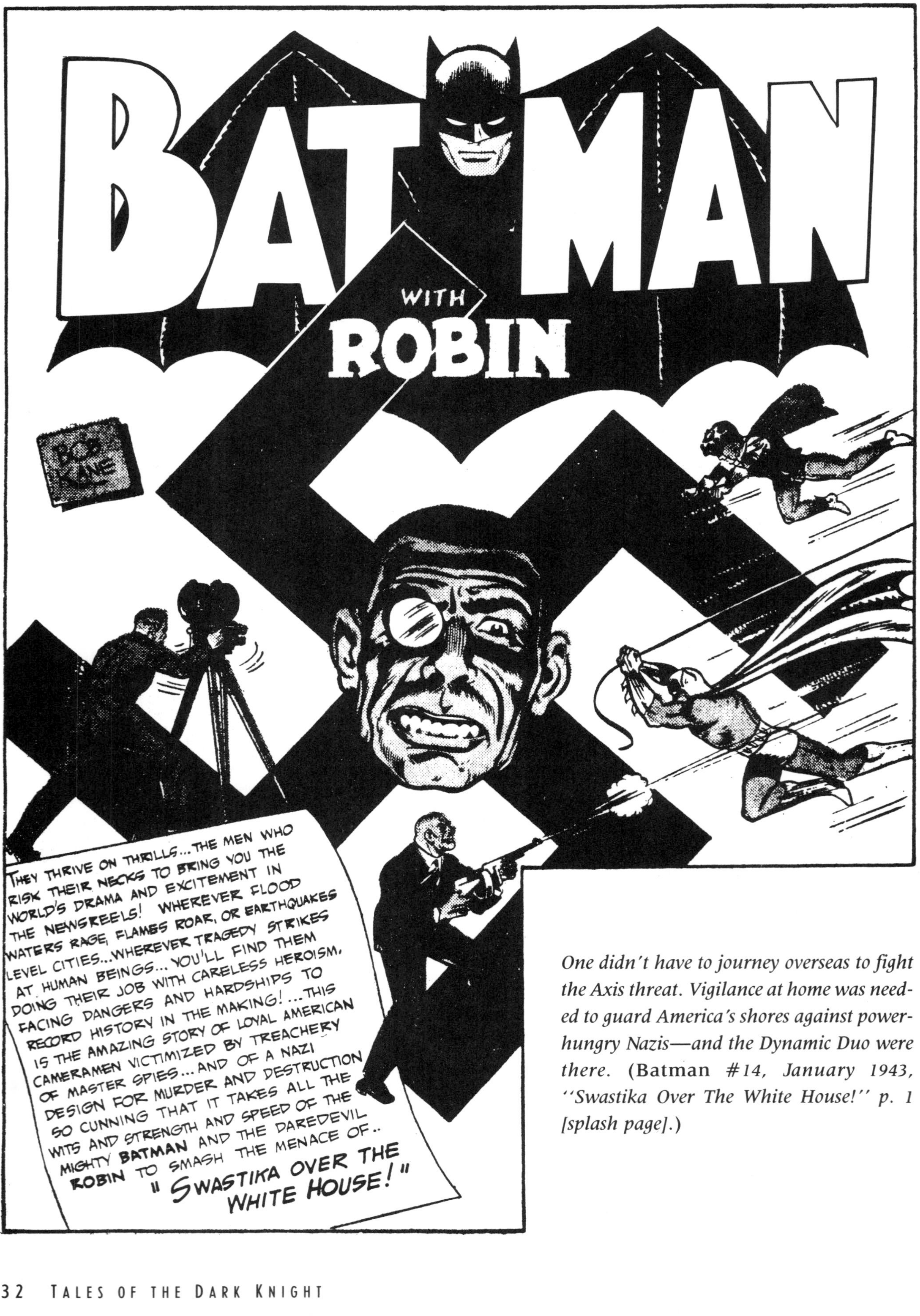
BATMAN
WITH ROBIN
BOB KANE
THEY THRIVE ON THRILLS... THE MEN WHO RISK THEIR NECKS TO BRING YOU THE WORLD'S DRAMA AND EXCITEMENT IN THE NEWSREELS! WHEREVER FLOOD WATERS RAGE, FLAMES ROAR, OR EARTHQUAKES LEVEL CITIES...WHEREVER TRAGEDY STRIKES AT HUMAN BEINGS... YOU'LL FIND THEM DOING THEIR JOB WITH CARELESS HEROISM, FACING DANGERS AND HARDSHIPS TO RECORD HISTORY IN THE MAKING! ...THIS IS THE AMAZING STORY OF LOYAL AMERICAN CAMERAMEN VICTIMIZED BY TREACHERY OF MASTER SPIES... AND OF A NAZI DESIGN FOR MURDER AND DESTRUCTION SO CUNNING THAT IT TAKES ALL THE WITS AND STRENGTH AND SPEED OF THE MIGHTY BATMAN AND THE DAREDEVIL ROBIN TO SMASH THE MENACE OF..
" SWASTIKA OVER THE WHITE HOUSE! "

One didn't have to journey overseas to fight the Axis threat. Vigilance at home was needed to guard America's shores against power-hungry Nazis—and the Dynamic Duo were there. (Batman *#14, January 1943, ''Swastika Over The White House!'' p. 1 [splash page].*)

CHAPTER 4

The Comic Book Front

DURING WORLD WAR II EVERYONE IN America was called to action. The folks who weren't overseas fighting in any of the global theaters of war still did their part by working in the weapons factories, buying war bonds and stamps, rationing gasoline and food, and planting victory gardens.

America's superheroes were also pressed into service. After all, it would have been a waste to let such omnipotent beings merely collar crooks at home while Axis troops were marching down the Champs Elysées, London was being bombed, and the Atlantic waters were teeming with German U-boats.

And there were always the persistent fears that the conflict would reach American soil or that Nazi saboteurs could cripple the war effort.

Given the strategic East Coast location of Gotham City, it was only natural that the State Department would be on the phone to Commissioner Gordon to shine the Bat Signal and call the Dynamic Duo into service.

Batman took to the patriotic calling with a surprising fervor. After all, only two years before, the "weird figure of the dark" was a grim, brutal loner busy with his own private war. Even Batman's public pose as a millionaire playboy given to skirt chasing and nightclub hopping was hardly the picture of the stalwart patriot.

But protect the home front, Batman and Robin certainly did. One of their biggest Nazi busts halted the plans of a Gotham-based spy ring that not only would have completely sabotaged the war effort, but would have turned the White House over to Adolf Hitler to use as the American headquarters of his evil empire (*Batman* 14/3, January 1943).

The Nazi spy ring during that case had even attempted to assassinate the Dynamic Duo with a drive-by shooting while the pair were publicizing the war bond campaign for the newsreel cameras.

In fact, the Dark Knight's patriotic, as well as crime-fighting, renown had led to an increasing number of civic ceremonials and similar exposures to danger.

There was the occasion (duly recorded in *Batman* 8/4, January 1942) when Batman and Robin went to the nation's capital at the request of the president to be honored with a ticker tape parade.

At the podium to accept the thanks of a grateful nation for his crime-busting efforts, Batman was almost shot dead by the Joker, who had been waiting on a rooftop overlooking the stage.

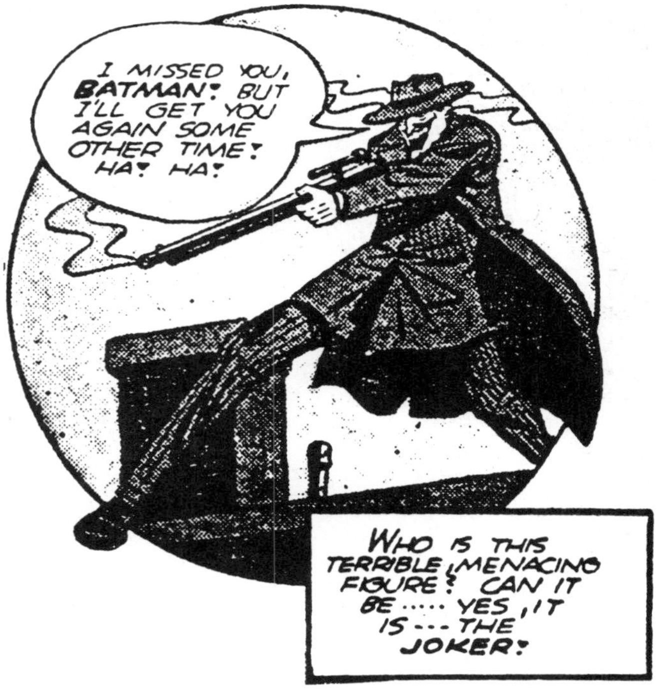
I MISSED YOU, BATMAN! BUT I'LL GET YOU AGAIN SOME OTHER TIME! HA! HA!
WHO IS THIS TERRIBLE, MENACING FIGURE? CAN IT BE..... YES, IT IS --- THE JOKER!

World War II's patriotic fervor often got Batman out of the shadows, into the sunlight—and into the gun sights of would-be assassins. (Batman *#8, January 1942, "The Cross Country Crimes!" p. 2 [panel].*)

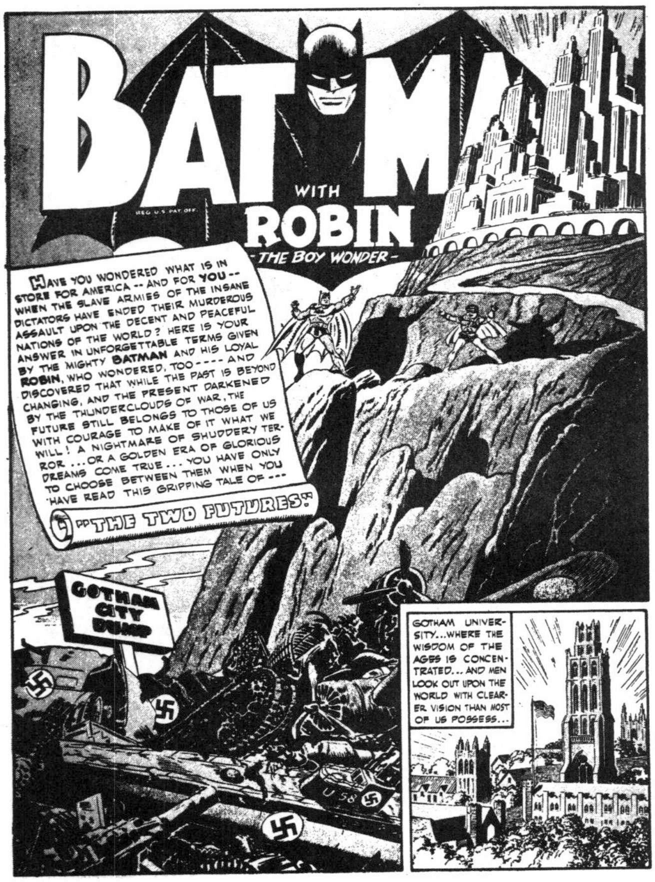
BATMAN
WITH ROBIN
-THE BOY WONDER-
HAVE YOU WONDERED WHAT IS IN STORE FOR AMERICA -- AND FOR YOU -- WHEN THE SLAVE ARMIES OF THE INSANE DICTATORS HAVE ENDED THEIR MURDEROUS ASSAULT UPON THE DECENT AND PEACEFUL NATIONS OF THE WORLD? HERE IS YOUR ANSWER IN UNFORGETTABLE TERMS GIVEN BY THE MIGHTY BATMAN AND HIS LOYAL ROBIN, WHO WONDERED, TOO---- AND DISCOVERED THAT WHILE THE PAST IS BEYOND CHANGING, AND THE PRESENT DARKENED BY THE THUNDERCLOUDS OF WAR, THE FUTURE STILL BELONGS TO THOSE OF US WITH COURAGE TO MAKE OF IT WHAT WE WILL! A NIGHTMARE OF SHUDDERY TERROR ... OR A GOLDEN ERA OF GLORIOUS DREAMS COME TRUE... YOU HAVE ONLY TO CHOOSE BETWEEN THEM WHEN YOU HAVE READ THIS GRIPPING TALE OF ---
"THE TWO FUTURES"
GOTHAM CITY DUMP
GOTHAM UNIVERSITY...WHERE THE WISDOM OF THE AGES IS CONCENTRATED... AND MEN LOOK OUT UPON THE WORLD WITH CLEARER VISION THAN MOST OF US POSSESS...

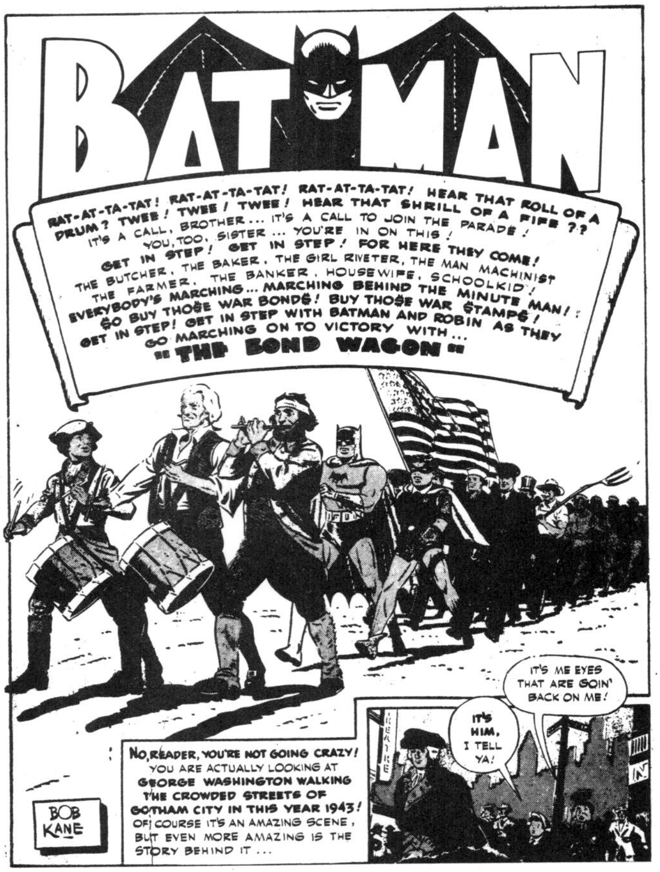
BATMAN
RAT-AT-TA-TAT! RAT-AT-TA-TAT! RAT-AT-TA-TAT! HEAR THAT ROLL OF A DRUM? TWEE! TWEE! TWEE! HEAR THAT SHRILL OF A FIFE?? IT'S A CALL, BROTHER... IT'S A CALL TO JOIN THE PARADE! YOU, TOO, SISTER ... YOU'RE IN ON THIS! GET IN STEP! GET IN STEP! FOR HERE THEY COME! THE BUTCHER, THE BAKER, THE GIRL RIVETER, THE MAN MACHINIST THE FARMER, THE BANKER, HOUSEWIFE, SCHOOLKID! EVERYBODY'S MARCHING... MARCHING BEHIND THE MINUTE MAN! GO BUY THOSE WAR BONDS! BUY THOSE WAR STAMPS! GET IN STEP! GET IN STEP WITH BATMAN AND ROBIN AS THEY GO MARCHING ON TO VICTORY WITH...
"THE BOND WAGON"
IT'S ME EYES THAT ARE GOIN' BACK ON ME!
IT'S HIM, I TELL YA!
NO, READER, YOU'RE NOT GOING CRAZY! YOU ARE ACTUALLY LOOKING AT GEORGE WASHINGTON WALKING THE CROWDED STREETS OF GOTHAM CITY IN THIS YEAR 1943! OF COURSE IT'S AN AMAZING SCENE, BUT EVEN MORE AMAZING IS THE STORY BEHIND IT ...
BOB KANE

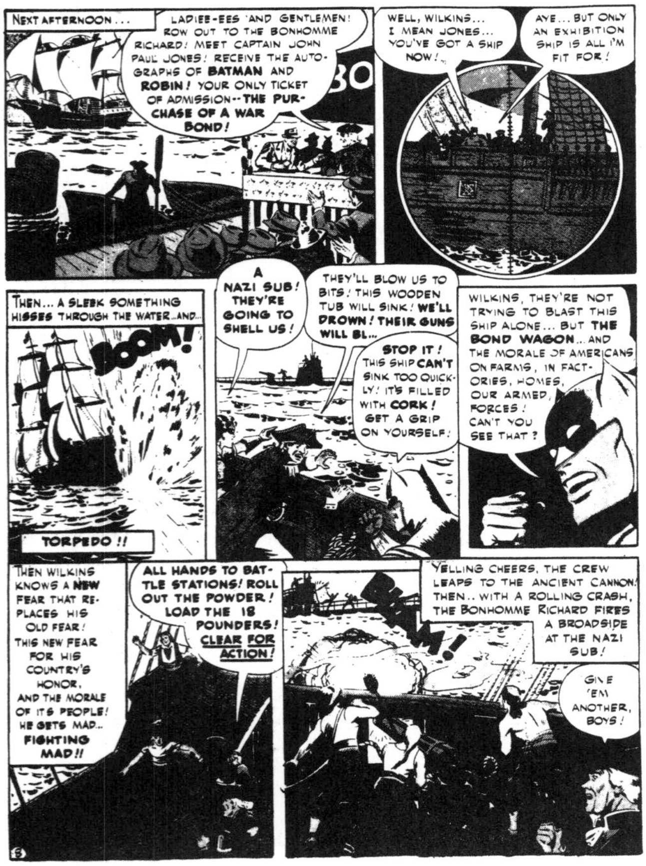
NEXT AFTERNOON...
LADIEE-EES AND GENTLEMEN! ROW OUT TO THE BONHOMME RICHARD! MEET CAPTAIN JOHN PAUL JONES! RECEIVE THE AUTOGRAPHS OF BATMAN AND ROBIN! YOUR ONLY TICKET OF ADMISSION -- THE PURCHASE OF A WAR BOND!
WELL, WILKINS... I MEAN JONES... YOU'VE GOT A SHIP NOW!
AYE... BUT ONLY AN EXHIBITION SHIP IS ALL I'M FIT FOR!
THEN... A SLEEK SOMETHING HISSES THROUGH THE WATER...AND...
BOOM!
TORPEDO !!
A NAZI SUB! THEY'RE GOING TO SHELL US!
THEY'LL BLOW US TO BITS! THIS WOODEN TUB WILL SINK! WE'LL DROWN! THEIR GUNS WILL BL...
STOP IT! THIS SHIP CAN'T SINK TOO QUICKLY! IT'S FILLED WITH CORK! GET A GRIP ON YOURSELF!
WILKINS, THEY'RE NOT TRYING TO BLAST THIS SHIP ALONE... BUT THE BOND WAGON... AND THE MORALE OF AMERICANS ON FARMS, IN FACTORIES, HOMES, OUR ARMED FORCES! CAN'T YOU SEE THAT?
THEN WILKINS KNOWS A NEW FEAR THAT REPLACES HIS OLD FEAR! THIS NEW FEAR FOR HIS COUNTRY'S HONOR, AND THE MORALE OF ITS PEOPLE! HE GETS MAD... FIGHTING MAD!!
ALL HANDS TO BATTLE STATIONS! ROLL OUT THE POWDER! LOAD THE 18 POUNDERS! CLEAR FOR ACTION!
YELLING CHEERS, THE CREW LEAPS TO THE ANCIENT CANNON! THEN.. WITH A ROLLING CRASH, THE BONHOMME RICHARD FIRES A BROADSIDE AT THE NAZI SUB!
GIVE 'EM ANOTHER, BOYS!

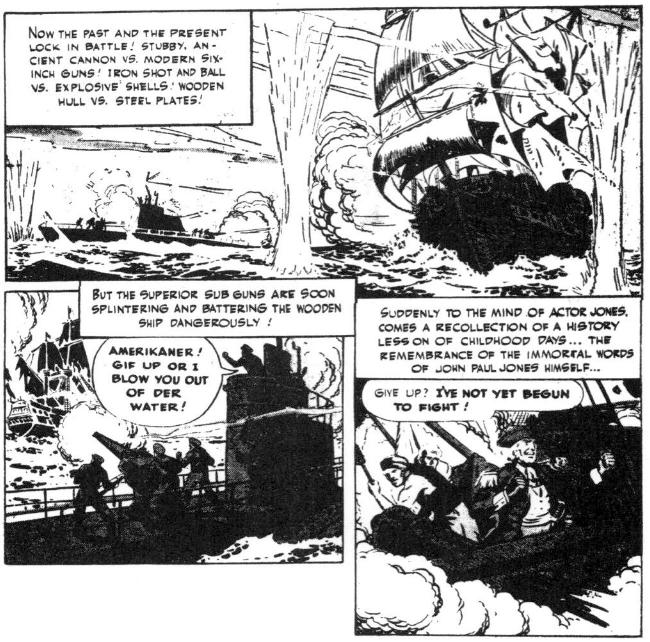
NOW THE PAST AND THE PRESENT LOCK IN BATTLE! STUBBY, ANCIENT CANNON VS. MODERN SIX-INCH GUNS! IRON SHOT AND BALL VS. EXPLOSIVE SHELLS! WOODEN HULL VS. STEEL PLATES!
BUT THE SUPERIOR SUB GUNS ARE SOON SPLINTERING AND BATTERING THE WOODEN SHIP DANGEROUSLY!
AMERIKANER! GIF UP OR I BLOW YOU OUT OF DER WATER!
SUDDENLY TO THE MIND OF ACTOR JONES, COMES A RECOLLECTION OF A HISTORY LESSON OF CHILDHOOD DAYS... THE REMEMBRANCE OF THE IMMORTAL WORDS OF JOHN PAUL JONES HIMSELF...
GIVE UP? I'VE NOT YET BEGUN TO FIGHT!

Top left: Batman #15, *February/March 1943, "The Two Futures," p. 1 [splash page]*. Top right: Detective #78, *August 1943, "The Bond Wagon," p. 1 [splash page]*. Bottom: Detective #78, *August 1943, "The Bond Wagon," pp. 8–9.*

(The brazen act in which G. Henry Mover, head of the nation's G-men, was wounded as he shook Batman's hand, led the president himself to order a nationwide dragnet for the evil crime jester.)

Batman was certainly out of his dark night element appearing at daytime speaking engagements and posing for "Buy Bonds" newsreel promo spots—and vulnerable to such assassination attempts from a Nazi spy, the Joker, or any hood holding a grudge and a gun.

Perhaps the constant danger, mixed with the unaccustomed adulation, was irresistible. At any rate, Batman's patriotic appearances increased as the war dragged on.

Batman and Robin became part of a special bond wagon effort that included a stop at Independence Hall in Philadelphia.

"Fellow Americans, you too, can sign a Declaration of Independence," Batman said during his appearance as Robin stood in the wings, looking on with pride. "Independence from slavery... for should the Axis win Americans WILL be slaves in bondage!

"Fellow Americans! Which is it to be be—bondage or war bonds?"

As the crowd filed out, heading for a table marked "Sign Here for War Bonds," Batman and Robin stood against the wall at attention, saluting them.[1]

Batman and Robin's war bonds promotions and patriotic messages graced many of their comic book covers. They posed for artists while parachuting out of military planes, the night sky around them lit up by searchlights. They drove past in a U.S. Army jeep and waved while Batman shouted with a grin, "War savings bonds and stamps KEEP 'EM ROLLING!" During one full moon they rode on the back of a giant eagle while flanked with an escort of two military planes, flashing the "V for Victory" sign and proclaiming: "Keep the American Eagle flying! Buy war bonds and stamps!"

They even risked their lives to make a pro-

1. "The Bond Wagon," *Detective Comics* 78 (August 1943).

No.12
TEN CENTS
A SUPERMAN DC PUBLICATION
BATMAN
AUG. SEPT.
WAR SAVINGS BONDS AND STAMPS KEEP 'EM ROLLING!
U.S.A.
ANNIVERSARY ISSUE

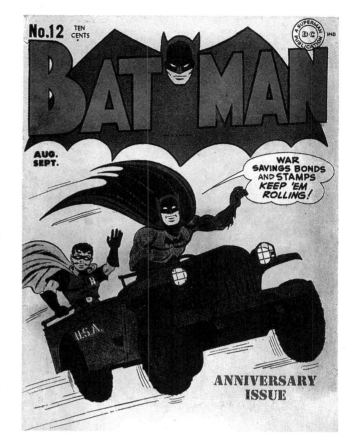

Batman *#12, August/September 1942, cover.*

BATMAN No.15
A SUPERMAN DC PUBLICATION
BATMAN
FEB. MAR.
10¢
R
KEEP THOSE BULLETS FLYING!
KEEP ON BUYING WAR BONDS & STAMPS!

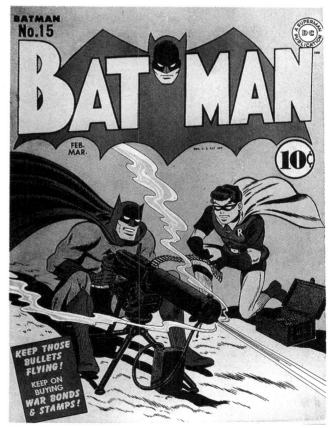

Batman *#15, February/March 1943, cover.*

No.13
A SUPERMAN DC PUBLICATION
TEN CENTS
BATMAN
OCT. NOV.

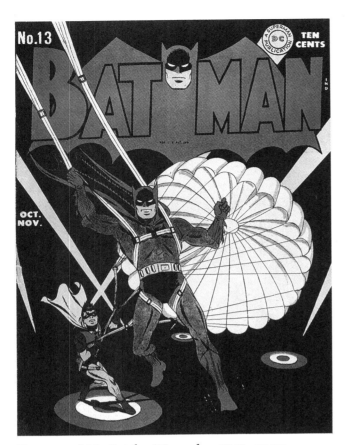

Batman #13, *October/November 1942, cover.*

No. 8 WINTER ISSUE
15¢
WORLD'S FINEST COMICS
96 PAGES
A SUPERMAN DC PUBLICATION
SINK THE JAPANAZIS WITH BONDS & STAMPS

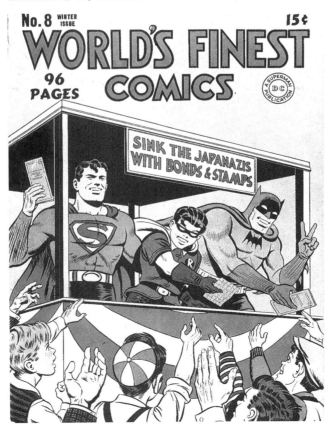

World's Finest Comics #8, *Winter issue 1942, cover.*

motional trip to the front (whether at the insistence of President or Mrs. Roosevelt is not known). With bullets whizzing around them, Batman held out a brand-new rifle to a GI.

"Here's a new gun from the folks back home, soldier!" Batman said as the dogface, whose own rifle had seen better days, smiled appreciatively.

And when Batman got close to a Nazi spy, he never held anything back.

"The only way to get the Nazi is by hitting him in the vital spots where it hurts most," he once said as he cracked a haymaker punch off a cornered Nazi. "Keep hammering away at him, keep socking until he just naturally falls apart! THAT'S THE WAY TO BEAT THE NAZI!!!"

All the Axis villains who sprouted from the Nazi nightmare to fall like a dark night's rain into the troubled comics world were nothing less than misanthropic demons.

The Japanese villains, with their devilish squints, enormous buck teeth, and spindly bodies, were madhouse versions of the evil Orientals of pulp tradition. The German Nazis were power-hungry brutes who desired to enslave the world in a death camp fever dream.

Small wonder that by the time the war had ended, many superheroes found it hard to go back to busting bank robbers after the intensity of halting the Axis aims of world conquest. Some, like Captain America, returned with fanfare to the home front (and some favored Cold War assignments from the State Department), but even Cap's patriotic luster dimmed a bit while he cooled his boots for a few years on the superhero unemployment rolls.

"The war in comic books despite its early promise, its compulsive flag waving, its incessant admonitions to keep 'em flying was, in the end, lost," Jules Feiffer wrote. "From Superman on down the old heroes gave up a lot of their edge. As I was growing up they were growing tiresome: more garrulous than I remembered them in the old days, a little show-offy about their winning of the war. Superman, The Shield, Captain America and the rest competed cattily to be photographed with the President; to be officially thanked for selling bonds, or catching spies, or opening up the second front."

And despite his tireless efforts on behalf of the Buy Bonds campaign, even the Batman, in Feiffer's estimation, had become "shrill."[2]

"World War II demolished (superhero) comics by sending all of its critters into the military," commiserates comics creator and entrepreneur Mike Friedrich.

In retrospect, Batman's wartime patriotism probably made him less the eerie figure of the dark in the eyes of the Gotham public and the comics readership.

But despite his patriotic efforts, the 1950s would see Batman vilified as a bad influence on American youth as the entire comics industry was threatened with censorship and falling sales.

2. Feiffer, *Comic Book Heroes,* p. 48.

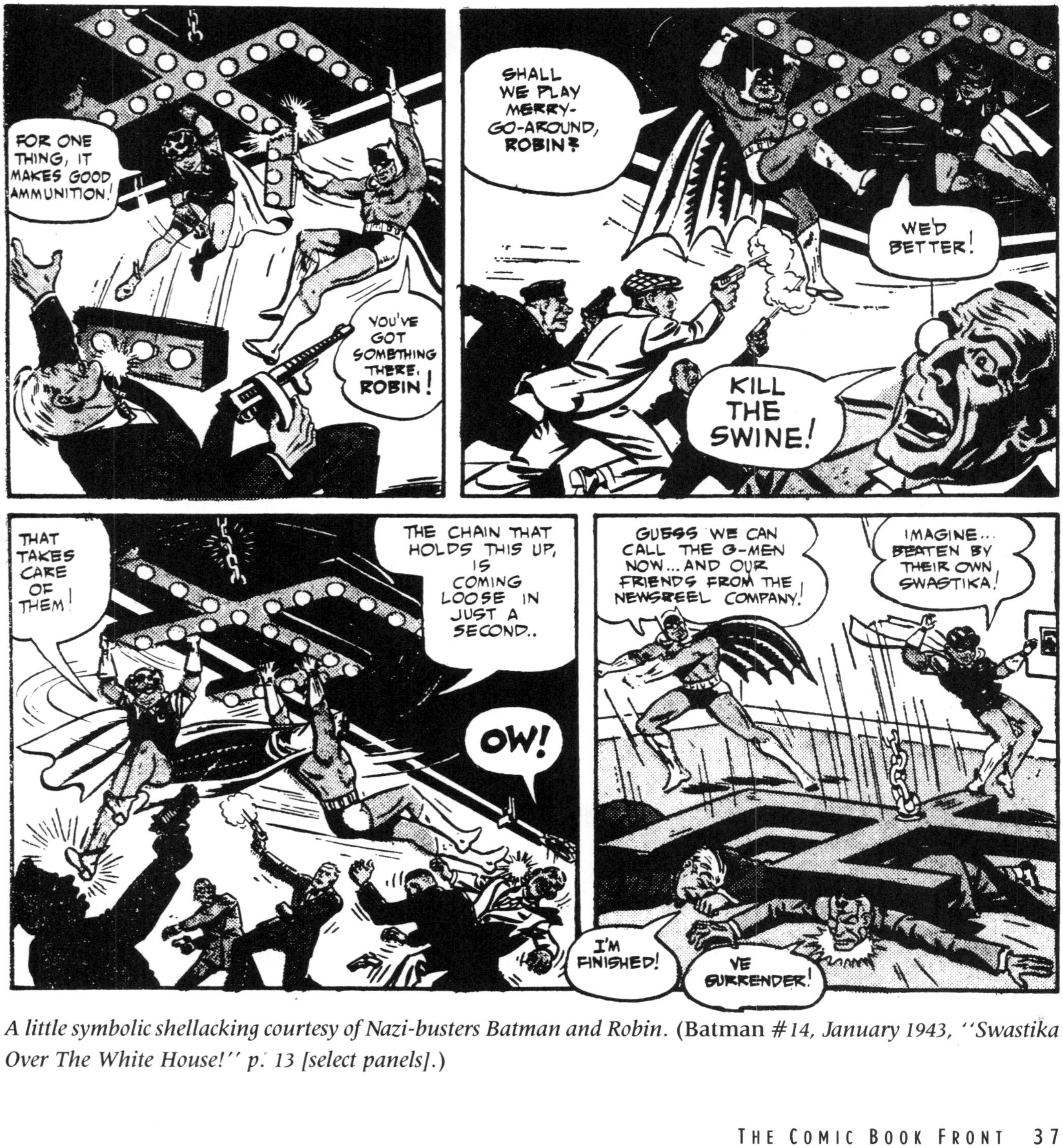
FOR ONE THING, IT MAKES GOOD AMMUNITION!
YOU'VE GOT SOMETHING THERE, ROBIN!
SHALL WE PLAY MERRY-GO-AROUND, ROBIN?
WE'D BETTER!
KILL THE SWINE!
THAT TAKES CARE OF THEM!
THE CHAIN THAT HOLDS THIS UP, IS COMING LOOSE IN JUST A SECOND..
OW!
GUESS WE CAN CALL THE G-MEN NOW... AND OUR FRIENDS FROM THE NEWSREEL COMPANY!
IMAGINE... BEATEN BY THEIR OWN SWASTIKA!
I'M FINISHED!
VE SURRENDER!

A little symbolic shellacking courtesy of Nazi-busters Batman and Robin. (Batman #14, *January 1943, ''Swastika Over The White House!'' p. 13 [select panels]*.)

DOSSIER 1

A BATMAN CHRISTMAS

In order to explain Batman's amazing longevity, we have to dig deep into our thick dossier of research on the Dark Knight.

There are many qualities that have contributed to Batman's celebrity: his aura of mystery, his physical power, his detective mastery, a strong supporting cast. But how many would consider the Dark Knight's compassion as a part of his success?

Mike Friedrich, who broke into comics with a Robin story penned for editor Julius Schwartz, considers Batman's sense of compassion an integral part of the Dark Knight legend.

"My favorite year for Batman was 1942—Batman had a real good combination of attitudes," Friedrich recalls. "He was a detective, and he was also a real mysterious character like the Shadow. He was someone people didn't know very much about. We as the readers were in on some of the secret, but you sort of had a sense we weren't in on all of it.

"Batman was involved in very bizarre conflicts, but at the same time he was involved in very ordinary life. It wasn't a totally fantastic world he was in, but a slightly twisted version of urban reality....

"The other sense was, he really cared for the little guys. There'd be a story where, say, an apple cart dealer got ripped off, and Batman would spend the whole story trying to solve that case."

Friedrich got the chance to wed Batman's feel for the average citizen with another great Batman theme, the annual Christmas story, when he wrote the 1970 tale "The Silent Night of the Batman" (partially reprinted herein). The upshot of the tale was that "maybe the spirit of Batman is the spirit of Christmas, that his was a positive presence on the city," Friedrich says.

At Christmas even the grim Dark Knight has been known to mellow a bit. He might take a break in a night patrol to join some of Commissioner's Gordon's men in singing a holiday carol, or give young Robin a fatherly lecture on the meaning of Christmas.

"Santa is real and always will be if we believe in the spirit he stands for—good cheer, unselfishness, and love of fellow man!" Batman once told Robin. "That's the real Santa Claus!"

"Golly!" Robin responded. "This almost does make me believe in Santa Claus, even if I do know he isn't real!"[1]

Even crime seemed to take a holiday (or at least slow down a little) when the winter solstice rolled around.

Gotham City itself was a less foreboding place after being frosted with the first Christmas snow. The Big City pace slowed as married couples recognized the treasure of their time together, as silent thanks were offered for the blessings of the year past, as children gleefully welcomed the season with a festival of snowmen and snowball fights. It was also a time that Gotham City opened its heart to the poor and suffering, so that those in need could have shelter from the cold, and food and drink to gladden the heart.

And if Batman had a case, it usually involved uniting a family or helping a lost soul find the strength to change his life for the good.

It might seem incongruous to an out-of-towner to imagine a Batman who would risk his life for the apple vendors of the world. What makes the news are the stories of a vigilante Batman, a warrior crime fighter whose sense of justice seems cold, swift, and brutal.

But there are many sides to the mysterious Batman, and one is the spirit of compassion that tempers his justice. And it is at Christmas that his compassion shines as bright as that legendary Christmas star.

---

1. "Merry Christmas 1941," *Batman* 9 (February/March 1941).

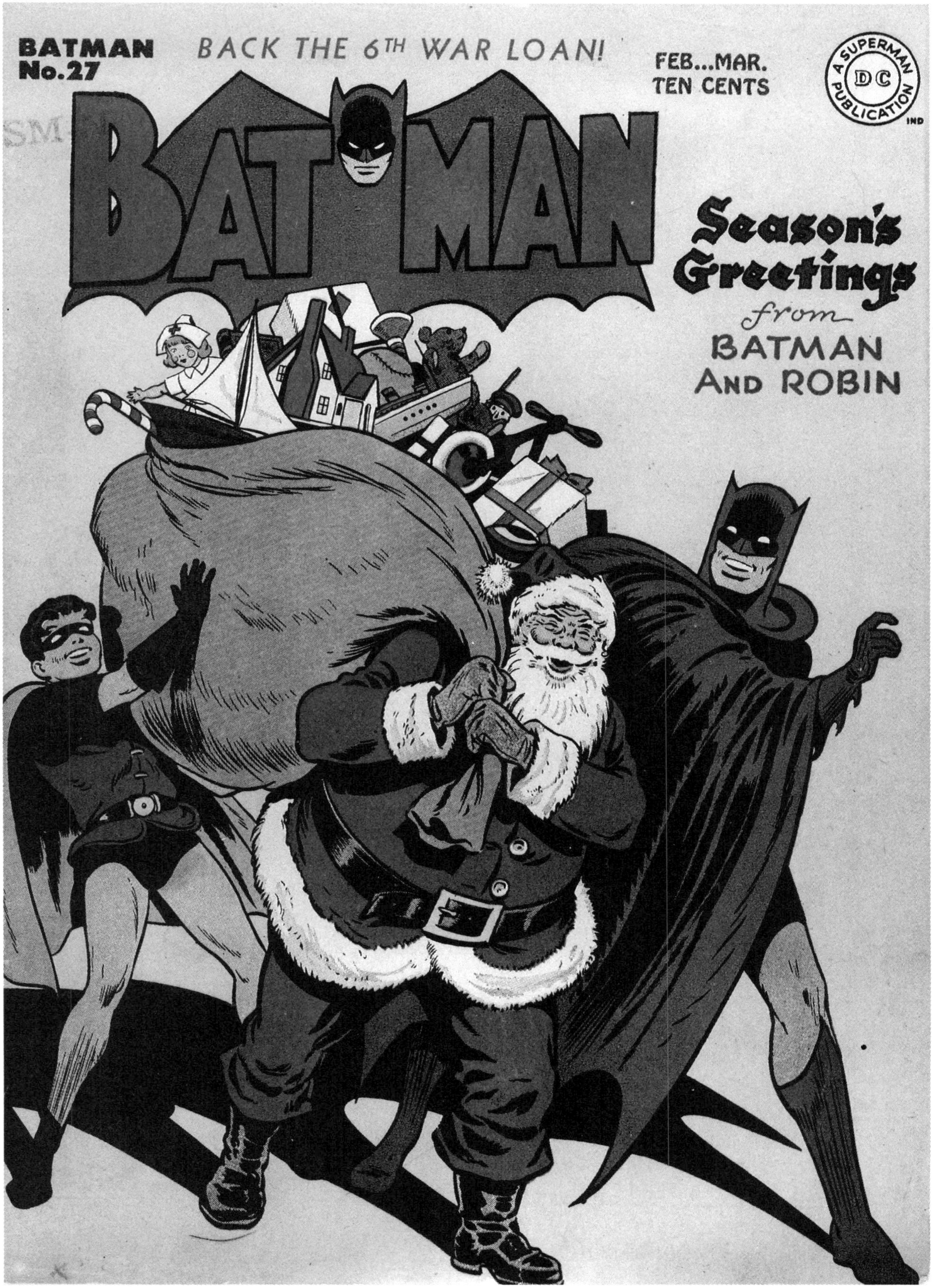
BATMAN
No.27
BACK THE 6TH WAR LOAN!
FEB...MAR.
TEN CENTS
A SUPERMAN DC PUBLICATION
BATMAN
Season's
Greetings
from
BATMAN
AND ROBIN

Batman *#27, February/March 1945, cover.*

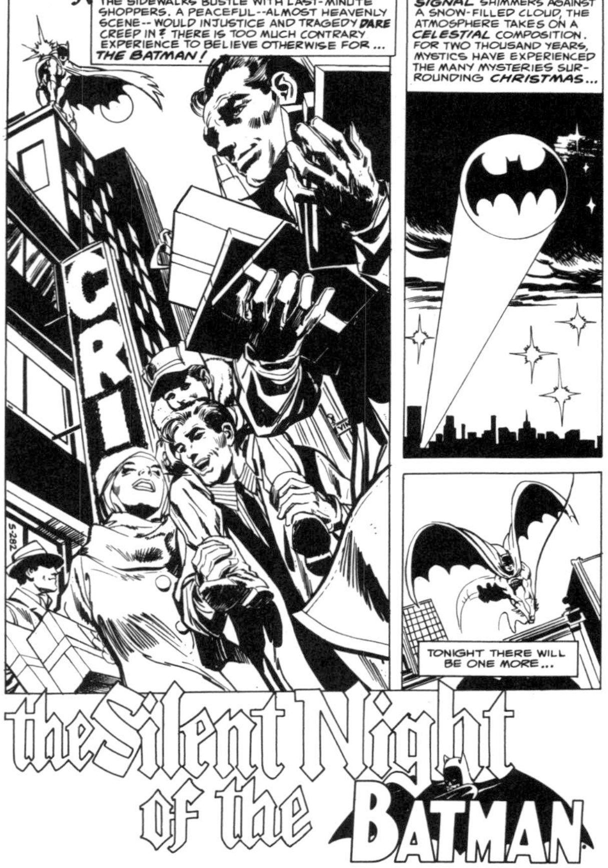
NIGHT FALLS ON CHRISTMAS EVE IN GOTHAM. THE SIDEWALKS BUSTLE WITH LAST-MINUTE SHOPPERS. A PEACEFUL--ALMOST HEAVENLY SCENE-- WOULD INJUSTICE AND TRAGEDY DARE CREEP IN? THERE IS TOO MUCH CONTRARY EXPERIENCE TO BELIEVE OTHERWISE FOR ... THE BATMAN!
CRI
THEN, AS THE EERIE BAT-SIGNAL SHIMMERS AGAINST A SNOW-FILLED CLOUD, THE ATMOSPHERE TAKES ON A CELESTIAL COMPOSITION. FOR TWO THOUSAND YEARS, MYSTICS HAVE EXPERIENCED THE MANY MYSTERIES SURROUNDING CHRISTMAS...
TONIGHT THERE WILL BE ONE MORE...
the Silent Night of the BATMAN

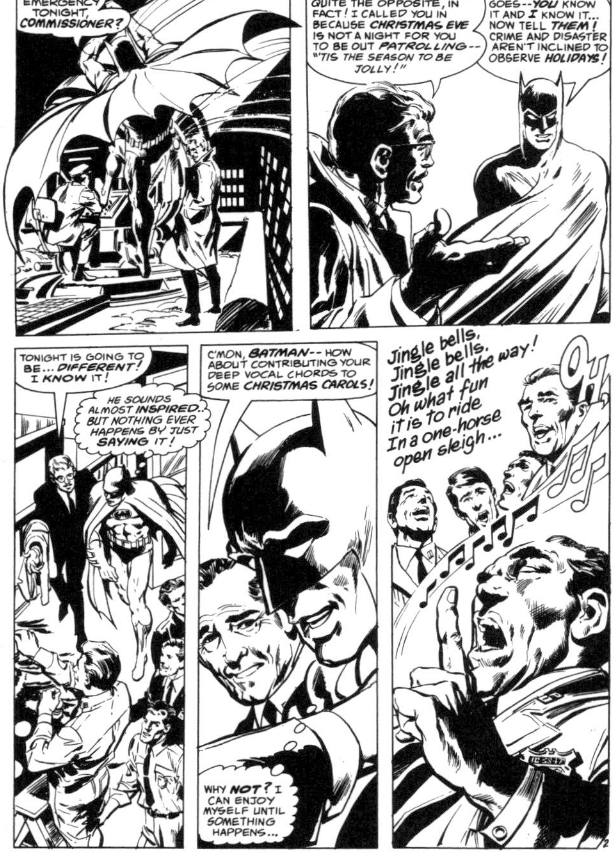
WHAT'S THE EMERGENCY TONIGHT, COMMISSIONER?
NO EMERGENCY, BATMAN! QUITE THE OPPOSITE, IN FACT! I CALLED YOU IN BECAUSE CHRISTMAS EVE IS NOT A NIGHT FOR YOU TO BE OUT PATROLLING-- "TIS THE SEASON TO BE JOLLY!"
LIKE THE SAYING GOES--YOU KNOW IT AND I KNOW IT... NOW TELL THEM! CRIME AND DISASTER AREN'T INCLINED TO OBSERVE HOLIDAYS!
TONIGHT IS GOING TO BE... DIFFERENT! I KNOW IT!
HE SOUNDS ALMOST INSPIRED.. BUT NOTHING EVER HAPPENS BY JUST SAYING IT!
C'MON, BATMAN-- HOW ABOUT CONTRIBUTING YOUR DEEP VOCAL CHORDS TO SOME CHRISTMAS CAROLS!
WHY NOT? I CAN ENJOY MYSELF UNTIL SOMETHING HAPPENS...
Jingle bells, Jingle bells, Jingle all the way! Oh what fun it is to ride In a one-horse open sleigh...

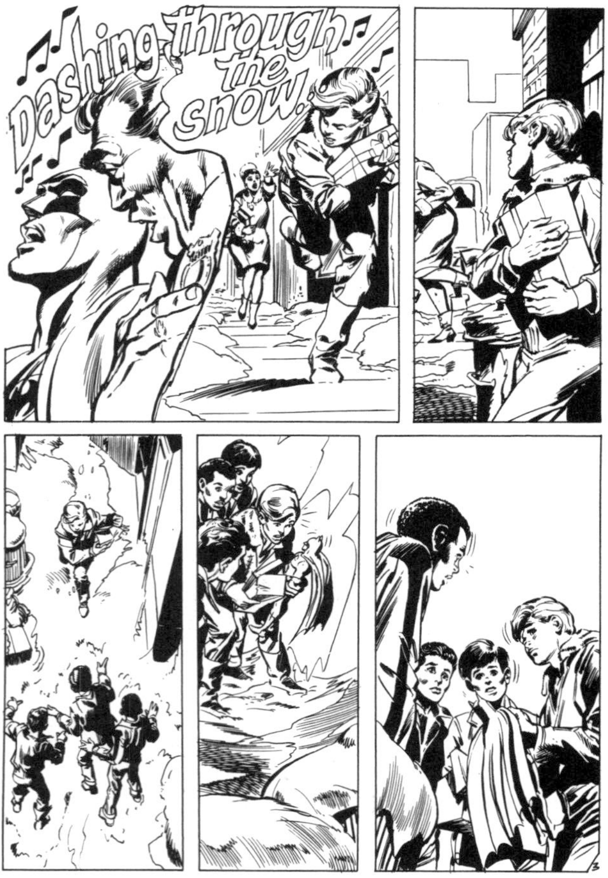
Dashing through the snow...

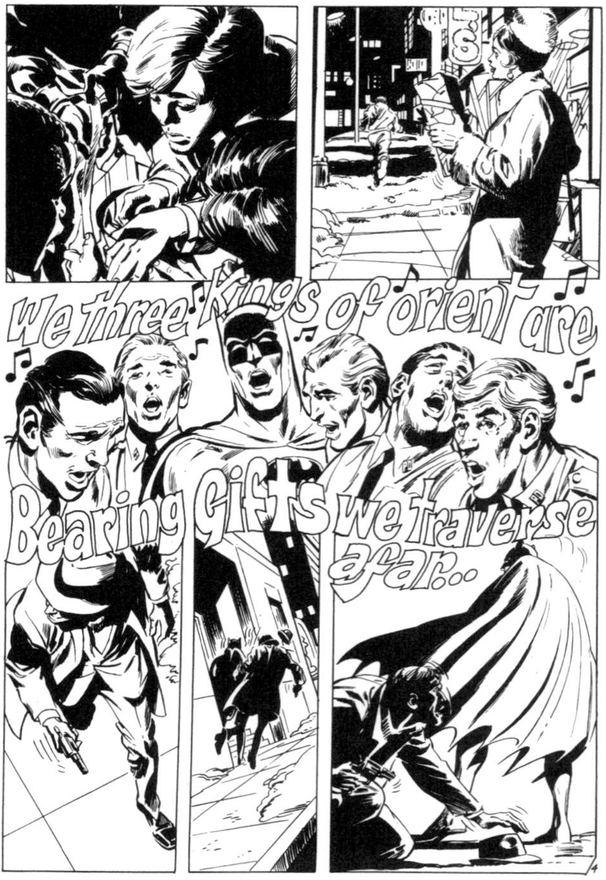
we three Kings of orient are
Bearing Gifts we traverse afar...

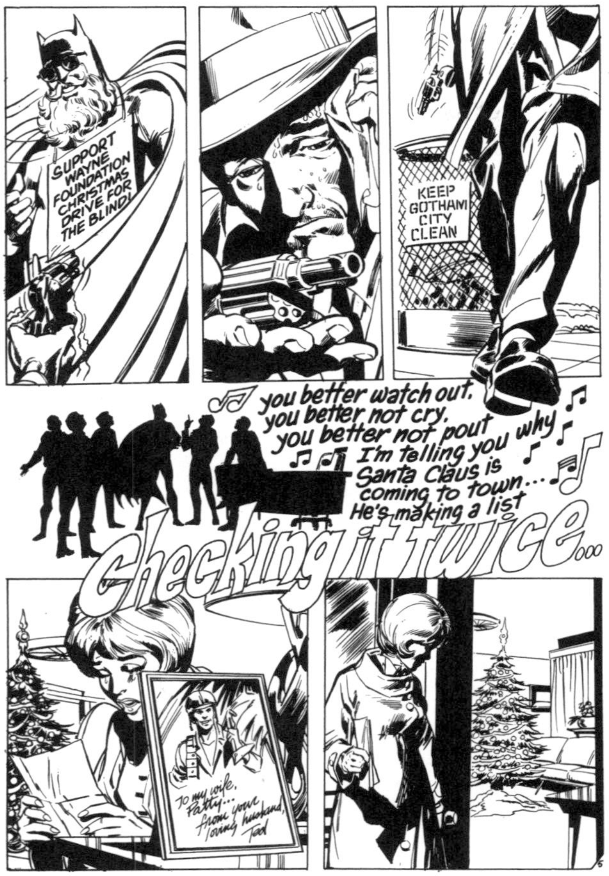
SUPPORT WAYNE FOUNDATION CHRISTMAS DRIVE FOR THE BLIND!
KEEP GOTHAM CITY CLEAN
you better watch out, you better not cry, you better not pout I'm telling you why Santa Claus is coming to town... He's making a list
Checking it twice...
To my wife, Patty... from your loving husband, Ted

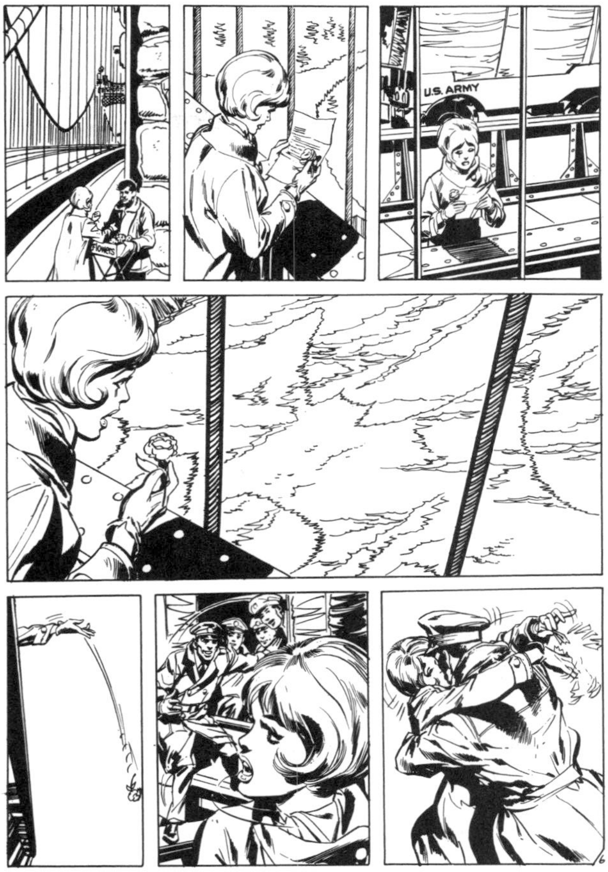
U.S. ARMY

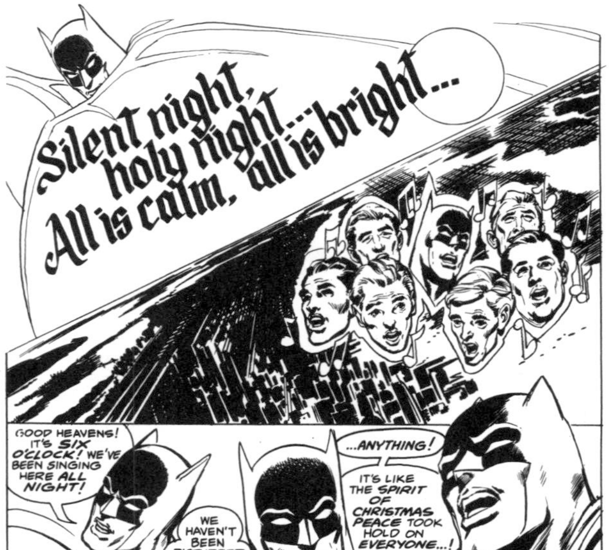
Silent night, holy night... All is calm, all is bright...
GOOD HEAVENS! IT'S SIX O'CLOCK! WE'VE BEEN SINGING HERE ALL NIGHT!
WE HAVEN'T BEEN DISTURBED BY ONE REPORT OF ROBBERY, MURDER, DRUG-PEDDLING...
...ANYTHING!
IT'S LIKE THE SPIRIT OF CHRISTMAS PEACE TOOK HOLD ON EVERYONE...!

Opposite and above: Batman #219, *February 1970, "The Silent Night of the Batman," pp. 1–7.*
Right: Batman #239, *February 1972, cover.*

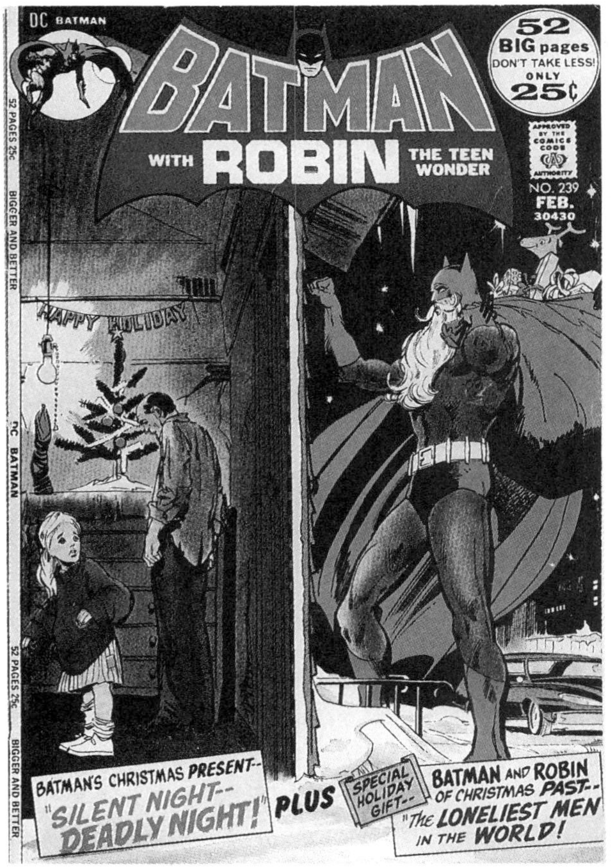
DC BATMAN
52 BIG pages DON'T TAKE LESS! ONLY 25¢
BATMAN
WITH ROBIN THE TEEN WONDER
APPROVED BY THE COMICS CODE AUTHORITY
NO. 239 FEB. 30430
52 PAGES 25¢ BIGGER AND BETTER
HAPPY HOLIDAY
BATMAN'S CHRISTMAS PRESENT-- "SILENT NIGHT-- DEADLY NIGHT!"
PLUS
SPECIAL HOLIDAY GIFT--
BATMAN AND ROBIN OF CHRISTMAS PAST-- "The LONELIEST MEN IN THE WORLD!"

CHAPTER 5

Comic Crackdown

Rose-colored nostalgia can certainly play tricks with history. A fond remembrance of the fifties, for example, might bring to the surface nothing more than visions of sock hops and soda fountains.

It was much more, of course. The post–World War II years, for example, ushered in the Big Chill between the United States and the Soviet Union. And one Joe McCarthy, senator from Wisconsin, took advantage of the tension by making red-baiting a particularly brutal weapon for achieving political power.

That the hardball, duplicitous tactics of the Wisconsin senator made him a national figure was not surprising—there was a lot of fear and anger loose in the land. McCarthy tapped that smoldering vein of postwar paranoia in the congressional witch hunts he led against supposed communists in the government. No matter how unfounded the accusation, or despite the absence of any evidence, to merely be called before one of McCarthy's high tribunals was usually enough to bring a career to ruin.

The paranoia went beyond concerns that spies of foreign powers were threatening America's national security. If you had any sort of liberal or progressive political background, it was

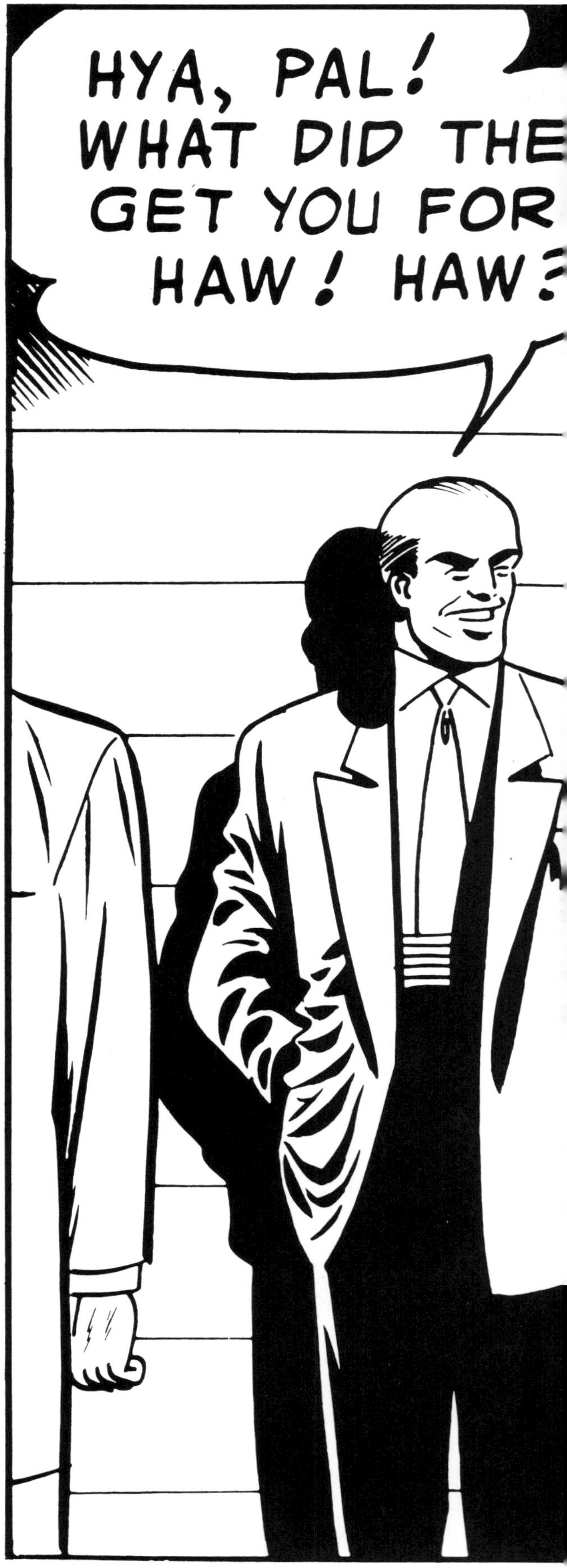
HYA, PAL! WHAT DID THE
GET YOU FOR
HAW! HAW

For a while it was Batman's worst nightmare—until it was revealed that the district attorney only jailed the Dark Knight to flush out the head of a dangerous criminal syndicate. ''I'd have done the same if I were you,'' a smiling Batman says to the district attorney at the end. Still, a mean ruse to pull on a legendary crimefighter and war hero. (Detective #240, *February 1957, ''The Outlaw Batman,'' p. 5 [panel]*).

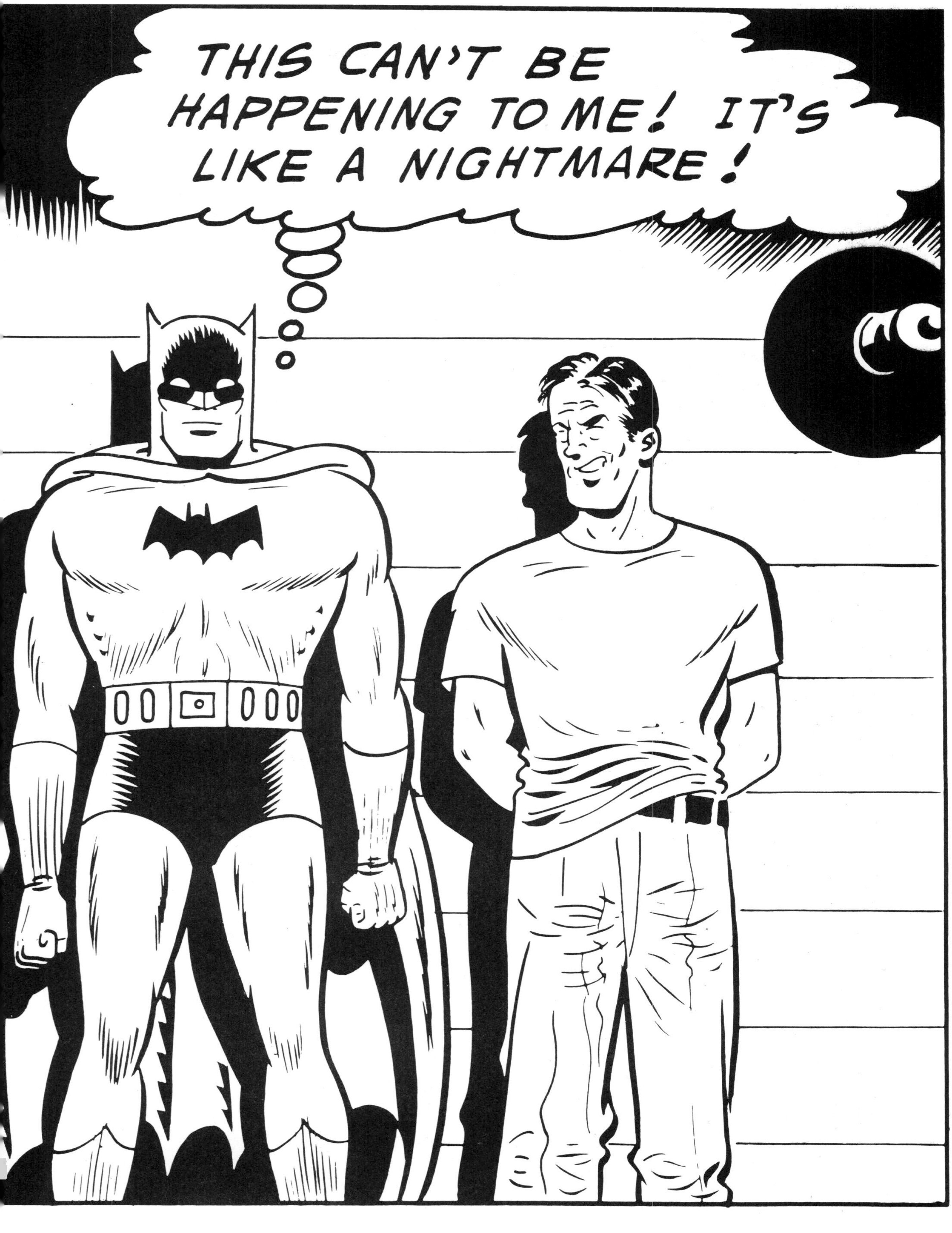
THIS CAN'T BE HAPPENING TO ME! IT'S LIKE A NIGHTMARE!

akin to being a traitorous, card-carrying Bolshevik from Mother Russia and worthy of condemnation.

These fears, and the resulting period of repression, affected the arts as well. The hunt was on for anything deemed provocative, from Salinger's *Catcher in the Rye* to the Beat Generation's hep poetry. And the lurid action of the comic books did not go unnoticed by procensorship groups.

In the early 1950s the comic book medium was still riding the crest of its amazing popularity. William Gaines, the son of comics pioneer Maxwell Gaines and president of Educational Comics (EC), remembers this time as "the heyday of comics." Ron Goulart, in his *Great History of Comic Books*, estimates that in 1952 there were about five hundred different comic book titles.[1]

Comic books were an indispensable part of the lives of most red-blooded American kids. The comics were as cherished a relic of youth as the first baseball mitt or bicycle. And since it would be years before television became the dominant medium of the culture, comics were the main source of entertainment for kids, providing an escape to fantastic worlds of warriors and superheroes, ghosts and crime busters.

But by the early fifties the legion of comic book haters began massing, ready to roll in like a storm on the pastoral reverie of kids reading comics on a summer day. The task of making the case against the comics, and leading the resulting comic crackdown, fell to an obscure senior psychiatrist for the New York Department of Hospitals named Dr. Frederic Wertham.

In 1954 Wertham's *Seduction of the Innocent* was published. The book contended that America's children were being manipulated to perverse ends by the comic books. The book, heralded as a sensational exposé by its publishers, led to the United States Senate investigating comics in 1954. Suddenly the comic books, once the province of childhood fun and escapism, were being used as fodder for a censorship battle that emulated the self-serving smear tactics of Senator McCarthy.

"It was the temper of the times which led both to McCarthy and the problems that comics were having," remembers William Gaines, whose titles suffered the fire and brimstone of the comic crackdown. "McCarthy didn't create the times, the times created McCarthy, and they also created a bad time for comics. It was just the way people were then—they were against everything, just the general population. They were convinced that comics were going to do terrible things to their children; they really believed it, and so did Wertham."[2]

Wertham even advanced one of the most incredible charges of that entire tumultuous period—that Batman and Robin were gay. But before we see how the Dynamic Duo were affected by the charges, we have to appreciate the anticomics paranoia that had been building years before Wertham wrote *Seduction of the Innocent*.

"Comics, radio, movies, and television—these are a part of our children's world today," wrote Josette Frank in a 1949 pamphlet. "They are among the ways by which words and ideas, our culture and our thinking, are being passed along to our children. Yet many view these new developments with misgivings, and yearn for the good old days when a child could sit down with a book without being distracted by the voice of the radio and the ever-present lure of a comics magazine."[3]

On the whole, Frank's pamphlet had none of the hysterical quality that would characterize the crackdown era. Although proclaiming there was "no substitute for parental vigilance!" she also quoted one Edwin J. Lukas, a director of the Society for the Prevention of Crime, who had been asked if there was any relationship between youngsters reading comics and juvenile delinquency.

"I am unaware of the existence of any scientifically established causal relationship between

1. Goulart, *Great History*, p. 274.
2. Dwight R. Decker and Gary Groth, "An Interview with William M. Gaines," *The Comics Journal*, May 1983, pp. 67, 72.
3. Josette Frank, *Comics, Radio, Movies—And Children* (New York: Public Affairs Committee, Inc., 1949), p. 1.

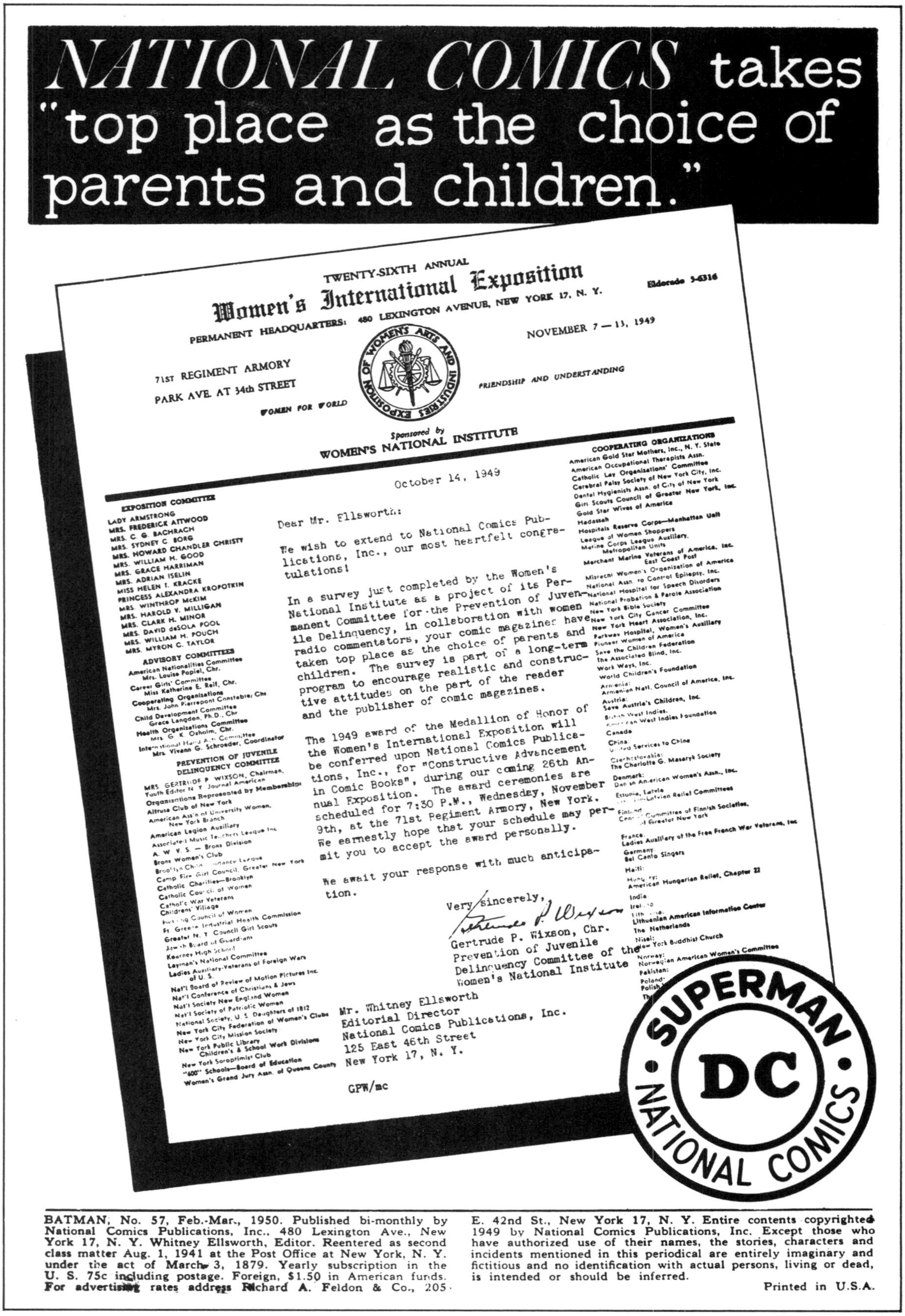

NATIONAL COMICS takes "top place as the choice of parents and children."

TWENTY-SIXTH ANNUAL

Women's International Exposition

PERMANENT HEADQUARTERS: 480 LEXINGTON AVENUE, NEW YORK 17, N. Y. Eldorado 5-6316

NOVEMBER 7 — 13, 1949

71ST REGIMENT ARMORY
PARK AVE. AT 34th STREET

EXPOSITION OF WOMEN'S ARTS AND INDUSTRIES

WOMEN FOR WORLD FRIENDSHIP AND UNDERSTANDING

Sponsored by
WOMEN'S NATIONAL INSTITUTE

EXPOSITION COMMITTEE
LADY ARMSTRONG
MRS. FREDERICK ATTWOOD
MRS. C. G. BACHRACH
MRS. SYDNEY C. BORG
MRS. HOWARD CHANDLER CHRISTY
MRS. WILLIAM H. GOOD
MRS. GRACE HARRIMAN
MRS. ADRIAN ISELIN
MISS HELEN T. KRACKE
PRINCESS ALEXANDRA KROPOTKIN
MRS. WINTHROP McKIM
MRS. HAROLD V. MILLIGAN
MRS. CLARK H. MINOR
MRS. DAVID deSOLA POOL
MRS. WILLIAM H. POUCH
MRS. MYRON C. TAYLOR

ADVISORY COMMITTEES
American Nationalities Committee
Mrs. Louise Popiel, Chr.
Career Girls' Committee
Miss Katherine E. Reif, Chr.
Cooperating Organizations
Mrs. John Pierrepont Constable, Chr.
Child Development Committee
Grace Langdon, Ph.D., Chr.
Health Organizations Committee
Mrs. G. K. Ozholm, Chr.
International Hand Arts Committee
Mrs. Vivann G. Schroeder, Coordinator

PREVENTION OF JUVENILE DELINQUENCY COMMITTEE
MRS. GERTRUDE P. WIXSON, Chairman,
Youth Editor N. Y. Journal American
Organizations Represented by Membership:
Altrusa Club of New York
American Ass'n of University Women,
New York Branch
American Legion Auxiliary
Associated Music Teachers League Inc.
A. W. V. S. — Bronx Division
Bronx Women's Club
Brooklyn Child Guidance League
Camp Fire Girl Council, Greater New York
Catholic Charities—Brooklyn
Catholic Council of Women
Catholic War Veterans
Childrens' Village
Flushing Council of Women
Ft. Greene Industrial Health Commission
Greater N. Y. Council Girl Scouts
Jewish Board of Guardians
Kearney High School
Layman's National Committee
Ladies Auxiliary-Veterans of Foreign Wars of U. S.
Nat'l Board of Review of Motion Pictures Inc.
Nat'l Conference of Christians & Jews
Nat'l Society New England Women
Nat'l Society of Patriotic Women
National Society, U. S. Daughters of 1812
New York City Federation of Women's Clubs
New York City Mission Society
New York Public Library
Children's & School Work Divisions
New York Soroptimist Club
"600" Schools—Board of Education
Women's Grand Jury Assn. of Queens County

COOPERATING ORGANIZATIONS
American Gold Star Mothers, Inc., N. Y. State
American Occupational Therapists Assn.
Catholic Lay Organizations' Committee
Cerebral Palsy Society of New York City, Inc.
Dental Hygienists Assn. of City of New York
Girl Scouts Council of Greater New York, Inc.
Gold Star Wives of America
Hadassah
Hospitals Reserve Corps—Manhattan Unit
League of Women Shoppers
Marine Corps League Auxiliary,
Metropolitan Units
Merchant Marine Veterans of America, Inc.
East Coast Post
Mizrachi Women's Organization of America
National Assn. to Control Epilepsy, Inc.
National Hospital for Speech Disorders
National Probation & Parole Association
New York Bible Society
New York City Cancer Committee
New York Heart Association, Inc.
Parkway Hospital, Women's Auxiliary
Pioneer Women of America
Save the Children Federation
The Associated Blind, Inc.
Work Ways, Inc.
World Children's Foundation
Armenia:
Armenian Natl. Council of America, Inc.
Austria:
Save Austria's Children, Inc.
British West Indies:
American West Indies Foundation
Canada
China:
United Services to China
Czechoslovakia:
The Charlotte G. Masaryk Society
Denmark:
Danish American Women's Assn., Inc.
Estonia, Latvia
Latvian Relief Committees
Finland:
Committee of Finnish Societies,
of Greater New York
France:
Ladies Auxiliary of the Free French War Veterans, Inc.
Germany:
Bel Canto Singers
Haiti:
Hungary:
American Hungarian Relief, Chapter 22
India:
Ireland
Lithuania:
Lithuanian American Information Center
The Netherlands
Nisei:
New York Buddhist Church
Norway:
Norwegian American Women's Committee
Pakistan:
Poland:
Polish

October 14, 1949

Dear Mr. Ellsworth:

We wish to extend to National Comics Publications, Inc., our most heartfelt congratulations!

In a survey just completed by the Women's National Institute as a project of its Permanent Committee for the Prevention of Juvenile Delinquency, in collaboration with women radio commentators, your comic magazines have taken top place as the choice of parents and children. The survey is part of a long-term program to encourage realistic and constructive attitudes on the part of the reader and the publisher of comic magazines.

The 1949 award of the Medallion of Honor of the Women's International Exposition will be conferred upon National Comics Publications, Inc., for "Constructive Advancement in Comic Books", during our coming 26th Annual Exposition. The award ceremonies are scheduled for 7:30 P.M., Wednesday, November 9th, at the 71st Regiment Armory, New York. We earnestly hope that your schedule may permit you to accept the award personally.

We await your response with much anticipation.

Very sincerely,

Gertrude P. Wixson, Chr.
Prevention of Juvenile
Delinquency Committee of the
Women's National Institute

Mr. Whitney Ellsworth
Editorial Director
National Comics Publications, Inc.
125 East 46th Street
New York 17, N. Y.

GPW/mc

SUPERMAN DC NATIONAL COMICS

BATMAN, No. 57, Feb.-Mar., 1950. Published bi-monthly by National Comics Publications, Inc., 480 Lexington Ave., New York 17, N. Y. Whitney Ellsworth, Editor. Reentered as second class matter Aug. 1, 1941 at the Post Office at New York, N. Y. under the act of March 3, 1879. Yearly subscription in the U. S. 75c including postage. Foreign, $1.50 in American funds. For advertising rates address Richard A. Feldon & Co., 205 E. 42nd St., New York 17, N. Y. Entire contents copyrighted 1949 by National Comics Publications, Inc. Except those who have authorized use of their names, the stories, characters and incidents mentioned in this periodical are entirely imaginary and fictitious and no identification with actual persons, living or dead, is intended or should be inferred.

Printed in U.S.A.

The DC line gets a clean bill of health from the Women's International Exposition during the pre-Comics Crackdown days. (Batman #57, *February/March 1950, inside front cover.*)

the reading of comic books and delinquency," Lukas had noted. "It is my feeling that efforts to link the two are an extension of the archaic impulse by which, through the ages, witchcraft, evil spirits, and other superstitious beliefs have in turn been blamed for anti-social behavior."[4]

Wertham, in fact, did not bother with traditional scientific methodologies to support his charges. Simply because many mentally disturbed youngsters read comic books was enough to suggest to him that the comics themselves were causing juvenile delinquency.

Certainly the comics featured some strong fare at times. Drug addicts were often presented in the hellish cold sweat of their frenzied withdrawals, horror stories had their share of bloody carnage, and the crime comics sometimes celebrated sadistic violence. (One famous crime comic cited by Wertham showed a gangland hit in which two hoods were tied to the back of a car and dragged over a gravel road. One of the hit men noted that there was nothing like a gravel road for "erasing faces.")

But Wertham and his fellow witch-hunters

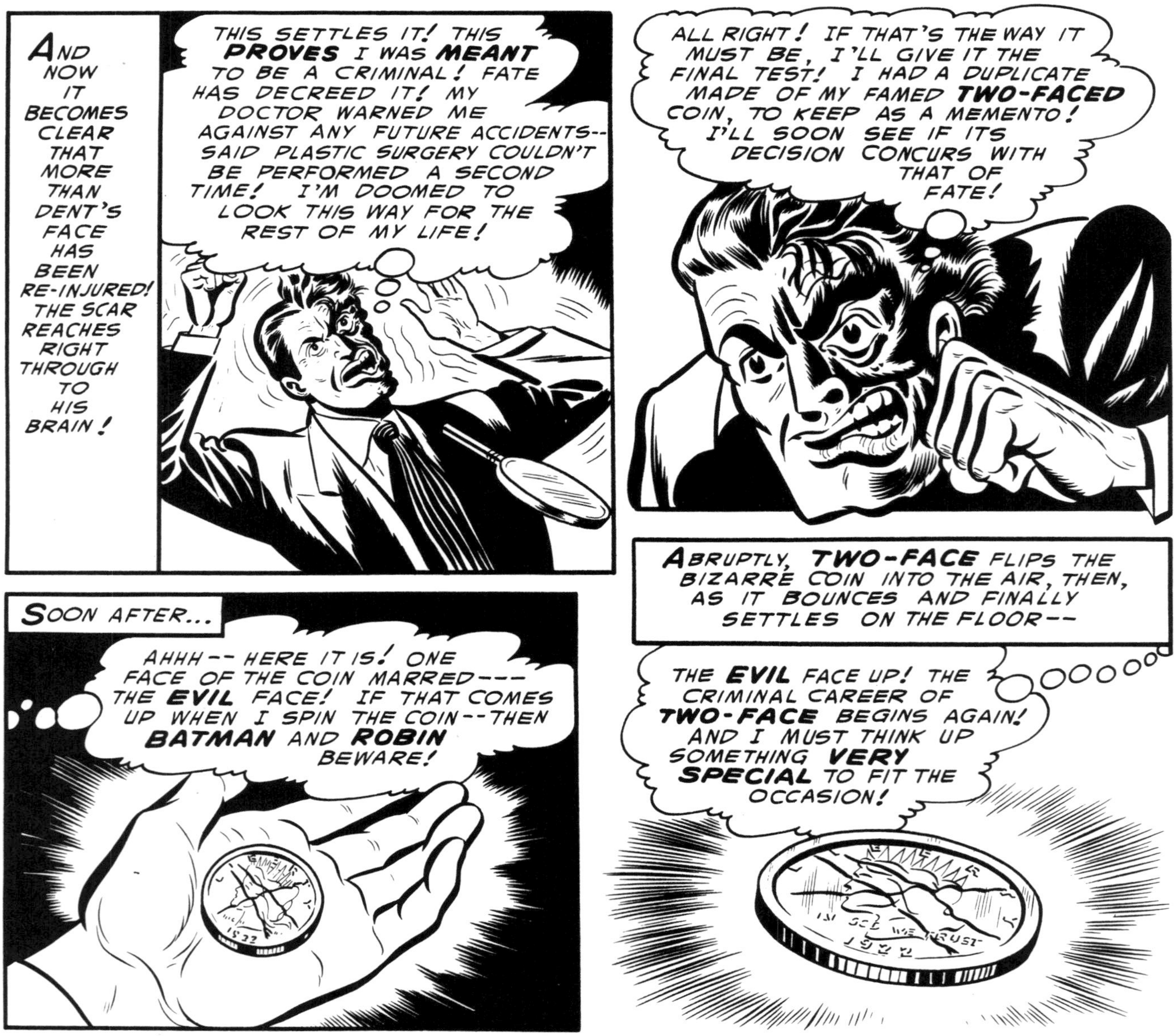
AND NOW IT BECOMES CLEAR THAT MORE THAN DENT'S FACE HAS BEEN RE-INJURED! THE SCAR REACHES RIGHT THROUGH TO HIS BRAIN!
THIS SETTLES IT! THIS PROVES I WAS MEANT TO BE A CRIMINAL! FATE HAS DECREED IT! MY DOCTOR WARNED ME AGAINST ANY FUTURE ACCIDENTS-- SAID PLASTIC SURGERY COULDN'T BE PERFORMED A SECOND TIME! I'M DOOMED TO LOOK THIS WAY FOR THE REST OF MY LIFE!
ALL RIGHT! IF THAT'S THE WAY IT MUST BE, I'LL GIVE IT THE FINAL TEST! I HAD A DUPLICATE MADE OF MY FAMED TWO-FACED COIN, TO KEEP AS A MEMENTO! I'LL SOON SEE IF ITS DECISION CONCURS WITH THAT OF FATE!
SOON AFTER...
AHHH -- HERE IT IS! ONE FACE OF THE COIN MARRED--- THE EVIL FACE! IF THAT COMES UP WHEN I SPIN THE COIN--THEN BATMAN AND ROBIN BEWARE!
ABRUPTLY, TWO-FACE FLIPS THE BIZARRE COIN INTO THE AIR, THEN, AS IT BOUNCES AND FINALLY SETTLES ON THE FLOOR--
THE EVIL FACE UP! THE CRIMINAL CAREER OF TWO-FACE BEGINS AGAIN! AND I MUST THINK UP SOMETHING VERY SPECIAL TO FIT THE OCCASION!

Face the nightmare of Harvey Dent: When a criminal's bomb blast reopens Harvey Dent's old wounds "the scar reaches right into his brain!" (Batman *#81, February 1954, "Two-Face Strikes Again!" p. 3 [select panels].)*

went beyond the bounds of the "parental vigilance" espoused by Josette Frank. In their own demonstration of perversity, they saw all manner of evil signs and subliminal horrors in the comics: vaginas hidden in the shadings on muscles, phallic symbols in background art, female breasts as provocative "headlights."

Wertham seemed to have a fascination with the perverse. Before *Seduction* he wrote an obscure collection of case histories entitled *Show of Violence* that makes the comics he criticized seem as benign as Peter Cottontail stories. The good doctor described such pleasantries as the gentleman who strangled a ten-year-old girl—and then ate her. There was the young widow who went after her children with an ax, and set them on fire, because she felt they were interfering with her career on a dance team. There was the mentally twisted sculptor who had committed some grisly murders in addition to performing a partial amputation of his penis. The sculptor was a special favorite of Wertham's, and *Show of Violence* took eighty-four pages to detail that prize case study.[5]

It was this kind of clinical voyeurism that irked Wertham's critics. Les Daniels, author of *Comix: A History of Comic Books in America,* opines that Wertham's success in marshaling his anti-comics crusade lay in the "subtle manipulation of his audience's most dread desires," which earned him free passage "into the mighty universe of the ladies' luncheon-club circuit."[6]

Wertham's charges that Batman and Robin were gay is a good example of the tactics used at the time to attack comics.

"Using his knowledge of morbid deviation, Dr. Wertham attempted to analyze fantasy-projections as though they were real people," Les Daniels writes. "Thus Batman and Robin, two crime fighters who shared the same quarters, were analyzed as homosexuals, despite the clear lack of overt evidence. If they had been actual men, they could have won a libel suit.[7]

Bob Kane has dismissed the notion of Batman and Robin as homosexuals, aghast that anyone would read into his characters some subliminal ode to homoeroticism. After all, Bruce Wayne regularly squired the most beautiful women in Gotham City and presumably had a healthy sex life. Even Dick Grayson, who showed no fear when battling crooks, would occasionally get all flustered and tongue-tied in the presence of a female classmate who had won his heart.

But the simple fact that Batman and Robin lived in the same rambling mansion was enough to make them homosexuals in Wertham's view. With the same eyes that saw phallic symbols in every drawing, the most seemingly innocent portrayal of the Gotham crime busters was enough to confirm his contentions. Thus, a picture of Robin standing with his legs spread and arms akimbo represented not the triumphant stance of a true martial artist but a flaunting of genitalia. And when Batman put his arm on Robin's shoulders, Wertham saw "proof" that their bond was a sexual one.

The unfounded rumors would shadow the Dynamic Duo for years. A decade later the Wertham charge even led Julius Schwartz, who had taken over the editorial duties on the Batman titles from old pro Jack Schiff in 1964, to kill loyal Alfred to placate the witch-hunting hordes!

"The reason I killed off Alfred was, there was a lot of talk about three men living in the same house," Schwartz recalls. "Many people were questioning why three males were living together. So I said, 'Okay, I'll kill off one of the males and put a woman in there!' And the woman turned out to be Aunt Harriet, the aunt of Dick Grayson....I guess that was pretty drastic, killing off Alfred."

It was sad that Wertham got so much mileage out of his unwarranted attacks on Batman. This was the same Batman who had fought Nazi spies and aided the War Bond effort (and was still get-

4. Ibid., p. 7

5. Frederic Wertham, M.D., *The Show of Violence* (Garden City, New York: Doubleday, 1949) pp. 72–94, 99–183, 211–38.

6. Les Daniels, *Comix: A History of Comic Books in America* (New York: Bonanza Books, 1971), p. 87.

7. Daniels, *Comix.*

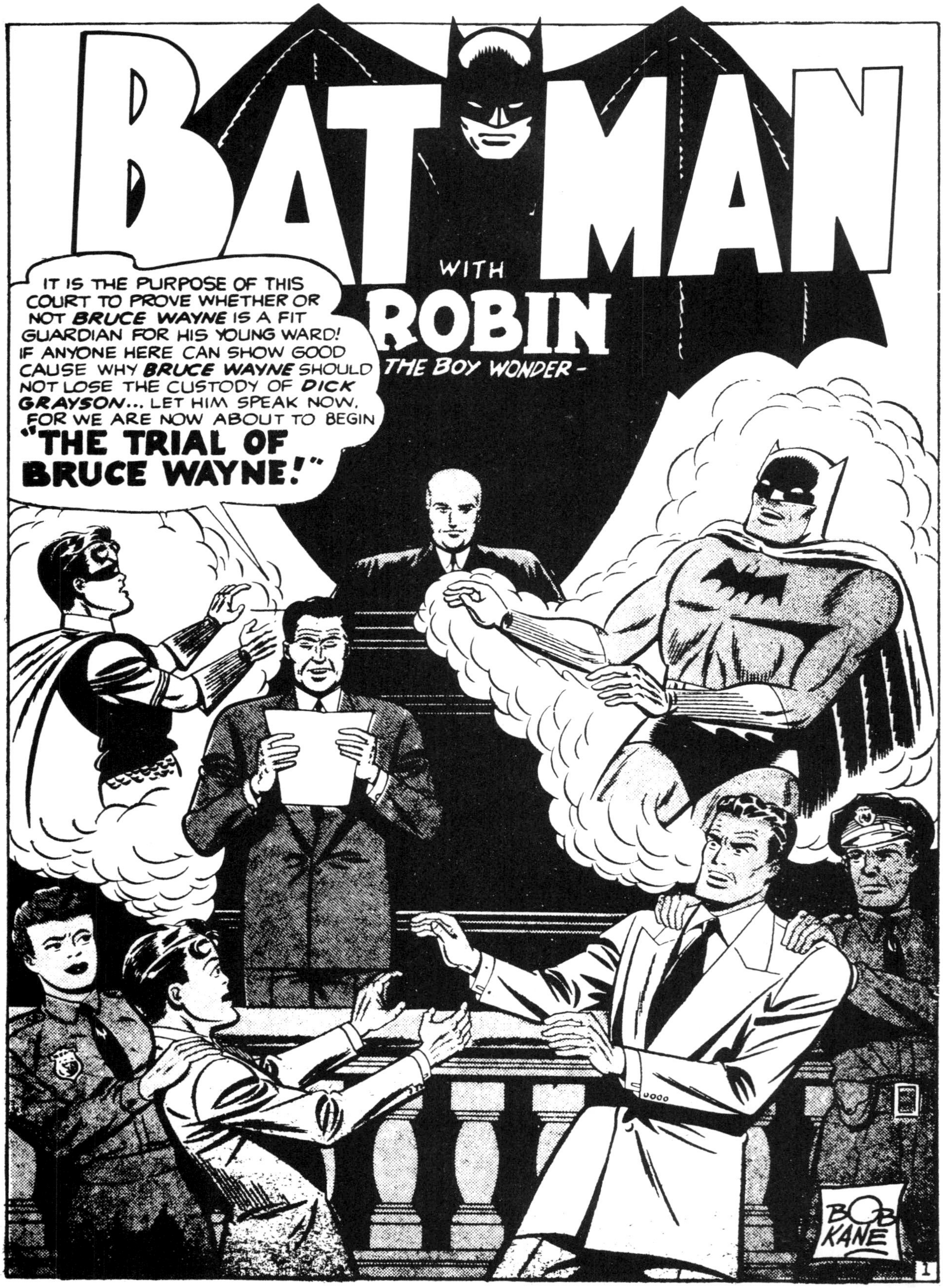
BATMAN
WITH
ROBIN
THE BOY WONDER -
IT IS THE PURPOSE OF THIS COURT TO PROVE WHETHER OR NOT BRUCE WAYNE IS A FIT GUARDIAN FOR HIS YOUNG WARD! IF ANYONE HERE CAN SHOW GOOD CAUSE WHY BRUCE WAYNE SHOULD NOT LOSE THE CUSTODY OF DICK GRAYSON... LET HIM SPEAK NOW, FOR WE ARE NOW ABOUT TO BEGIN "THE TRIAL OF BRUCE WAYNE!"
BOB KANE
1

A cornerstone of Batman bashing during the Comics Crackdown era was all that talk about Bruce and Dick's uh . . . relationship. And even in the comic book dimension their friendship was under siege. (*Batman* #57, *February/March 1950, "The Trial of Bruce Wayne!" p. 1 [splash page].*)

ting calls for special assignments from the State Department in the 1950s), bestowed an annual "Merry Christmas" message to the people of Gotham City, and even lectured kids on how to be courteous on a bus, or on the importance of racial equality—in the 1950s no less!

"Batman was fairly liberal in his thinking," notes Jack Schiff, who, while DC's managing editor from the 1940s through the 1960's, was in charge of all the Batman titles. "He had a heart! In many of the stories we tried to show him caring for oppressed people.... That's missing now in comics, this feeling of having some kind of concern about people and teaching moral values."

Batman did take on more of what Denny O'Neil has referred to as a "benign scoutmaster" personality during the comic crackdown period. There he was, the former "weird figure of the night," too often waltzing around Gotham in the light of day. Even the evil Joker, who hadn't murdered any innocent people for years, became

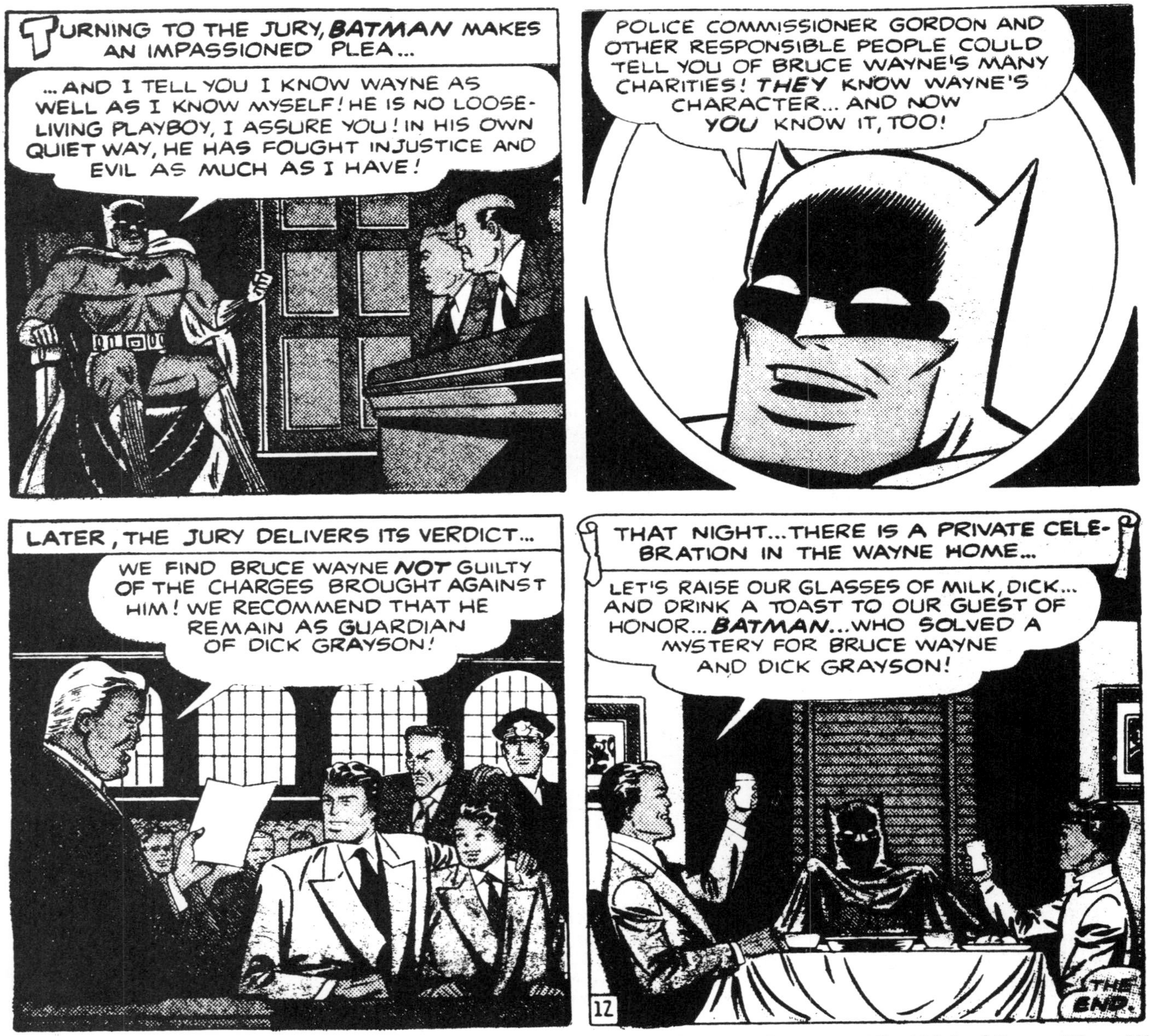

TURNING TO THE JURY, BATMAN MAKES AN IMPASSIONED PLEA...
...AND I TELL YOU I KNOW WAYNE AS WELL AS I KNOW MYSELF! HE IS NO LOOSE-LIVING PLAYBOY, I ASSURE YOU! IN HIS OWN QUIET WAY, HE HAS FOUGHT INJUSTICE AND EVIL AS MUCH AS I HAVE!
POLICE COMMISSIONER GORDON AND OTHER RESPONSIBLE PEOPLE COULD TELL YOU OF BRUCE WAYNE'S MANY CHARITIES! THEY KNOW WAYNE'S CHARACTER... AND NOW YOU KNOW IT, TOO!
LATER, THE JURY DELIVERS ITS VERDICT...
WE FIND BRUCE WAYNE NOT GUILTY OF THE CHARGES BROUGHT AGAINST HIM! WE RECOMMEND THAT HE REMAIN AS GUARDIAN OF DICK GRAYSON!
THAT NIGHT...THERE IS A PRIVATE CELEBRATION IN THE WAYNE HOME...
LET'S RAISE OUR GLASSES OF MILK, DICK... AND DRINK A TOAST TO OUR GUEST OF HONOR... BATMAN...WHO SOLVED A MYSTERY FOR BRUCE WAYNE AND DICK GRAYSON!
12
THE END.

Batman clears Bruce Wayne's good name. (Batman #57, February/March 1950, "The Trial of Bruce Wayne!" p. 12 [select panels].)

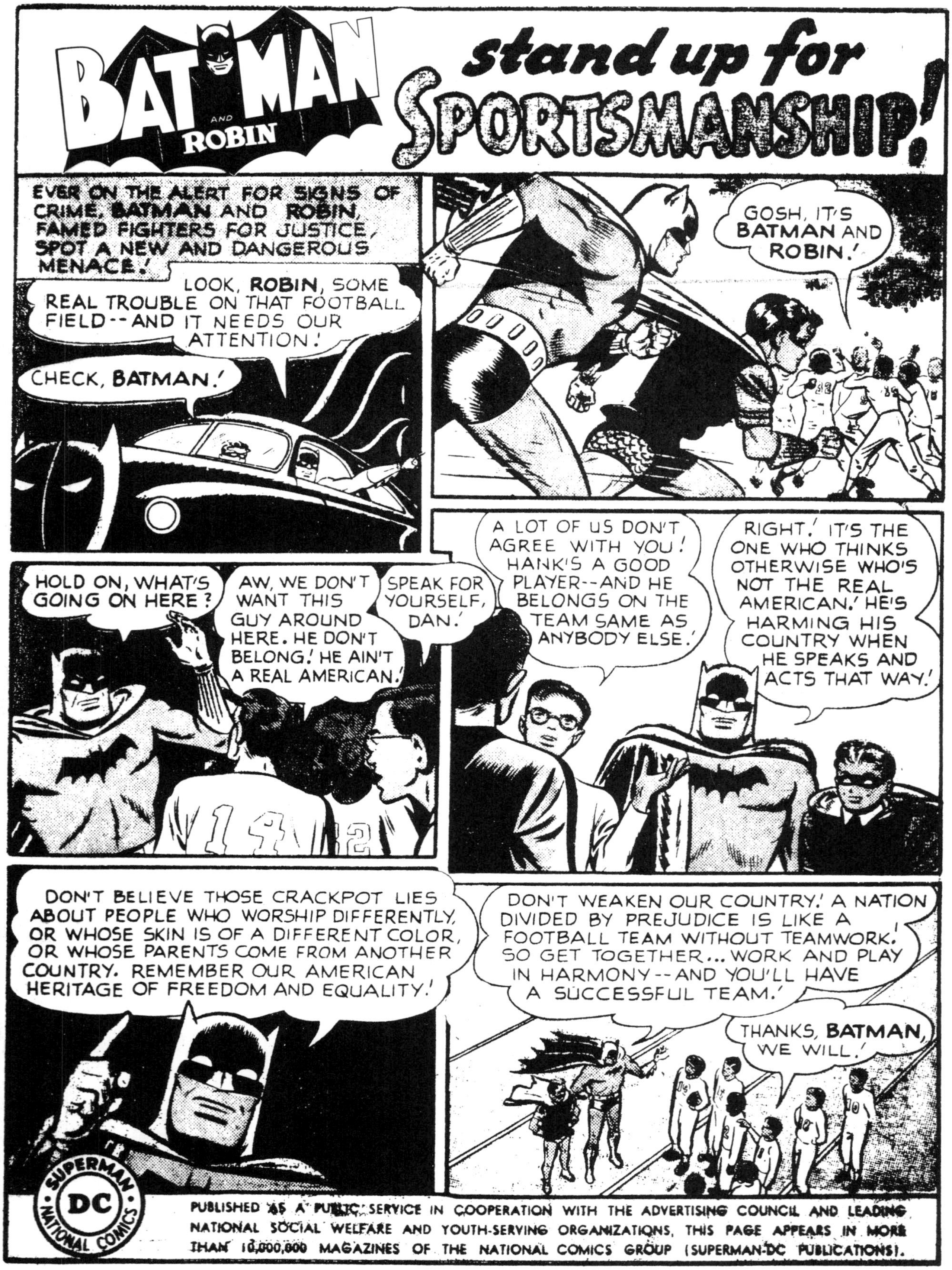
BATMAN AND ROBIN
stand up for SPORTSMANSHIP!
EVER ON THE ALERT FOR SIGNS OF CRIME, BATMAN AND ROBIN, FAMED FIGHTERS FOR JUSTICE, SPOT A NEW AND DANGEROUS MENACE!
LOOK, ROBIN, SOME REAL TROUBLE ON THAT FOOTBALL FIELD--AND IT NEEDS OUR ATTENTION!
CHECK, BATMAN!
GOSH, IT'S BATMAN AND ROBIN!
HOLD ON, WHAT'S GOING ON HERE?
AW, WE DON'T WANT THIS GUY AROUND HERE. HE DON'T BELONG! HE AIN'T A REAL AMERICAN!
SPEAK FOR YOURSELF, DAN!
A LOT OF US DON'T AGREE WITH YOU! HANK'S A GOOD PLAYER--AND HE BELONGS ON THE TEAM SAME AS ANYBODY ELSE!
RIGHT! IT'S THE ONE WHO THINKS OTHERWISE WHO'S NOT THE REAL AMERICAN! HE'S HARMING HIS COUNTRY WHEN HE SPEAKS AND ACTS THAT WAY!
DON'T BELIEVE THOSE CRACKPOT LIES ABOUT PEOPLE WHO WORSHIP DIFFERENTLY, OR WHOSE SKIN IS OF A DIFFERENT COLOR, OR WHOSE PARENTS COME FROM ANOTHER COUNTRY. REMEMBER OUR AMERICAN HERITAGE OF FREEDOM AND EQUALITY!
DON'T WEAKEN OUR COUNTRY! A NATION DIVIDED BY PREJUDICE IS LIKE A FOOTBALL TEAM WITHOUT TEAMWORK! SO GET TOGETHER... WORK AND PLAY IN HARMONY--AND YOU'LL HAVE A SUCCESSFUL TEAM!
THANKS, BATMAN, WE WILL!
SUPERMAN DC NATIONAL COMICS
PUBLISHED AS A PUBLIC SERVICE IN COOPERATION WITH THE ADVERTISING COUNCIL AND LEADING NATIONAL SOCIAL WELFARE AND YOUTH-SERVING ORGANIZATIONS, THIS PAGE APPEARS IN MORE THAN 10,000,000 MAGAZINES OF THE NATIONAL COMICS GROUP (SUPERMAN-DC PUBLICATIONS).

Citizen Batman settles a racial dispute with a civics lesson. Batman *#57, February/March 1950, ''Batman and Robin Stand up for Sportsmanship!'' last page of magazine.*

merely a wacky, ribald nuisance.

During the decade Batman tales moved away from the original formula of darkness and menace that had set the tone in the Golden Age. Batman cases emphasized his detective qualities, or involved globetrotting adventures (anything to get out of town). By the end of the decade Batman stories would be so full of science fiction that DC editors years later would remember the time as "the monster fad."

Wertham's tactics not only roughed up the Dynamic Duo, but changed the prosperous outlook of the entire comics industry. His crusade had led to congressional hearings (which did not legislate against comics but helped to legitimize the anticomics forces) and book burnings.

The repression resulted in hundreds of titles disappearing from the newsstands as entire publishing houses vanished overnight. The surviving publishers surrendered and, in September of 1954, formed the Comics Code Authority. The little logo bearing the legend "Approved by the Comics Code Authority" carried a divine weight until the 1980s, when a new era of creativity would relax such censorship guidelines.

The editorial standards of the Code were so restrictive that the comics lost the zip and verve that had made them so entertaining. As comics became boring, and television began asserting itself as the prime entertainment medium, sales fell even more.

EC alone, boasting such in-house talent as Harvey Kurtzman, Wallace Wood, Al Williamson, Jack Davis, Joe Orlando, and Johnny Craig, was virtually driven out of business. The only revenge for publisher Gaines was that he was able to safely steer his satirical *Mad Magazine* through the dangerous period.

"I didn't live through that (the comic crackdown period), except as a child, but people lost their professions, people committed suicide—it was a very sad time," says artist Neal Adams, whose Batman work would enliven the Dark Knight saga in the 1970s. "One of my favorite artists for a good deal of the time worked as a night watchman. Other artists moved on, became assistants on comic strips, or went out to California to get into the animation field. There was very little to do, and that was the way it was."

To put the crackdown in perspective, Adams, who is in his late forties, estimates that no one working in the field today is five years his junior, or five years his senior. In other words, the Wertham era created a ten-year period in which no new creators entered the field.

That Batman survived at all is a credit to the compelling nature of the character. Batman fans who had enjoyed the Gotham crime buster during the wild Golden Age party were willing to stick with their hero during the dark days of the comic crackdown.

But fans would have a long wait before the Caped Crusader regained his original stature as the dreaded avenger of the dark streets of Gotham.

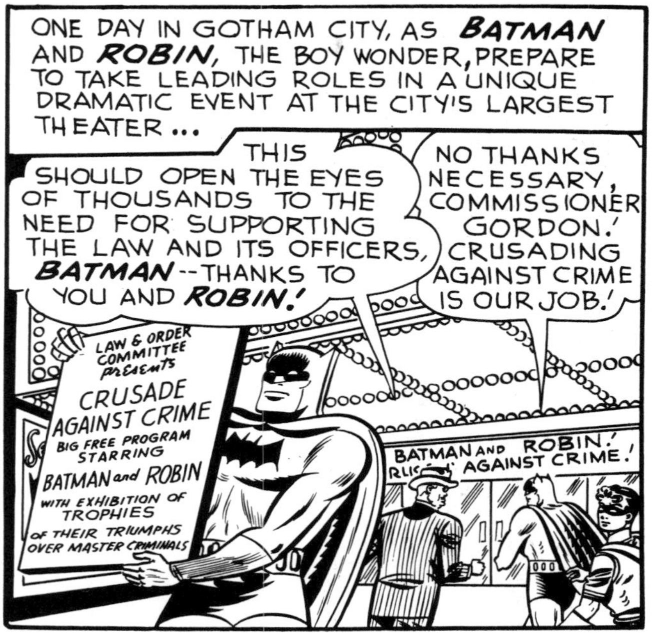
ONE DAY IN GOTHAM CITY, AS BATMAN AND ROBIN, THE BOY WONDER, PREPARE TO TAKE LEADING ROLES IN A UNIQUE DRAMATIC EVENT AT THE CITY'S LARGEST THEATER...
THIS SHOULD OPEN THE EYES OF THOUSANDS TO THE NEED FOR SUPPORTING THE LAW AND ITS OFFICERS, BATMAN--THANKS TO YOU AND ROBIN!
NO THANKS NECESSARY, COMMISSIONER GORDON! CRUSADING AGAINST CRIME IS OUR JOB!
LAW & ORDER COMMITTEE PRESENTS CRUSADE AGAINST CRIME BIG FREE PROGRAM STARRING BATMAN and ROBIN WITH EXHIBITION OF TROPHIES OF THEIR TRIUMPHS OVER MASTER CRIMINALS
BATMAN AND ROBIN!
AGAINST CRIME!

Detective #187, September 1952, "The Double-Crimes of Two-Face!" p. 2 [panel].

CHAPTER 6

ROBIN, THE BOY WONDER!

Batman's move away from his hard-line approach was signaled by the introduction of Robin, the Boy Wonder . . . . Robin was to relieve the gloom of isolation, demanding by his very presence that the bitter Batman become more sympathetic, more human. He also provided an opportunity for some needed dialogue, and gave younger readers a character with whom they could identify. The bright colors of his red, yellow and green costume lightened the dark tone of the entire series, and set a major precedent for later heroes, very few of which would spring up without a kid companion in tow.

—*Les Daniels in* Comix: A History of Comic Books in America[1] *(E.P. Dutton, Inc. Copyright © 1971 by Les Daniels and Mad Peck Studios)*

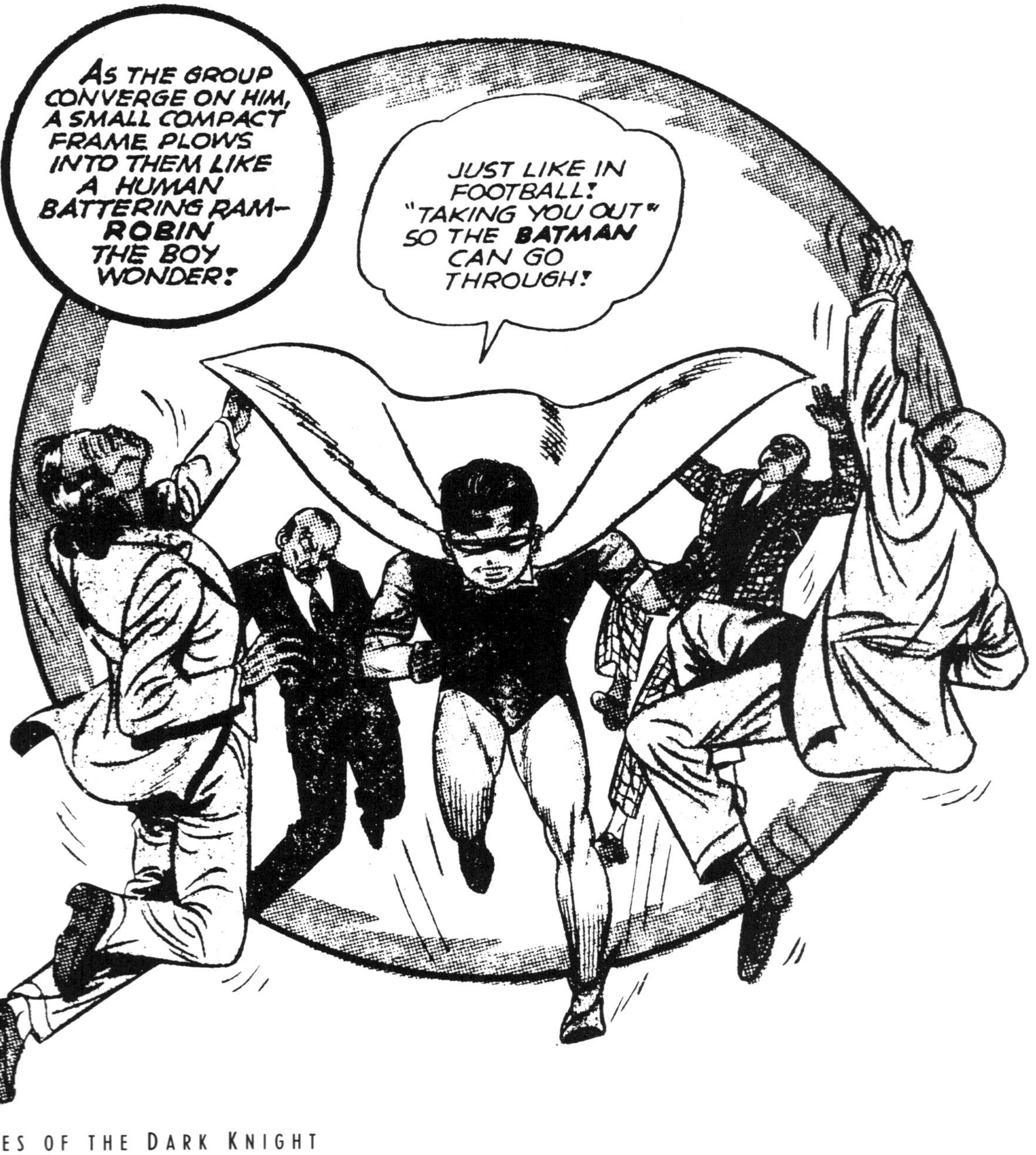
AS THE GROUP CONVERGE ON HIM, A SMALL COMPACT FRAME PLOWS INTO THEM LIKE A HUMAN BATTERING RAM—ROBIN THE BOY WONDER!
JUST LIKE IN FOOTBALL! "TAKING YOU OUT" SO THE BATMAN CAN GO THROUGH!

BY ALL ACCOUNTS THE BROODING, VIGILANTE Batman of 1939 was in need of a lighter touch. But just before the Batman took too sinister a turn, the Dark Knight met a circus kid named Dick Grayson, who, teamed with his parents, formed the Flying Graysons trapeze act. The night of his fateful meeting with Batman, Dick had seen his parents fall to their death when their ropes snapped during a high-wire act under the big top.

But Dick discovered that the ropes had been weakened with acid and that his parents' death had been the penalty exacted by Gotham crime lord "Boss" Zucco for the refusal of the circus manager to pay protection money.

Batman, still suspicious of the police and the hold Zucco might have over them, appeared to Grayson like a dark angel and warned him against going to the authorities. Perhaps recognizing a kindred spirit, Batman couldn't say no when the boy insisted they team up to avenge his parents' death.

As Batman and Robin, they broke "Boss" Zucco's hold on the city. In response the governor promised to use the power of his office to see that Gotham City politics stayed clean. (Buried in the back pages of the Gotham papers would be the notice that millionaire socialite Bruce Wayne had legally adopted as his ward the tragic orphan Dick Grayson.)

Not all Batman fans were pleased that this "laughing, fighting, young daredevil" had joined forces with the darkest, grimmest crime buster since the Shadow.

"I couldn't stand boy companions," writes Jules Feiffer. "... The super *grownups* were the ones I identified with. They were versions of me in the future. There was still time to prepare. But Robin the Boy Wonder was my own age. One need only look at him to see he could fight better, swing from a rope better, play ball better, eat better, and live better—for while I lived in the east Bronx, Robin lived in a mansion, and while I was trying, somehow, to please my mother—and getting it all wrong, Robin was rescuing Batman and getting the gold medals."[2]

And of course, there would come Dr. Wertham's accusations that the legal papers giving Bruce custody over Dick were really a cover for their licentious relationship.

The sly sneers aside, the fact is, Batman and Robin had a blood brother closeness. Theirs was a spiritual intimacy forged from the stress of countless battles fought side by side. But Batman was also a mentor, protector, and father-figure. In their crime-fighting roles, Batman served as the field general during battle, while as Dick Grayson's guardian, he saw to it that the boy grew up with something at least close to a normal childhood.

When Robin first appeared in *Detective Comics* 38, the splash page announced:

"The Batman, that amazing weird figure of night, at last takes under his protecting mantle, an ally in his relentless fight against crime...."

In Robin Batman had a lively pupil who seemed far more resilient in responding to the death of his parents than had the young, obsessed Bruce Wayne. Dick Grayson's enthusiasm helped bring a smile to Batman's lips. Robin helped make fighting crime FUN!

As father figure Batman was like a dad priming his favorite son to eventually take over the

1. Daniels, *Comix,* pp. 12–13.
2. Feiffer, *Comic Book Heroes,* pp. 42–43.

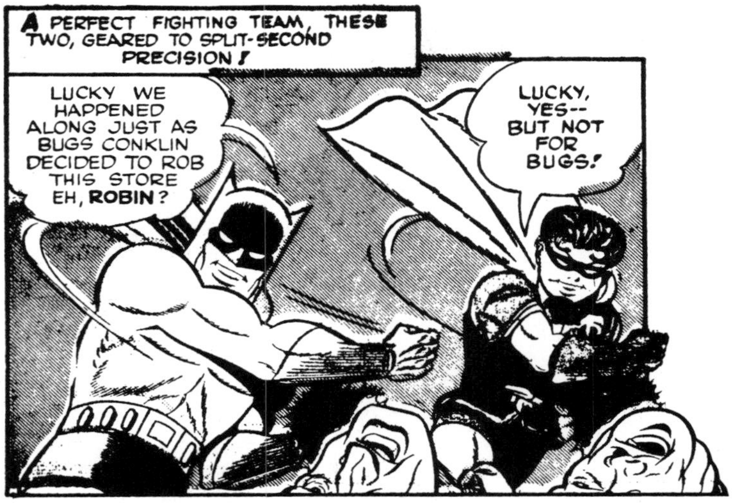
A PERFECT FIGHTING TEAM, THESE TWO, GEARED TO SPLIT-SECOND PRECISION!
LUCKY WE HAPPENED ALONG JUST AS BUGS CONKLIN DECIDED TO ROB THIS STORE EH, ROBIN?
LUCKY, YES-- BUT NOT FOR BUGS!

Above: Batman #23, *June/July 1944, "Damsel in Distress!" p. 2 [panel].* Left: Detective #45, *November 1940, "The Case of the Laughing Death!" p. 13 [panel].*

family business. One day you'll outgrow your Robin uniform, he would sometimes say. One day I'll be retired and you'll carry on the tradition as Batman II.

In many ways Dick Grayson was a quicker study of the crime fighter's art than Bruce Wayne. After all, it took Bruce Wayne fifteen years to prepare, while Dick Grayson was turned into a topflight crime fighter within months. (Of course, Dick had the greatest teacher an aspiring young crusader could ask for.)

Dick Grayson may even have been the purer athlete. He certainly didn't need a tragedy as the impetus to go out and get into shape. At an early age he was already a superb gymnast and a star on the flying trapeze.

Dick Grayson's life as a circus performer gave him the philosophical, worldly experience he needed to bounce back emotionally from the tragedy of his parents' death. Whereas young Bruce Wayne had been born into comfort and privilege, Dick Grayson had always lived a more vagabond life. Constant traveling with the circus to hundreds of strange new towns had demanded constant emotional adjustments.

Any fan of the finer points of crime fighting

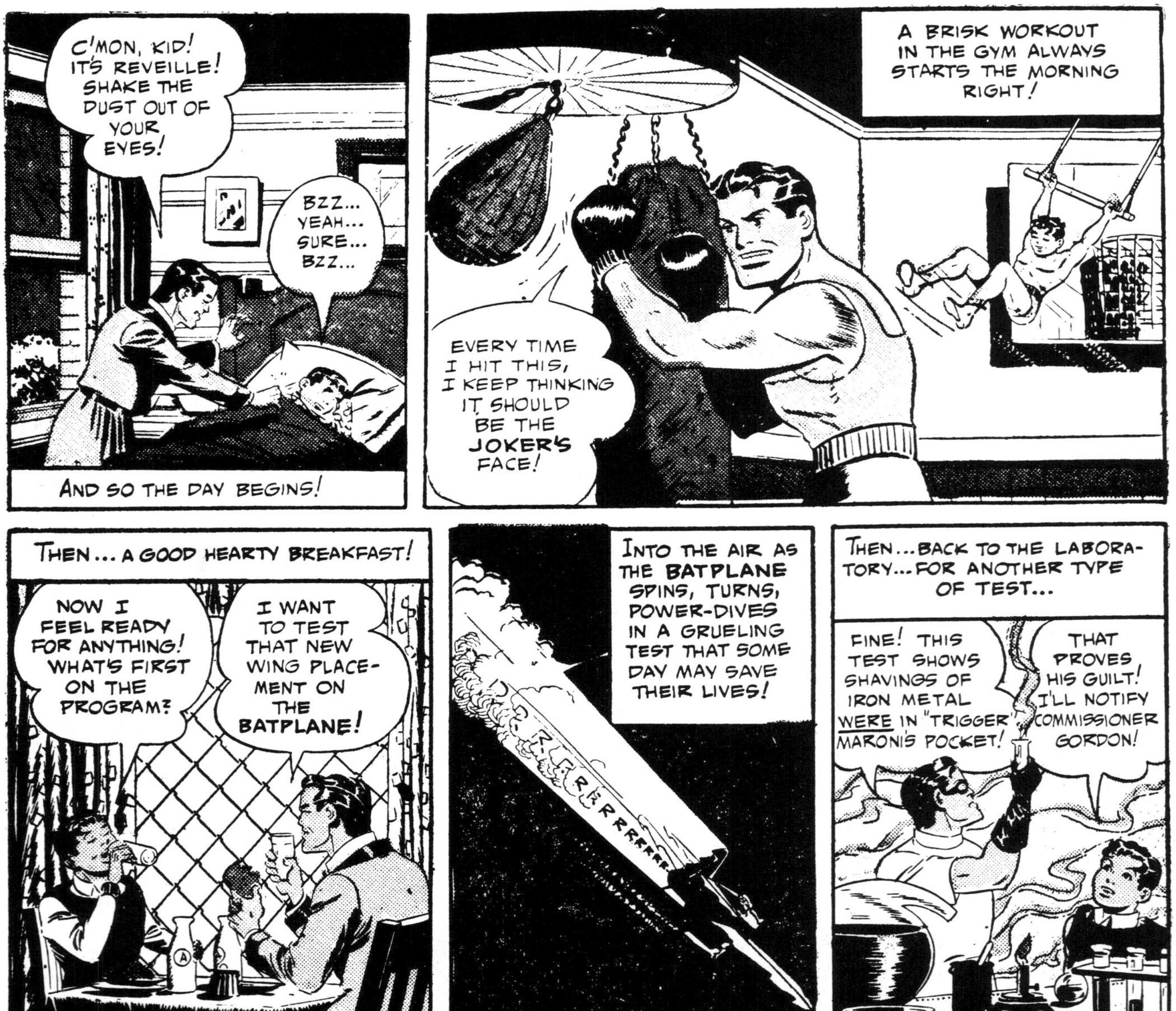
C'MON, KID! IT'S REVEILLE! SHAKE THE DUST OUT OF YOUR EYES!
BZZ... YEAH... SURE... BZZ...
AND SO THE DAY BEGINS!
A BRISK WORKOUT IN THE GYM ALWAYS STARTS THE MORNING RIGHT!
EVERY TIME I HIT THIS, I KEEP THINKING IT SHOULD BE THE JOKER'S FACE!
THEN ... A GOOD HEARTY BREAKFAST!
NOW I FEEL READY FOR ANYTHING! WHAT'S FIRST ON THE PROGRAM?
I WANT TO TEST THAT NEW WING PLACEMENT ON THE BATPLANE!
INTO THE AIR AS THE BATPLANE SPINS, TURNS, POWER-DIVES IN A GRUELING TEST THAT SOME DAY MAY SAVE THEIR LIVES!
THEN...BACK TO THE LABORATORY...FOR ANOTHER TYPE OF TEST...
FINE! THIS TEST SHOWS SHAVINGS OF IRON METAL WERE IN "TRIGGER" MARONI'S POCKET!
THAT PROVES HIS GUILT! I'LL NOTIFY COMMISSIONER GORDON!

Starting the day the Batman and Robin way. (Batman *#12, August-September 1942, "Around The Clock With The Batman!" p. 3 [select panels].*)

has to give Robin his due. His own natural discipline helped him stay in control during the most dangerous situations, his heroism often carried the fight, and his gritty determination saved the Dark Knight's life many times.

Robin has been an inspiration to many Batman fans over the years. One of Robin's biggest fans was the late Jimmy Jacobs, who, with his partner, Bill Cayton, managed four boxing champs, including powerhouse heavyweight Mike Tyson.

Jacobs had been a great athlete himself, winning the U.S. Handball Association singles and doubles championships six times each from 1955 to 1968. During the intensity of handball competition, Jacobs often turned to Robin for inspiration, no small compliment considering Jacobs was so plugged in to the superhero mythos that his collection of half a million comic books has been considered the largest in the world.

"All of us are susceptible to our emotions when under stress," Jacobs once said, "and when I was younger, I would think, What would Robin do? Instead of succumbing to nervous ap-

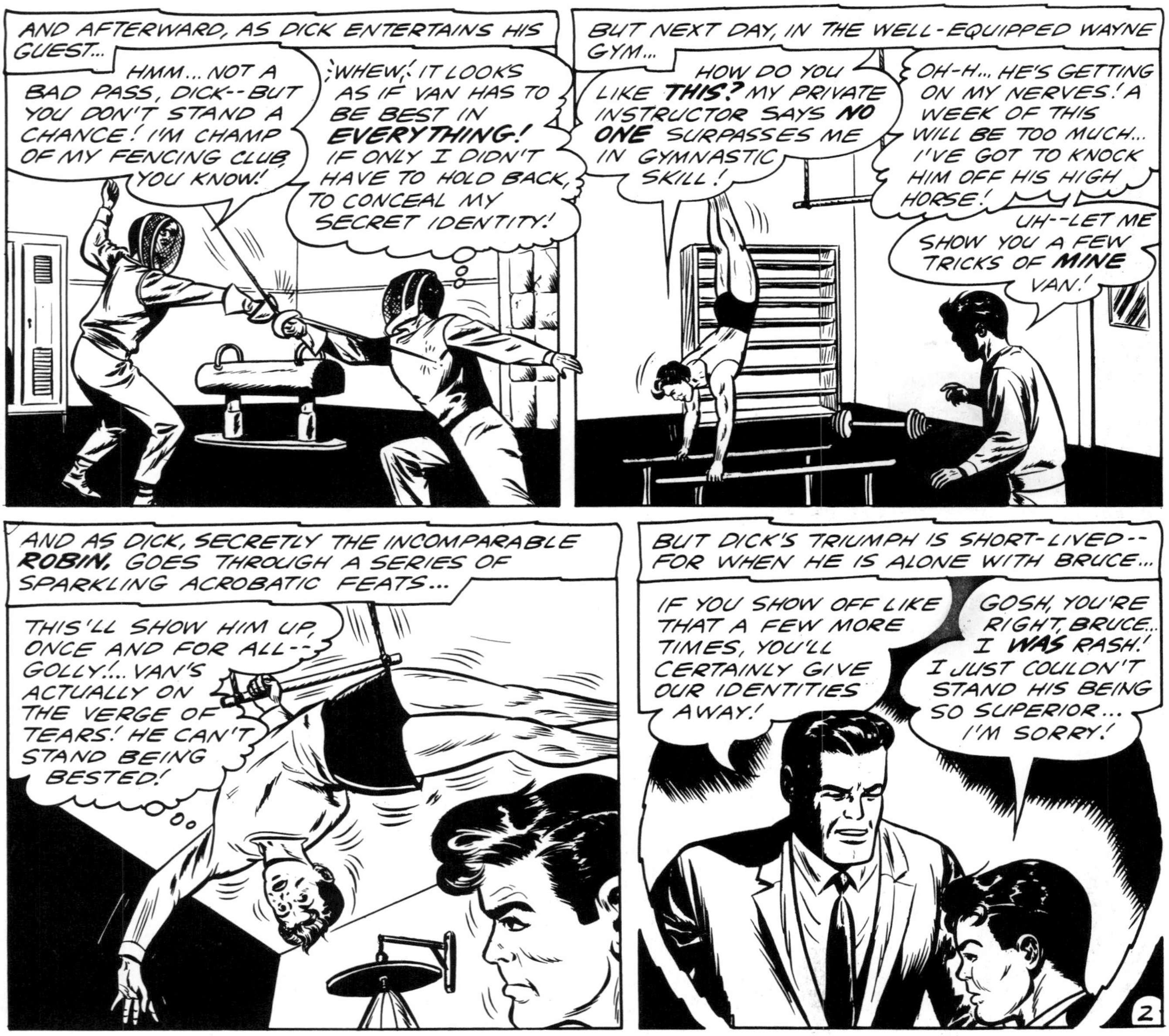
AND AFTERWARD, AS DICK ENTERTAINS HIS GUEST...
HMM... NOT A BAD PASS, DICK--BUT YOU DON'T STAND A CHANCE! I'M CHAMP OF MY FENCING CLUB, YOU KNOW!
WHEW! IT LOOKS AS IF VAN HAS TO BE BEST IN EVERYTHING! IF ONLY I DIDN'T HAVE TO HOLD BACK, TO CONCEAL MY SECRET IDENTITY!
BUT NEXT DAY, IN THE WELL-EQUIPPED WAYNE GYM...
HOW DO YOU LIKE THIS? MY PRIVATE INSTRUCTOR SAYS NO ONE SURPASSES ME IN GYMNASTIC SKILL!
OH-H... HE'S GETTING ON MY NERVES! A WEEK OF THIS WILL BE TOO MUCH... I'VE GOT TO KNOCK HIM OFF HIS HIGH HORSE!
UH--LET ME SHOW YOU A FEW TRICKS OF MINE VAN!
AND AS DICK, SECRETLY THE INCOMPARABLE ROBIN, GOES THROUGH A SERIES OF SPARKLING ACROBATIC FEATS...
THIS'LL SHOW HIM UP, ONCE AND FOR ALL--
GOLLY!... VAN'S ACTUALLY ON THE VERGE OF TEARS! HE CAN'T STAND BEING BESTED!
BUT DICK'S TRIUMPH IS SHORT-LIVED--FOR WHEN HE IS ALONE WITH BRUCE...
IF YOU SHOW OFF LIKE THAT A FEW MORE TIMES, YOU'LL CERTAINLY GIVE OUR IDENTITIES AWAY!
GOSH, YOU'RE RIGHT, BRUCE... I WAS RASH! I JUST COULDN'T STAND HIS BEING SO SUPERIOR... I'M SORRY!
2

The major drawback of a dual identity for Dick Grayson were those times when he had to keep his superior abilities under wraps ("If I look too good someone may suspect my secret Robin identity!"). (Batman *#148, June 1962, "The Boy Who Was Robin," p. 2 [select panels].)*

Here Dick Grayson's early acrobatic training pays off as he catches the crooks (and a Batman compliment!). (Batman #162, March 1964, ''Robin's New Secret Identity!'' p. 3 [select panels].)

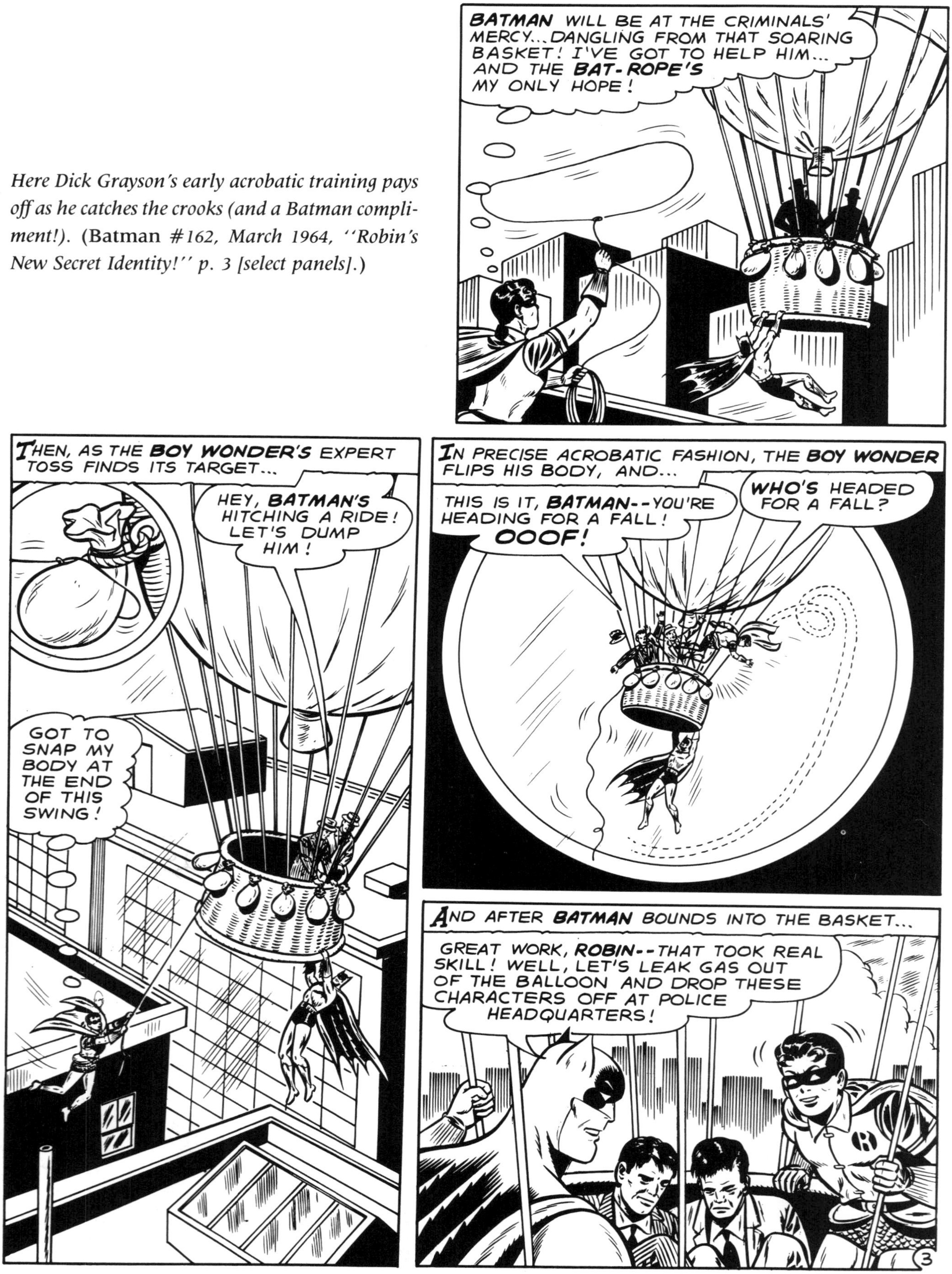
BATMAN WILL BE AT THE CRIMINALS' MERCY...DANGLING FROM THAT SOARING BASKET! I'VE GOT TO HELP HIM... AND THE BAT-ROPE'S MY ONLY HOPE!
THEN, AS THE BOY WONDER'S EXPERT TOSS FINDS ITS TARGET...
HEY, BATMAN'S HITCHING A RIDE! LET'S DUMP HIM!
GOT TO SNAP MY BODY AT THE END OF THIS SWING!
IN PRECISE ACROBATIC FASHION, THE BOY WONDER FLIPS HIS BODY, AND...
THIS IS IT, BATMAN--YOU'RE HEADING FOR A FALL! OOOF!
WHO'S HEADED FOR A FALL?
AND AFTER BATMAN BOUNDS INTO THE BASKET...
GREAT WORK, ROBIN--THAT TOOK REAL SKILL! WELL, LET'S LEAK GAS OUT OF THE BALLOON AND DROP THESE CHARACTERS OFF AT POLICE HEADQUARTERS!
3

prehension, I would transform myself into this other character."[3]

It was always a stirring sight to see the Dynamic Duo as they fought crime with a grin, dealing roundhouse rights and tandem wisecracks in equal measure. They used their brains, they used their brawn, they were a team.

But one day Robin would grow up, leave Wayne Manor, and go to college. He would have girlfriends, would begin to grow apart from Batman....

But perhaps that's getting ahead of the story.

For the nonce let's raise our glasses of milk, Robin's favorite beverage, and toast the Boy Wonder. We can pay Robin no finer tribute than to remember his first case, when he single-handedly took on the ruthless "Boss" Zucco and his men. ("W-why it's only a KID!" the crooks exclaimed as Robin plowed through them like a scythe through weeds.)

"Okay, you reckless young squirt, I ought to whale you for jumping those men alone," a smiling Bruce Wayne said to his young ward after the adventure. "Why didn't you wait for me?"

"Aw! I didn't want to miss any of the fun," Dick Grayson grinned in return. "Say, I can hardly wait till we go on our next case. I bet it'll be a corker!"

3. Robert H. Boyle, "A Champ Who Helped Mold Champs," *Sports Illustrated,* April 4, 1988, p. 22.

I'LL... PHHHFT!
I DIDN'T QUITE GET WHAT YOU SAID!
A-NOTHER THUNDER-BOLT BLOW--THEN
HO HUM!
THE FRIGHTENED MEN SHOW THEIR TRUE COLOR!
HEY--WHERE ARE YOU BOYS GOING?-- LETS PLAY SOME MORE!
N-NO! DON'T HIT ME AGAIN! I QUIT--YOU WIN!
T-TAKE IT EASY KID!

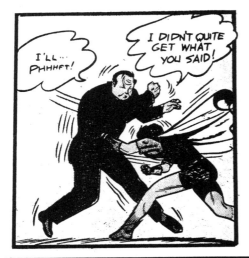

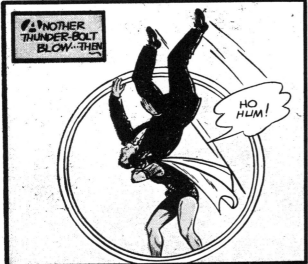

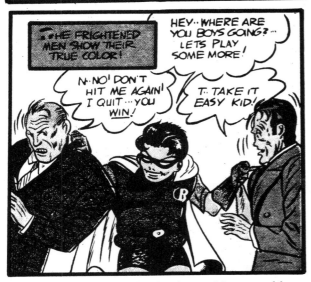

Above: *From the very beginning Robin proved he was a great fighter—and that crooks were yellow!* (Batman *#1 Spring 1940, untitled story, p. 9 [select panels].*) Right: Batman *#137, February 1961, "Robin's New Boss," p. 10 [panel].*

YES, WE'RE TOGETHER AGAIN --AS A TEAM!
C'MON, ROBIN-- DINNER'S WAITING... LET'S GO HOME!
THE END

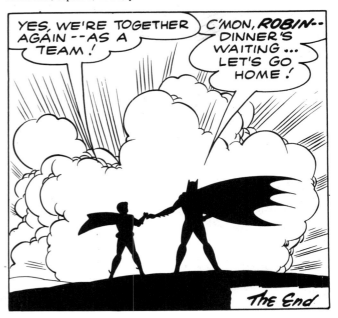

CHAPTER 7

THE STRANGE LIVES OF BATMAN AND ROBIN

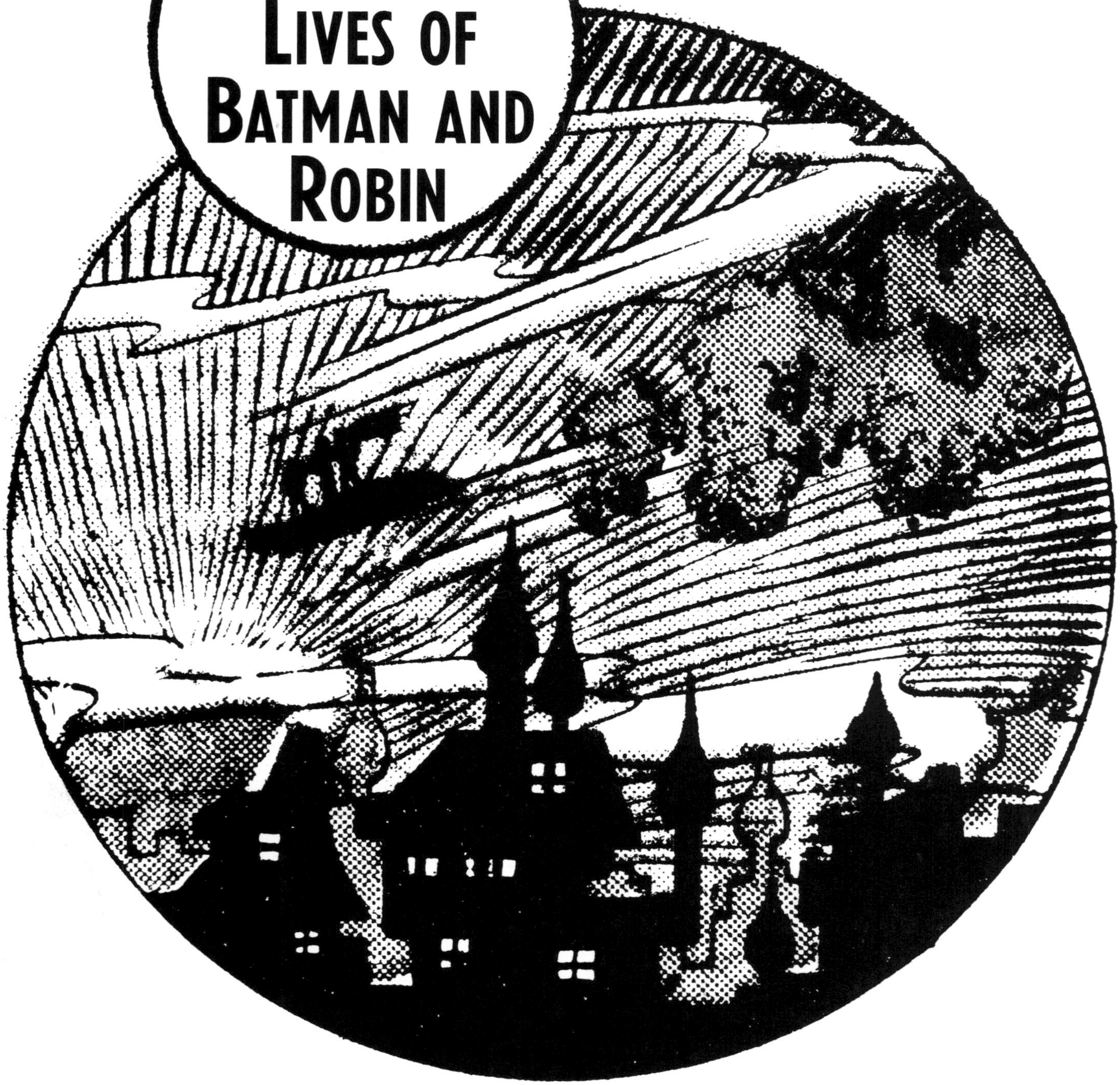

THE DARK KNIGHT HAS NEVER BEEN AFRAID to take one step beyond the province of reality. Back in the Golden Age, for example, the Dark Knight once battled witches and giants in an enchanted dimension and slayed vampires in Hungary.[1]

But much to the chagrin of many Bat-fans, the adventures took a decided turn toward science fiction in the late 1950s. (Comic book historians Will Jacobs and Gerard Jones mark the

1. References: "Book of Enchantment," *Batman* 5 (Spring 1941); Untitled vampire story, *Detective Comics* 32 (October 1939).

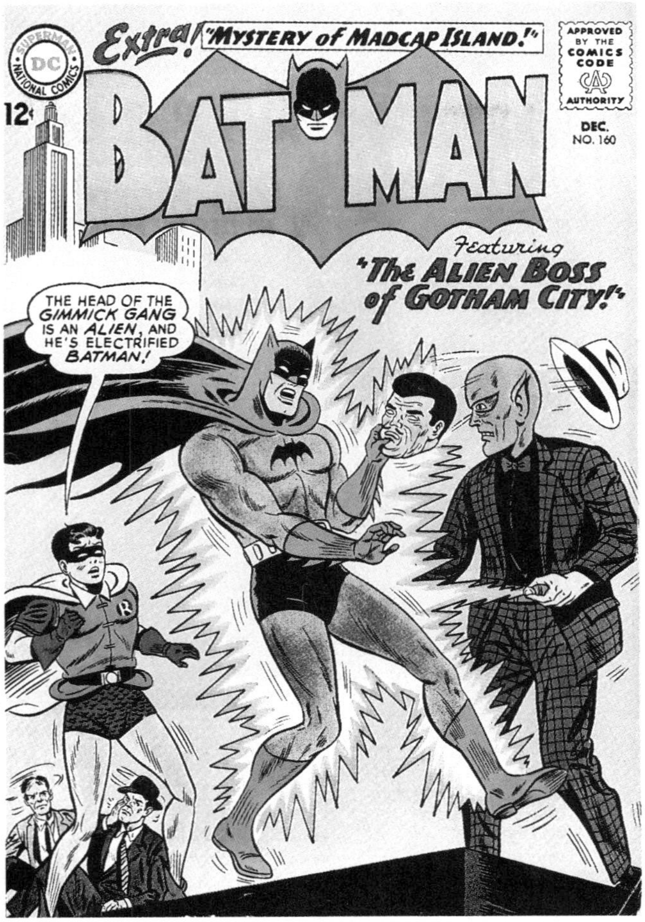
Extra! "MYSTERY of MADCAP ISLAND!"
APPROVED BY THE COMICS CODE AUTHORITY
12¢
BATMAN
DEC. NO. 160
Featuring "The ALIEN BOSS of GOTHAM CITY!"
THE HEAD OF THE GIMMICK GANG IS AN ALIEN, AND HE'S ELECTRIFIED BATMAN!

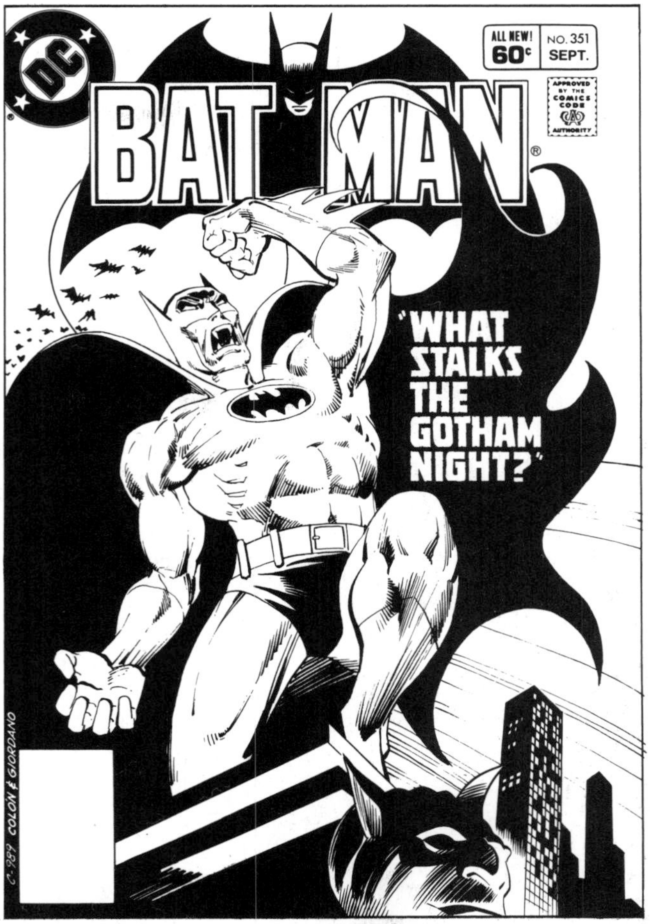
ALL NEW! 60¢
NO. 351 SEPT.
APPROVED BY THE COMICS CODE AUTHORITY
BATMAN
"WHAT STALKS THE GOTHAM NIGHT?"

Left: *One of the last science fiction covers marking the close of Jack Schiff's editorial duties on the Batman titles. (Julius Schwartz took over the helm with* Batman *#164 and* Detective *#327.)* (Batman *#160, December 1963, cover.*) **Right:** Batman *#351, September 1982, cover.* **Opposite:** *Batman has never been a stranger to the world of fantasy adventure. Here the Dynamic Duo take a Golden Age magic carpet ride.* (Batman *#5, Spring 1941, ''Book of Enchantment,'' p. 13 [panel].*)

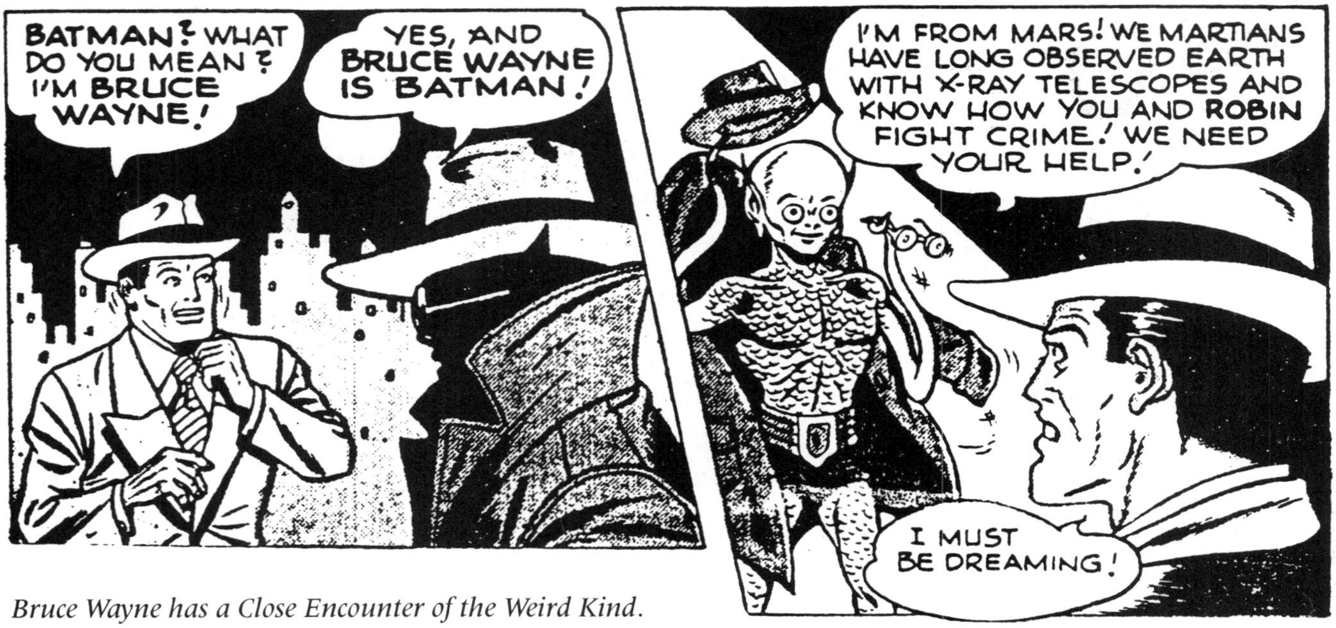
BATMAN? WHAT DO YOU MEAN? I'M BRUCE WAYNE!
YES, AND BRUCE WAYNE IS BATMAN!
I'M FROM MARS! WE MARTIANS HAVE LONG OBSERVED EARTH WITH X-RAY TELESCOPES AND KNOW HOW YOU AND ROBIN FIGHT CRIME! WE NEED YOUR HELP!
I MUST BE DREAMING!

Bruce Wayne has a Close Encounter of the Weird Kind.
(Batman *#41, June/July 1947, ''Batman, Interplanetary Policeman!'' p. 2 [select panels].*)

debut of the Dark Knight's sci-fi era with *Detective Comics* 250, December 1957, when Batman battled an alien hood from the planet Skar.)

"During the early 1950s, Batman and Robin spent more and more time traveling the world and donning exotic disguises, yet still their adventures remained squarely in the realm of what was plausible for a costumed master-sleuth without special powers," Jacobs and Jones write in *The Comic Book Heroes*. "But beginning in 1957 . . . science fiction came to Gotham City, and during the next few years the Dynamic Duo went haywire . . . .

"Suddenly Batman and Robin were wrenched from their world of dark alleys and rooftops and hurled to other dimensions and distant solar systems."[2]

2. Will Jacobs and Gerard Jones, *The Comic Book Heroes* (New York: Crown, 1985), pp. 30–31.

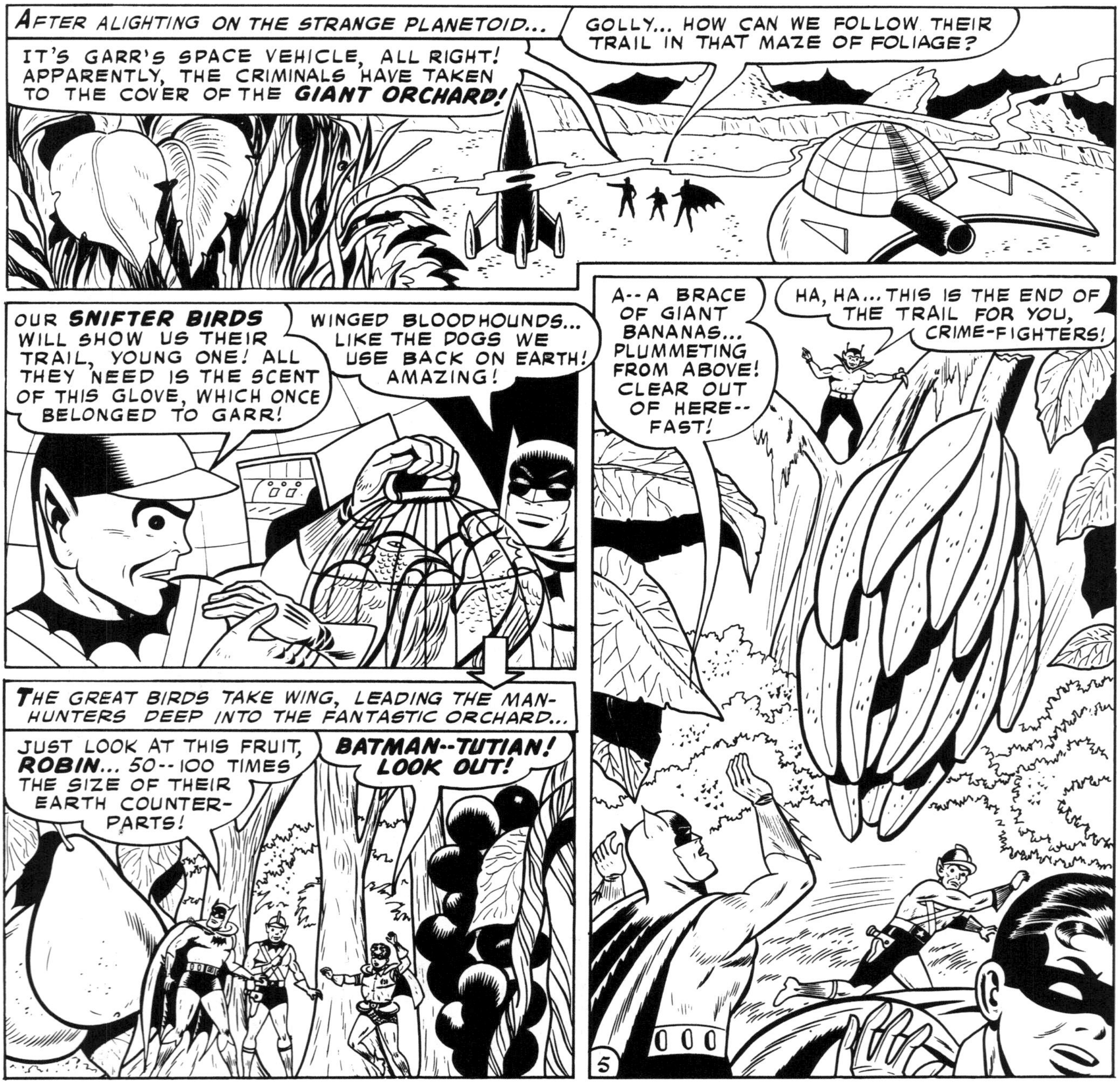
AFTER ALIGHTING ON THE STRANGE PLANETOID...
IT'S GARR'S SPACE VEHICLE, ALL RIGHT! APPARENTLY, THE CRIMINALS HAVE TAKEN TO THE COVER OF THE GIANT ORCHARD!
GOLLY... HOW CAN WE FOLLOW THEIR TRAIL IN THAT MAZE OF FOLIAGE?
OUR SNIFTER BIRDS WILL SHOW US THEIR TRAIL, YOUNG ONE! ALL THEY NEED IS THE SCENT OF THIS GLOVE, WHICH ONCE BELONGED TO GARR!
WINGED BLOODHOUNDS... LIKE THE DOGS WE USE BACK ON EARTH! AMAZING!
THE GREAT BIRDS TAKE WING, LEADING THE MAN-HUNTERS DEEP INTO THE FANTASTIC ORCHARD...
JUST LOOK AT THIS FRUIT, ROBIN... 50--100 TIMES THE SIZE OF THEIR EARTH COUNTER-PARTS!
BATMAN--TUTIAN! LOOK OUT!
HA, HA...THIS IS THE END OF THE TRAIL FOR YOU, CRIME-FIGHTERS!
A--A BRACE OF GIANT BANANAS... PLUMMETING FROM ABOVE! CLEAR OUT OF HERE-- FAST!
5

The Dynamic Duo avoid a truly ignominious end—being crushed to death by giant bananas—during an outer space caper. (Batman #117, *August 1958, "Manhunt in Outer Space," p. 5. [select panels].*)

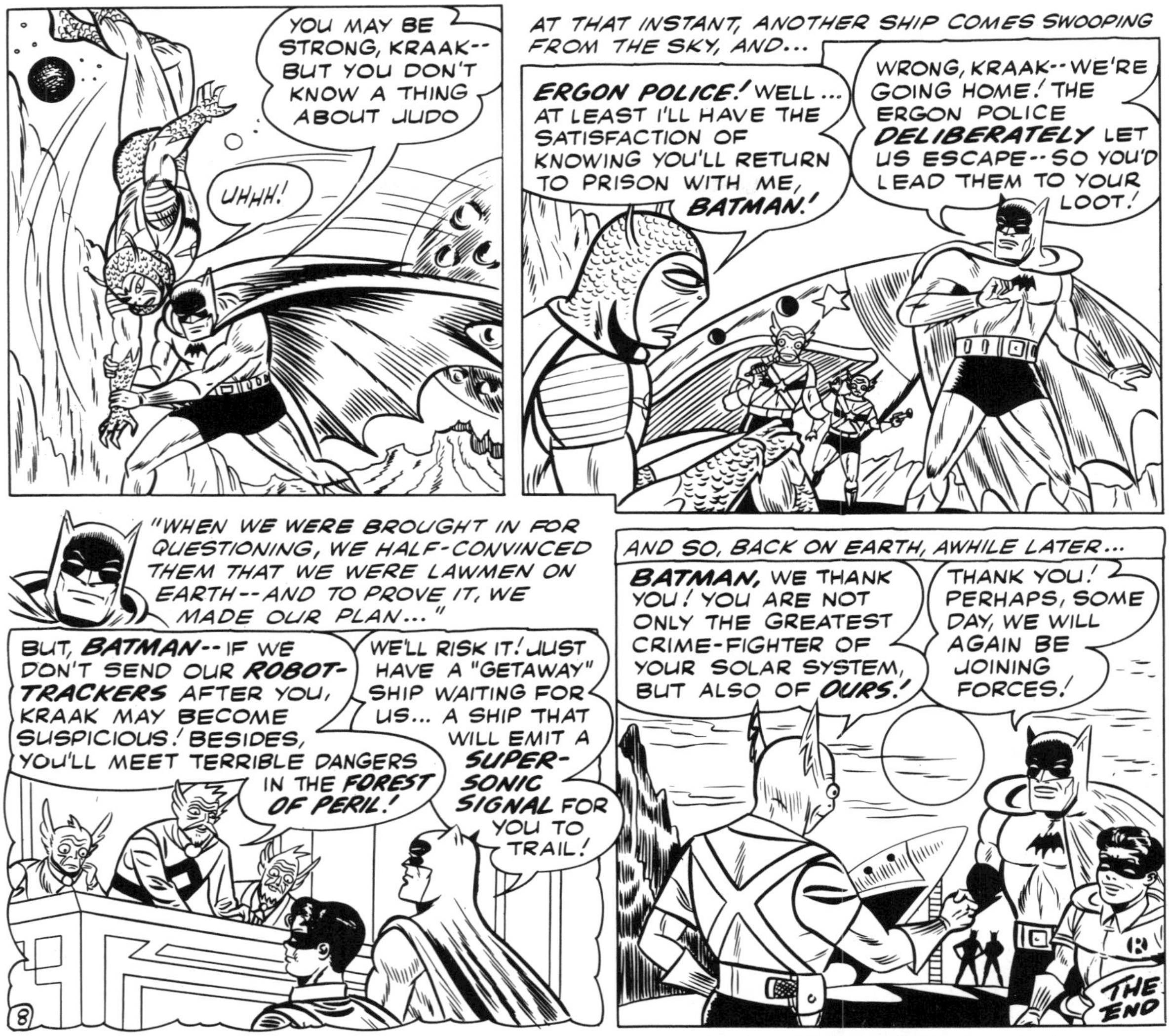
YOU MAY BE STRONG, KRAAK-- BUT YOU DON'T KNOW A THING ABOUT JUDO
UHHH!
AT THAT INSTANT, ANOTHER SHIP COMES SWOOPING FROM THE SKY, AND...
ERGON POLICE! WELL... AT LEAST I'LL HAVE THE SATISFACTION OF KNOWING YOU'LL RETURN TO PRISON WITH ME, BATMAN!
WRONG, KRAAK-- WE'RE GOING HOME! THE ERGON POLICE DELIBERATELY LET US ESCAPE-- SO YOU'D LEAD THEM TO YOUR LOOT!
"WHEN WE WERE BROUGHT IN FOR QUESTIONING, WE HALF-CONVINCED THEM THAT WE WERE LAWMEN ON EARTH--AND TO PROVE IT, WE MADE OUR PLAN..."
BUT, BATMAN-- IF WE DON'T SEND OUR ROBOT-TRACKERS AFTER YOU, KRAAK MAY BECOME SUSPICIOUS! BESIDES, YOU'LL MEET TERRIBLE DANGERS IN THE FOREST OF PERIL!
WE'LL RISK IT! JUST HAVE A "GETAWAY" SHIP WAITING FOR US... A SHIP THAT WILL EMIT A SUPER-SONIC SIGNAL FOR YOU TO TRAIL!
8
AND SO, BACK ON EARTH, AWHILE LATER...
BATMAN, WE THANK YOU! YOU ARE NOT ONLY THE GREATEST CRIME-FIGHTER OF YOUR SOLAR SYSTEM, BUT ALSO OF OURS!
THANK YOU! PERHAPS, SOME DAY, WE WILL AGAIN BE JOINING FORCES!
THE END

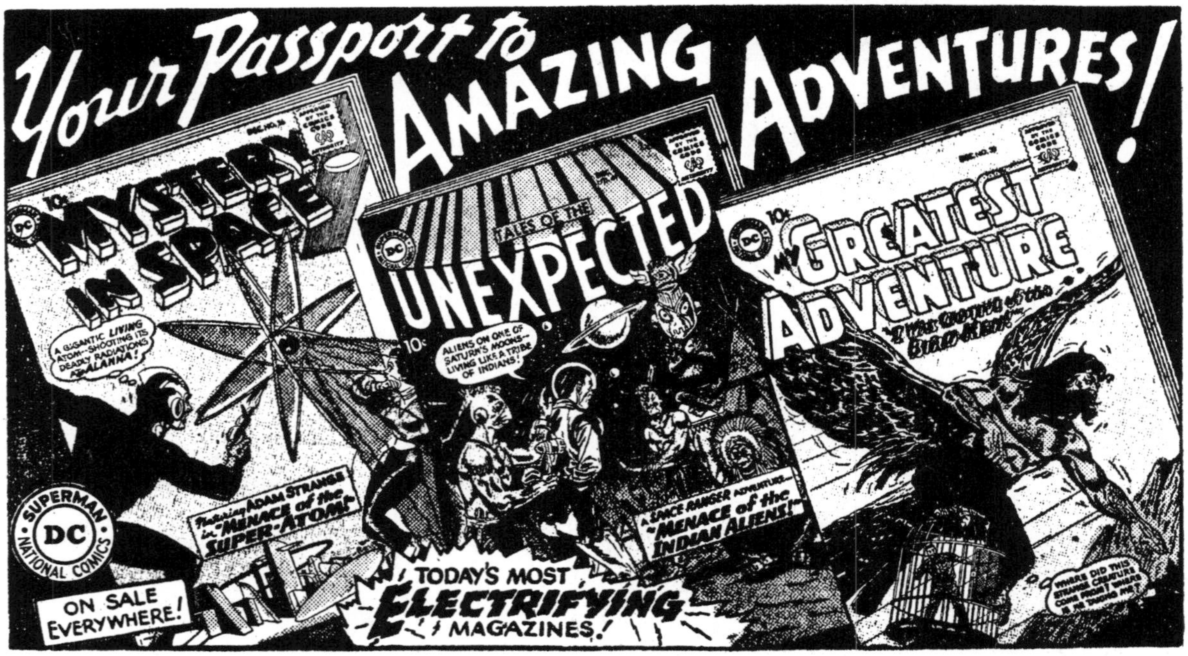
Your Passport to AMAZING ADVENTURES!
MYSTERY IN SPACE
A GIGANTIC LIVING ATOM--SHOOTING ITS DEADLY RADIATIONS AT ALANNA!
Featuring ADAM STRANGE in "MENACE of the SUPER-ATOM!"
TALES OF THE UNEXPECTED
ALIENS ON ONE OF SATURN'S MOONS-- LIVING LIKE A TRIBE OF INDIANS!
A SPACE RANGER ADVENTURE... "MENACE of the INDIAN ALIENS!"
MY GREATEST ADVENTURE
SUPERMAN DC NATIONAL COMICS
ON SALE EVERYWHERE!
TODAY'S MOST ELECTRIFYING MAGAZINES!

Batman's mastery of earthly martial arts helps subdue an alien foe. (Note the ad for the DC science fiction titles popular at the time.) (Batman *#128, December 1959, "The Interplanetary Batman!" p. 8.*)

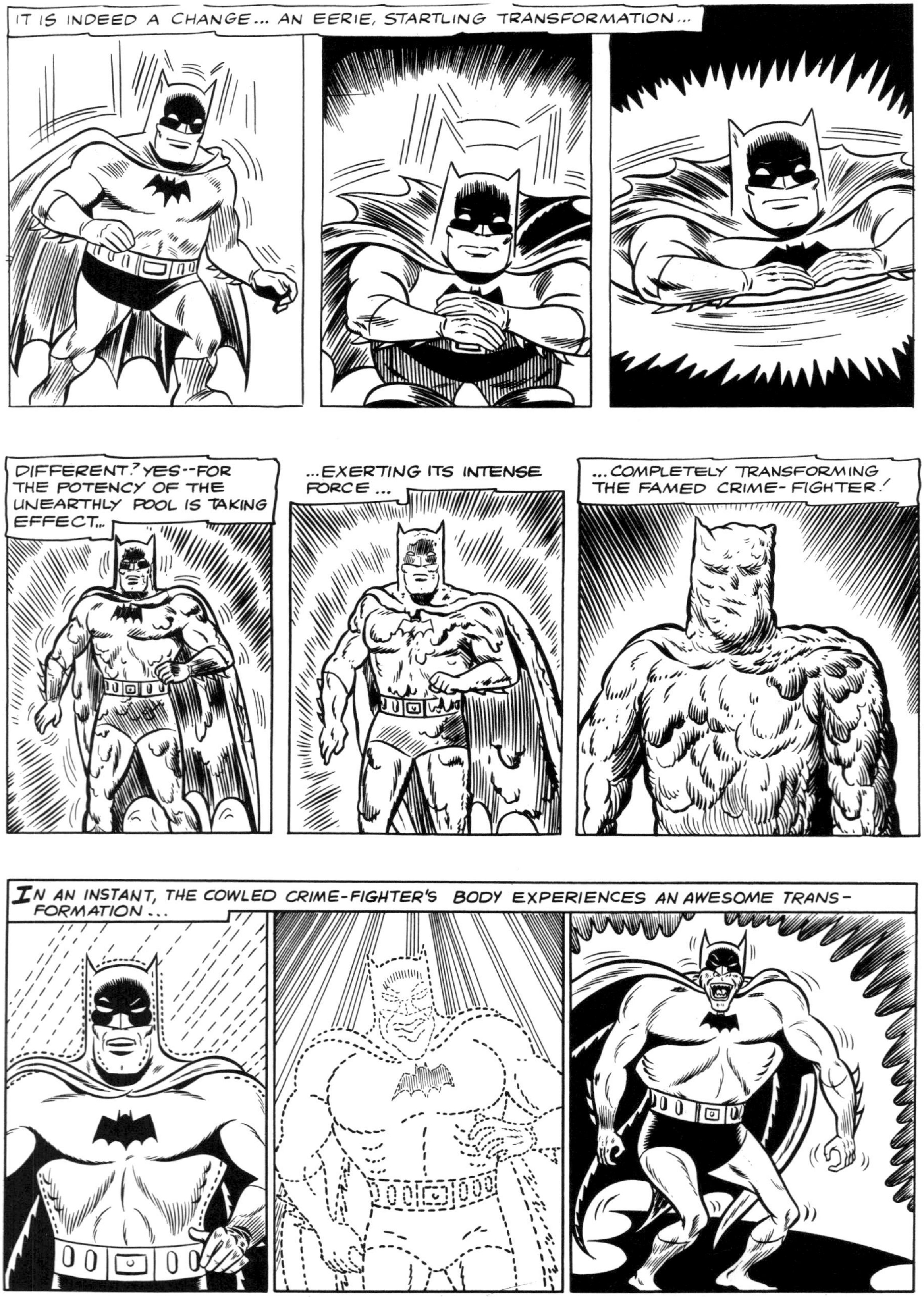
IT IS INDEED A CHANGE... AN EERIE, STARTLING TRANSFORMATION...
DIFFERENT? YES--FOR THE POTENCY OF THE UNEARTHLY POOL IS TAKING EFFECT...
...EXERTING ITS INTENSE FORCE...
...COMPLETELY TRANSFORMING THE FAMED CRIME-FIGHTER!
IN AN INSTANT, THE COWLED CRIME-FIGHTER'S BODY EXPERIENCES AN AWESOME TRANS-FORMATION...

During his science fiction/monster period, the Dark Knight was subjected to many startling transformations. (Top: World's Finest *#128, September 1962, ''The Power That Transformed Batman,'' p. 8.* Middle: Detective *#312, February 1963, ''The Secret of Clayface's Power,'' p. 10.* Bottom: Batman *#162, March 1964, ''The Batman Creature!'' p. 9 [select panels throughout].)*

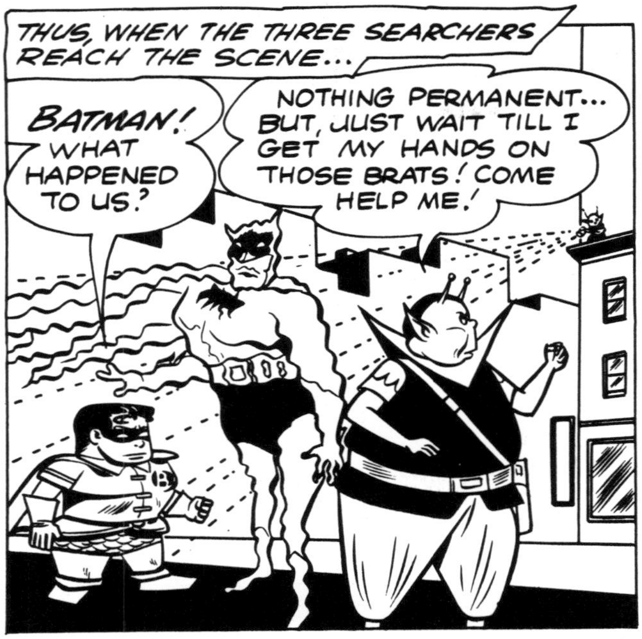
THUS, WHEN THE THREE SEARCHERS REACH THE SCENE...
BATMAN! WHAT HAPPENED TO US?
NOTHING PERMANENT... BUT, JUST WAIT TILL I GET MY HANDS ON THOSE BRATS! COME HELP ME!

Top: *Weird transformations meets outer space themes in this strange scene*. . . (Batman *#137, February 1961, "Teacher from the Stars," p. 6* [panel].) Bottom: *Batman Genie*. . . . (Detective *#322, February 1961, "The Bizarre Batman Genie," p. 5 [select panels].*)

The emphasis on fantastic story lines, a change dictated by the DC front office of the time, is remembered by then Batman editor Jack Schiff as "the monster fad." He hated it.

Besides alien encounters, Batman underwent bizarre physical transformations during the monster fad phase. Most of these changes were triggered when the normally alert Caped Crusader just happened to walk in front of deadly, atom-altering rays devised by aliens or criminal scientists, or was hit with the freakish force of a chemical explosion.

During the ensuing years Batman would become a giant (and even a giant genie), an invisible man, a "human fish" who for a time could only breathe underwater, a phantom, a human buzz saw, a gorillalike monster, and dozens of other wild incarnations.

The Dynamic Duo didn't have to journey to outer space for a little science fiction action—Gotham City during this period was a popular

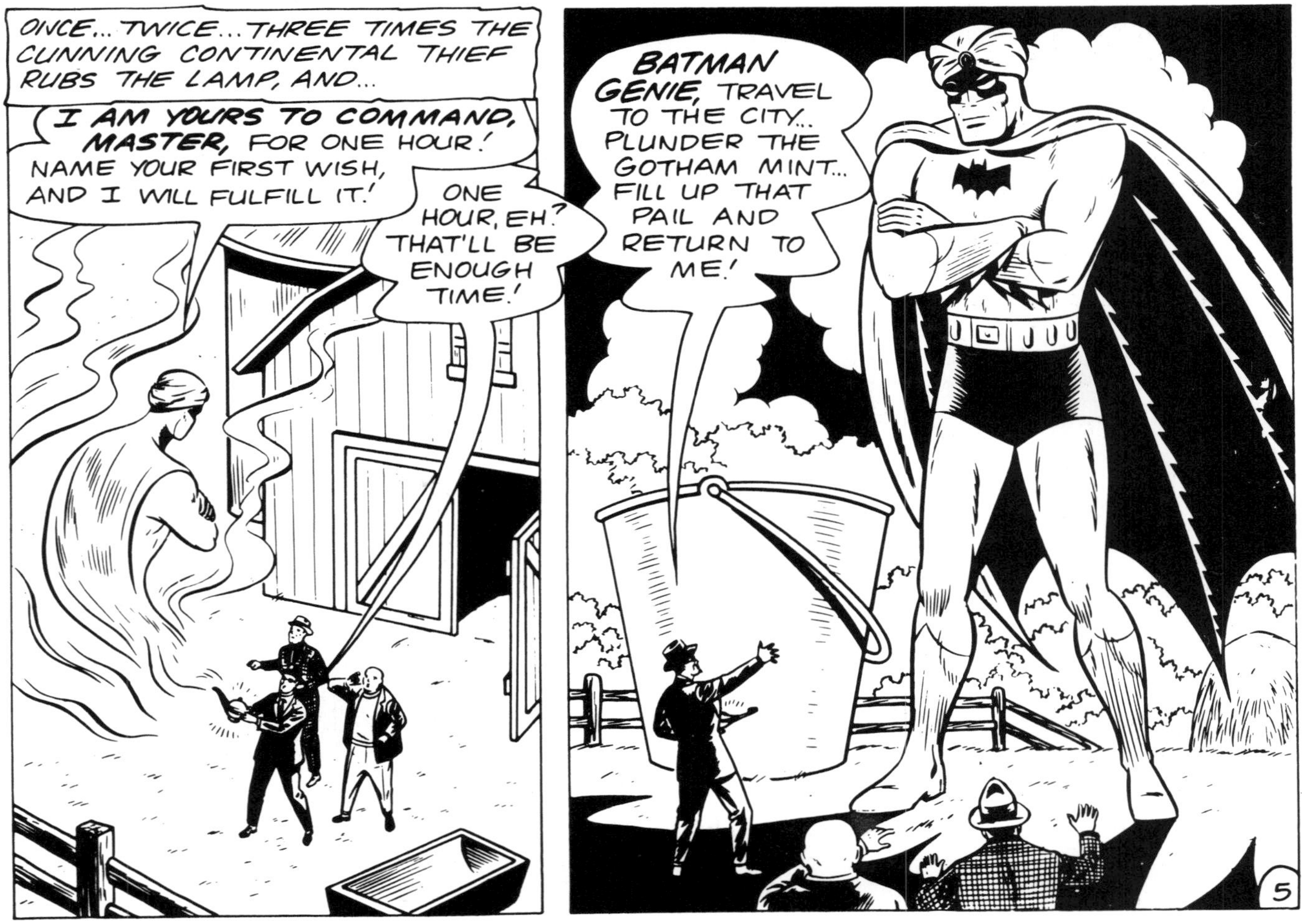
ONCE... TWICE... THREE TIMES THE CUNNING CONTINENTAL THIEF RUBS THE LAMP, AND...
I AM YOURS TO COMMAND, MASTER, FOR ONE HOUR! NAME YOUR FIRST WISH, AND I WILL FULFILL IT!
ONE HOUR, EH? THAT'LL BE ENOUGH TIME!
BATMAN GENIE, TRAVEL TO THE CITY... PLUNDER THE GOTHAM MINT... FILL UP THAT PAIL AND RETURN TO ME!
5

landing point for beings from other planets and dimensions.

Bat-Mite, a bumbling, albeit lovable, elf from another dimension, made periodic appearances in his little bat costume to help the Dynamic Duo fight crime. Batman considered the imp "a pest."[3]

Batman's sci-fi trend of the 1950s was influenced by the mesmeric quality of science's accelerating pace. The atomic bomb was simultaneously showing promise as a source of unlimited energy and threatening the planet with total destruction, while the Soviet launching of Sputnik was pointing the way to the stars and increasing Cold War fears.

In their book *The Fifties,* authors Douglas T. Miller and Marion Nowak claim that official government assurances of the safety of nuclear power were accepted as a way "Americans avoided seeing the nuclear issue straight on." But the fear of this brave new world was still running silent but deep in the national psyche.

"Their (Americans) fears did emerge more indirectly," Miller and Nowak write. "The fiction of holocaust and deformity was one expression of such fears. The novels and comics that predicted genetic monsters represent a degree of rebellion against officialdom. By fantasizing a

This page: *Batman and Robin sometimes had the opportunity to watch someone else go through a fantastic transformation.* (Batman *#154, March 1963, "The Strange Experiment of Doctor Dorn," p. 6 [select panels].*) Right: *Not every crimefighter got to put up with a hero-worshipping imp from another dimension (Superman had an adversarial relationship with the other dimensional Mr. Mxyzptlk). Here Bat-mite pops in to make life miserable for the Dynamic Duo.* (Batman *#136, December 1960, "The Case of the Crazy Crimes," p. 8 [select panels].*)

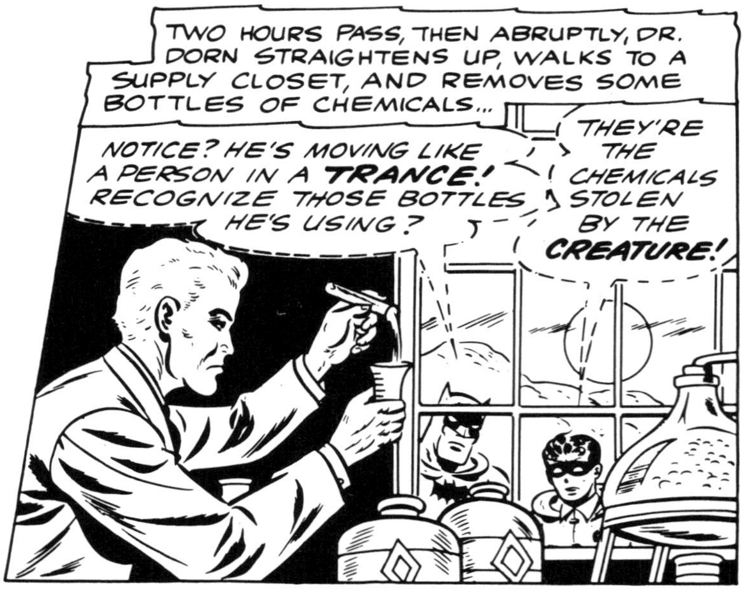
TWO HOURS PASS, THEN ABRUPTLY, DR. DORN STRAIGHTENS UP, WALKS TO A SUPPLY CLOSET, AND REMOVES SOME BOTTLES OF CHEMICALS...
NOTICE? HE'S MOVING LIKE A PERSON IN A TRANCE! RECOGNIZE THOSE BOTTLES HE'S USING?
THEY'RE THE CHEMICALS STOLEN BY THE CREATURE!

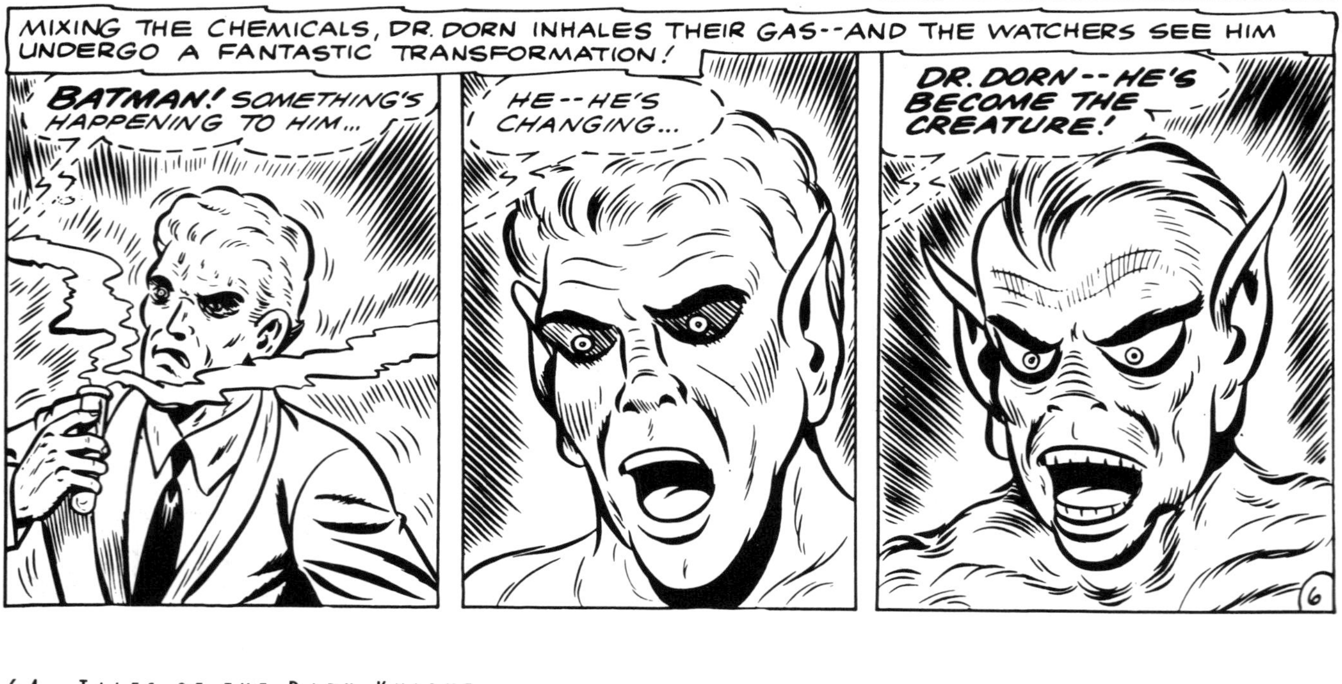
MIXING THE CHEMICALS, DR. DORN INHALES THEIR GAS--AND THE WATCHERS SEE HIM UNDERGO A FANTASTIC TRANSFORMATION!
BATMAN! SOMETHING'S HAPPENING TO HIM...
HE--HE'S CHANGING...
DR. DORN--HE'S BECOME THE CREATURE!
6

future filled with freaks and horrors, Americans rejected the nuclear safety message."[4]

Whether the Dark Knight's strange transformations and science fiction tales of the era represented public rejection of nuclear and other scientific breakthroughs is debatable. But science fiction and weird science movies were certainly popular, a number of them of the radiation-created monster variety, including *The Beast, The Blob, The Creature from the Black Lagoon, Godzilla,* and *The Thing.*

In the mid-sixties the editorial pendulum would swing away from fantastic story lines and into Batman's "New Look"—which actually marked a return to traditional crime fighting in good old Gotham City.

The change would occur none too soon for the Dark Knight. After years of weird transmutations and bewildering battles with aliens and monsters, there was the incident where Batman, ready to battle another monster foe, finally blurted out in exasperation:

"Great Scott! Another bizarre creature with a fantastic weapon!" (*Detective* 287, January 1961, Cover)

---

3. Fleisher, *Batman,* p. 134.
4. Douglas T. Miller and Marion Nowak, *The Fifties* (Garden City, New York: Doubleday, 1977), p. 65.

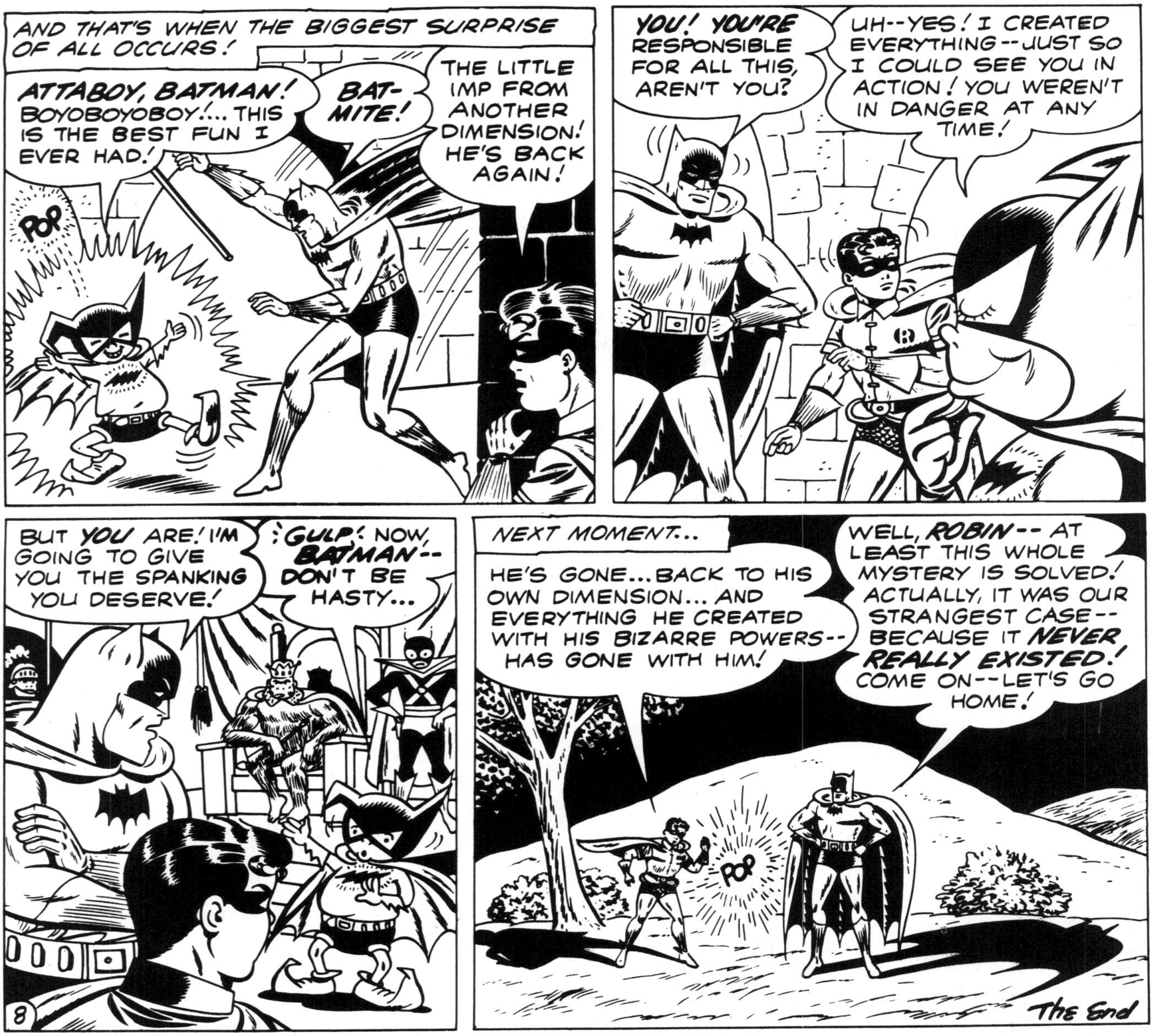
AND THAT'S WHEN THE BIGGEST SURPRISE OF ALL OCCURS!
ATTABOY, BATMAN! BOYOBOYOBOY!... THIS IS THE BEST FUN I EVER HAD!
BAT-MITE!
THE LITTLE IMP FROM ANOTHER DIMENSION! HE'S BACK AGAIN!
POP
YOU! YOU'RE RESPONSIBLE FOR ALL THIS, AREN'T YOU?
UH--YES! I CREATED EVERYTHING--JUST SO I COULD SEE YOU IN ACTION! YOU WEREN'T IN DANGER AT ANY TIME!
BUT YOU ARE! I'M GOING TO GIVE YOU THE SPANKING YOU DESERVE!
GULP! NOW, BATMAN--DON'T BE HASTY...
8
NEXT MOMENT...
HE'S GONE... BACK TO HIS OWN DIMENSION... AND EVERYTHING HE CREATED WITH HIS BIZARRE POWERS--HAS GONE WITH HIM!
WELL, ROBIN--AT LEAST THIS WHOLE MYSTERY IS SOLVED! ACTUALLY, IT WAS OUR STRANGEST CASE--BECAUSE IT NEVER REALLY EXISTED! COME ON--LET'S GO HOME!
POP
The End

DOSSIER 2
BATMAN'S BIG CITY BEAT

Gotham City is the enduring stage for the tales of the Dark Knight. Although in the early days New York was identified as Batman's Big City Beat, by *Batman* 4 the venue was Gotham City. Although it was meant to be a fictional place, it was—and is—clearly modeled after New York.

"My standard definition of Gotham City is, it's New York below Fourteenth Street after eleven o'clock at night," says Batman editor Denny O'Neil. "Recognizably New York, but with emphasis on the grimmer aspects of the city."

For those not familiar with New York, this includes the environs of Greenwich Village, SoHo, the Bowery, Little Italy, and Chinatown, as well as the mighty Brooklyn and Manhattan bridges.

Like New York, Gotham City has its ethnic neighborhoods, its enclaves of bohemia, its business and financial centers, and fashionable avenues. But, unlike New York, Gotham has a Batman, and evidence of the Dark Knight's renown can be seen everywhere.

Rising out of the bright blue Gotham Bay waters is the Batman Lighthouse, one of many monuments throughout the city erected at public expense by a grateful populace. The lifelike, three-hundred-foot tall Batman statue holds in its raised right hand the incandescent torch beacon that sheds the light to guide merchant ships safely through the straits of Gotham Bay to the docks of Gotham's wharf.

The delta and inland conduits of the bay waters are full of hidden Batman-lore. One A. K. Barnaby owns his own island, which he has turned into his personal Batman Island, complete with Batman and Robin monuments and a Batman film library. And in a watery cove is Madcap Island, where wealthy eccentrics have built their summer homes and dishware manu-

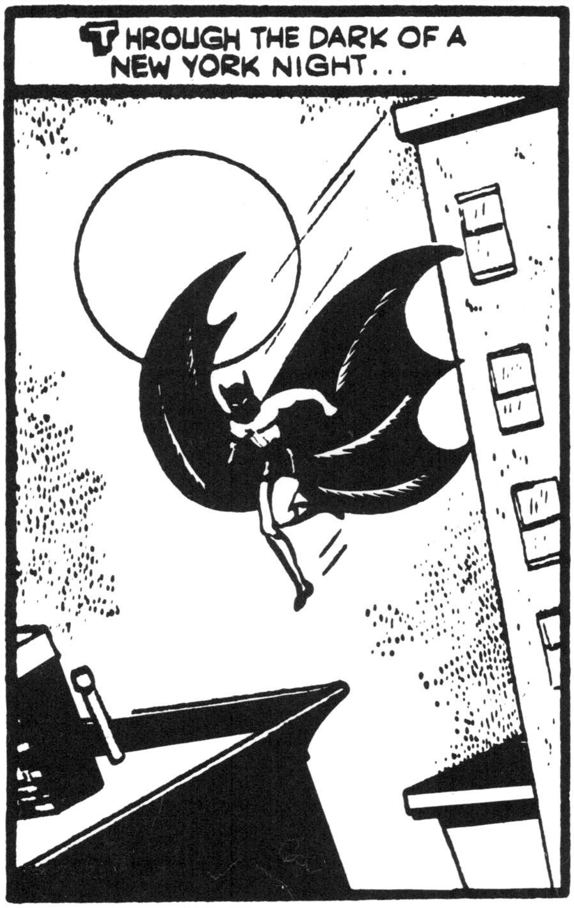
THROUGH THE DARK OF A NEW YORK NIGHT...

New York was Batman's Big City Beat in the early chronicles. (Detective *#31, September 1939, untitled story, p. 1 [panel].*)

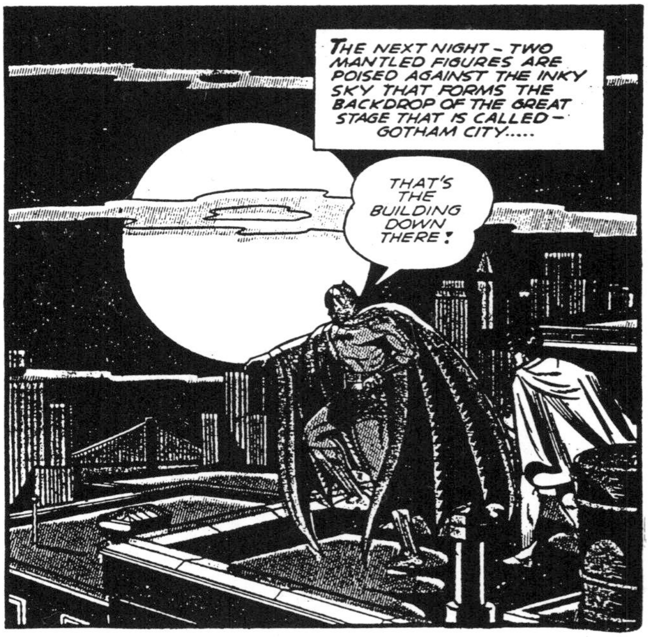
THE NEXT NIGHT - TWO MANTLED FIGURES ARE POISED AGAINST THE INKY SKY THAT FORMS THE BACKDROP OF THE GREAT STAGE THAT IS CALLED - GOTHAM CITY.....
THAT'S THE BUILDING DOWN THERE!

The first mention of Gotham City. . . . (Batman *#4, Winter 1941, ''Batman Scores a Touchdown,'' last story, p. 5 [panel].*)

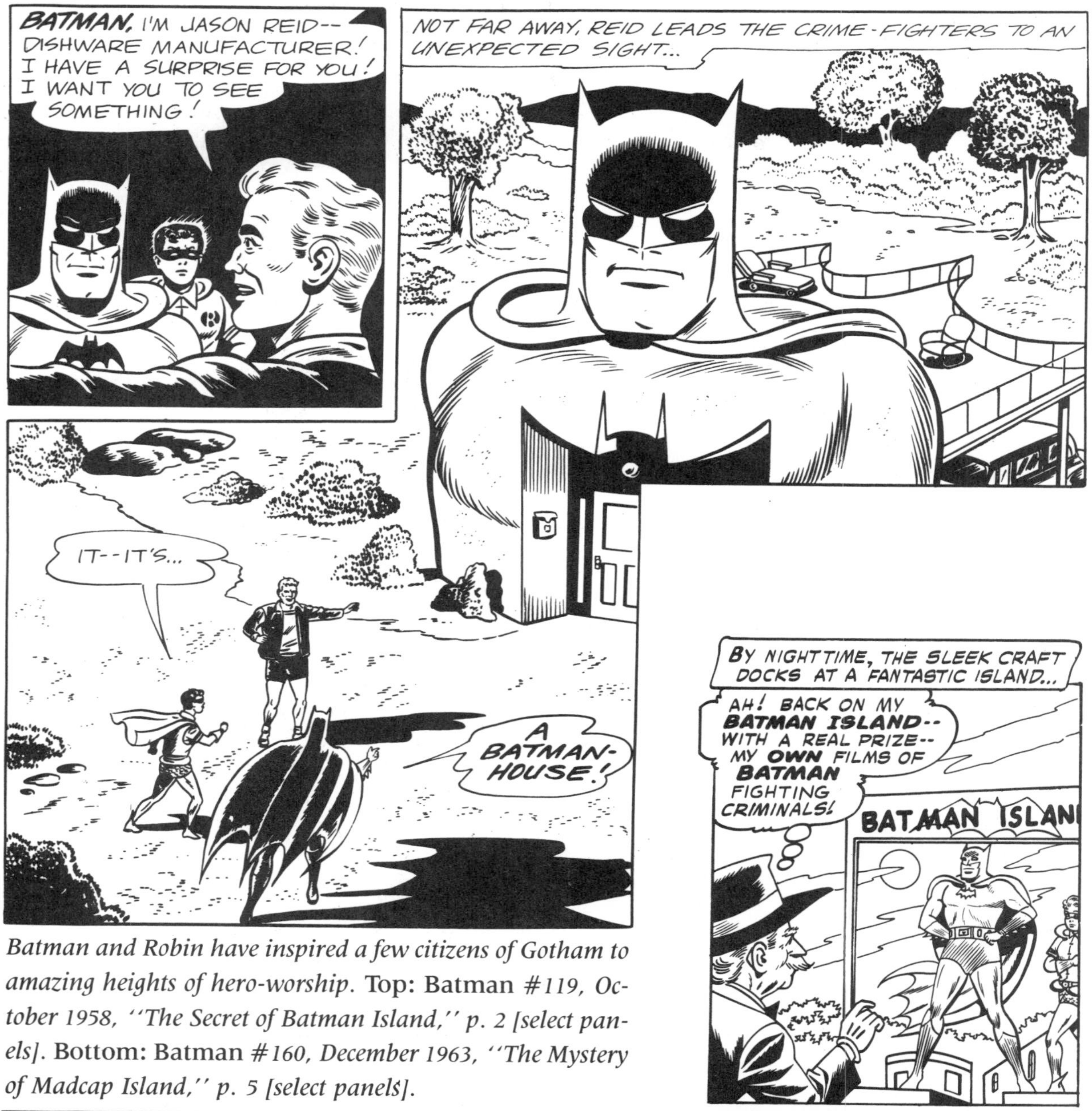
BATMAN, I'M JASON REID-- DISHWARE MANUFACTURER! I HAVE A SURPRISE FOR YOU! I WANT YOU TO SEE SOMETHING!
NOT FAR AWAY, REID LEADS THE CRIME-FIGHTERS TO AN UNEXPECTED SIGHT...
IT--IT'S...
A BATMAN-HOUSE!
BY NIGHTTIME, THE SLEEK CRAFT DOCKS AT A FANTASTIC ISLAND...
AH! BACK ON MY BATMAN ISLAND-- WITH A REAL PRIZE-- MY OWN FILMS OF BATMAN FIGHTING CRIMINALS!

Batman and Robin have inspired a few citizens of Gotham to amazing heights of hero-worship. Top: Batman #119, *October 1958, ''The Secret of Batman Island,'' p. 2 [select panels].* Bottom: Batman #160, *December 1963, ''The Mystery of Madcap Island,'' p. 5 [select panel$].*

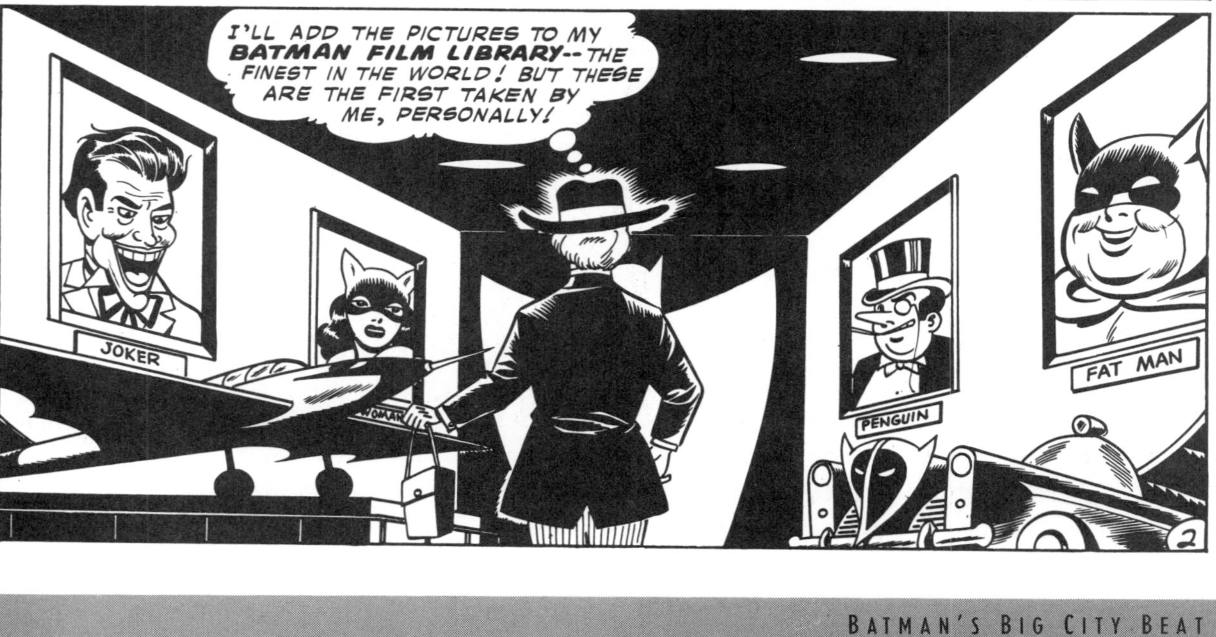
I'LL ADD THE PICTURES TO MY BATMAN FILM LIBRARY-- THE FINEST IN THE WORLD! BUT THESE ARE THE FIRST TAKEN BY ME, PERSONALLY!
JOKER
PENGUIN
FAT MAN

facturer Jason Reid has constructed a Batman House.[1]

There is the Batman Museum, popular with the Gotham citizenry as well as the tourist trade.

Of course, the ultimate front-row seat for a Gotham City view is the outdoor observation deck on the hundredth floor of the Gotham State Building. From this dizzying height one can see the forested jewel of Central Park, the bay, the East River, the Gotham Bridge, as well as a notable curiosity that makes Gotham unique among the big cities of the world—the number of over-size advertising props that adorn many Gotham buildings.

With the aid of the high-powered observation deck telescope, one can identify the prominent businesses by these particular items: giant coffee cups, diamonds rings, golf clubs....

Many of the props themselves are of historic interest, their rooftop sites the scenes of many of Batman's skirmishes with the underworld.

Even Mount Gotham, which looms outside the city environs, has been marked with a Batman monument—the giant head of the Caped

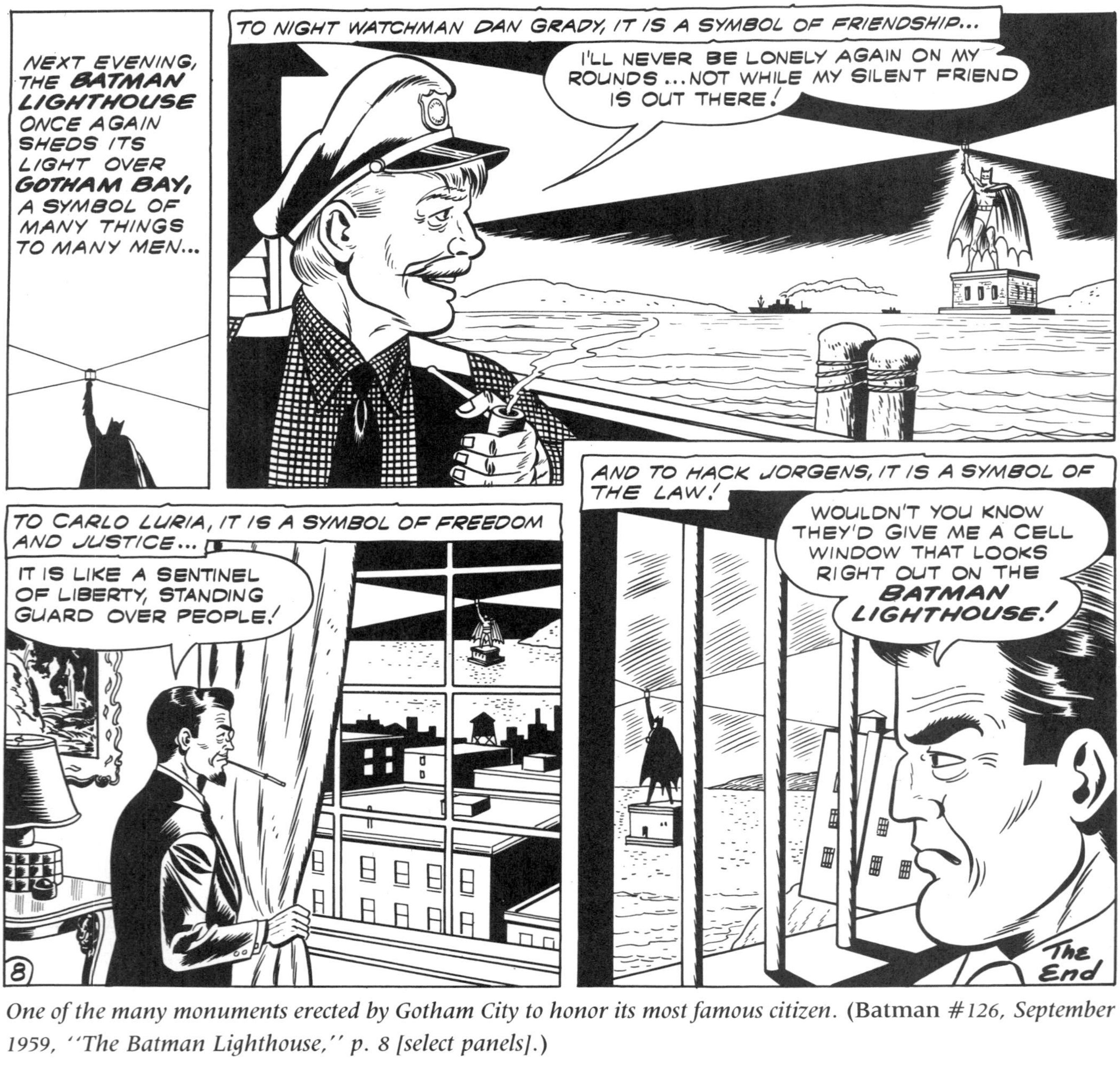
NEXT EVENING, THE BATMAN LIGHTHOUSE ONCE AGAIN SHEDS ITS LIGHT OVER GOTHAM BAY, A SYMBOL OF MANY THINGS TO MANY MEN...
TO NIGHT WATCHMAN DAN GRADY, IT IS A SYMBOL OF FRIENDSHIP...
I'LL NEVER BE LONELY AGAIN ON MY ROUNDS ... NOT WHILE MY SILENT FRIEND IS OUT THERE!
TO CARLO LURIA, IT IS A SYMBOL OF FREEDOM AND JUSTICE...
IT IS LIKE A SENTINEL OF LIBERTY, STANDING GUARD OVER PEOPLE!
8
AND TO HACK JORGENS, IT IS A SYMBOL OF THE LAW!
WOULDN'T YOU KNOW THEY'D GIVE ME A CELL WINDOW THAT LOOKS RIGHT OUT ON THE BATMAN LIGHTHOUSE!
The End

One of the many monuments erected by Gotham City to honor its most famous citizen. (Batman *#126, September 1959, ''The Batman Lighthouse,'' p. 8 [select panels].*)

Crusader carved out of the rock. A particularly memorable case, literally a cliff-hanger, ended there.

The case had begun when notorious criminal Bart Magan tried to use an experimental skin rejuvenation ray to remove a prominent facial scar and instead obliterated all his facial features. Driven insane by the maiming, Magan, now known as Dr. No-Face, began destroying anything with a face on it. His rampage culminated in his attempt to sandblast Mount Gotham's huge Batman face. When Batman and Robin appeared, Dr. No-Face sandblasted Batman's Bat-Rope as he attempted to swing down on the deranged criminal. With Batman hanging from the lip of his sculpted face, it took Robin's quick thinking to wrench the sandblaster loose before Dr. No-Face turned its explosive force on Batman's own masked face.[2]

For Batman the entire city has been one big prop, a piece of movable theater. It's a landscape full of moods and symbols as well as heights and angles. Thus, a battle atop a clock tower only tells the criminal time is running out, a bridge serves as a strategic observation perch, and a sculpted gargoyle projecting from a downtown building becomes a perfect spot to anchor and swing on the Bat-Rope.

If Gotham City is justly famous for the exploits of Batman, it is also known for its extraordinary nightscapes. If Paris is the City of Lights, then Gotham is the City of Moonlit Nights. Batman would not be the "weird figure of the dark" he is without those Gotham nights.

"We were always striving for mood," Jerry Robinson remembers of Batman's Golden Age days. "That was one of the things I was most intrigued in when I started doing the inking—getting very moody and casting long shadows."

Batman artist Dick Sprang expounds on the visual dynamics that go into producing adventure on a Batman scale.

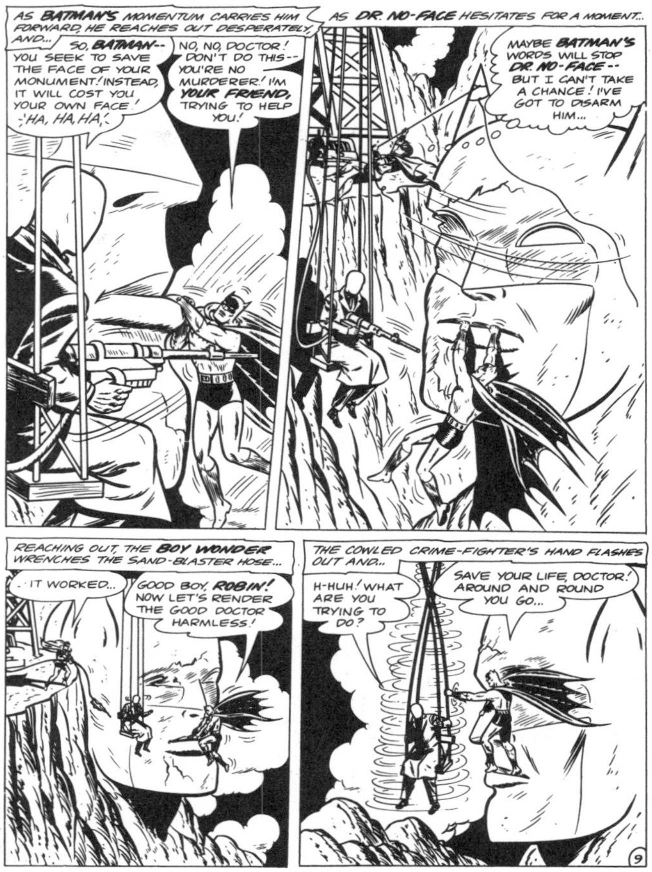
AS BATMAN'S MOMENTUM CARRIES HIM FORWARD, HE REACHES OUT DESPERATELY, AND...
SO, BATMAN-- YOU SEEK TO SAVE THE FACE OF YOUR MONUMENT! INSTEAD, IT WILL COST YOU YOUR OWN FACE! HA, HA, HA!
NO, NO, DOCTOR! DON'T DO THIS-- YOU'RE NO MURDERER! I'M YOUR FRIEND, TRYING TO HELP YOU!
AS DR. NO-FACE HESITATES FOR A MOMENT...
MAYBE BATMAN'S WORDS WILL STOP DR. NO-FACE-- BUT I CAN'T TAKE A CHANCE! I'VE GOT TO DISARM HIM...
REACHING OUT, THE BOY WONDER WRENCHES THE SAND-BLASTER HOSE...
..IT WORKED...
GOOD BOY, ROBIN! NOW LET'S RENDER THE GOOD DOCTOR HARMLESS!
THE COWLED CRIME-FIGHTER'S HAND FLASHES OUT AND...
H-HUH! WHAT ARE YOU TRYING TO DO?
SAVE YOUR LIFE, DOCTOR! AROUND AND ROUND YOU GO...
9

Some of Batman's most dramatic contests have been decided in the shadow of his own monuments. **Detective** *#319, September 1963, "The Fantastic Dr. No-Face," p. 9.*

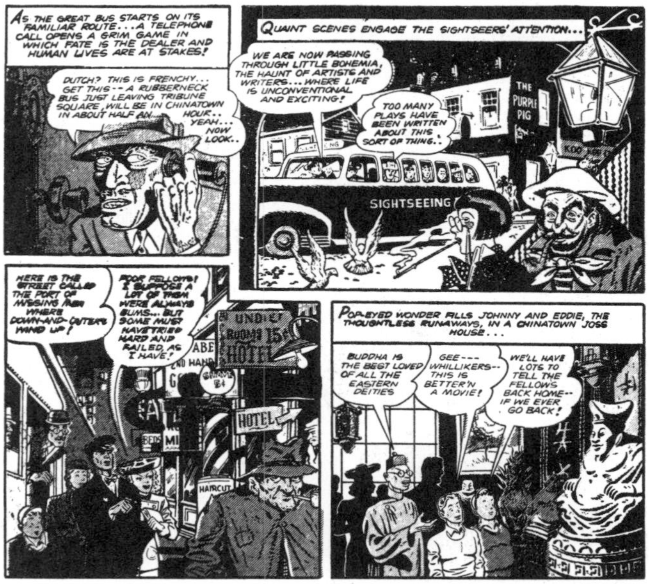
AS THE GREAT BUS STARTS ON ITS FAMILIAR ROUTE...A TELEPHONE CALL OPENS A GRIM GAME IN WHICH FATE IS THE DEALER AND HUMAN LIVES ARE AT STAKES!
DUTCH? THIS IS FRENCHY... GET THIS--A RUBBERNECK BUS JUST LEAVING TRIBUNE SQUARE, WILL BE IN CHINATOWN IN ABOUT HALF AN... HOUR.. YEAH... NOW LOOK..
QUAINT SCENES ENGAGE THE SIGHTSEERS' ATTENTION...
WE ARE NOW PASSING THROUGH LITTLE BOHEMIA, THE HAUNT OF ARTISTS AND WRITERS... WHERE LIFE IS UNCONVENTIONAL AND EXCITING!
TOO MANY PLAYS HAVE BEEN WRITTEN ABOUT THIS SORT OF THING.
THE PURPLE PIG
SIGHTSEEING
HERE IS THE STREET CALLED THE PORT OF MISSING MEN WHERE DOWN-AND-OUTERS WIND UP!
POOR FELLOWS! I SUPPOSE A LOT OF THEM WERE ALWAYS BUMS... BUT SOME MUST HAVE TRIED HARD AND FAILED AS I HAVE!
HOTEL
HAIRCUT
POP-EYED WONDER FILLS JOHNNY AND EDDIE, THE THOUGHTLESS RUNAWAYS, IN A CHINATOWN JOSS HOUSE...
BUDDHA IS THE BEST LOVED OF ALL THE EASTERN DEITIES
GEE--- WHILLIKERS-- THIS IS BETTER'N A MOVIE!
WE'LL HAVE LOTS TO TELL THE FELLOWS BACK HOME-- IF WE EVER GO BACK!

Take a tour of Golden Age Gotham from Little Bohemia ("where life is unconventional and exciting!") to Chinatown. **(Detective** *#93, November 1944, "One Night of Crime," p. 4 [select panels].***)**

---

1. "The Secret of Batman Island," *Batman* 119 (October 1958); "The Mystery of Madcap Island," *Batman* 160 (December 1963).
2. "The Fantastic Dr. No-Face," *Detective Comics* 319 (September 1963).

BATMAN AND ROBIN—By Bob Kane

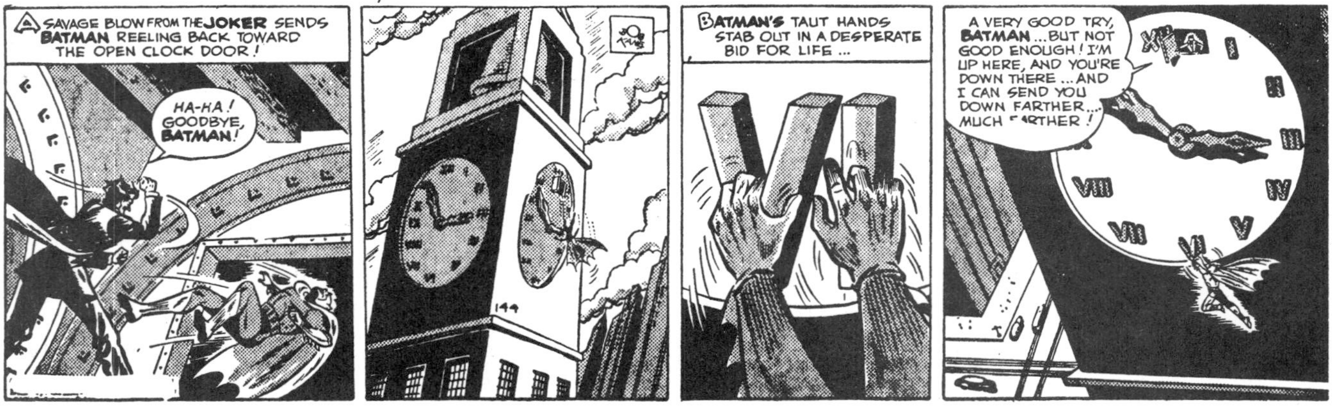
A SAVAGE BLOW FROM THE JOKER SENDS BATMAN REELING BACK TOWARD THE OPEN CLOCK DOOR!
HA-HA! GOODBYE, BATMAN!
BATMAN'S TAUT HANDS STAB OUT IN A DESPERATE BID FOR LIFE ...
A VERY GOOD TRY, BATMAN ... BUT NOT GOOD ENOUGH! I'M UP HERE, AND YOU'RE DOWN THERE ... AND I CAN SEND YOU DOWN FARTHER ... MUCH

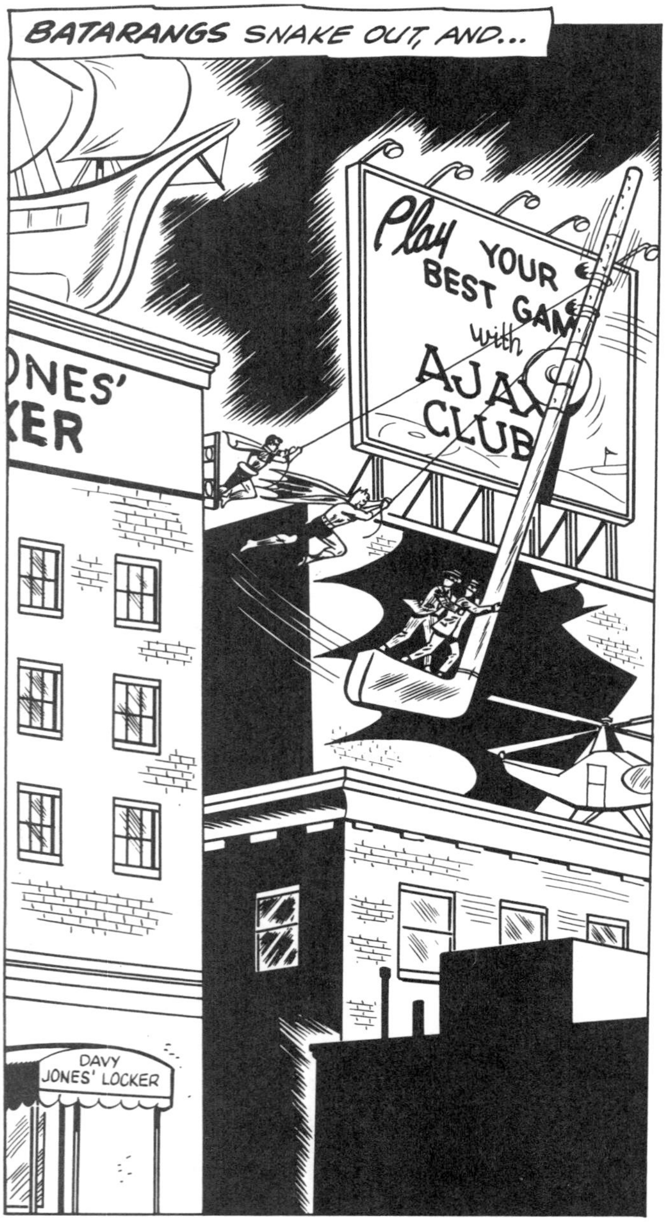
BATARANGS SNAKE OUT, AND...
Play YOUR BEST GAM
with
CLUB
ONES'
KER
DAVY JONES' LOCKER

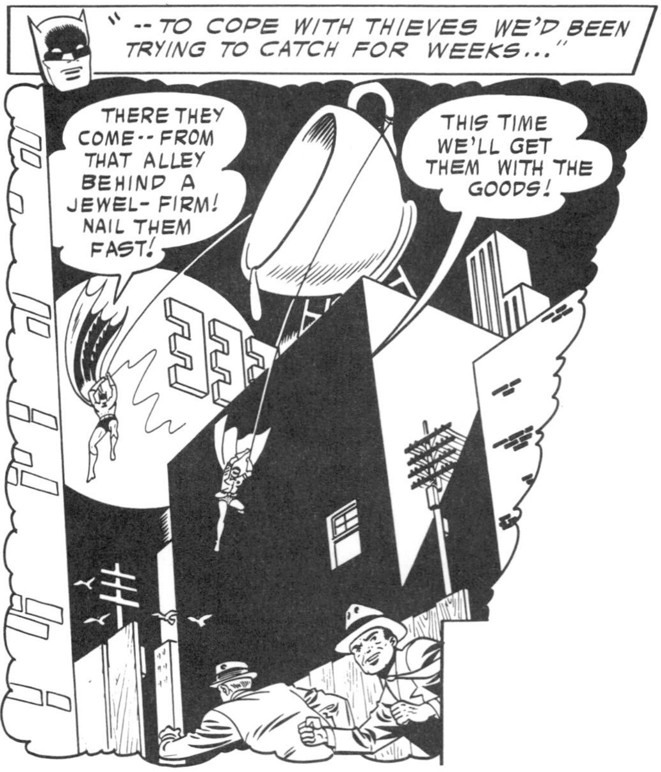
" --TO COPE WITH THIEVES WE'D BEEN TRYING TO CATCH FOR WEEKS..."
THERE THEY COME -- FROM THAT ALLEY BEHIND A JEWEL-FIRM! NAIL THEM FAST!
THIS TIME WE'LL GET THEM WITH THE GOODS!

Top: *Even a seemingly ordinary fixture such as a clock tower can become a prop in Batman's theater of crime-fighting. In this dramatic sequence Batman hangs on for dear life—but time runs out on the Joker.* (Batman and Robin, *newspaper strip, 1944.*) **Left:** *Gotham City has always been famed for the gigantic advertising props scattered across its skyline.* (Batman *#141, August 1961, ''The Crimes of The Clockmaster,'' p. 4 [panel].*) **Right:** Batman *#109, August 1957, ''The 1,001 Inventions of Batman,'' p. 3 [panel].*

"Tricky perspectives, aerial shots, worm's-eye views, compositional variation from panel to panel, the knack for drama, are primary to interpreting the script of an action story," Sprang says. "You have to be able to draw anything from any angle, dramatically. To do this you probe, as a movie camera probes, searching for the best ways to shoot a scene. Unlike a movie, you're working in a static medium; your panels, in movie terms, are frozen frames. Into them you strive for the peak action, mood, and suspense which carry interest to the next panel."

DC vice president for editorial Dick Giordano, who as a kid in the Bronx was awestruck by the 1940s Batman and years later would find himself drawing his hero, also uses film techniques when drawing Batman action.

"My normal way of drawing a story is to run through a sequence in my own mind as if it were being filmed, and then stopping at an appropriate place for the panel," Giordano explains. "While I'm there in a freeze-frame, I move around to see what the best angle is. I move the 'camera' around. So in my own mind I'm acting out all the parts to get this run-through in my mind."

"I think all illustrators project themselves into their characters to some degree," agrees Jerry Robinson. "We have to visualize how the heroes would feel and move. In my own work I try to get each character acting synchronistically.... The traditional thing is that in doing a comic

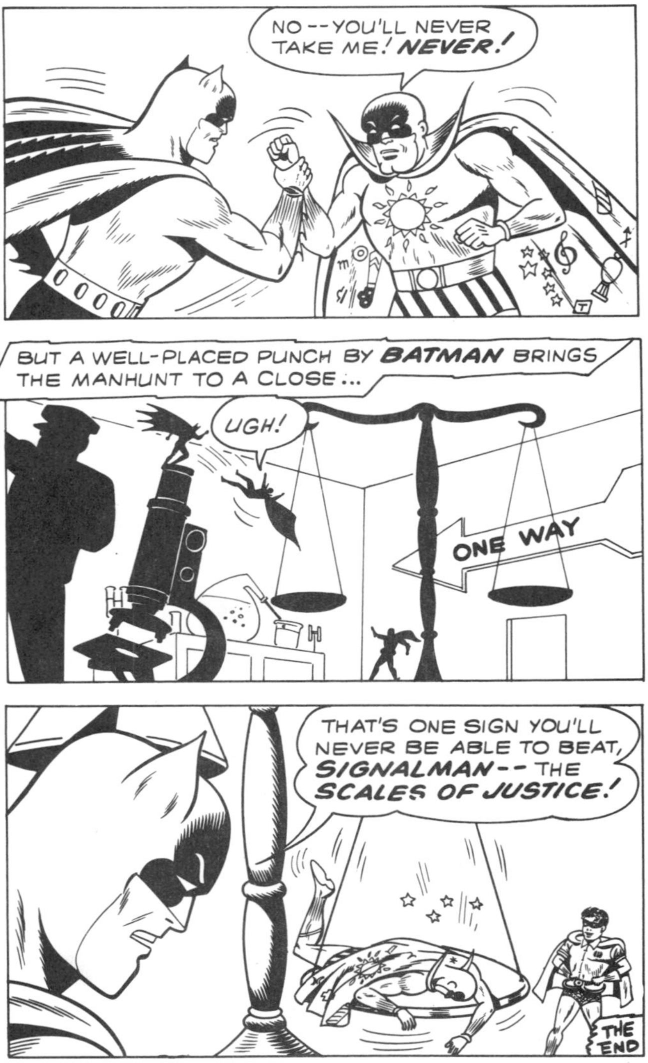

NO--YOU'LL NEVER TAKE ME! NEVER!
BUT A WELL-PLACED PUNCH BY BATMAN BRINGS THE MANHUNT TO A CLOSE...
UGH!
ONE WAY
THAT'S ONE SIGN YOU'LL NEVER BE ABLE TO BEAT, SIGNALMAN-- THE SCALES OF JUSTICE!
THE END

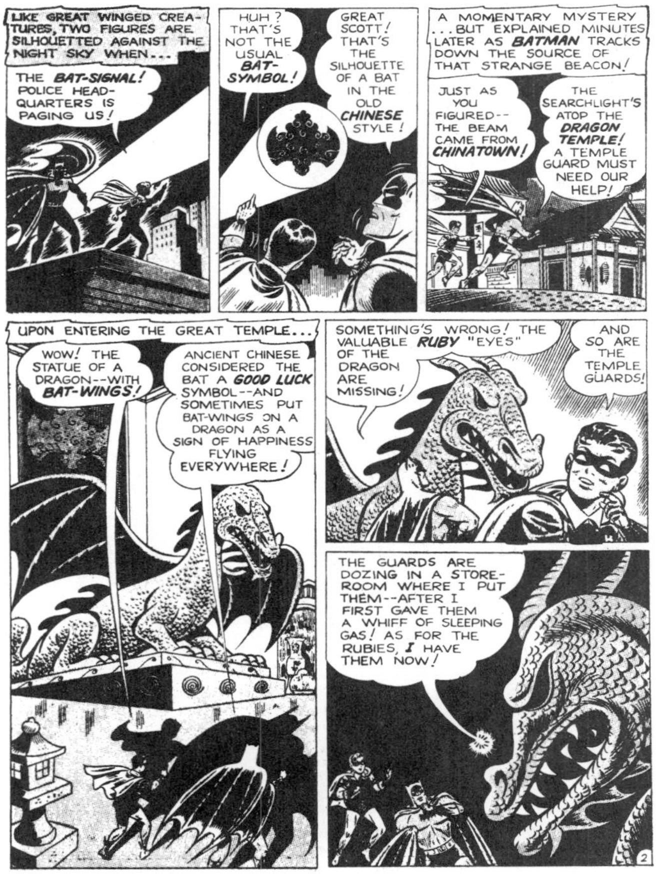

LIKE GREAT WINGED CREATURES, TWO FIGURES ARE SILHOUETTED AGAINST THE NIGHT SKY WHEN...
THE BAT-SIGNAL! POLICE HEADQUARTERS IS PAGING US!
HUH? THAT'S NOT THE USUAL BAT-SYMBOL!
GREAT SCOTT! THAT'S THE SILHOUETTE OF A BAT IN THE OLD CHINESE STYLE!
A MOMENTARY MYSTERY ...BUT EXPLAINED MINUTES LATER AS BATMAN TRACKS DOWN THE SOURCE OF THAT STRANGE BEACON!
JUST AS YOU FIGURED-- THE BEAM CAME FROM CHINATOWN!
THE SEARCHLIGHT'S ATOP THE DRAGON TEMPLE! A TEMPLE GUARD MUST NEED OUR HELP!
UPON ENTERING THE GREAT TEMPLE...
WOW! THE STATUE OF A DRAGON--WITH BAT-WINGS!
ANCIENT CHINESE CONSIDERED THE BAT A GOOD LUCK SYMBOL--AND SOMETIMES PUT BAT-WINGS ON A DRAGON AS A SIGN OF HAPPINESS FLYING EVERYWHERE!
SOMETHING'S WRONG! THE VALUABLE RUBY "EYES" OF THE DRAGON ARE MISSING!
AND SO ARE THE TEMPLE GUARDS!
THE GUARDS ARE DOZING IN A STOREROOM WHERE I PUT THEM--AFTER I FIRST GAVE THEM A WHIFF OF SLEEPING GAS! AS FOR THE RUBIES, I HAVE THEM NOW!

Left: *Not all the over-sized props adorned the outside of Gotham buildings—many were inside buildings as well.* (Batman #124, *June 1959, "The Return of Signalman," p. 8 [select panels].*) Right: Batman #155, *May 1963, "The Return of the Penguin," p. 2.*

strip, you're the screenwriter, you're the producer, director, the casting director, the actor, the set and costume designer—you're performing all those roles. That's what makes it exciting. You're producing your own movie.

"When I was doing Batman, Fred Ray [another DC artist of the period] and I first saw Orson Welles's *Citizen Kane,* and it absolutely blew our minds, the things he was doing dramatically. A lot of the things we were trying to do on paper, Welles was doing on film.

"Somewhere one of us read that he was a fan of the comics. We felt legitimized! We had never thought of ourselves on that level of talent.

" 'See—we were right!' we said to ourselves. 'Even Orson Welles is doing this—he saw it in the comics!' "

But it wasn't only the atmospheric, moody, nocturnal Gotham city vistas that were key to Batman's adventures. Bill Finger's scripts echoed the dark look of the series.

Of all the architects of Batman's world, it was Bill Finger who for a long time was "the unsung hero of Batman," according to Bob Kane. Kane has credited Finger, who passed away in 1974,

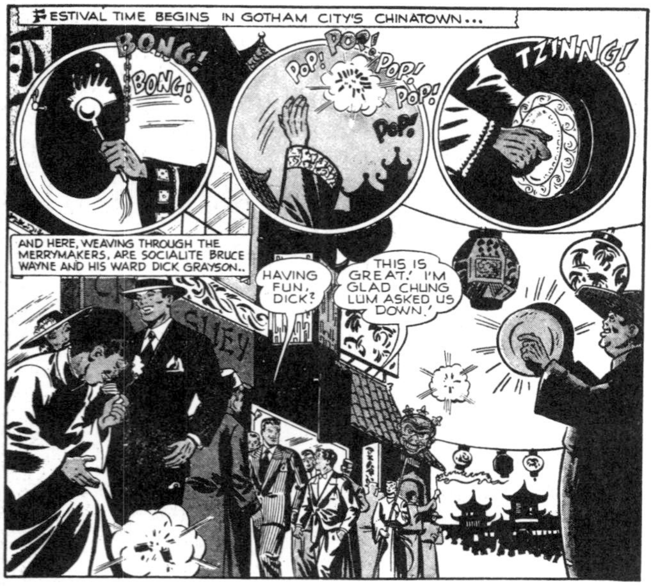
FESTIVAL TIME BEGINS IN GOTHAM CITY'S CHINATOWN...
BONG! BONG!
POP! POP! POP! POP! POP!
TZINNG!
AND HERE, WEAVING THROUGH THE MERRYMAKERS, ARE SOCIALITE BRUCE WAYNE AND HIS WARD DICK GRAYSON..
HAVING FUN, DICK?
THIS IS GREAT! I'M GLAD CHUNG LUM ASKED US DOWN!

Gotham's Chinatown provided an exotic, dangerous backdrop to many Batman adventures. (World's Finest *#42, September–October 1949, "The Amazing Adventure of Batman and Marco Polo!" p. 2 [panel].*)

with helping him refine the look and mood of the strip. The special flavor of Gotham City, particularly the oversize props, was a Finger trademark, for example.[3]

"I regret that I did not give Bill a byline, which he richly deserved, but somehow the policy in those days was to give credit only to the original creator and not to the writers who came in after the fact," Kane recently wrote. "Bill, I wish you were around now for me to give your just dues for your invaluable input into Batman. I thank you now and God bless you eternally."[4]

All the creators who helped build the Batman added luster to the mythos with the care by which they erected the Gotham skyline, by the way they brought on the night, parted the midnight clouds, and revealed the moon. And when they seeded that midnight urban tableau with the denizens of the underworld, they also gave to the people of Gotham an avenger who knew the ways of the dark night, who could protect the innocent and bring the guilty to justice.

We are not as lucky as those good citizens of Gotham City. Our world is more complex, and often we can only dream for that guardian figure of compassion, that messenger of justice.

"All cities are Gotham City, warrens of malice where the entreaties of the lost are an inconvenience, where shrieks of children are ignored, where innocents are slain on a whim," Denny O'Neil writes. "Yet we live here, in Gotham, and occasionally we prosper. We raise our young, we laugh, we celebrate, we brave the terrors and sometimes, at our best, we deny them with acts of kindness, decency, love.

"It would be nice if we had heroes to help us. I have often walked through Gotham City and every time I wished someone strong, cunning and compassionate was walking with me."[5]

Gotham City has that hero, and every night he walks his Big City beat.

---

3. "Bill Finger: The Darknight Detective Emerges," *Fifty Who Made DC Great* (New York: DC Comics, Inc., 1985), p. 11.
4. Kane, *History of the DC Universe,* p. 15.
5. Denny O'Neil, "Bat-Signals," *Batman* 401 (November 1986).

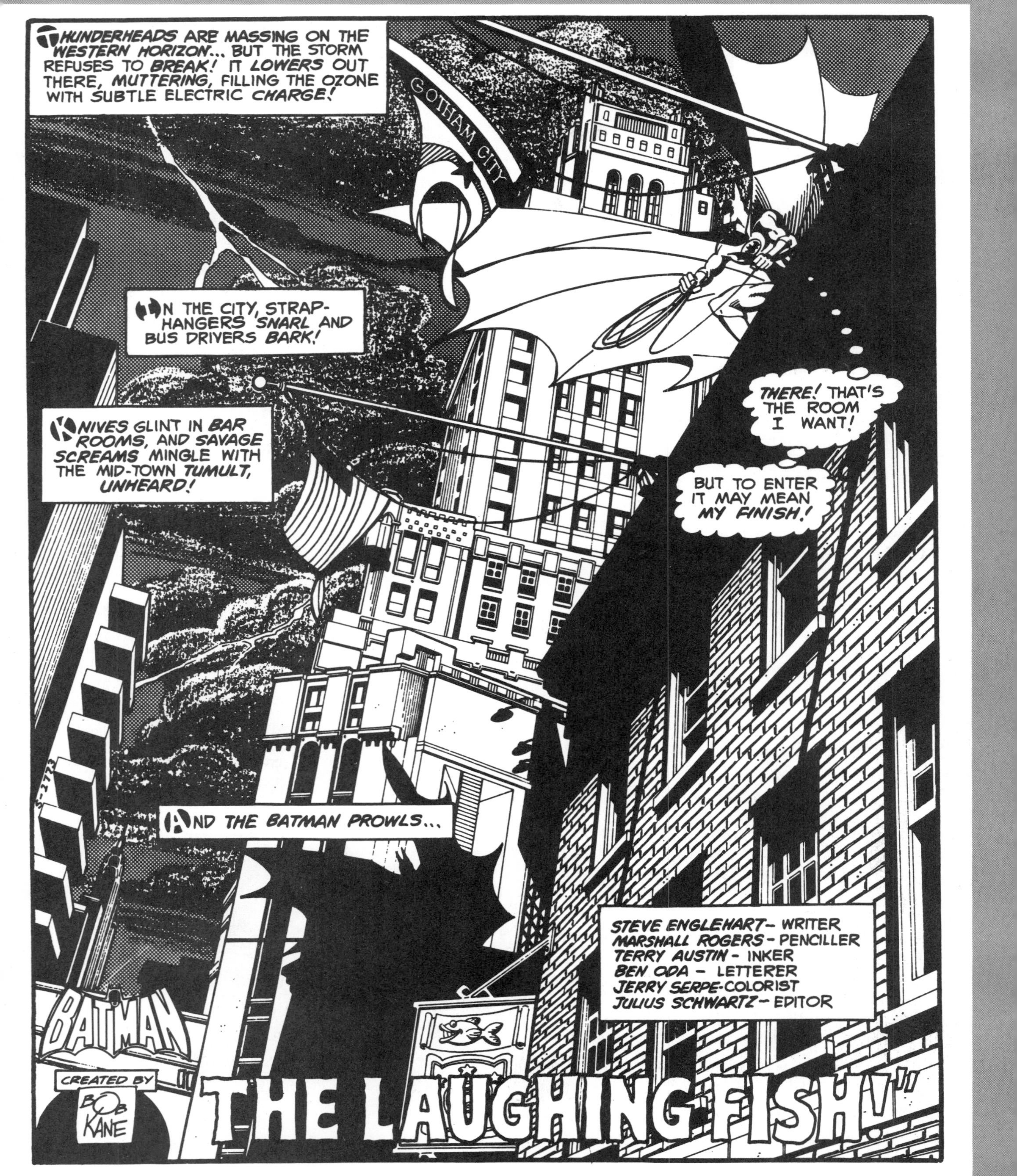
THUNDERHEADS ARE MASSING ON THE WESTERN HORIZON... BUT THE STORM REFUSES TO BREAK! IT LOWERS OUT THERE, MUTTERING, FILLING THE OZONE WITH SUBTLE ELECTRIC CHARGE!
GOTHAM CITY
IN THE CITY, STRAP-HANGERS SNARL AND BUS DRIVERS BARK!
KNIVES GLINT IN BAR ROOMS, AND SAVAGE SCREAMS MINGLE WITH THE MID-TOWN TUMULT, UNHEARD!
THERE! THAT'S THE ROOM I WANT!
BUT TO ENTER IT MAY MEAN MY FINISH!
AND THE BATMAN PROWLS...
STEVE ENGLEHART- WRITER
MARSHALL ROGERS- PENCILLER
TERRY AUSTIN- INKER
BEN ODA - LETTERER
JERRY SERPE-COLORIST
JULIUS SCHWARTZ- EDITOR
BATMAN
CREATED BY BOB KANE
"THE LAUGHING FISH!"

Detective #475, *February 1978, "The Laughing Fish," p. 1 (splash page).*

CHAPTER 8

Around the World with Batman

BATMAN STROVE FOR HIS VISION OF JUSTICE ever since the night his parents were slain on the beautiful boulevard that would later be known as "Crime Alley." That horrible tragedy lit an obsession that could never be satiated by the millions he inherited or dimmed by the unforgiving passage of time.

And such a passion, unleashed after fifteen years of preparation, could not be constrained by the borders of even his beloved Gotham City.

Batman has always had an explorer's pure love of exotic locales. Over the decades a succession of Batplanes, built and maintained with the Wayne fortune, has taken the Dynamic Duo from the shadow of Big Ben to the stormy heights of the Himalayas, from the mysterious Sargasso sea to the living legend of Atlantis.

Gotham City will always be the Batman's home, but the wanderlust in him will always push him to the secret places beyond the horizon.

Because the entire world is in need of justice.

But the secrets of the planet are not enough to satisfy Batman's wanderlust. When the door to the infinite mysteries has swung open periodically, both Batman and Robin have never shirked from passing through the magical gates leading to complete Unknown. And thanks to the time-travel devices of the mysterious Professor Nichols, they have often had that chance.

GIANT
G73
GIANT BATMAN
AUG.
NO. 223
BATMAN
25¢
BATMAN AND ROBIN FACE DANGER
CRIME IN CANADA
TROUBLE IN TIBET
MYSTERY IN MEXICO
EVIL IN ENGLAND
AROUND THE WORLD!
HAZARD IN HOLLAND

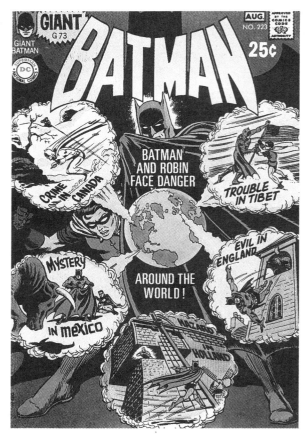

Batman *#223 July/August 1970, cover.*

Detective Comics
STARRING
BATMAN
541
75¢
THE NEW
THERE'S NO STOPPING US NOW.
ANTARCTIC NIGHTMARE!

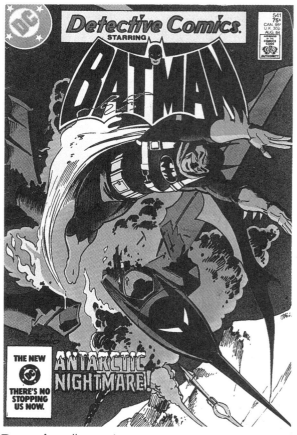

Detective *#541, August 1984, cover.*

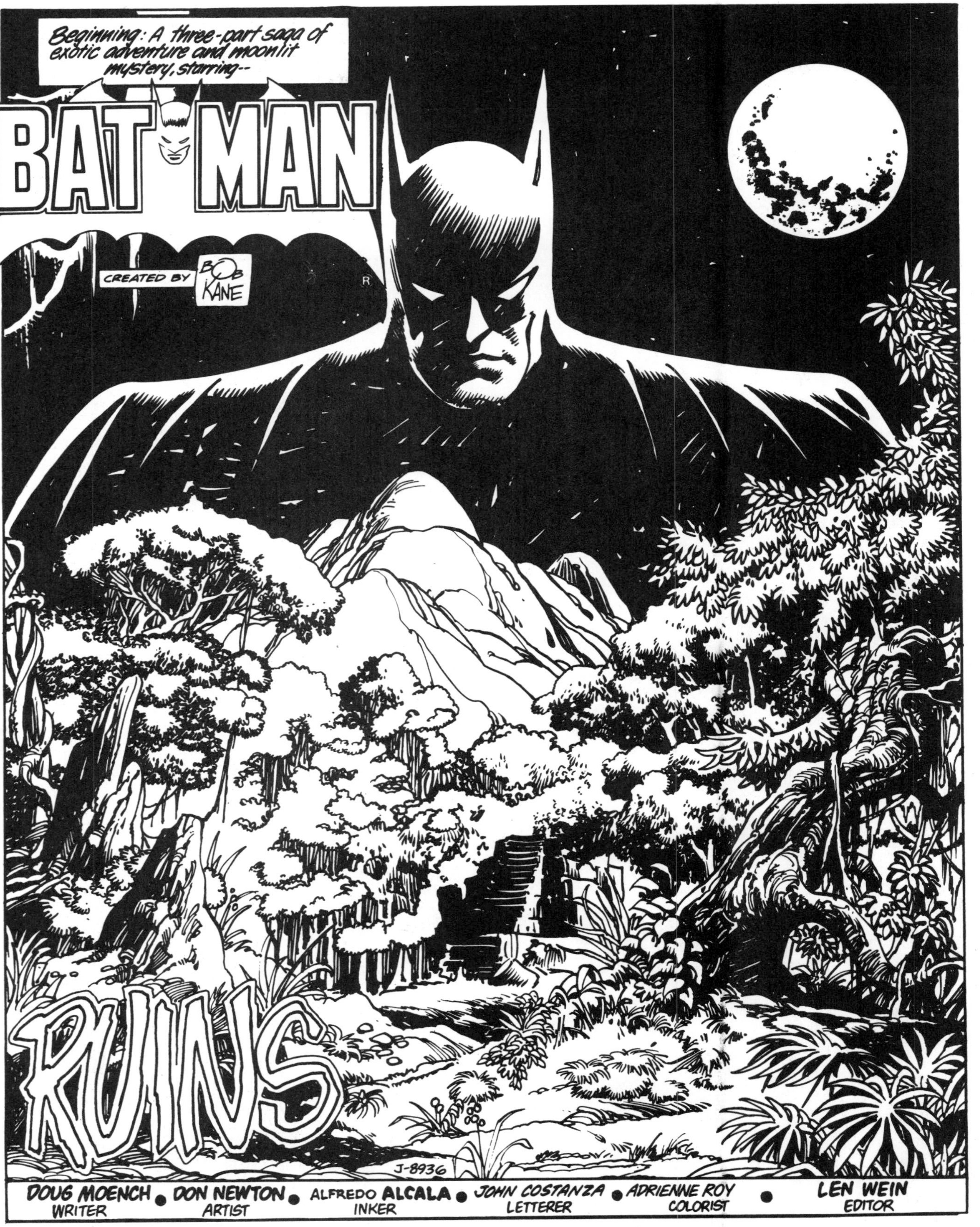
Beginning: A three-part saga of exotic adventure and moonlit mystery, starring--
BATMAN
CREATED BY BOB KANE
RUINS
J-8936
DOUG MOENCH WRITER • DON NEWTON ARTIST • ALFREDO ALCALA INKER • JOHN COSTANZA LETTERER • ADRIENNE ROY COLORIST • LEN WEIN EDITOR

Batman *#365, November 1983, "Ruins," p. 1 (splash page).*

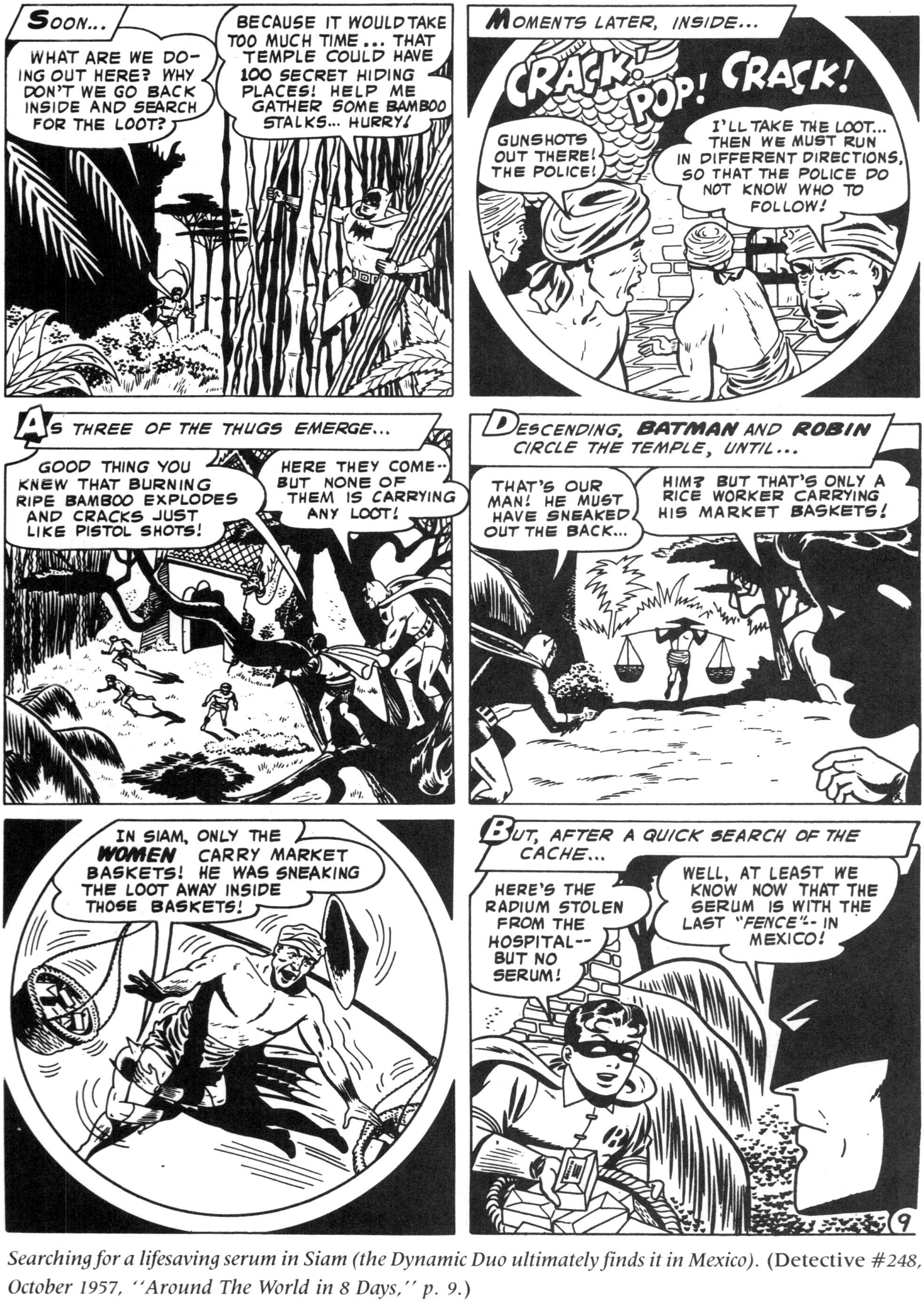
SOON...
WHAT ARE WE DOING OUT HERE? WHY DON'T WE GO BACK INSIDE AND SEARCH FOR THE LOOT?
BECAUSE IT WOULD TAKE TOO MUCH TIME ... THAT TEMPLE COULD HAVE 100 SECRET HIDING PLACES! HELP ME GATHER SOME BAMBOO STALKS... HURRY!
MOMENTS LATER, INSIDE...
CRACK! POP! CRACK!
GUNSHOTS OUT THERE! THE POLICE!
I'LL TAKE THE LOOT... THEN WE MUST RUN IN DIFFERENT DIRECTIONS, SO THAT THE POLICE DO NOT KNOW WHO TO FOLLOW!
AS THREE OF THE THUGS EMERGE...
GOOD THING YOU KNEW THAT BURNING RIPE BAMBOO EXPLODES AND CRACKS JUST LIKE PISTOL SHOTS!
HERE THEY COME-- BUT NONE OF THEM IS CARRYING ANY LOOT!
DESCENDING, BATMAN AND ROBIN CIRCLE THE TEMPLE, UNTIL...
THAT'S OUR MAN! HE MUST HAVE SNEAKED OUT THE BACK...
HIM? BUT THAT'S ONLY A RICE WORKER CARRYING HIS MARKET BASKETS!
IN SIAM, ONLY THE WOMEN CARRY MARKET BASKETS! HE WAS SNEAKING THE LOOT AWAY INSIDE THOSE BASKETS!
BUT, AFTER A QUICK SEARCH OF THE CACHE...
HERE'S THE RADIUM STOLEN FROM THE HOSPITAL-- BUT NO SERUM!
WELL, AT LEAST WE KNOW NOW THAT THE SERUM IS WITH THE LAST "FENCE"-- IN MEXICO!
9

Searching for a lifesaving serum in Siam (the Dynamic Duo ultimately finds it in Mexico). (Detective #248, *October 1957, "Around The World in 8 Days," p. 9.*)

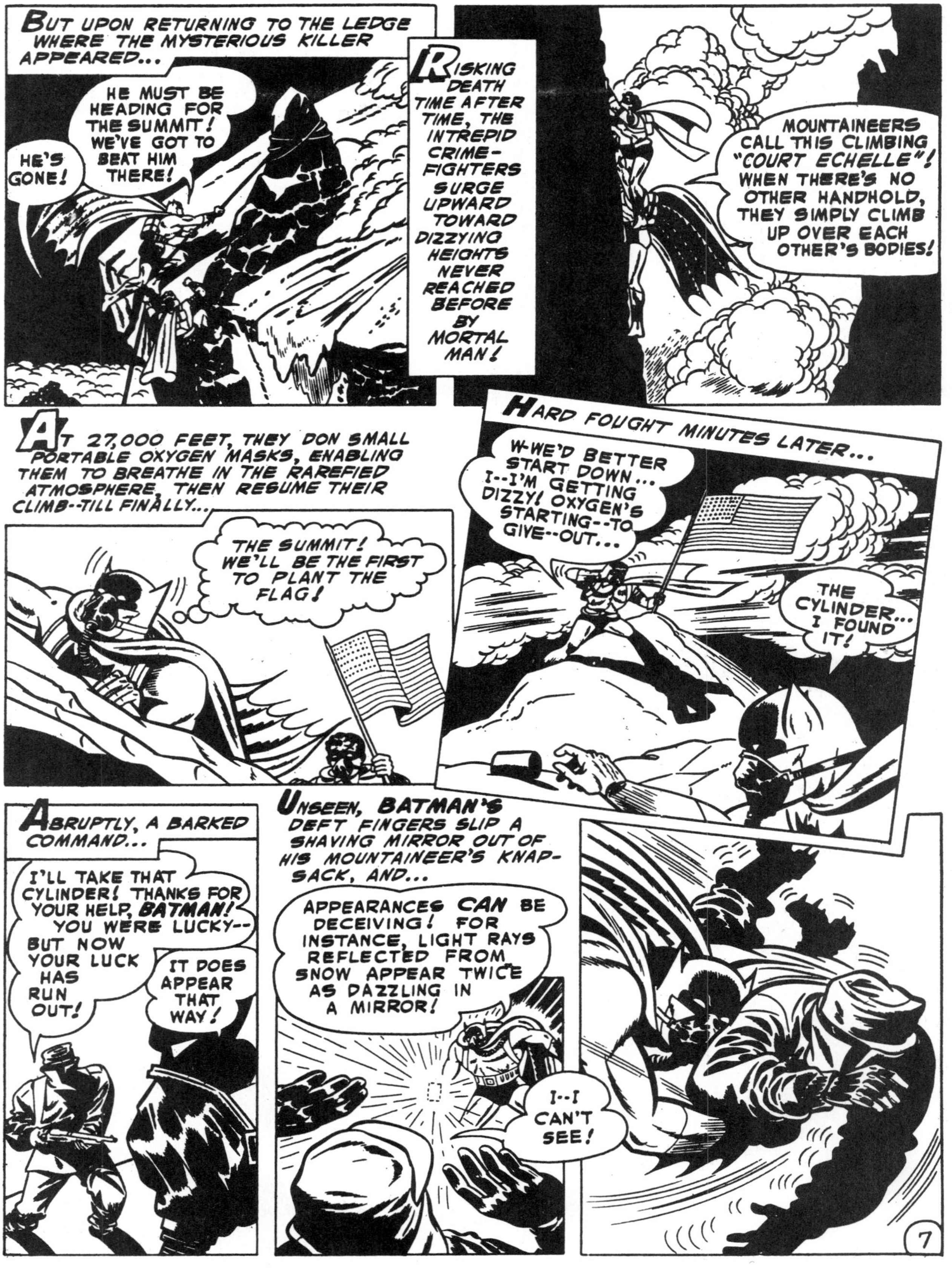
BUT UPON RETURNING TO THE LEDGE WHERE THE MYSTERIOUS KILLER APPEARED...
HE'S GONE!
HE MUST BE HEADING FOR THE SUMMIT! WE'VE GOT TO BEAT HIM THERE!
RISKING DEATH TIME AFTER TIME, THE INTREPID CRIME-FIGHTERS SURGE UPWARD TOWARD DIZZYING HEIGHTS NEVER REACHED BEFORE BY MORTAL MAN!
MOUNTAINEERS CALL THIS CLIMBING "COURT ECHELLE"! WHEN THERE'S NO OTHER HANDHOLD, THEY SIMPLY CLIMB UP OVER EACH OTHER'S BODIES!
AT 27,000 FEET, THEY DON SMALL PORTABLE OXYGEN MASKS, ENABLING THEM TO BREATHE IN THE RAREFIED ATMOSPHERE, THEN RESUME THEIR CLIMB--TILL FINALLY...
THE SUMMIT! WE'LL BE THE FIRST TO PLANT THE FLAG!
HARD FOUGHT MINUTES LATER...
W-WE'D BETTER START DOWN... I--I'M GETTING DIZZY! OXYGEN'S STARTING--TO GIVE--OUT...
THE CYLINDER... I FOUND IT!
ABRUPTLY, A BARKED COMMAND...
I'LL TAKE THAT CYLINDER! THANKS FOR YOUR HELP, BATMAN! YOU WERE LUCKY--BUT NOW YOUR LUCK HAS RUN OUT!
IT DOES APPEAR THAT WAY!
UNSEEN, BATMAN'S DEFT FINGERS SLIP A SHAVING MIRROR OUT OF HIS MOUNTAINEER'S KNAP-SACK, AND...
APPEARANCES CAN BE DECEIVING! FOR INSTANCE, LIGHT RAYS REFLECTED FROM SNOW APPEAR TWICE AS DAZZLING IN A MIRROR!
I--I CAN'T SEE!
7

The Dynamic Duo conquer the Himalayas—and a wanted criminal—during their ''Journey to the Top of the World!'' (Batman #93, *August 1955, ''Journey to the Top of the World!'' p. 7.*)

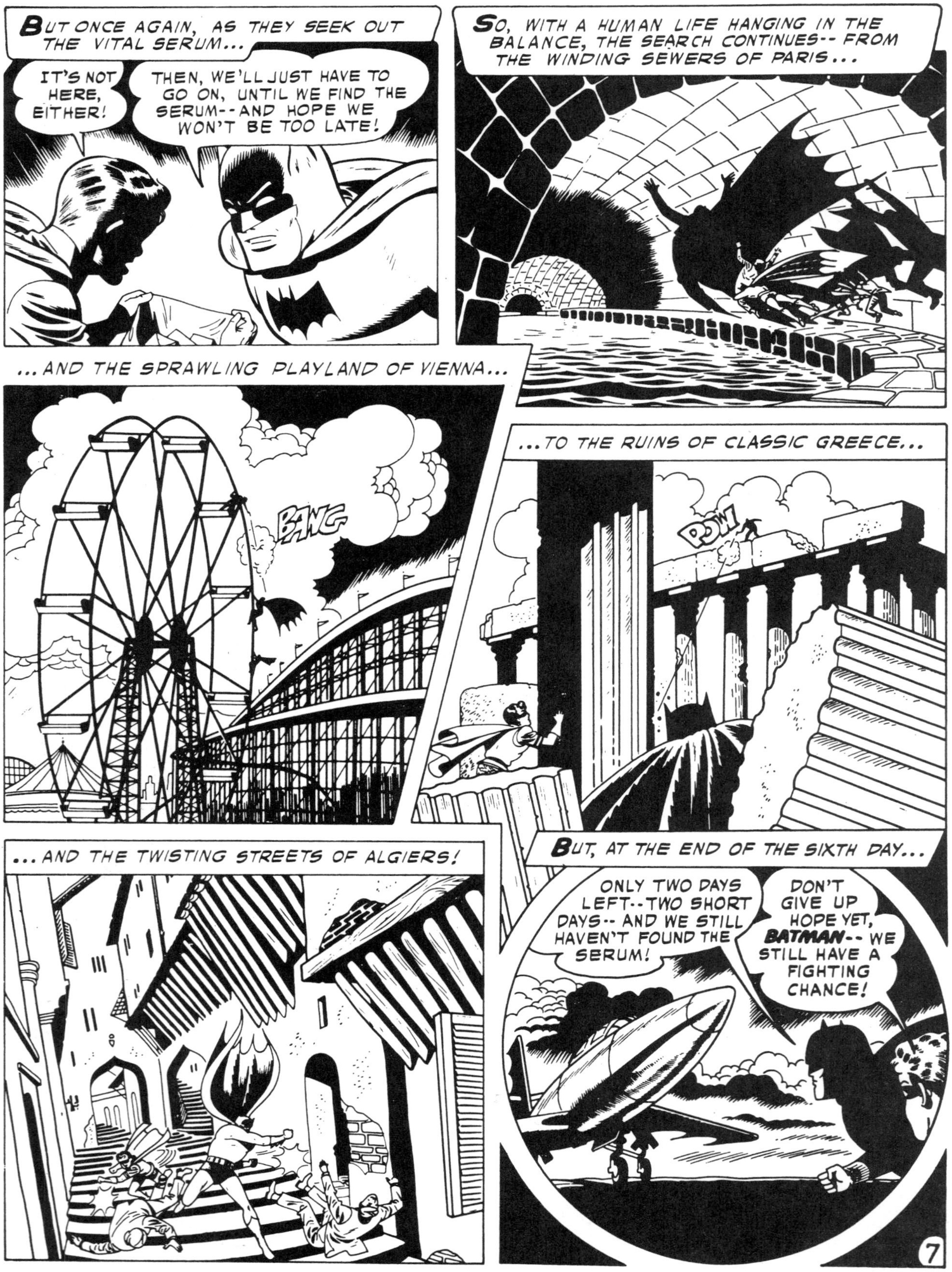
BUT ONCE AGAIN, AS THEY SEEK OUT THE VITAL SERUM...
IT'S NOT HERE, EITHER!
THEN, WE'LL JUST HAVE TO GO ON, UNTIL WE FIND THE SERUM--AND HOPE WE WON'T BE TOO LATE!
SO, WITH A HUMAN LIFE HANGING IN THE BALANCE, THE SEARCH CONTINUES-- FROM THE WINDING SEWERS OF PARIS...
...AND THE SPRAWLING PLAYLAND OF VIENNA...
BANG
...TO THE RUINS OF CLASSIC GREECE...
POW
...AND THE TWISTING STREETS OF ALGIERS!
BUT, AT THE END OF THE SIXTH DAY...
ONLY TWO DAYS LEFT--TWO SHORT DAYS-- AND WE STILL HAVEN'T FOUND THE SERUM!
DON'T GIVE UP HOPE YET, BATMAN-- WE STILL HAVE A FIGHTING CHANCE!
7

Take a whirlwind global crimefighting tour with the Dynamic Duo . . . (Detective *#248, October 1957, ''Around The World in 8 Days,'' p. 7.*)

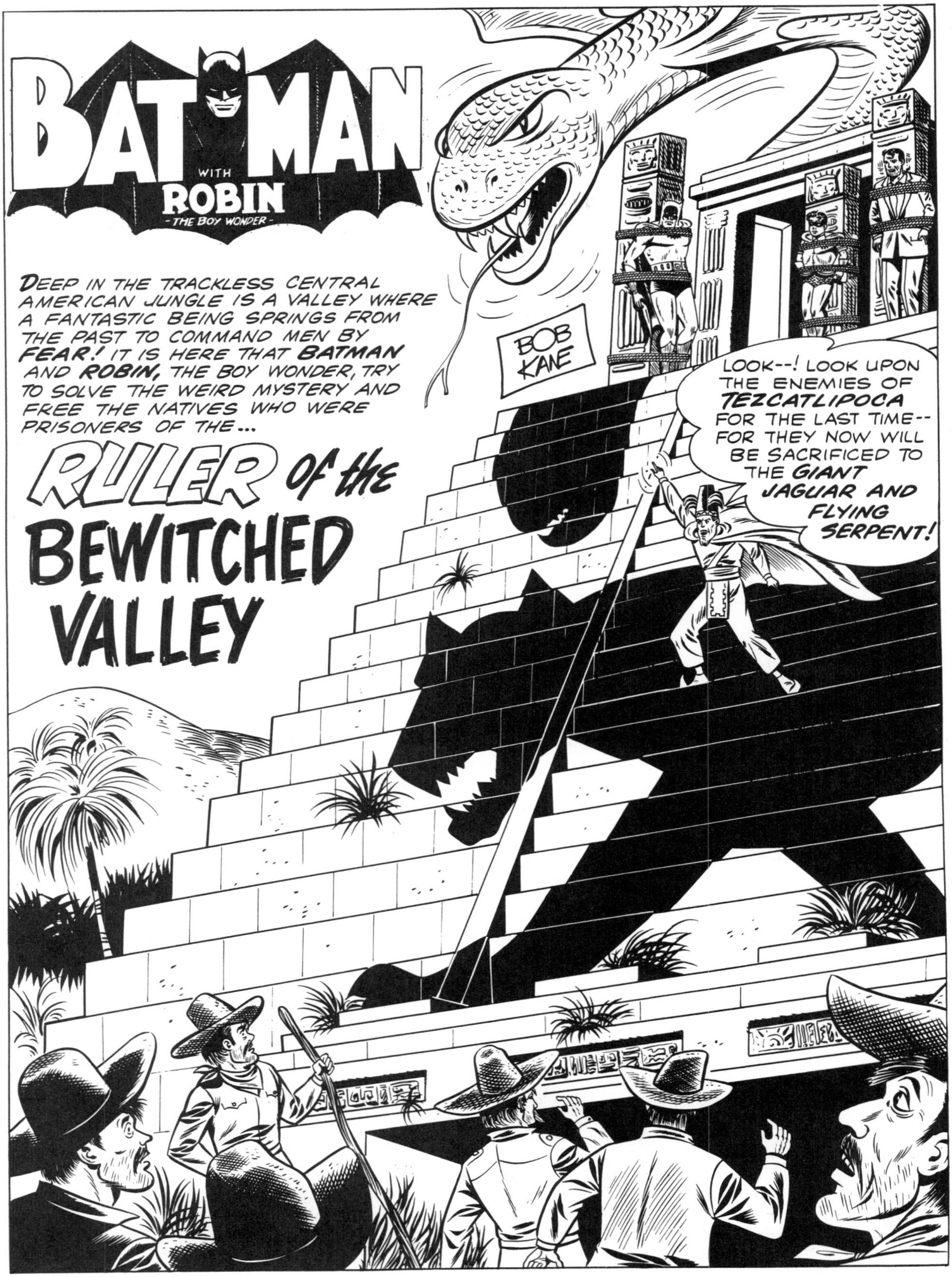
BATMAN
WITH
ROBIN
-THE BOY WONDER-
DEEP IN THE TRACKLESS CENTRAL AMERICAN JUNGLE IS A VALLEY WHERE A FANTASTIC BEING SPRINGS FROM THE PAST TO COMMAND MEN BY FEAR! IT IS HERE THAT BATMAN AND ROBIN, THE BOY WONDER, TRY TO SOLVE THE WEIRD MYSTERY AND FREE THE NATIVES WHO WERE PRISONERS OF THE...
RULER of the BEWITCHED VALLEY
BOB KANE
LOOK--! LOOK UPON THE ENEMIES OF TEZCATLIPOCA FOR THE LAST TIME--FOR THEY NOW WILL BE SACRIFICED TO THE GIANT JAGUAR AND FLYING SERPENT!

Ancient ruins sometimes provided a dramatic backdrop for a global episode. (Batman #142, September 1961, *''Ruler of the Bewitched Valley,'' p. 1 [splash page].*)

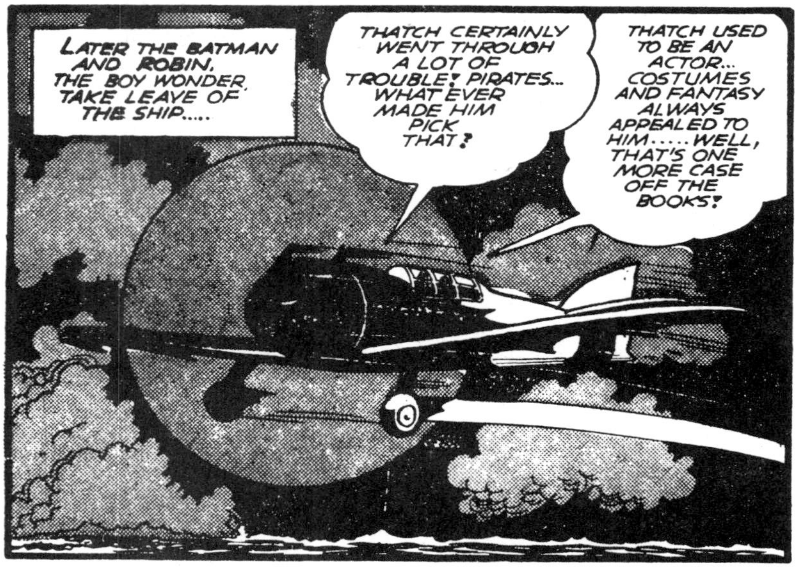
LATER THE BATMAN AND ROBIN, THE BOY WONDER, TAKE LEAVE OF THE SHIP.....
THATCH CERTAINLY WENT THROUGH A LOT OF TROUBLE! PIRATES... WHAT EVER MADE HIM PICK THAT?
THATCH USED TO BE AN ACTOR... COSTUMES AND FANTASY ALWAYS APPEALED TO HIM.....WELL, THAT'S ONE MORE CASE OFF THE BOOKS!

Left: *The Batplane was the vehicle of choice for many of Batman's global adventures.* (**Batman** *#4, Winter 1941, ''Blackbeard's Crew and the Yacht Society,'' p. 13 [panel].*) **Below:** *No spot on earth was too mysterious or remote to escape the Dynamic Duo's detection.* (**Batman** *#122, March 1959, ''Prisoners of the Sargasso Sea,'' p. 2 [select panels].*)

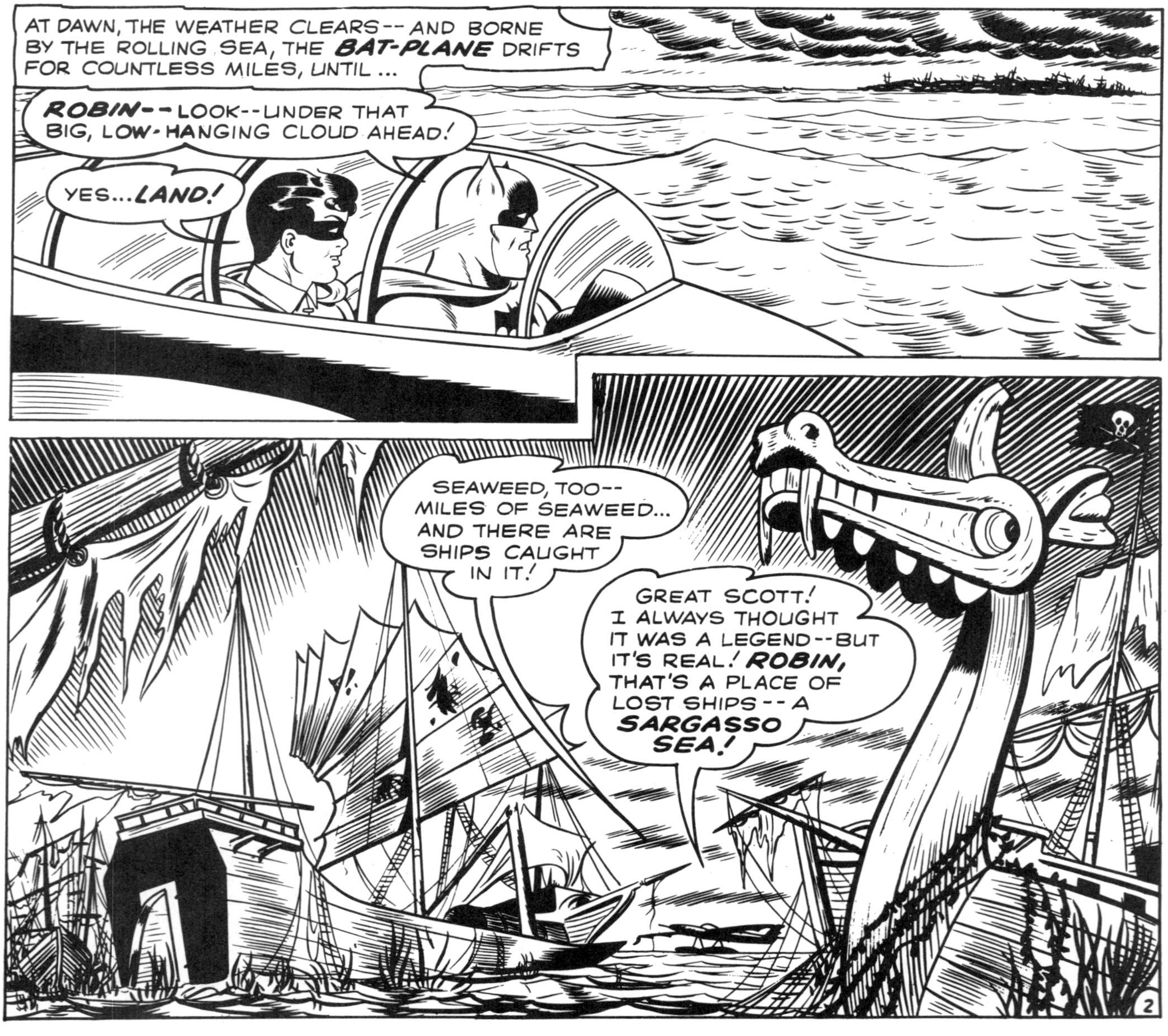
AT DAWN, THE WEATHER CLEARS-- AND BORNE BY THE ROLLING SEA, THE BAT-PLANE DRIFTS FOR COUNTLESS MILES, UNTIL ...
ROBIN--LOOK--UNDER THAT BIG, LOW-HANGING CLOUD AHEAD!
YES...LAND!
SEAWEED, TOO-- MILES OF SEAWEED... AND THERE ARE SHIPS CAUGHT IN IT!
GREAT SCOTT! I ALWAYS THOUGHT IT WAS A LEGEND--BUT IT'S REAL! ROBIN, THAT'S A PLACE OF LOST SHIPS--A SARGASSO SEA!
2

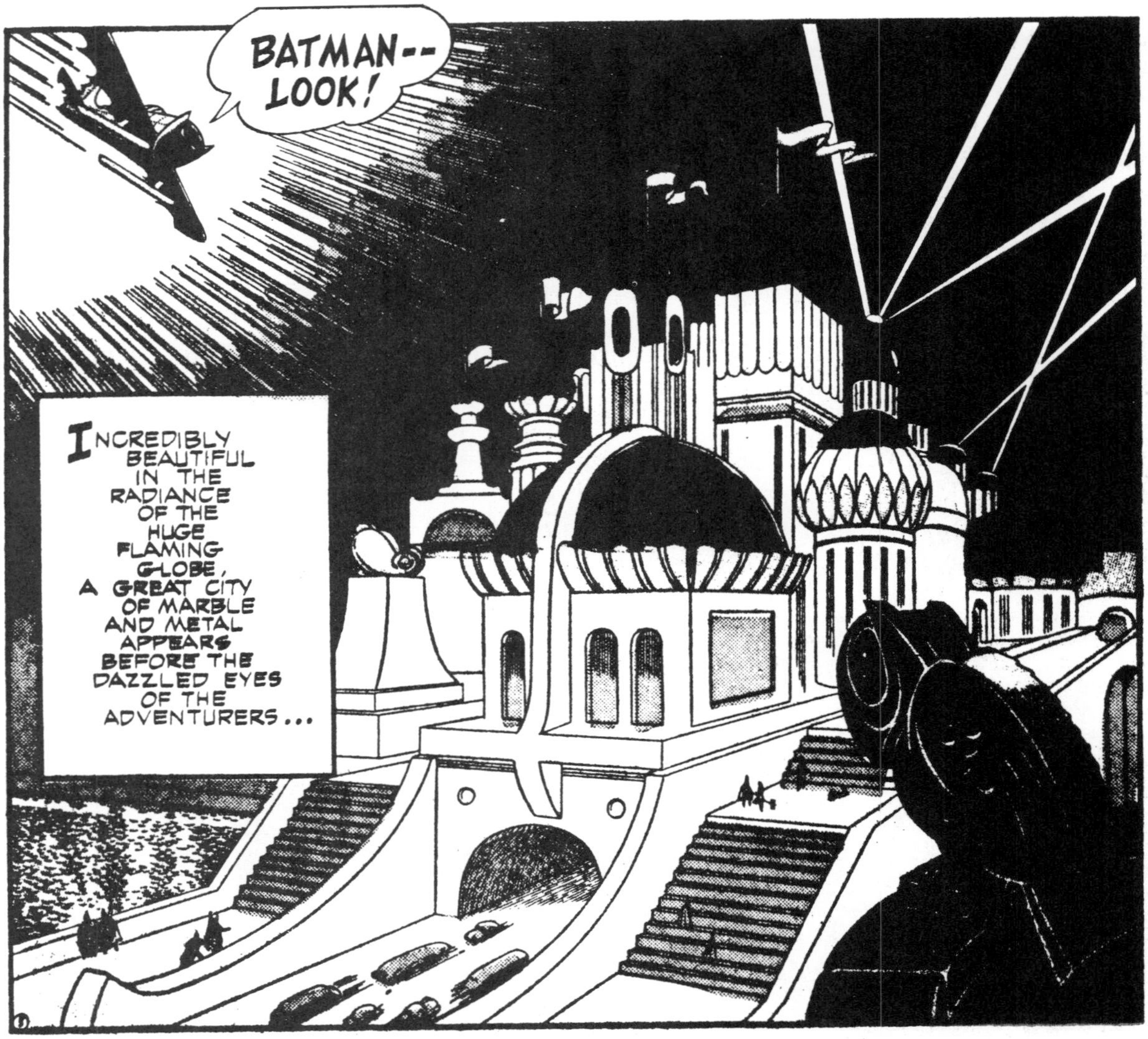
BATMAN-- LOOK!
INCREDIBLY BEAUTIFUL IN THE RADIANCE OF THE HUGE FLAMING GLOBE, A GREAT CITY OF MARBLE AND METAL APPEARS BEFORE THE DAZZLED EYES OF THE ADVENTURERS...

Top: *Atlantis revealed.* (Batman #19, *October/November 1943, "Atlantis Goes to War!" p. 5 [panel].*)
Bottom: *Batman and Robin journey to the South American jungles to help Ted Carter prove his father's fantastic tale of a lost golden city—and gain him admission to the Inner Circle of Gotham's prestigious Explorer's Club.* (Batman #158, *September 1963, "The Secret of the Impossible Perils," p. 8 [select panels].*)

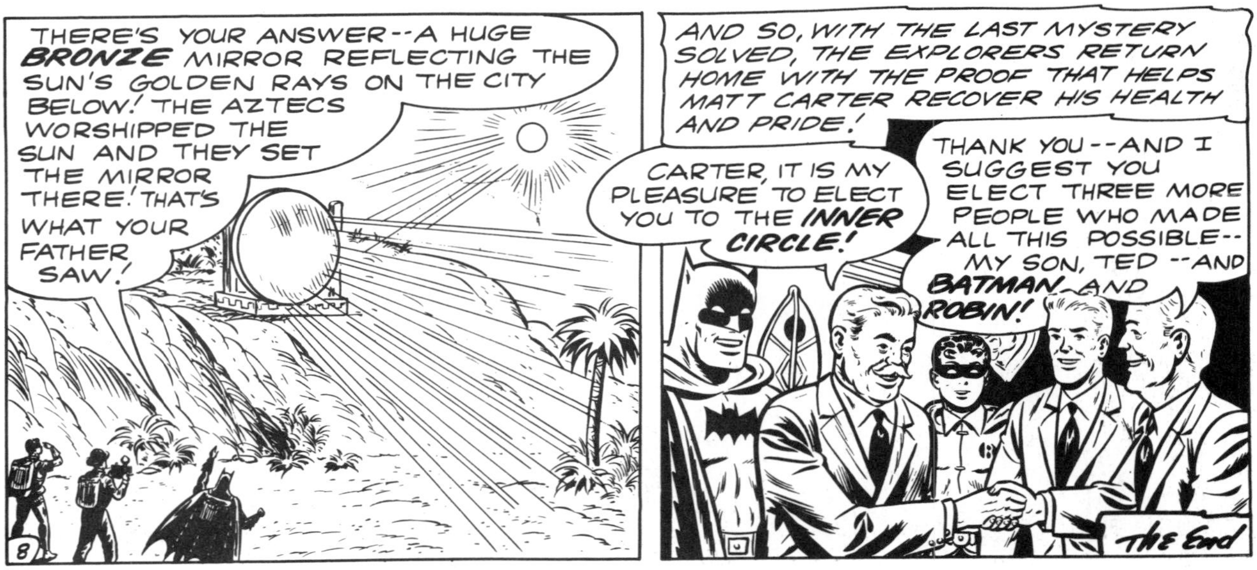
THERE'S YOUR ANSWER--A HUGE BRONZE MIRROR REFLECTING THE SUN'S GOLDEN RAYS ON THE CITY BELOW! THE AZTECS WORSHIPPED THE SUN AND THEY SET THE MIRROR THERE! THAT'S WHAT YOUR FATHER SAW!
8
AND SO, WITH THE LAST MYSTERY SOLVED, THE EXPLORERS RETURN HOME WITH THE PROOF THAT HELPS MATT CARTER RECOVER HIS HEALTH AND PRIDE!
CARTER, IT IS MY PLEASURE TO ELECT YOU TO THE INNER CIRCLE!
THANK YOU--AND I SUGGEST YOU ELECT THREE MORE PEOPLE WHO MADE ALL THIS POSSIBLE--MY SON, TED--AND BATMAN AND ROBIN!
THE END

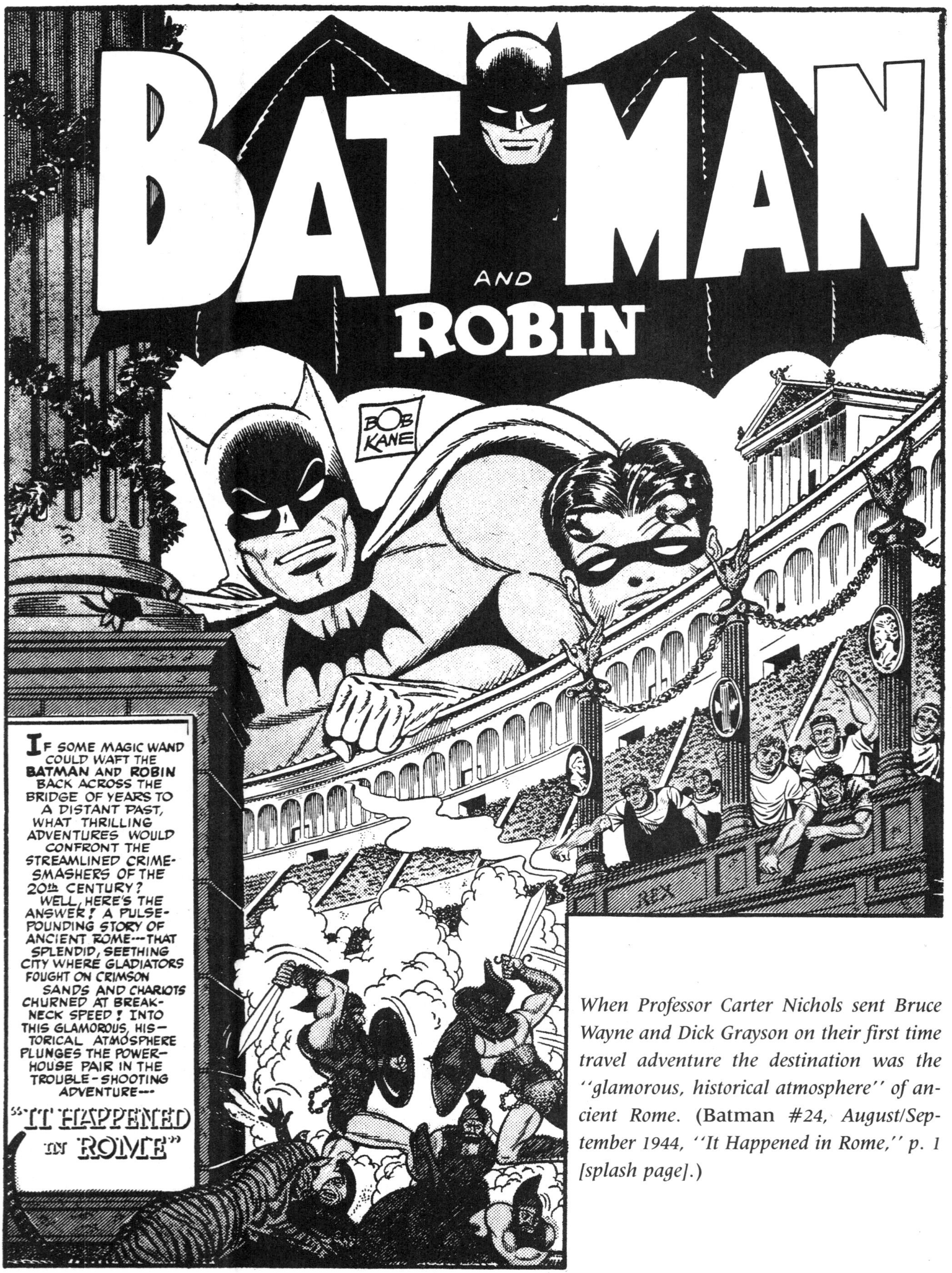
BATMAN
AND
ROBIN
BOB KANE
IF SOME MAGIC WAND COULD WAFT THE BATMAN AND ROBIN BACK ACROSS THE BRIDGE OF YEARS TO A DISTANT PAST, WHAT THRILLING ADVENTURES WOULD CONFRONT THE STREAMLINED CRIME-SMASHERS OF THE 20th CENTURY? WELL, HERE'S THE ANSWER! A PULSE-POUNDING STORY OF ANCIENT ROME---THAT SPLENDID, SEETHING CITY WHERE GLADIATORS FOUGHT ON CRIMSON SANDS AND CHARIOTS CHURNED AT BREAK-NECK SPEED! INTO THIS GLAMOROUS, HIS-TORICAL ATMOSPHERE PLUNGES THE POWER-HOUSE PAIR IN THE TROUBLE-SHOOTING ADVENTURE---
"IT HAPPENED IN ROME"
REX

When Professor Carter Nichols sent Bruce Wayne and Dick Grayson on their first time travel adventure the destination was the ''glamorous, historical atmosphere'' of ancient Rome. (Batman *#24, August/September 1944, ''It Happened in Rome,'' p. 1 [splash page].)*

CHAPTER 9
DARK KNIGHT IN TIME

WHEN BATMAN ARTIST DICK SPRANG left New York for Arizona, he was drawn by his desire to explore the remote canyons and rivers of the Southwest. In that timeless, rugged land he could retrace the trails of the early expeditions that first opened the region.

In those isolated canyons he could also see even more ancient examples of human activity: the petroglyphs of ancient tribes, evoking the mystery of an age forever lost in time.

Given his explorations of ageless territory, it's not surprising when Sprang reveals that it was a special joy to illustrate a Batman time-travel tale.

"I enjoyed researching and drawing historical architecture, costumes, and all manner of exotic props," Sprang explains. "Whitney Ellsworth, the executive editor who gave me my break on Batman, said of these historical pieces, 'Let's make them accurate, every bit and piece of the environment, so that the readers are exposed to the real thing, not faked-up alternates.' I believe I carried out his wish because I was given a considerable number of these stories, most of them written by the superlative Bill Finger."

The engineer of Batman's time-travel adventures in the comic books was a famed Gotham City scientist and historian named Professor Carter Nichols.

The time-travel adventures began as a special interest of Bruce Wayne. Although Nichols was renowned as the world's foremost authority on time travel, his experiments with Wayne (who never revealed his dual identity to the scientist) were seemingly conducted in secret. If the Gotham press had gotten wind of the mysterious experiments, it would no doubt have characterized them as an eccentric millionaire's bizarre in-

dulgence. Later on, the Dynamic Duo, ostensibly referred to Nichols by their good friend Bruce Wayne, would take time-travel trips.

The Dynamic Duo's epic voyages have taken them to ancient China and Arabia, Greece and Rome. They've met such historical figures as Leonardo da Vinci, Marco Polo, Cleopatra, and Jules Verne.

Their travels have taken them fifty thousand years in the past (where they learned how to prevent an alien invasion of Earth), as well as to A.D. 2050 (experienced during a mistake in Nichols's time transportation technique).

Although Nichols let others experience the time-travel thrill, he once took the risks himself as the subject for the "mighty force streams" from his time-ray projector, his most dangerous time-travel innovation up to that point. He landed in ancient Rome and was captured by King Phorbus of Rhodes, who tried to force him to fashion "magic weapons" for both king and army.

Fortunately, Bruce Wayne and Dick Grayson had made a check of Nichols's lab. When the scientist hadn't returned at the appointed hour, they rode to Rhodes on the streams of the time-ray as Batman and Robin.

After rescuing the professor, and safely on the way back to their own era, Nichols turned to Batman and gratefully acknowledged that "I never want to go to the past again! I'll send Bruce Wayne and his ward, instead!"[1]

Professor Nichols, usually dressed in a white lab coat and black bow tie, has always been pictured with the intense look of a dedicated scientist. His large, glistening pate seems to boast an advanced cranium, while the eyeglasses set

---

1. Fleisher, *Batman,* p. 289. All other Nichols references in Chapter 9 taken from Fleisher book, pages 286–90.

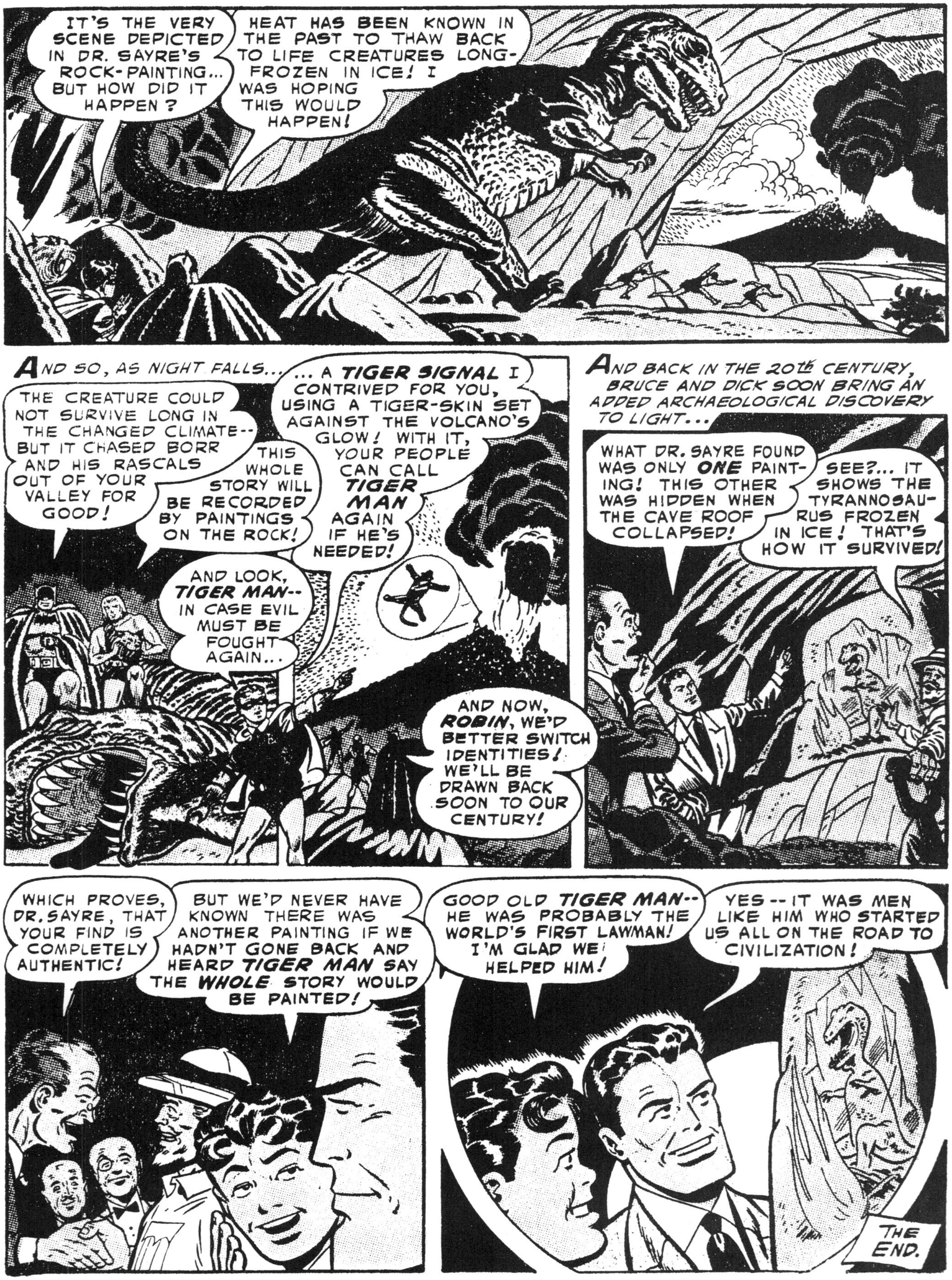

IT'S THE VERY SCENE DEPICTED IN DR. SAYRE'S ROCK-PAINTING... BUT HOW DID IT HAPPEN?
HEAT HAS BEEN KNOWN IN THE PAST TO THAW BACK TO LIFE CREATURES LONG-FROZEN IN ICE! I WAS HOPING THIS WOULD HAPPEN!
AND SO, AS NIGHT FALLS...
THE CREATURE COULD NOT SURVIVE LONG IN THE CHANGED CLIMATE-- BUT IT CHASED BORR AND HIS RASCALS OUT OF YOUR VALLEY FOR GOOD!
THIS WHOLE STORY WILL BE RECORDED BY PAINTINGS ON THE ROCK!
... A TIGER SIGNAL I CONTRIVED FOR YOU, USING A TIGER-SKIN SET AGAINST THE VOLCANO'S GLOW! WITH IT, YOUR PEOPLE CAN CALL TIGER MAN AGAIN IF HE'S NEEDED!
AND LOOK, TIGER MAN-- IN CASE EVIL MUST BE FOUGHT AGAIN...
AND NOW, ROBIN, WE'D BETTER SWITCH IDENTITIES! WE'LL BE DRAWN BACK SOON TO OUR CENTURY!
AND BACK IN THE 20th CENTURY, BRUCE AND DICK SOON BRING AN ADDED ARCHAEOLOGICAL DISCOVERY TO LIGHT...
WHAT DR. SAYRE FOUND WAS ONLY ONE PAINTING! THIS OTHER WAS HIDDEN WHEN THE CAVE ROOF COLLAPSED!
SEE?... IT SHOWS THE TYRANNOSAURUS FROZEN IN ICE! THAT'S HOW IT SURVIVED!
WHICH PROVES, DR. SAYRE, THAT YOUR FIND IS COMPLETELY AUTHENTIC!
BUT WE'D NEVER HAVE KNOWN THERE WAS ANOTHER PAINTING IF WE HADN'T GONE BACK AND HEARD TIGER MAN SAY THE WHOLE STORY WOULD BE PAINTED!
GOOD OLD TIGER MAN-- HE WAS PROBABLY THE WORLD'S FIRST LAWMAN! I'M GLAD WE HELPED HIM!
YES -- IT WAS MEN LIKE HIM WHO STARTED US ALL ON THE ROAD TO CIVILIZATION!
THE END.

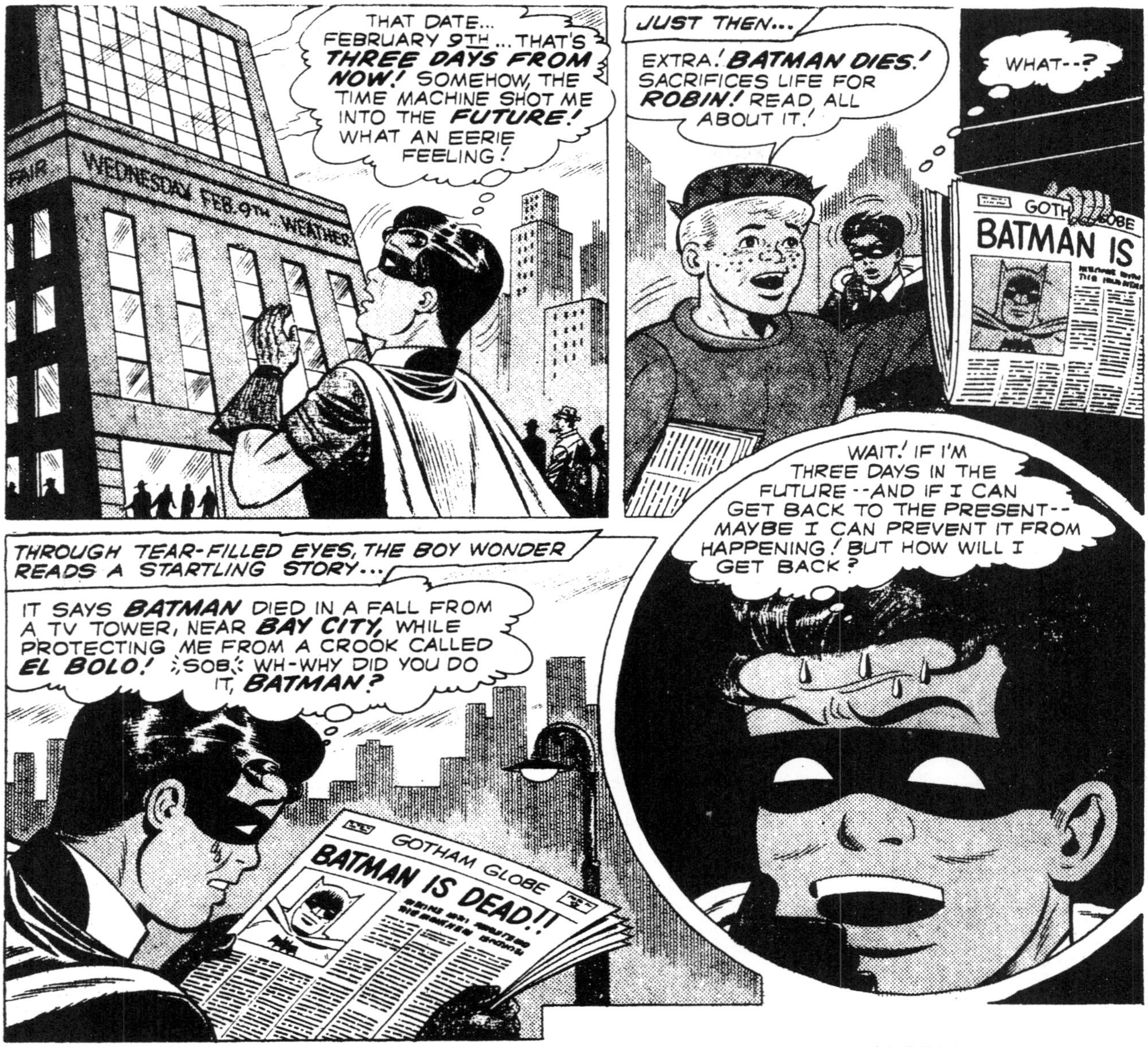
THAT DATE... FEBRUARY 9TH ...THAT'S **THREE DAYS FROM NOW!** SOMEHOW, THE TIME MACHINE SHOT ME INTO THE **FUTURE!** WHAT AN EERIE FEELING!
FAIR WEDNESDAY FEB. 9TH WEATHER
JUST THEN...
EXTRA! **BATMAN DIES!** SACRIFICES LIFE FOR **ROBIN!** READ ALL ABOUT IT!
WHAT--?
GOTH GLOBE
BATMAN IS
WAIT! IF I'M THREE DAYS IN THE FUTURE--AND IF I CAN GET BACK TO THE PRESENT--MAYBE I CAN PREVENT IT FROM HAPPENING! BUT HOW WILL I GET BACK?
THROUGH TEAR-FILLED EYES, THE BOY WONDER READS A STARTLING STORY...
IT SAYS **BATMAN** DIED IN A FALL FROM A TV TOWER, NEAR **BAY CITY,** WHILE PROTECTING ME FROM A CROOK CALLED **EL BOLO!** SOB! WH-WHY DID YOU DO IT, **BATMAN?**
GOTHAM GLOBE
BATMAN IS DEAD!!

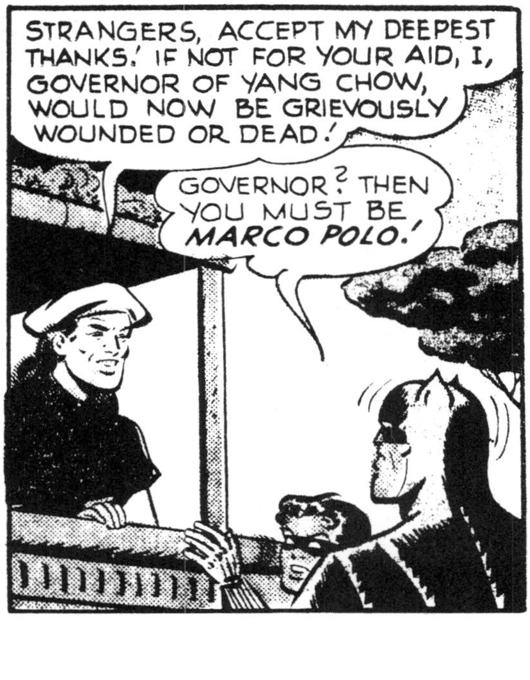
STRANGERS, ACCEPT MY DEEPEST THANKS! IF NOT FOR YOUR AID, I, GOVERNOR OF YANG CHOW, WOULD NOW BE GRIEVOUSLY WOUNDED OR DEAD!
GOVERNOR? THEN YOU MUST BE **MARCO POLO!**

Above: *Time travel wasn't as simple as takin' the ''A'' train. Here, Robin jumps ahead to read about the death of Batman. (Not to worry—the ''Batman Is Dead'' headline turns out to be inaccurate. But since when did you believe everything you read in the* Gotham Globe*?)* (Batman #*125, August 1959, ''The Last Days of Batman,'' p. 3 [select panels].*) Right: *Batman saves the life, and enjoys the hospitality, of the famed Venetian explorer Marco Polo.* (World's Finest #*42, September/October 1949, ''The Amazing Adventure of Batman and Marco Polo!'' p. 4 [panel].*) Left: *Batman battles a Tyrannosaurus Rex, solves an archeological mystery, and meets a prehistoric crimefighter in this time-bending adventure.* (Batman #*93, August 1955,''The Caveman Batman,'' p. 8.*)

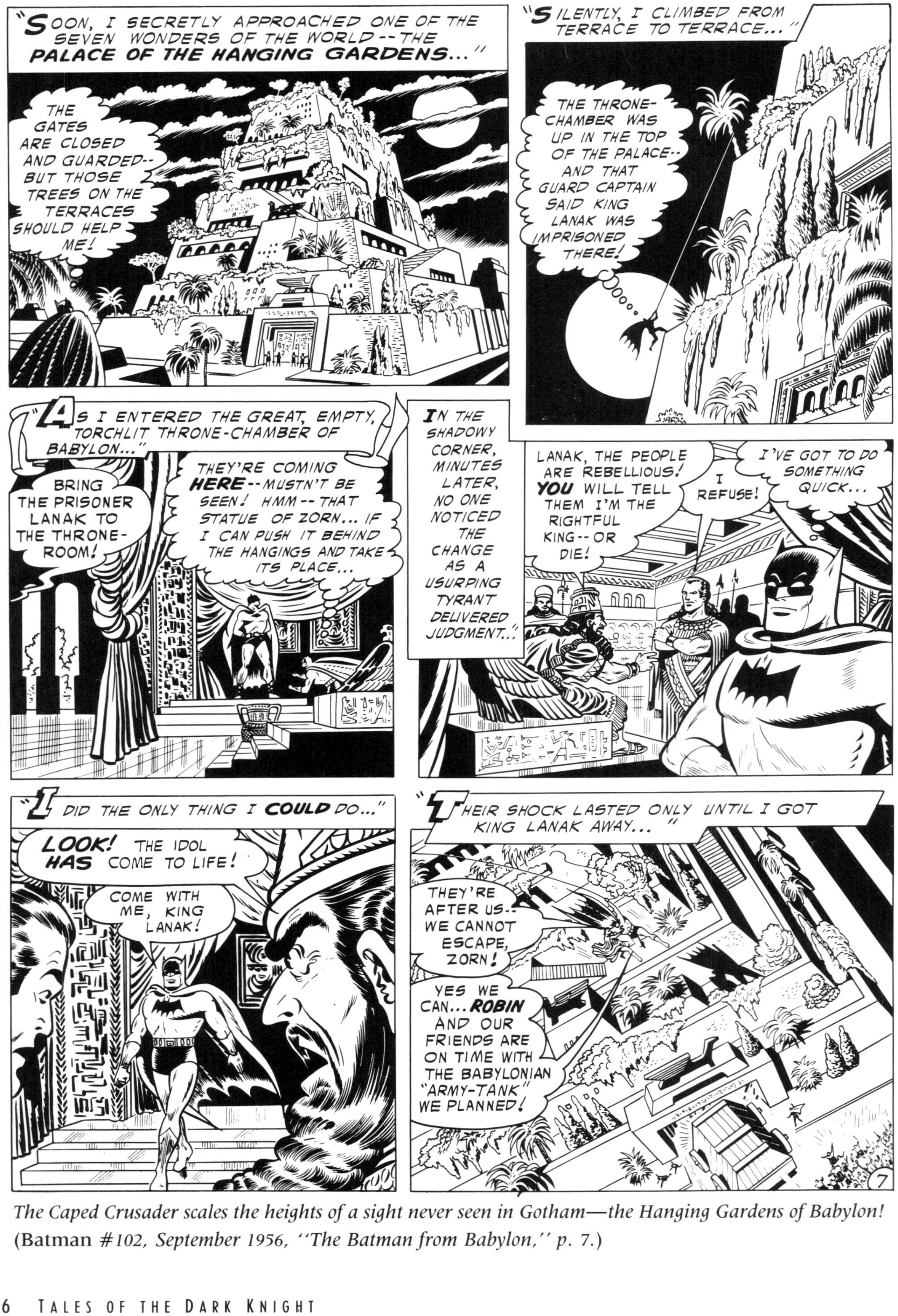
"SOON, I SECRETLY APPROACHED ONE OF THE SEVEN WONDERS OF THE WORLD--THE PALACE OF THE HANGING GARDENS..."
THE GATES ARE CLOSED AND GUARDED--BUT THOSE TREES ON THE TERRACES SHOULD HELP ME!
"SILENTLY, I CLIMBED FROM TERRACE TO TERRACE..."
THE THRONE-CHAMBER WAS UP IN THE TOP OF THE PALACE--AND THAT GUARD CAPTAIN SAID KING LANAK WAS IMPRISONED THERE!
"AS I ENTERED THE GREAT, EMPTY, TORCHLIT THRONE-CHAMBER OF BABYLON..."
BRING THE PRISONER LANAK TO THE THRONE-ROOM!
THEY'RE COMING HERE--MUSTN'T BE SEEN! HMM--THAT STATUE OF ZORN... IF I CAN PUSH IT BEHIND THE HANGINGS AND TAKE ITS PLACE...
IN THE SHADOWY CORNER, MINUTES LATER, NO ONE NOTICED THE CHANGE AS A USURPING TYRANT DELIVERED JUDGMENT..."
LANAK, THE PEOPLE ARE REBELLIOUS! YOU WILL TELL THEM I'M THE RIGHTFUL KING--OR DIE!
I REFUSE!
I'VE GOT TO DO SOMETHING QUICK...
"I DID THE ONLY THING I COULD DO..."
LOOK! THE IDOL HAS COME TO LIFE!
COME WITH ME, KING LANAK!
"THEIR SHOCK LASTED ONLY UNTIL I GOT KING LANAK AWAY..."
THEY'RE AFTER US--WE CANNOT ESCAPE, ZORN!
YES WE CAN... ROBIN AND OUR FRIENDS ARE ON TIME WITH THE BABYLONIAN "ARMY-TANK" WE PLANNED!
7

The Caped Crusader scales the heights of a sight never seen in Gotham—the Hanging Gardens of Babylon! (**Batman** *#102, September 1956, ''The Batman from Babylon,'' p. 7.)*

on his thin face give him an owlish look.

His time-travel methods grew out of his studies into the mysteries of the subconscious mind. During his first time-travel experiment he sent Bruce Wayne and Dick Grayson to ancient Rome using his own special hypnosis technique (which he has never revealed in detail).

Even though Wayne and Grayson were both physically slumped in chairs in Nichols's home during this deep hypnosis, upon awakening, they reported they had been physically, as well as mentally, present in the time of the Caesars.

His role as the initiator of the experience did seem to involve subtle mental linkups with his time-travel subjects. When Bruce Wayne and Dick Grayson were once transported one hundred years into the future, instead of the original destination of one hunded years in the past, Nichols realized the deadly mistake was due to his own subconscious preoccupations with the possibilities of future time travel.

Seeking to avoid such mistakes, and ensure greater control over the experiment, Nichols developed a technique involving both hypnosis and a time machine contraption.

He had Bruce Wayne and his young ward sit in chairs geared to the controls of his time machine, and then hypnotized them. Upon their successful return, the two described a strange ringing in their ears followed by the "sensation of dropping off into a bottomless abyss, being caught up in a giant whirlpool of blackness" and a violent spinning that only stopped when the darkness cleared and they discovered themselves in the appointed time zone.

The breakthrough innovation was Nichols's development of a time-ray complete with an automatic control bringing the subject back at a set time. A further advance was his creation of a portable time-box which the traveler could activate at any point in order to return to the present.

Given Batman and Robin's willing participation in these experiments, it can be said that the Dynamic Duo helped Nichols develop and perfect time travel—as well as take the Batman legend into new frontiers of adventure.

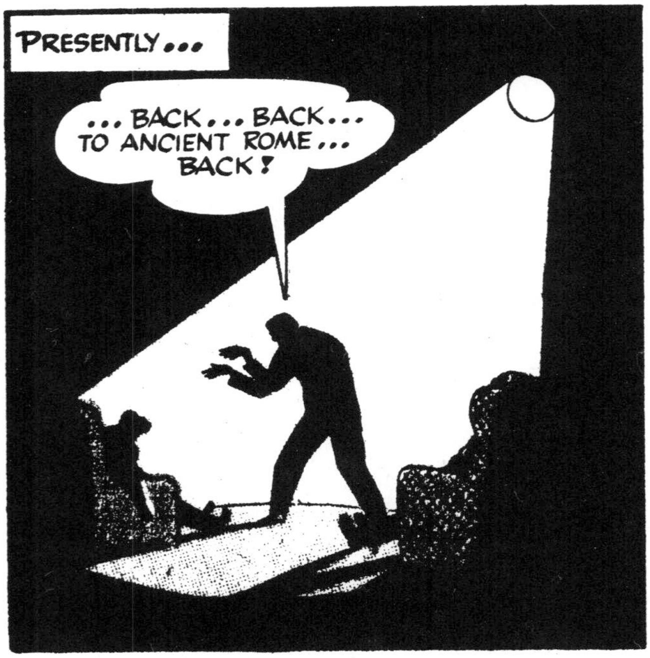
PRESENTLY...
...BACK...BACK... TO ANCIENT ROME... BACK!

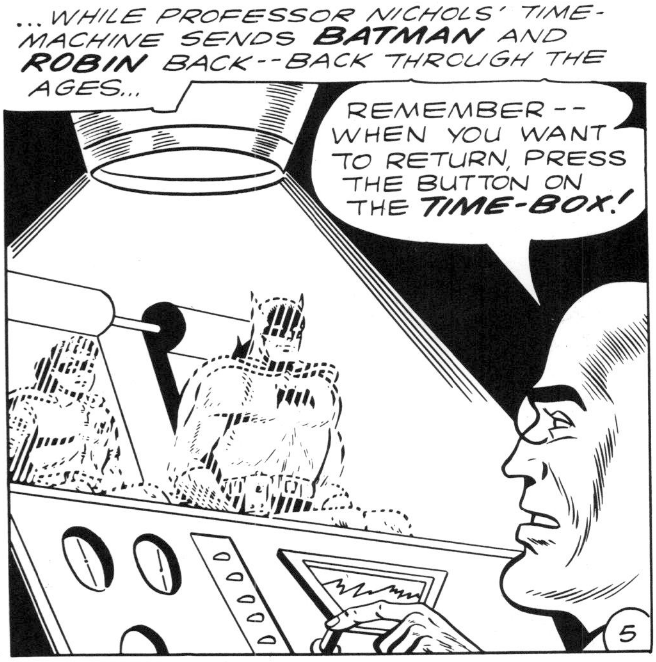
...WHILE PROFESSOR NICHOLS' TIME-MACHINE SENDS BATMAN AND ROBIN BACK--BACK THROUGH THE AGES...
REMEMBER-- WHEN YOU WANT TO RETURN, PRESS THE BUTTON ON THE TIME-BOX!
5

Left: *Professor Nichols originally used a mysterious, deep hypnosis technique to send the Dynamic Duo back into time.* (Batman *#24, August/September 1944, "It Happened in Rome," p. 3 [panel].)* Right: *Later time travel innovations included the addition of the "time-box."* (World's Finest *#135, August 1963, "Menace of The Future Man," p. 5 [panel].)*

CHAPTER 10

Pop Goes the Batman

There's no escape. It's all over the place. Madness! Supermadness! The entertainment world offers it on all sides, and the public gobbles it up. Batman conquers TV. *Kids swing Batman capes in the backyard, and Bat products are everywhere.*

—Life, *March 11, 1966*

After the troublesome years following the comics crackdown and flagging comic book sales of the 1950s, the superhero was in real danger of going the way of the pulp heroes of old.

The super shot in the arm for the genre was provided by the Batman TV show, which debuted on ABC-TV on Wednesday, January 12, 1966. For most of its three-year run, thirty million viewers tuned in to the twice-weekly episodes, placing the series consistently in the Nielsen top twenty rated shows. (In the final season the program was aired only once a week.)

How Bat-Mad did the country go in 1966? Well, a *Life* magazine cover featured series star Adam West, in full Batman regalia, the first such honor for a comic book superhero.

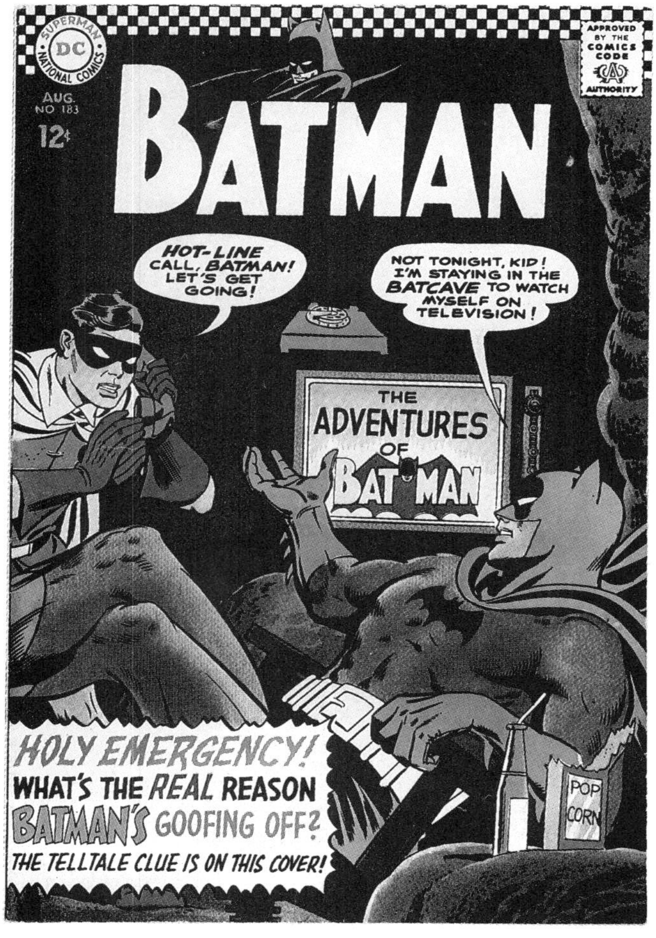
SUPERMAN DC NATIONAL COMICS
AUG. NO 183
12¢
APPROVED BY THE COMICS CODE AUTHORITY
BATMAN
HOT-LINE CALL, BATMAN! LET'S GET GOING!
NOT TONIGHT, KID! I'M STAYING IN THE BATCAVE TO WATCH MYSELF ON TELEVISION!
THE ADVENTURES OF BATMAN
HOLY EMERGENCY!
WHAT'S THE REAL REASON BATMAN'S GOOFING OFF?
THE TELLTALE CLUE IS ON THIS COVER!
POP CORN

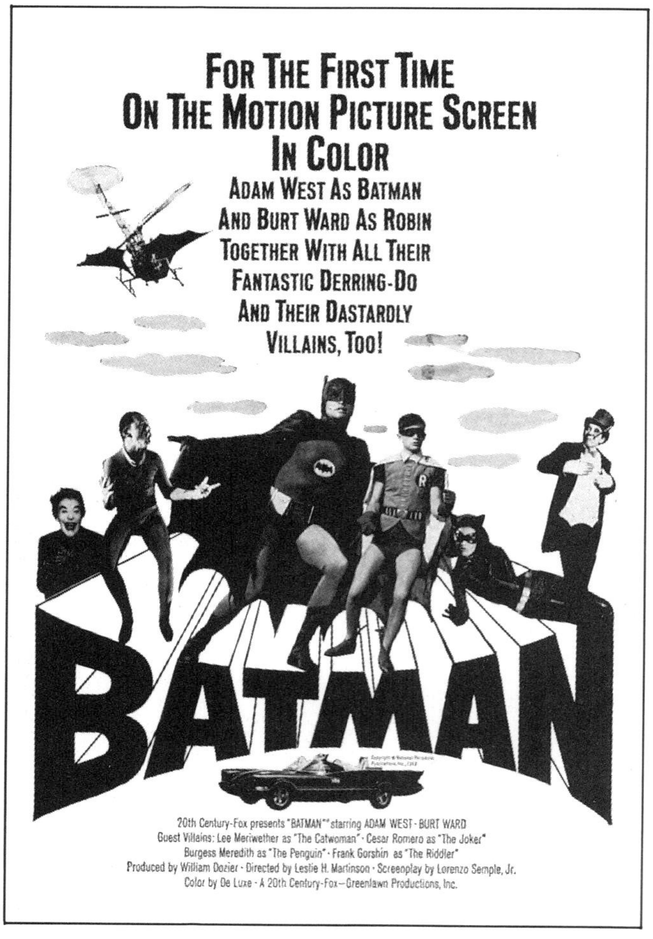
FOR THE FIRST TIME
ON THE MOTION PICTURE SCREEN
IN COLOR
ADAM WEST AS BATMAN
AND BURT WARD AS ROBIN
TOGETHER WITH ALL THEIR
FANTASTIC DERRING-DO
AND THEIR DASTARDLY
VILLAINS, TOO!
BATMAN
20th Century-Fox presents "BATMAN" starring ADAM WEST - BURT WARD
Guest Villains: Lee Meriwether as "The Catwoman" · Cesar Romero as "The Joker"
Burgess Meredith as "The Penguin" · Frank Gorshin as "The Riddler"
Produced by William Dozier · Directed by Leslie H. Martinson · Screenplay by Lorenzo Semple, Jr.
Color by De Luxe - A 20th Century-Fox—Greenlawn Productions, Inc.

Left: *The Splashy Pop Art spirit of the Batman TV show affected the chronicles themselves. (The Batman on this cover is an imposter—he's without the yellow chest insignia that marked Batman's "New Look" period.)* (Batman #183, *August 1966, cover.*) Right: *Promo for the 1966 "Batman" movie.* (Detective #356, *October 1966, movie ad, inside front cover.*)

Batman helped create the era of "pop," which Lawrence Alloway, then curator of New York's Guggenheim Museum, termed: "an affectionate way of referring to mass culture, the whole man-made environment."

Pop was the fashion in cities from London to New York. Pop artists such as Roy Lichtenstein were becoming wealthy and famous with their evocations of the comic book world.

And through it all, Batmania raged like a wildfire through the parched fields of mass culture. There was the nightclub outside San Francisco known as "Wayne Manor," where guests could buy their tickets from Batman at the front door, be seated by a Joker maître d', and enjoy drinks served by Wonder Woman while girls dressed like Robin (!) danced behind a plate glass screen and led revelers in the Batusi. A Detroit hairdresser invented the Bat Cut, while a veteran Cleveland cop named Gilbert Batman became a local celebrity and helped stimulate blood bank donations by donating his own blood—while costumed as his fabled namesake. Batman was even applauded by the National Safety Council because of his constant vigilance in making sure Robin was safely seat-belted before the Batmobile roared off after the week's evil villain.

"This is the biggest thing that's ever happened in licensing," Jay Emmett, president of the Licensing Corp. of America, told *Newsweek* of their handling of the selling of Batman. Mere months after Batman battled the Riddler on the first show, some one thousand Batman items had

SUPERMAN DC NATIONAL COMICS
APPROVED BY THE COMICS CODE AUTHORITY
BATMAN
12¢
HOLY CLIFF-HANGER! THE CAPED CRUSADER IN THE GRIP OF THE ONE VILLAIN HE IS COMPELLED TO FEAR!
FRIGHT OF THE SCARECROW!

HOLY HOBBY KITS!
IF YOU DIG BATMAN, FEATURE THESE NEW AURORA MODELS IN YOUR BATCAVE
THE BATMOBILE!
THE BATPLANE!
coming soon
ROBIN!
BUILD THEM...ADD THEM TO YOUR COLLECTION—
they assemble as fast as a Batarang—and show them off to your friends!
98c each wherever toys and hobby products are sold
models can be painted as shown. Kits do not include paint or cement.
© 1966 AURORA PLASTICS CORP., WEST HEMPSTEAD, NEW YORK
The World's Largest Manufacturer of Hobby Products
Aurora products are manufactured entirely in the U.S. for distribution in America; in Canada for the Commonwealth nations; and in Holland for Europe and Africa.
AURORA

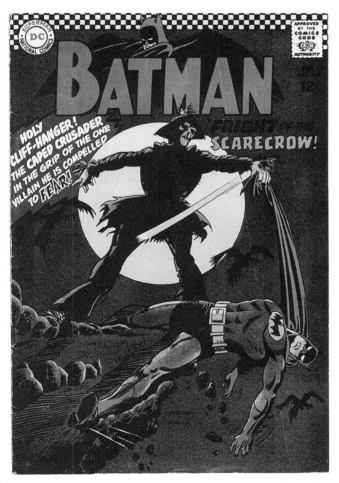

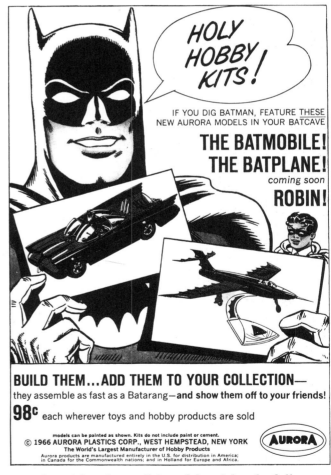

Left: *Despite the overtones of parody in the mid-Sixties Batman chronicles, the tradition of the night, the full moon, evil villains, and menace did not entirely disappear.* (Batman *#189, February 1967, cover.*) Right: *Holy merchandise—hundreds of millions of dollars worth in the Bat-crazed mid-Sixties.* (Detective *#356, October 1966, back cover.*)

been licensed, including mask-and-cape sets, sport jackets, toiletries, and posters (often hung as examples of true pop art).

With Batmania kicking up such a ruckus, the social theorists and arbiters of public taste weighed in with their own pop pronouncements.

Poet W. H. Auden feared that a cultural Gresham's law was in effect, with bad culture driving out good culture.

Media expert Marshall McLuhan felt the comics evoked "a pastoral world of primal innocence from which young America has clearly graduated.... There was still adolescence in those days, and there were still remote ideals and private dreams, and visualizable goals."[1]

"Many people, it seems, have seen the future—and prefer the past," Newsweek concluded. "When the Gemini 8 astronauts were in trouble and the networks interrupted their programming to switch to NASA headquarters, thousands of calls flooded the networks, complaining, in effect, about the cancellation of their fantasy universe. They were watching ABC's 'Batman' and, ironically, CBS's 'Lost in Space.'"[2]

The "Batman" show, with the first weekly episode always ending on a cliff-hanger note, evoked the thrilling world of the old movie serials, which had often featured Golden Age superheroes.

"The importance of comic strips in our lives [to a youngster of the thirties or forties] can't be overestimated, and in the serials we actually saw in action the people we read about in the comics," write movie serial historians Ken Weiss and Ed Goodgold. "And not just the comic characters themselves, but the trapdoors, secret passageways, death rays, and the complicated scientific devices."[3]

Two fifteen-episode Batman serials were produced by Columbia Pictures in 1943 and 1949. In the first Batman, the Dynamic Duo stopped the evil Dr. Daka, who was transforming people into zombies on behalf of the Axis powers. In Batman and Robin (1949), the pair crushed the criminal career of a cloaked, hooded figure known as "the Wizard."

The Batman serials were forgettable, even offensive. (The 1943 film is full of racial stereotypes.) Batman artist Jerry Robinson remembers flying out to Los Angeles from New York to provide some technical advice to the writers and director. Once in the land of dreams and tinsel, he realized firsthand the difficulty of translating characters from one medium to another.

"I was still very young, a kid, and I remember sitting down and the writers were plotting a story and they didn't know how to get out of the situation," Robinson recalls. "They had ideas we wouldn't even consider comic-book-worthy. It was so amateurish. I remember suggesting a couple of ideas, just ordinary things we were doing in the comic books every day, and they thought I was a boy genius. They just didn't know how to plot it."

That "Batman" even made it to TV was a lucky break. William Dozier, the executive producer of the show, has recalled that Batman trailed Superman and Dick Tracy on a short list of potential development properties.

Various conflicts prevented the development of Superman or Dick Tracy projects, so Batman received a serious look. On a flight from New York to Los Angeles, the fifty-eightish Dozier settled in for the long ride with "seven or eight" vintage Batman comics.

"I felt a little bit like an idiot," Dozier explains in The Official Batman Batbook. "Then I digested all of those books.... Then I had just the simple idea of overdoing it, of making it so square and so serious that adults would find it amusing. I knew kids would go for the derring-do, the adventure, but the trick would be to find adults who would either watch it with their kids or, to hell with the kids, and watch it anyway."[4]

A week later Dozier was back in New York presenting the Batman TV show concept to ABC's top brass. With the executives seated around a huge table, Dozier recounted the tale of a young boy, his parents murdered by a criminal, who had vowed to spend his life avenging their deaths as the Batman.

Dozier received a green light to develop a

Batman show. The next stop was Madrid, where writer Lorenzo Semple was working at the time. Over lunch and three bottles of Spanish wine, they plotted the pilot film. Semple then wrote it, while Dozier produced and cast it.

At first there were concerns that "Batman" would be a bomb. Preview audiences had given the show lukewarm ratings. But ABC wanted something different for its 7:30 P.M. slot and ordered the first thirteen episodes.

Such precurtain jitters become part of show biz legend when your program is a hit. But although Batman was a smash with the network and the Nielsens, the tongue-in-cheek interpretation of the Dark Knight did not meet with universal acclaim.

"While it was fun, I thought they were burlesquing it too much—you can only do so much of that and it's gone," Jerry Robinson remarks. "It could have been handled a little differently and been a bigger property, like James Bond or Tarzan, where the concept was kept consistent. They didn't satirize a satire."

"He (Dozier) explained at the time that... they'd sort of play around with it a little," remembers then Batman editor Julius Schwartz. "At the time we didn't know exactly what he was getting at. I guess I could use the words 'alarmed' and 'horrified' when we saw what came on over the screen."

Schwartz was an old hand from the Golden Age who had also been a literary agent for such sci-fi and weird tale legends as Ray Bradbury, Alfred Bester, Robert Bloch, and H. P. Lovecraft. When he took over the Batman titles in 1964, he ushered in Batman's "New Look."

Schwartz had replaced Jack Schiff, who had edited Batman for almost a quarter century. Schiff had managed to weather Batman's monster/sci-fi period, and had begun bringing back the old villains: the Penguin returned; the Mad Hatter made a comeback; Clayface had a new incarnation as Matt Hagen, whose brown, claylike body (achieved after a dip in a hidden pool possessed of a "strange liquid protoplasm") allowed him to change into other forms; and the Joker himself was again making regular visits to Gotham City.

Schwartz continued, and expanded upon, the renewal of the Batman tradition of twisted villains. In a major transition, Bob Kane was no longer in charge of providing the finished artwork. Artists like Carmine Infantino took up pen and brush and helped illustrate the New Look. Batman was equipped with a new, streamlined Batmobile and Batplane. The old twisting staircase that had descended into the Bat Cave from Wayne Manor was replaced with an automatic elevator. The work area in the Bat Cave itself was modernized with the latest crimefighting technology. The crowning touch, and Schwartz's own editorial signature, was his enclosing the black bat image on Batman's chest in a yellow moon.

Schwartz had always been as precise as a diamond cutter at reviving and updating the careers of old, out-of-work crime fighters. One of his most successful superhero reclamation efforts was the Flash, whom he outfitted with a new identity, origin, and costume. But there were some built-in restrictions on how far and fast he could play with the Batman mythos.

"With the Flash there was a whole new generation [who hadn't read the long-gone Golden Age–era Flash], so I could do anything I wanted," Schwartz explains. "But I couldn't take over a continuing series like Batman and say, 'Hey! We've got to change the uniform.' It just wouldn't work."

The TV show, however, exerted a strong influence on the comic book.

At Dozier's request, Schwartz had Barbara Gordon, a librarian and daughter of Police Commissioner Gordon, suit up as the Batgirl. (The TV show had needed a female interest.)

1. "The Story of Pop," *Newsweek,* April 25, 1966, p. 61.
2. Ibid.
3. Ken Weiss and Ed Goodgold, *To Be Continued . . .* (New York: Bonanza Books, 1972), p. ix.
4. Joel Eisner, *The Official Batman Batbook* (Chicago: Contemporary Books, Inc., 1986), p. 6.

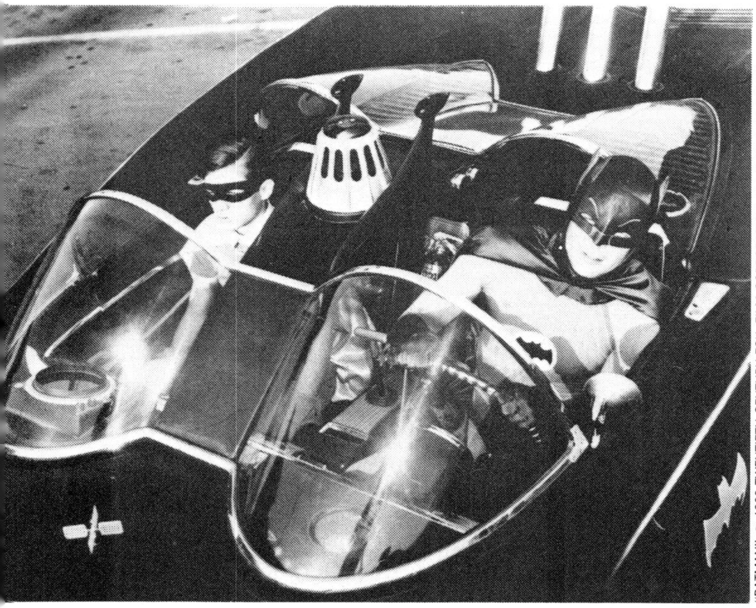

The Dynamic Duo revved up the Batmobile for 120 episodes during their TV career. Twenty-one years later it's still "Battime" on the "Batchannels" that syndicate the legendary top hit.

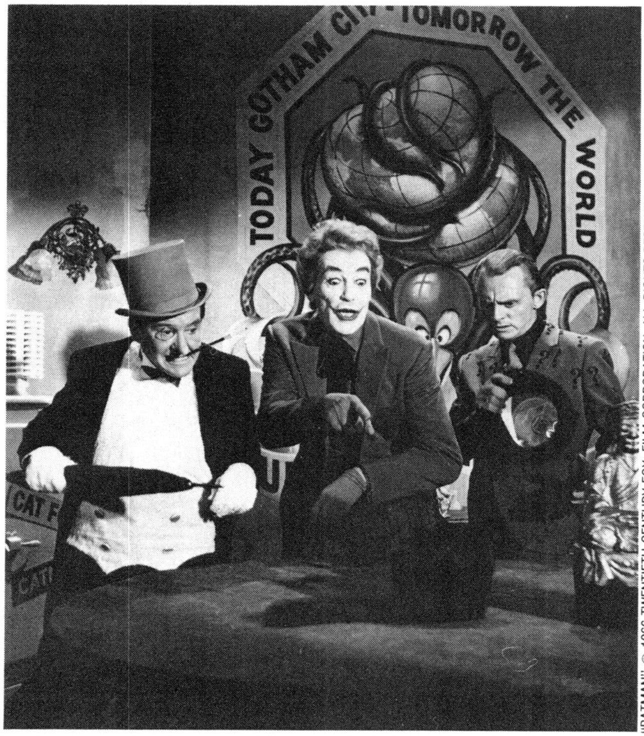
TODAY GOTHAM
TOMORROW THE WORLD

It was the height of Hollywood hip for an actor to land a coveted "Batman" guest villain spot. Three that kept coming back to bedevil Batman were the Penguin (Burgess Meredith), the Joker (Cesar Romero), and the Riddler (Frank Gorshin).

BATMAN: THE MOVIE

Batman, the Warner Bros. movie, released in fitting fashion on Batman's fiftieth anniversary, ushered in a wave of Batmania that had baby boomers and TV-cultists recalling the explosive Batman-TV show era of the 1960s.

But while the campy TV program epitomized psychedelic flash and pop panache, the movie was a serious, big-budget mix of comic book fantasy, film noir, and grand opera.

Batman, hailed by many film critics as a visionary work of art, also found phenomenal favor with film fans as well. *Batman* became the first film in history to sell $100.2 million worth of tickets in just ten days.

Batman was more than a film, it was an event. The international media had been ballyhooing *Batman* from the moment the production began filming on the spectacular sets recreating downtown Gotham City on the back lot of Pinewood Studios in England (said to be the biggest movie sets since *Cleopatra* in 1963). Months before the film opened Batman merchandising, with potential sales of hundreds of millions of dollars, began flooding the market, helping to fuel the phenomenon.

Rock star Prince's *Batman Motion Picture Soundtrack* began jamming the air waves and the rock video shows two weeks before the film's June 23rd nationwide release. The Hollywood premiere, attended by movie industry stars and fans, many of whom had camped out for days to buy the 1,000 tickets available to the public, also drew 10,000 onlookers. Vice President Dan Quayle announced his plans to attend the Washington premiere before stopping at a reception at the National Zoo—for the opening of a batcave exhibit.

Newsweek characterized 1989 Batmania as "a summer struggle for the dark soul of a mythic American hero," wistfully recalling how the Batman legend "started so simply in the spring of 1939, when comics cost a dime and the bad guys only came out at night."[1]

The good news for Batman fans was that the film did indeed evoke the spirit of that bygone Golden Age of comic books. Producers Jon Peters and Peter Guber and director Tim Burton promised from the start of the production that *Batman* would be played straight, not be a TV show swipe. Creator Bob Kane served as consultant, keeping the film makers true to the Batman tradition. Screenwriter Sam Hamm was a comics fan from childhood and knew how to translate the comic book mythos to a big-screen, live-action production. (Hamm's already legendary first drafts helped give momentum to a project that had been languishing since it was first optioned as a film property in 1979.)

"The idea Tim [Burton] and I had was to do a Batman story which was just as good as the Batman stories we remembered," Hamm says. "Yet, rather than just going back through individual stories to find plot situations I was trying to do a story that captured the interesting premise and paradox of a millionaire who can have anything he wants yet is compelled to dress up in a batsuit and fight crime."

There is a scene in *Batman* where Vicki Vale, Bruce Wayne's love interest, has just been ushered into the inner sanctum of the Bat Cave to confront Bruce about his crime-fighting identity. His body armor bat-suit is in an airtight vault—without it Wayne is just another guy, albeit a wealthy and well-traveled one. Wayne is anxious to transform into Batman for his climactic duel against the Joker, but Vicki is anxious to know what makes him do it.

"Why? Because nobody else can," Wayne says, looking off into the distance. He's got that steely eyed look now. "It's just something I have to do."

The body armor then goes on and the troubled, sensitive man named Bruce Wayne becomes the Dark Knight, and it's time to go to work.

THE OFFICIAL COMIC ADAPTATION OF THE WARNER BROS. MOTION PICTURE
BATMAN
DENNIS O'NEIL and JERRY ORDWAY with STEVE OLIFF
No.1 1989
A MOVIE SPECIAL
BATMAN
DENNIS O'NEIL
JERRY ORDWAY
STEVE OLIFF

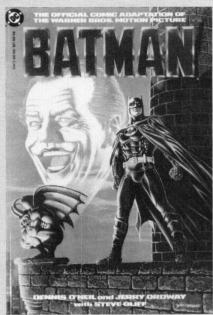

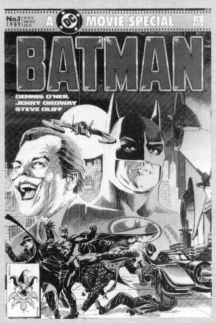

Batman: The Official Comic Adaptation of the Warner Bros. Motion Picture, *1989, cover* (Top: *Prestige Format edition;* bottom: *comic edition*).

1. "Batmania," *Newsweek* June 26, 1989, p. 70

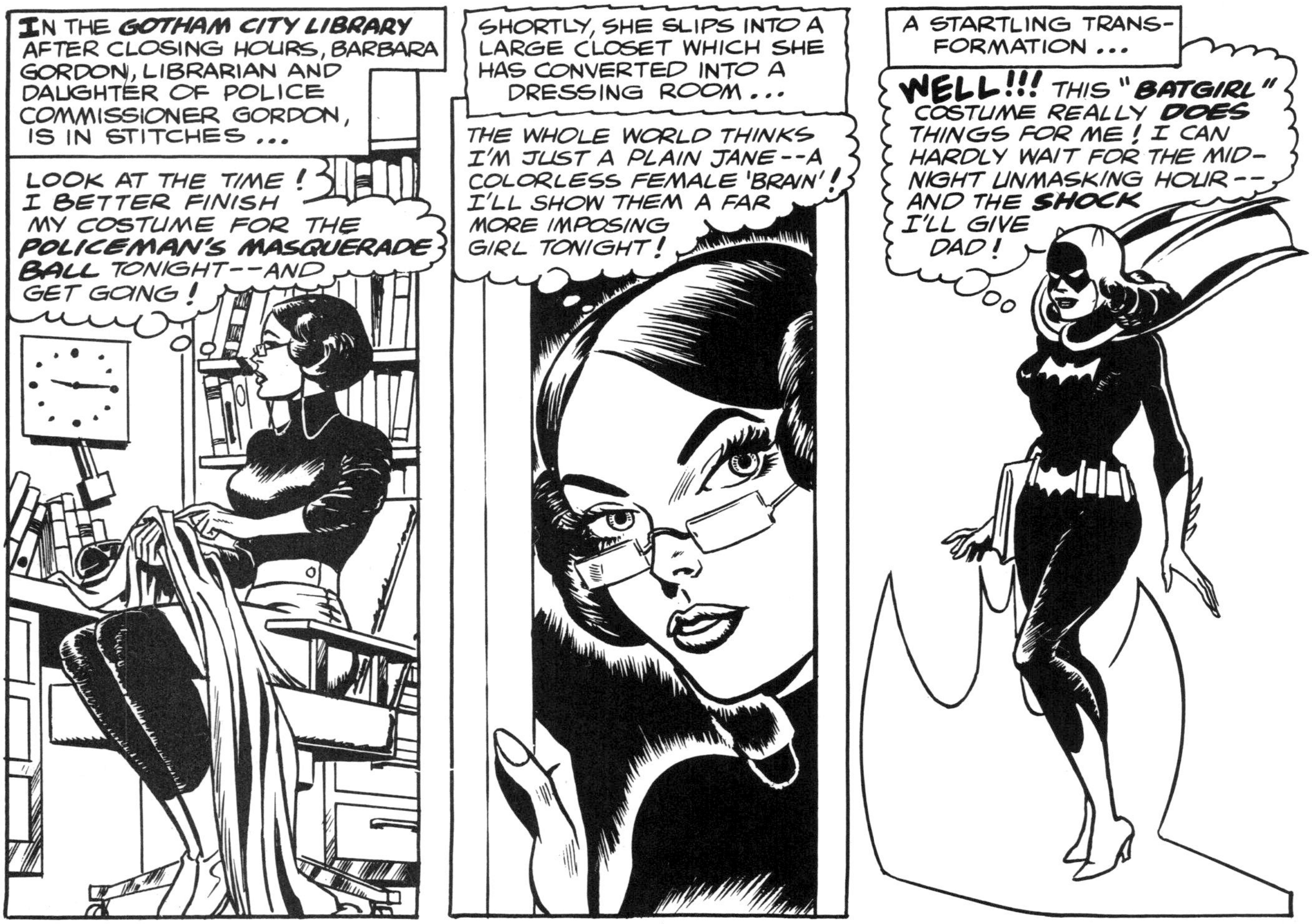
IN THE GOTHAM CITY LIBRARY AFTER CLOSING HOURS, BARBARA GORDON, LIBRARIAN AND DAUGHTER OF POLICE COMMISSIONER GORDON, IS IN STITCHES ...
LOOK AT THE TIME! I BETTER FINISH MY COSTUME FOR THE POLICEMAN'S MASQUERADE BALL TONIGHT--AND GET GOING!
SHORTLY, SHE SLIPS INTO A LARGE CLOSET WHICH SHE HAS CONVERTED INTO A DRESSING ROOM ...
THE WHOLE WORLD THINKS I'M JUST A PLAIN JANE--A COLORLESS FEMALE 'BRAIN'! I'LL SHOW THEM A FAR MORE IMPOSING GIRL TONIGHT!
A STARTLING TRANSFORMATION ...
WELL!!! THIS "BATGIRL" COSTUME REALLY DOES THINGS FOR ME! I CAN HARDLY WAIT FOR THE MIDNIGHT UNMASKING HOUR--AND THE SHOCK I'LL GIVE DAD!

Betty Kane, the original Batgirl of the early 1960s, only occasionally graced the Batman chronicles. When the Batman *TV series became a success, the producers asked Batman editor Julius Schwartz to come up with a new Batgirl. The lovely result was Barbara Gordon, the Police Commissioner's own daughter, who presumedly found more excitement as a crimefighter than as a librarian.* (Detective *#359, Janauary 1967, ''The Million Dollar Debut of Batgirl!'' p. 2 [select panels].*)

The TV show also wanted loyal Alfred in Wayne Manor once again serving tea and sage advice to Batman and Robin. That was a problem since Schwartz had killed off Alfred a few years before (crushed to death under the weight of a giant boulder) as a sacrificial offering to all the whispers about three single men living in a millionaire's manse.

"It became a very difficult situation when they (the "Batman" producers) wanted Alfred there and they wanted me to bring him back," Schwartz admits. "I said, 'But he's dead!' They said, 'You can think of a way.' "

What Schwartz did was take the Outsider, a continuing villain whose identity was unknown, and unmask the mysterious foe as Alfred. It made for one of the most bizarre bring-'em-back-alive tales in the annals of comic book superheroes.

In "Inside Story of the Outsider!" (*Detective* 356, October 1966) a scientific genius named Brandon Crawford, on a nighttime walk through a cemetery in search of a rare insect, picks up on his supersensitive audiometer the sounds of moaning coming from the mausoleum in which Alfred has been buried. Rushing into the crypt, the scientist discovers Alfred still barely alive in his coffin. Noting that the body had not been embalmed ("so there's still a chance!"), Crawford takes Alfred to his secret laboratory to see if he can be saved with a shot of the rays from an untested cell-regeneration device. Alfred is

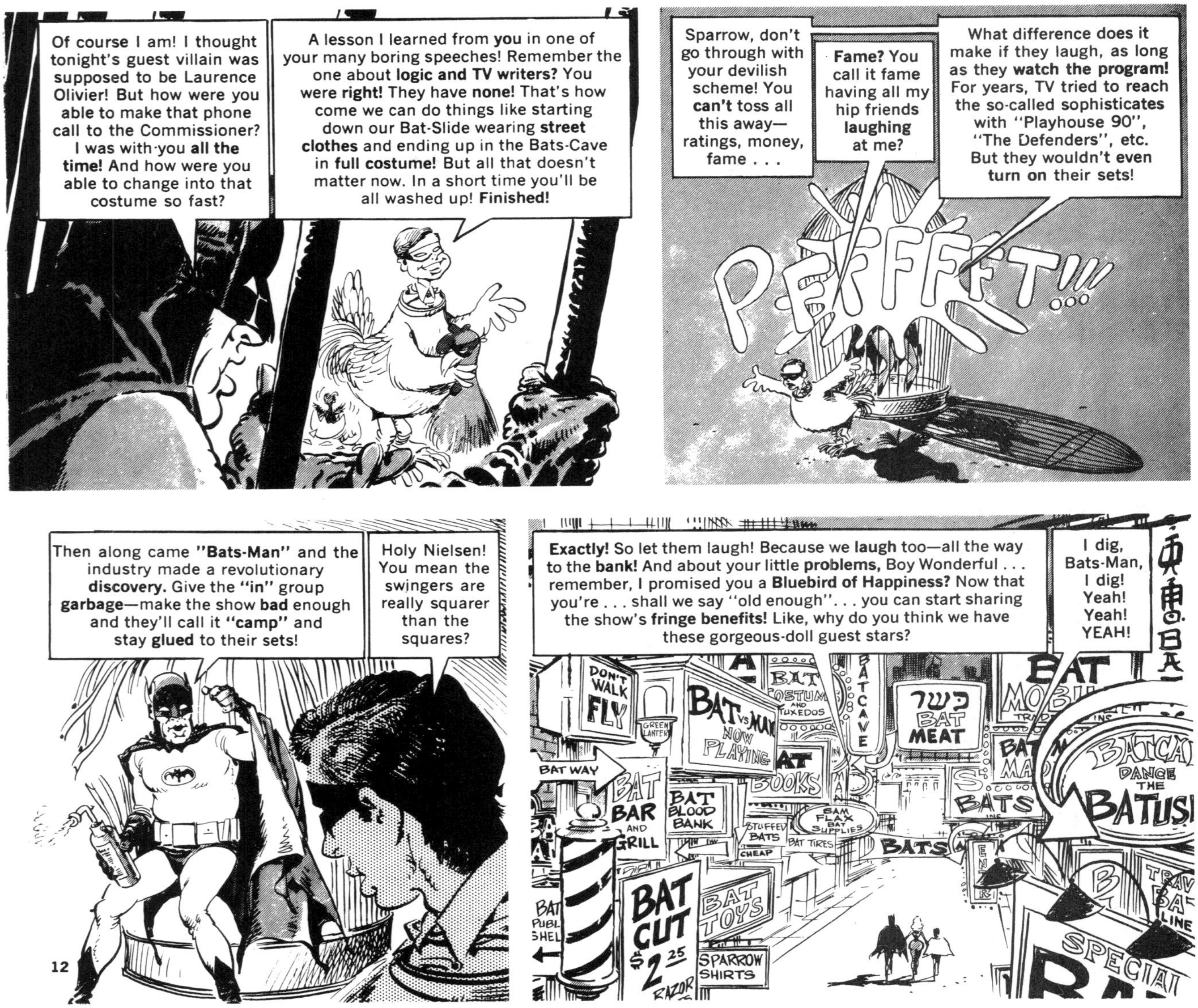
Of course I am! I thought tonight's guest villain was supposed to be Laurence Olivier! But how were you able to make that phone call to the Commissioner? I was with you all the time! And how were you able to change into that costume so fast?
A lesson I learned from you in one of your many boring speeches! Remember the one about logic and TV writers? You were right! They have none! That's how come we can do things like starting down our Bat-Slide wearing street clothes and ending up in the Bats-Cave in full costume! But all that doesn't matter now. In a short time you'll be all washed up! Finished!
Sparrow, don't go through with your devilish scheme! You can't toss all this away— ratings, money, fame . . .
Fame? You call it fame having all my hip friends laughing at me?
What difference does it make if they laugh, as long as they watch the program! For years, TV tried to reach the so-called sophisticates with "Playhouse 90", "The Defenders", etc. But they wouldn't even turn on their sets!
PFFFFT!!!
Then along came "Bats-Man" and the industry made a revolutionary discovery. Give the "in" group garbage—make the show bad enough and they'll call it "camp" and stay glued to their sets!
Holy Nielsen! You mean the swingers are really squarer than the squares?
Exactly! So let them laugh! Because we laugh too—all the way to the bank! And about your little problems, Boy Wonderful . . . remember, I promised you a Bluebird of Happiness? Now that you're . . . shall we say "old enough". . . you can start sharing the show's fringe benefits! Like, why do you think we have these gorgeous-doll guest stars?
I dig, Bats-Man, I dig! Yeah! Yeah! YEAH!
BAT MEAT
BAT BAR AND GRILL
BAT BLOOD BANK
BAT CUT $2.25
BAT TOYS
SPARROW SHIRTS
BATCAVE
BAT WAY
12

Mad *goes to camp in this parody of the ''Batman'' TV show—which was itself a parody!* (Mad *#105, September 1966, ''Bats-Man,'' p. 12 [select panels].*)

revived—but as the twisted, amnesic, Batman-hating Outsider. After being defeated by Batman, another shot of cell-regeneration juice reverses the process and restores Alfred—but leaving him with no memory of his Outsider activities.

But despite the story lines so often directly dictated by network needs, the biggest influence the TV show had on the comic book was making Batman a campy, lighthearted figure.

"As long as it was so popular on television, we said, 'Let's do it in comics, too!'" Schwartz recalls. "We were told to do it—I can't come up with the exact answer as to who came up with the idea—but I did it anyway. And it was successful as long as the show was successful. And once that was enough, the readers wanted the previous-type Batman."

The "previous-type Batman" was that grim crime fighter driven by an obsession born of tragedy, that Dark Knight who patrolled the nighttime streets of Gotham City, haunting the underworld and bringing justice to the urban jungle.

Writer Denny O'Neil and artist Neal Adams came together at this critical juncture to take Batman into his postpop period—and back to his Dark Knight beginnings.

DOSSIER 3

DESCENT INTO THE BAT CAVE

It was said that one might wander days and nights together through its intricate tangle of rifts and chasms, and never find the end of the cave; and that he might go down and down, and still down, into the earth, and it was just the same—labyrinth underneath labyrinth, and no end to any of them. No man ''knew'' the cave. That was an impossible thing.

—The Adventures of Tom Sawyer
Mark Twain

The Bat Cave, located in a subterranean cavern below the sprawling estate of Wayne Manor, has always represented the dark, mysterious side of the Batman. With its labyrinthian tunnels and the rustling of bats flying up into the stalactite heights, this cave is Batman's seat of power, nerve center, and command post for his war on crime.

When he first began utilizing the Bat Cave, an electric-lit main chamber stored his crime-fighting files and supplies, his Batmobile, and a small laboratory. Over the years the Bat Cave has expanded to include an updated laboratory and garage, a computer bank, a Hall of Trophies, a hangar built to hold the Batplane and Batcopter, and other high-tech innovations.

Though the Bat Cave might seem one of the eternal elements of Batman's world, it was years after the character first appeared before Batman even discovered the Bat Cave.

In the beginning Batman used an old barn on his estate as the secret entrance to Wayne Manor. A hidden stairway inside led to an underground tunnel, with a flight of stairs at the end ascending to an entrance into the mansion.

The Batplane and other heavy artillery were always stored in unnamed, nondescript places during this early period.

But one day, while Bruce Wayne was testing the barn's rotted floorboards, they gave way, and Bruce fell into the hidden cavern. After collecting himself from the fall, which had been cushioned

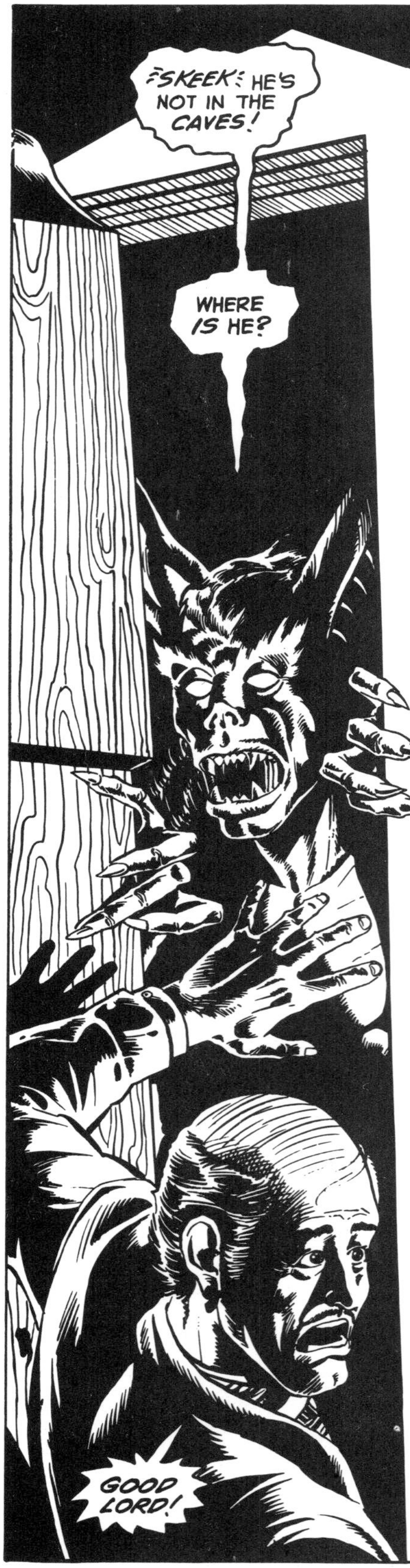
SKEEK! HE'S NOT IN THE CAVES!
WHERE IS HE?
GOOD LORD!

Alfred has a chilling encounter with Professor Kirk Langstrom's Manbat metamorphosis. (Detective #527, *June 1983, ''Avatars of Vengeance,'' p. 11 [panel].*)

by hay from the barn that had fallen with him, Wayne surveyed a vast, bat-filled cave.

Like everything connected with his role as a crime fighter, from the bedside vow after his parents' death to the sight of a bat flying through an open window of Wayne Manor, this fateful tumble had the feel of destiny intervening to further shape his "Batman" persona.

The cave itself had a colorful history. During the colonial period it served as the base of operations for Jeremy Coe, who led counterattacks against the Indians who originally populated the area. During the Civil War the place was known as Anderson's Cave, a favored hideout for Confederate spies. And years before Wayne Manor was even constructed, the cave served as the hideout for a gangster named Whitey Weir.

Perhaps the shadows of this submerged kingdom are a comfort to one such as the Batman. Just above is Wayne Manor, symbol of a world of comfort and respectability. But it is in this foreboding subterranean lair that Bruce Wayne is most at home and where he can plot his midnight prowls. Deep in the earth and lost in the shadows, with only the bats for company, he can be his true self; he can be the Batman....

THERE THEY GO! —TOWARD THAT OLD BARN!
WE'VE GOT 'EM CORNERED —C'MON!
......AFTER WHAT SEEMS HOURS TO THE WEARY GUNMEN, THE BATMAN AND ROBIN LEAD THEIR PURSUERS TO AN OPEN FIELD AT THE EDGE OF TOWN....
BUT WHEN THE GANGSTERS ENTER THE BARN.....
GONE! THERE'S NOBODY HERE!
FINE! THAT'S BRUCE WAYNE'S HOME OVER THERE! I PLANTED SOME BOYS THERE EARLIER THIS EVENING IN CASE THIS SHOULD HAPPEN!
THEY MUST'VE GONE THROUGH THE WINDOW!

"PERHAPS YOU ARE WONDERING HOW THE BATMAN MANAGED TO GET INTO THE HOUSE WITHOUT BEING SEEN BY THE THUGS?... IT'S ALL VERY SIMPLE......"
"WHEN THE BATMAN DARTED INTO THE BARN, HE RAISED A CLEVERLY HIDDEN TRAPDOOR WHICH LEADS TO A TUNNEL BELOW......"
"THIS TUNNEL RAN DIRECTLY TO THE WAYNE HOUSE WHERE THE BATMAN MOUNTED STEPS, AND SLIPPED THROUGH A SECRET PANEL INTO HIS HOME......."
"THEN, HE SIMPLY DISCARDED HIS COSTUME AND OPENED THE FRONT DOOR!"

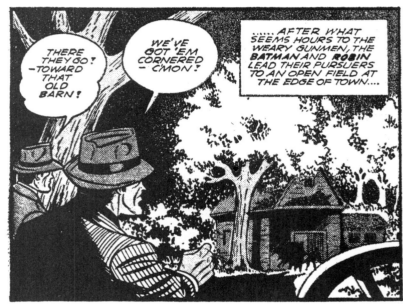

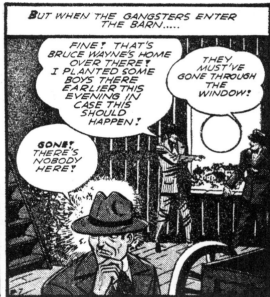

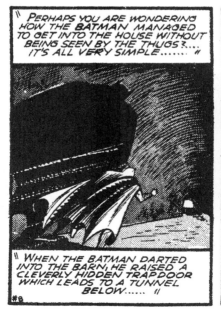

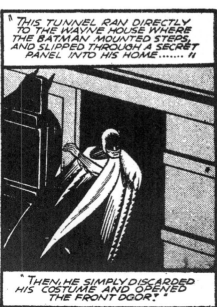

In the early days Batman used this underground tunnel to secretly slip back into Wayne Manor—his discovery of the Bat Cave was still years away. (Batman #4, *Winter 1941, untitled story, pp. 7-8 [select panels].*)

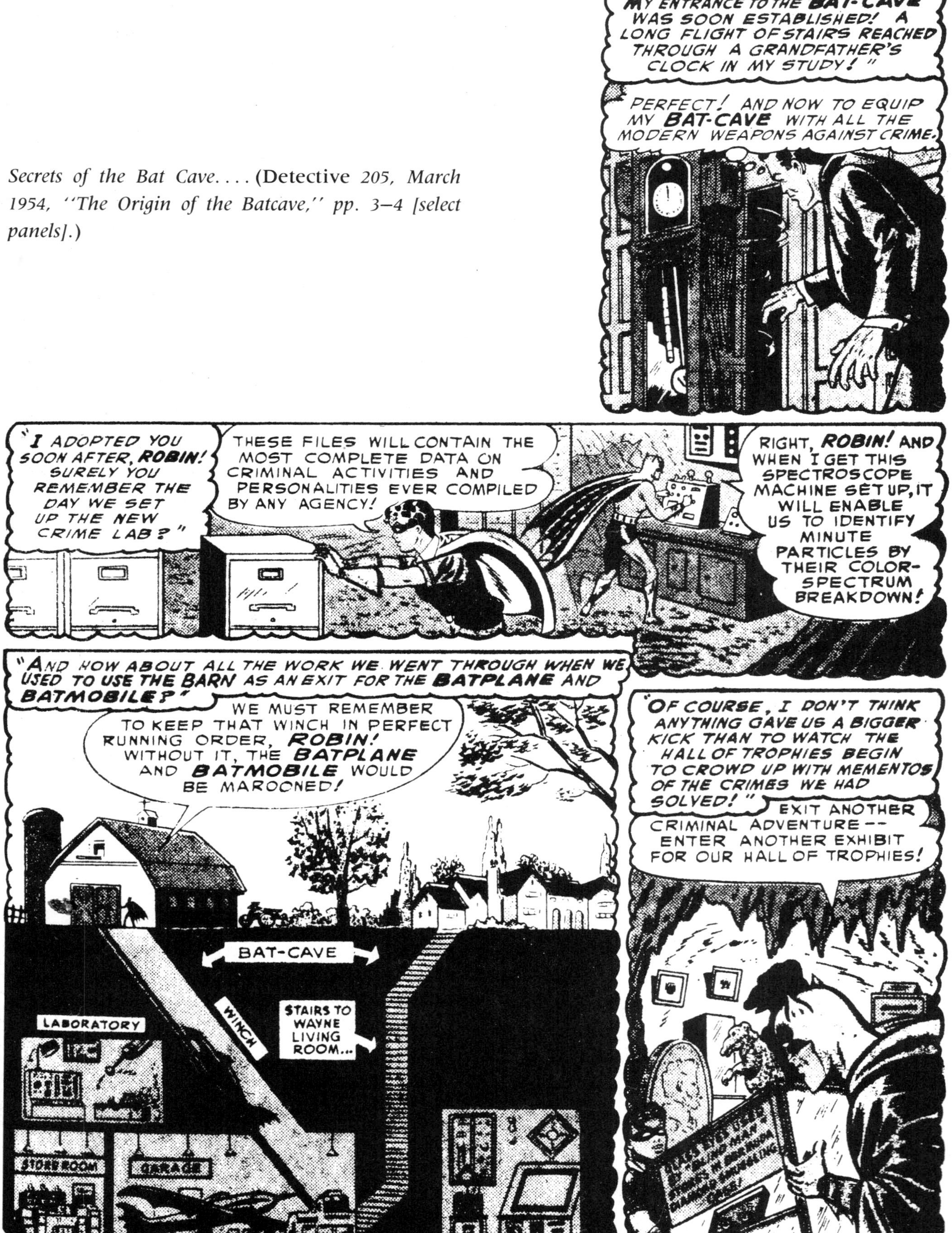
"MY ENTRANCE TO THE BAT-CAVE WAS SOON ESTABLISHED! A LONG FLIGHT OF STAIRS REACHED THROUGH A GRANDFATHER'S CLOCK IN MY STUDY!"
PERFECT! AND NOW TO EQUIP MY BAT-CAVE WITH ALL THE MODERN WEAPONS AGAINST CRIME.
"I ADOPTED YOU SOON AFTER, ROBIN! SURELY YOU REMEMBER THE DAY WE SET UP THE NEW CRIME LAB?"
THESE FILES WILL CONTAIN THE MOST COMPLETE DATA ON CRIMINAL ACTIVITIES AND PERSONALITIES EVER COMPILED BY ANY AGENCY!
RIGHT, ROBIN! AND WHEN I GET THIS SPECTROSCOPE MACHINE SET UP, IT WILL ENABLE US TO IDENTIFY MINUTE PARTICLES BY THEIR COLOR-SPECTRUM BREAKDOWN!
"AND HOW ABOUT ALL THE WORK WE WENT THROUGH WHEN WE USED TO USE THE BARN AS AN EXIT FOR THE BATPLANE AND BATMOBILE?"
WE MUST REMEMBER TO KEEP THAT WINCH IN PERFECT RUNNING ORDER, ROBIN! WITHOUT IT, THE BATPLANE AND BATMOBILE WOULD BE MAROONED!
BAT-CAVE
WINCH
STAIRS TO WAYNE LIVING ROOM...
LABORATORY
STOREROOM
GARAGE
"OF COURSE, I DON'T THINK ANYTHING GAVE US A BIGGER KICK THAN TO WATCH THE HALL OF TROPHIES BEGIN TO CROWD UP WITH MEMENTOS OF THE CRIMES WE HAD SOLVED!"
EXIT ANOTHER CRIMINAL ADVENTURE -- ENTER ANOTHER EXHIBIT FOR OUR HALL OF TROPHIES!

Secrets of the Bat Cave. . . . (Detective *205, March 1954, ''The Origin of the Batcave,'' pp. 3–4 [select panels].*)

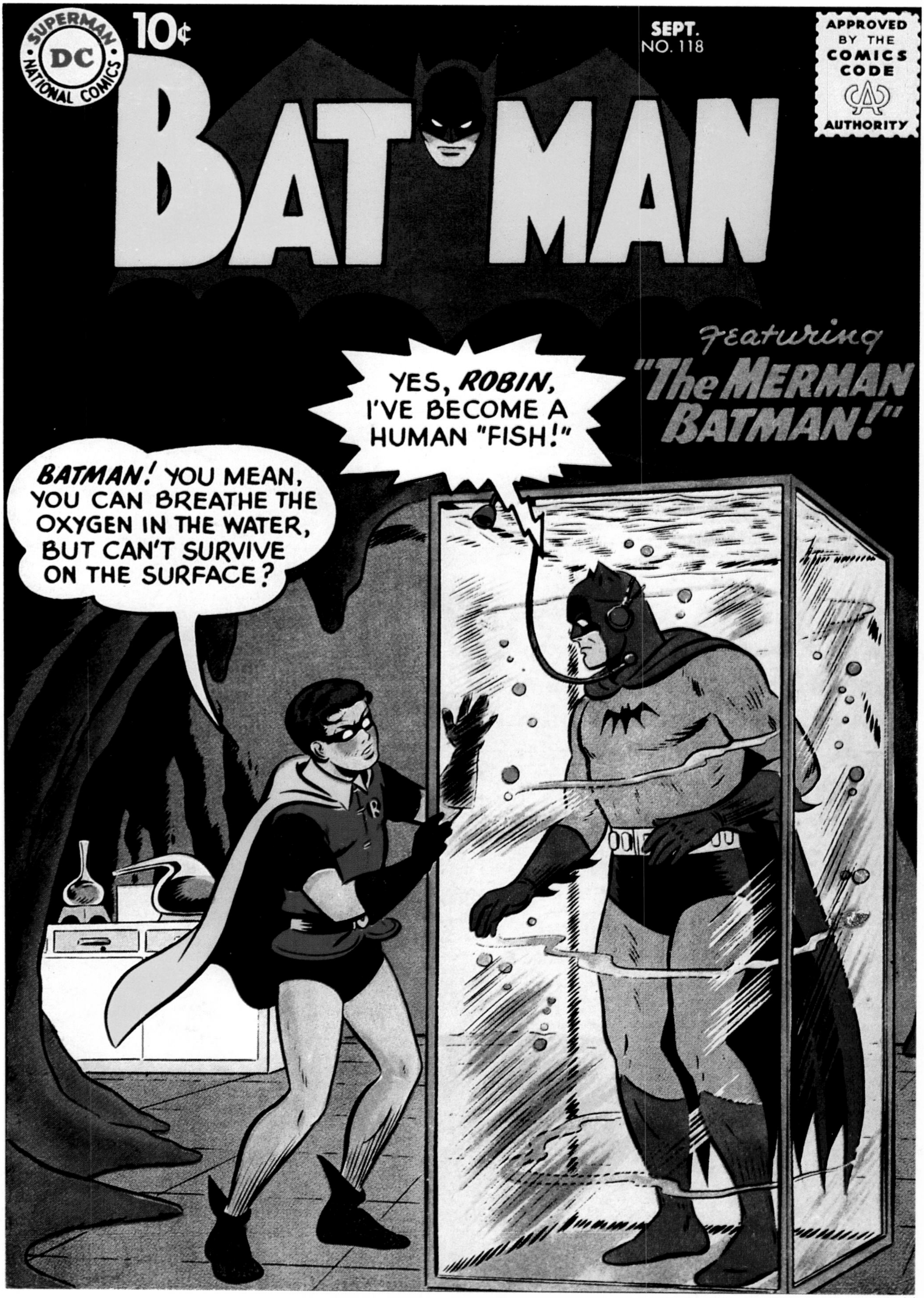
SUPERMAN DC NATIONAL COMICS
10¢
SEPT.
NO. 118
APPROVED BY THE COMICS CODE AUTHORITY
BATMAN
Featuring "The MERMAN BATMAN!"
BATMAN! YOU MEAN, YOU CAN BREATHE THE OXYGEN IN THE WATER, BUT CAN'T SURVIVE ON THE SURFACE?
YES, ROBIN, I'VE BECOME A HUMAN "FISH!"

BATMAN #118, September 1958 (Curt Swan, pencils; Stan Kaye, inks)

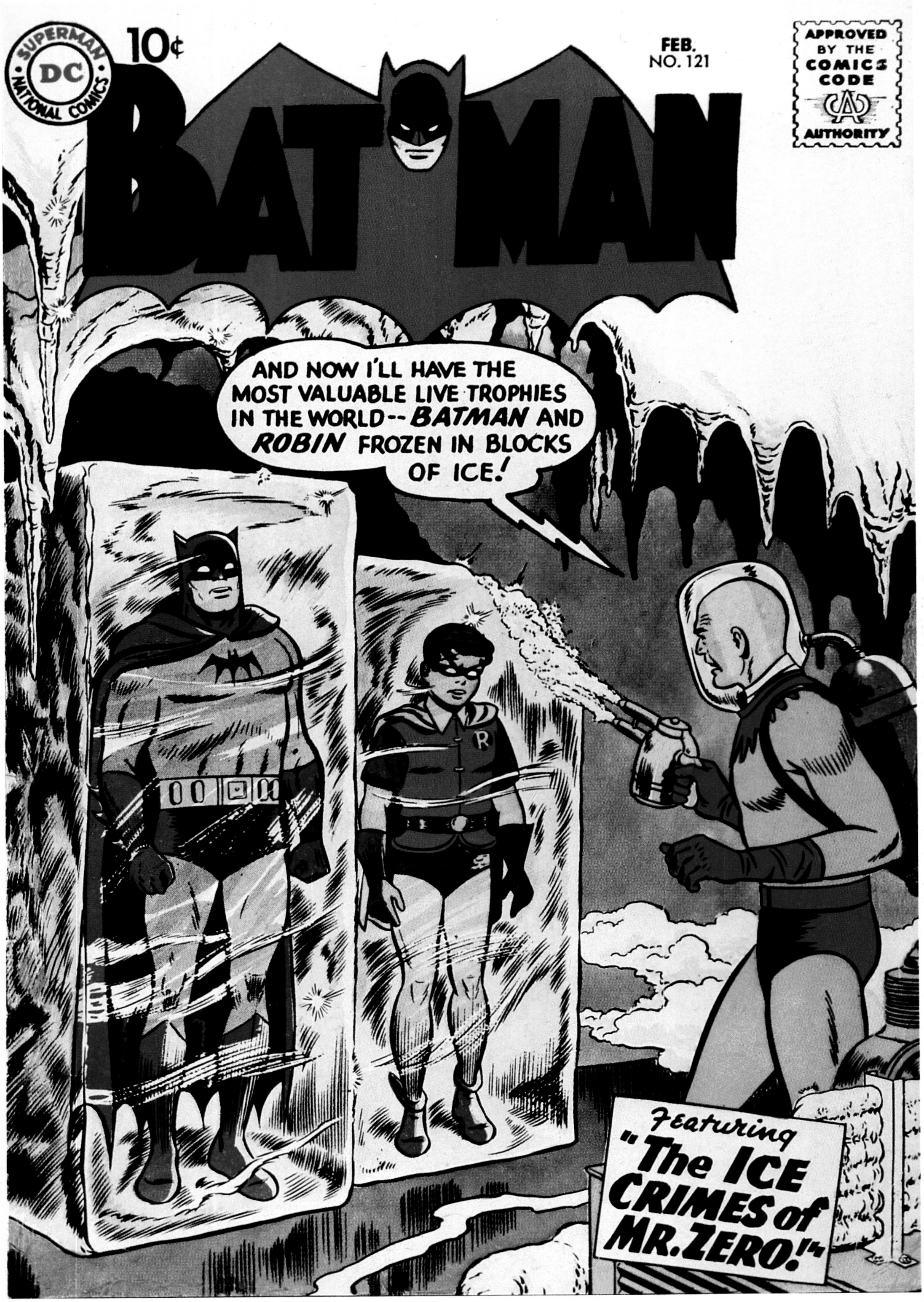
SUPERMAN DC NATIONAL COMICS
10¢
FEB.
NO. 121
APPROVED BY THE COMICS CODE AUTHORITY
BATMAN
AND NOW I'LL HAVE THE MOST VALUABLE LIVE TROPHIES IN THE WORLD--BATMAN AND ROBIN FROZEN IN BLOCKS OF ICE!
Featuring "The ICE CRIMES of MR. ZERO!"

BATMAN #121, February 1959 (Curt Swan, pencils; Stan Kaye, inks)

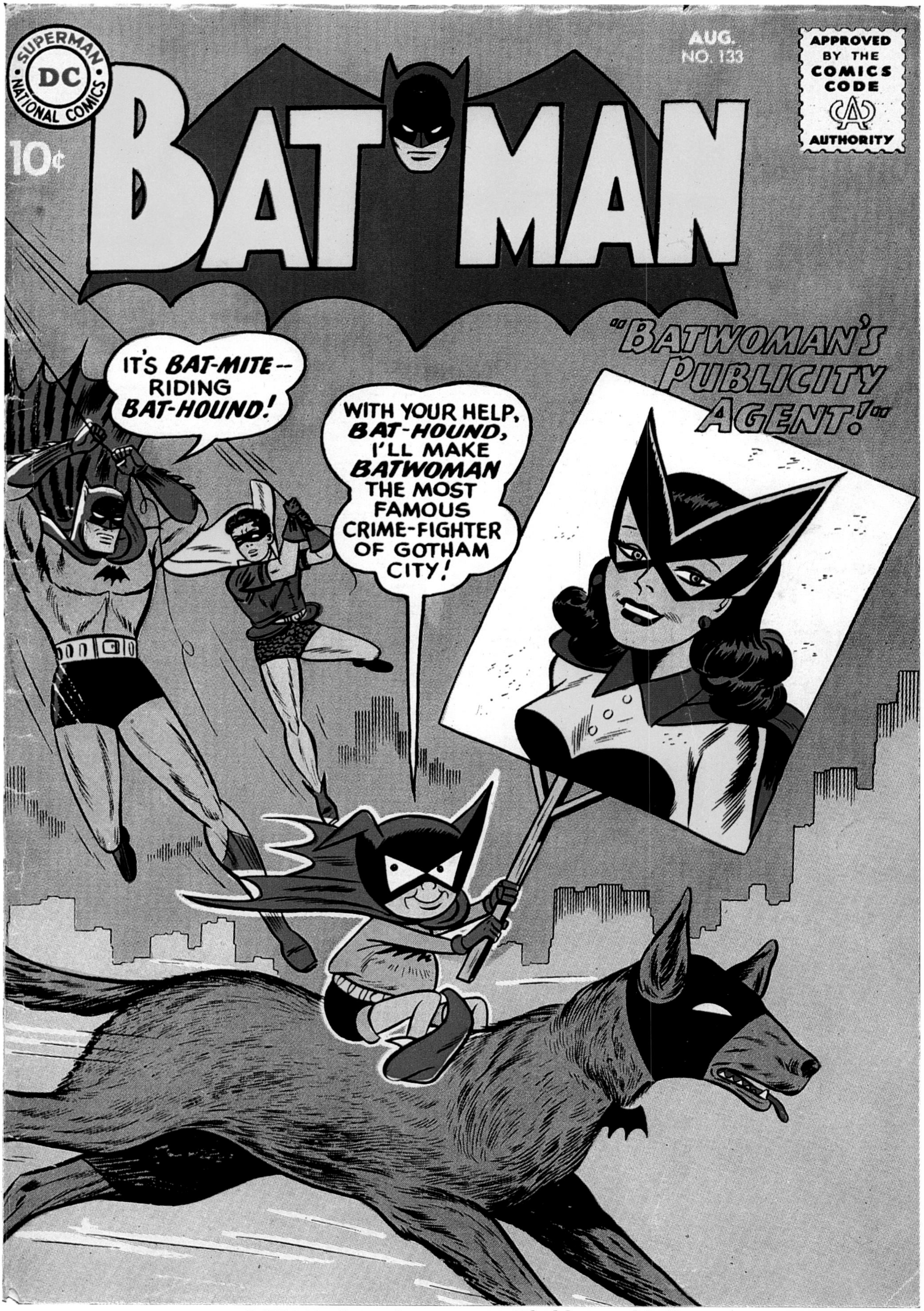
SUPERMAN DC NATIONAL COMICS
10¢
AUG. NO. 133
APPROVED BY THE COMICS CODE AUTHORITY
BATMAN
"BATWOMAN'S PUBLICITY AGENT!"
IT'S BAT-MITE-- RIDING BAT-HOUND!
WITH YOUR HELP, BAT-HOUND, I'LL MAKE BATWOMAN THE MOST FAMOUS CRIME-FIGHTER OF GOTHAM CITY!

BATMAN #133, August 1960 (Sheldon Moldoff)

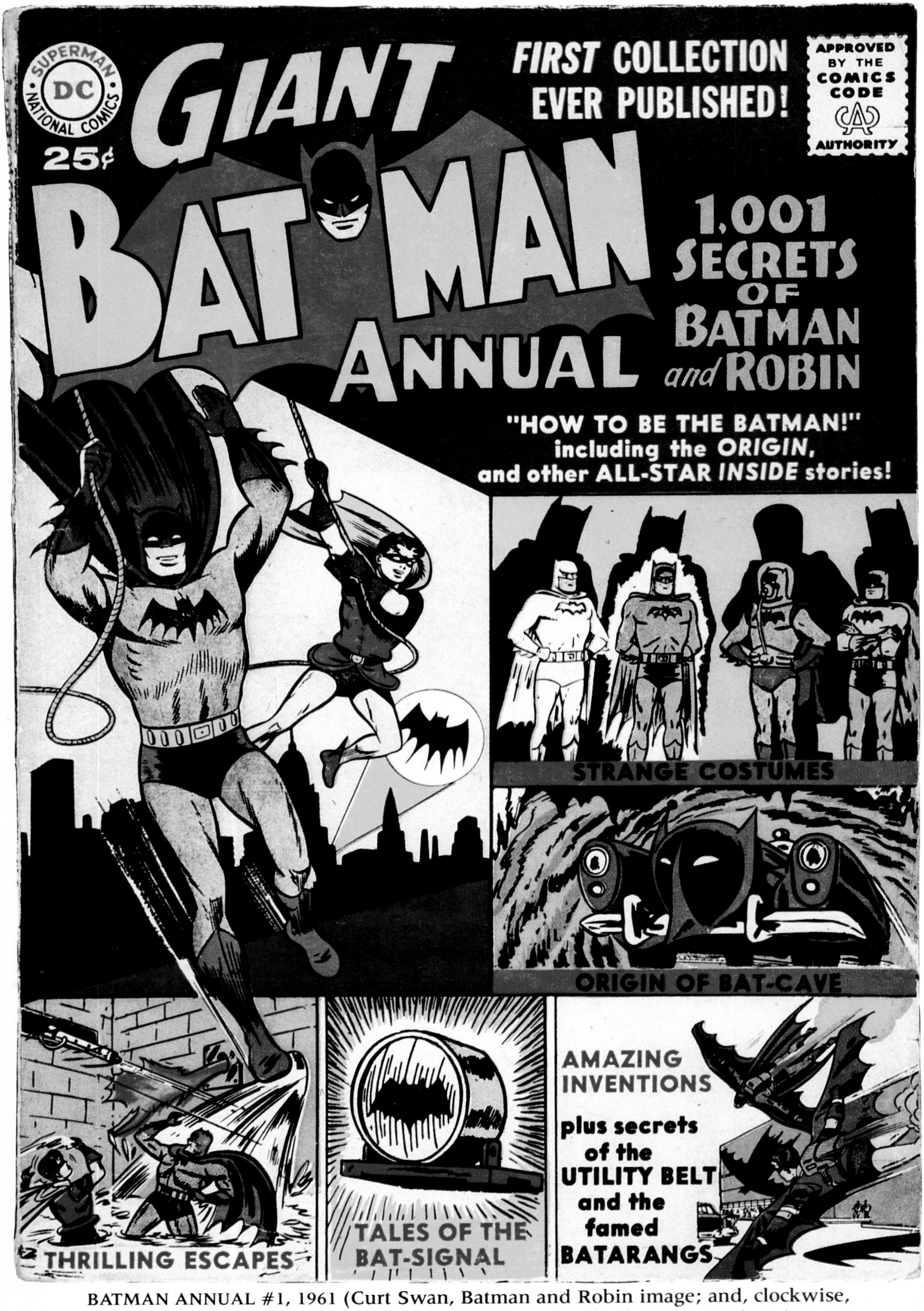
SUPERMAN DC NATIONAL COMICS
25¢
GIANT
FIRST COLLECTION EVER PUBLISHED!
APPROVED BY THE COMICS CODE AUTHORITY
BATMAN
ANNUAL
1,001 SECRETS OF BATMAN and ROBIN
"HOW TO BE THE BATMAN!" including the ORIGIN, and other ALL-STAR INSIDE stories!
STRANGE COSTUMES
ORIGIN OF BAT-CAVE
THRILLING ESCAPES
TALES OF THE BAT-SIGNAL
AMAZING INVENTIONS
plus secrets of the UTILITY BELT and the famed BATARANGS

BATMAN ANNUAL #1, 1961 (Curt Swan, Batman and Robin image; and, clockwise, Dick Sprang, Sheldon Moldoff, Dick Sprang, Sheldon Moldoff, Sheldon Moldoff)

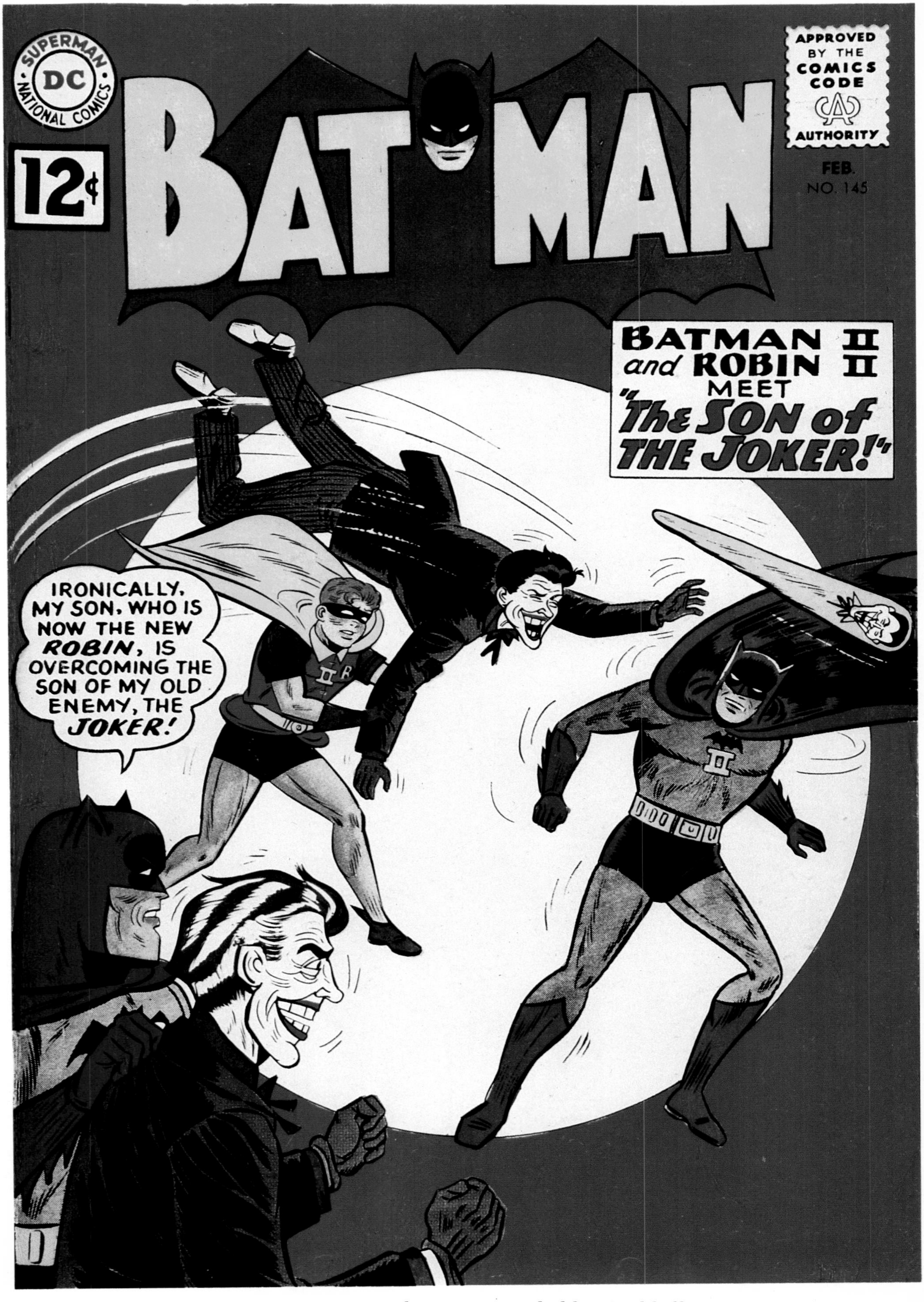
SUPERMAN DC NATIONAL COMICS
12¢
BATMAN
APPROVED BY THE COMICS CODE AUTHORITY
FEB. NO. 145
BATMAN II and ROBIN II MEET "The SON of THE JOKER!"
IRONICALLY, MY SON, WHO IS NOW THE NEW ROBIN, IS OVERCOMING THE SON OF MY OLD ENEMY, THE JOKER!

BATMAN #145, February 1962 (Sheldon Moldoff)

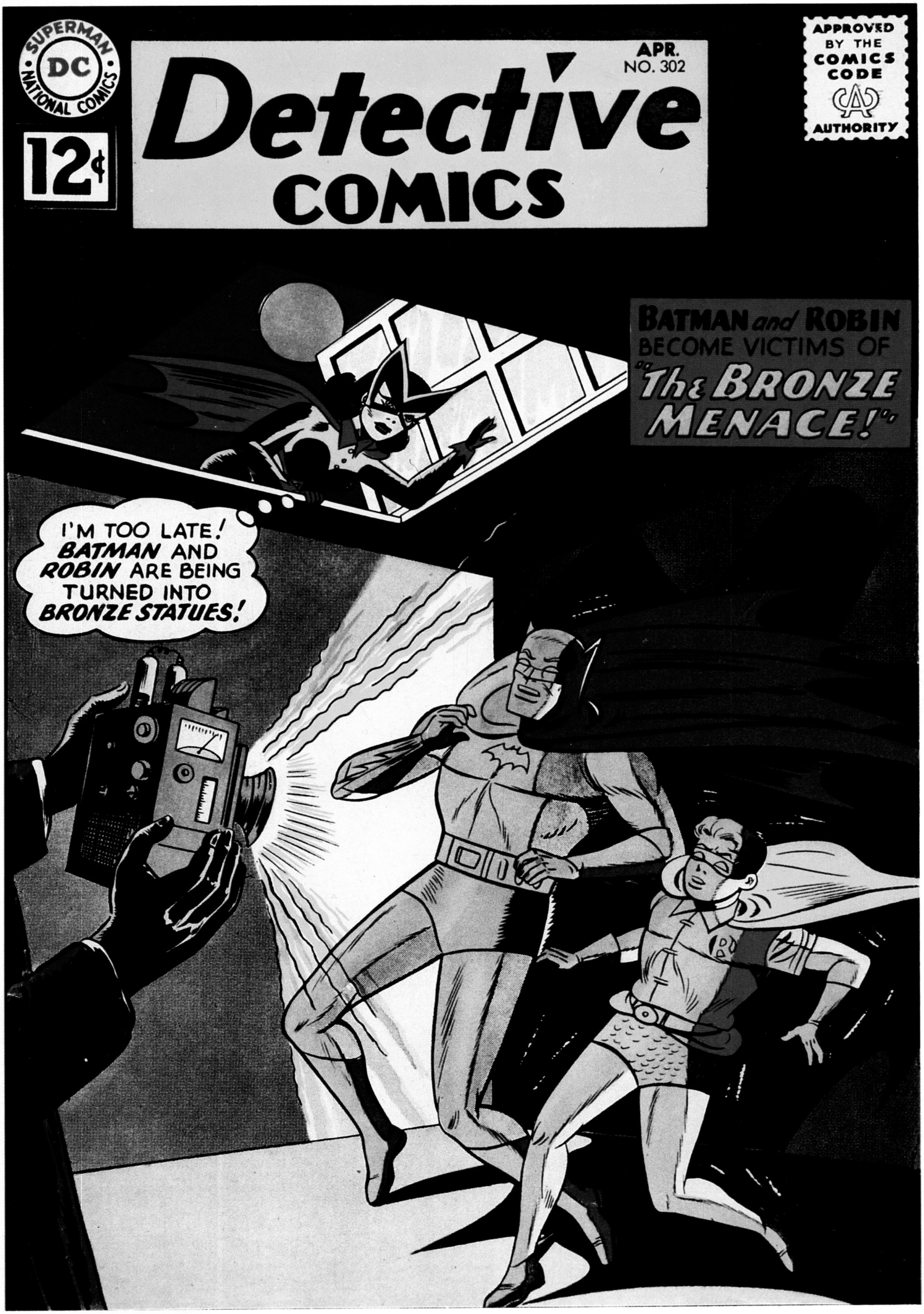
SUPERMAN DC NATIONAL COMICS
12¢
APR. NO. 302
Detective COMICS
APPROVED BY THE COMICS CODE AUTHORITY
BATMAN and ROBIN BECOME VICTIMS OF "The BRONZE MENACE!"
I'M TOO LATE! BATMAN AND ROBIN ARE BEING TURNED INTO BRONZE STATUES!

DETECTIVE #302, April 1962 (Sheldon Moldoff)

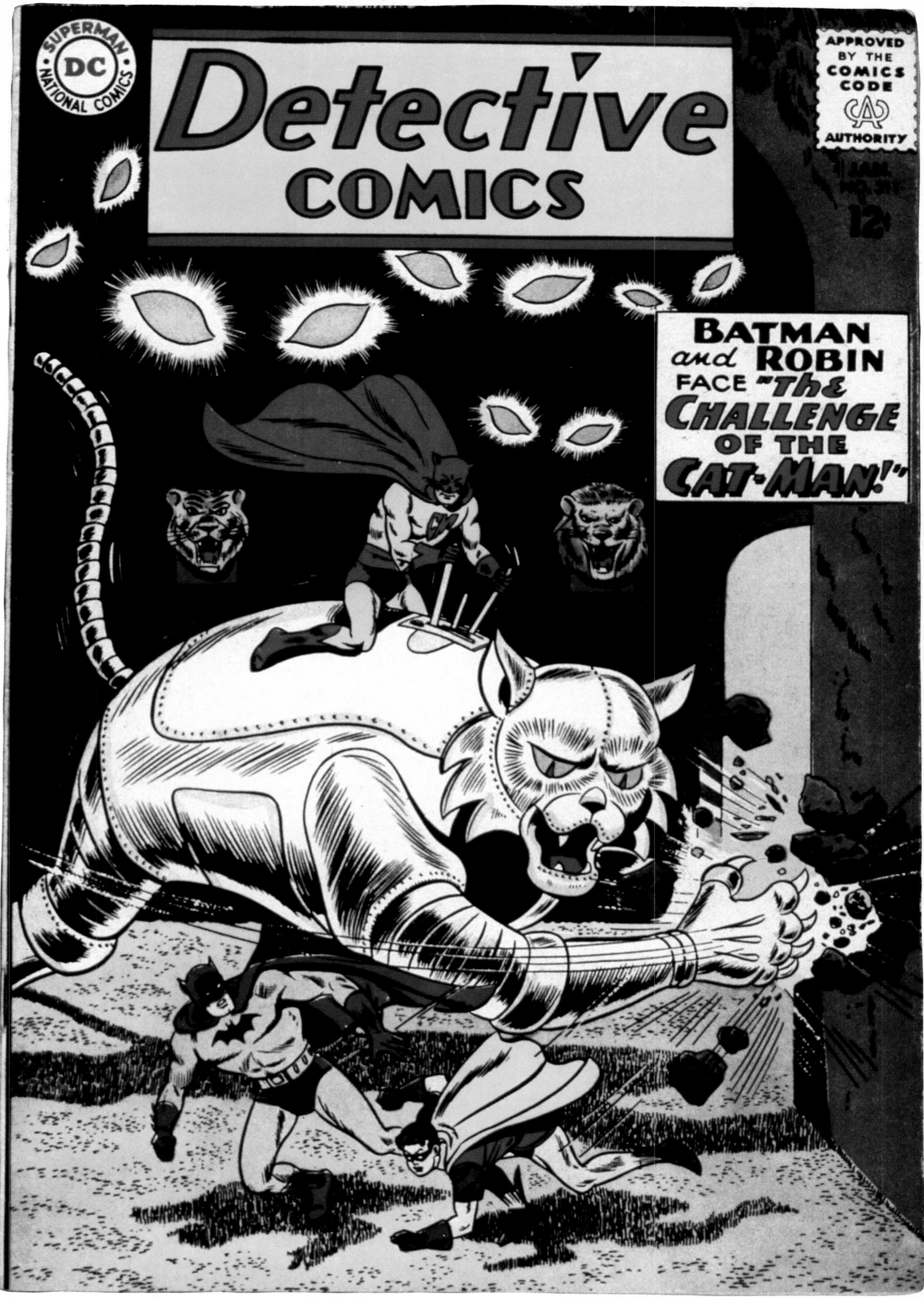
SUPERMAN
DC
NATIONAL COMICS
Detective
COMICS
APPROVED BY THE COMICS CODE AUTHORITY
JAN.
12¢
BATMAN and ROBIN FACE "The CHALLENGE OF THE CAT-MAN!"

DETECTIVE #311, January 1963 (Jim Mooney)

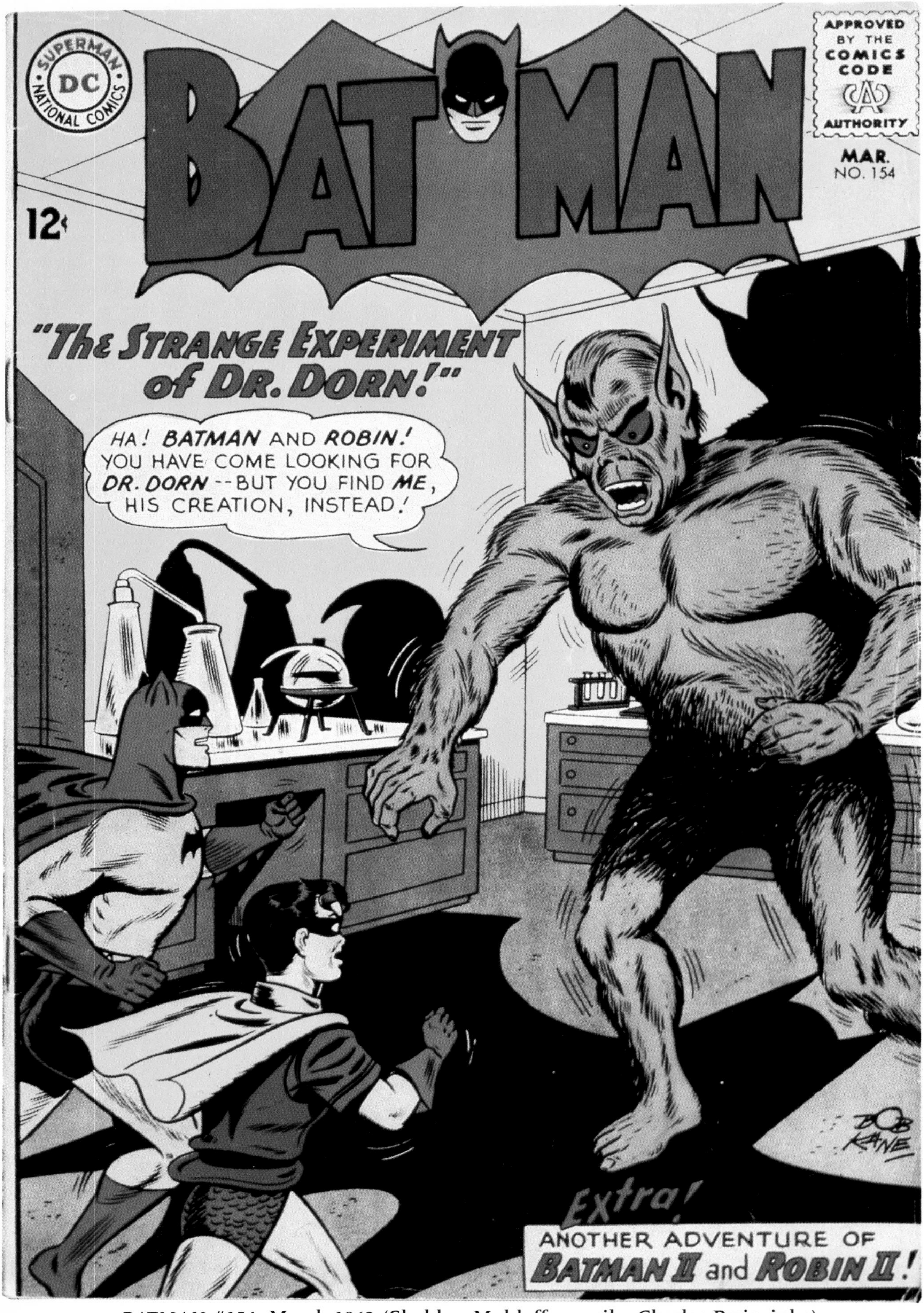
SUPERMAN DC NATIONAL COMICS
BATMAN
APPROVED BY THE COMICS CODE AUTHORITY
MAR. NO. 154
12¢
"The STRANGE EXPERIMENT of DR. DORN!"
HA! BATMAN AND ROBIN! YOU HAVE COME LOOKING FOR DR. DORN--BUT YOU FIND ME, HIS CREATION, INSTEAD!
BOB KANE
Extra!
ANOTHER ADVENTURE OF BATMAN II and ROBIN II!

BATMAN #154, March 1963 (Sheldon Moldoff, pencils; Charles Paris, inks)

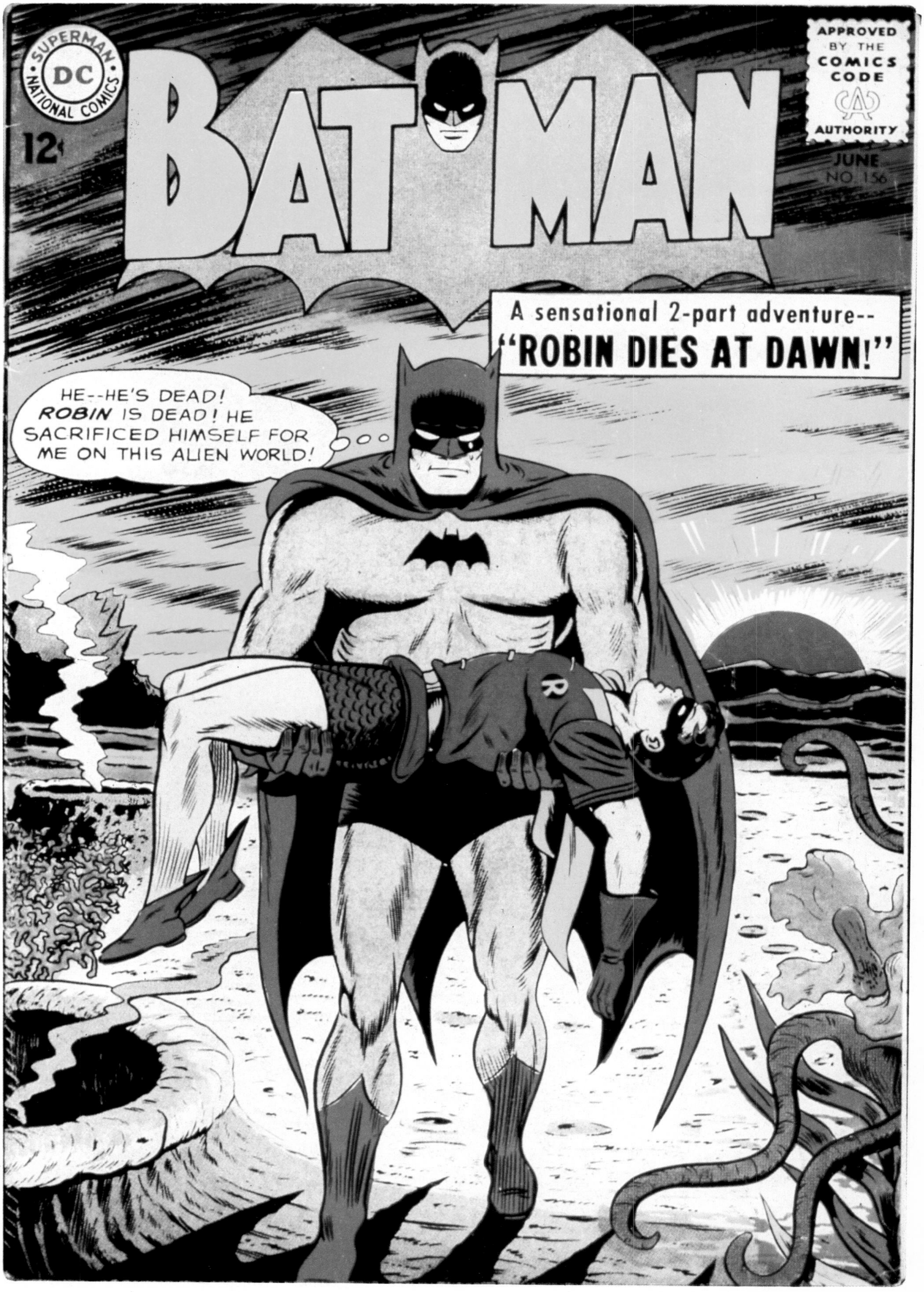
SUPERMAN DC NATIONAL COMICS
12¢
BATMAN
APPROVED BY THE COMICS CODE AUTHORITY
JUNE NO. 156
A sensational 2-part adventure--
"ROBIN DIES AT DAWN!"
HE--HE'S DEAD! ROBIN IS DEAD! HE SACRIFICED HIMSELF FOR ME ON THIS ALIEN WORLD!

BATMAN #156, June 1963 (Sheldon Moldoff, pencils; Charles Paris, inks)

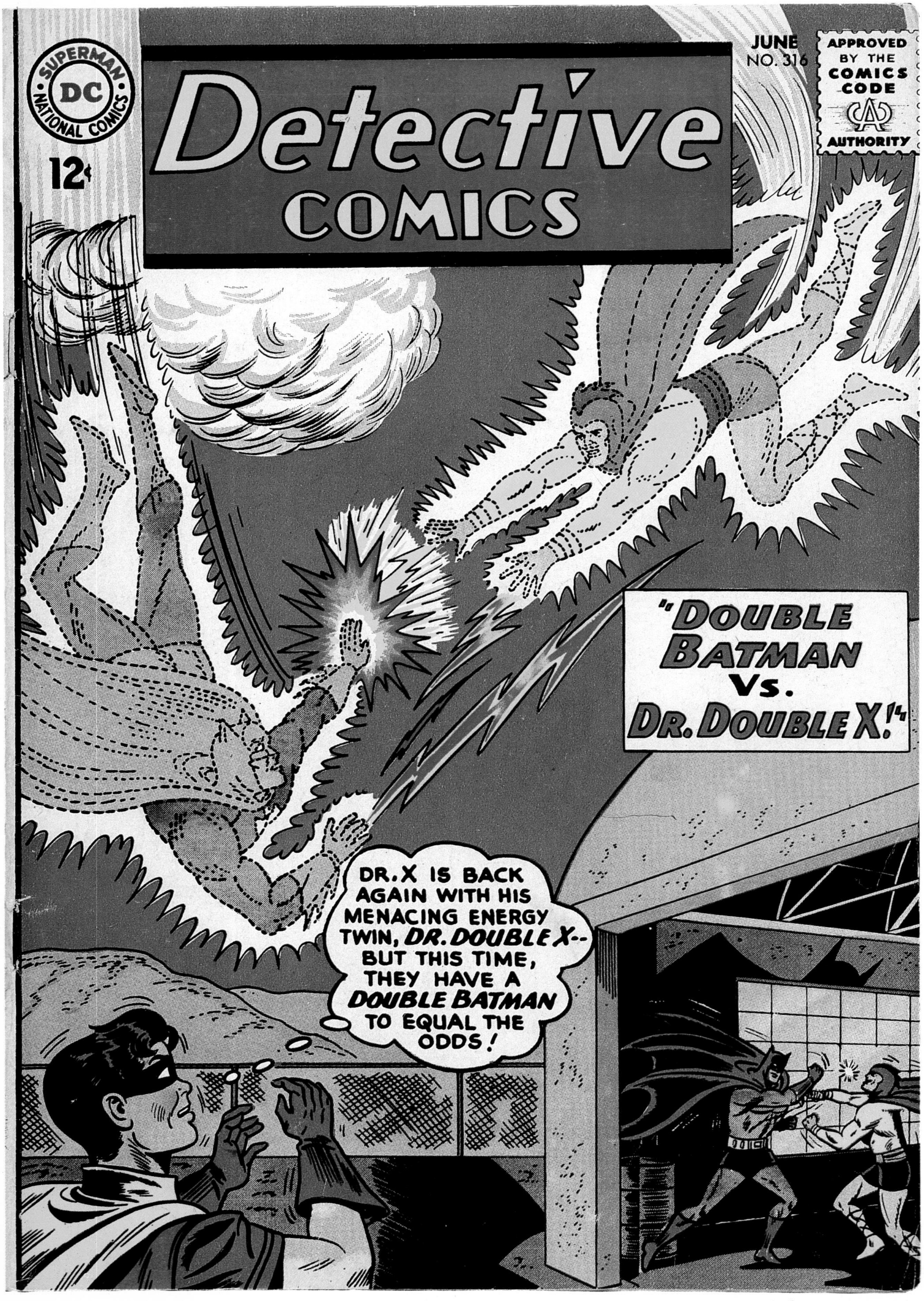

SUPERMAN DC NATIONAL COMICS
12¢
Detective COMICS
JUNE NO. 316
APPROVED BY THE COMICS CODE AUTHORITY
"DOUBLE BATMAN VS. DR. DOUBLE X!"
DR. X IS BACK AGAIN WITH HIS MENACING ENERGY TWIN, DR. DOUBLE X-- BUT THIS TIME, THEY HAVE A DOUBLE BATMAN TO EQUAL THE ODDS!

DETECTIVE #316, June 1963 (Sheldon Moldoff, pencils; Charles Paris, inks)

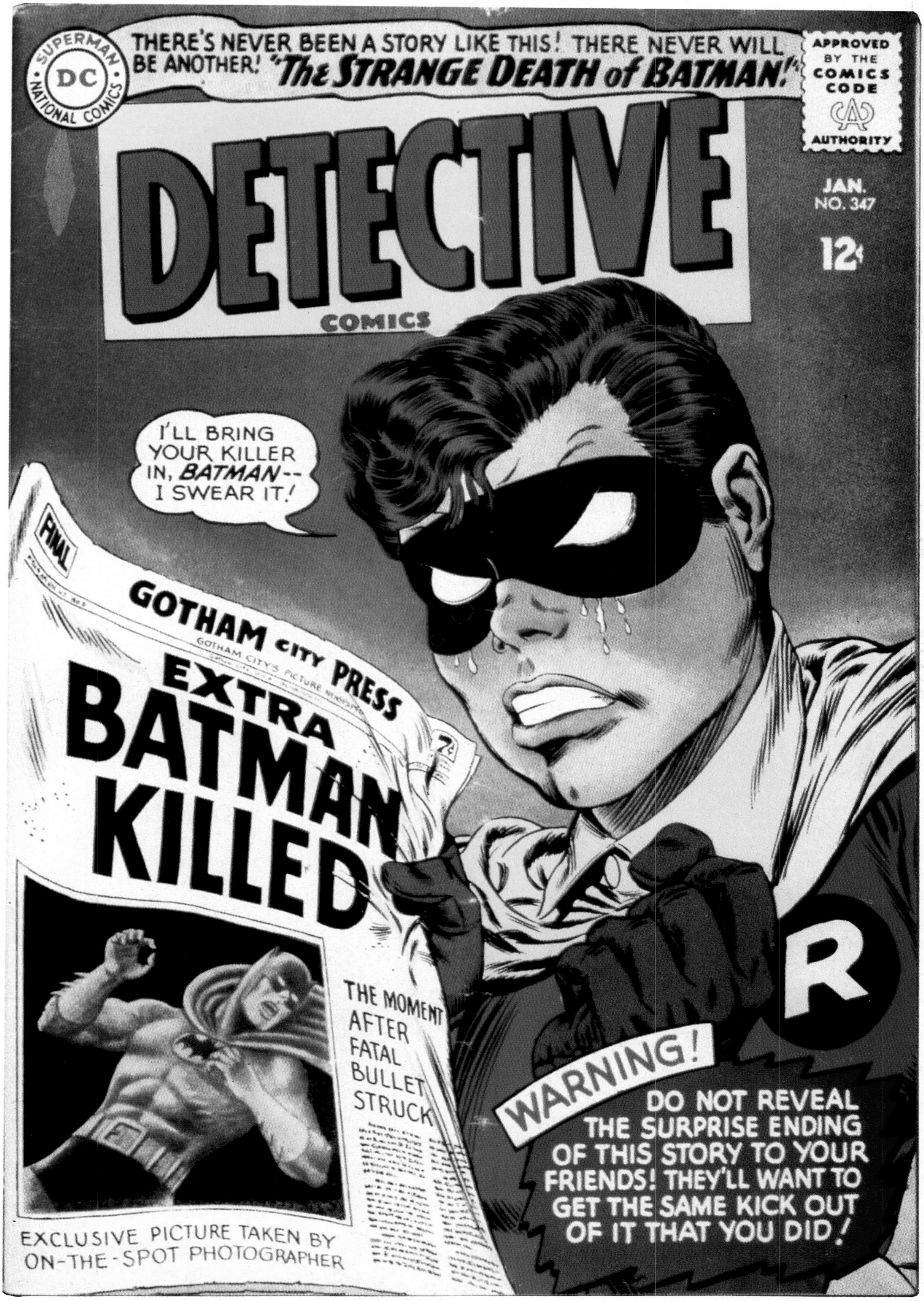

SUPERMAN DC NATIONAL COMICS
THERE'S NEVER BEEN A STORY LIKE THIS! THERE NEVER WILL BE ANOTHER! "The STRANGE DEATH of BATMAN!"
APPROVED BY THE COMICS CODE AUTHORITY
DETECTIVE COMICS
JAN. NO. 347
12¢
I'LL BRING YOUR KILLER IN, BATMAN-- I SWEAR IT!
FINAL
GOTHAM CITY PRESS
GOTHAM CITY'S PICTURE NEWSPAPER
EXTRA
BATMAN KILLED
7¢
THE MOMENT AFTER FATAL BULLET STRUCK
EXCLUSIVE PICTURE TAKEN BY ON-THE-SPOT PHOTOGRAPHER
R
WARNING!
DO NOT REVEAL THE SURPRISE ENDING OF THIS STORY TO YOUR FRIENDS! THEY'LL WANT TO GET THE SAME KICK OUT OF IT THAT YOU DID!

DETECTIVE #347, January 1966 (Carmine Infantino, pencils; Murphy Anderson, inks)

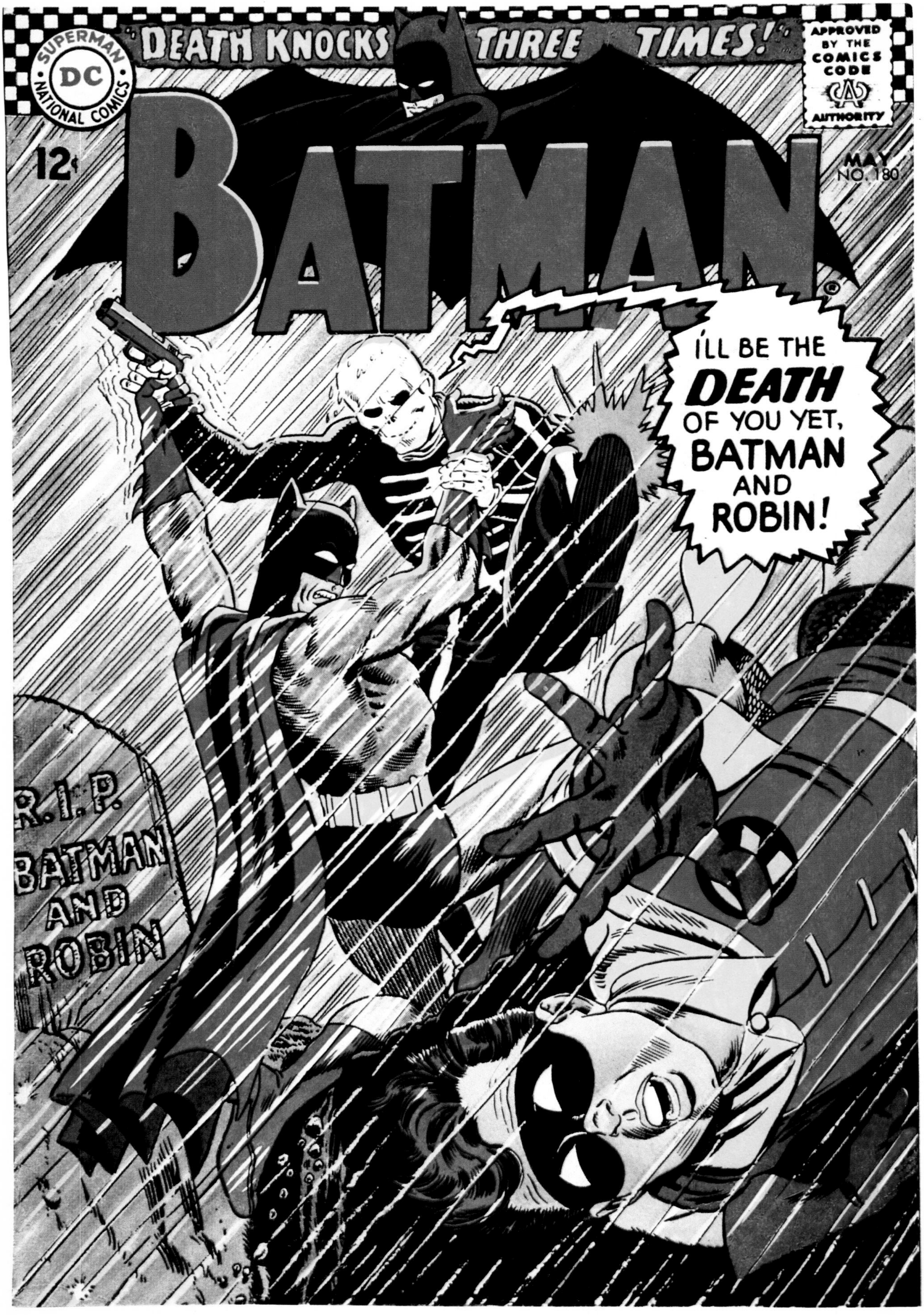

"DEATH KNOCKS THREE TIMES!"
SUPERMAN DC NATIONAL COMICS
APPROVED BY THE COMICS CODE AUTHORITY
12¢
BATMAN
MAY NO. 180
I'LL BE THE DEATH OF YOU YET, BATMAN AND ROBIN!
R.I.P. BATMAN AND ROBIN

BATMAN #180, May 1966 (Gil Kane, pencils; Murphy Anderson, inks)

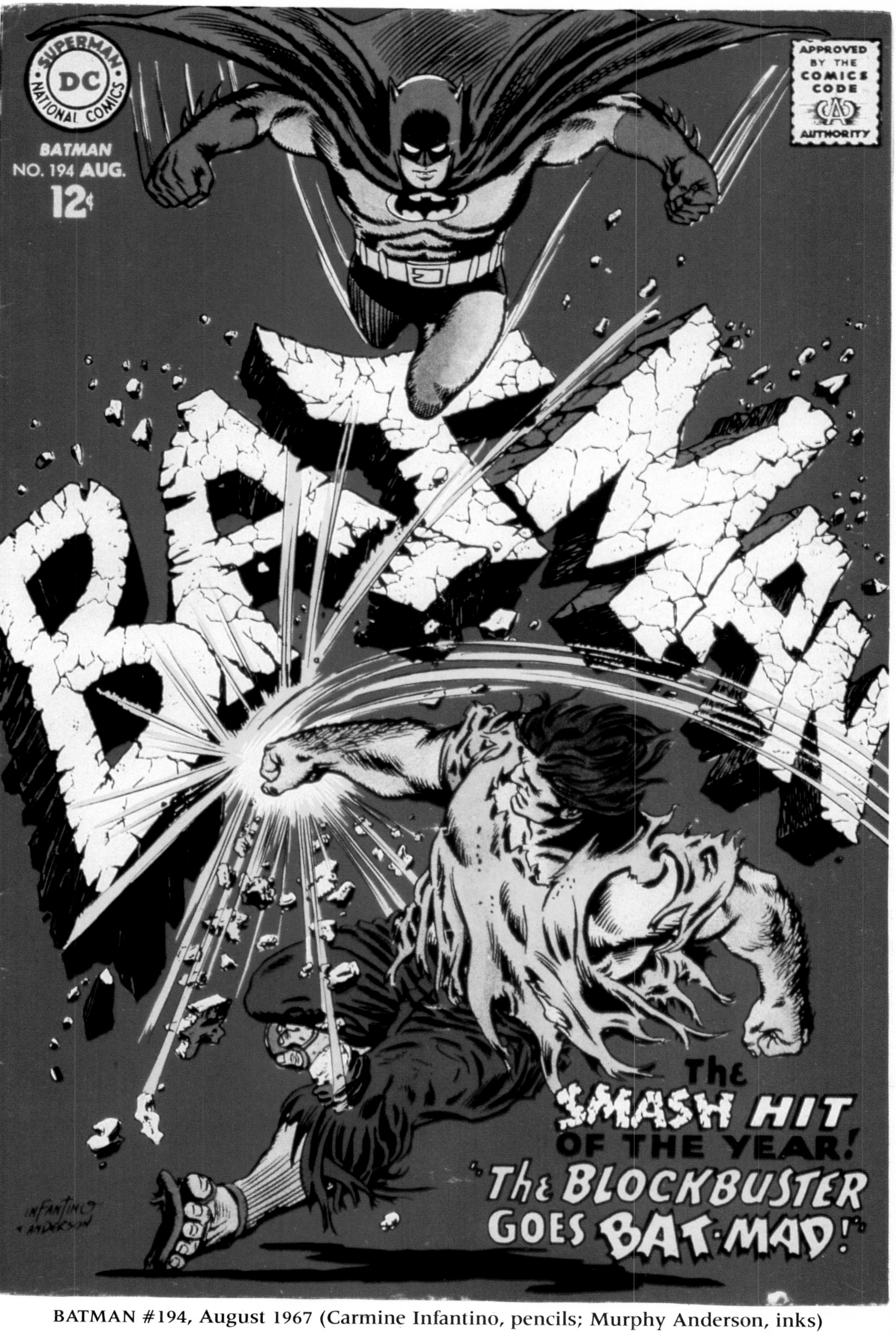
SUPERMAN DC NATIONAL COMICS
BATMAN
NO. 194 AUG.
12¢
APPROVED BY THE COMICS CODE AUTHORITY
BAM
The SMASH HIT OF THE YEAR!
"The BLOCKBUSTER GOES BAT-MAD!"
INFANTINO + ANDERSON

BATMAN #194, August 1967 (Carmine Infantino, pencils; Murphy Anderson, inks)

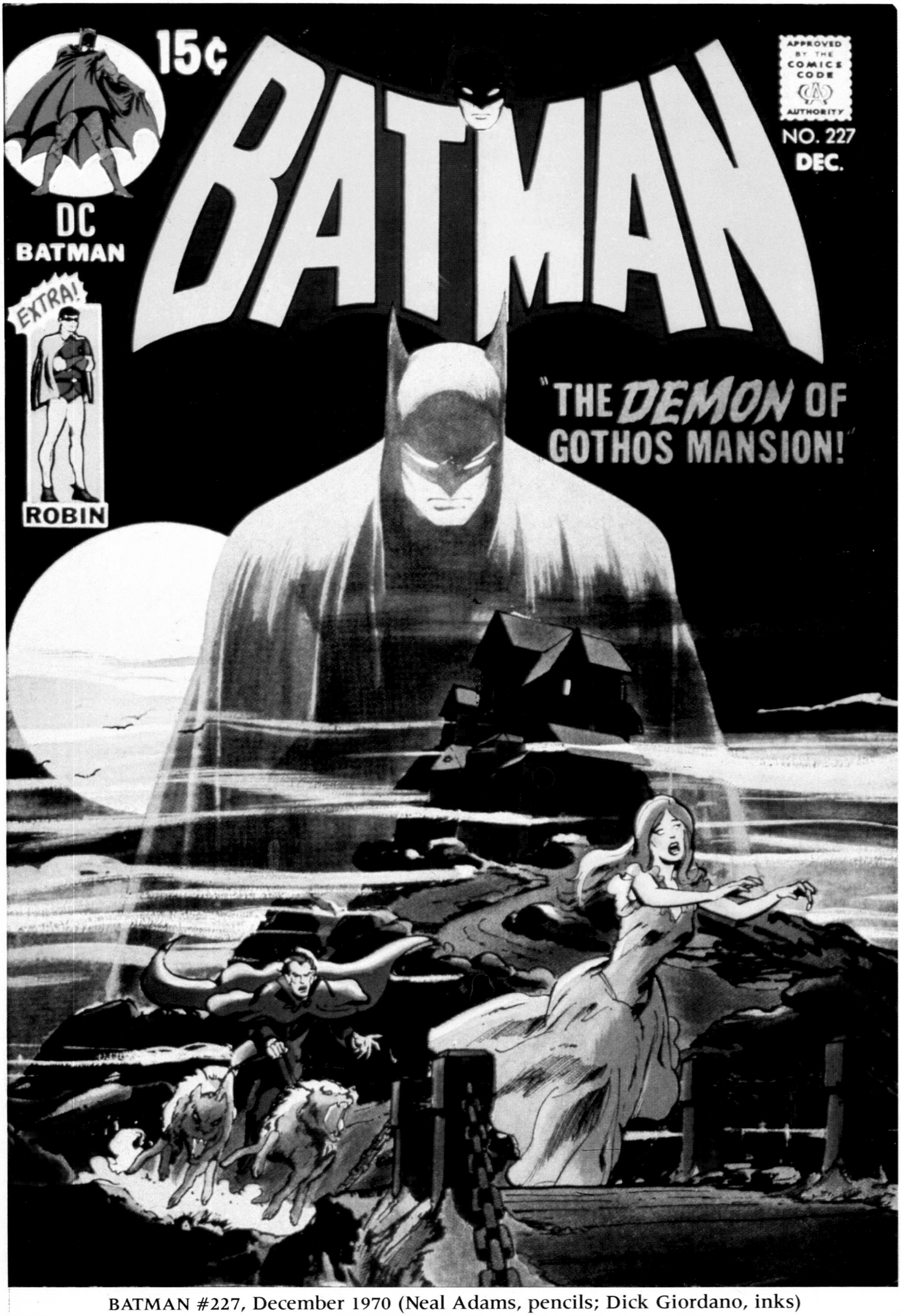
15¢
BATMAN
APPROVED BY THE COMICS CODE AUTHORITY
NO. 227
DEC.
DC
BATMAN
EXTRA!
ROBIN
"THE DEMON OF GOTHOS MANSION!"

BATMAN #227, December 1970 (Neal Adams, pencils; Dick Giordano, inks)

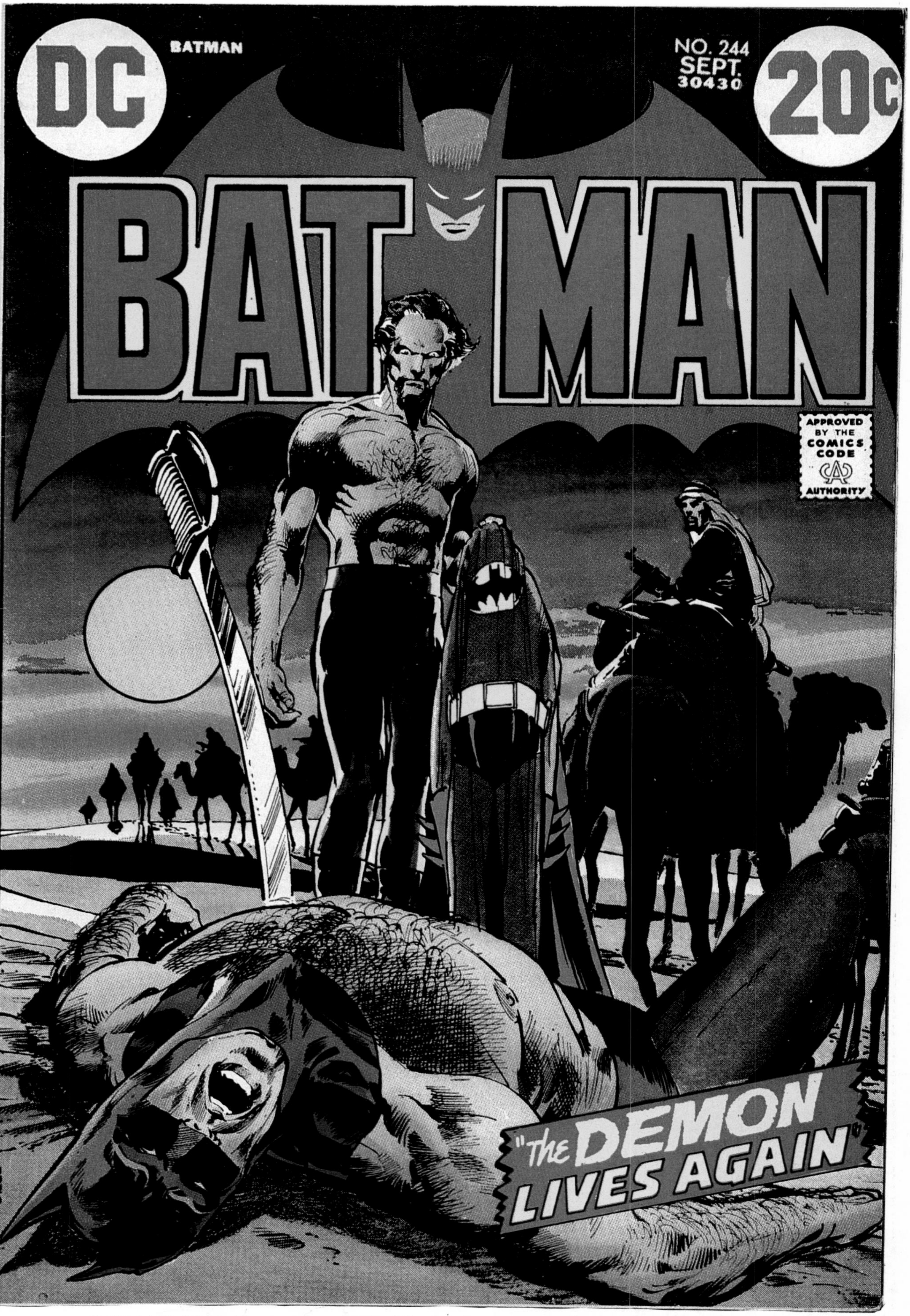
DC
BATMAN
NO. 244
SEPT.
30430
20c
BATMAN
APPROVED
BY THE
COMICS
CODE
AUTHORITY
"The DEMON
LIVES AGAIN"

BATMAN #244, September 1972 (Neal Adams, pencils; Dick Giordano, inks)

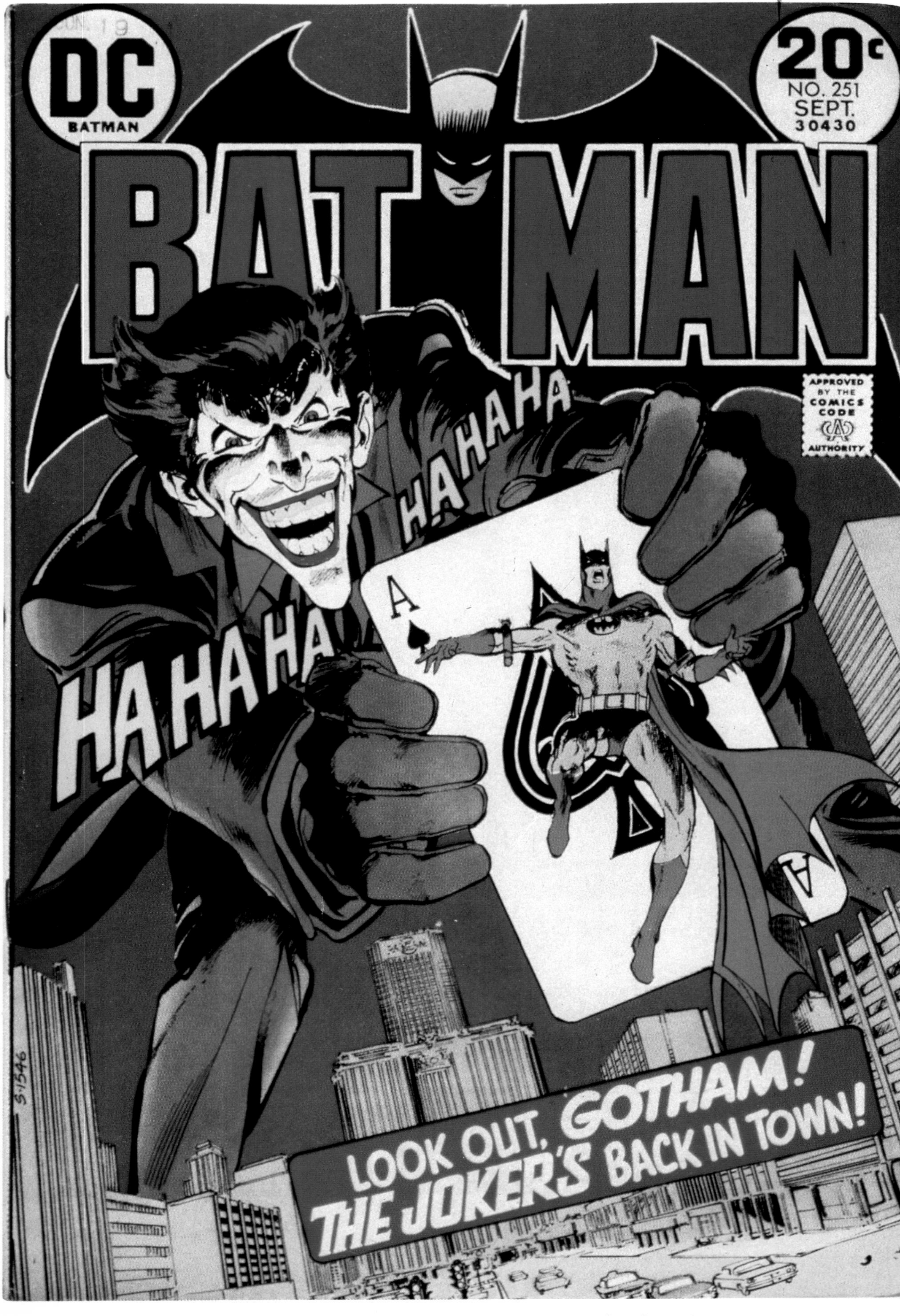
DC
BATMAN
20¢
NO. 251
SEPT.
30430
BATMAN
APPROVED BY THE COMICS CODE AUTHORITY
HAHAHA
HA
HA HA HA
LOOK OUT, GOTHAM!
THE JOKER'S BACK IN TOWN!

BATMAN #251, September 1973 (Neal Adams)

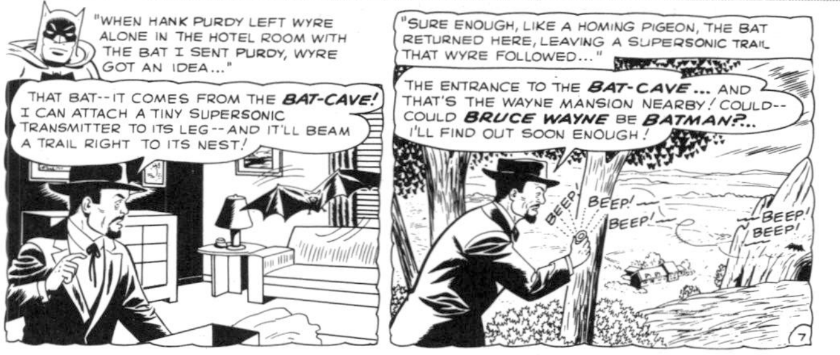
"WHEN HANK PURDY LEFT WYRE ALONE IN THE HOTEL ROOM WITH THE BAT I SENT PURDY, WYRE GOT AN IDEA..."
THAT BAT--IT COMES FROM THE BAT-CAVE! I CAN ATTACH A TINY SUPERSONIC TRANSMITTER TO ITS LEG--AND IT'LL BEAM A TRAIL RIGHT TO ITS NEST!
"SURE ENOUGH, LIKE A HOMING PIGEON, THE BAT RETURNED HERE, LEAVING A SUPERSONIC TRAIL THAT WYRE FOLLOWED..."
THE ENTRANCE TO THE BAT-CAVE... AND THAT'S THE WAYNE MANSION NEARBY! COULD--COULD BRUCE WAYNE BE BATMAN?.. I'LL FIND OUT SOON ENOUGH!
BEEP! BEEP! BEEP!
BEEP! BEEP!
7

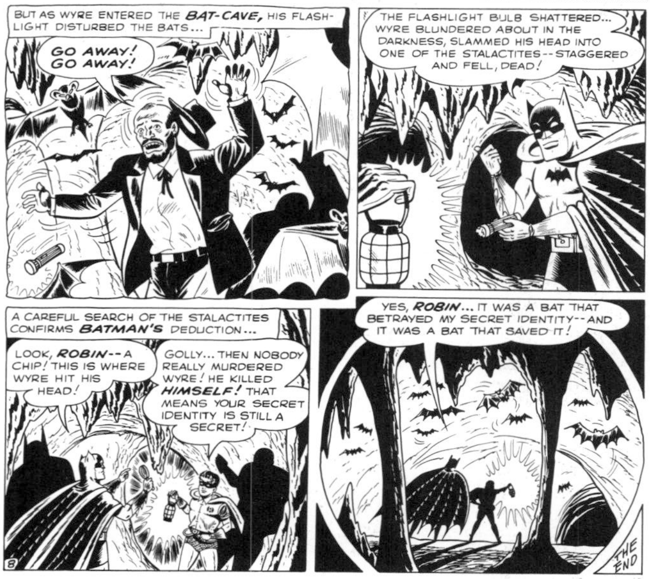
BUT AS WYRE ENTERED THE BAT-CAVE, HIS FLASHLIGHT DISTURBED THE BATS...
GO AWAY! GO AWAY!
THE FLASHLIGHT BULB SHATTERED... WYRE BLUNDERED ABOUT IN THE DARKNESS, SLAMMED HIS HEAD INTO ONE OF THE STALACTITES--STAGGERED AND FELL, DEAD!
A CAREFUL SEARCH OF THE STALACTITES CONFIRMS BATMAN'S DEDUCTION...
LOOK, ROBIN--A CHIP! THIS IS WHERE WYRE HIT HIS HEAD!
GOLLY... THEN NOBODY REALLY MURDERED WYRE! HE KILLED HIMSELF! THAT MEANS YOUR SECRET IDENTITY IS STILL A SECRET!
8
YES, ROBIN... IT WAS A BAT THAT BETRAYED MY SECRET IDENTITY--AND IT WAS A BAT THAT SAVED IT!
THE END

Top: *The mysterious Bat Cave has seen a few unwanted intruders over the years. Some of them ended up like the unfortunate Alec Wyre, pictured here.* (Batman #*121, February 1959, ''The Body in the Bat-cave,'' pp. 7–8 [select panels].*) **Bottom Left:** *The pulse-pounding moment when Alfred Pennyworth discovers that his masters Bruce Wayne and Dick Grayson are really the crimefighting Dynamic Duo.* (The Untold Legend of the Batman #*2, August 1980, ''With Friends Like These . . . ,'' p. 14.*) **Bottom Right:** *The limits of technology: Even the Bat Cave's super computer can't answer the riddle of the Joker.* (The Killing Joke, *1988, p. 11.)*

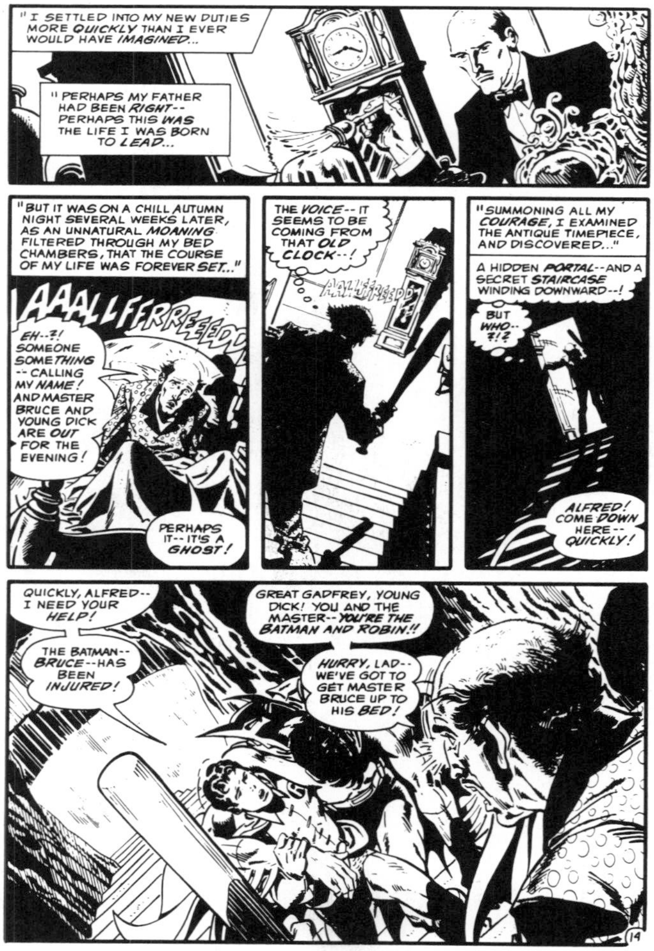
"I SETTLED INTO MY NEW DUTIES MORE QUICKLY THAN I EVER WOULD HAVE IMAGINED...
"PERHAPS MY FATHER HAD BEEN RIGHT--PERHAPS THIS WAS THE LIFE I WAS BORN TO LEAD...
"BUT IT WAS ON A CHILL AUTUMN NIGHT SEVERAL WEEKS LATER, AS AN UNNATURAL MOANING FILTERED THROUGH MY BED CHAMBERS, THAT THE COURSE OF MY LIFE WAS FOREVER SET..."
AAALLFFRREEEDD
EH--?! SOMEONE SOMETHING--CALLING MY NAME! AND MASTER BRUCE AND YOUNG DICK ARE OUT FOR THE EVENING!
PERHAPS IT--IT'S A GHOST!
THE VOICE--IT SEEMS TO BE COMING FROM THAT OLD CLOCK--!
"SUMMONING ALL MY COURAGE, I EXAMINED THE ANTIQUE TIMEPIECE, AND DISCOVERED..."
A HIDDEN PORTAL--AND A SECRET STAIRCASE WINDING DOWNWARD--!
BUT WHO--?!?
ALFRED! COME DOWN HERE--QUICKLY!
QUICKLY, ALFRED--I NEED YOUR HELP!
THE BATMAN--BRUCE--HAS BEEN INJURED!
GREAT GADFREY, YOUNG DICK! YOU AND THE MASTER--YOU'RE THE BATMAN AND ROBIN!!
HURRY, LAD--WE'VE GOT TO GET MASTER BRUCE UP TO HIS BED!
14

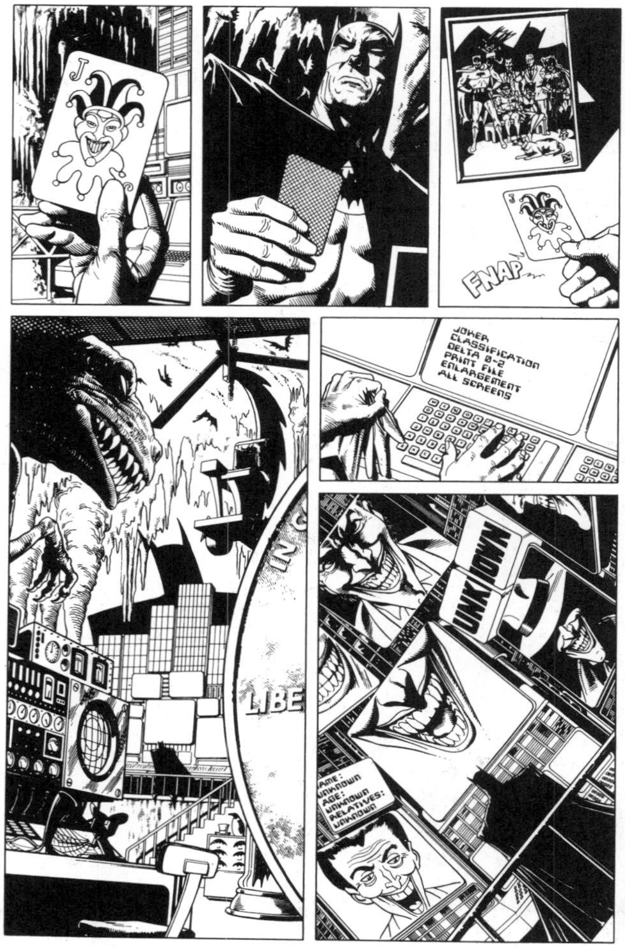
FNAP
JOKER
CLASSIFICATION
DELTA 8-2
PRINT FILE
ENLARGEMENT
ALL SCREENS
UNKNOWN
LIBE

THE HALL OF TROPHIES

More than one thousand trophies are displayed in this famous addition to the Bat Cave. Many of the items, souvenirs from completed assignments, are secured behind temperature-controlled glass cases.

Some of the most famous items include the giant Lincoln-head penny from the "Penny Plunder Case," and the colossal dinosaur model from the "Dinosaur Island Case."

But one of the most prized items in the Hall is the old Batman costume Bruce Wayne once saw his father wear to a masquerade ball. In later years Bruce Wayne would credit that old, subconscious childhood memory with resurfacing the fateful day a bat flew in the window of Wayne Manor.

"Now I realize I adopted a Batman costume because I remembered my father wearing one," Batman once told Robin. (Batman once told Alfred the old costume was the most precious thing he has ever owned.)

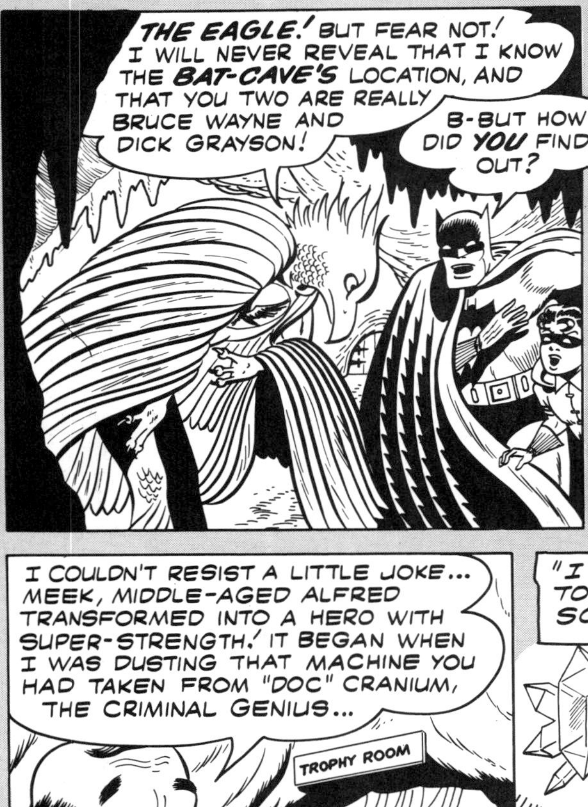
THE EAGLE! BUT FEAR NOT! I WILL NEVER REVEAL THAT I KNOW THE BAT-CAVE'S LOCATION, AND THAT YOU TWO ARE REALLY BRUCE WAYNE AND DICK GRAYSON!
B-BUT HOW DID YOU FIND OUT?

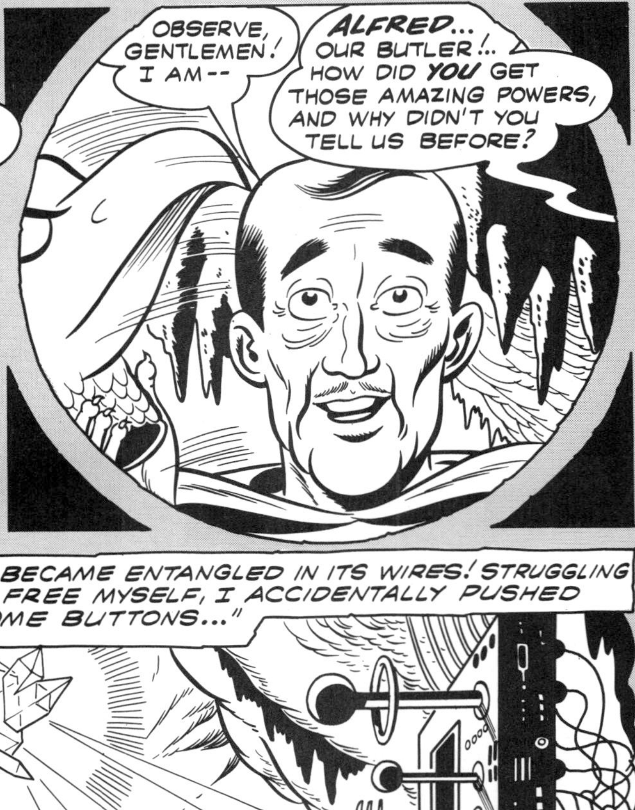
OBSERVE, GENTLEMEN! I AM--
ALFRED... OUR BUTLER!.. HOW DID YOU GET THOSE AMAZING POWERS, AND WHY DIDN'T YOU TELL US BEFORE?

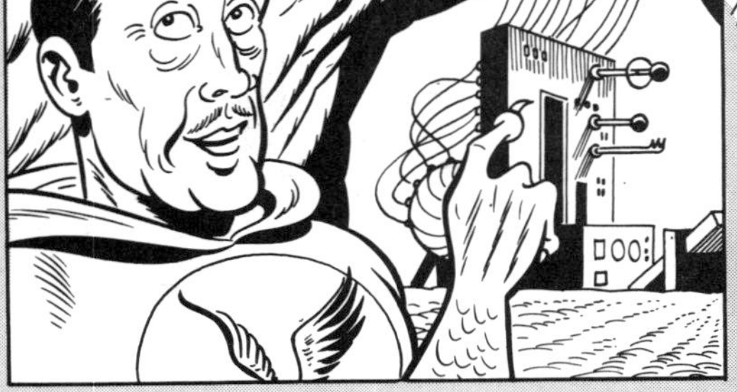
I COULDN'T RESIST A LITTLE JOKE... MEEK, MIDDLE-AGED ALFRED TRANSFORMED INTO A HERO WITH SUPER-STRENGTH! IT BEGAN WHEN I WAS DUSTING THAT MACHINE YOU HAD TAKEN FROM "DOC" CRANIUM, THE CRIMINAL GENIUS...
TROPHY ROOM

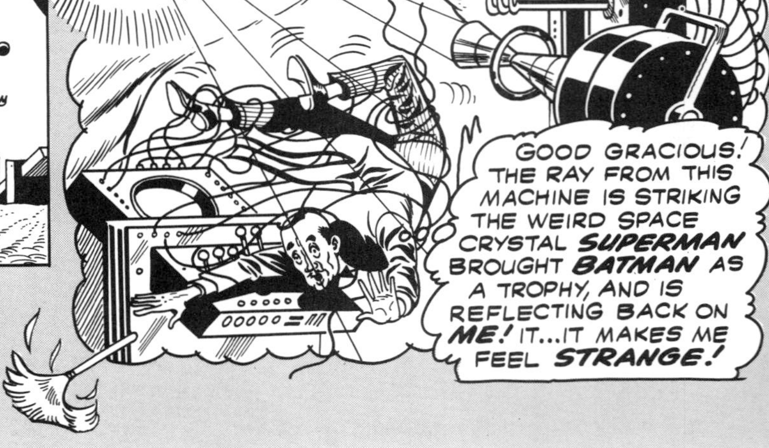
"I BECAME ENTANGLED IN ITS WIRES! STRUGGLING TO FREE MYSELF, I ACCIDENTALLY PUSHED SOME BUTTONS..."
GOOD GRACIOUS! THE RAY FROM THIS MACHINE IS STRIKING THE WEIRD SPACE CRYSTAL SUPERMAN BROUGHT BATMAN AS A TROPHY, AND IS REFLECTING BACK ON ME! IT...IT MAKES ME FEEL STRANGE!

Alfred enjoys the brief spell of super powers as "The Eagle." (Batman *#127, October 1959, "Batman's Super-Partner," p. 4 [select panels].)*

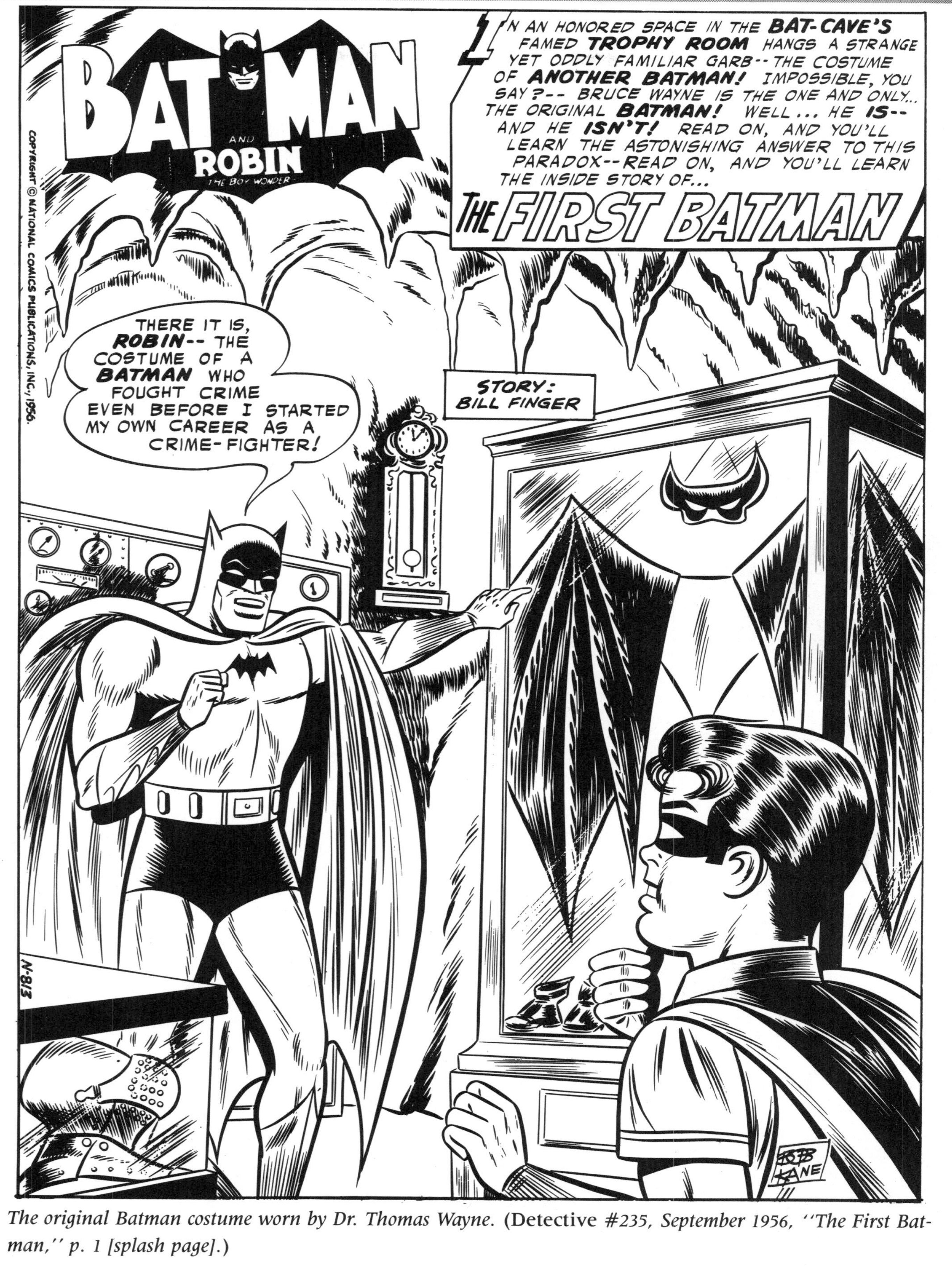
BATMAN AND ROBIN THE BOY WONDER
COPYRIGHT © NATIONAL COMICS PUBLICATIONS, INC., 1956.
IN AN HONORED SPACE IN THE BAT-CAVE'S FAMED TROPHY ROOM HANGS A STRANGE YET ODDLY FAMILIAR GARB-- THE COSTUME OF ANOTHER BATMAN! IMPOSSIBLE, YOU SAY?-- BRUCE WAYNE IS THE ONE AND ONLY... THE ORIGINAL BATMAN! WELL ... HE IS-- AND HE ISN'T! READ ON, AND YOU'LL LEARN THE ASTONISHING ANSWER TO THIS PARADOX--READ ON, AND YOU'LL LEARN THE INSIDE STORY OF...
THE FIRST BATMAN
THERE IT IS, ROBIN-- THE COSTUME OF A BATMAN WHO FOUGHT CRIME EVEN BEFORE I STARTED MY OWN CAREER AS A CRIME-FIGHTER!
STORY: BILL FINGER
N-813
BOB KANE

The original Batman costume worn by Dr. Thomas Wayne. (Detective #235, *September 1956, ''The First Batman,'' p. 1 [splash page].*)

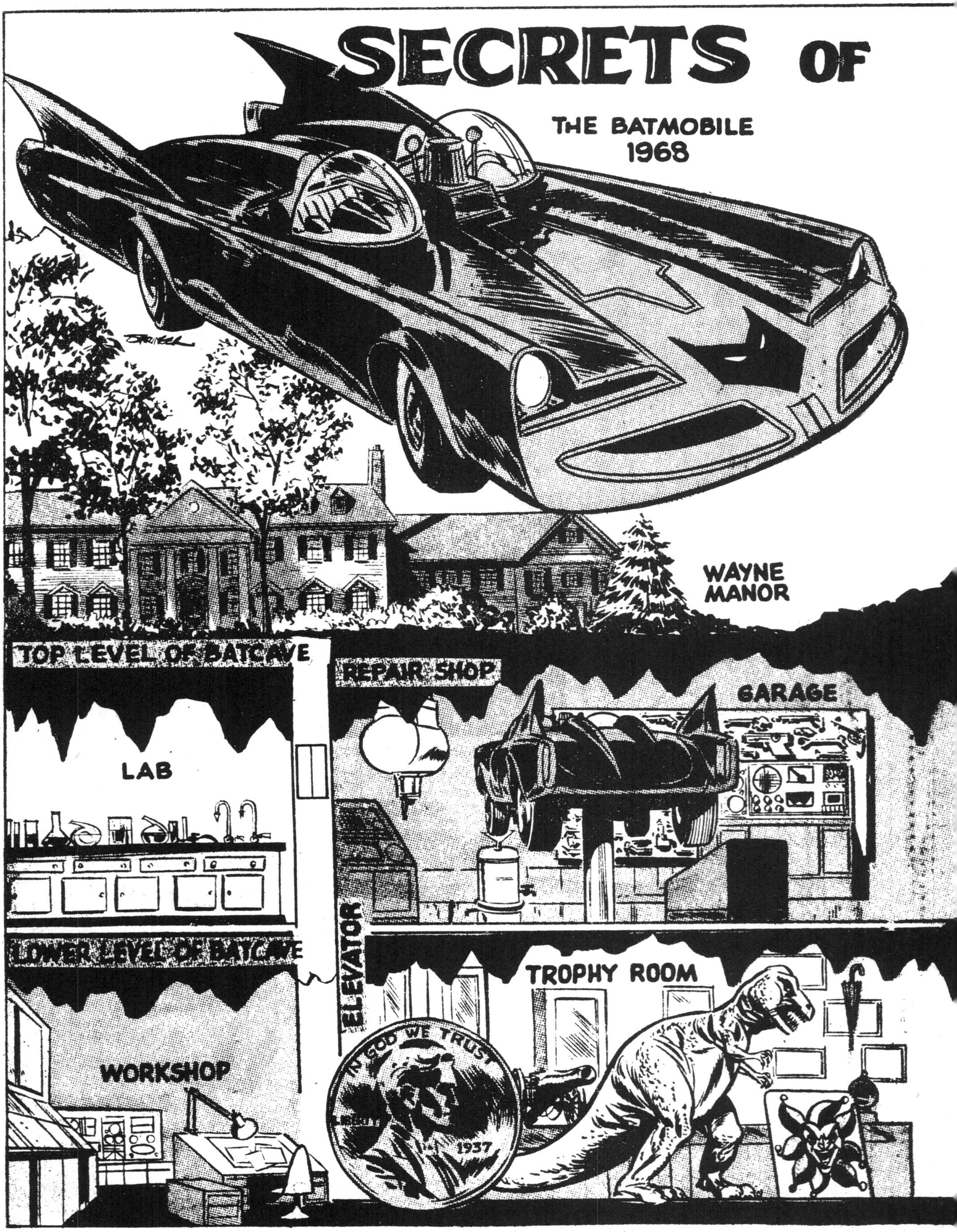
SECRETS OF
THE BATMOBILE
1968
WAYNE
MANOR
TOP LEVEL OF BATCAVE
REPAIR SHOP
GARAGE
LAB
ELEVATOR
LOWER LEVEL OF BATCAVE
TROPHY ROOM
WORKSHOP
IN GOD WE TRUST
LIBERTY
1937

Batman 80-page Giant *#203, August 1968, ''Secrets of the Batcave—1968,'' pp. 28–29.*

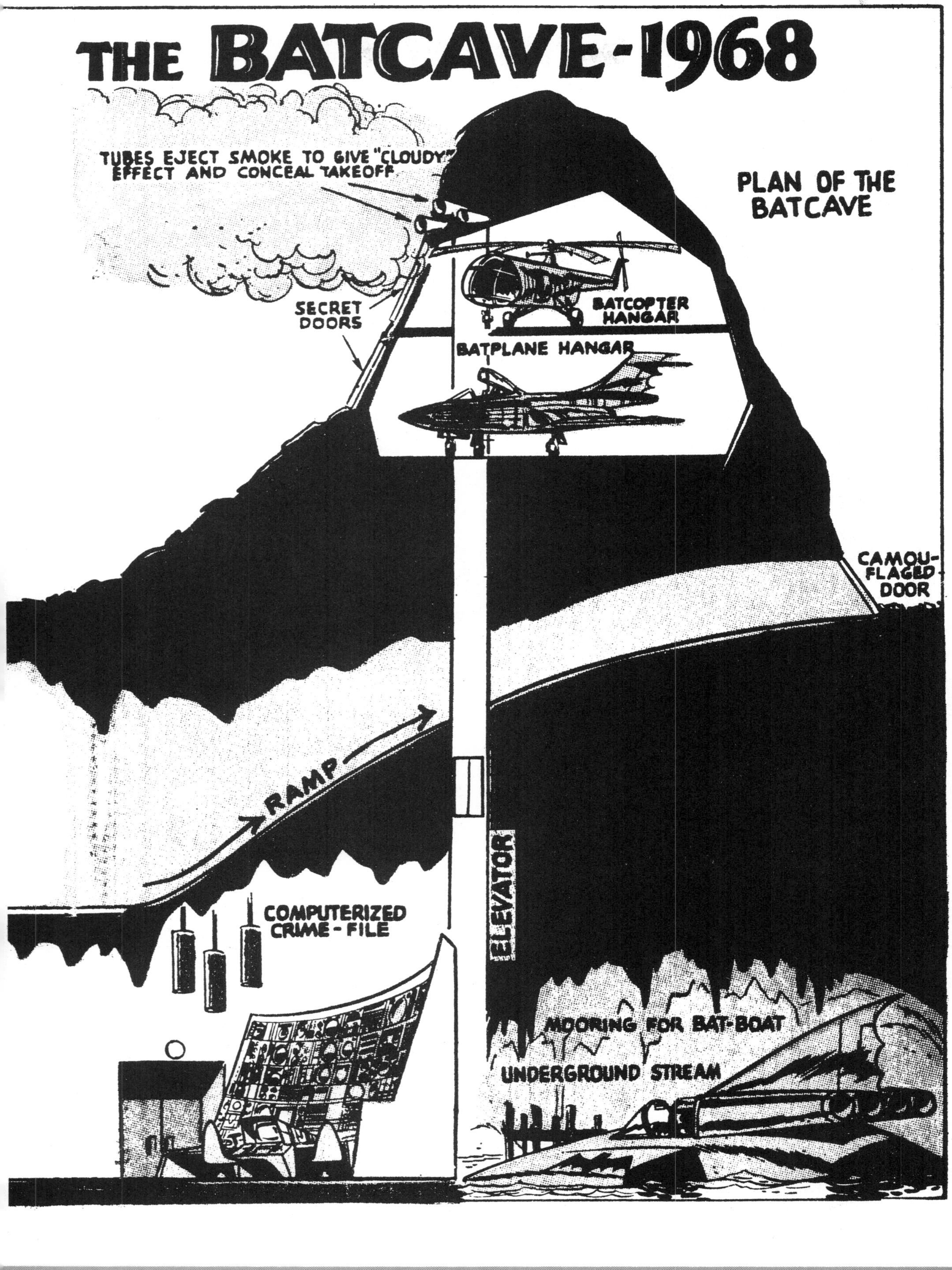
THE BATCAVE-1968
TUBES EJECT SMOKE TO GIVE "CLOUDY" EFFECT AND CONCEAL TAKEOFF
PLAN OF THE BATCAVE
BATCOPTER HANGAR
SECRET DOORS
BATPLANE HANGAR
CAMOU-FLAGED DOOR
RAMP
ELEVATOR
COMPUTERIZED CRIME-FILE
MOORING FOR BAT-BOAT
UNDERGROUND STREAM

CHAPTER 11
DETECTIVE SCIENCE

DURING A 1987 CASE IN LONDON, THE DYnamic Duo, assisted by the Elongated Man and an aging Golden Age private eye named Slam Bradley, halted an assassination attempt on the royal family. The case closed with a historic meeting between the Batman and a legendary figure wearing a trademark deerstalker cap, an elegant pipe clenched in his teeth, and a familiar, proud profile—none other than a still spry and very much alive Sherlock Holmes!

The elevated climate of Tibet, where he kept his primary residence, and a special diet accounted for his remarkable longevity, Holmes explained (although one suspects that the esoteric spiritual practices of that fabled land played some part as well).

As the Elongated Man gushed and Slam Bradley and the rest just gawked, Batman stood silently to the side in deference to Holmes. And Holmes, gazing upon Batman, didn't need to waste words—his twinkling eyes and wise smile spoke volumes on the respect he had for Batman.[1]

It's important that Sherlock Holmes, whose very name is synonymous with the art of deductive reasoning, would have such respect for the hero who has been dubbed "the Darknight Detective." Whether decoding the cryptic crime messages of the Riddler, solving a murder mystery, or divining the crime patterns of a Joker or Two-Face, a major part of Batman's appeal has been his brilliance as a detective.

"I still remember the ritual of shining shoes for a dime, or collecting six soda pop bottles for the twelve cents deposit they would bring," Mark Hamill (Luke Skywalker of *Star Wars* fame) writes in his introduction to the *Son of the Demon* Batman book. "That would buy a comic book,

through which I could be instantly transported to the Batcave and watch the world's greatest detective in action.... Batman's world was dark, mysterious and challenging. Oh, how I agonized over the panel that asked the reader to guess how Batman had solved the crime! Should I go back and examine everything in detail or just turn the damn page and get it over with? Show me, Batman, tell me how you did it. And he would, of course, patiently explaining the methods of his deduction as if each and every one of us were Robin (and we *were*)."[2]

Batman's greatness as a detective comes from his renaissance approach to criminology. The Dark Knight is adept at the mechanics of crime fighting, whether dusting for fingerprints or processing an important clue by chemical analysis. He is a superb master of disguise, has an eye for detail and a command of language from the most obscure dialect of distant lands to the underworld's street slang. His mind is not locked into one pattern of logic but is fluid and flexible. Even if a life hangs on the outcome of his reasonings, Batman can shrug off the pressures and mentally sift through the data of a case until the saving truth emerges. To top it off, the Dark Knight has an almost supernatural sense of intuition.

"I often think of him as an obsessed artist," Jenette Kahn reasons. "He has an artist's purity and commitment to his art.... He has incredible discipline, fire, and ferocity in his commitment."

"You would assume that he does not concern himself with crimes that the cop on the beat can solve," says Denny O'Neil. "He would concern

---

1. "The Doomsday Book," *Detective Comics* 572 (March 1987), pp. 52–53.
2. Mark Hamill, "Introduction," in *Batman: Son of the Demon* (New York: DC Comics, Inc., 1987), pp. 1–2.

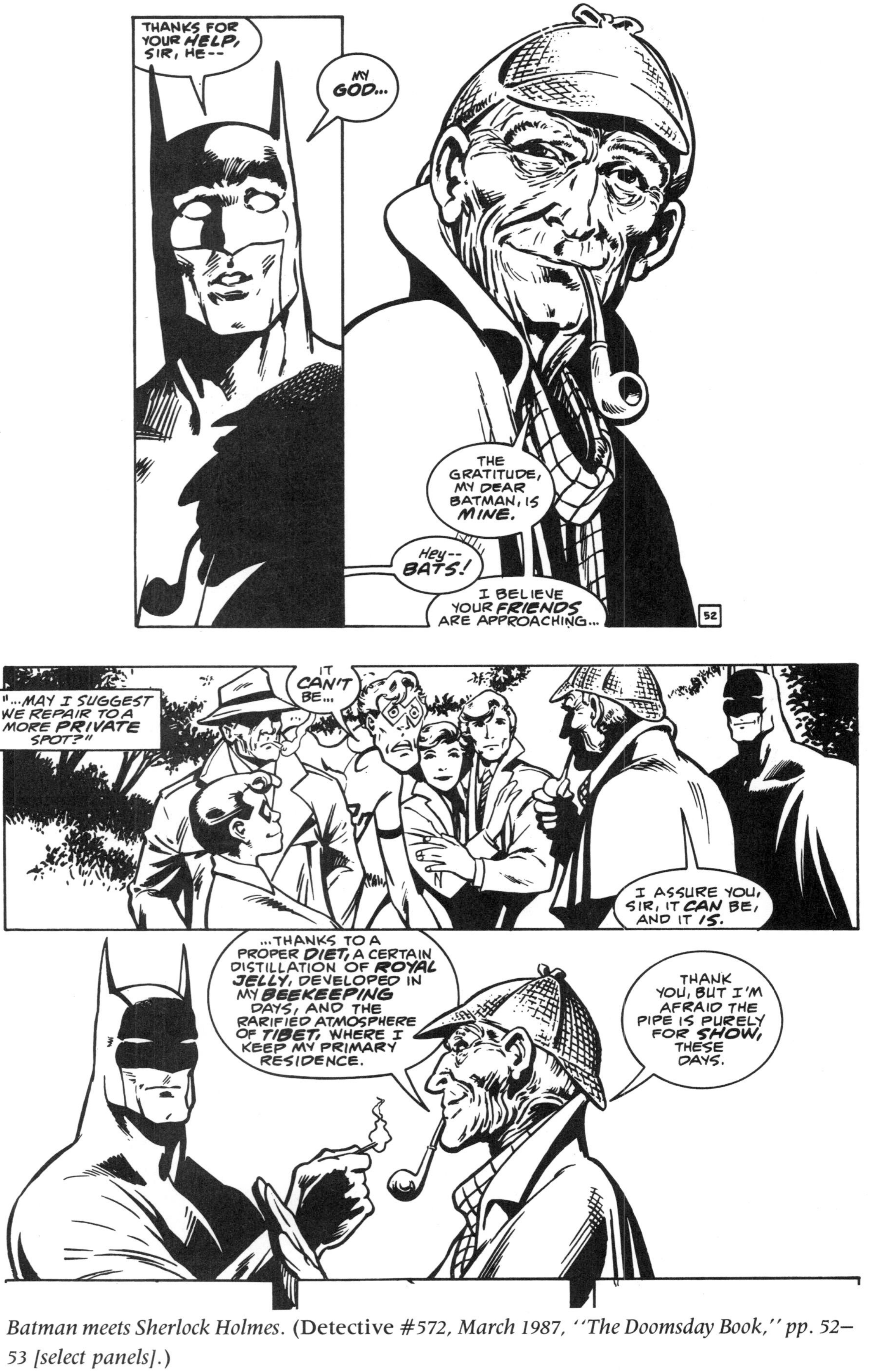
THANKS FOR YOUR HELP, SIR, HE--
MY GOD...
THE GRATITUDE, MY DEAR BATMAN, IS MINE.
Hey-- BATS!
I BELIEVE YOUR FRIENDS ARE APPROACHING...
52
"...MAY I SUGGEST WE REPAIR TO A MORE PRIVATE SPOT?"
IT CAN'T BE...
I ASSURE YOU, SIR, IT CAN BE, AND IT IS.
...THANKS TO A PROPER DIET, A CERTAIN DISTILLATION OF ROYAL JELLY, DEVELOPED IN MY BEEKEEPING DAYS, AND THE RARIFIED ATMOSPHERE OF TIBET, WHERE I KEEP MY PRIMARY RESIDENCE.
THANK YOU, BUT I'M AFRAID THE PIPE IS PURELY FOR SHOW, THESE DAYS.

Batman meets Sherlock Holmes. (Detective #572, *March 1987, ''The Doomsday Book,'' pp. 52–53 [select panels]*.)

himself with crimes that wouldn't fall under simple police procedure. It's an idea that's in Rex Stout's Nero Wolfe novels where Wolfe is constantly saying, 'I am an artist or I am nothing,' operating as much by intuition as logic, which, oddly enough, makes him a scientific crime fighter. . . . If you're a scientific crime fighter, you're going to operate by intuition."

O'Neil, who prior to his comic book career was a newspaper reporter assigned to the crime beat, recalls how often a cop's gut feelings cracked a case or uncovered an important lead—a special intuitive awareness shared by Batman.

When Denny O'Neil teamed with Neal Adams to return Batman to his Dark Knight roots in the post-TV show years, not only the art of detection but the tradition of mystery once again became a featured part of Batman's repertoire.

"When the TV show went out of business suddenly, they couldn't sell camp anymore and

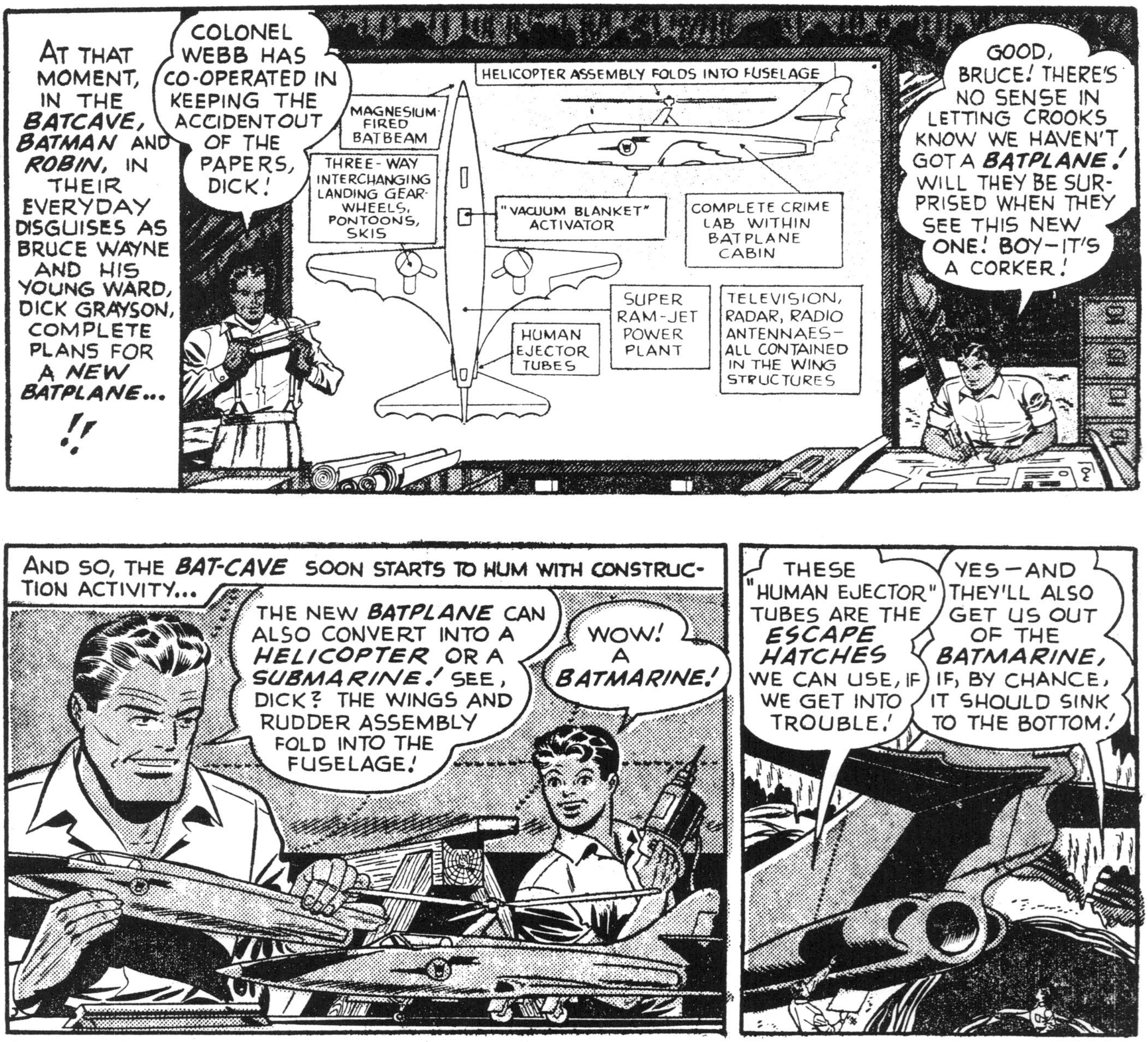

AT THAT MOMENT, IN THE BATCAVE, BATMAN AND ROBIN, IN THEIR EVERYDAY DISGUISES AS BRUCE WAYNE AND HIS YOUNG WARD, DICK GRAYSON, COMPLETE PLANS FOR A NEW BATPLANE... !!
COLONEL WEBB HAS CO-OPERATED IN KEEPING THE ACCIDENT OUT OF THE PAPERS, DICK!
HELICOPTER ASSEMBLY FOLDS INTO FUSELAGE
MAGNESIUM-FIRED BATBEAM
THREE-WAY INTERCHANGING LANDING GEAR-WHEELS, PONTOONS, SKIS
"VACUUM BLANKET" ACTIVATOR
COMPLETE CRIME LAB WITHIN BATPLANE CABIN
SUPER RAM-JET POWER PLANT
HUMAN EJECTOR TUBES
TELEVISION, RADAR, RADIO ANTENNAES—ALL CONTAINED IN THE WING STRUCTURES
GOOD, BRUCE! THERE'S NO SENSE IN LETTING CROOKS KNOW WE HAVEN'T GOT A BATPLANE! WILL THEY BE SURPRISED WHEN THEY SEE THIS NEW ONE! BOY—IT'S A CORKER!
AND SO, THE BAT-CAVE SOON STARTS TO HUM WITH CONSTRUCTION ACTIVITY...
THE NEW BATPLANE CAN ALSO CONVERT INTO A HELICOPTER OR A SUBMARINE! SEE, DICK? THE WINGS AND RUDDER ASSEMBLY FOLD INTO THE FUSELAGE!
WOW! A BATMARINE!
THESE "HUMAN EJECTOR" TUBES ARE THE ESCAPE HATCHES WE CAN USE, IF WE GET INTO TROUBLE!
YES—AND THEY'LL ALSO GET US OUT OF THE BATMARINE, IF, BY CHANCE, IT SHOULD SINK TO THE BOTTOM!

Thanks to his engineering brilliance—and the family fortune—Bruce Wayne has always been able to maintain a high-tech edge against Gotham's evil underworld. (Batman *#61, October/November 1950, "The Birth of Batplane II," pp. 5, 7 [select panels].)*

they [the DC editorial side], came to me and said, What can you do with Batman?" Denny O'Neil recalls.

"At that point I was willing, even anxious, to do it. When I talked about it with editor Julius Schwartz, we decided we could not possibly do better than to go back to the basics—figure out what really constitutes this character."

"Batman in both of our minds was this Darknight Detective, a combination of the best athlete in the world and Sherlock Holmes, whose parents were killed by a thief in the night in front of his eyes, and who grew up with a kind of schizoid paranoia that made him believe it was his role in life to track down—and at times even maim—the villains of the world," Neal Adams remembers of his early Batman story line discussions with O'Neil.

"...I believe any character that's any good represents the deeper parts of human beings in general," Adams continues. "...The idea of being able to figure out from very small clues how the world works, and becoming Sherlock Holmes, is very attractive to people. People put themselves in the part. Skulking around at night is part of every child's past. You know, going into the darkness and sneaking around and scaring people—that's a real solid, deep thing for human beings. It should be no surprise that Batman is a popular character. The surprise is when they don't make the most of it."

To Adams, "they" represented the editorial decisions prompted by television's pop-comedy opera depiction of Batman. When Julius Schwartz teamed Adams, who had been earning rave reviews for his realistic depiction of Batman during the character's regular appearances in *The Brave and the Bold*, with writer Denny O'Neil (with Dick Giordano providing much of the inking), some of the landmark Batman tales resulted.

For instance, in one story line the team not only created one of the most memorable and original of villains in Ra's Al Ghul, but introduced as compelling a female character (and love interest for Batman) as has ever graced a comic book story—Ra's's beautiful daughter, Talia.

The O'Neil/Adams formula was a return to the spirit of the Dark Knight version of Bob Kane and Bill Finger. And with the same intuitive fire as Batman's own crime-fighting artistry, O'Neil and Adams played off each other in fashioning their Dark Knight tales. And they didn't need to hold a lot of meetings to decide their direction. As was the style of the early 1970's, O'Neil would generally turn in a completed script to editor Schwartz, and then Adams would get the script and go to work with his pencils.

"Oddly enough, I probably worked less closely with Neal than almost anybody, and almost always got what I wanted...sometimes better," O'Neil remembers.

"I believe the best Batman stories I did were with Denny O'Neil," Adams says. "...It was just fortunate that we got together at that time."

Batman's world changed in many ways after the demise of the television show. For one, Batman finally decided to modernize his crime-fighting operation by sealing up the Wayne Manor Bat Cave and moving the Dark Knight's operations to another cave in the underground depths of Gotham City itself.

"ROBIN AND I RETURNED TO THE BATCAVE AND BEGAN AT ONCE TO PLAN A NEW BAT-SIGNAL, ONE THAT WOULD STAND UP TO ANY EMERGENCY..."
BULLET-PROOF GLASS. HAND-GROUND FOR CLARITY
IN THE PAST, HEAVY FOG HAS STYMIED THE USE OF THE BAT-SIGNAL. THAT'S ONE OF THE CONDITIONS THIS NEW MODEL WILL CORRECT!
SUPER-CARBON ARC FILAMENTS
ELECTRONIZED SILVER REFLECTOR
NEW CHANGEABLE CARRIAGE
YELLOW FOG FILTER
BATSLIDE
LARGER, MORE POWERFUL LAMPMOBILE WITH NEW CARRIAGE
OUTER CASING OF DURALUMINUM COVERED WITH BULLET-PROOF GLASS

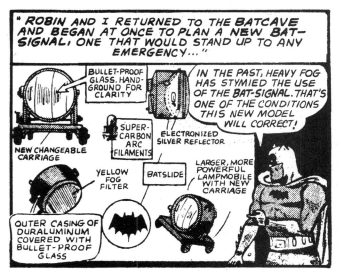

A hallmark of Batman's career has been his ceaseless search for an edge against the underworld. He's maintained that edge by constantly upgrading and modernizing his crimefighting devices. Here, Batman creates a new, improved Bat Signal. (Detective *#164, October 1950, "Untold Tales of The Bat Signal!" p. 7 [panel].)*

The new Bat Cave was actually an abandoned Depression-era subway station located below the Wayne Foundation building. And this was a new Bruce Wayne—no longer the idle rich cover for his Batman pursuits, but a wealthy, powerful, politically ambitious man as obsessed in his Foundation boardroom during the day as his crime-fighter persona would continue to be at night.

And then there was the matter of Dick Grayson growing up. The Dynamic Duo was finally breaking up so that Dick could attend Hudson University. By now Dick was no longer a boy, but a young man who stood tall and lean, with a chiseled profile that would set the hearts of Hudson coeds fluttering.

In that special tale (*Batman* 217), we saw Dick standing in the mansion foyer in his white Hudson University jacket over his turtle neck sweater and slacks. He was all grins waiting for the taxi

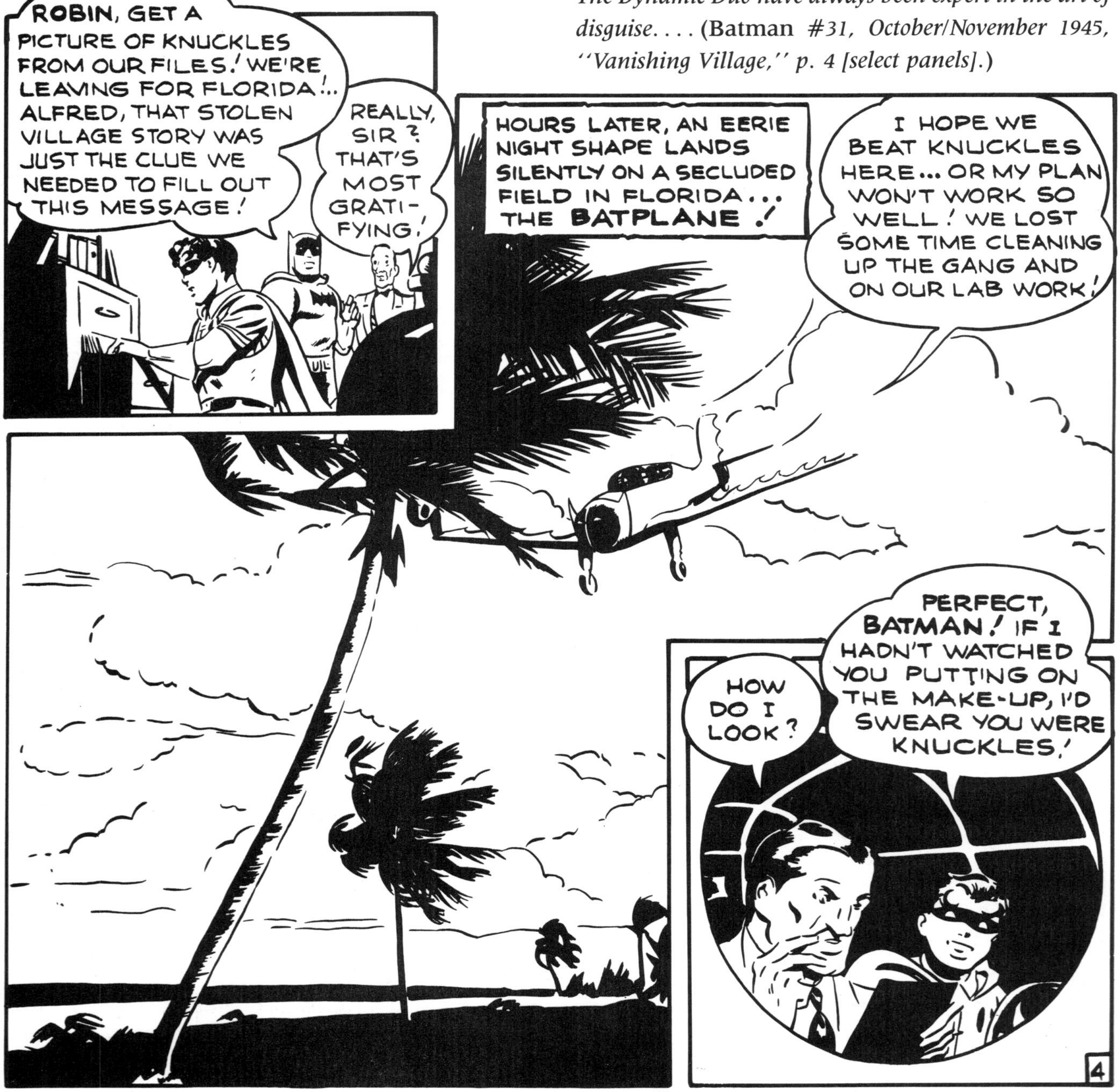

ROBIN, GET A PICTURE OF KNUCKLES FROM OUR FILES! WE'RE LEAVING FOR FLORIDA!.. ALFRED, THAT STOLEN VILLAGE STORY WAS JUST THE CLUE WE NEEDED TO FILL OUT THIS MESSAGE!
REALLY, SIR? THAT'S MOST GRATI-FYING!
HOURS LATER, AN EERIE NIGHT SHAPE LANDS SILENTLY ON A SECLUDED FIELD IN FLORIDA... THE BATPLANE!
I HOPE WE BEAT KNUCKLES HERE... OR MY PLAN WON'T WORK SO WELL! WE LOST SOME TIME CLEANING UP THE GANG AND ON OUR LAB WORK!
HOW DO I LOOK?
PERFECT, BATMAN! IF I HADN'T WATCHED YOU PUTTING ON THE MAKE-UP, I'D SWEAR YOU WERE KNUCKLES!
4

The Dynamic Duo have always been expert in the art of disguise. . . . (Batman *#31, October/November 1945, ''Vanishing Village,'' p. 4 [select panels].*)

that would take him to the airport. But Bruce looked grim, and Alfred was losing a valiant battle to hold back tears.

"Aw, c'mon, fellas—we're all grown up now!" Dick said. "Stop acting like you're attending my funeral!

"I know it's going to be pretty rough on you guys—in the beginning!" Dick continued as the cab drove up. "Guess it's kinda hard for you to dig that only yesterday I was your 'young Master Dick,' Alfie, and your 'kid who needed a big-brother image,' Bruce.

"But—I'm a man now! 'Least that's what my draft-card says plus my acceptance at Hudson University. So...I'd prefer to go to the airport alone...."

With barely a look back, he stepped into the taxi. But once inside and safely driving away, a

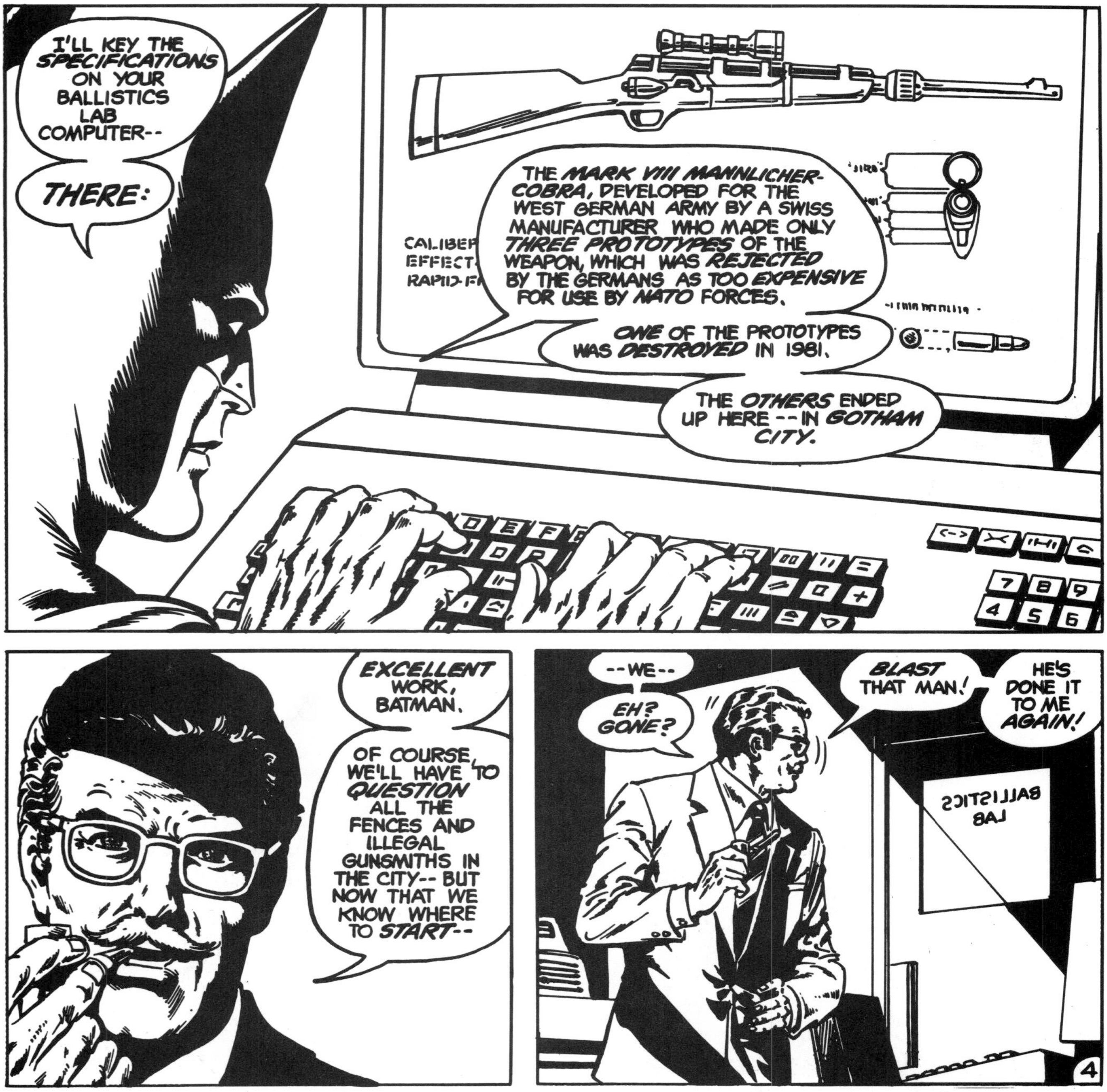

I'LL KEY THE SPECIFICATIONS ON YOUR BALLISTICS LAB COMPUTER--
THERE:
THE MARK VIII MANNLICHER-COBRA, DEVELOPED FOR THE WEST GERMAN ARMY BY A SWISS MANUFACTURER WHO MADE ONLY THREE PROTOTYPES OF THE WEAPON, WHICH WAS REJECTED BY THE GERMANS AS TOO EXPENSIVE FOR USE BY NATO FORCES.
ONE OF THE PROTOTYPES WAS DESTROYED IN 1981.
THE OTHERS ENDED UP HERE--IN GOTHAM CITY.
EXCELLENT WORK, BATMAN.
OF COURSE, WE'LL HAVE TO QUESTION ALL THE FENCES AND ILLEGAL GUNSMITHS IN THE CITY-- BUT NOW THAT WE KNOW WHERE TO START--
--WE--
EH? GONE?
BLAST THAT MAN!
HE'S DONE IT TO ME AGAIN!
4

Whether glancing through a magnifying glass or working a crime lab computer, Batman will find a way to wrest clues from murder weapons. (Batman *#358, April 1983, "Don't Mess With Killer Croc!" p. 4 [select panels].*)

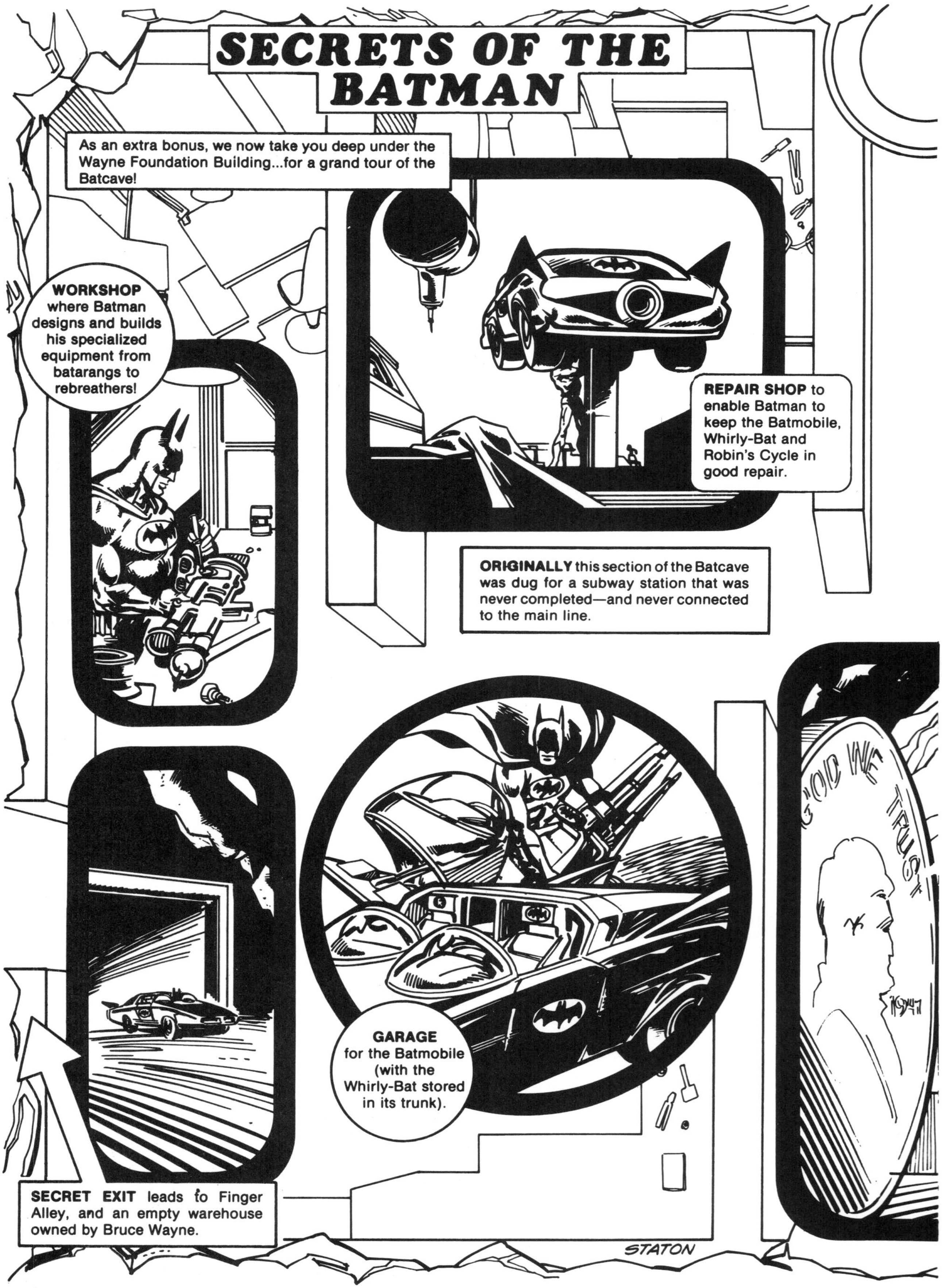
SECRETS OF THE BATMAN
As an extra bonus, we now take you deep under the Wayne Foundation Building...for a grand tour of the Batcave!
WORKSHOP where Batman designs and builds his specialized equipment from batarangs to rebreathers!
REPAIR SHOP to enable Batman to keep the Batmobile, Whirly-Bat and Robin's Cycle in good repair.
ORIGINALLY this section of the Batcave was dug for a subway station that was never completed—and never connected to the main line.
GARAGE for the Batmobile (with the Whirly-Bat stored in its trunk).
GOD WE TRUST
SECRET EXIT leads to Finger Alley, and an empty warehouse owned by Bruce Wayne.
STATON

The Untold Legend of the Batman *#3, September 1980, ''Secrets of the Batman,'' pp. 1–3.*

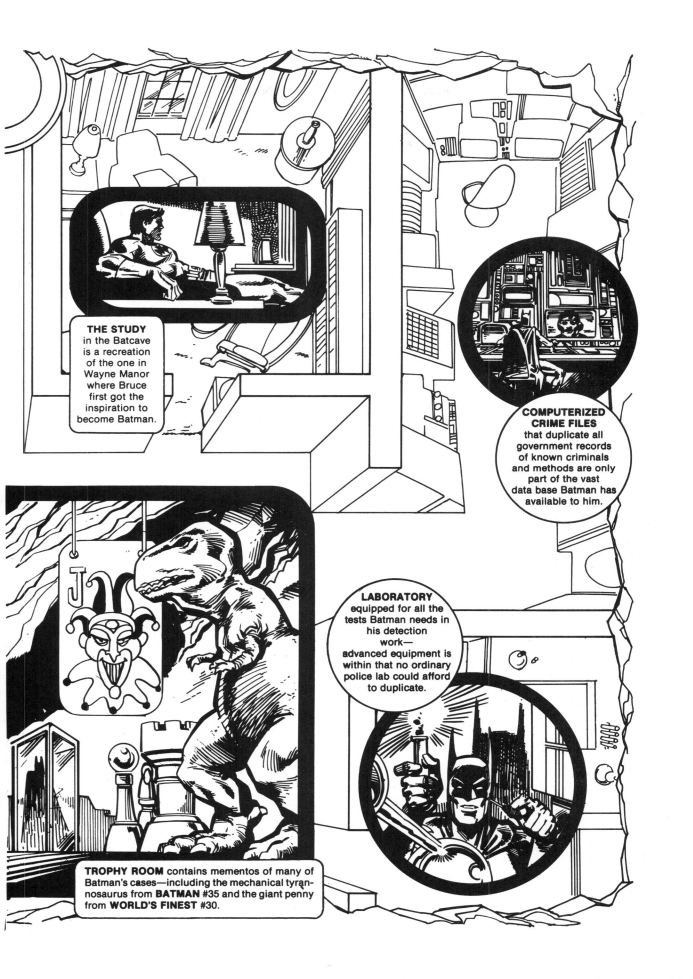

THE STUDY in the Batcave is a recreation of the one in Wayne Manor where Bruce first got the inspiration to become Batman.

COMPUTERIZED CRIME FILES that duplicate all government records of known criminals and methods are only part of the vast data base Batman has available to him.

LABORATORY equipped for all the tests Batman needs in his detection work—advanced equipment is within that no ordinary police lab could afford to duplicate.

TROPHY ROOM contains mementos of many of Batman's cases—including the mechanical tyrannosaurus from **BATMAN** #35 and the giant penny from **WORLD'S FINEST** #30.

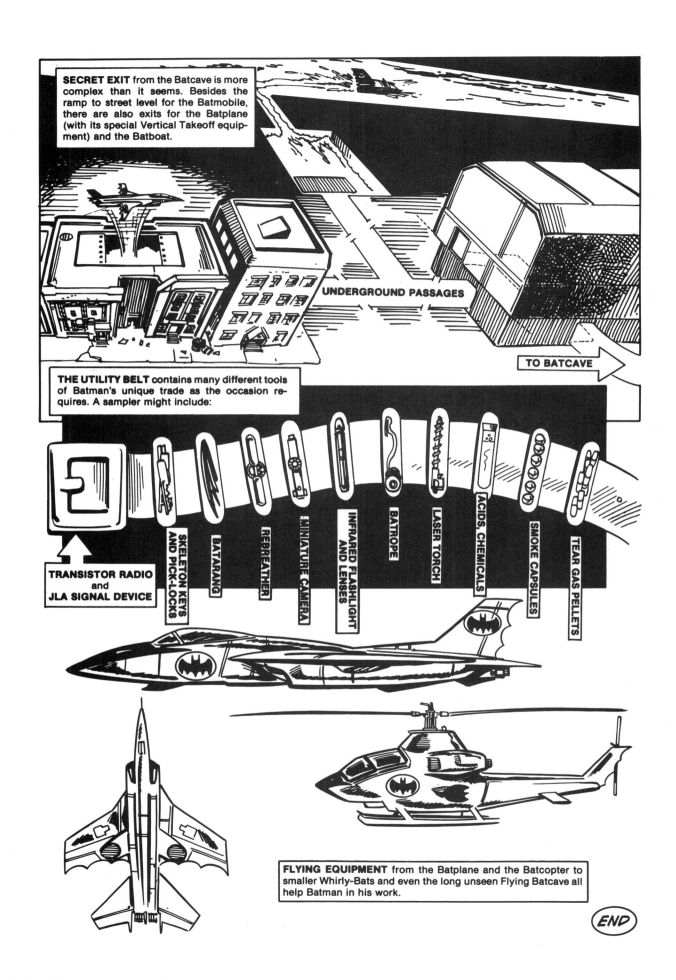

SECRET EXIT from the Batcave is more complex than it seems. Besides the ramp to street level for the Batmobile, there are also exits for the Batplane (with its special Vertical Takeoff equipment) and the Batboat.

UNDERGROUND PASSAGES

TO BATCAVE

THE UTILITY BELT contains many different tools of Batman's unique trade as the occasion requires. A sampler might include:

TRANSISTOR RADIO and JLA SIGNAL DEVICE

SKELETON KEYS AND PICK-LOCKS

BATARANG

REBREATHER

MINIATURE CAMERA

INFRARED FLASHLIGHT AND LENSES

BATROPE

LASER TORCH

ACIDS, CHEMICALS

SMOKE CAPSULES

TEAR GAS PELLETS

FLYING EQUIPMENT from the Batplane and the Batcopter to smaller Whirly-Bats and even the long unseen Flying Batcave all help Batman in his work.

END

tear trickled down the cheek of a manchild more comfortable battling an evil villain than dealing with the heartache of a long good-bye.

Once back inside the house, Bruce revealed, to Alfred's astonishment, his plan to close down the Bat Cave and move the entire Batman operation to Gotham City.

"Dick's leaving brought home the stark fact that our private world has changed," Bruce said with a grim determination previously seen only when he was outfitted in his Batman costume. "We're in grave danger of becoming outmoded! Obsolete dodos of the mod world outside! Our best chance for survival is to close up shop here!"

"Oh-h... no, Master Bruce!" Alfred interjected. "H-how will—er—we function as the crimefighters of old?"

"By becoming new—streamlining the operation," Bruce answers. "By discarding the paraphernalia of the past and functioning with the clothes on our backs... the wits in our heads! By re-establishing this trademark of the 'old' Batman—to strike new fear into the new breed of gangsterism sweeping the world!

"Today this new breed of rat uses the modern weapons of 'phony respectability,' 'big business fronts,' 'legal cover-ups,' and hides in the fortress towers of Gotham's metropolis. We're moving out of this suburban sanctuary, to live in the heart of that sprawling urban blight—to dig them out where they live and fatten on the innocent....

"We suffer great pain over true justice—'rights of the individual,' 'innocent until proven guilty'— all for the accused parties! But what about the 'proven' innocent—the victims?

"Innocent victims such as Dick and I were—when our parents were brutally slain! Their deaths were the births of Batman and Robin! We were in the fortunate position to claim justice for ourselves—but what of the less fortunates?"

Almost in the same breath a determined Bruce Wayne described his vision of Wayne Foundation lobbying for public funds to aid victims of crime.[3]

This was a Batman renewal, a rededication to his "Crime Does Not Pay" idealism of the Golden Age.

But despite these changes of the late sixties and seventies (a time when the watchword was "relevance"), the thrills and chills would continue. Some things never change.

And that, of course, meant the constant challenge of those terrible traps.

3. "One Bullet Too Many," *Batman* 217 (December 1969), pp. 1–6.

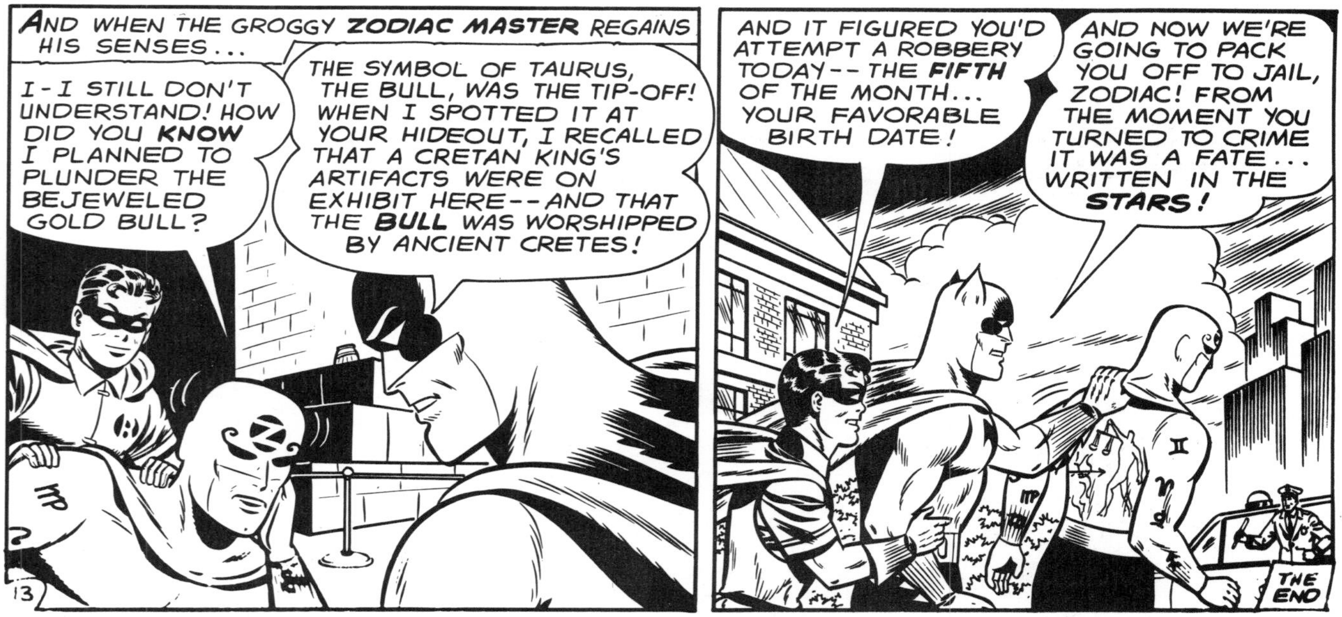

AND WHEN THE GROGGY ZODIAC MASTER REGAINS HIS SENSES...
I-I STILL DON'T UNDERSTAND! HOW DID YOU KNOW I PLANNED TO PLUNDER THE BEJEWELED GOLD BULL?
THE SYMBOL OF TAURUS, THE BULL, WAS THE TIP-OFF! WHEN I SPOTTED IT AT YOUR HIDEOUT, I RECALLED THAT A CRETAN KING'S ARTIFACTS WERE ON EXHIBIT HERE--AND THAT THE BULL WAS WORSHIPPED BY ANCIENT CRETES!
13
AND IT FIGURED YOU'D ATTEMPT A ROBBERY TODAY--THE FIFTH OF THE MONTH... YOUR FAVORABLE BIRTH DATE!
AND NOW WE'RE GOING TO PACK YOU OFF TO JAIL, ZODIAC! FROM THE MOMENT YOU TURNED TO CRIME IT WAS A FATE... WRITTEN IN THE STARS!
THE END

In any war of wits with the underworld, bet on Batman to be holding the trump card at the end game. (*Detective #323, January 1964, "The Zodiac Master!" p. 13 [select panels].*)

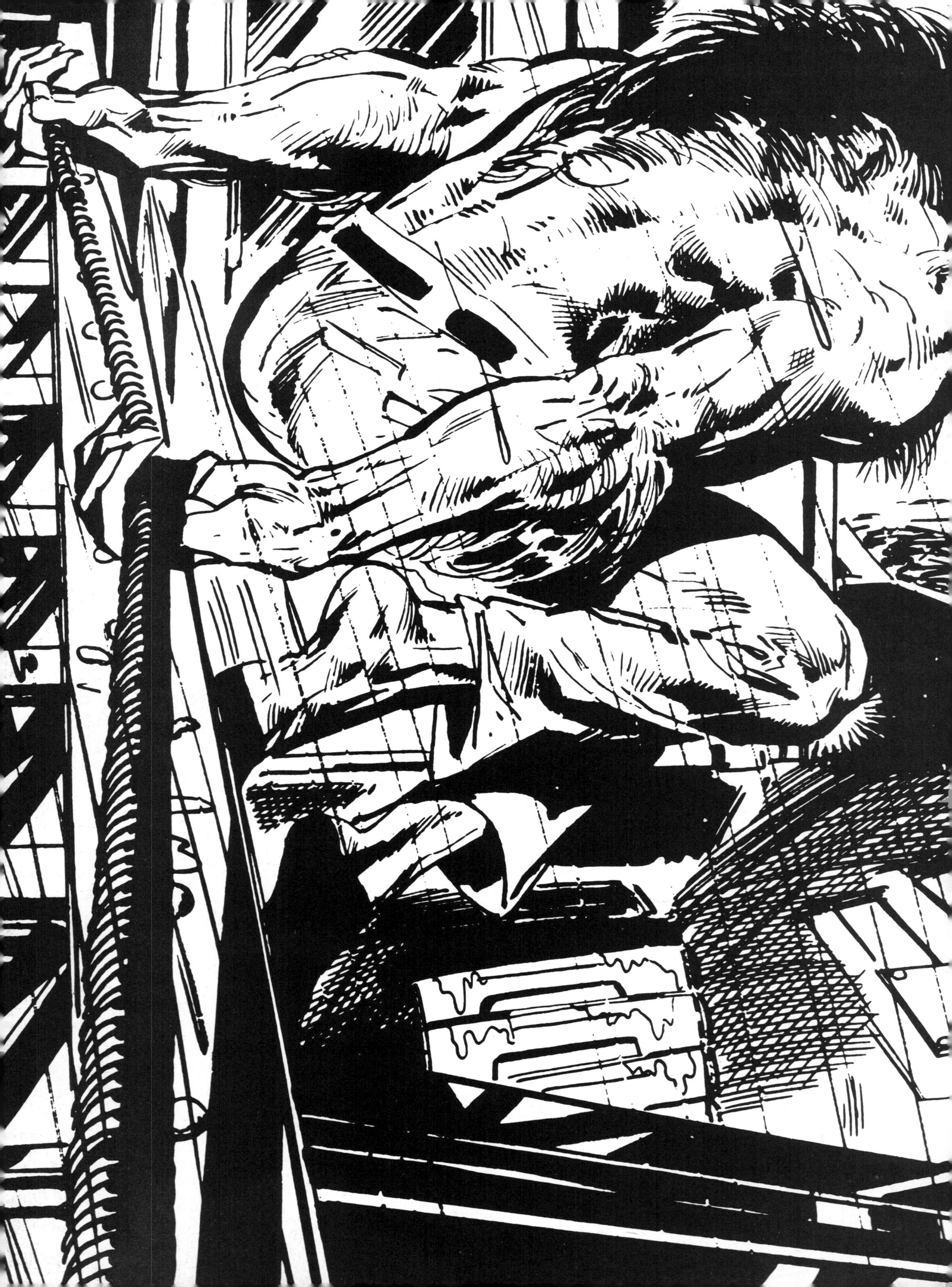

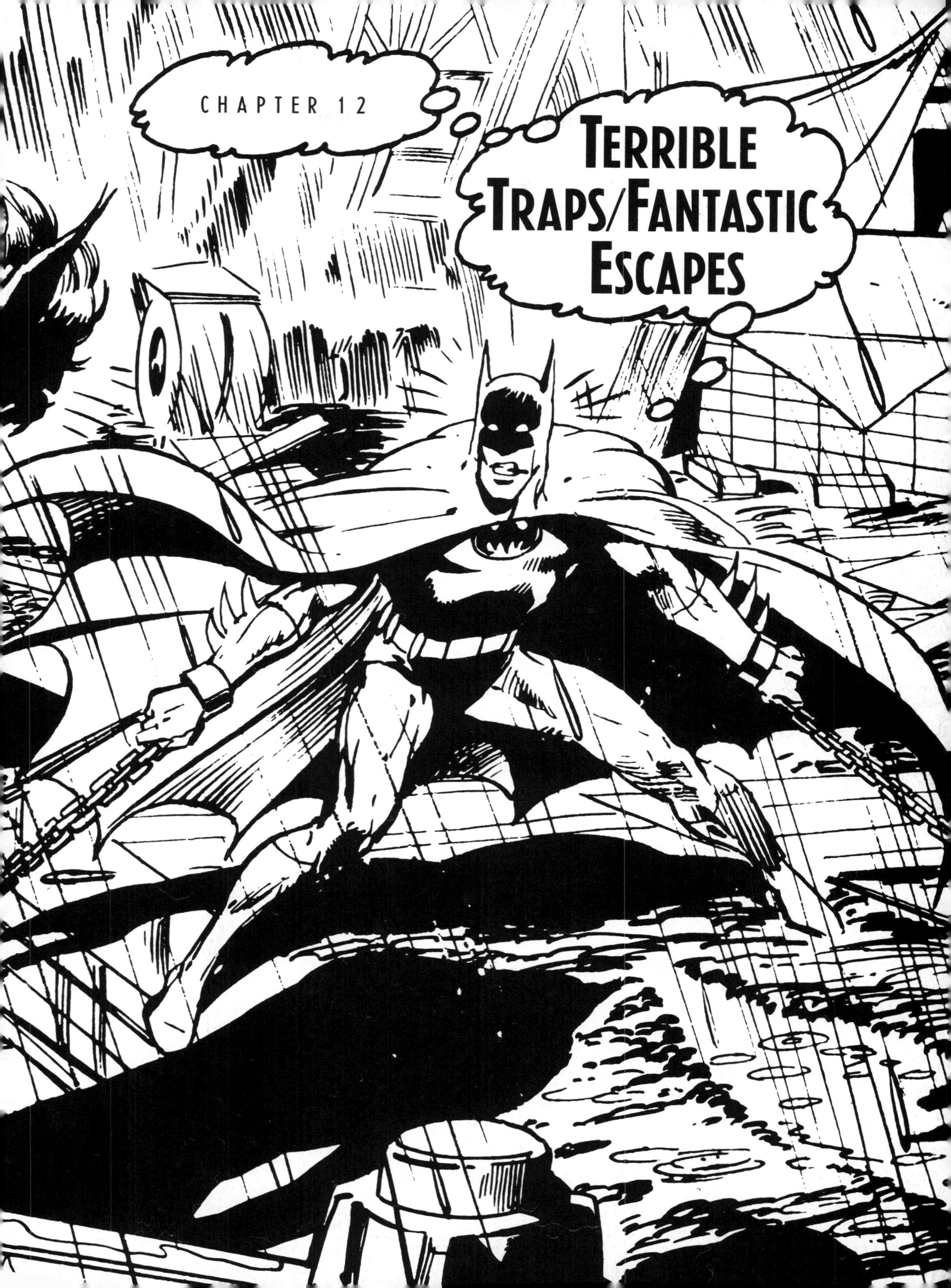
CHAPTER 12
TERRIBLE TRAPS/FANTASTIC ESCAPES

IMAGINE BEING SHACKLED WITH CHAINS AT a construction site while above you a monstrous werewolf gets set to pounce. Maybe you're locked in a mechanical prison as a deadly gas begins to pour in through unseen vents. Perhaps, in some horrible nightmare, you find yourself struggling in a pit that is filling up with water, the buoyancy lifting you up to a mounted machine gun blasting away overhead.

Such scenarios would surely mean death to us but are just a few of the on-the-job hazards the Dark Knight has survived.

The superhero who does not have the talent for trap busting will have a very short career, indeed. For a mortal crime fighter like Batman, it means that he must use his brain to figure a way out, while his willpower must eliminate any paralyzing panic as the seconds tick away and death gets closer.

"With Batman the hard part was getting him into a very clever trap and then having him do a more clever thing to get out of the trap," Julius Schwartz remembers. "It's like in the movies where boy meet girl, boy gets girl, boy loses girl, boy gets her back: Batman goes after villain, Batman gets caught in trap, escapes, and captures villain."

The difficulty the creators have in engineering a Batman deathtrap escape is the same factor that makes the Dark Knight prey to villainous ambushes: his mortal vulnerability.

Batman can't vibrate his atoms at superspeed to pass through containing walls, or use laser vision to cut through ropes, or punch through the offending obstacle with a mighty fist.

It's just the trap and Batman, with life or death in the bargain. Sometimes the Dark Knight's muscles or an adroitly mixed batch of chemicals from his utility belt have sprung him. But usually it has been his logic that figured a way to save the day. As Batman himself has said: "Every trap contains its own escape."

Let's once again thrill to Batman's incomparable escape techniques.

WHILE, ACROSS THE STREET, A DRIVING RAIN STIRS A BAT-CLOAKED FIGURE TO AWARENESS ONCE AGAIN...
UUNNHH-- DON'T KNOW WHAT LUPUS DRUGGED ME WITH-- BUT MY HEAD FEELS LIKE A HALF-CRAZED RHINO HAS BEEN DANCING ON--!
HEY-- WHAT IS THIS? CHAINED-- IN A CONSTRUCTION SITE--?
WHAT KIND OF WARPED REASON COULD LUPUS HAVE FOR DOING THIS?
I CAN FIGURE THAT AFTER I FREE MYSELF FROM THESE THINGS--
HAFTA PICK IT UP WITH MY TEETH-- BUT BEGGARS CAN'T BE PARTICULAR!
--AND I SPY A TWISTED COTTER PIN THAT SHOULD BE PERFECT TO HELP ME UNLOCK THEM!
GOT IT! TASTES TERRIBLE-- BUT I'M NOT GOING TO EAT IT-- JUST--
RRAAARRGGH!
WHAT IN--?
HIM AGAIN?
IN SOME TWISTED FASHION, THIS IS BEGINNING TO MAKE SENSE!

THIS CHARACTER IS DEFINITELY NOT WEARING A MASK--
--AND I GET THE UNPLEASANT FEELING LUPUS SET ME UP TO BE ITS DINNER!
WELL, I HATE TO DISAPPOINT HIM...
--BUT I DON'T PLAN ON BEING THE MAIN COURSE ON ANYBODY'S-- UNNFF!
AND HE WORKS VERY FAST INDEED--FOR THE CAPED CRUSADER HAS SPENT MANY HOURS FOR MANY YEARS LEARNING HOW TO PICK THE MOST COMPLICATED LOCKS WITH THE MOST OUTLANDISH TOOLS...
WHEW! --IT WORKED! MY EARS ARE RINGING FROM THAT SHOT-- BUT SHAGGY FARED WORSE!
HE SHOULD STAY DAZED LONG ENOUGH FOR ME TO PICK THESE BLASTED LOCKS --IF I WORK FAST!
HE'S UP AGAIN-- IN LESS THAN HALF THE TIME I FIGURED!

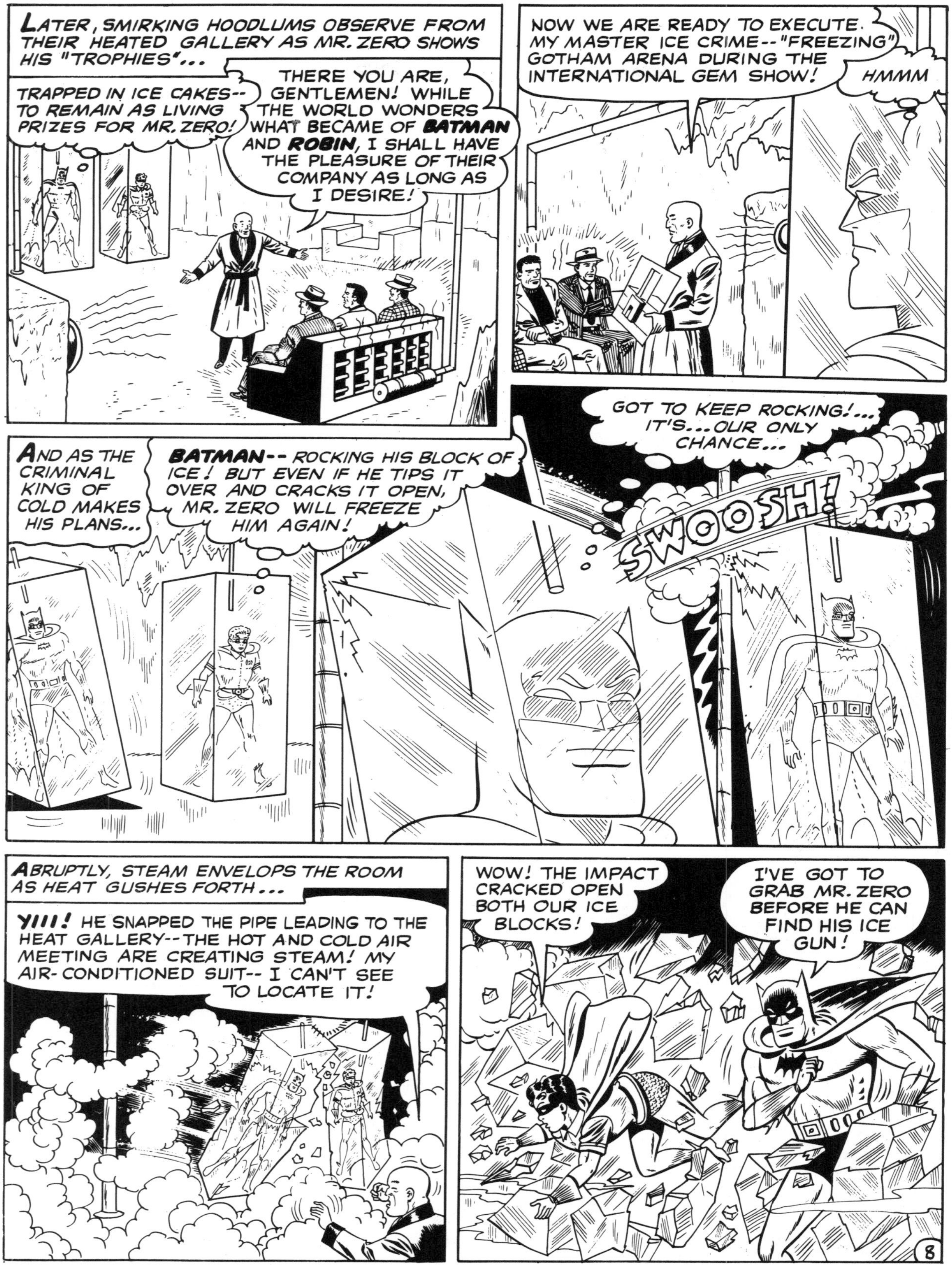
LATER, SMIRKING HOODLUMS OBSERVE FROM THEIR HEATED GALLERY AS MR. ZERO SHOWS HIS "TROPHIES"...
TRAPPED IN ICE CAKES-- TO REMAIN AS LIVING PRIZES FOR MR. ZERO!
THERE YOU ARE, GENTLEMEN! WHILE THE WORLD WONDERS WHAT BECAME OF BATMAN AND ROBIN, I SHALL HAVE THE PLEASURE OF THEIR COMPANY AS LONG AS I DESIRE!
NOW WE ARE READY TO EXECUTE MY MASTER ICE CRIME--"FREEZING" GOTHAM ARENA DURING THE INTERNATIONAL GEM SHOW!
HMMM
AND AS THE CRIMINAL KING OF COLD MAKES HIS PLANS...
BATMAN-- ROCKING HIS BLOCK OF ICE! BUT EVEN IF HE TIPS IT OVER AND CRACKS IT OPEN, MR. ZERO WILL FREEZE HIM AGAIN!
GOT TO KEEP ROCKING!... IT'S...OUR ONLY CHANCE...
SWOOSH!
ABRUPTLY, STEAM ENVELOPS THE ROOM AS HEAT GUSHES FORTH...
YIII! HE SNAPPED THE PIPE LEADING TO THE HEAT GALLERY--THE HOT AND COLD AIR MEETING ARE CREATING STEAM! MY AIR-CONDITIONED SUIT-- I CAN'T SEE TO LOCATE IT!
WOW! THE IMPACT CRACKED OPEN BOTH OUR ICE BLOCKS!
I'VE GOT TO GRAB MR. ZERO BEFORE HE CAN FIND HIS ICE GUN!
8

Above: *Batman cracks the Big Chill trap of Mr. Zero.* (**Batman** *#121, February 1959, ''The Ice Crimes of Mr. Zero,'' p. 8.*) **Left:** *A hungry werewolf adds a bit of tension as Batman tries to unshackle himself (Houdini never had to deal with this kind of pressure!).* (**Batman** *#255, March/April 1974, ''Moon of the Wolf,'' pp. 15–16.*)

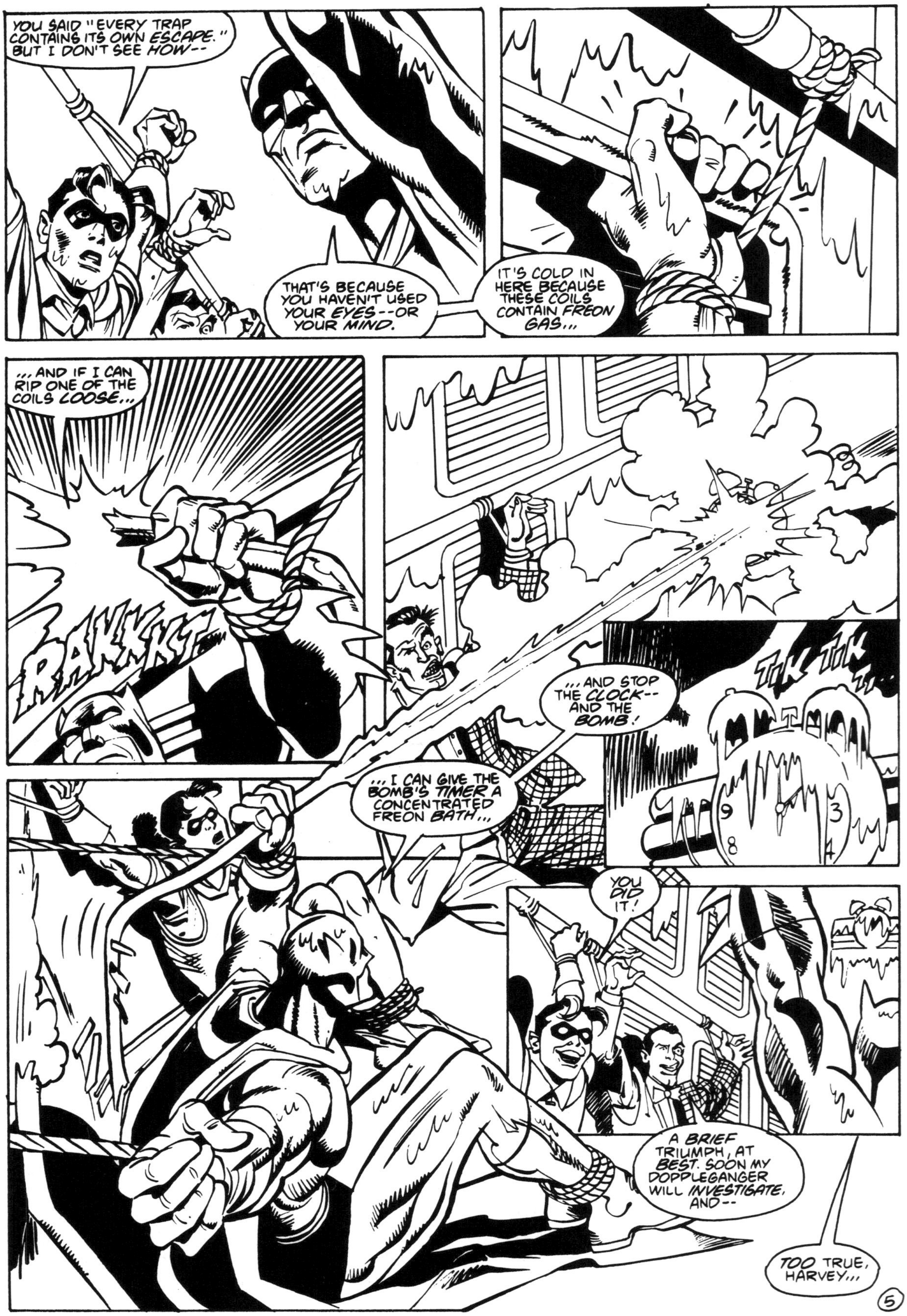
YOU SAID "EVERY TRAP CONTAINS ITS OWN ESCAPE." BUT I DON'T SEE HOW--
THAT'S BECAUSE YOU HAVEN'T USED YOUR EYES--OR YOUR MIND.
IT'S COLD IN HERE BECAUSE THESE COILS CONTAIN FREON GAS...
...AND IF I CAN RIP ONE OF THE COILS LOOSE...
RAKKK
...I CAN GIVE THE BOMB'S TIMER A CONCENTRATED FREON BATH...
...AND STOP THE CLOCK--AND THE BOMB!
TIK TIK
YOU DID IT!
A BRIEF TRIUMPH, AT BEST. SOON MY DOPPLEGANGER WILL INVESTIGATE, AND--
TOO TRUE, HARVEY...
5

The Jason Todd Robin and Harvey Dent happily experience the Dark Knight's masterful escape technique. (**Detective** *#581, December 1987, ''One Out of Two . . . Isn't Bad . . . ,''p. 5.*)

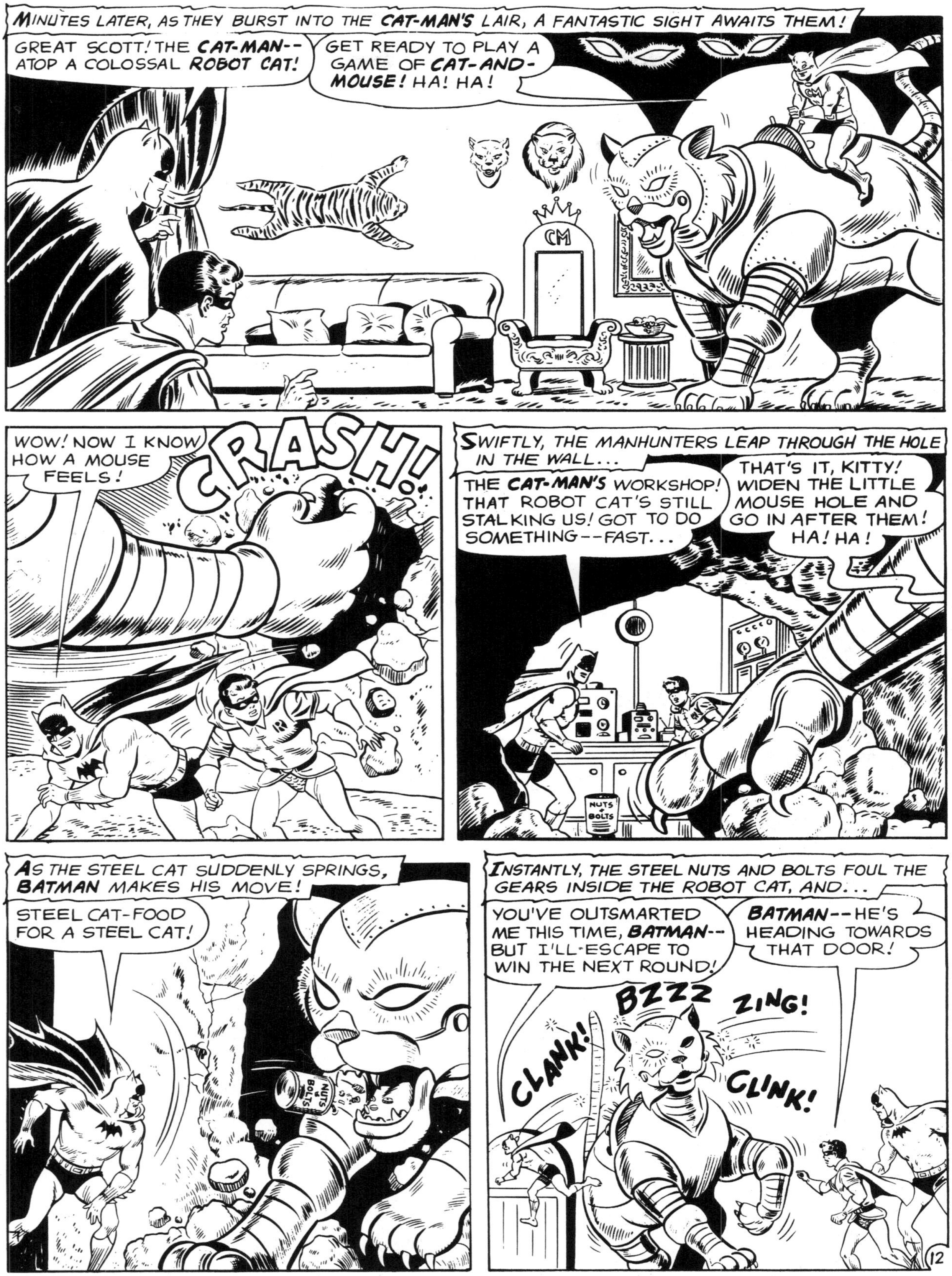
MINUTES LATER, AS THEY BURST INTO THE CAT-MAN'S LAIR, A FANTASTIC SIGHT AWAITS THEM!
GREAT SCOTT! THE CAT-MAN-- ATOP A COLOSSAL ROBOT CAT!
GET READY TO PLAY A GAME OF CAT-AND-MOUSE! HA! HA!
CM
WOW! NOW I KNOW HOW A MOUSE FEELS!
CRASH!
SWIFTLY, THE MANHUNTERS LEAP THROUGH THE HOLE IN THE WALL...
THE CAT-MAN'S WORKSHOP! THAT ROBOT CAT'S STILL STALKING US! GOT TO DO SOMETHING--FAST...
THAT'S IT, KITTY! WIDEN THE LITTLE MOUSE HOLE AND GO IN AFTER THEM! HA! HA!
NUTS & BOLTS
AS THE STEEL CAT SUDDENLY SPRINGS, BATMAN MAKES HIS MOVE!
STEEL CAT-FOOD FOR A STEEL CAT!
INSTANTLY, THE STEEL NUTS AND BOLTS FOUL THE GEARS INSIDE THE ROBOT CAT, AND...
YOU'VE OUTSMARTED ME THIS TIME, BATMAN-- BUT I'LL ESCAPE TO WIN THE NEXT ROUND!
BATMAN--HE'S HEADING TOWARDS THAT DOOR!
BZZZ
ZING!
CLANK!
CLINK!
12

Batman's talent of keeping his head in a crisis has helped him find a way out of the most dangerous situation. Here a well-thrown bucket of bolts stops Catman's robot monster. (Detective *#311, January 1963, "Challenge of the Cat-Man," p. 12.*)

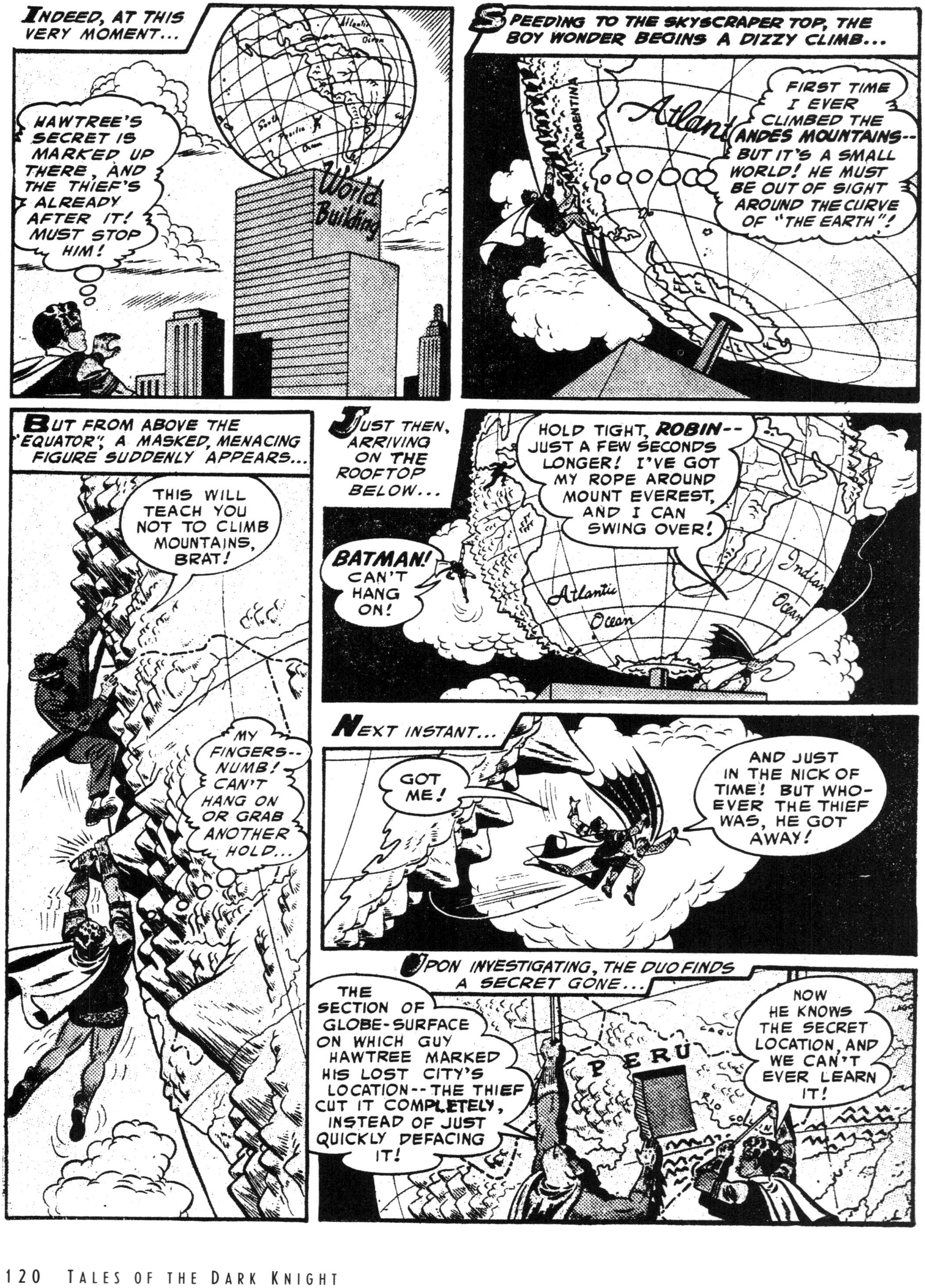
INDEED, AT THIS VERY MOMENT...
HAWTREE'S SECRET IS MARKED UP THERE, AND THE THIEF'S ALREADY AFTER IT! MUST STOP HIM!
World Building
SPEEDING TO THE SKYSCRAPER TOP, THE BOY WONDER BEGINS A DIZZY CLIMB...
FIRST TIME I EVER CLIMBED THE ANDES MOUNTAINS-- BUT IT'S A SMALL WORLD! HE MUST BE OUT OF SIGHT AROUND THE CURVE OF "THE EARTH"!
ARGENTINA
BUT FROM ABOVE THE "EQUATOR", A MASKED, MENACING FIGURE SUDDENLY APPEARS...
THIS WILL TEACH YOU NOT TO CLIMB MOUNTAINS, BRAT!
MY FINGERS-- NUMB! CAN'T HANG ON OR GRAB ANOTHER HOLD...
JUST THEN, ARRIVING ON THE ROOFTOP BELOW...
HOLD TIGHT, ROBIN-- JUST A FEW SECONDS LONGER! I'VE GOT MY ROPE AROUND MOUNT EVEREST, AND I CAN SWING OVER!
BATMAN! CAN'T HANG ON!
Atlantic Ocean
Indian Ocean
NEXT INSTANT...
GOT ME!
AND JUST IN THE NICK OF TIME! BUT WHO-EVER THE THIEF WAS, HE GOT AWAY!
UPON INVESTIGATING, THE DUO FINDS A SECRET GONE...
THE SECTION OF GLOBE-SURFACE ON WHICH GUY HAWTREE MARKED HIS LOST CITY'S LOCATION--THE THIEF CUT IT COMPLETELY, INSTEAD OF JUST QUICKLY DEFACING IT!
NOW HE KNOWS THE SECRET LOCATION, AND WE CAN'T EVER LEARN IT!
PERU

Right: *Hey kids! Stick with those science classes and you too can master the best-laid traps of evil villains!* (Batman #8, *December/January 1942, "Stone Walls Do Not a Prison Make!" p. 11 [panel].*) **Bottom:** *The Dynamic Duo will defeat even this seemingly unbeatable trap.* (Detective #309, *August 1962, "The Wizard of 1,000 Menaces," p. 9 [select panels].*) **Left:** *Another cliff-hanging predicament—another thrilling escape.* (Batman #91, *April 1955, "The Map of Mystery!" p. 6.*)

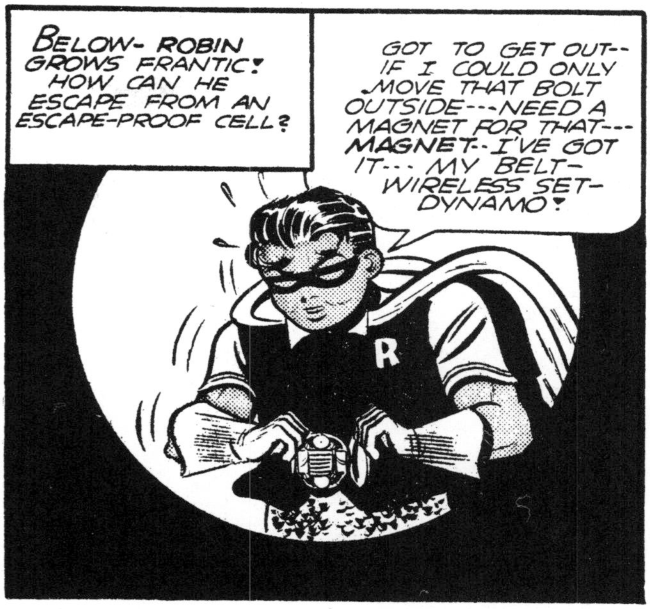
BELOW- ROBIN GROWS FRANTIC! HOW CAN HE ESCAPE FROM AN ESCAPE-PROOF CELL?
GOT TO GET OUT-- IF I COULD ONLY MOVE THAT BOLT OUTSIDE---NEED A MAGNET FOR THAT--- MAGNET--I'VE GOT IT--- MY BELT-WIRELESS SET-DYNAMO!
R

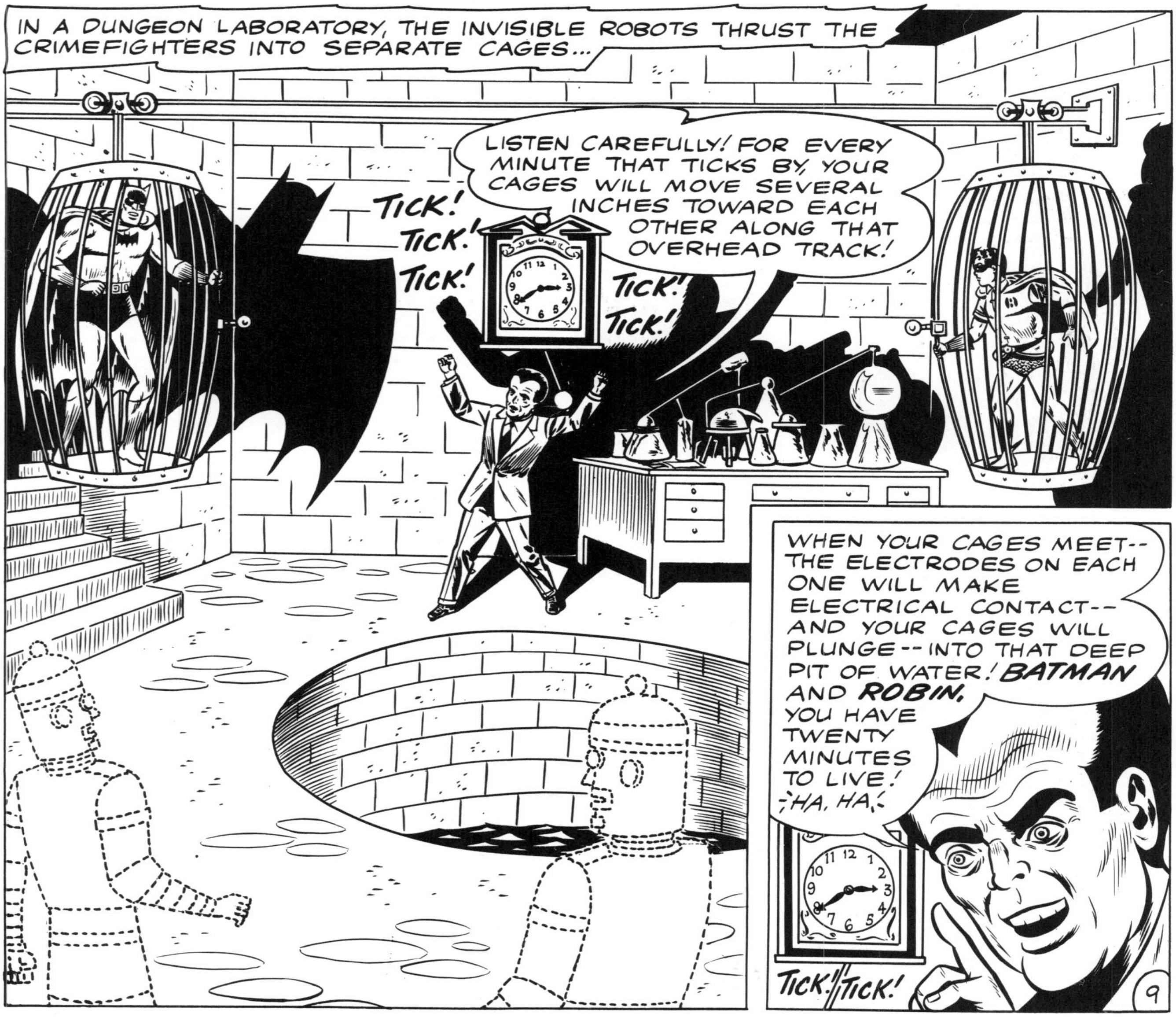
IN A DUNGEON LABORATORY, THE INVISIBLE ROBOTS THRUST THE CRIMEFIGHTERS INTO SEPARATE CAGES...
LISTEN CAREFULLY! FOR EVERY MINUTE THAT TICKS BY, YOUR CAGES WILL MOVE SEVERAL INCHES TOWARD EACH OTHER ALONG THAT OVERHEAD TRACK!
TICK! TICK! TICK!
TICK! TICK!
WHEN YOUR CAGES MEET-- THE ELECTRODES ON EACH ONE WILL MAKE ELECTRICAL CONTACT-- AND YOUR CAGES WILL PLUNGE--INTO THAT DEEP PIT OF WATER! BATMAN AND ROBIN, YOU HAVE TWENTY MINUTES TO LIVE! HA, HA!
TICK! TICK!
9

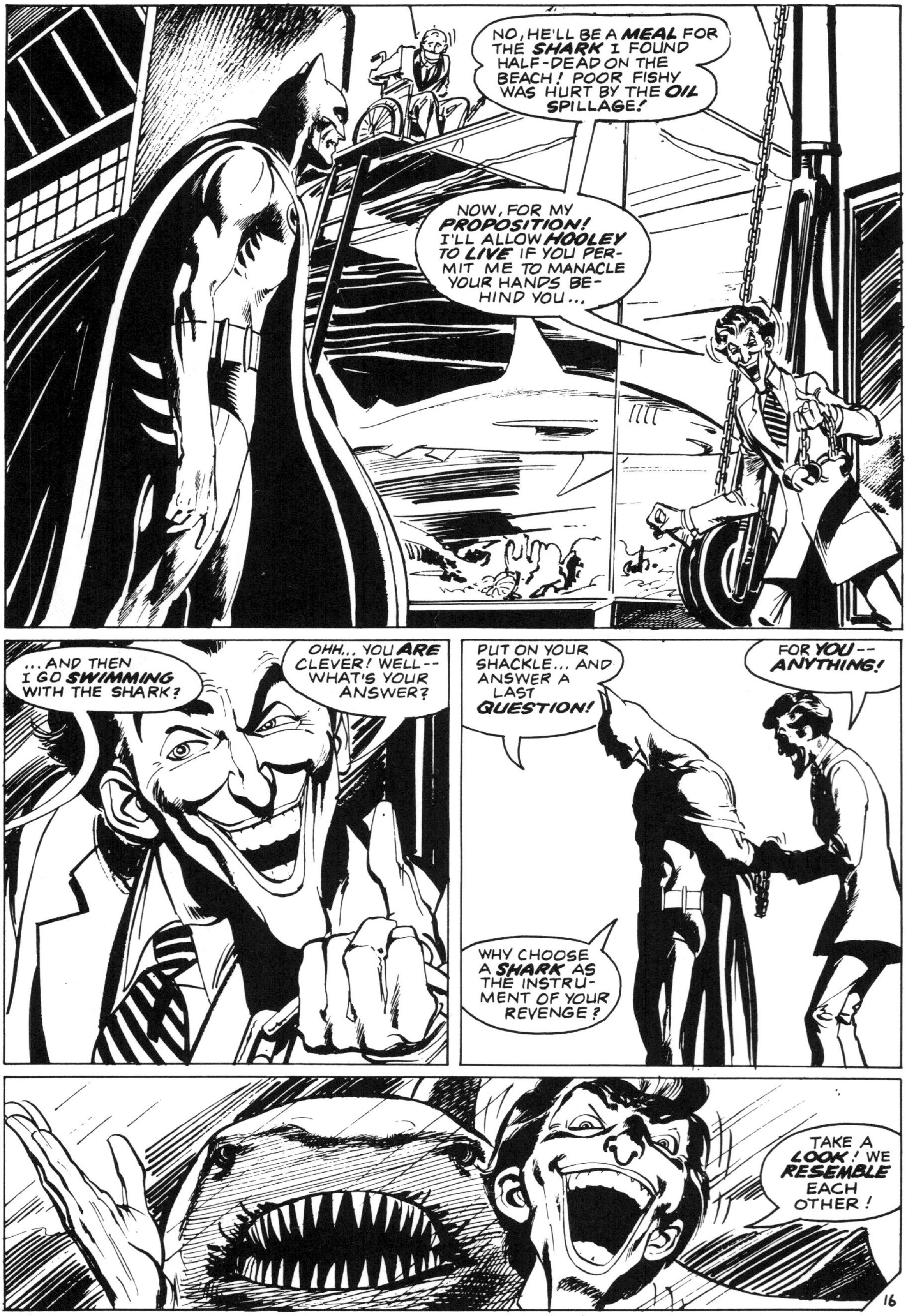
NO, HE'LL BE A MEAL FOR THE SHARK I FOUND HALF-DEAD ON THE BEACH! POOR FISHY WAS HURT BY THE OIL SPILLAGE!
NOW, FOR MY PROPOSITION! I'LL ALLOW HOOLEY TO LIVE IF YOU PERMIT ME TO MANACLE YOUR HANDS BEHIND YOU...
...AND THEN I GO SWIMMING WITH THE SHARK?
OHH... YOU ARE CLEVER! WELL-- WHAT'S YOUR ANSWER?
PUT ON YOUR SHACKLE... AND ANSWER A LAST QUESTION!
FOR YOU-- ANYTHING!
WHY CHOOSE A SHARK AS THE INSTRUMENT OF YOUR REVENGE?
TAKE A LOOK! WE RESEMBLE EACH OTHER!
16

Of all Batman's foes, the Joker has consistently set the deadliest traps. Thrill to this Joker masterpiece—and say a prayer for the Dark Knight. (**Batman** *#251, September 1973, "The Joker's Five-Way Revenge!" pp. 16–20.*)

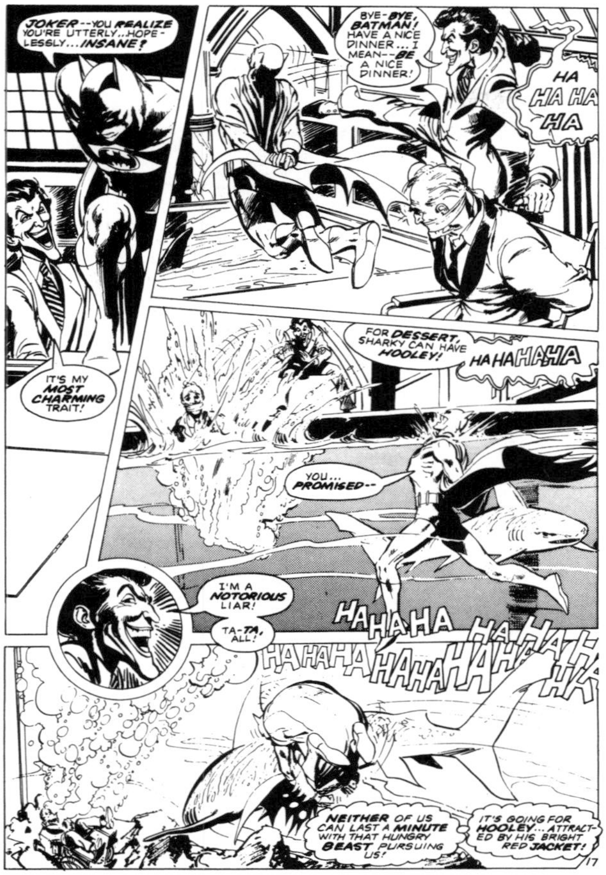
JOKER--YOU REALIZE YOU'RE UTTERLY...HOPE-LESSLY...INSANE?
BYE-BYE, BATMAN! HAVE A NICE DINNER... I MEAN--BE A NICE DINNER!
HA HA HA HA HA
IT'S MY MOST CHARMING TRAIT!
FOR DESSERT, SHARKY CAN HAVE HOOLEY!
HAHAHAHAHA
YOU... PROMISED--
I'M A NOTORIOUS LIAR!
TA-TA, ALL!
HAHAHA HAHAHA HAHAHAHAHAHAHAHA
NEITHER OF US CAN LAST A MINUTE WITH THAT HUNGRY BEAST PURSUING US!
IT'S GOING FOR HOOLEY... ATTRACT-ED BY HIS BRIGHT RED JACKET!
17

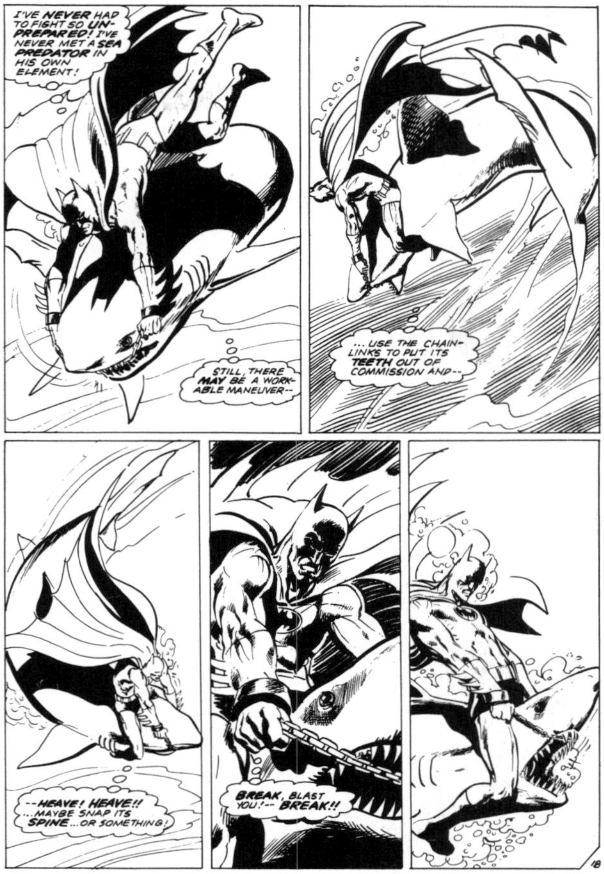
I'VE NEVER HAD TO FIGHT SO UN-PREPARED! I'VE NEVER MET A SEA PREDATOR IN HIS OWN ELEMENT!
STILL, THERE MAY BE A WORK-ABLE MANEUVER--
...USE THE CHAIN-LINKS TO PUT ITS TEETH OUT OF COMMISSION AND--
--HEAVE! HEAVE!! ...MAYBE SNAP ITS SPINE...OR SOMETHING!
BREAK, BLAST YOU!--BREAK!!
18

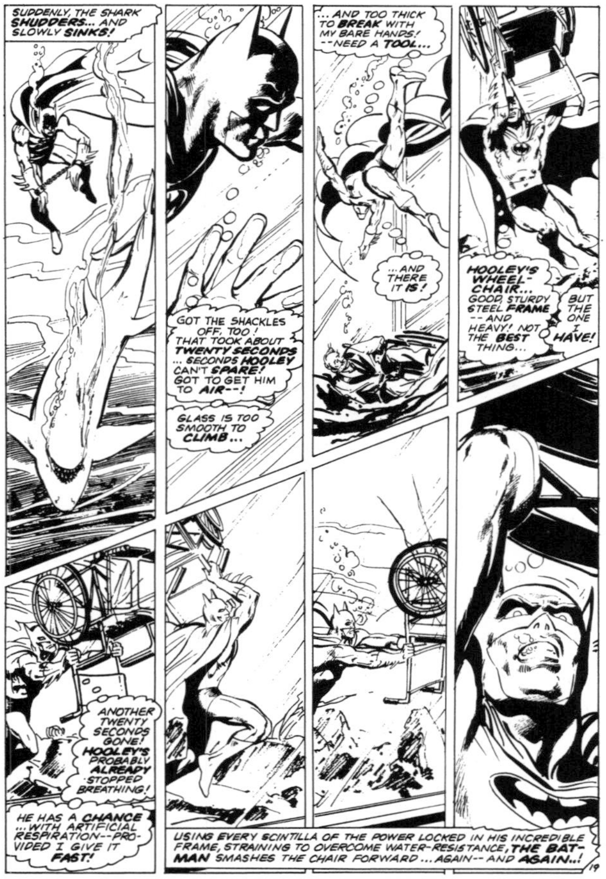
SUDDENLY, THE SHARK SHUDDERS... AND SLOWLY SINKS!
...AND TOO THICK TO BREAK WITH MY BARE HANDS! --NEED A TOOL...
...AND THERE IT IS!
HOOLEY'S WHEEL-CHAIR... GOOD, STURDY STEEL FRAME --AND HEAVY! NOT THE BEST THING...
BUT THE ONE I HAVE!
GOT THE SHACKLES OFF, TOO! THAT TOOK ABOUT TWENTY SECONDS ...SECONDS HOOLEY CAN'T SPARE! GOT TO GET HIM TO AIR--!
GLASS IS TOO SMOOTH TO CLIMB...
ANOTHER TWENTY SECONDS GONE! HOOLEY'S PROBABLY ALREADY STOPPED BREATHING!
HE HAS A CHANCE ...WITH ARTIFICIAL RESPIRATION--PRO-VIDED I GIVE IT FAST!
USING EVERY SCINTILLA OF THE POWER LOCKED IN HIS INCREDIBLE FRAME, STRAINING TO OVERCOME WATER-RESISTANCE, THE BATMAN SMASHES THE CHAIR FORWARD...AGAIN--AND AGAIN...!
19

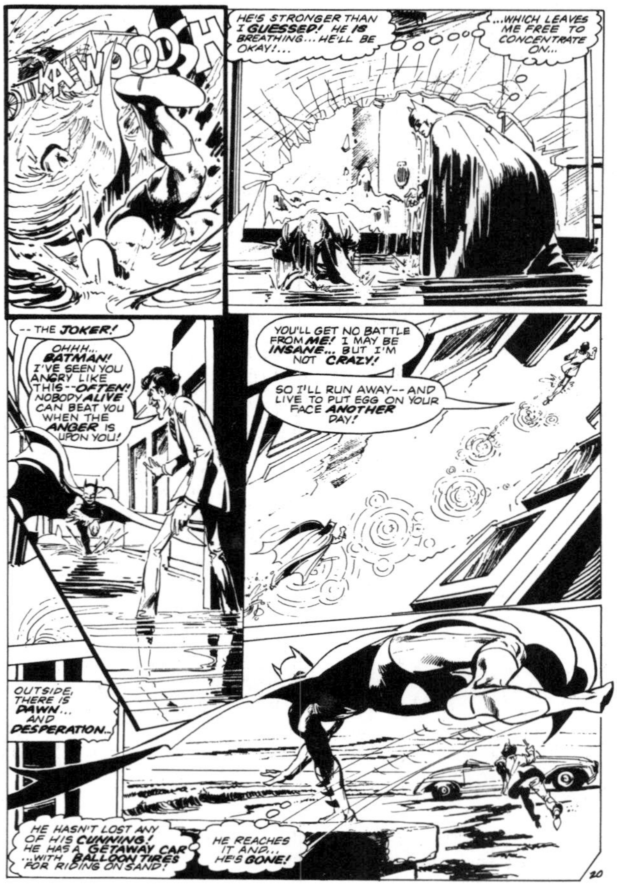
KAWOOOSH
HE'S STRONGER THAN I GUESSED! HE IS BREATHING... HE'LL BE OKAY!...
...WHICH LEAVES ME FREE TO CONCENTRATE ON...
--THE JOKER!
OHHH... BATMAN! I'VE SEEN YOU ANGRY LIKE THIS--OFTEN! NOBODY ALIVE CAN BEAT YOU WHEN THE ANGER IS UPON YOU!
YOU'LL GET NO BATTLE FROM ME! I MAY BE INSANE... BUT I'M NOT CRAZY!
SO I'LL RUN AWAY--AND LIVE TO PUT EGG ON YOUR FACE ANOTHER DAY!
OUTSIDE, THERE IS DAWN... AND DESPERATION...
HE HASN'T LOST ANY OF HIS CUNNING! HE HAS A GETAWAY CAR ...WITH BALLOON TIRES FOR RIDING ON SAND!
HE REACHES IT AND... HE'S GONE!
20

CHAPTER 13
THE LOVES OF BATMAN

Beneath the dark denim of that stern figure of the night . . . Batman! . . . beats a tender, generous heart! A heart that can be merciful to the unfortunate . . . and that can soften to the whispers of love!

—Batman 15, February/March 1943

FOR A VIRILE, PASSIONATE MAN SUCH AS Batman, it must be frustrating to steel himself against love's siren call, giving himself totally to his crime-fighting obsession. Part of that frustration stems from Bruce Wayne's millionaire playboy role, which has invited the attention of the most beautiful women in Gotham City.

Some students of the chronicles have read all sorts of hidden meanings into the bachelorhood of Batman/Bruce Wayne.

"The sudden, violent loss of his mother while he was still a boy, during the period of his childhood when his psyche was grappling with the complexity of his affectional and erotic feelings for her, left Bruce Wayne with a deep reservoir of unconscious hostility toward women," opines writer Michael L. Fleisher. "Like many orphaned children, he saw the death of his mother as a personal desertion. He loved and needed his mother, and yet she left him."[1]

It's perhaps more to the point that the Caped Crusader's only negative attitude toward women has been an old-fashioned chivalrous manner around the ladies. And although the Batman side has often inhibited the flowering of love, his crime-fighting vow did not prevent Bruce Wayne from romantic entanglements.

Early in his crime-fighting career, Bruce Wayne was briefly betrothed to Julie Madison, a raven-haired high-society beauty who constantly compared idle Bruce to the exciting Batman,

1. Fleisher, *Batman*, p. 95.

THIS IS MY FINISH. I GUESS I.... LOVED YOU ALL THE TIME. MR. BRUCE WAYNE. I'M GOING..... PLEASE, KISS ME...KISS ME BEFORE IT'S TOO LATE-
SHE KNEW I WAS BRUCE WAYNE??
THANKS-- OHH--
DEAD....
I--I DO LOVE YOU! I NEVER WANTED TO ADMIT IT BEFORE...
OH, BATMAN...
OH, I'M SO GLAD YOU'RE ALL RIGHT! I WAS SO WORRIED ABOUT YOU...
GOSH! YOU WERE? GEE, BAT-GIRL... I--I...
MMMMMMM!

Top: Batman #5, *Spring 1941, "The Riddle of the Missing Card," p. 11 [select panels]*. Bottom: *Well—what do you expect when crimefighters double date?* (Batman #*153, February 1963, "Prisoners of Three Worlds," pp. 16; 20 [select panels]*.)

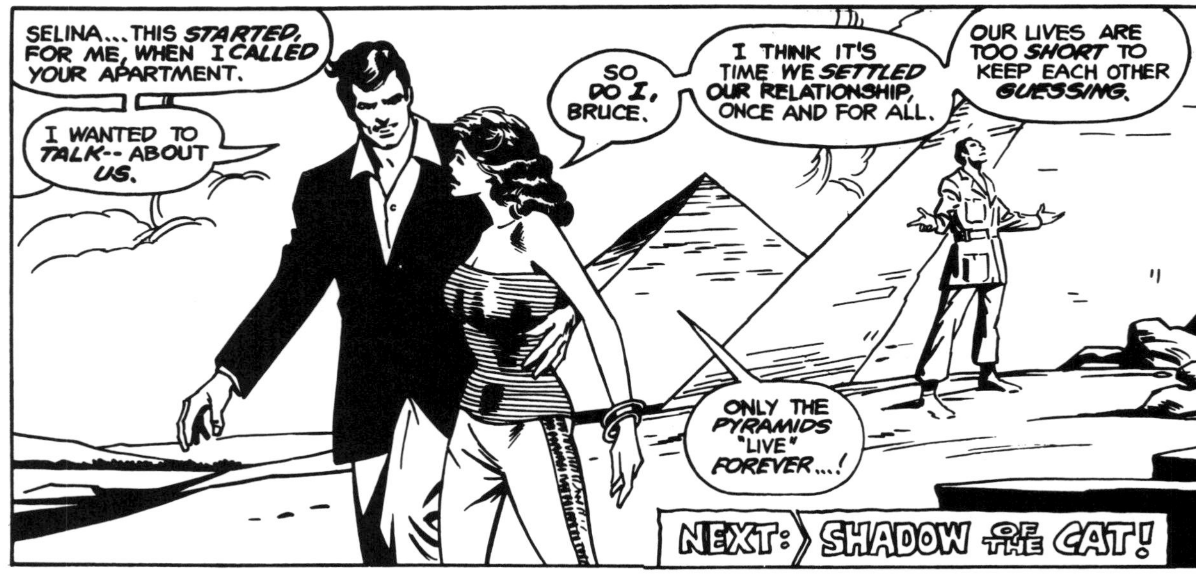

SELINA...THIS STARTED, FOR ME, WHEN I CALLED YOUR APARTMENT.
I WANTED TO TALK-- ABOUT US.
SO DO I, BRUCE.
I THINK IT'S TIME WE SETTLED OUR RELATIONSHIP, ONCE AND FOR ALL.
OUR LIVES ARE TOO SHORT TO KEEP EACH OTHER GUESSING.
ONLY THE PYRAMIDS "LIVE" FOREVER....!
NEXT: SHADOW OF THE CAT!

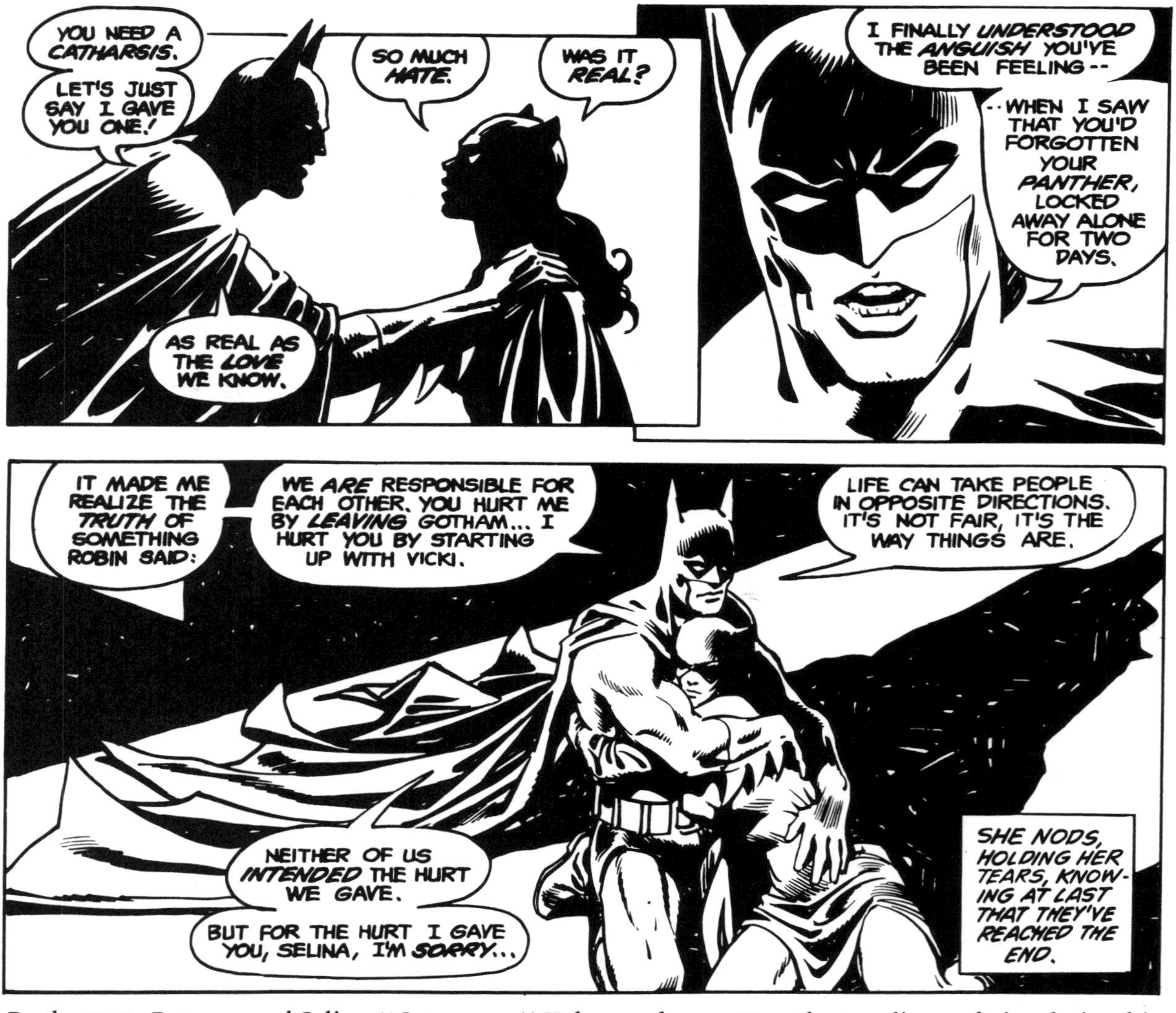

YOU NEED A CATHARSIS.
LET'S JUST SAY I GAVE YOU ONE!
SO MUCH HATE.
WAS IT REAL?
AS REAL AS THE LOVE WE KNOW.
I FINALLY UNDERSTOOD THE ANGUISH YOU'VE BEEN FEELING--
--WHEN I SAW THAT YOU'D FORGOTTEN YOUR PANTHER, LOCKED AWAY ALONE FOR TWO DAYS.
IT MADE ME REALIZE THE TRUTH OF SOMETHING ROBIN SAID:
WE ARE RESPONSIBLE FOR EACH OTHER. YOU HURT ME BY LEAVING GOTHAM... I HURT YOU BY STARTING UP WITH VICKI.
LIFE CAN TAKE PEOPLE IN OPPOSITE DIRECTIONS. IT'S NOT FAIR, IT'S THE WAY THINGS ARE.
NEITHER OF US INTENDED THE HURT WE GAVE.
BUT FOR THE HURT I GAVE YOU, SELINA, I'M SORRY...
SHE NODS, HOLDING HER TEARS, KNOWING AT LAST THAT THEY'VE REACHED THE END.

By the 1980s Batman and Selina ''Catwoman'' Kyle were lovers. Here the two discuss their relationship in the shadow of the pyramids. (Top: Detective *#508, November 1981, ''Secret of the Sphinx Sinister!'' p. 19 [panel].* Bottom: Batman *#355, January 1983, ''Never Scratch A Cat,'' p. 23 [select panels].*)

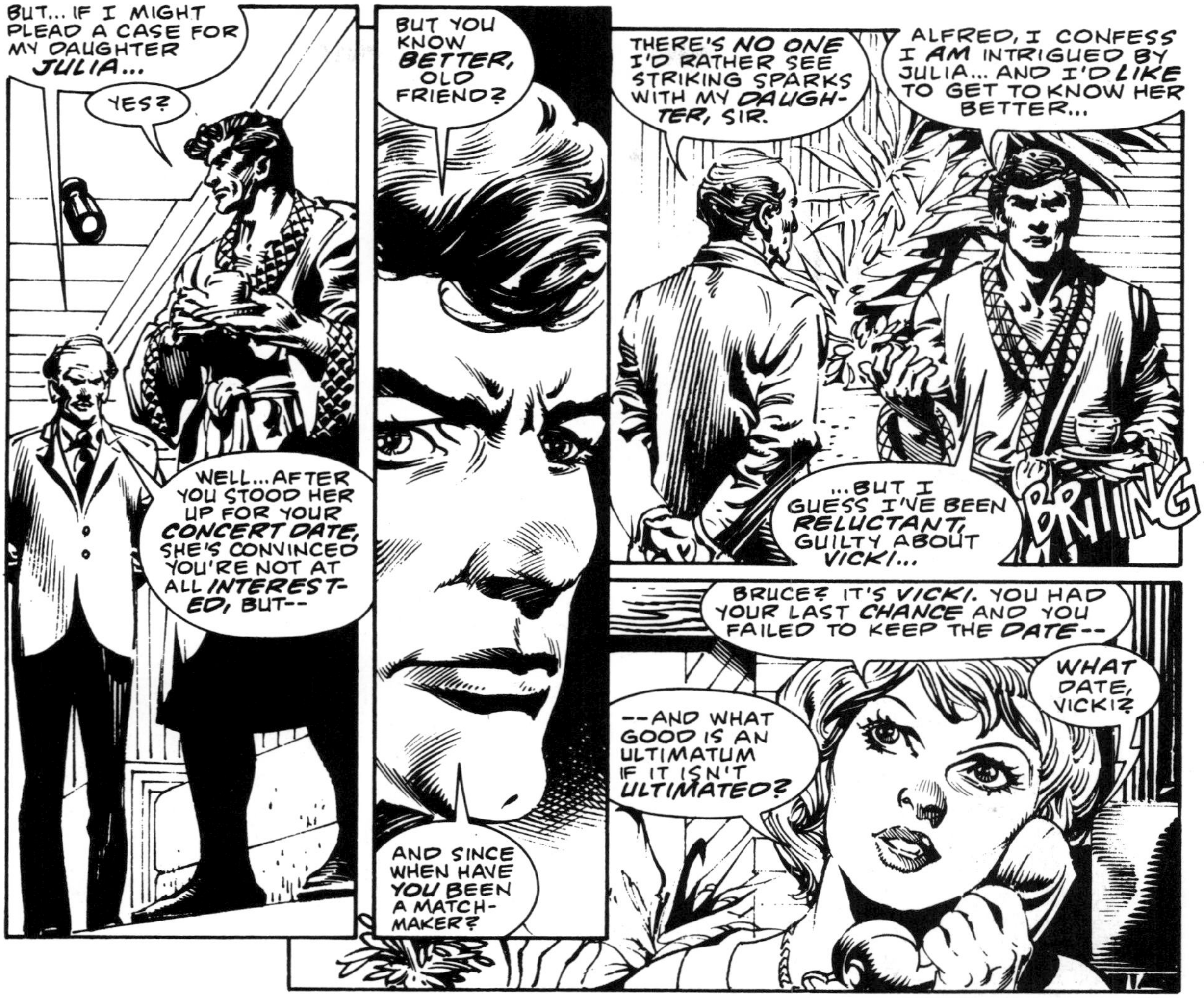
BUT... IF I MIGHT PLEAD A CASE FOR MY DAUGHTER JULIA...
YES?
WELL... AFTER YOU STOOD HER UP FOR YOUR CONCERT DATE, SHE'S CONVINCED YOU'RE NOT AT ALL INTEREST-ED, BUT--
BUT YOU KNOW BETTER, OLD FRIEND?
AND SINCE WHEN HAVE YOU BEEN A MATCH-MAKER?
THERE'S NO ONE I'D RATHER SEE STRIKING SPARKS WITH MY DAUGH-TER, SIR.
ALFRED, I CONFESS I AM INTRIGUED BY JULIA... AND I'D LIKE TO GET TO KNOW HER BETTER...
...BUT I GUESS I'VE BEEN RELUCTANT, GUILTY ABOUT VICKI...
BRIIING
BRUCE? IT'S VICKI. YOU HAD YOUR LAST CHANCE AND YOU FAILED TO KEEP THE DATE--
WHAT DATE, VICKI?
--AND WHAT GOOD IS AN ULTIMATUM IF IT ISN'T ULTIMATED?

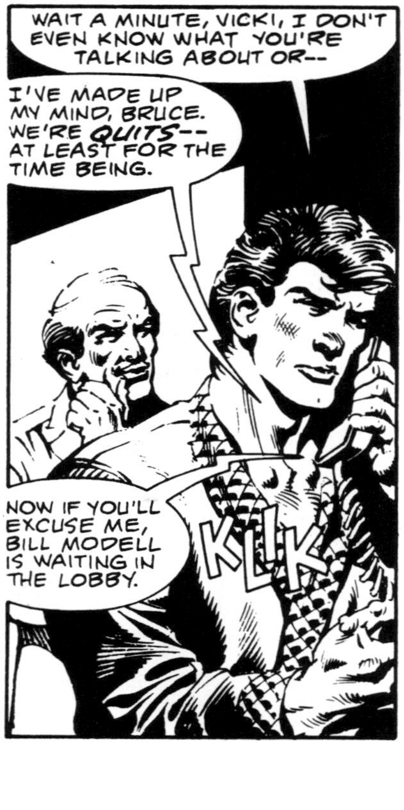
WAIT A MINUTE, VICKI, I DON'T EVEN KNOW WHAT YOU'RE TALKING ABOUT OR--
I'VE MADE UP MY MIND, BRUCE. WE'RE QUITS-- AT LEAST FOR THE TIME BEING.
NOW IF YOU'LL EXCUSE ME, BILL MODELL IS WAITING IN THE LOBBY.
KLIK

Alfred broaches the matter of his daughter's interest in Bruce Wayne. . . . (Batman *#384, June 1985, ''Broken Dates,'' p. 13 [select panels].*)

and eventually left Wayne because of her disapproval of his playboy ways.

There was Linda Page, the daughter of a wealthy oilman, who was Bruce Wayne's love interest after the dissolution of his relationship with Julie Madison. But Page also compared Bruce to Batman—and found her handsome, but lazy, playboy wanting.

News photographer Vicki Vale had a long relationship with Bruce Wayne—but here, too, the specter of Batman has interfered, as Vicki often sought to prove her suspicions that Bruce Wayne was Batman.

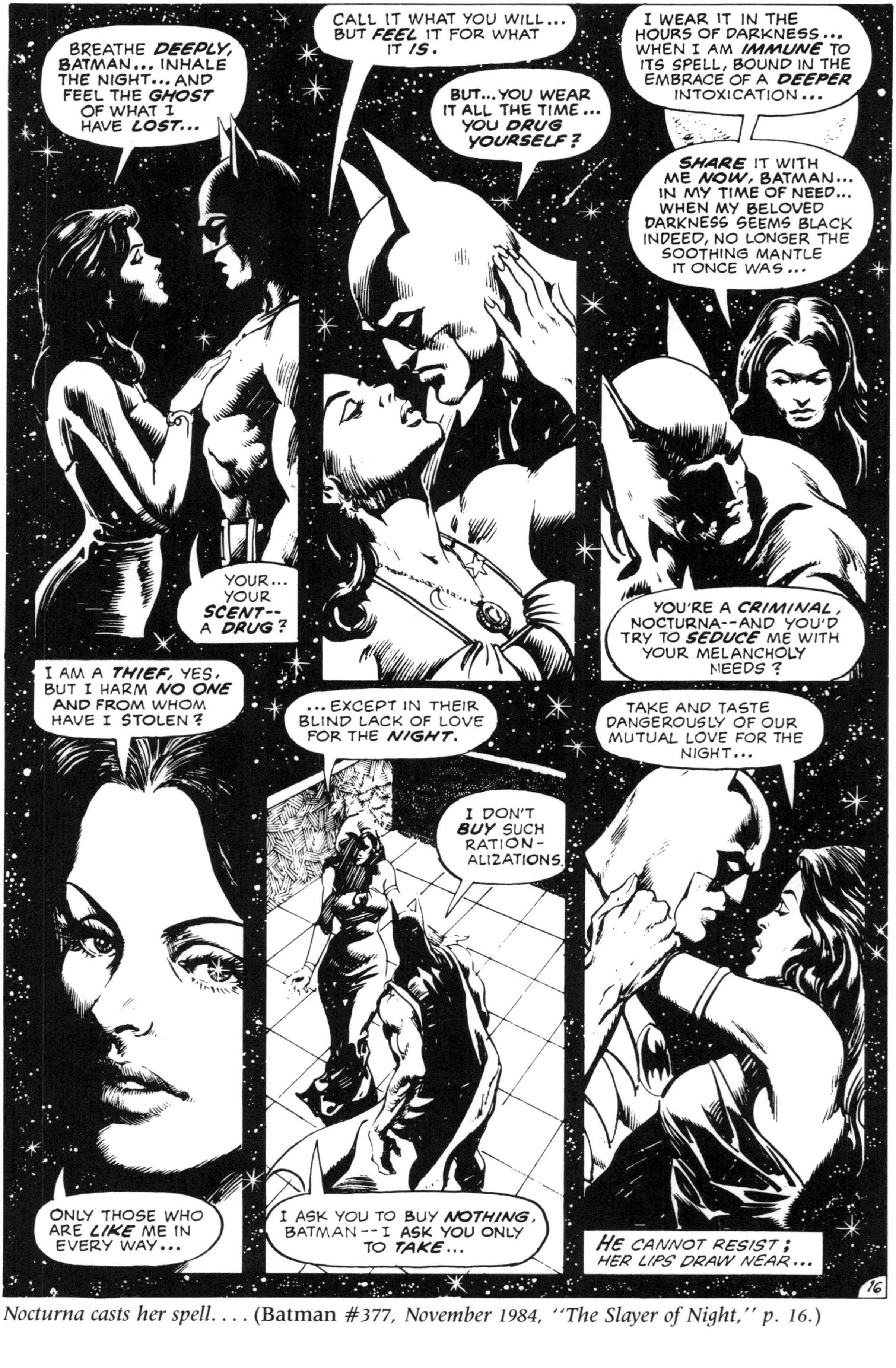
BREATHE DEEPLY, BATMAN... INHALE THE NIGHT... AND FEEL THE GHOST OF WHAT I HAVE LOST...
YOUR... YOUR SCENT-- A DRUG?
CALL IT WHAT YOU WILL... BUT FEEL IT FOR WHAT IT IS.
BUT... YOU WEAR IT ALL THE TIME... YOU DRUG YOURSELF?
I WEAR IT IN THE HOURS OF DARKNESS... WHEN I AM IMMUNE TO ITS SPELL, BOUND IN THE EMBRACE OF A DEEPER INTOXICATION...
SHARE IT WITH ME NOW, BATMAN... IN MY TIME OF NEED... WHEN MY BELOVED DARKNESS SEEMS BLACK INDEED, NO LONGER THE SOOTHING MANTLE IT ONCE WAS...
YOU'RE A CRIMINAL, NOCTURNA--AND YOU'D TRY TO SEDUCE ME WITH YOUR MELANCHOLY NEEDS?
I AM A THIEF, YES, BUT I HARM NO ONE AND FROM WHOM HAVE I STOLEN?
ONLY THOSE WHO ARE LIKE ME IN EVERY WAY...
...EXCEPT IN THEIR BLIND LACK OF LOVE FOR THE NIGHT.
I DON'T BUY SUCH RATION-ALIZATIONS.
I ASK YOU TO BUY NOTHING, BATMAN--I ASK YOU ONLY TO TAKE...
TAKE AND TASTE DANGEROUSLY OF OUR MUTUAL LOVE FOR THE NIGHT...
HE CANNOT RESIST; HER LIPS DRAW NEAR...
16

Nocturna casts her spell. . . . (**Batman** *#377, November 1984, "The Slayer of Night," p. 16.*)

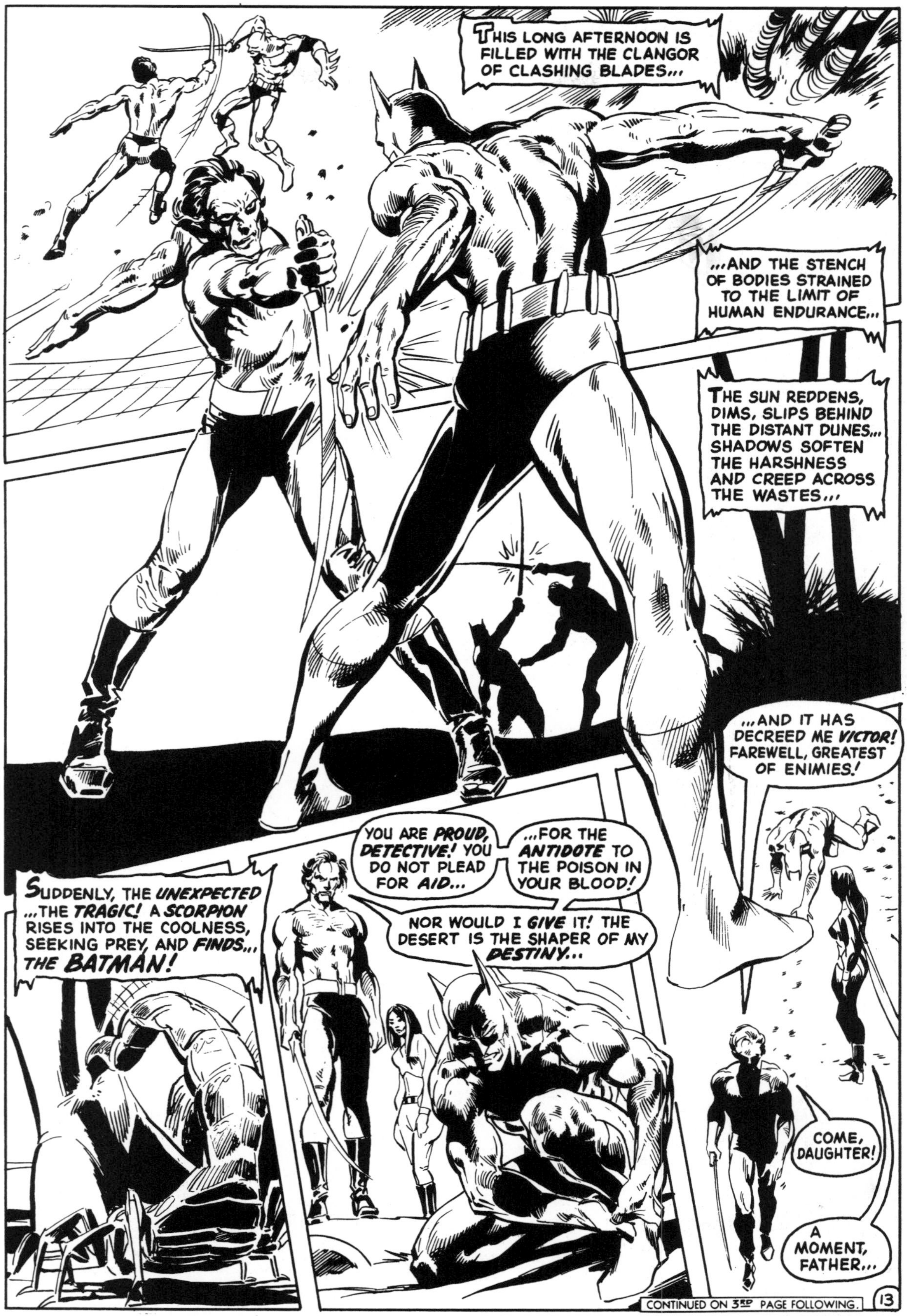
THIS LONG AFTERNOON IS FILLED WITH THE CLANGOR OF CLASHING BLADES...
...AND THE STENCH OF BODIES STRAINED TO THE LIMIT OF HUMAN ENDURANCE...
THE SUN REDDENS, DIMS, SLIPS BEHIND THE DISTANT DUNES... SHADOWS SOFTEN THE HARSHNESS AND CREEP ACROSS THE WASTES...
SUDDENLY, THE UNEXPECTED ...THE TRAGIC! A SCORPION RISES INTO THE COOLNESS, SEEKING PREY, AND FINDS... THE BATMAN!
YOU ARE PROUD, DETECTIVE! YOU DO NOT PLEAD FOR AID...
...FOR THE ANTIDOTE TO THE POISON IN YOUR BLOOD!
NOR WOULD I GIVE IT! THE DESERT IS THE SHAPER OF MY DESTINY...
...AND IT HAS DECREED ME VICTOR! FAREWELL, GREATEST OF ENIMIES!
COME, DAUGHTER!
A MOMENT, FATHER...
CONTINUED ON 3RD PAGE FOLLOWING.
13

From a duel in the desert to Talia's sweet surrender. (Batman *#244, September 1972, ''The Demon Lives Again!'' pp. 13–15.*)

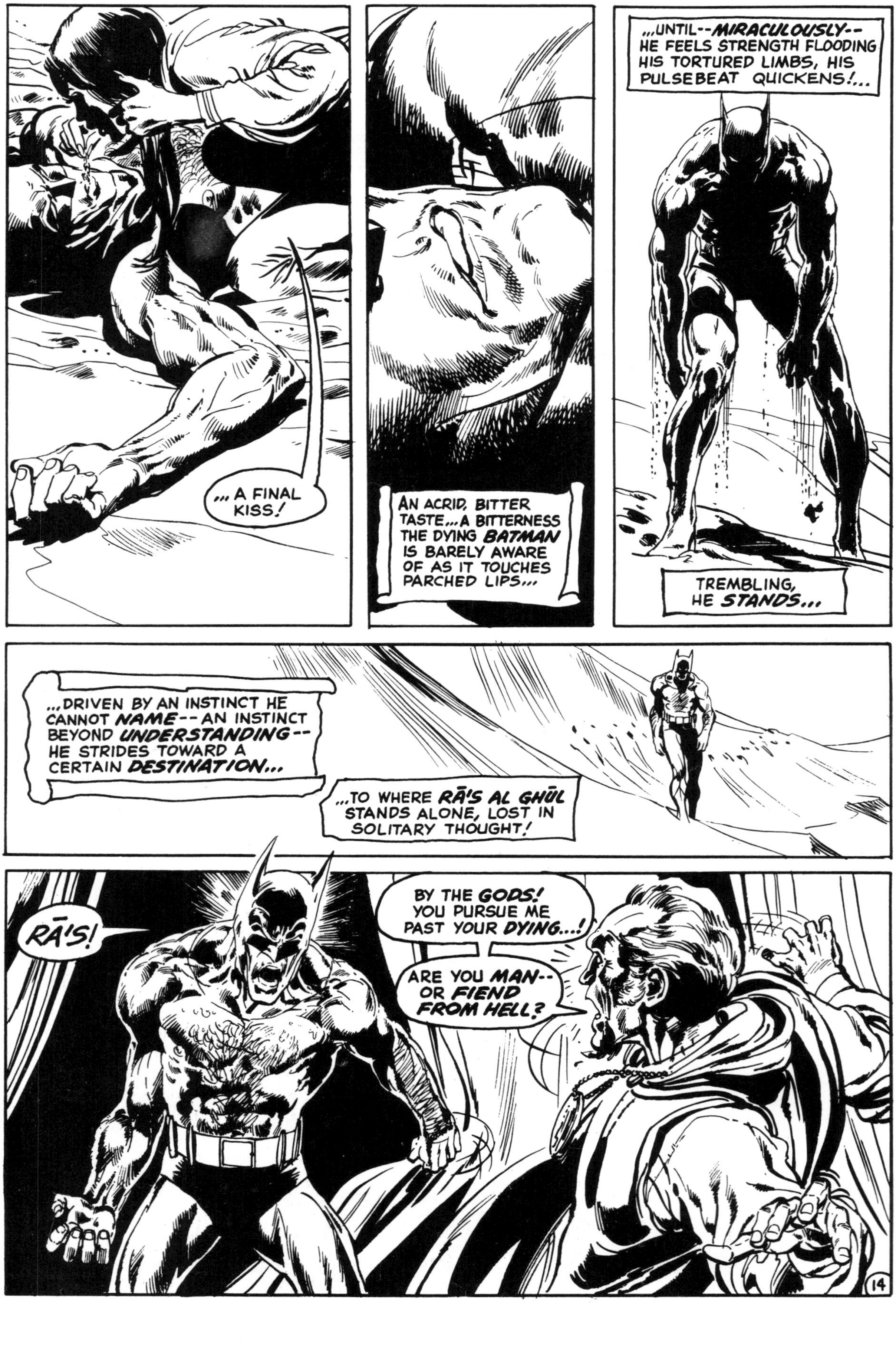
...A FINAL KISS!
AN ACRID, BITTER TASTE...A BITTERNESS THE DYING BATMAN IS BARELY AWARE OF AS IT TOUCHES PARCHED LIPS...
...UNTIL--MIRACULOUSLY--HE FEELS STRENGTH FLOODING HIS TORTURED LIMBS, HIS PULSEBEAT QUICKENS!...
TREMBLING, HE STANDS...
...DRIVEN BY AN INSTINCT HE CANNOT NAME--AN INSTINCT BEYOND UNDERSTANDING--HE STRIDES TOWARD A CERTAIN DESTINATION...
...TO WHERE RĀ'S AL GHŪL STANDS ALONE, LOST IN SOLITARY THOUGHT!
RĀ'S!
BY THE GODS! YOU PURSUE ME PAST YOUR DYING...!
ARE YOU MAN--OR FIEND FROM HELL?
14

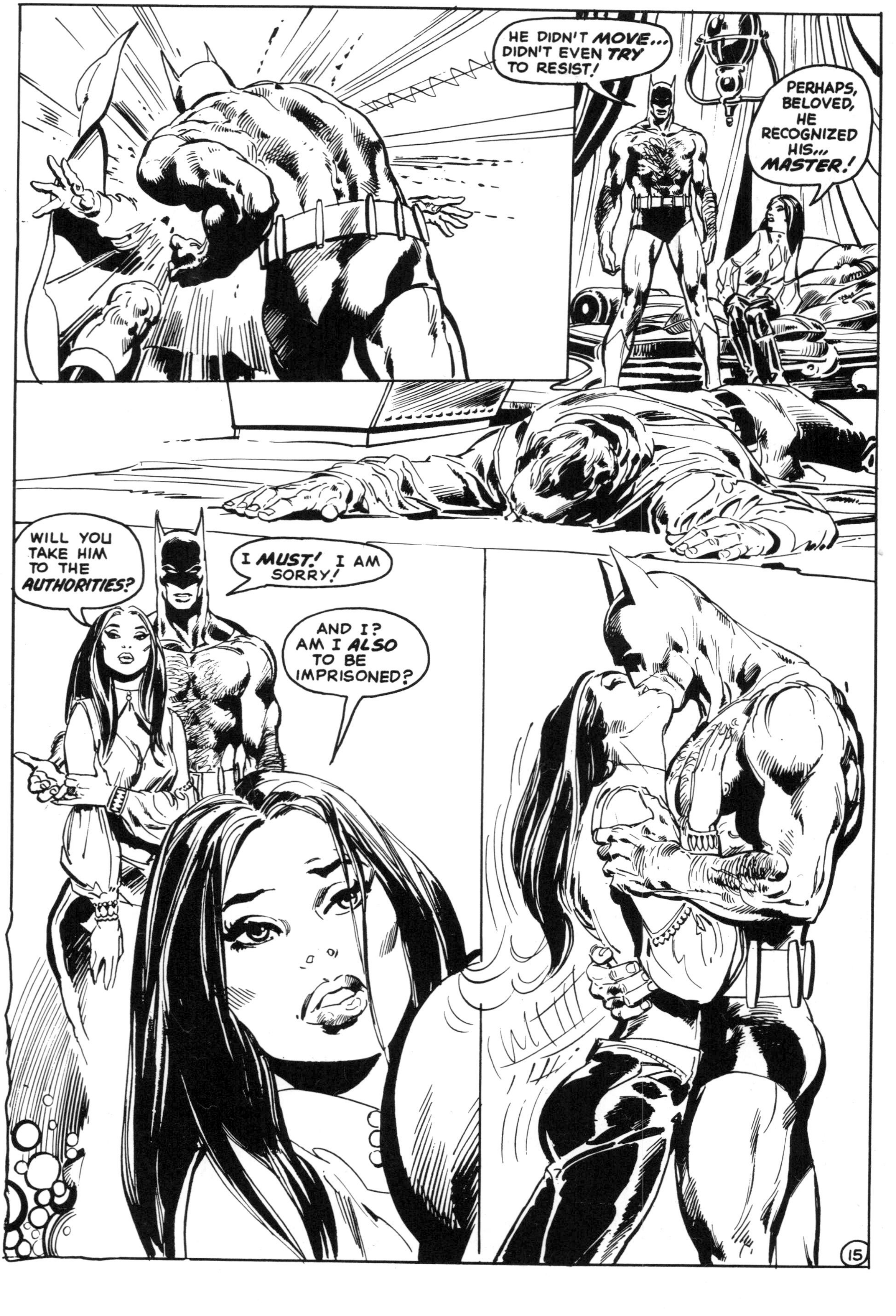
HE DIDN'T MOVE... DIDN'T EVEN TRY TO RESIST!
PERHAPS, BELOVED, HE RECOGNIZED HIS... MASTER!
WILL YOU TAKE HIM TO THE AUTHORITIES?
I MUST! I AM SORRY!
AND I? AM I ALSO TO BE IMPRISONED?
15

The dual identity business has been a tight-rope walk for Batman. The stress only intensified as Bruce Wayne matured into the hard-driving head of the Wayne Foundation and the leading philanthropist in Gotham. But it was still his Batman identity, and the call of the night, that would rule his being.

"The Batman...becomes alive with the night," Jenette Kahn has written. "It is then that he can drop all pretense, then that he can stalk his prey. When he pursues criminals, his senses are at their keenest, his reflexes most acutely tuned, his mind a cutting edge, his courage and daring and stamina untinged by fear.

"How then, could a woman compete with the exhilaration of these nights? Especially when the women are attracted to Bruce Wayne, the inconsequential beard for the complex detective avenger...how can an ordinary woman, no matter how beautiful or cultured or rich excite a man who craves to have every fiber in his being challenged? Out of that necessity we all have to be appreciated for our true selves, he is drawn irresistibly to those women who, because they live on the razor's edge as he does, sense the Batman within Bruce Wayne. So, too, are these women drawn to him. Both know they have met their match."[2]

Women "on the razor's edge" that Batman himself has dallied with, particularly in the 1980s, include the wealthy Natasha "Nocturna" Knight (known for her seductive charm, unnatural pallor, and penchant for "classy crimes") and Selina "Catwoman" Kyle (who has been a sweet temptation to Batman ever since the Golden Age).

In the 1980s his Bruce Wayne persona would be romantically occupied by a stormy relationship with Vicki Vale. The appearance of Alfred's daughter, Julia, who would fall in love with Bruce Wayne, would further muddle an already complicated romantic picture.

And then there was Talia, the daughter of Ra's al Ghul, the man whose name means "demon's head" in Arabic. Given the formidable challenge of dueling Ra's al Ghul, Batman was initially wary of Talia's advances.

The mission of the Demon's Head is to purify a polluted planet, to restore nature to the dominion abridged by the human species. While he works to achieve his dream, Ra's al Ghul is drawn to wastelands of limitless emptiness. There his heart can find solace, unrestrained by the arbitrary physical and spiritual borders humankind erects.

For the Dark Knight the Demon's dream was just another disastrous bid for world conquest.

But despite his opposition to Ra's, there can be no denying his attraction to Talia. With the body of an Olympic sprinter and a face sculpted with high cheekbones and framed with swirling tresses, moist, pouting lips and emerald eyes alive with an enchanting, childlike gaze, her charms are considerable.

Talia is something more than just another beautiful woman: at once innocent and regal, she is also a warrior who has stared through the portals of death, having brought her father back from the dead many times through the power of the rejuvenating Lazarus Pit.

It's perhaps the love she has for her obsessed father that has given her the understanding to unlock the heart of Batman, the one she calls "beloved."

Of all the loves who tried to win the heart of Batman, from Vicki Vale to Batwoman to Catwoman, it was Talia whom the Dark Knight agreed to wed. They were married in the tradition of Ra's al Ghul's own country, where only the consent of the bride was needed to institute a marriage. Their union would be brief, but beautiful.[3]

But all the women Batman has known have helped soften the brutal edge of his obsessed life. None of their sweet songs of love have captured the heart of the Dark Knight—but they will always haunt him.

2. Jenette Kahn, correspondence with Mark Canton of Warner Brothers, Inc., October 18, 1982.
3. *Batman: Son of the Demon*, 1987.

Opposite: *The Dark Knight surrenders to Talia.* (Batman: Son of The Demon, *1987, p. 31.*)

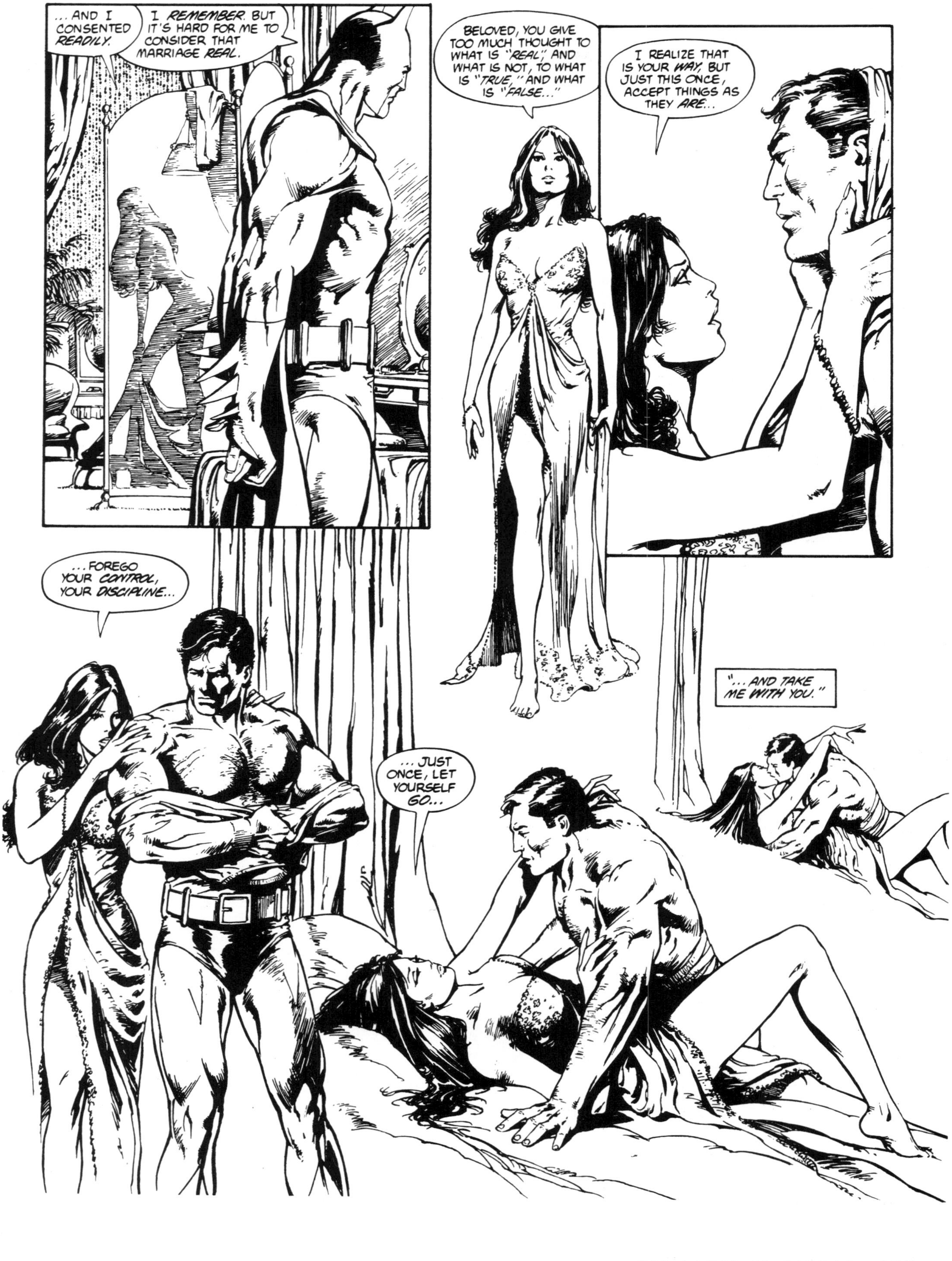
...AND I CONSENTED READILY.
I REMEMBER. BUT IT'S HARD FOR ME TO CONSIDER THAT MARRIAGE REAL.
BELOVED, YOU GIVE TOO MUCH THOUGHT TO WHAT IS "REAL," AND WHAT IS NOT, TO WHAT IS "TRUE," AND WHAT IS "FALSE..."
I REALIZE THAT IS YOUR WAY, BUT JUST THIS ONCE, ACCEPT THINGS AS THEY ARE...
...FOREGO YOUR CONTROL, YOUR DISCIPLINE...
...JUST ONCE, LET YOURSELF GO...
"...AND TAKE ME WITH YOU."

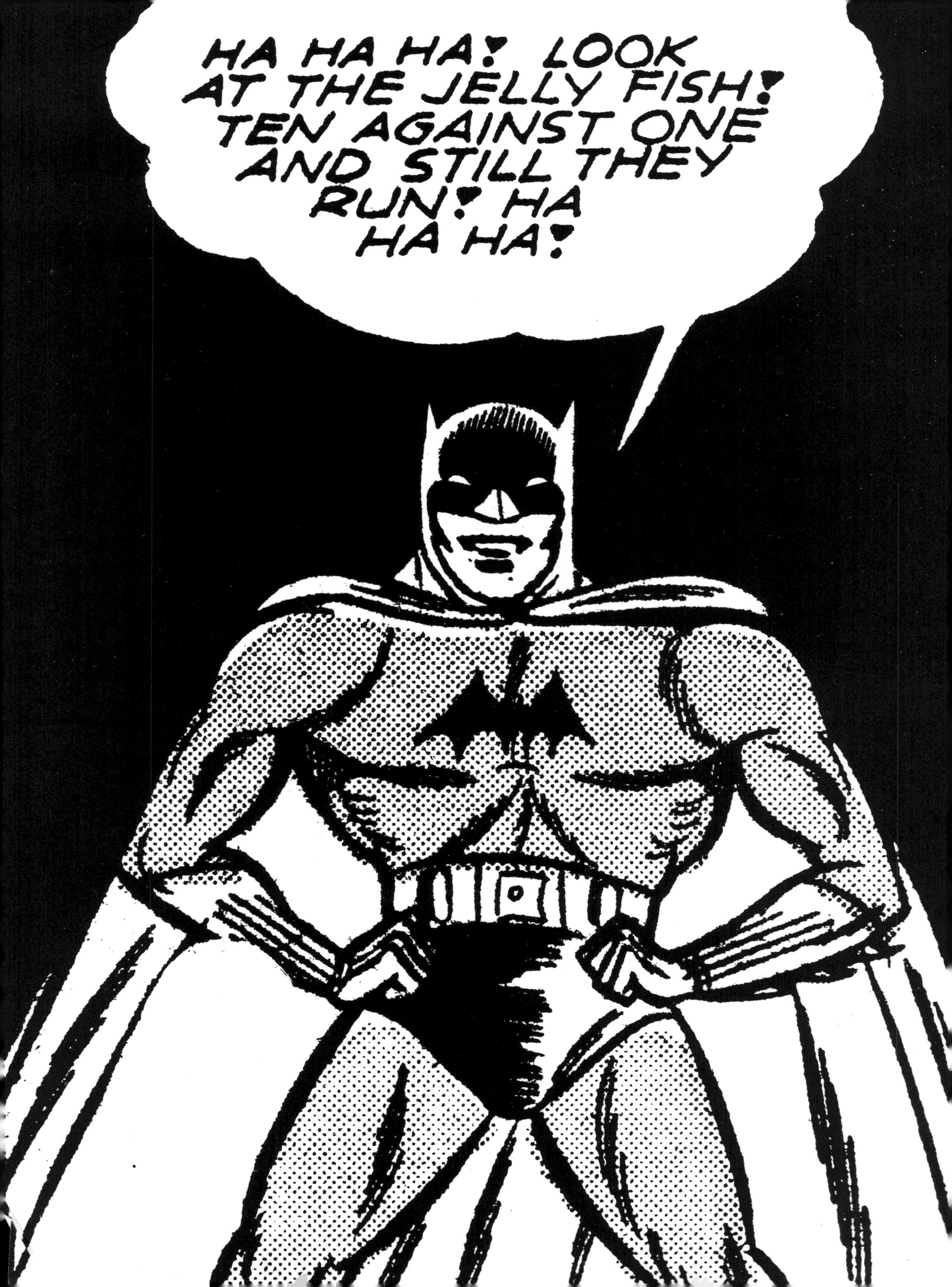
HA HA HA! LOOK AT THE JELLY FISH! TEN AGAINST ONE AND STILL THEY RUN! HA HA HA!

CHAPTER 14
THE WARRIOR BATMAN

I N *THE UNTOLD LEGEND OF THE BATMAN,* A three-part 1980 miniseries, there is a sequence in which the Dark Knight is heading straight into the heart of the underworld to get information, and God help the guilty. This Batman is a pure, primal fighting machine. The Warrior Batman.

He drives to the Gotham oceanfront, bringing the Batmobile to a screeching halt in front of The Last Resort, a weathered-looking bar that long ago lost its battle against the elements.

Inside, the place is thick with longshoremen, seedy drifters, and tough-looking cutthroats sipping beers, smoking cigarettes, and conducting hushed conversations. But all talk stops as the Dark Knight makes his entrance and heads for the bar.

The men seated on the bar stools move away, opening a path to a hopped-up man at the bar dressed in a white suit and wearing a white fedora. He's alternating between sips from his cocktail and drags from a cigarette that will soon join the mess of stamped-out butts filling the ashtray in front of him.

The man turns with a jittery start to face the Dark Knight. He has a thin, haggard face that hasn't seen a razor blade in days. And despite the late hour, he's wearing dark glasses.

"I figured I'd find you here, Snitch," Batman says, a stern edge in his voice.

"Hey, I—I been keepin' my nose clean, Batman! Whaddaya want from me?"

"What I always want, Snitch—information," the Batman says, leaning forward, taking

Opposite: *The young warrior often taunted his mismatched opponents. (Batman #4, Winter 1941, "Blackbeard's Crew and the Yacht Society," p. 11 [panel].)*

Snitch's cigarette and dropping it into his drink.

As they talk, a man tries to sneak behind the Dark Knight, a blackjack in his right hand. The man raises the blackjack and is ready to bring it crashing against Batman's skull when Batman inexplicably turns and grabs the attacker's wrist.

"If you want to play rough, punk—you picked a bad night for it!" Batman growls as, in one smooth motion, he lifts the man up and sends him over the bar with a crash.

"That wasn't very smart, Snitch," Batman says angrily, walking toward the cowering man who has just fallen off his bar stool. "I just wanted to talk—but now I'll get my answers another way!"

"Stay away from me, Batman—I'm warning you," the shaken Snitch cries as he pulls himself up by the bar and reaches inside his jacket. With a trembling hand he pulls out a gun and points it at Batman.

"Keep back—or I'll blow you away!!"

"You dare!?! You DARE to pull a gun on me?!" the Dark Knight demands.

And in a blur of motion the Batman has his right hand gripped on Snitch's jacket, his other hand knocking the weapon loose.

"Don't you EVER point a gun at me again!" Batman shouts, his left hand slapping the hood's face, sending the dark glasses flying after the lost gun.

"Never, do you hear me?" the Batman almost screams, another clap crashing against Snitch's cheeks.

"Never!!" the Dark Knight shouts with yet a third punishing slap.

"That's enough," comes a voice from the other end of the bar. It's Robin, who has followed the Batman to The Last Resort.

"Just protecting your back, Batman," Robin

says grimly. "Don't you think you've done enough here?"

"Y-yes, of course," Batman says in a slow voice. "There's nothing more this punk can tell me."

He removes his fist from Snitch's jacket, and the man falls to the floor. The bar crowd watches with a combination of hatred, respect, and relief as the Dynamic Duo turn and leave.[1]

That scene provides a rare, but revealing, look at the Warrior Batman. Rare because it is one of the few times that Batman has come close to losing control. Revealing because it shows the awesome physical strength of an unleashed Dark Knight.

Another, even bloodier, battle took place way back in the Golden Age (*Batman* 5, Spring 1941), when Batman discovered a wounded Robin and believed his faithful friend and sidekick had been murdered by the underworld.

"For the first time, the Batman knows rage, bleak, grim rage," went the text. "Woe to all criminals, for now, the Batman has become a terrible figure of vengeance!"

Sure enough, when Batman tracked the offending criminals to their lair, he made it clear he was in no mood to be messed with. He splintered open the door to their hideout with his shoulders and, despite taking a bullet in the shoulder (no more than a "flea bite" to the furious crime fighter), proceeded to toss the crooks around like rag dolls.

For decades Batman has been taking criminals with the surprise, if not always the ferocity, of his brutal interrogation at The Last Resort and the Robin reprisal. Many a Batman bust has caught criminals in the middle of a heist, dropping them before they have a chance to go for their guns. Many an underworld poker game has been interrupted by Batman crashing down through a hideout skylight, demanding information or the return of ill-gotten gains.

How such unexpected attacks have sent shivers of fear throughout the criminal underworld! But such has been Batman's strategy from the beginning. Criminals are "a superstitious, cowardly lot" to him. And like the virtuoso crime fighter he is, Batman jams his imagery of darkness and retribution into the mainline of their fear.

His mastery of instilling a psychology of fear, his supreme sense of strategy, and his physical

1. *The Untold Legend of the Batman* 2 (August 1980).

DON'T YOU EVER POINT A GUN AT ME AGAIN!
WAK
NEVER, DO YOU HEAR ME?
WOK
NEVER!!

The Untold Legend of the Batman *#2, August 1980, "With Friends Like These. . . . ," p. 3 [select panels].*

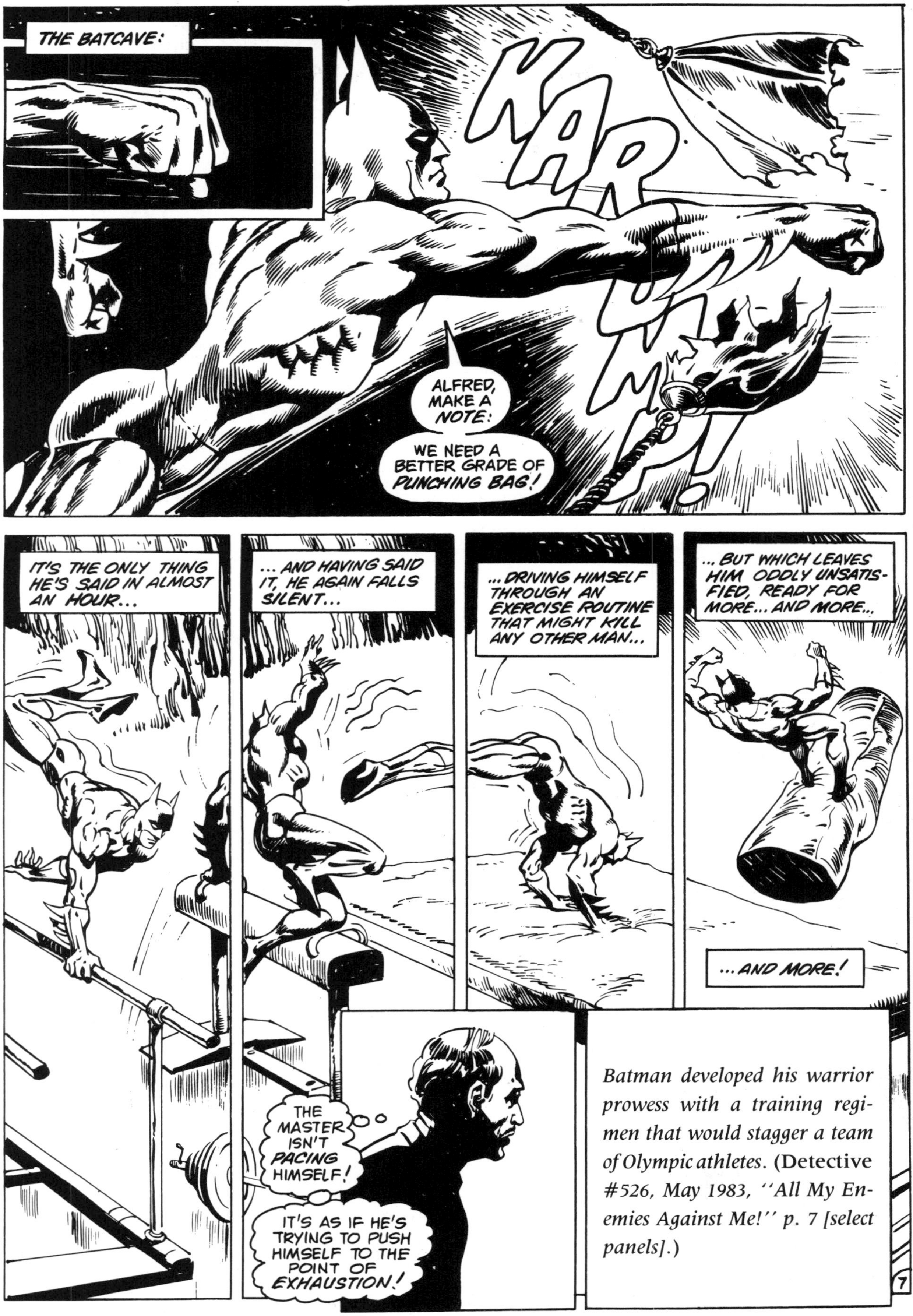
THE BATCAVE:
KARUMMP!
ALFRED, MAKE A NOTE:
WE NEED A BETTER GRADE OF PUNCHING BAG!
IT'S THE ONLY THING HE'S SAID IN ALMOST AN HOUR...
...AND HAVING SAID IT, HE AGAIN FALLS SILENT...
...DRIVING HIMSELF THROUGH AN EXERCISE ROUTINE THAT MIGHT KILL ANY OTHER MAN...
...BUT WHICH LEAVES HIM ODDLY UNSATIS-FIED, READY FOR MORE... AND MORE...
...AND MORE!
THE MASTER ISN'T PACING HIMSELF!
IT'S AS IF HE'S TRYING TO PUSH HIMSELF TO THE POINT OF EXHAUSTION!
7

Batman developed his warrior prowess with a training regimen that would stagger a team of Olympic athletes. (Detective *#526, May 1983, ''All My Enemies Against Me!'' p. 7 [select panels].*)

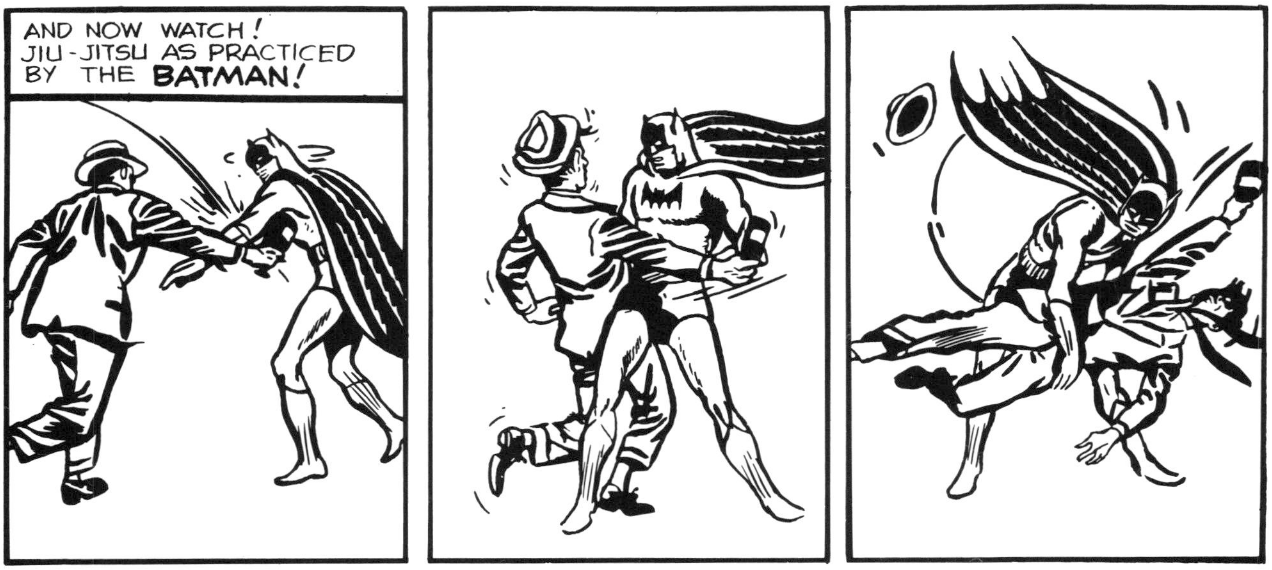
AND NOW WATCH! JIU-JITSU AS PRACTICED BY THE BATMAN!

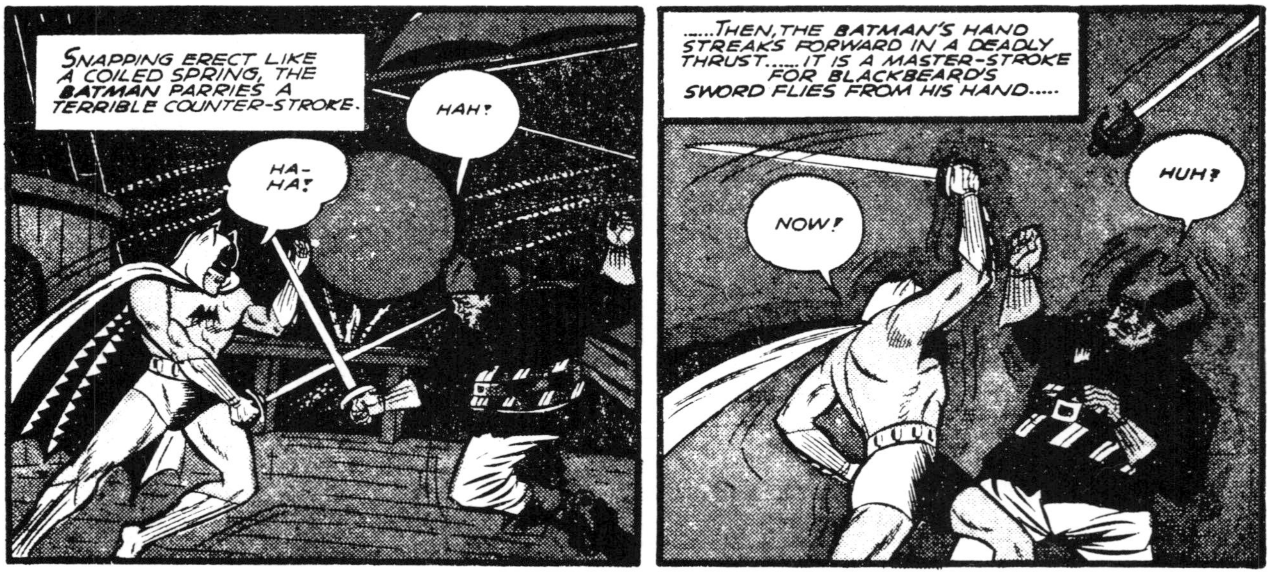
SNAPPING ERECT LIKE A COILED SPRING, THE BATMAN PARRIES A TERRIBLE COUNTER-STROKE.
HAH?
HA-HA!
.....THEN, THE BATMAN'S HAND STREAKS FORWARD IN A DEADLY THRUST.....IT IS A MASTER-STROKE FOR BLACKBEARD'S SWORD FLIES FROM HIS HAND.....
HUH?
NOW!

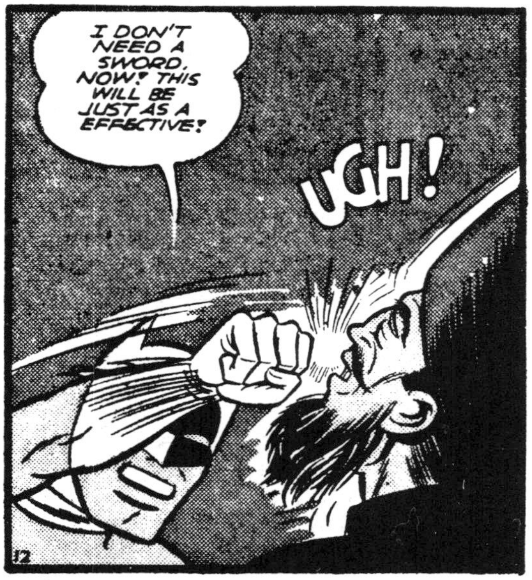
I DON'T NEED A SWORD, NOW! THIS WILL BE JUST AS EFFECTIVE!
UGH!

Left: *The Dark Knight has always had a talent for swordplay. Here he disarms a modern-day buccaneer.* **(Batman #4,** *Winter 1941, ''Blackbeard's Crew and the Yacht Society,'' p. 12 [select panels].*) **Above: Batman #31,** *October/November 1945, ''Trade Marks of Crime!'' p. 5 (select panels).* **Right:** *The Warrior Batman.* **(Batman #393,** *March 1986, ''The Dark Rider,'' p. 12*)

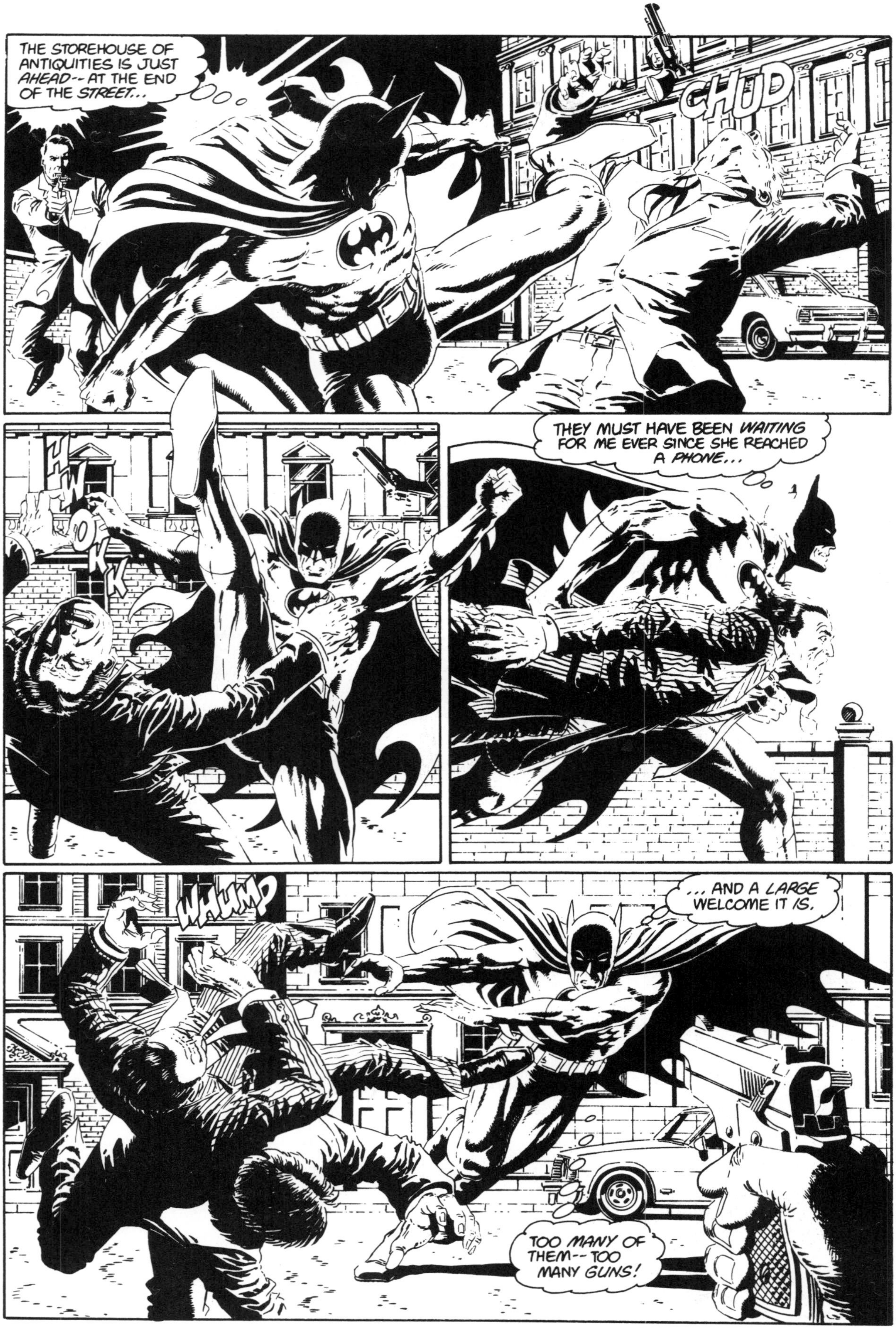
THE STOREHOUSE OF ANTIQUITIES IS JUST AHEAD-- AT THE END OF THE STREET...
CHUD
THEY MUST HAVE BEEN WAITING FOR ME EVER SINCE SHE REACHED A PHONE...
WHUMP
... AND A LARGE WELCOME IT IS.
TOO MANY OF THEM-- TOO MANY GUNS!

power emulate the samurai and ninjutsu of feudal Japan, the adepts of Shaolin Temple, and other well-rounded warrior cultures of old.

But the Batman's very renown as a warrior crime fighter has caused many foes to battle him just for the thrill of dueling the best. The Joker has been known to not only match wits, but stand his ground and exchange punches with the Dark Knight. Many foes in the 1980s, such as the deadly Croc, have the muscle to pose a physical threat to Batman.

But the deadliest, most ruthless killer the Dark Knight has faced in the eighties must surely be the KGB agent known as the Beast. The cybernetically enhanced martial artist and weapons master put the Dark Knight to the test in the four-part "Ten Nights of the Beast" series (*Batman* 417–420, 1988).

As the story goes, when the Beast slips into Gotham without the approval of his Soviet superiors to begin systematically eliminating the American architects of the Reagan administration's Star Wars program, Batman jumps into the case.

But the Beast is always one step ahead of the Dark Knight. Whenever Batman arrives on the scene of a Beast strike, it's to get the body count, not save the day.

And when they finally do battle, the Beast comes close to defeating Batman.

"I've finally run into someone who's better at this game than I am," Batman thinks after their first battle.[2]

In their final sequence the Beast is on the run through the maze of the Gotham City sewer system with Batman in pursuit. The Beast has tried gunfire and tear gas, but each time the Dark Knight has parried the attacks. The Beast runs through the sewer's dark passages looking for a new position.

2. "Ten Nights of the Beast," *Batman* 418 (April 1988).

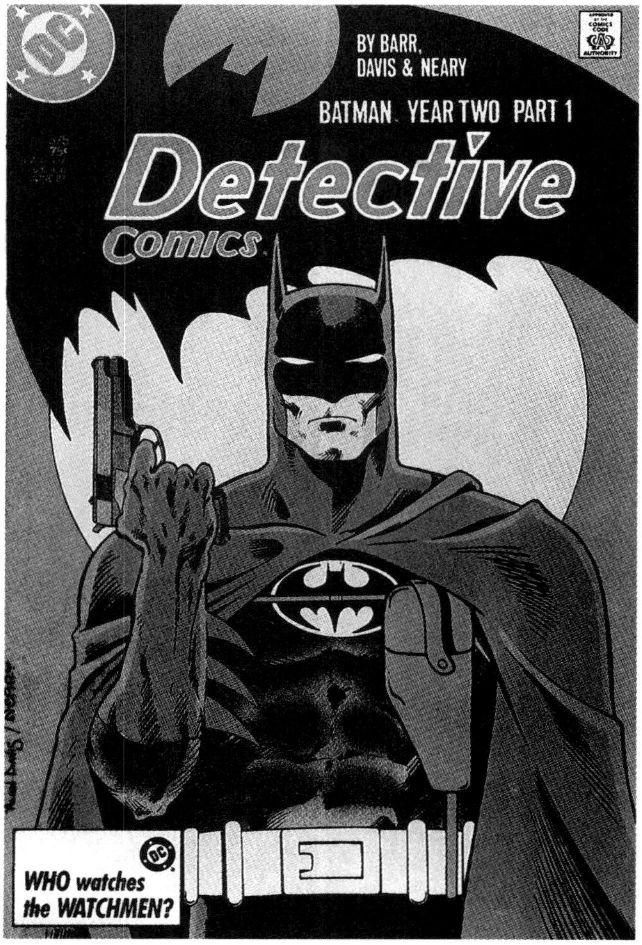
BY BARR,
DAVIS & NEARY
BATMAN. YEAR TWO PART 1
Detective
Comics
WHO watches the WATCHMEN?

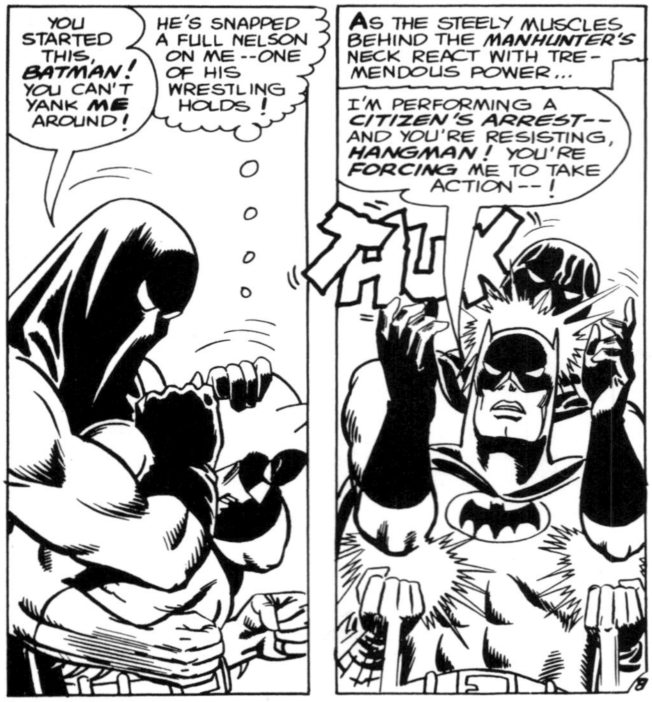
YOU STARTED THIS, BATMAN! YOU CAN'T YANK ME AROUND!
HE'S SNAPPED A FULL NELSON ON ME--ONE OF HIS WRESTLING HOLDS!
AS THE STEELY MUSCLES BEHIND THE MANHUNTER'S NECK REACT WITH TREMENDOUS POWER...
I'M PERFORMING A CITIZEN'S ARREST--AND YOU'RE RESISTING, HANGMAN! YOU'RE FORCING ME TO TAKE ACTION--!
TALK

Left: *In 1987 there was a special look back on Batman's gun-wielding days.* (Detective *#575, June 1987, cover.*) **Right:** *Batman uses a martial artist's sense of leverage and angles to break the holds of this muscular assailant.* (Detective *#355, September 1966, "Hate of the Hooded Hangman!" p. 8 [select panels].*)

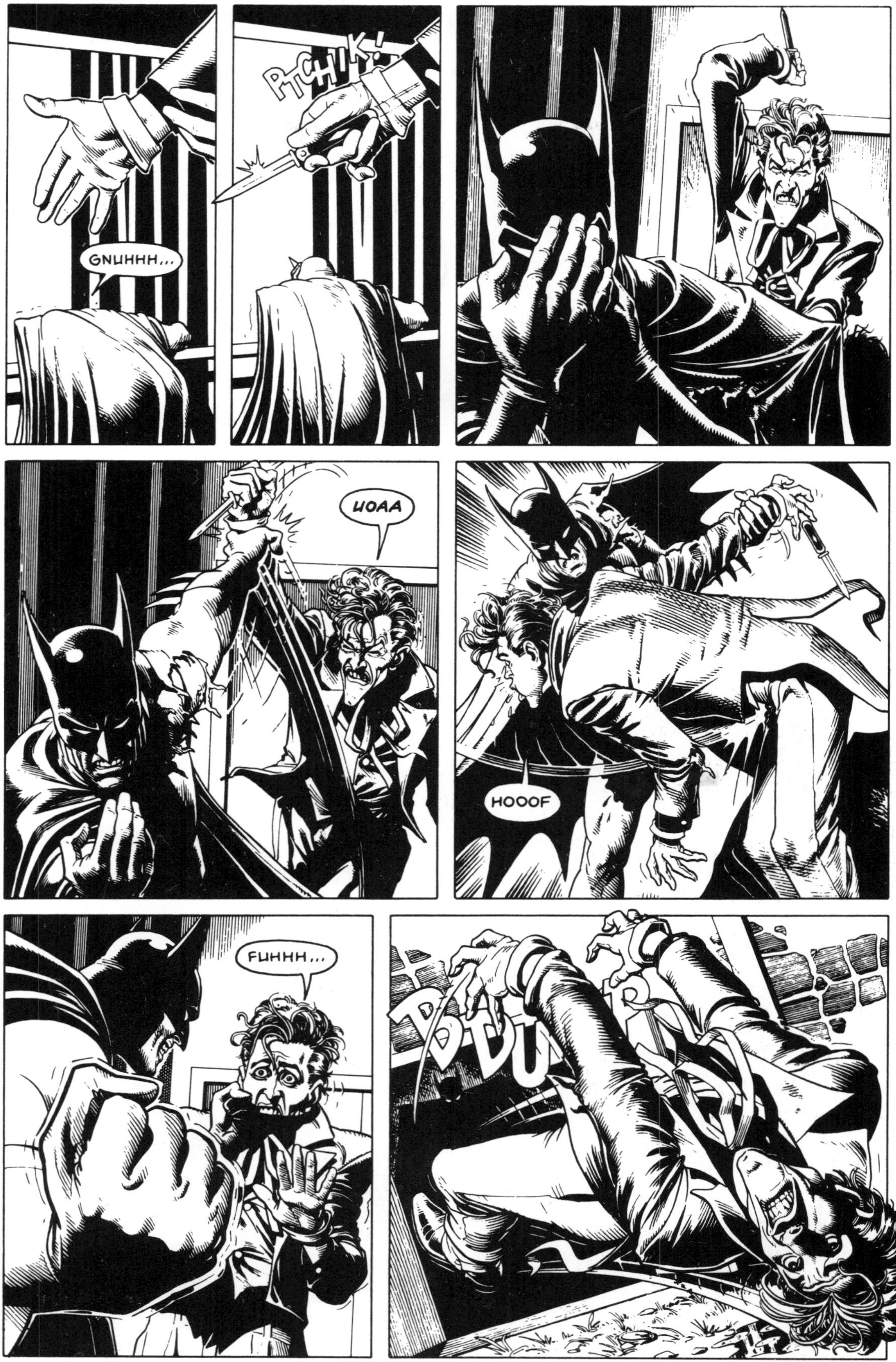
GNUHHH...
PTCHIK!
UOAA
HOOOF
FUHHH...

Here the Joker gets a taste of Batman's swift, deadly reflexes. (The Killing Joke, *1988, p. 43.*)

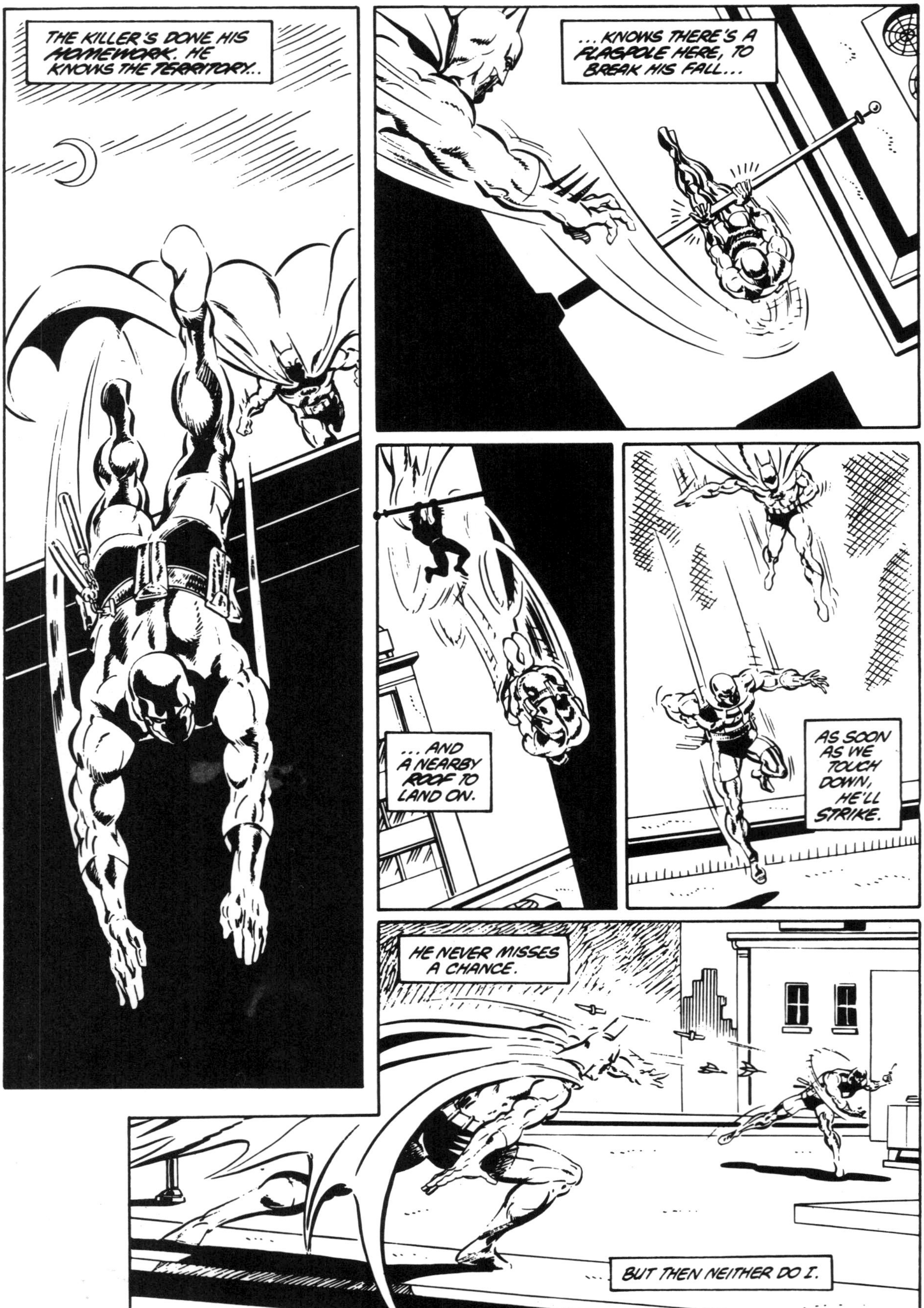
THE KILLER'S DONE HIS HOMEWORK. HE KNOWS THE TERRITORY...
...KNOWS THERE'S A FLAGPOLE HERE, TO BREAK HIS FALL...
...AND A NEARBY ROOF TO LAND ON.
AS SOON AS WE TOUCH DOWN, HE'LL STRIKE.
HE NEVER MISSES A CHANCE.
BUT THEN NEITHER DO I.
20

Batman and the Beast in a deadly dance of death. (Batman *#418, April 1988, ''Ten Nights of the*

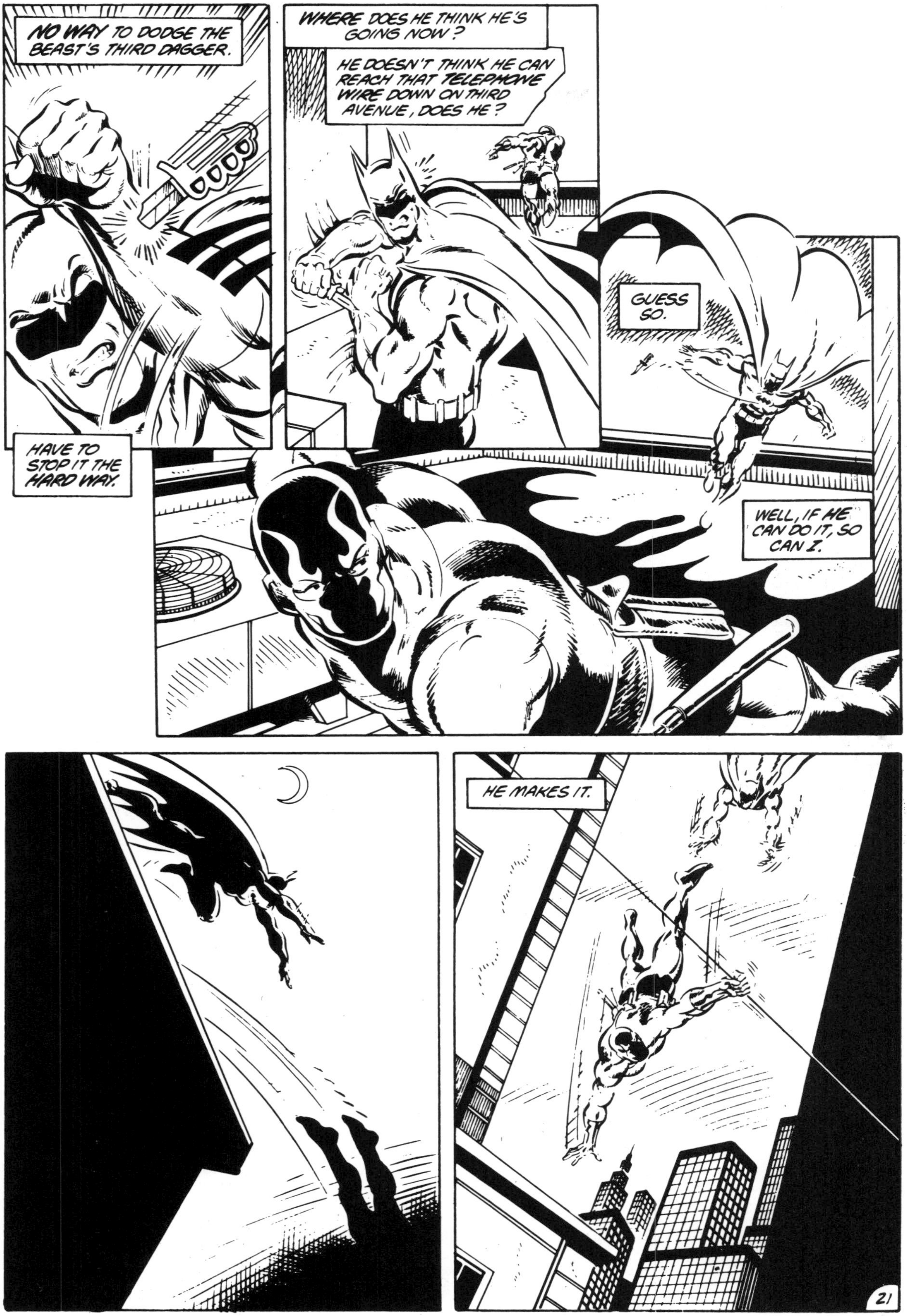
NO WAY TO DODGE THE BEAST'S THIRD DAGGER.
HAVE TO STOP IT THE HARD WAY.
WHERE DOES HE THINK HE'S GOING NOW?
HE DOESN'T THINK HE CAN REACH THAT TELEPHONE WIRE DOWN ON THIRD AVENUE, DOES HE?
GUESS SO.
WELL, IF HE CAN DO IT, SO CAN I.
HE MAKES IT.
21

Beast,'' Part II, pp. 20–22.)

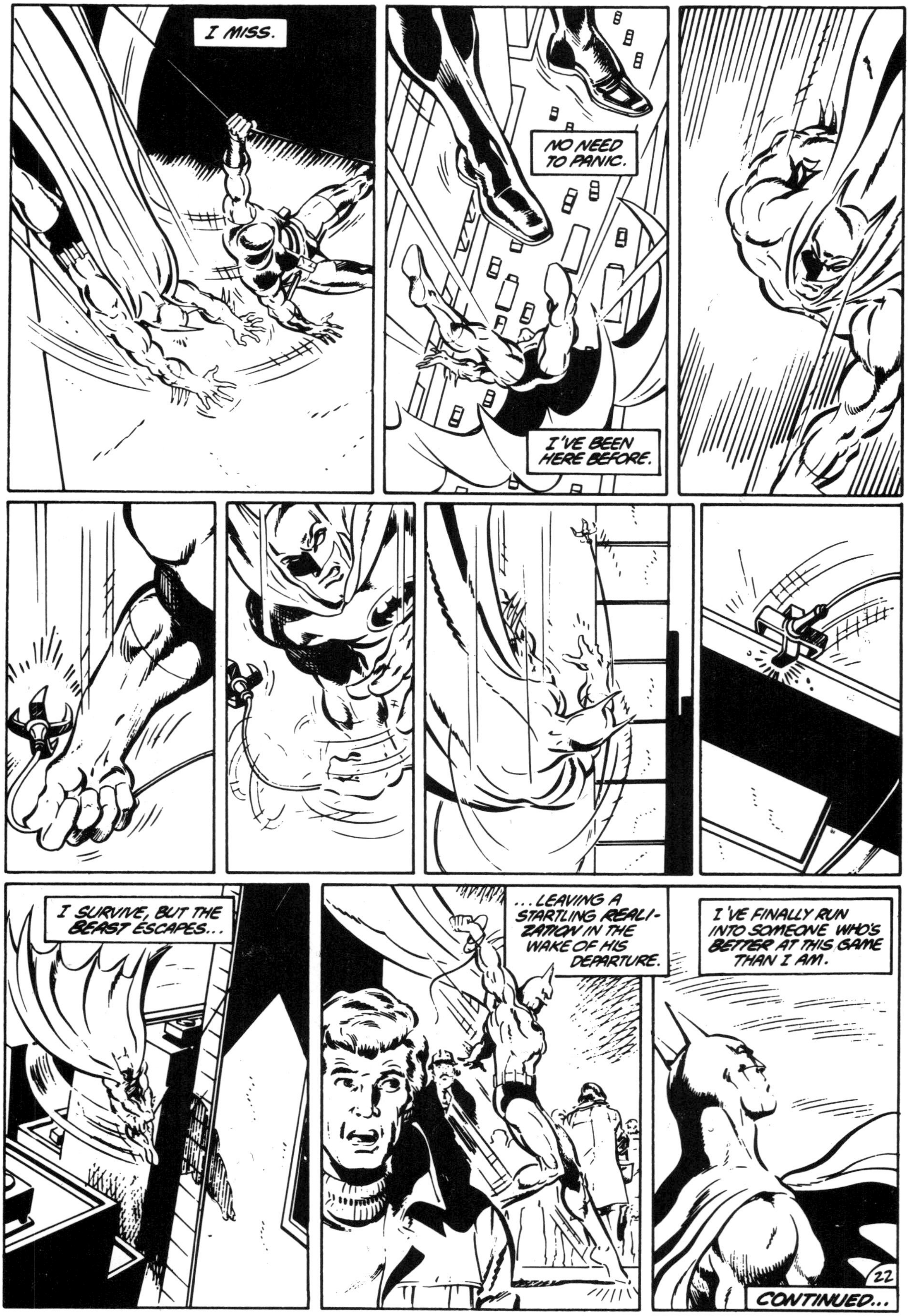
I MISS.
NO NEED TO PANIC.
I'VE BEEN HERE BEFORE.
I SURVIVE, BUT THE BEAST ESCAPES...
...LEAVING A STARTLING REALIZATION IN THE WAKE OF HIS DEPARTURE.
I'VE FINALLY RUN INTO SOMEONE WHO'S BETTER AT THIS GAME THAN I AM.
22
CONTINUED...

Batman sees the Beast running toward a steel door and slows down, knowing it only leads to a dead end.

When the Dark Knight approaches and stands in the doorway, he finds the Beast brandishing a wicked length of lead pipe. At last the two evenly matched warriors face each other. But how will the Dark Knight survive, much less humble and apprehend this killing machine?

"Well, my worthy opponent, a time of reckoning is upon us," the Beast says. "Time for us to find out which of us is the best—the best at this game of life and death."

The Batman, a faceless shadow framed in the doorway, says nothing.

"What are you waiting for?" the Beast demands. "Come! Let us play out this black game!"

"Why should I?" comes the voice of the Dark Knight. "A few years ago I would have jumped at this chance to test myself against you. But time has taught me many valuable lessons."

And we watch, mesmerized, as the Dark Knight begins to slowly close the steel door.

"There's no reason for me to risk my life, coming in there after you. It would neither accomplish nor prove anything worthwhile," the Dark Knight says, closing the door, jamming it tight.

And with the sounds of the Beast frantically pounding on the door of his prison, the Dark Knight turns and slowly walks away into the darkness.

"Sometimes you have to ignore the rules," the Dark Knight whispers, revealing his true warrior's sense of strategy. "Sometimes circumstances are such that the rules pervert justice.

"I'm not in this business to protect the rules. I serve justice."[3]

> Enact strategy broadly, correctly and openly.
>
> Then you will come to think of things in a wide sense and, taking the void as the Way, you will see the Way as void.
>
> In the void is virtue, and no evil. Wisdom has existence, principle has existence, the Way has existence, spirit is nothingness.
>
> —Miyamoto Musashi.[4]

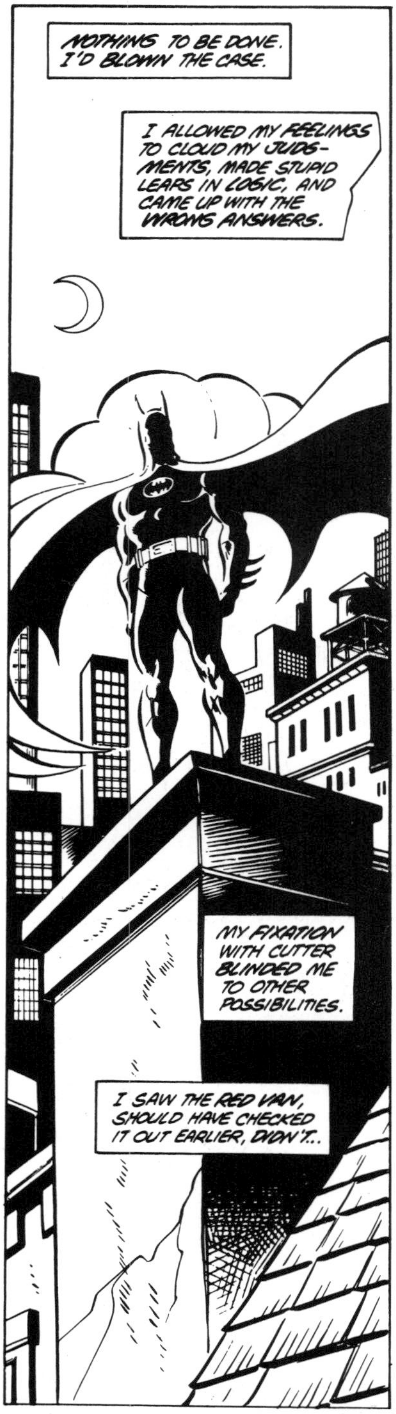
NOTHING'S TO BE DONE. I'D BLOWN THE CASE.
I ALLOWED MY FEELINGS TO CLOUD MY JUDG-MENTS, MADE STUPID LEAPS IN LOGIC, AND CAME UP WITH THE WRONG ANSWERS.
MY FIXATION WITH CUTTER BLINDED ME TO OTHER POSSIBILITIES.
I SAW THE RED VAN, SHOULD HAVE CHECKED IT OUT EARLIER, DIDN'T...

Batman always had a sense of strategy to go with his muscles and intuition. (Batman *#414, December 1987, "Victims!" p. 22 [panel].*)

3. "Ten Nights of the Beast," *Batman* 420 (June 1988).

4. Miyamoto Musashi, *A Book of Five Rings* (Woodstock, New York: The Overlook Press, 1982), p. 95.

DOSSIER 4

BAT-NOIR

The word *noir,* whether used in connection with a work of film or literature, has come to stand for a dark, fatal vision. The world of noir (French for black and gloomy) can claim its victims in many ways: it's a suicidal drive to the bad side of town; it's the stray bullet that hits you when you think the game is won; it's the caper gone sour; it's the unexpected betrayal, the false accusation, the deadly seduction, the endgame.

Noir, particularly in film, is a vision of a nocturnal urban inferno. In this bleak landscape no one is safe, everyone is doomed. Even when the hero of a noir piece emerges triumphant, some price, usually the early loss of a loved one, has been paid.

The Batman mythos has been steeped in such noir traditions from the very beginning.

"I remember Batman as being very dark and ominous and quirky," notes screenwriter Sam Hamm, who wrote a very noir *Batman* screenplay for Warner Brothers. "...That really makes the strongest impression on you when you're a kid...Just how basic a level does the character tap into some intriguing myth?...

"Batman is a mysterious guy; he's essentially a vigilante, and he's a fairly disturbed character. His whole gimmick is, he wants to be menacing, he wants to be frightening, he wants to be shadowy."

Batman's noir world has always been troubling. Since fate plays no favorites in this domain, even a handsome, heroic figure such as district attorney Harvey Dent can become transformed into the evil Two-Face. Even a young, wealthy couple, such as Thomas and Martha Wayne, can end up as just another homicide statistic.

Batman can only try to tip the scales for justice. He can never promise salvation. Although Batman lives by a strict code of ethics, he is such a part of these shadows that even he often feels the pull of the dark side.

Even during the days when Batman and Robin battled aliens, received civic citations from a grateful populace, or grinned their way through another round of gangster bashing, there was the sense of darker streams running just below the surface. (Certainly, the murder of his parents would forever cast over Batman's landscape that hint of primal evil lurking in the shadows.)

This noir menace is the glue that holds the whole of the Batman oeuvre together. Noir is the element that transforms the ordinary into the extraordinary—or nightmarish.

In the following commentary writer Foster Hirsch describes the essential elements of film noir. It just as easily describes Batman's world.

"Dramas of people in crisis, noir illuminated the night world of the other self that bedevils us all," Hirsch writes. "...In the verve and collo-

BUT NO ONE KNOWS, EXCEPT YOU AND ME... AND NOTHING MATTERS NOW BUT THE TWO OF US...
JUST YOU AND ME... MEANT FOR EACH OTHER...
NO, SWEETHEART... YOU'VE GOT ME ALL WRONG!
THAT'S NOT HOW I OPERATE!
KLICK

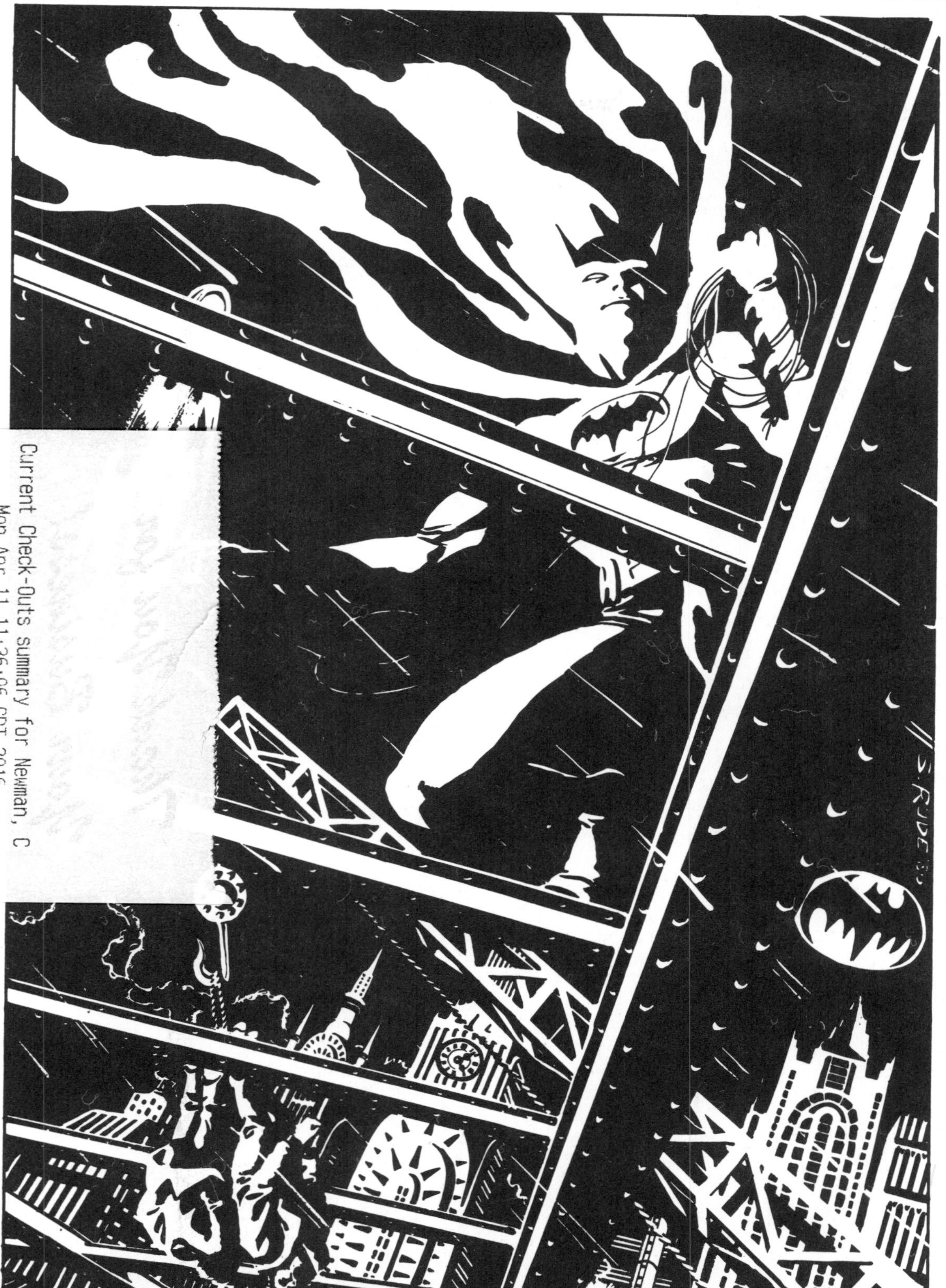

Above: Batman *#400, October 1986 (Steve Rude pin-up, last page of book)*. Left: *Batman and Terry Tremayne evoke Sam Spade and Brigid O'Shaughnessy in this homage to Dashiell Hammett.* (Batman *#269, November 1975, ''The Daily Death of Terry Tremayne,'' p. 18 [select panels].)*

quial tanginess of its dialogue, in its range of provocative themes, in its gallery of taut performances, its studied compositions in light and shadow, its creation of sustained suspense, and its dramatic use of the city ... film noir seizes and peneterates a universal heart of darkness."[1]

The Batman penetrates this "heart of darkness" during his ceaseless forays into Gotham's criminal underworld. Waiting for him, in every rat-infested corner of this land of noir, are plenty of gangsters, thugs, and two-bit hoods. But deeper into that endless darkness are even deadlier embodiments of evil.

From the very beginning the Dark Knight has been shadowed by twisted, maniacal supervillains. They represent the "night world of the other self" that the Dark Knight faces every time he plunges deep into the underworld.

1. Foster Hirsch, Film Noir (New York: Da Capo Press, Inc., 1981), p. 209.

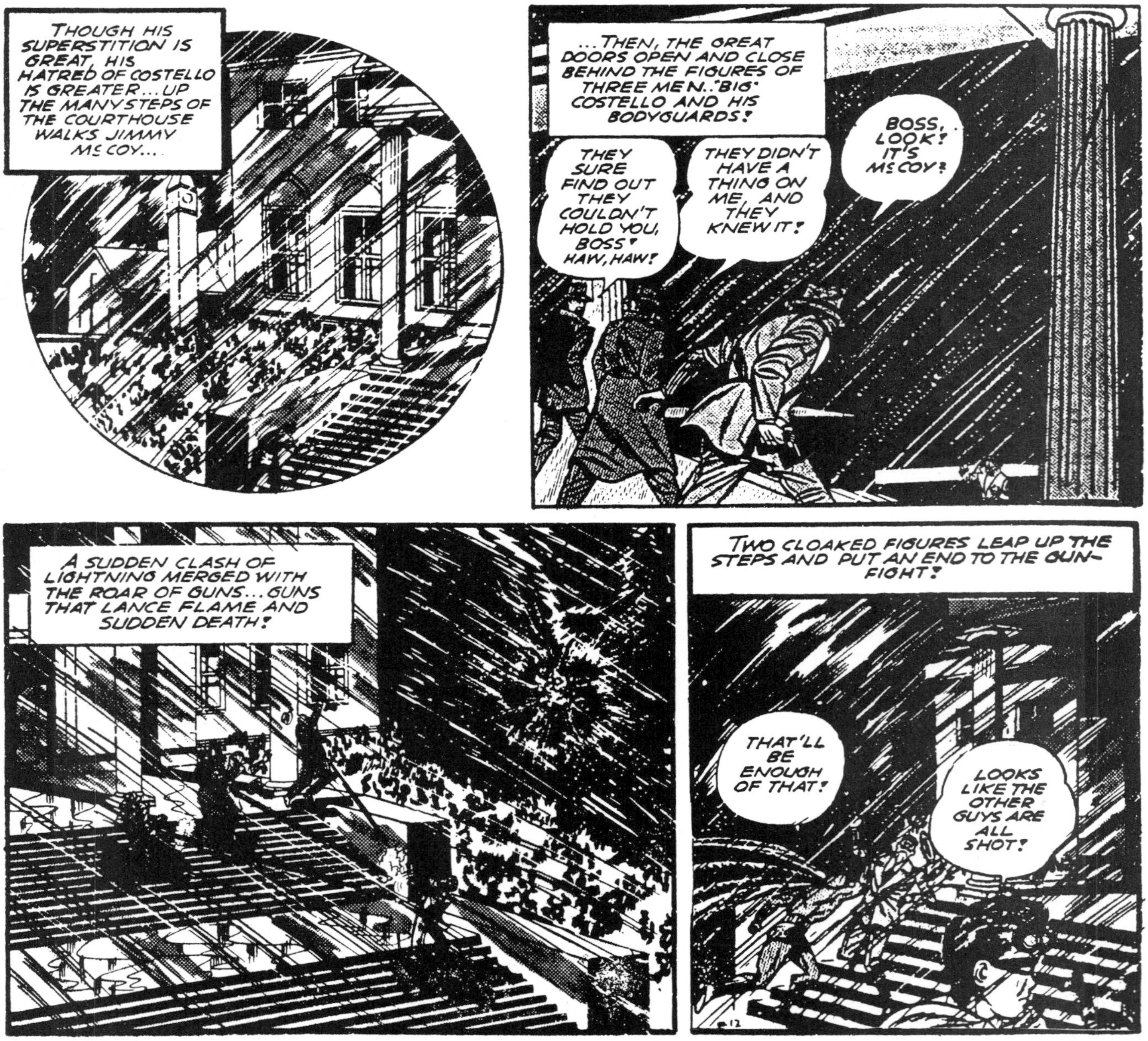
THOUGH HIS SUPERSTITION IS GREAT, HIS HATRED OF COSTELLO IS GREATER... UP THE MANY STEPS OF THE COURTHOUSE WALKS JIMMY McCOY...
...THEN, THE GREAT DOORS OPEN AND CLOSE BEHIND THE FIGURES OF THREE MEN.."BIG" COSTELLO AND HIS BODYGUARDS!
THEY SURE FIND OUT THEY COULDN'T HOLD YOU, BOSS! HAW, HAW!
THEY DIDN'T HAVE A THING ON ME, AND THEY KNEW IT!
BOSS, LOOK! IT'S McCOY!
A SUDDEN CLASH OF LIGHTNING MERGED WITH THE ROAR OF GUNS... GUNS THAT LANCE FLAME AND SUDDEN DEATH!
TWO CLOAKED FIGURES LEAP UP THE STEPS AND PUT AN END TO THE GUN-FIGHT!
THAT'LL BE ENOUGH OF THAT!
LOOKS LIKE THE OTHER GUYS ARE ALL SHOT!

The Golden Age saga of gangster Jimmy McCoy (based on James Cagney's "The Public Enemy"), made it clear that it's a doomed man who takes up a crime career. (Batman #4, *Winter 1941, "Public Enemy No. 1," pp. 12 [select panels] and 13.*)

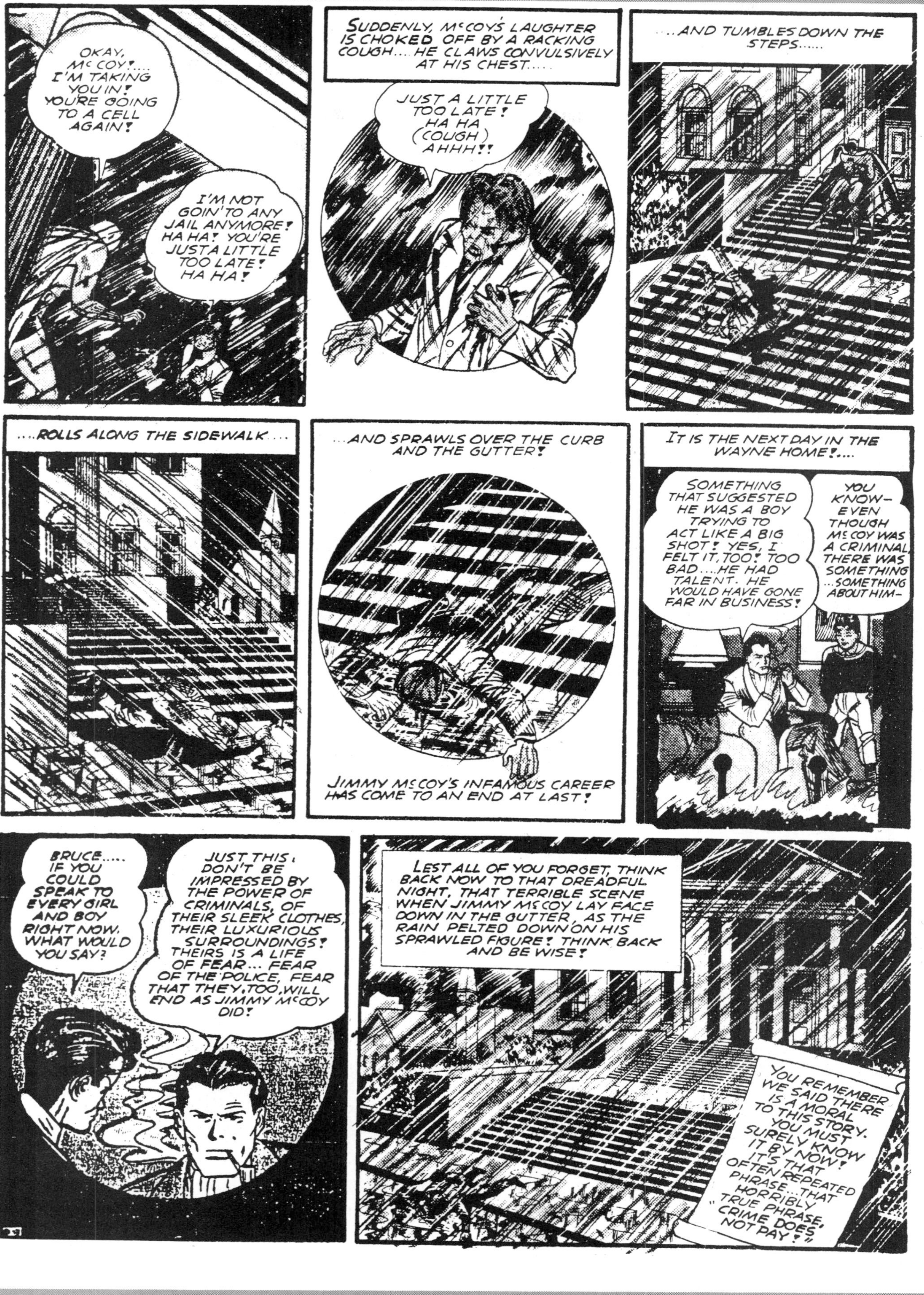

OKAY, McCOY!... I'M TAKING YOU IN! YOU'RE GOING TO A CELL AGAIN!
I'M NOT GOIN' TO ANY JAIL ANYMORE! HA HA! YOU'RE JUST A LITTLE TOO LATE! HA HA!
SUDDENLY, McCOY'S LAUGHTER IS CHOKED OFF BY A RACKING COUGH.... HE CLAWS CONVULSIVELY AT HIS CHEST.....
JUST A LITTLE TOO LATE! HA HA (COUGH) AHHH!!
....AND TUMBLES DOWN THE STEPS......
....ROLLS ALONG THE SIDEWALK....
...AND SPRAWLS OVER THE CURB AND THE GUTTER!
JIMMY McCOY'S INFAMOUS CAREER HAS COME TO AN END AT LAST!
IT IS THE NEXT DAY IN THE WAYNE HOME!....
YOU KNOW- EVEN THOUGH McCOY WAS A CRIMINAL THERE WAS SOMETHING ...SOMETHING ABOUT HIM-
SOMETHING THAT SUGGESTED HE WAS A BOY TRYING TO ACT LIKE A BIG SHOT! YES, I FELT IT, TOO! TOO BAD....HE HAD TALENT. HE WOULD HAVE GONE FAR IN BUSINESS!
BRUCE..... IF YOU COULD SPEAK TO EVERY GIRL AND BOY RIGHT NOW, WHAT WOULD YOU SAY?
JUST THIS: DON'T BE IMPRESSED BY THE POWER OF CRIMINALS, OF THEIR SLEEK CLOTHES, THEIR LUXURIOUS SURROUNDINGS! THEIRS IS A LIFE OF FEAR... FEAR OF THE POLICE, FEAR THAT THEY, TOO, WILL END AS JIMMY McCOY DID!
LEST ALL OF YOU FORGET, THINK BACK NOW TO THAT DREADFUL NIGHT, THAT TERRIBLE SCENE WHEN JIMMY McCOY LAY FACE DOWN IN THE GUTTER, AS THE RAIN PELTED DOWN ON HIS SPRAWLED FIGURE! THINK BACK AND BE WISE!
YOU REMEMBER WE SAID THERE IS A MORAL TO THIS STORY. YOU MUST SURELY KNOW IT BY NOW! IT'S THAT OFTEN REPEATED PHRASE...THAT HORRIBLY TRUE PHRASE, "CRIME DOES NOT PAY!"

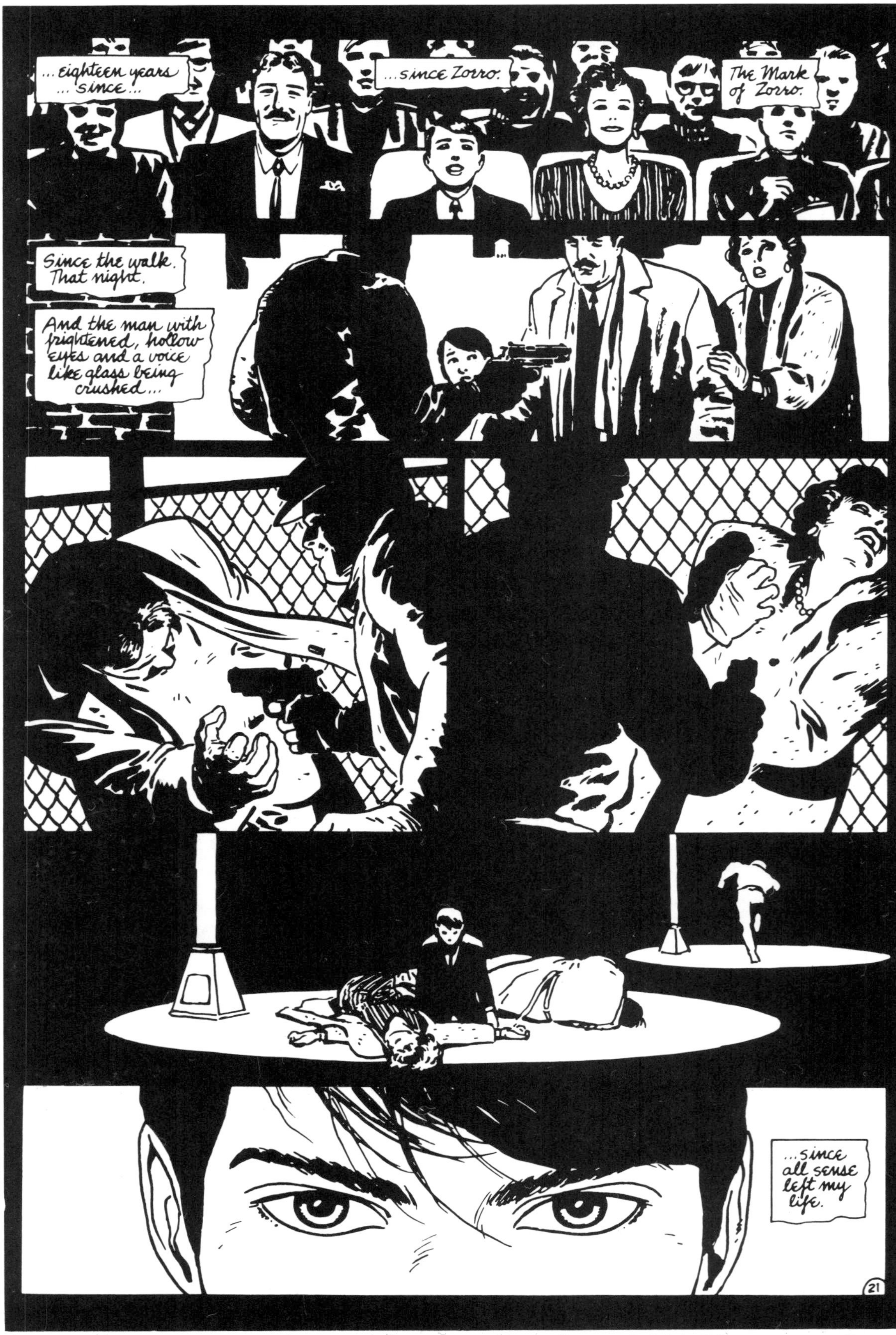

...eighteen years ...since...
...since Zorro.
The Mark of Zorro.
Since the walk. That night.
And the man with frightened, hollow eyes and a voice like glass being crushed...
...since all sense left my life.
21

Bruce Wayne would never forget that dark moment when all sense left his life. (Batman #404, *February 1987, "Batman Year One, Chapter One," p. 21.*)

As of this writing Tumbleweed Crossing may not even exist. When Batman arrived in 1973, that place in Arizona was a virtual ghost town on the edge of rugged, and uncharted, southwestern terrain. But the piece of an Arizona map found during a counterfeiting bust had brought the Dark Knight to the desolate place. The bogus bills were so perfect, only a master counterfeiting operation could be at work. For Batman it was worth the gamble to find out if Tumbleweed Crossing might be the base for a sophisticated national operation.

But someone else was interested, also. In Gotham City he also found the lead that would bring him to dusty Tumbleweed. Or rather, he had made a lead by hypnotizing one of the busted counterfeiters into revealing the name of the fateful town.

The mystery man shadowed Batman throughout the adventure. On the trail the Dark Knight would find dazed hoodlums babbling about the creature in the hat and long coat with the eyes that burned holes into their skulls, or Batman might hear a snatch of that eerie, unmistakable laugh and wonder if HE had finally returned.

After Batman had busted the operation hidden in the ruins of the ancient cliff dwellers and captured the operation's kingpin—a crafty old-timer who ran Tumbleweed Crossing's broken-down hotel—the Dark Knight received a mysterious note from the invisible man who had been pursuing the case with him.

It was at midnight in the Gotham freight yards ("when dawn is no more than a distant promise") that Batman met the Shadow. Batman asked the dark figure why he had followed him throughout the case.

"I was curious!" the Shadow replied. "I wished to determine if you deserve your splendid reputation! I am happy to state you fulfilled my greatest expectations!"

"I consider that a magnificent compliment," Batman answered. "I've never told anyone this, but you were my biggest inspiration! I'd be honored to shake your hand!"

"The honor is mine," the Shadow replied as they exchanged a firm handshake.

And then the Shadow, with a cackling laugh, disappeared back into the darkness, leaving Batman alone with the night.

—As recorded in "Who Knows What Evil—?" *Batman* 253, November 1973.

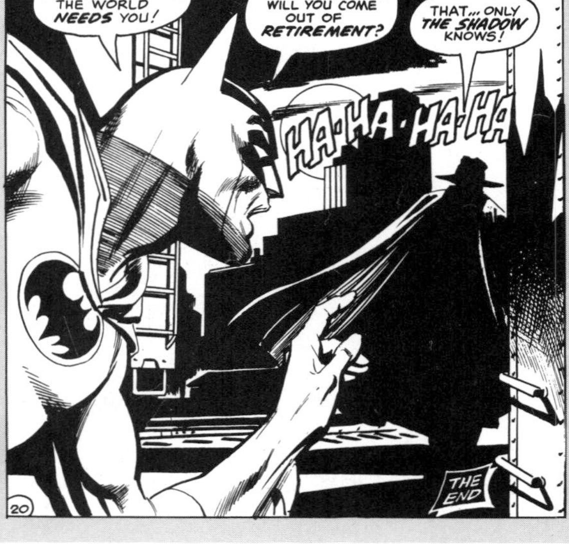
NO! DON'T LEAVE! THE WORLD NEEDS YOU!
WILL YOU HELP? WILL YOU COME OUT OF RETIREMENT?
THAT... ONLY THE SHADOW KNOWS!
HA-HA-HA-HA
20
THE END

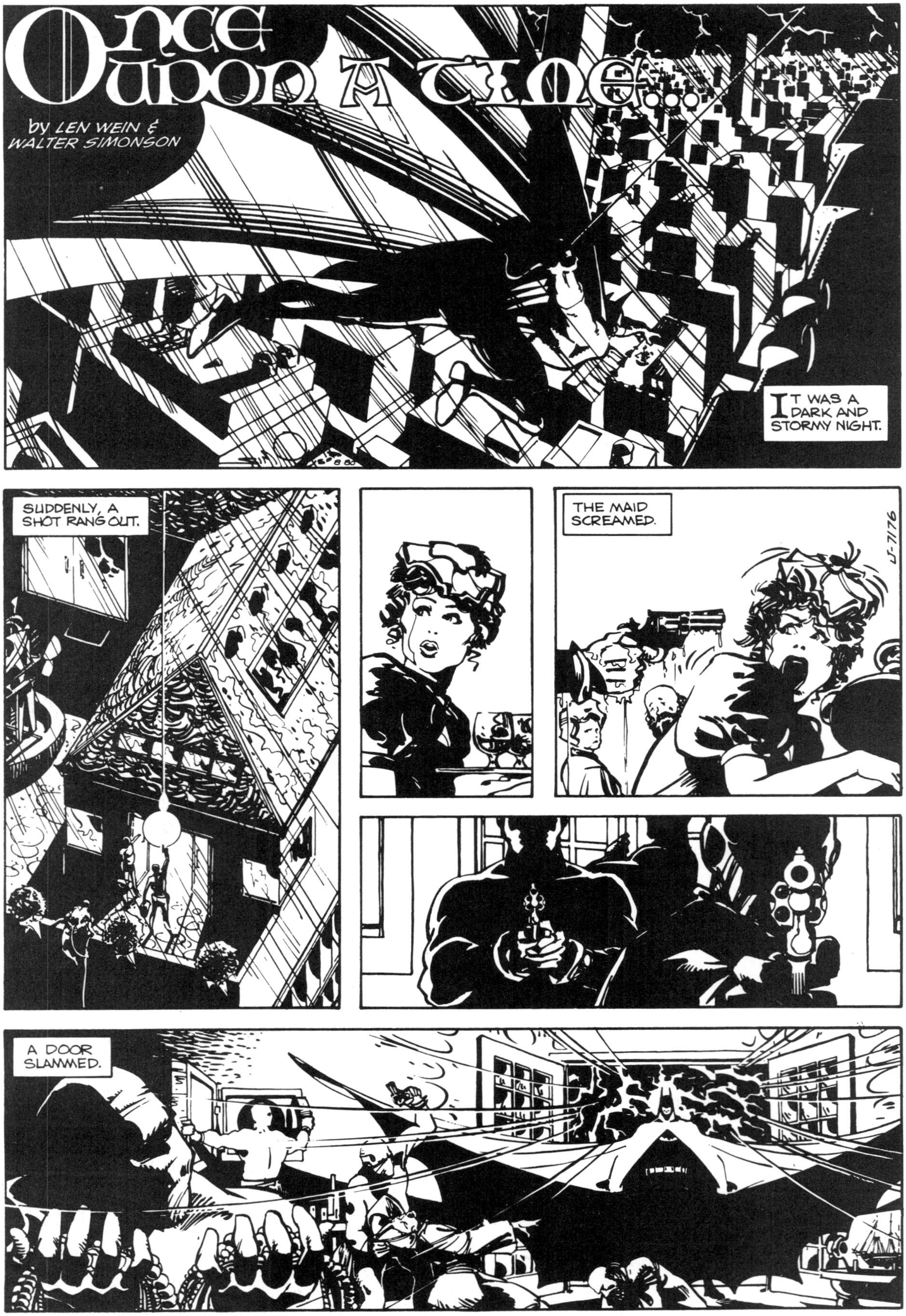
ONCE UPON A TIME...
by LEN WEIN & WALTER SIMONSON
IT WAS A DARK AND STORMY NIGHT.
SUDDENLY, A SHOT RANG OUT.
THE MAID SCREAMED.
A DOOR SLAMMED.

Detective #500, *March 1981, "Once Upon A Time . . . ," pp. 1–2.*

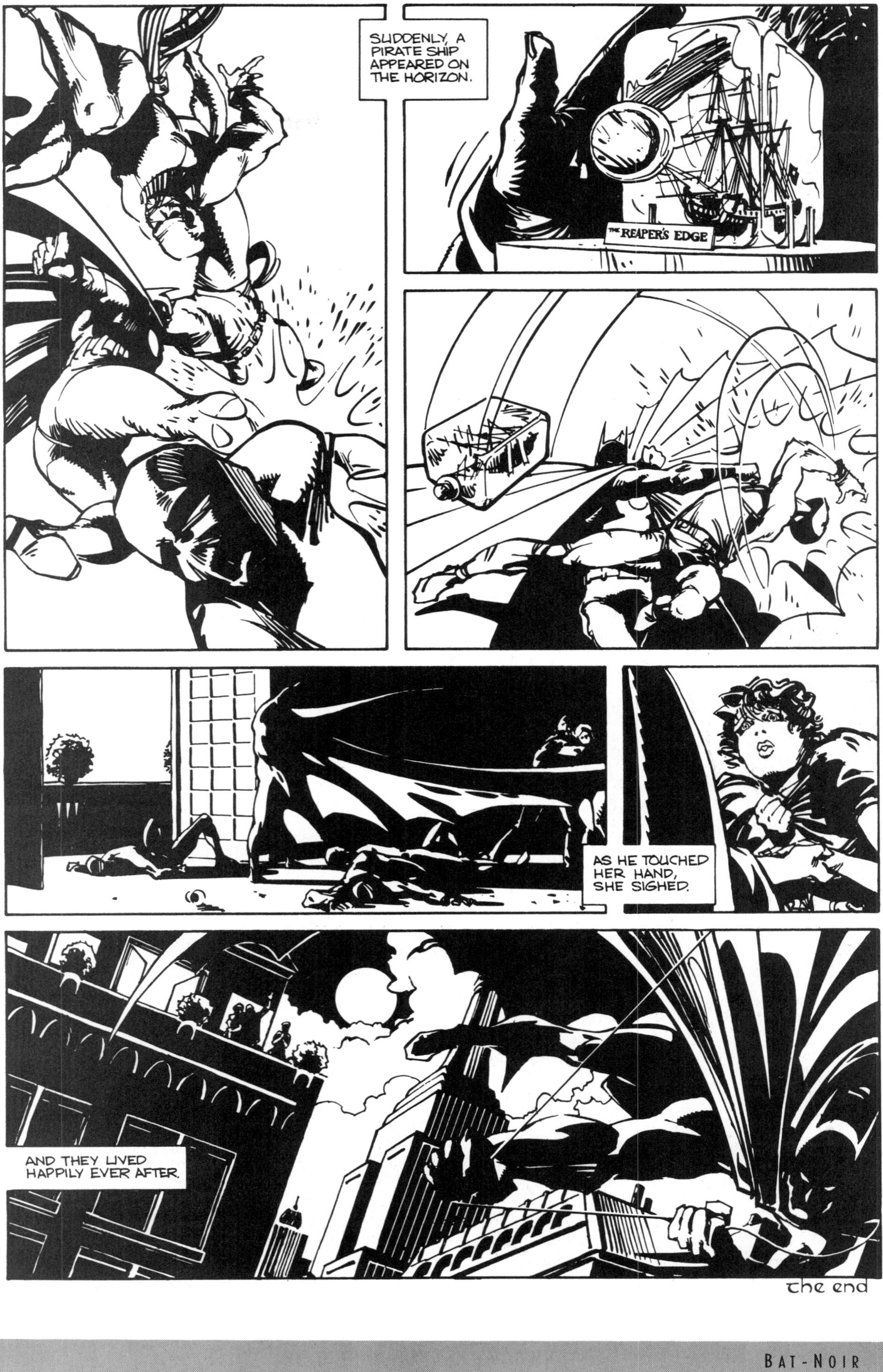
SUDDENLY, A PIRATE SHIP APPEARED ON THE HORIZON.
THE REAPER'S EDGE
AS HE TOUCHED HER HAND, SHE SIGHED.
AND THEY LIVED HAPPILY EVER AFTER.
the end

CHAPTER 15

INTO THE UNDERWORLD

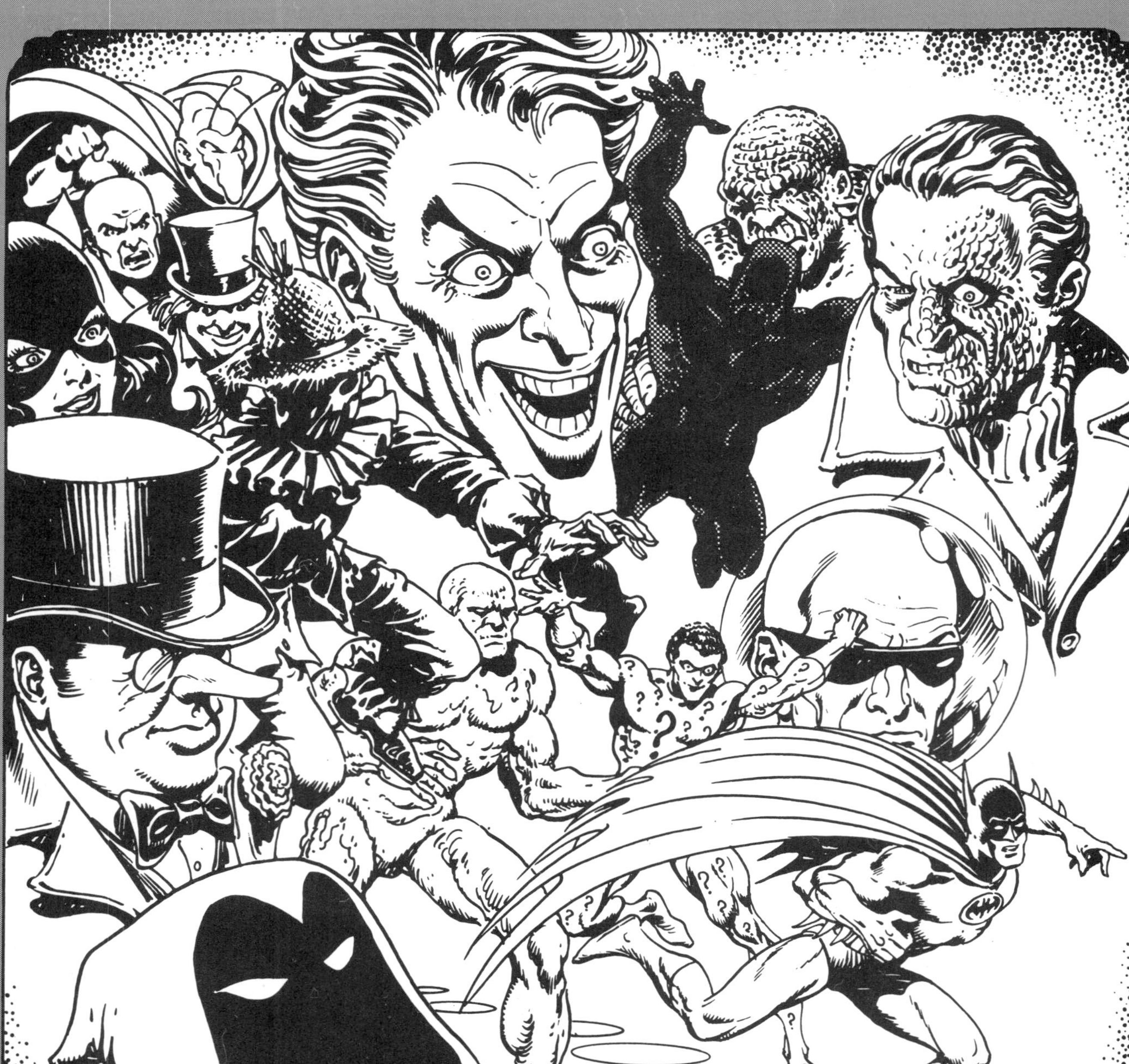
"... ALWAYS LURKING AND WAITING AND HATING AND HOUNDING ME ... TRYING TO DESTROY ME..."
19

Batman *#380, February 1985, "End of The Bat," p. 19 (panel).*

N JIM STARLIN AND BERNI WRIGHTSON'S *The Cult,* the chilling four-part psychodrama opens with a fevered dream tormenting the Batman.

In his dark dream landscape Batman sees himself as a young boy, not yet devastated by the Crime Alley tragedy to come, exploring the sprawling grounds of Wayne Estates.

Suddenly he comes upon a foreboding house atop a hill. Despite its aura of danger and death, he enters the decaying, deserted house. He feels a sweaty fear as he walks down a hall where shadows play across walls lined with dusty and forgotten swords, shields, battle-axes, crossbows, and other ancient weapons. But young Bruce shrugs off the fear that tries to envelop him like the shadows he walks through.

"I'm young and invulnerable," he thinks.

At the end of the hall he finds a door. Somehow his feeling of confidence begins to waver, even as his hand hovers above the door handle. Something inside him screams to turn and run from the place—but something else makes him open the door.

A long flight of medieval stone steps takes him deep into the earth, "closer to the fear." At the bottom he finds a trapdoor, where, locked away, the fear awaits.

Suddenly the trapdoor bursts open, and the Joker pops out like a macabre jack-in-the-box.

"No matter where you run, fear will seek you out," the young boy thinks at the sight of the cackling, demonic apparition.[1]

For fifty years the Dark Knight has been facing fear in the form of the most maniacal foes any hero has ever encountered. Indeed, if his dream sequence had continued, a whole army of grotesques could have popped out from the underworld to stand alongside the Joker, including Two-Face, the Penguin, Clayface, Doctor Death, Hugo Strange, Killer Moth, the Mad Hatter, the Scarecrow, and the Riddler.

If by the 1980s Batman has grown noticeably more withdrawn, at times downright irritable, it's because decades of fighting such a villainous lineup would furrow the brow of the most su-perpowered hero, much less a mortal crime buster.

When it gets down to bragging rights over which hero has been tested by the villainous best, most superbeings can only boast of one or two archfoes—Batman has dozens. (Even Superman's gallery of evil starts getting lean after Lex Luthor and Brainiac. The Man of Steel's crime-stopping casebook is heavy with hopelessly overmatched, low-rent criminal opponents.)

Dick Tracy, one of the few crime fighters who could stay up all night with Batman swapping tales of frightful foes, has a pantheon of villains that differs in many respects from Batman's own rogue's gallery. For one, Dick Tracy's enemies usually didn't survive their initial encounters with the square-jawed detective—if some accident didn't kill them, Tracy (licensed to pack a gun and not loath to use it) sometimes dispatched them in a final, furious shootout. But since Batman has vowed never to take a life, and Gotham's jails have never been able to permanently incarcerate Joker, Penguin, Two-Face, et al., the Dark Knight finds himself glued to a mad merry-go-round where the villains he battles, captures, and jails usually return to fight again another day.

And despite the similarly bizarre portraits of villainy in both *Batman* and *Dick Tracy,* each world of evil is unique, concludes Max Allan Collins, a man who should know—he scripts the continuing Dick Tracy comic strip and wrote a series of Batman adventures in the 1980s.

"While Bob Kane admits that Batman was to a degree a costumed version of Dick Tracy, it is unfair to suggest that the larger-than-life villains in the former derive from the latter," Collins wrote. "In fact, the Joker predates most of Tracy's grotesque foes; prior to the appearance of the Mole in 1941, (Chester) Gould's villains had been primarily gangsters and outlaws patterned after the Capones and Dillingers of the day."[2]

Not all of Batman's foes have been misshapen

---

1. "Ordeal," *The Cult,* Book One, 1988.
2. Max Allan Collins, "The Dick Tracy/Batman Connection; Part Two: The Galleries of Grotesques," *Batman* 403 (December 1986).

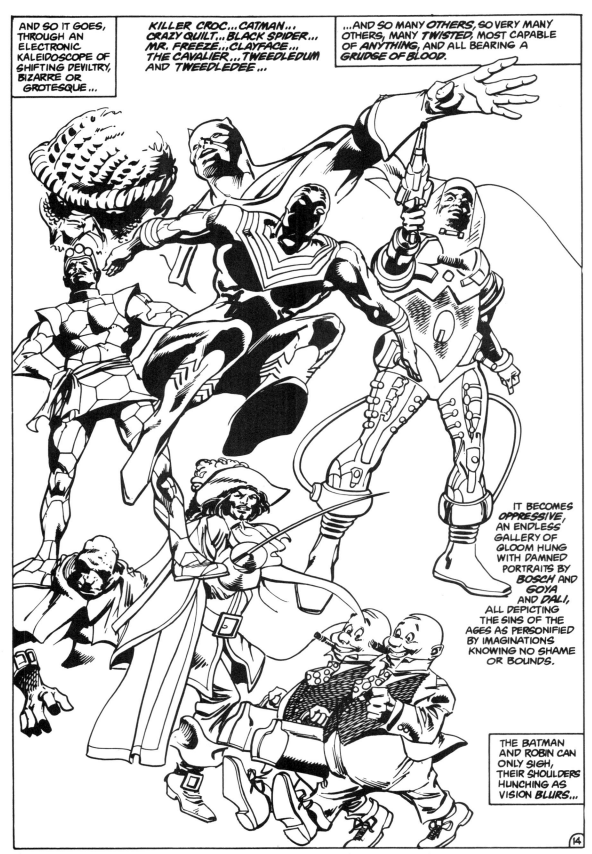

AND SO IT GOES, THROUGH AN ELECTRONIC KALEIDOSCOPE OF SHIFTING DEVILTRY, BIZARRE OR GROTESQUE...

KILLER CROC...CATMAN... CRAZY QUILT...BLACK SPIDER... MR. FREEZE...CLAYFACE... THE CAVALIER...TWEEDLEDUM AND TWEEDLEDEE...

...AND SO MANY OTHERS, SO VERY MANY OTHERS, MANY TWISTED, MOST CAPABLE OF ANYTHING, AND ALL BEARING A GRUDGE OF BLOOD.

IT BECOMES OPPRESSIVE, AN ENDLESS GALLERY OF GLOOM HUNG WITH DAMNED PORTRAITS BY BOSCH AND GOYA AND DALI, ALL DEPICTING THE SINS OF THE AGES AS PERSONIFIED BY IMAGINATIONS KNOWING NO SHAME OR BOUNDS.

THE BATMAN AND ROBIN CAN ONLY SIGH, THEIR SHOULDERS HUNCHING AS VISION BLURS...

The Bat Cave's computer files yield more portraits of villainy than just The Joker, Penguin, and Two-Face. Here's a glimpse at a few of the denizens of Gotham's underworld who've given Batman nightmares. (Detective #566, September 1986, ''Know Your Foes,'' p. 14.)

Batman foes are noted for their mastery of ingenious gadgetry. Here Mr. Zero (forced to wear a suit that maintains zero-degree temperatures after an accident with an experimental freezing solution), puts a pursuing patrol car on ice. (Batman *#121, February 1959, ''The Ice Crimes of Mr. Zero,'' p. 7 [select panels].)*

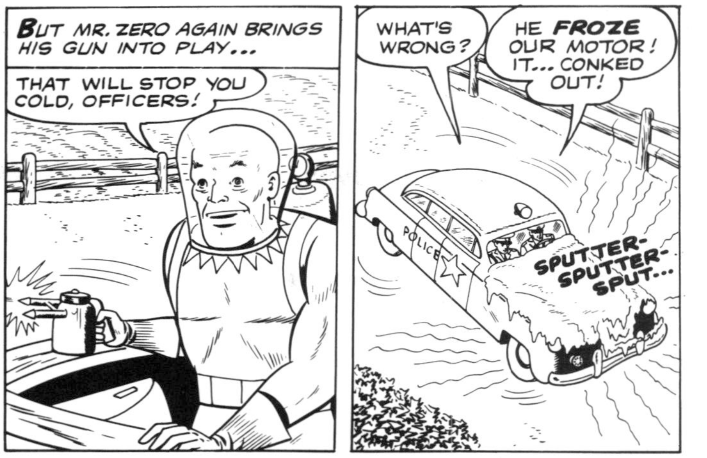
BUT MR. ZERO AGAIN BRINGS HIS GUN INTO PLAY...
THAT WILL STOP YOU COLD, OFFICERS!
WHAT'S WRONG?
HE FROZE OUR MOTOR! IT... CONKED OUT!
POLICE
SPUTTER-SPUTTER-SPUT...

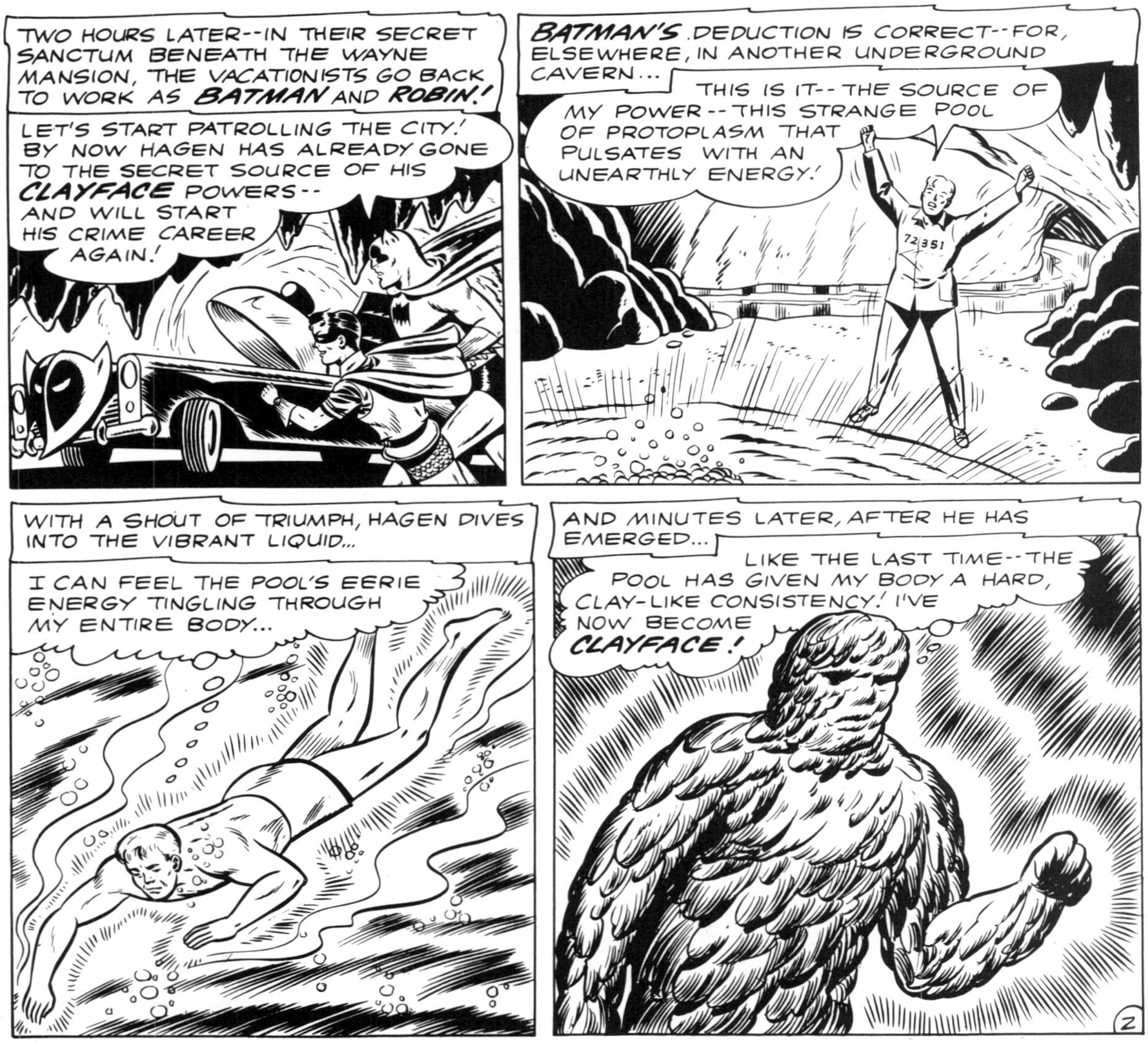
TWO HOURS LATER--IN THEIR SECRET SANCTUM BENEATH THE WAYNE MANSION, THE VACATIONISTS GO BACK TO WORK AS BATMAN AND ROBIN!
LET'S START PATROLLING THE CITY! BY NOW HAGEN HAS ALREADY GONE TO THE SECRET SOURCE OF HIS CLAYFACE POWERS-- AND WILL START HIS CRIME CAREER AGAIN!
BATMAN'S DEDUCTION IS CORRECT--FOR, ELSEWHERE, IN ANOTHER UNDERGROUND CAVERN...
THIS IS IT--THE SOURCE OF MY POWER--THIS STRANGE POOL OF PROTOPLASM THAT PULSATES WITH AN UNEARTHLY ENERGY!
72351
WITH A SHOUT OF TRIUMPH, HAGEN DIVES INTO THE VIBRANT LIQUID...
I CAN FEEL THE POOL'S EERIE ENERGY TINGLING THROUGH MY ENTIRE BODY...
AND MINUTES LATER, AFTER HE HAS EMERGED...
LIKE THE LAST TIME--THE POOL HAS GIVEN MY BODY A HARD, CLAY-LIKE CONSISTENCY! I'VE NOW BECOME CLAYFACE!
2

Unlike such permanently disfigured underworld kingpins as The Joker and Two-Face, Matt Hagen willingly exchanges his handsome physique for the grotesque, but super-powered, form of Clayface in order to commit crimes. (Hagen marks the second of three incarnations of the Clayface namesake. In the 1940s there was the crazed actor Basil Karlo, and in the Eighties there is the monstrous Preston Payne Clayface—''Of the three, [Payne is] easily the craziest and the most dangerous,'' Batman has concluded.) (Detective *#312, February 1963, ''The Secret of Clayface's Power,'' p. 2 [select panels].)*

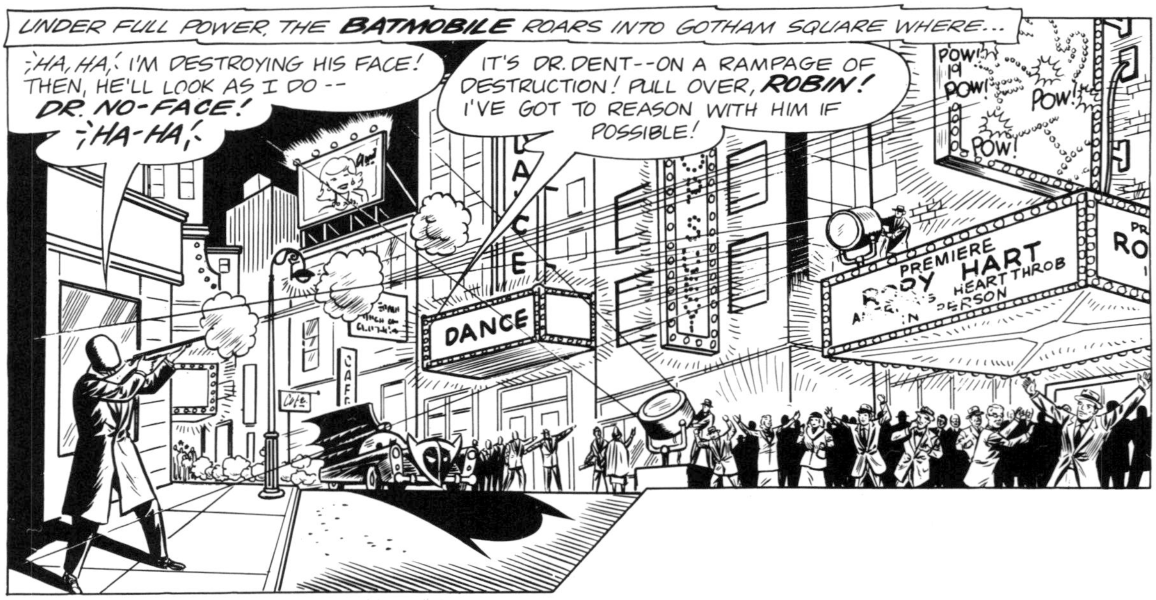
UNDER FULL POWER, THE BATMOBILE ROARS INTO GOTHAM SQUARE WHERE...
¡HA, HA,! I'M DESTROYING HIS FACE! THEN, HE'LL LOOK AS I DO -- DR. NO-FACE! ¡HA-HA!
IT'S DR. DENT--ON A RAMPAGE OF DESTRUCTION! PULL OVER, ROBIN! I'VE GOT TO REASON WITH HIM IF POSSIBLE!
POW! POW! POW! POW!
DANCE
PREMIERE
HEART THROB

Top: *Most superheroes contend with criminals seeking plunder or power. But in Batman's world an alarming number of evildoers are prone to nothing more than psychotic rampages. Here we see a frenzied Dr. No-Face performance in Gotham Square.* (**Detective** *#319, September 1963, "The Fantastic Dr. No-Face," p. 3 [panel].*) **Bottom:** *His retirement a thing of the past, the Penguin demonstrates he hasn't lost the touch that made him arguably one of Batman's greatest foes (second only to The Joker).* (**Batman** *#169, February 1965, "Partners in Plunder!" p. 5 [select panels].*)

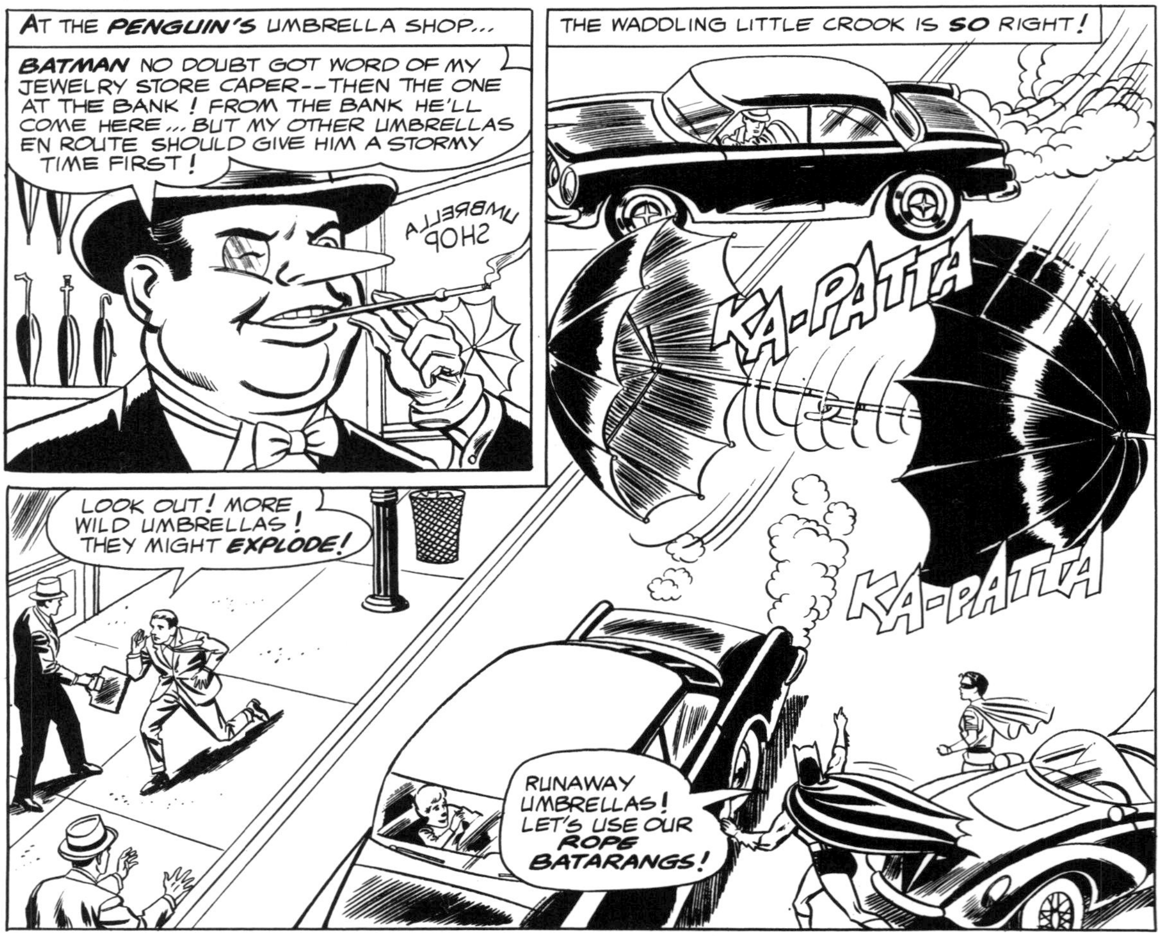
AT THE PENGUIN'S UMBRELLA SHOP...
BATMAN NO DOUBT GOT WORD OF MY JEWELRY STORE CAPER--THEN THE ONE AT THE BANK! FROM THE BANK HE'LL COME HERE... BUT MY OTHER UMBRELLAS EN ROUTE SHOULD GIVE HIM A STORMY TIME FIRST!
UMBRELLA SHOP
THE WADDLING LITTLE CROOK IS SO RIGHT!
KA-PATTA
KA-PATTA
LOOK OUT! MORE WILD UMBRELLAS! THEY MIGHT EXPLODE!
RUNAWAY UMBRELLAS! LET'S USE OUR ROPE BATARANGS!

creatures from the darkness. Lovely, leggy females such as Catwoman, Poison Ivy, and Nocturna have not only provided criminal conflicts, but sexual tension.

Selina Kyle, in her Catwoman identity, has been Batman's longest-lived female foil, having first appeared in *Batman* 1. Although considered a wily, dangerous opponent, Catwoman's effectiveness as an archcriminal was hampered by her romantic feelings for the Dark Knight. For decades Catwoman crimes, and the thrill of the resulting chase by Batman, served as a kind of courtship. In the 1980s the two finally had a brief, and overdue, romance.

The feline theme was carried on in deadlier fashion by Selina's brother, Karl, who had a brief criminal career as the King of the Cats (*Batman* 69/3), and Tom Blake, a trapper of jungle cats who took up crime in the early to mid-1960s as the deadly Cat-Man.

The trademark of many Batman foes is this almost pathological adherence to elaborate identities and crime themes.

The Penguin, often ranked only behind the Joker as the archnemesis of the Dynamic Duo, has long delighted in bird-theme crimes. The physical appearance of the Penguin has always been a caricature of a human being—the waddling, chubby, ski-nosed fellow always wears gloves, a high silk hat, and sports a monocle. The Penguin has a fondness for umbrellas, Shakespeare, and Keats. But there civility ends—in his early days, particularly, the Penguin was a death-dealing criminal who, like the Joker, viewed crime as the ultimate art form. (Even the seemingly innocuous and humorous looks of those roly-poly twins Tweedledum and Tweedledee disguised a ruthless criminality.)

The modus operandi of Edward Nigma, popularly known as the Riddler, has always been to tip Batman to a planned crime with cryptic riddles and puzzles. As it is with most of Batman's archfoes, ill-gotten gains were less important than winning a game of wits with the Darknight Detective.

"Could it be that I actually respect the Batman—and look forward to our periodic contests?" the Calendar Man, the Dark Knight's sometime foe, once mused. "Of course it could. And were I to kill the Batman—red-letter day aside . . . the rest of my days could well be blank boxes! With the Batman dead, would I have any reason to live?"[3]

But there is another level of Batman superfoes who have no such compunction about killing the Dynamic Duo. Many such opponents have long since given themselves up totally to a violent madness.

There is the brilliant, but twisted, Jonathan Crane, who has periodically carried out his theories of the psychology of terror in his guise as

3. "Broken Dates," *Batman* 384 (June 1985), p. 4.

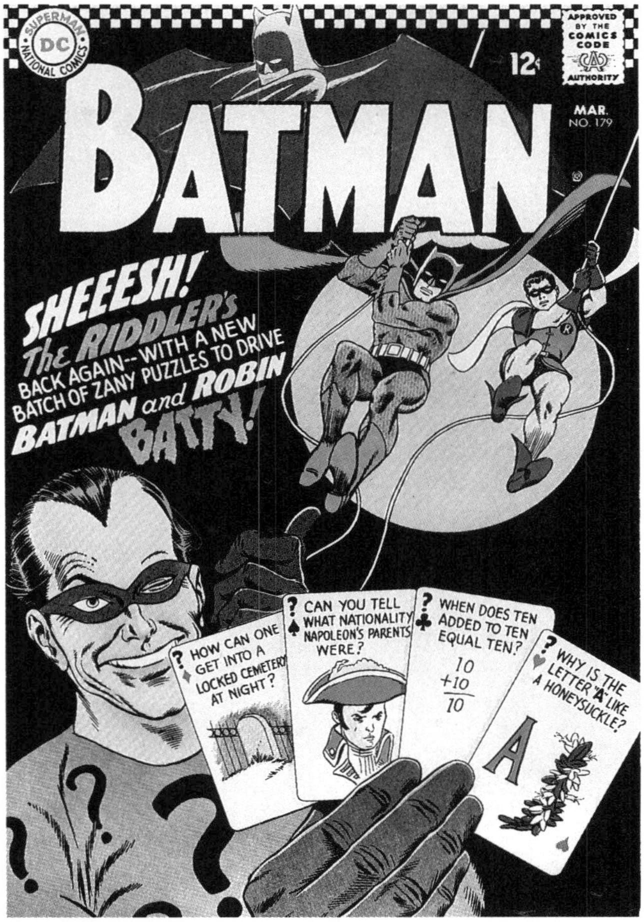

SUPERMAN DC NATIONAL COMICS
APPROVED BY THE COMICS CODE AUTHORITY
12¢
BATMAN
MAR. NO. 179
SHEEESH! The RIDDLER'S BACK AGAIN--WITH A NEW BATCH OF ZANY PUZZLES TO DRIVE BATMAN and ROBIN BATTY!
HOW CAN ONE GET INTO A LOCKED CEMETERY AT NIGHT?
CAN YOU TELL WHAT NATIONALITY NAPOLEON'S PARENTS WERE?
WHEN DOES TEN ADDED TO TEN EQUAL TEN?
10 +10 10
WHY IS THE LETTER 'A' LIKE A HONEYSUCKLE?
A

Riddle me this! Which villain had the honor of battling the Dynamic Duo in the first Batman-TV episode? None other than Edward "Riddler" Nigma who has been riddling Gotham City with crime since 1948. (Batman *#179, March 1966, cover.*)

the criminal Scarecrow. And Jervis "Mad Hatter" Tetch's hat-theme crimes were so outlandish, readers could only conclude he was indeed as crazy as his *Alice in Wonderland* namesake.

In a 1988 tale, the insane Cornelius Stirk captured and tortured his victims for the express purpose of extracting the chemicals in their bodies released during the feverish height of their terror.

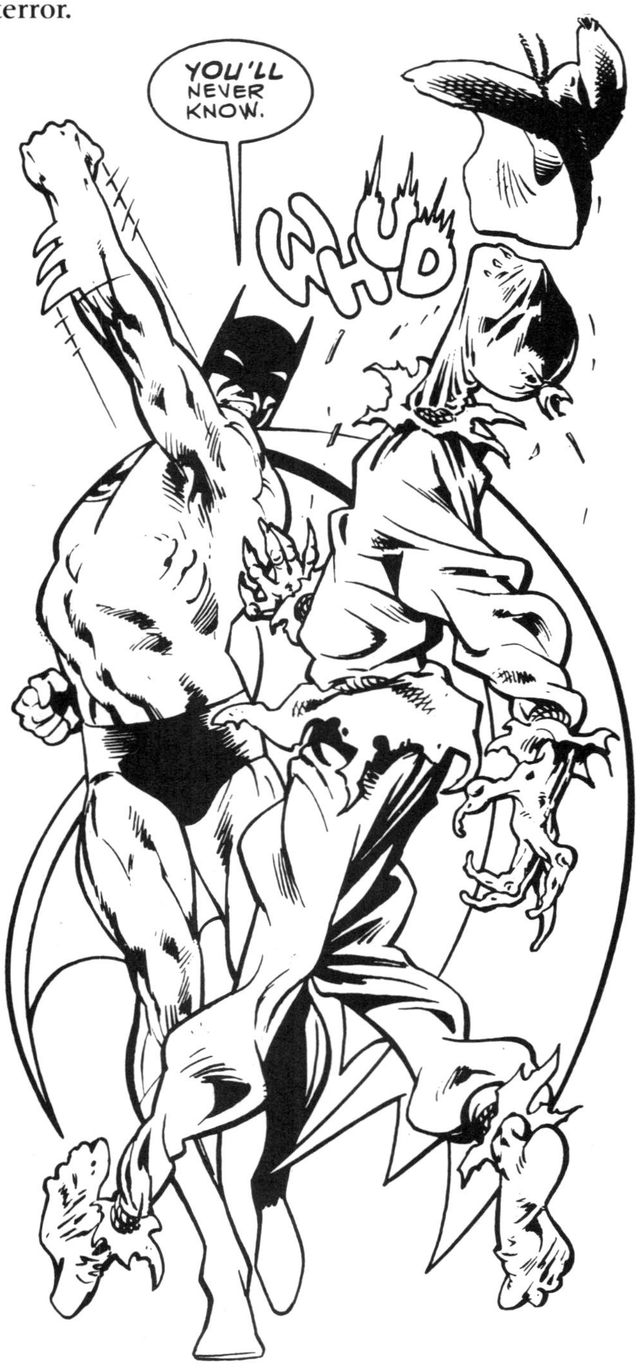
YOU'LL NEVER KNOW.
WHUD

The Dark Knight hammers the Scarecrow. (Detective *#571, February 1987, "Fear For Sale," p. 21 [panel].*)

"I need your fear," Stirk told a captured Batman, moments before the Dark Knight broke loose to capture him. "I need it to remain sane. I need its norepinephrine, surging like flames in your blood! I need its adrenocorticotrophic hormones."[4]

But the most famous study in madness in Batman's casebook must be Two-Face. The grim saga of the handsome, crusading district attorney Harvey Dent (identified as Harvey Kent in the early episodes), whose acid-scarred face suffered at the hands of a gangster he was prosecuting marked his descent into crime and madness, stands as an apotheosis in Batman's noir-tinged tradition.

With one side of his face retaining his perfectly chiseled good looks, the other side a monstrous mask of ravaged and wasted skin tissue, Two-Face's outer appearance perfectly captured the theme of the inner Jekyll/Hyde struggle. Two-Face even heeded the conflicting calls of his dual nature by the flip of a former lucky piece: if the scarred side of the coin came up, he'd follow his criminal nature; if the clean side appeared, he would abide by his law-abiding instincts.

And there have been those pathological foes with the physical abilities to give even a supreme athlete like Batman a fight. One of the most dangerous of these is Killer Croc, a gargantuan criminal with the strength, and the desire, to grip Batman in a fatal, spine-cracking bear hug.

Madness has taken every conceivable form in the villains who have risen up from the underworld to battle the Dark Knight. Batman foes have exemplified the most perverse possibilities lurking in the dark side of human nature, from the Savage Skull, a crazed ex-cop whose dismissal from the force drove him to a grisly rampage of killing Gotham policemen (*Batman* 360, June 1983), to the Dark Rider, a zealous foreign terrorist who immersed himself in deadly plutonium and attempted to throw himself into the Gotham reservoir to poison the city's water supply (*Batman* 394, April 1986).

4. "The Fear, Part Two: Dairy of a Madman," *Detective* 593 (December 1988), p. 12.

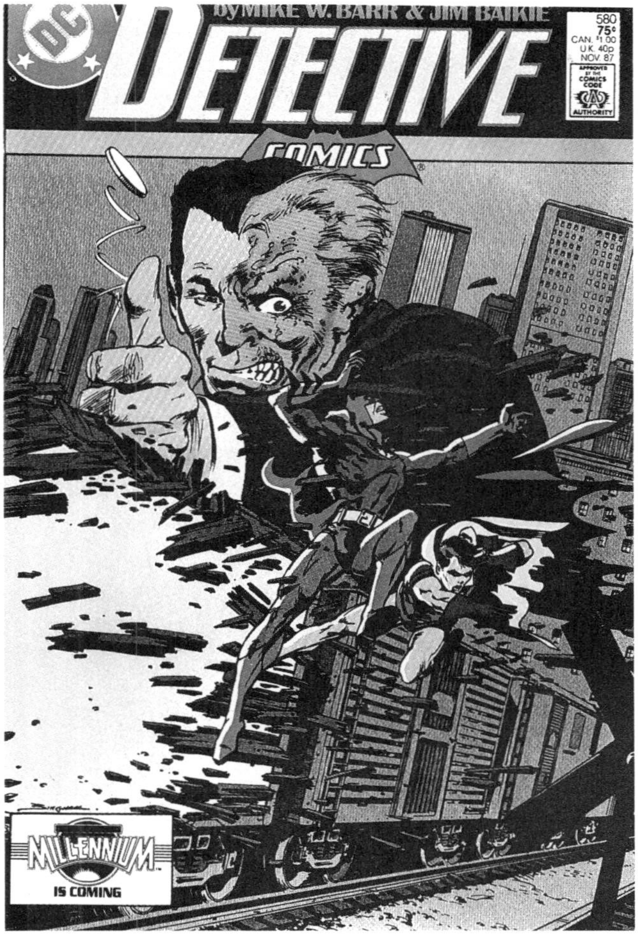
by MIKE W. BARR & JIM BAIKIE
DETECTIVE
COMICS
580
75¢
CAN. $1.00
U.K. 40p
NOV. 87
APPROVED BY THE COMICS CODE AUTHORITY
MILLENNIUM
IS COMING

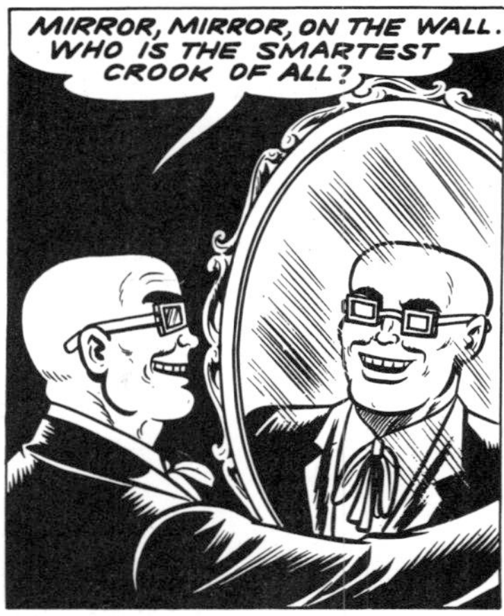
MIRROR, MIRROR, ON THE WALL... WHO IS THE SMARTEST CROOK OF ALL?

Left: *Detective #580, November 1987, cover.* Right: *Despite his confidence and cunning, the Mirror-Man's crime plans have always been busted by Batman. But one Mirror-Man attempt to prove that Batman was Bruce Wayne did come perilously close to unmasking the Dark Knight.* (Batman *#157, August 1963, "The Hunt For Batman's Secret Identity," p. 10 [panel].*) Below: *The Black Mask's trademark coup de grace is administered to a doomed Wayne Foundation executive—a mask holding a toxic compound that causes a hideous face-shriveling death.* (Detective *#553, August 1985, "The False Face Society of Gotham City," pp. 3-4 [select panels].*)

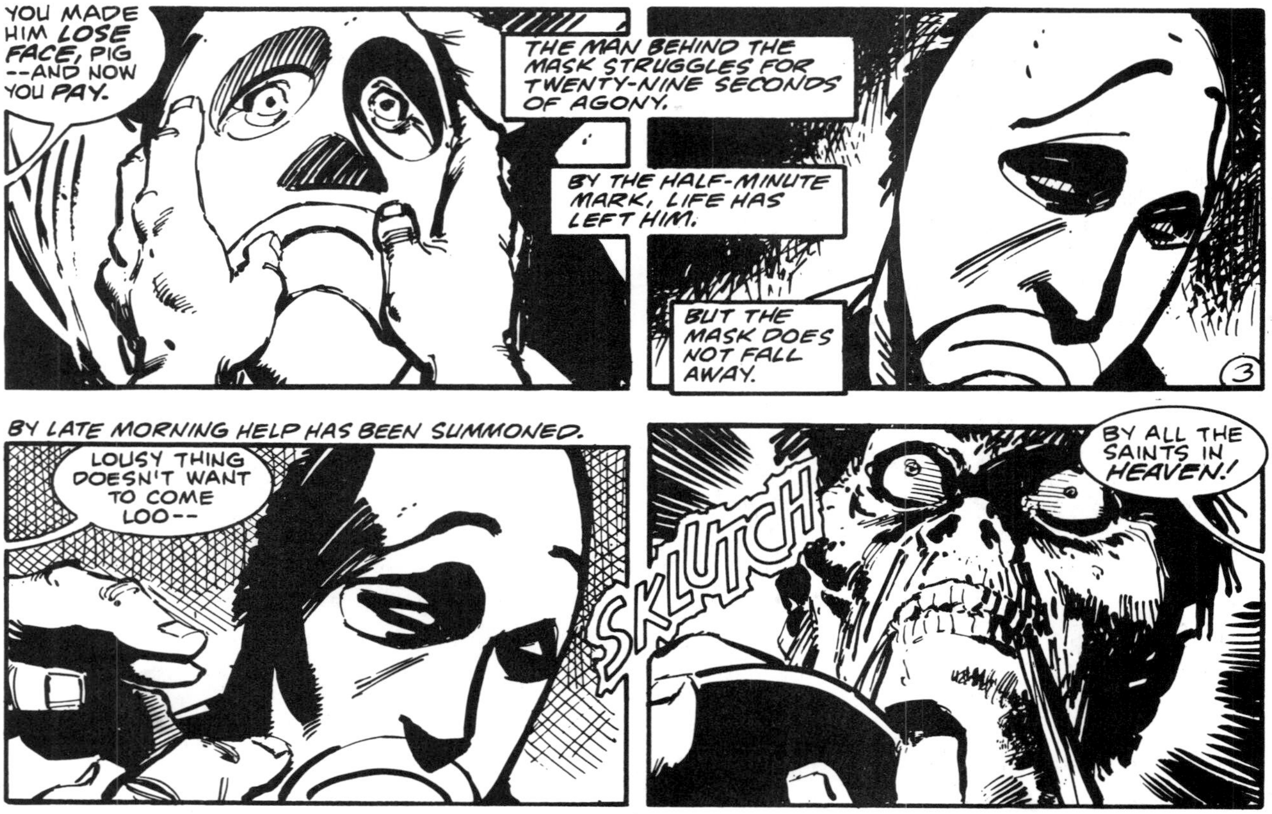
YOU MADE HIM LOSE FACE, PIG --AND NOW YOU PAY.
THE MAN BEHIND THE MASK STRUGGLES FOR TWENTY-NINE SECONDS OF AGONY.
BY THE HALF-MINUTE MARK, LIFE HAS LEFT HIM.
BUT THE MASK DOES NOT FALL AWAY.
3
BY LATE MORNING HELP HAS BEEN SUMMONED.
LOUSY THING DOESN'T WANT TO COME LOO--
SKLUTCH
BY ALL THE SAINTS IN HEAVEN!

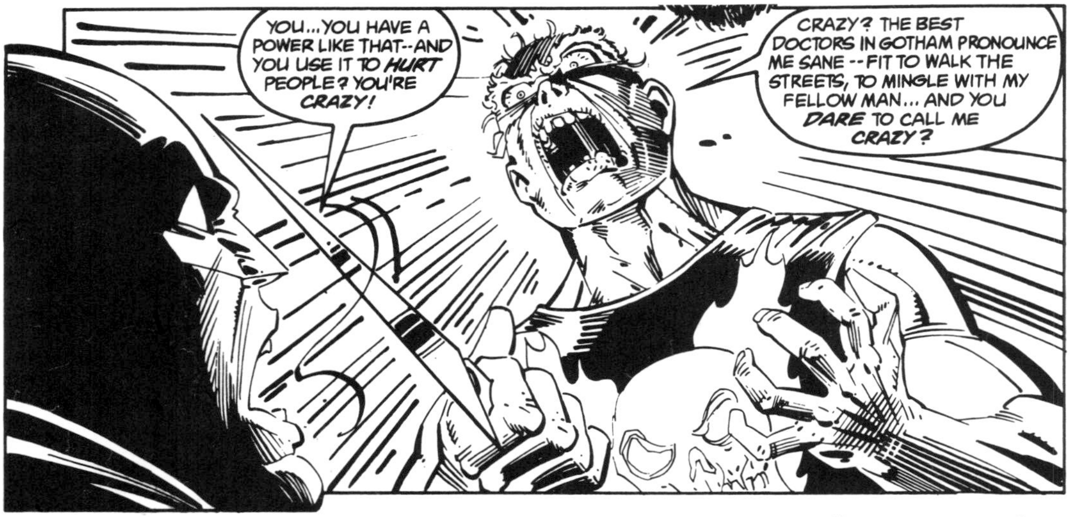
YOU...YOU HAVE A POWER LIKE THAT--AND YOU USE IT TO HURT PEOPLE? YOU'RE CRAZY!
CRAZY? THE BEST DOCTORS IN GOTHAM PRONOUNCE ME SANE --FIT TO WALK THE STREETS, TO MINGLE WITH MY FELLOW MAN... AND YOU DARE TO CALL ME CRAZY?

Top: *Cornelius Stirk is having another bad day—much to Batman's dismay.* (Detective *#593, December 1988, ''The Fear, Part Two: Diary of a Madman,'' p. 11 [panel].*) Bottom: *The Dark Rider, an obsessed foreign agent, soaks himself in deadly plutonium and attempts to throw himself into the Gotham reservoir to poison the city's water supply.* (Batman *#394, April 1986, ''At The Heart of Stone,'' p. 19 [select panels].*)

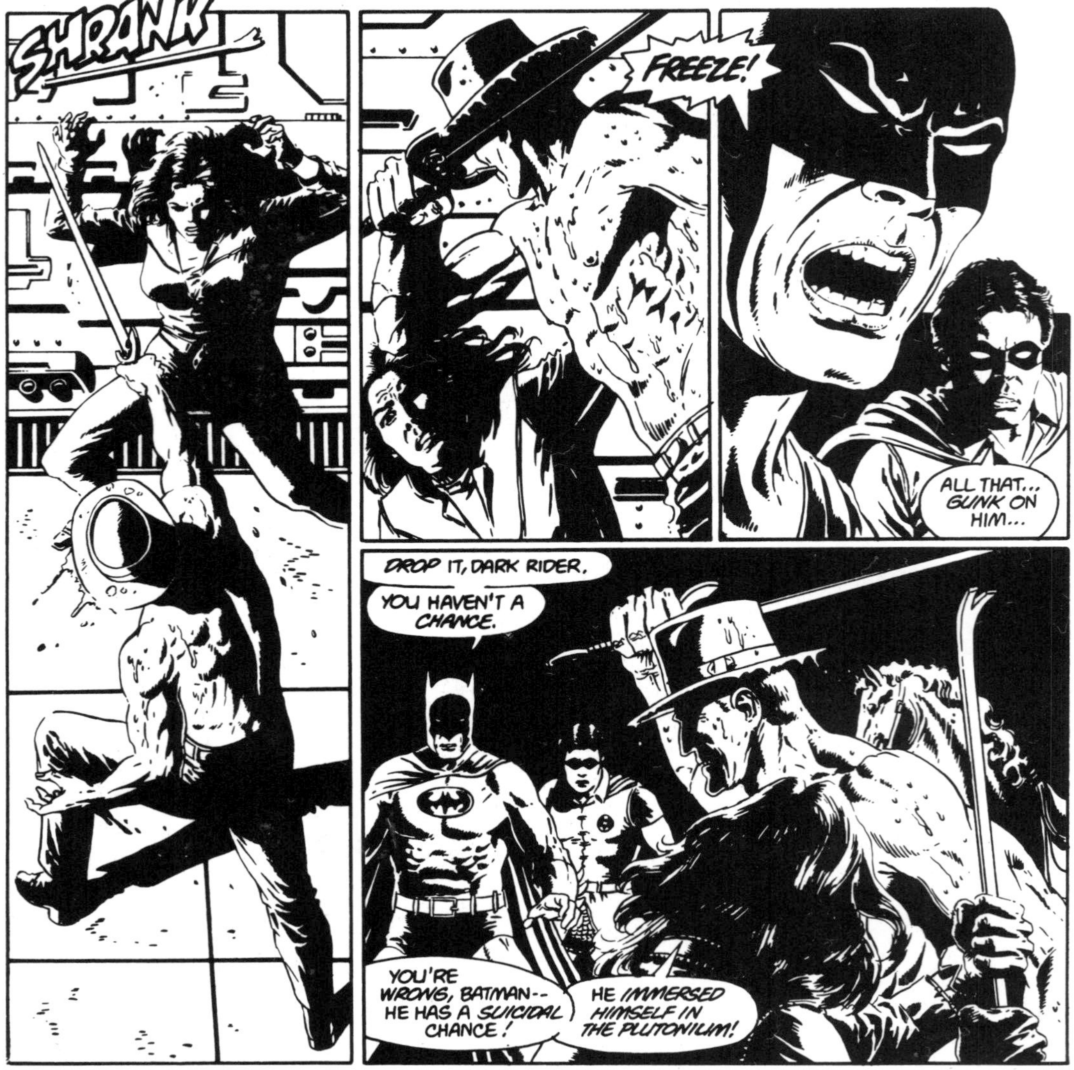
SHRANK
FREEZE!
ALL THAT... GUNK ON HIM...
DROP IT, DARK RIDER.
YOU HAVEN'T A CHANCE.
YOU'RE WRONG, BATMAN-- HE HAS A SUICIDAL CHANCE!
HE IMMERSED HIMSELF IN THE PLUTONIUM!

Detective Comics
566
75¢
SEPT 86
STARRING
BATMAN
BY
DOUG MOENCH
GENE COLAN
& BOB SMITH
PROWL THE DARK KNIGHT'S ROGUES GALLERY ...IF YOU DARE!
WHO watches the WATCHMEN?

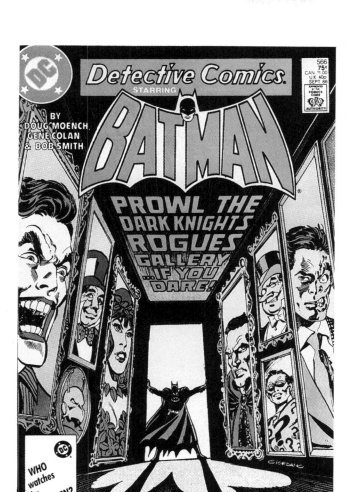

And while Batman's nightmare world has offered up such monsters as the deformed Clayface, the height of physical horror arguably was reached with the introduction of the Man-Bat. Once a scientist named Kirk Langstrom, who had developed an experimental bat gland extract in an effort to gain a bat's highly developed sonar abilities, the doomed scientist had injected himself with his untested formula—and was transformed into the gruesome half man/half bat monster.

But of all these deadly foes, it is the Joker who stands alone as Batman's supreme nemesis. And while the Calendar Man debates whether he should kill Batman, it is the Joker who has had dozens of opportunities to kill, or at the very least unmask, the Dark Knight. Each time the Joker has passed on these chances.

The Batman/Joker conflict goes much deeper than the battles Batman wages with the scores of other criminals who seek to outwit him. The decades-long rivalry between Batman and the Joker represents a supreme obsession—and a war that could only lead to death for both of them.

Top: Detective *#566, September 1986, cover.* Bottom: *The haunting of Batman.* (Batman *#180, May, 1966, ''Death Knocks Three Times!'' p. 20 [select panels].*)

THAT SAME NIGHT--THE MASKED PURSUER FINDS HIMSELF THE PURSUED-- IN A NIGHTMARE ...
FOOL! DO YOU REALLY THINK YOU'VE CAPTURED ME?
YOU CAUGHT NOTHING BUT THE BLACK SHADOW OF DEATH--I CAN DRIFT RIGHT BETWEEN YOUR FINGERS LIKE SMOKE-- ANYTIME I WISH!
HA-HA-HA!

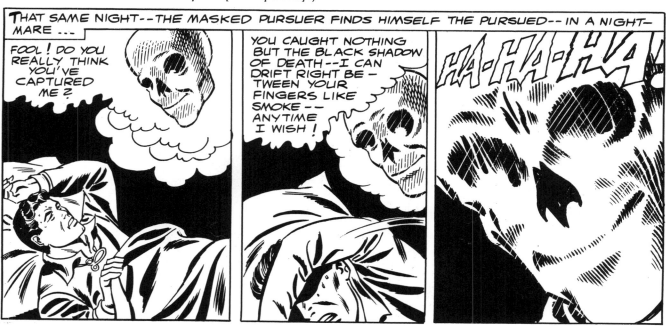

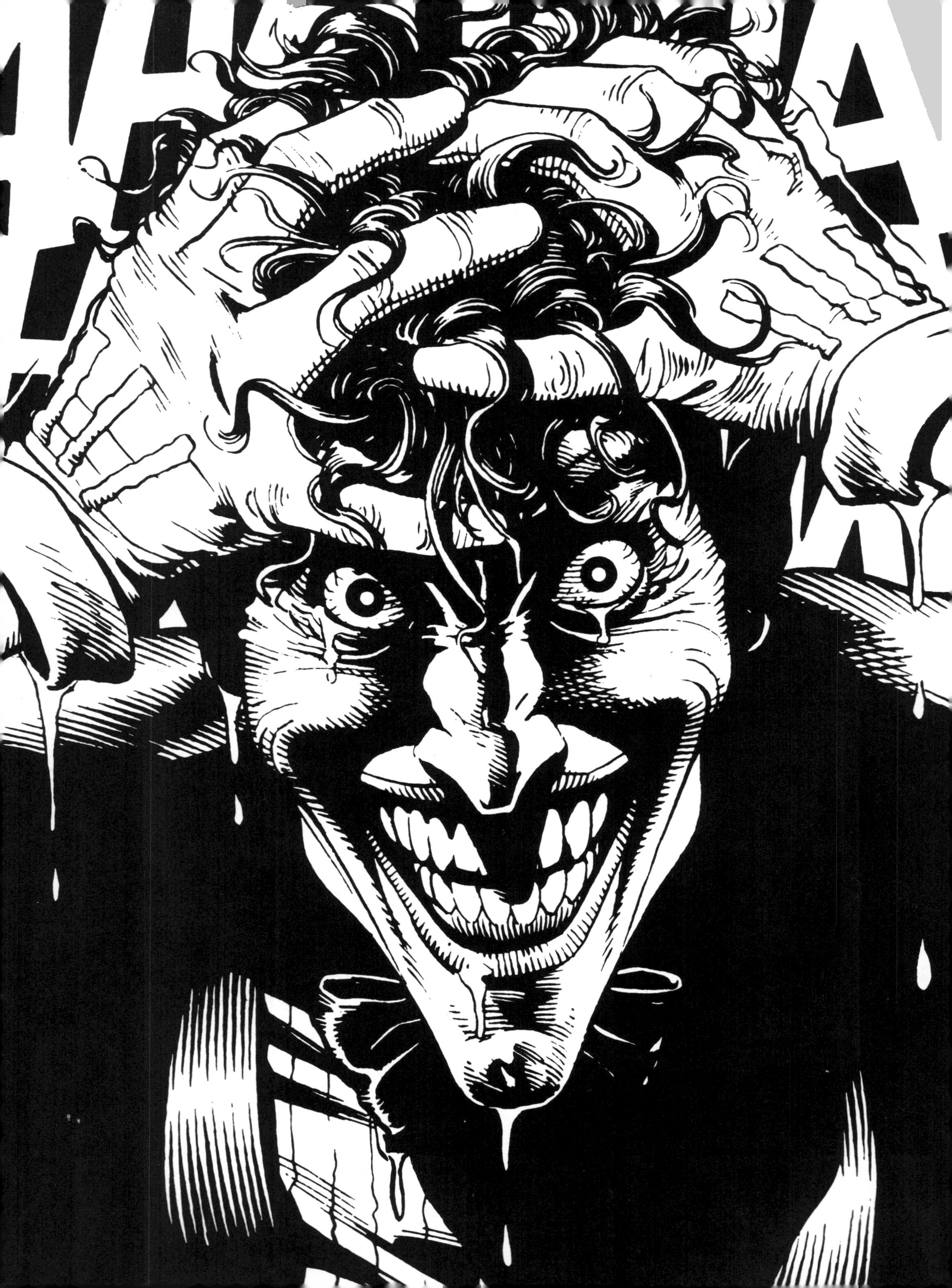

CHAPTER 16
OBSESSION

BATMAN HAS BEEN CALLED AN "OB-sessed artist" for his renaissance approach to crime fighting. He is always seeking an edge, whether by pushing the limits of what is physically possible, or by developing some new technological innovation for his war on crime. And Batman brings to his art a warrior's ferocity, a scientist's brilliance, a feel for the streets, and a millionaire's sense of elegance.

Of all the foes who have been his foils for decades, it is the Joker who best emulates Batman's artistic obsession. In Gotham's world of menace, they both need each other: the Joker to create beautiful crimes (often embroidered with death dealt in a delicious manner), the Batman to stop them by figuring out the crime pattern and shattering it.

The Joker's crime motifs have been multi-leveled crime mandalas, maniacal masterpieces of thematic crimemaking.

One Joker pattern was a cross-country spree that forced Batman to anticipate which state the Joker would hit next. There was a series of crimes based on the royal flush of diamonds. Another time he announced crimes before committing them—crimemaking in reverse. Once he committed crimes based on famous comedy characters of fiction. During one uncharacteristically uninspired period he even hired underworld gag writers to plan crimes for him that would garner big rewards while making the Dynamic Duo look like fools.

Joker crimes might seem to be wild and wacky episodes, but there is a disquieting tone about them. Their nonsensical patterns have the colorful flair of an amusement park ride—but with a homicidal bite.

The Joker's first crime, the robbery and mur-der of Gotham millionaire Henry Claridge (*Batman* 1, 1940), made it clear that he was a crazed genius who would kill if it added a beautiful tone and texture to a successful heist.

In that episode, the Joker broke into the morning broadcast of a Gotham radio station, promising he would kill Claridge and rob him of his fabled Claridge diamond at the coming midnight hour. Even though a cordon of police officers surrounded the millionaire, at the stroke of twelve, Claridge mysteriously crumpled to the floor, dead. To the horror of the assembled officers, Claridge's facial muscles then contorted into a hideous death grin.

The psychological effect on the police was devastating. It was as if the Joker had moved through them like a vengeful ghost to claim his victim. And when the police opened the safe, they discovered the diamond had been stolen and replaced with a phony glass one—and the taunting Joker playing card.

The Joker had broken into the Claridge mansion the midnight before, injected the sleeping millionaire with a lethal solution that would take a full twenty-four hours to kill (and leave the victim with that ghastly death grin), and stole the diamond, replacing it with a glass copy.[1]

The killing heist gave the Joker the satisfaction of having won a battle of wits against the police. But the Joker considered the law enforcement agencies bungling bureaucracies beneath his contempt. When Batman and Robin soon appeared to halt his first crime spree, it was a godsend to the crime jester. Here was an opponent who would provide him with a supreme challenge.

With his chalk-white face, bright red lips,

---

1. Untitled Joker story, *Batman* 1 (Spring 1940).

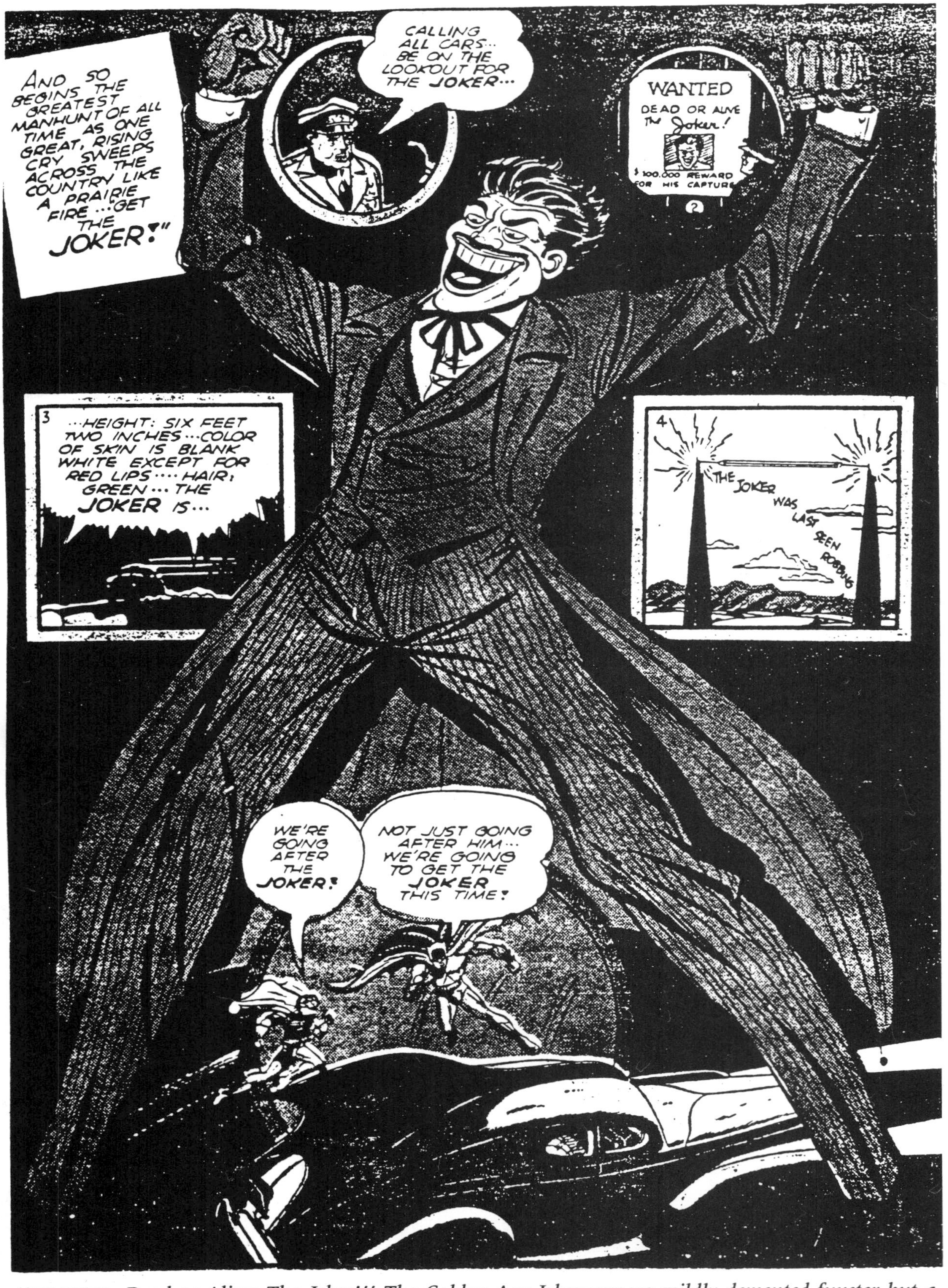
AND SO BEGINS THE GREATEST MANHUNT OF ALL TIME AS ONE GREAT, RISING CRY SWEEPS ACROSS THE COUNTRY LIKE A PRAIRIE FIRE ... GET THE JOKER!"
CALLING ALL CARS... BE ON THE LOOKOUT FOR THE JOKER...
WANTED
DEAD OR ALIVE
The Joker!
$100,000 REWARD FOR HIS CAPTURE
2
3
...HEIGHT: SIX FEET TWO INCHES... COLOR OF SKIN IS BLANK WHITE EXCEPT FOR RED LIPS.... HAIR: GREEN... THE JOKER IS...
4
THE JOKER WAS LAST SEEN ROBBING
WE'RE GOING AFTER THE JOKER!
NOT JUST GOING AFTER HIM... WE'RE GOING TO GET THE JOKER THIS TIME!

''WANTED: Dead or Alive: The Joker!'' The Golden Age Joker was no mildly demented funster but a maniacal killer. Here we see law enforcement around the nation mobilizing for a Joker manhunt. (Batman #8, *January 1942, ''The Cross-Country Crimes!'' p. 3.*)

and wavy green hair, the Joker has the perfect nightmare looks to reign as the underworld's top Batman antagonist. It's a position he relishes—and will defend against any pretender to the throne. (The Joker's competitive desire to be recognized as Batman's number one foe has even led him to conflict with such fellow criminals as the Penguin in the 1940s, Clayface in the 1960's, Two-Face in the 1970s, and Croc in the 1980s.)

The Joker's pride is legendary. The Batman once told the press that the Joker was "a supreme egoist advertising his crimes like a fool." In one inspired case the Joker launched Joker Film Productions, Inc., in which he and his henchmen made live-action films of their own crimes and then sold them to their underworld contacts as "educational films for criminals."

It is his madness that makes the Joker great. For decades the Joker has been willing to take the plunge over the line that separates good and evil in Batman's shadowy world. Deep in that chasm of darkness, he calls up to the Dark Knight with his chilling, cackling laugh, challenging the Batman to give it up and join him. The Joker may be damned, but he's comfortable in this hell. He know his own darkness is just a deeper shade of the shadows "normal" people pretend don't exist.

"Madness is the emergency exit," he has said (*The Killing Joke,* 1988). "You can just step outside, and close the door on all those dreadful things that happened. You can lock them away—forever. . . .

"My point is, I went crazy. When I saw what a black, awful joke the world was, I went crazy as a coot! I admit it! . . . You must see the reality of the situation. Do you know how many times we've come close to World War Three over a flock of geese on a computer screen? Do you know what triggered the last world war? An argument over how many telegraph poles Germany owed its war debt creditors! Telegraph poles! Ha, ha, ha, ha, HA!"

It is that grim despair that has so frustrated the Batman. The Dark Knight had overcome his own personal nightmare to dedicate himself to justice—you could even call it public service, but the Joker would have another wild, cackling laugh over that one.

To Batman, ever idealistic that criminals can be reformed, the Joker represents the ultimate challenge. To make the demented Joker a law-abiding member of society would be a personal triumph for the Caped Crusader and an affirmation of his vaunted rehabilitation methods. Perhaps such a feat would finally lay to rest the

WHUNK
FOR YEARS, YOU'VE SNEERED AND LAUGHED AT EVERYTHING DECENT...
WHAP
...BUT NO MORE, DO YOU HEAR ME?
NO MORE!
BATMAN, STOP...!

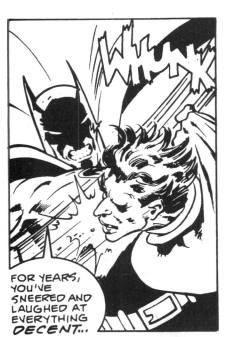

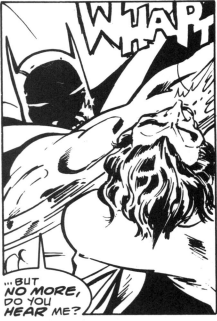

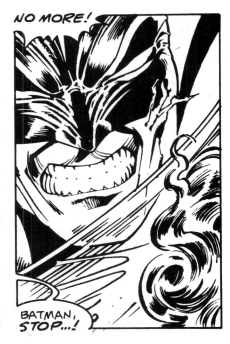

Detective #570, *January 1987, "The Last Laugh," p. 22 (select panels.)*

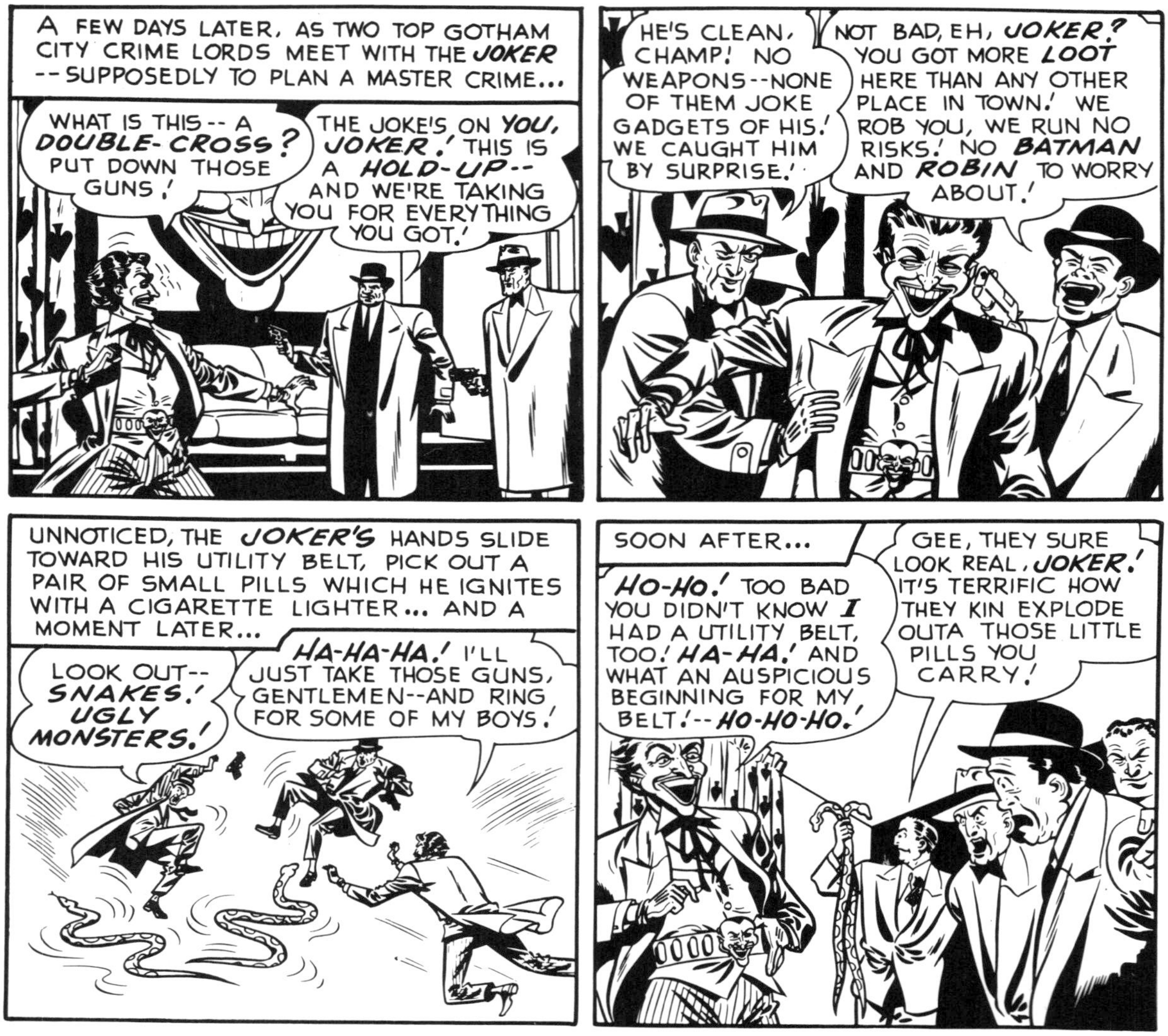
A FEW DAYS LATER, AS TWO TOP GOTHAM CITY CRIME LORDS MEET WITH THE JOKER --SUPPOSEDLY TO PLAN A MASTER CRIME...
WHAT IS THIS-- A DOUBLE-CROSS? PUT DOWN THOSE GUNS!
THE JOKE'S ON YOU, JOKER! THIS IS A HOLD-UP-- AND WE'RE TAKING YOU FOR EVERYTHING YOU GOT!
HE'S CLEAN, CHAMP! NO WEAPONS--NONE OF THEM JOKE GADGETS OF HIS! WE CAUGHT HIM BY SURPRISE!
NOT BAD, EH, JOKER? YOU GOT MORE LOOT HERE THAN ANY OTHER PLACE IN TOWN! WE ROB YOU, WE RUN NO RISKS! NO BATMAN AND ROBIN TO WORRY ABOUT!
UNNOTICED, THE JOKER'S HANDS SLIDE TOWARD HIS UTILITY BELT, PICK OUT A PAIR OF SMALL PILLS WHICH HE IGNITES WITH A CIGARETTE LIGHTER... AND A MOMENT LATER...
LOOK OUT-- SNAKES! UGLY MONSTERS!
HA-HA-HA! I'LL JUST TAKE THOSE GUNS, GENTLEMEN--AND RING FOR SOME OF MY BOYS!
SOON AFTER...
HO-HO! TOO BAD YOU DIDN'T KNOW I HAD A UTILITY BELT, TOO! HA-HA! AND WHAT AN AUSPICIOUS BEGINNING FOR MY BELT!--HO-HO-HO!
GEE, THEY SURE LOOK REAL, JOKER! IT'S TERRIFIC HOW THEY KIN EXPLODE OUTA THOSE LITTLE PILLS YOU CARRY!

Top: *Depending on the era, and his mood swings, the Joker has acted as either criminal prankster—or ruthless killer. Here, the Joker pulls the old snake trick.* (Batman *#73, October/November 1952, "The Joker's Utility Belt," p. 4 [select panels.*) Bottom: *The Joker's ego often led him to battle against criminal competitors for the number one spot as Batman's greatest foe.* (Batman *#159, November 1963, "The Great Clayface—Joker Feud," p. 5 [select panels].*)

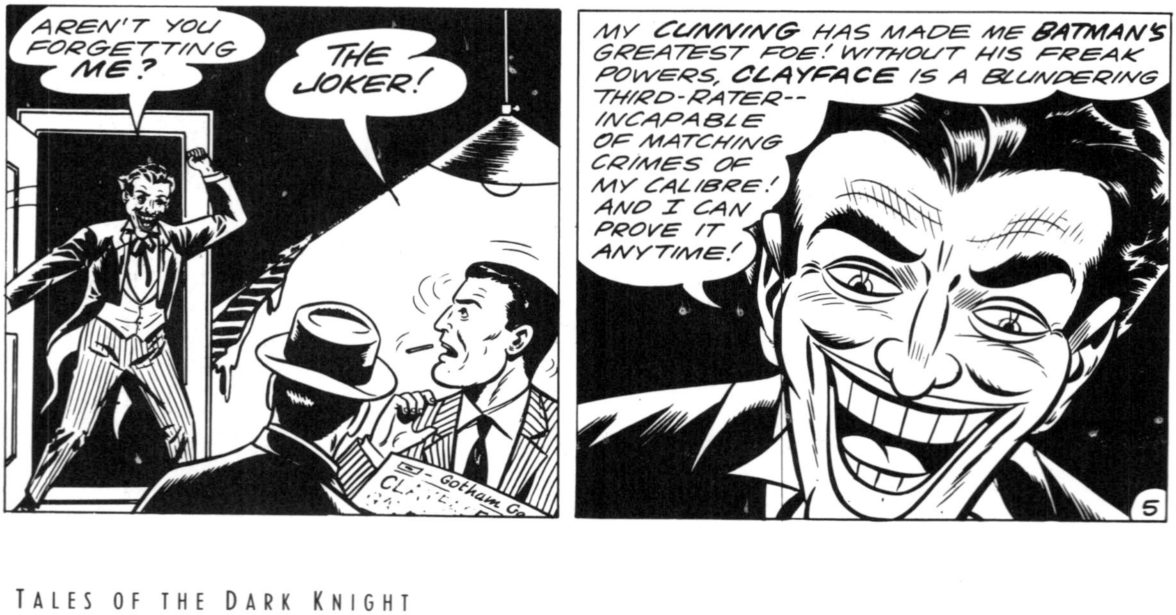
AREN'T YOU FORGETTING ME?
THE JOKER!
MY CUNNING HAS MADE ME BATMAN'S GREATEST FOE! WITHOUT HIS FREAK POWERS, CLAYFACE IS A BLUNDERING THIRD-RATER-- INCAPABLE OF MATCHING CRIMES OF MY CALIBRE! AND I CAN PROVE IT ANYTIME!
5

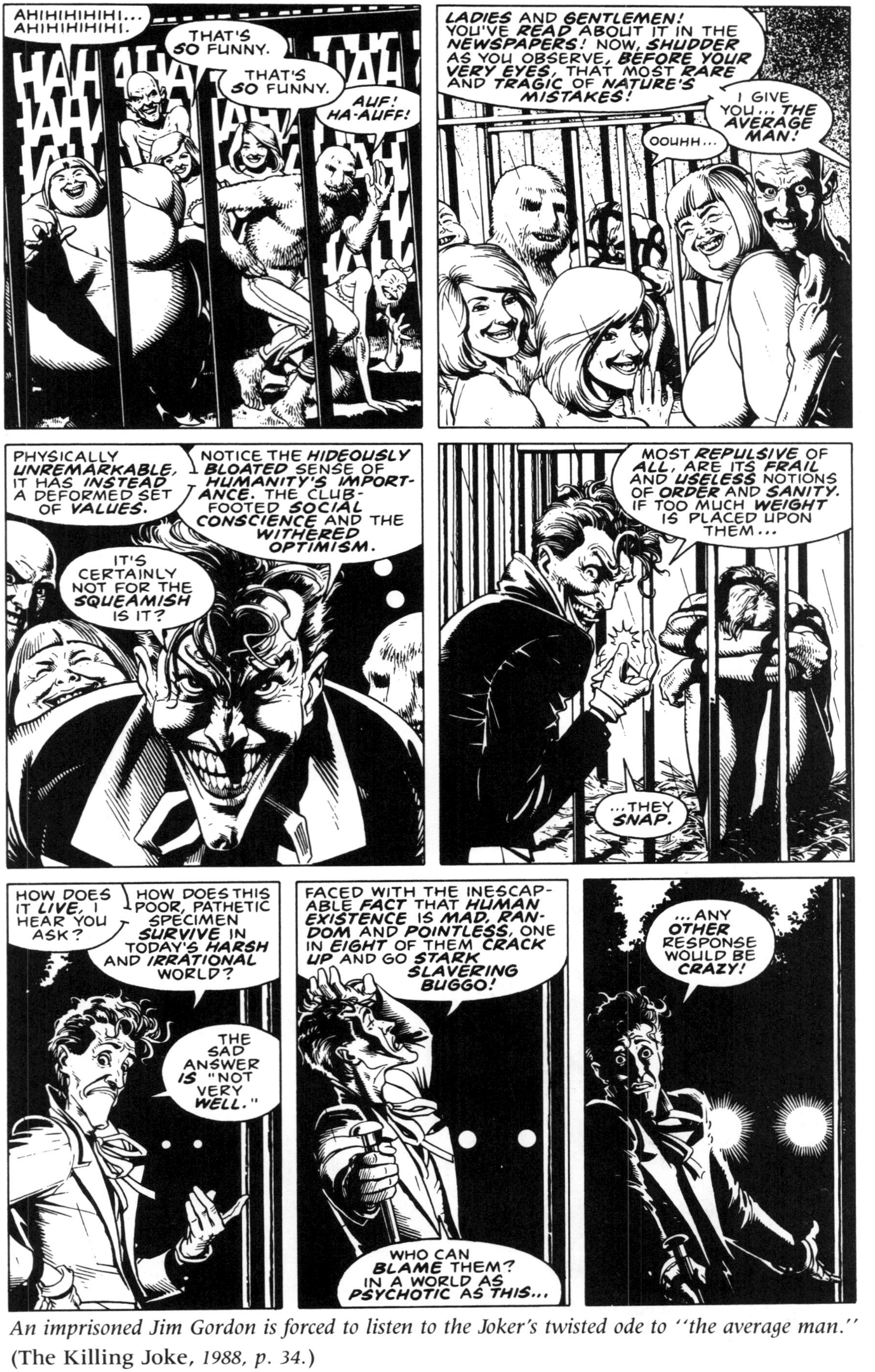
AHIHIHIHIHI...
AHIHIHIHIHI.
THAT'S SO FUNNY.
THAT'S SO FUNNY.
AUF! HA-AUFF!
LADIES AND GENTLEMEN! YOU'VE READ ABOUT IT IN THE NEWSPAPERS! NOW, SHUDDER AS YOU OBSERVE, BEFORE YOUR VERY EYES, THAT MOST RARE AND TRAGIC OF NATURE'S MISTAKES!
I GIVE YOU... THE AVERAGE MAN!
OOUHH...
PHYSICALLY UNREMARKABLE, IT HAS INSTEAD A DEFORMED SET OF VALUES.
NOTICE THE HIDEOUSLY BLOATED SENSE OF HUMANITY'S IMPORTANCE. THE CLUB-FOOTED SOCIAL CONSCIENCE AND THE WITHERED OPTIMISM.
IT'S CERTAINLY NOT FOR THE SQUEAMISH IS IT?
MOST REPULSIVE OF ALL, ARE ITS FRAIL AND USELESS NOTIONS OF ORDER AND SANITY. IF TOO MUCH WEIGHT IS PLACED UPON THEM...
...THEY SNAP.
HOW DOES IT LIVE, I HEAR YOU ASK?
HOW DOES THIS POOR, PATHETIC SPECIMEN SURVIVE IN TODAY'S HARSH AND IRRATIONAL WORLD?
THE SAD ANSWER IS "NOT VERY WELL."
FACED WITH THE INESCAPABLE FACT THAT HUMAN EXISTENCE IS MAD, RANDOM AND POINTLESS, ONE IN EIGHT OF THEM CRACK UP AND GO STARK SLAVERING BUGGO!
WHO CAN BLAME THEM? IN A WORLD AS PSYCHOTIC AS THIS...
...ANY OTHER RESPONSE WOULD BE CRAZY!

An imprisoned Jim Gordon is forced to listen to the Joker's twisted ode to "the average man." (The Killing Joke, *1988, p. 34.*)

demons of Crime Alley that still haunt the Dark Knight.

"I don't want to hurt you," Batman says to a subdued Joker he has just captured in a deserted amusement park at the end of *The Killing Joke.* It is a strange comment since the Joker has outdone even himself in terms of vicious, demented crimemaking: he's left Barbara Gordon paralyzed with a bullet through the spine and kidnapped Jim Gordon, stripped him naked, and forced him onto one of the amusement park's rides to view giant photographs of his helpless, naked daughter.

"I don't want either of us to end up killing the other, but we're both running out of alternatives—and we both know it," Batman continues in his imploring tone.

"Maybe it all hinges on tonight. Maybe this is our last chance to sort this bloody mess out. If you don't take it, then we're locked on a suicide course. BOTH of us. To the death.

"It doesn't have to end like that. I don't know what it was that bent your life out of shape, but who knows? Maybe I've been there too. Maybe I can help. We could work together. I could rehabilitate you. You needn't be out there on the edge any more. You needn't be alone. We don't have to kill each other. What do you say?"

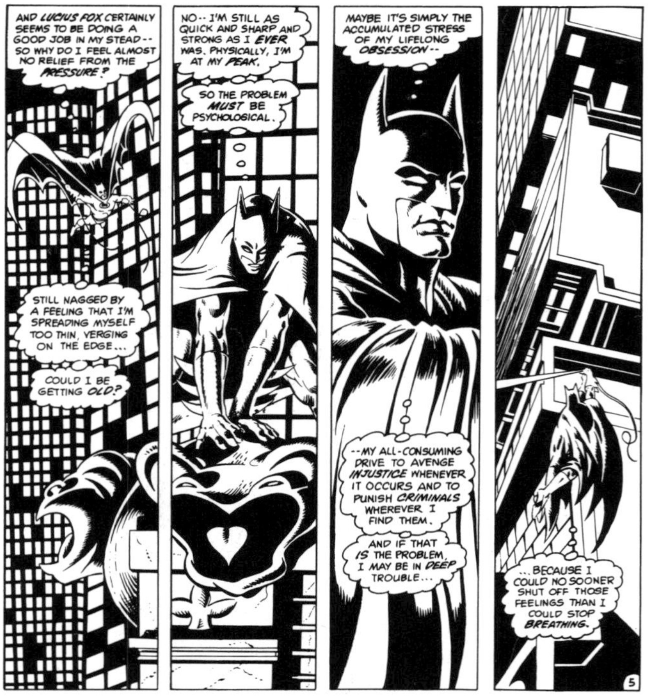
AND LUCIUS FOX CERTAINLY SEEMS TO BE DOING A GOOD JOB IN MY STEAD-- SO WHY DO I FEEL ALMOST NO RELIEF FROM THE PRESSURE?
STILL NAGGED BY A FEELING THAT I'M SPREADING MYSELF TOO THIN, VERGING ON THE EDGE...
COULD I BE GETTING OLD?
NO-- I'M STILL AS QUICK AND SHARP AND STRONG AS I EVER WAS. PHYSICALLY, I'M AT MY PEAK.
SO THE PROBLEM MUST BE PSYCHOLOGICAL.
MAYBE IT'S SIMPLY THE ACCUMULATED STRESS OF MY LIFELONG OBSESSION--
--MY ALL-CONSUMING DRIVE TO AVENGE INJUSTICE WHENEVER IT OCCURS AND TO PUNISH CRIMINALS WHEREVER I FIND THEM.
AND IF THAT IS THE PROBLEM, I MAY BE IN DEEP TROUBLE...
...BECAUSE I COULD NO SOONER SHUT OFF THOSE FEELINGS THAN I COULD STOP BREATHING.
5

Detective #527, *June 1983, "Avatars of Vengeance," p. 5 [select panels].*

The Dark Knight is silent as his old foe turns to look at him. It is a dark night, and a blustery storm is sending down a cold rain.

"No. I'm sorry, but... no," the Joker says, the rain streaking down his face. "It's too late for that, far too late. Y'know, it's funny... this situation reminds me of a joke....

"See, there were these two guys in a lunatic asylum and one night, one night they decide they don't like living in an asylum any more. They decide they're going to escape!

"So, like, they get up on the roof, and there, just across this narrow gap, they see the rooftops of the town, stretching away in the moonlight ... stretching away to freedom.

"Now, the first guy, he jumps right across with no problem. But his friend, his friend daredn't make the leap. Y'see... y'see, he's afraid of falling.

"So then, the first guy has an idea... he says, 'Hey! I have my flashlight with me! I'll shine it across the gap between the buildings. You can walk along the beam and join me!'

"B-but the second guy just shakes his head. He suh-says... he says 'Wh-what do you think I am? Crazy? You'd turn it off when I was half way across!' "

The Joker's shoulders begin to shake, and he struggles to hold back his cackling laughter. And then the Dark Knight, who has listened with a grim expression throughout, lets a chuckle escape, and then a laugh....

And then the two old foes begin to laugh together, the sounds of approaching police sirens adding a background drone.

This night will bring no resolution to their decades-long obsession. Perhaps that's the way they want it. Perhaps this dance of theirs is an arrangement that gives sense and a kind of order to their dark universe.

And then the rain begins to fall in all its fury.... [2]

---

2. Situation and dialogue taken from *The Killing Joke,* 1988.

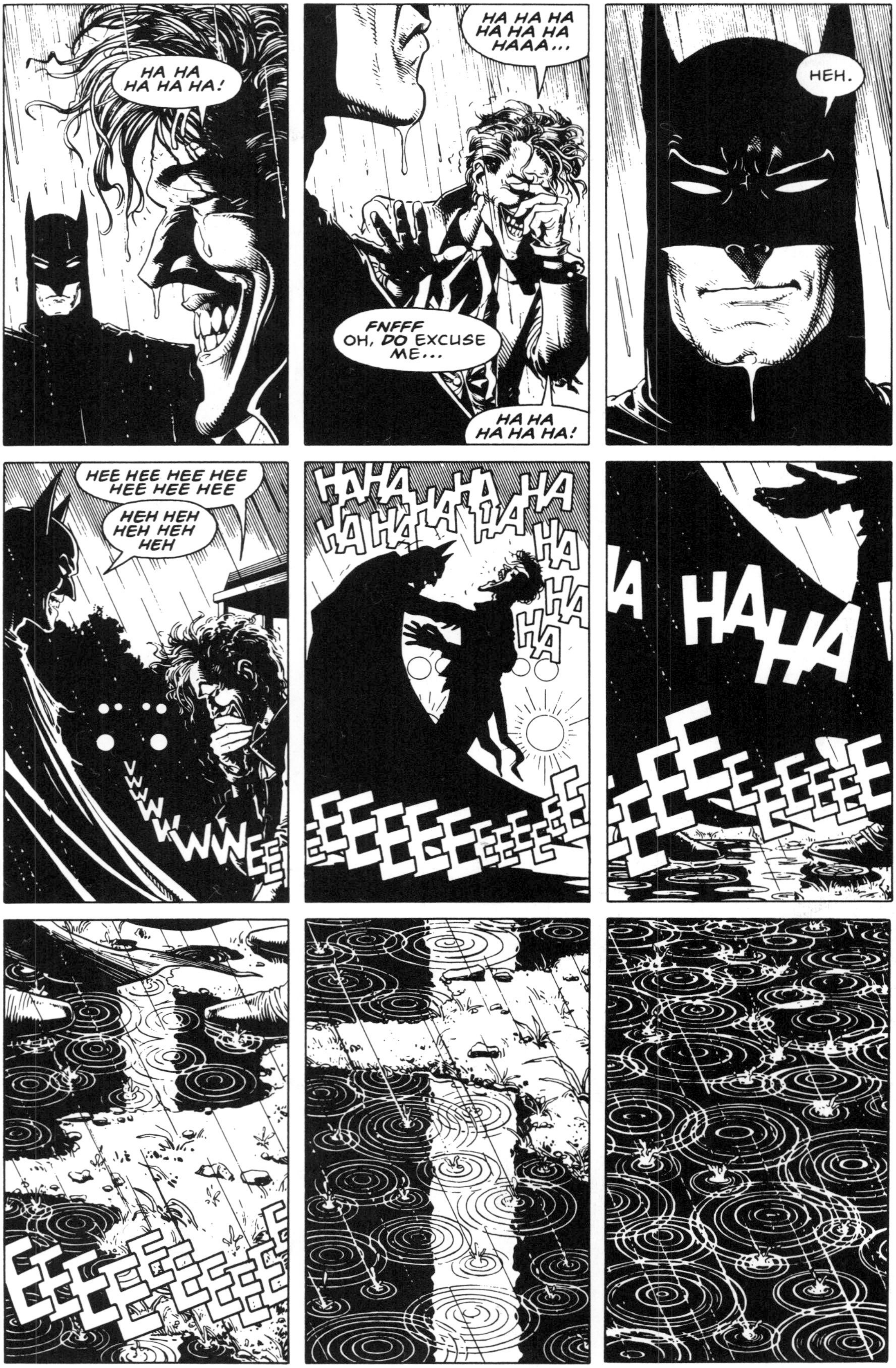
HA HA
HA HA HA!
HA HA HA
HA HA HA
HAAA...
FNFFF
OH, DO EXCUSE
ME...
HA HA
HA HA HA!
HEH.
HEE HEE HEE HEE
HEE HEE HEE
HEH HEH
HEH HEH
HEH

The Killing Joke, *1988, p. 47.*

Ace of Knaves, the Clown of Crime, the Harlequin of Hate, the Jester of Crime, the Madman of Mirth, and Prince of Pranksters, are a few of the over forty monikers accorded the Joker during his career.

The Joker's bizarre features—chalk-white face, red lips, green hair—were never explained until 1951. It was revealed that the Joker had once had normal features. He had been a masked criminal known as the Red Hood who had escaped a botched robbery at the Monarch Playing Card Company by diving into a catch basin for the plant's chemical wastes and following the flow out to the river. When he removed his mask, he discovered the hideous disfigurement that, because he resembled the joker of a playing card deck, gave him a new criminal identity.

It is believed that this hideous accident drove the Joker insane.

The Joker is a master at escaping prisons—and certain death: "He's cheated death so often, you just can't trust that guy!" Batman once remarked to Robin.

Over the years the Joker has come close to unmasking, and even killing, Batman. He has never followed through because it would have been the end of their battle of wits.

It has been a rare event, but occasionally the Joker has teamed up with other criminals, such as the Penguin—and Lex Luthor to battle both Superman and Batman.

In the summer of 1940 Batman planned to kidnap a wounded Joker from the hospital where he was staying to take his foe "to a famous brain specialist for an operation, so that he can be cured and turned into a valuable citizen." The plot never came to fruition.

The tales have never identified the Joker with a proper surname.

Opposite: *It was meant to be a simple burglary—but an unnamed, novice crook hadn't counted on a retreat through a stream of chemical wastes, hadn't counted on becoming . . . THIS!* (The Killing Joke, *1988, p. 33.*)

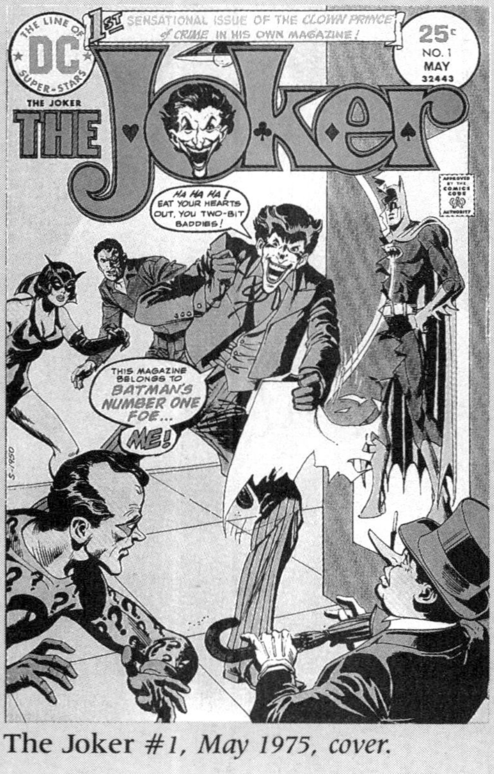
1ST SENSATIONAL ISSUE OF THE CLOWN PRINCE OF CRIME IN HIS OWN MAGAZINE!
25¢ NO. 1 MAY
THE JOKER
THE Joker
HA HA HA! EAT YOUR HEARTS OUT, YOU TWO-BIT BADDIES!
THIS MAGAZINE BELONGS TO BATMAN'S NUMBER ONE FOE... ME!

The Joker *#1, May 1975, cover.*

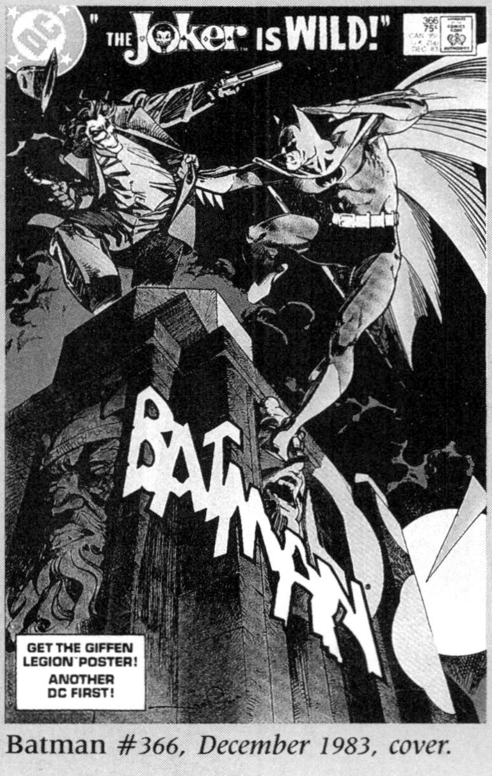
"THE Joker IS WILD!"
BATMAN
GET THE GIFFEN LEGION POSTER! ANOTHER DC FIRST!

Batman *#366, December 1983, cover.*

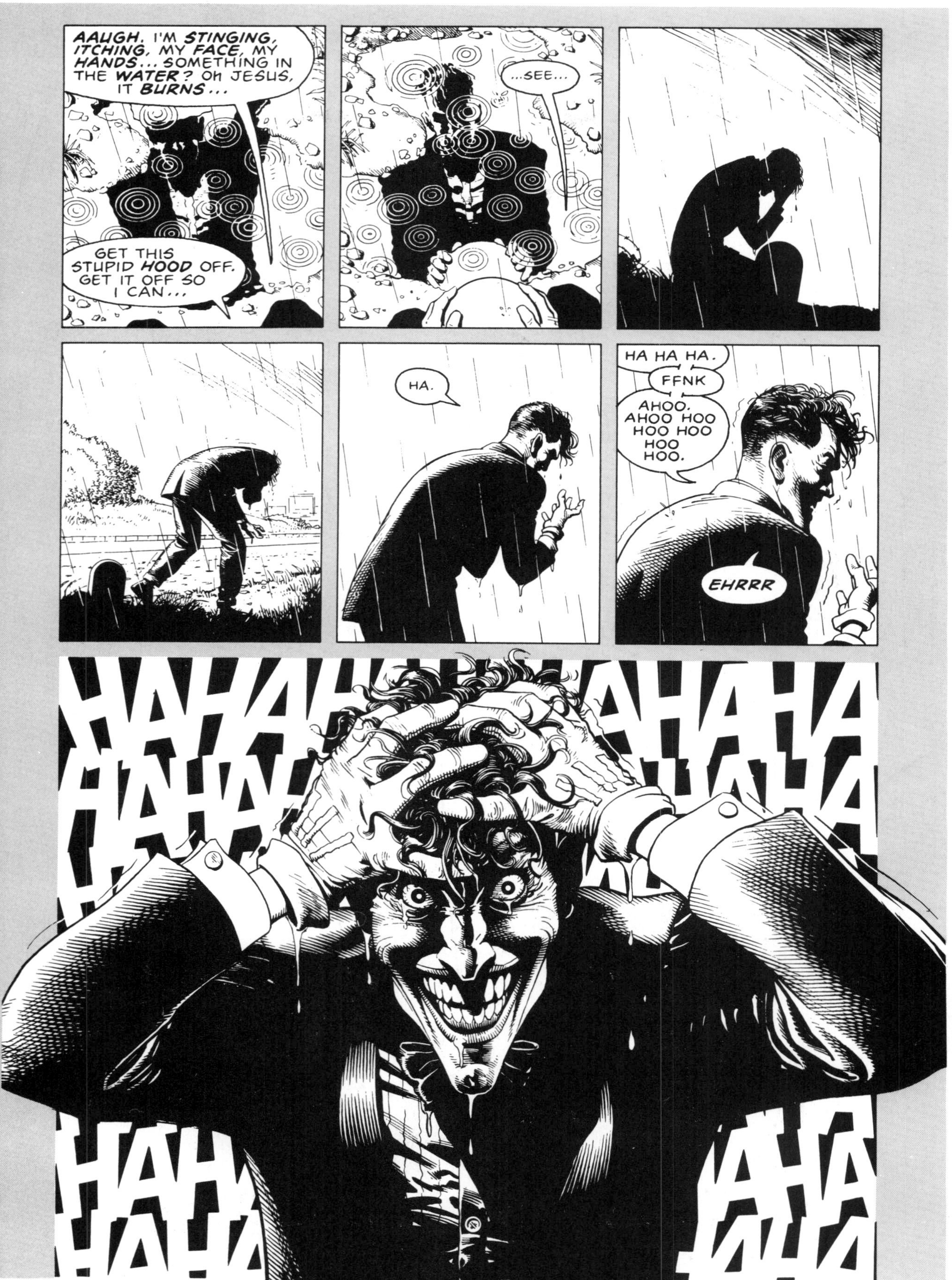
AAUGH. I'M STINGING, ITCHING, MY FACE, MY HANDS... SOMETHING IN THE WATER? Oh JESUS, IT BURNS...
GET THIS STUPID HOOD OFF. GET IT OFF SO I CAN...
...SEE...
HA.
HA HA HA.
FFNK
AHOO. AHOO HOO HOO HOO HOO HOO.
EHRRR

CHAPTER 17
DARK KNIGHT OF THE EIGHTIES

FROM THE VERY BEGINNING OF FRANK Miller's *Batman: The Dark Knight Returns,* Miller makes it clear that he is taking the Batman mythos over the line into new terrain of apocalyptic darkness.

In one of the opening scenes we are beckoned to join a nighttime walk in Gotham City. The city is darker, grittier, than we've ever seen it. An unsettling heat wave coats the town with a smoky, toxic texture. The streets are gridlocked with automobiles, and the sidewalks are choked with pedestrians walking in a jittery daze.

But one middle-aged man stands out from the crowd. It's Bruce Wayne, and we catch sight of him as he walks past two lost souls who are clutching posters scrawled with "We Are Damned." His aura of primal athleticism still remains, but his girth has thickened a bit, his hair has turned gray, and deep furrows of worry cut across his forehead.

"I walk the streets of this city I'm learning to hate, the city that's given up, like the whole world seems to have," Bruce Wayne thinks.

It's troubling for Batman fans to read such thoughts. We've never heard such words of despair from the Dark Knight before. This is a Batman who is wrestling with the muddled ebb and flow of his two identities. In this scene his Batman identity is a separate force, an urban siren song calling him to the place where it all began— the once elegant boulevard where his parents were murdered in front of his eyes, the place now known as Crime Alley.

We then see Bruce standing in the dull circle of light from an old lamppost at THE spot. The first breeze of night pulls at his tie and sends litter scuttling along the sidewalk and gutters. This used to be one of the most prestigious streets in all of Gotham. Now it is deserted, its buildings boarded up, parking lots gleaming with broken glass, and abandoned save for the metal hulls of rotting cars.

"Once again, He's brought me back—to show me how little it has changed," Bruce Wayne muses. "It's older, dirtier, but—it could have happened yesterday. It could be happening right now. They could be lying at your feet, twitching, bleeding . . . and the man who stole all sense from your life, he could be standing right over there . . . ."

For the first time, Bruce Wayne's face becomes animated as his eyes open in shock. Approaching him are two young, masked members of the cult gang the Mutants. The gang is the twisted, maniacal Greek chorus for this Gotham of the damned. In the Mutants' code, there is no future, love and compassion are obsolete, and it's pro forma to kill for kicks.

They pull out knives as long as their forearms. As they sneer about slicing and dicing, we see Bruce turning to face them, his fists clenching, his eyes squinting with the intensity of a lifetime of focused fury.

"It is Him, it is, and we know so many ways to HURT him, so many lovely ways to PUNISH him," race his thoughts.

"I don't know," hisses one of the Mutants. "Look at him. He's into it—can't do murders when they're into it."

"Let's hit the arcade, man," the other Mutant hums. "Always a good time at the arcade . . . ."

"No, it's NOT Him," Bruce Wayne thinks. "Not him. He flinched when he pulled the trigger. He was sick and guilty over what he did. All he wanted was money. I was naive enough to think him the lowest sort of man."

He looks out at the mutants walking off in-

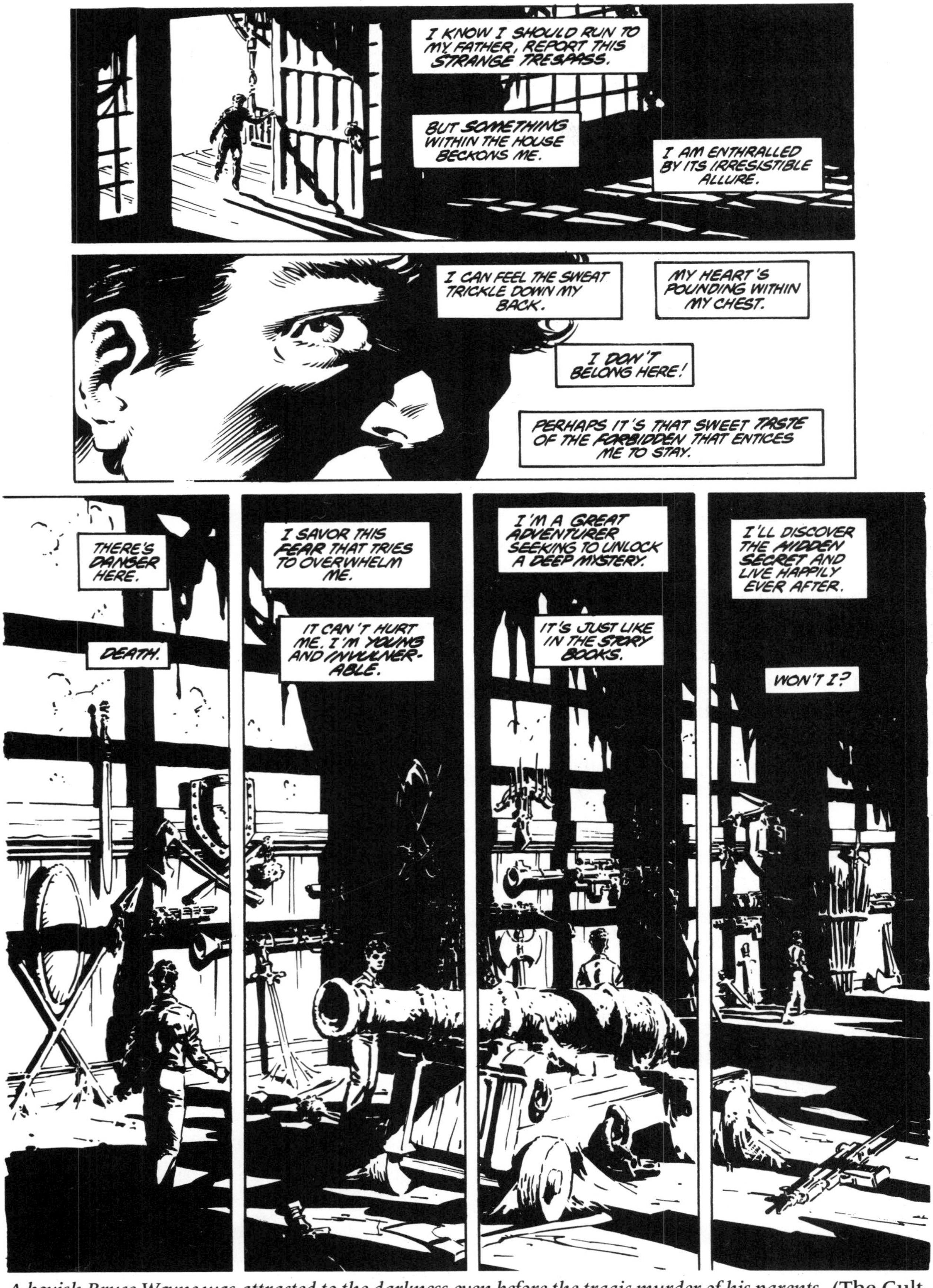
I KNOW I SHOULD RUN TO MY FATHER, REPORT THIS STRANGE TRESPASS.
BUT SOMETHING WITHIN THE HOUSE BECKONS ME.
I AM ENTHRALLED BY ITS IRRESISTIBLE ALLURE.
I CAN FEEL THE SWEAT TRICKLE DOWN MY BACK.
MY HEART'S POUNDING WITHIN MY CHEST.
I DON'T BELONG HERE!
PERHAPS IT'S THAT SWEET TASTE OF THE FORBIDDEN THAT ENTICES ME TO STAY.
THERE'S DANGER HERE.
DEATH.
I SAVOR THIS FEAR THAT TRIES TO OVERWHELM ME.
IT CAN'T HURT ME. I'M YOUNG AND INVULNER-ABLE.
I'M A GREAT ADVENTURER SEEKING TO UNLOCK A DEEP MYSTERY.
IT'S JUST LIKE IN THE STORY BOOKS.
I'LL DISCOVER THE HIDDEN SECRET AND LIVE HAPPILY EVER AFTER.
WON'T I?

A boyish Bruce Wayne was attracted to the darkness even before the tragic murder of his parents. (The Cult, *Book One, 1988, "Ordeal," p. 3.*)

to the darkness. A pang of despair constricts around his chest, choking him, shaking him with the truth that his war against crime was lost long ago, perhaps even doomed from the start.

"These—these are his children," he thinks. "A purer breed...and this world is theirs."[1]

Such scenes made Miller's four-part series a sensation when it was first published in 1986. Never before had the psychodrama possibilities of Batman been taken to such literate, and artistic, heights.

"I was involved in a hands-on way with *Dark Knight,* which brought a few people up short because it was clear that it was a futuristic story and may not have ever really happened, or may not really ever happen," admits DC vice president Dick Giordano. "But we did some things in there that startled a few people because we got away from the squeaky-clean image of Batman that had preceded it and got a little grittier and a little dirtier with the character and—I hope I'm not deluding myself—a little more literate."

Miller's script and explosive drawings, with Klaus Janson assisting on inks and Lynn Varley providing "colors and visual effects," were packaged in a revolutionary new format dubbed the "Prestige Format." The power and popularity of the production caused the mainstream media to take notice.

Rolling Stone hailed the saga for "radically rewriting several of the myths and archetypes that are at the heart of comics tradition itself and placing them in the context of fearful modern events... In Miller's hands Batman is bigger than a comics icon: he is a violent symbol of American dissolution and American idealism."[2]

James Wolcott, in *Vanity Fair,* called the epic "Batman seen through a film noir lens....

"Perhaps comic art will never receive the brainy scrutiny in this country that comic strips—*bandes dessinées*—receive in France, but the reception given *Dark Knight* offers a leg up from the fan-mag ghetto of kiddies and collectors."[3]

Miller's *Dark Knight* has had its share of crit-

ics. Most have had praise for Miller's storytelling power but decry the use he made of Batman. To many a Batman purist, Miller took the character over the line that had separated him from the criminal element, in the process causing the fabled crime fighter to lose the luster of his Dark Knight nobility.

But Miller had definite reasons for presenting a grimmer, more brutal Batman.

"Batman only makes sense as a response to the world being a basically screwed-up place, where all the wrong people are in charge and justice is not served," Miller, who was mugged twice during a ten-year residence in Manhattan, told *Rolling Stone.* "...You see, Batman's basic conflict in the story is to decide whether there's a purpose for his kind of force in the world. In a sense, it's a classic case of a hero whose function is to make himself obsolete.... He essentially harbors a death wish—much like a warrior who goes into battle one last time to find peace."[4]

While Miller's work stands out as a powerful moment in the whole of Batman lore, other creators in the 1980s were providing their own dark Batman visions.

The long list of artists with Batman work in this decade include Don Newton (whose work Dick Sprang credits as the apex of "Batman's physical image"), Alfredo Alcala, Gene Colan, Paul Gulacy, David Mazzucchelli, Jim Aparo, Berni Wrightson, Alan Davis and Paul Neary, Brian Bolland, Jerry Bingham, Norm Breyfogle, and Mike Mignola.

Writers during this period have included Doug Moench, Gerry Conway, Max Allan Collins, Jim Starlin, Mike Barr, and Alan Moore.

Antecedent, and influential, to these creators has been the work of Denny O'Neil, Neal Adams, Dick Giordano, Steve Englehart, and Marshall Rogers.

---

1. Situation and dialogue taken from *The Dark Knight Returns,* Book One, 1986.

2. Mikal Gilmore, "Comic Genius," *Rolling Stone,* March 27, 1986, p. 129.

3. James Wolcott, "Mixed Media," *Vanity Fair,* September 1986, pp. 56–57.

4. Gilmore, "Comic Genius," p. 129.

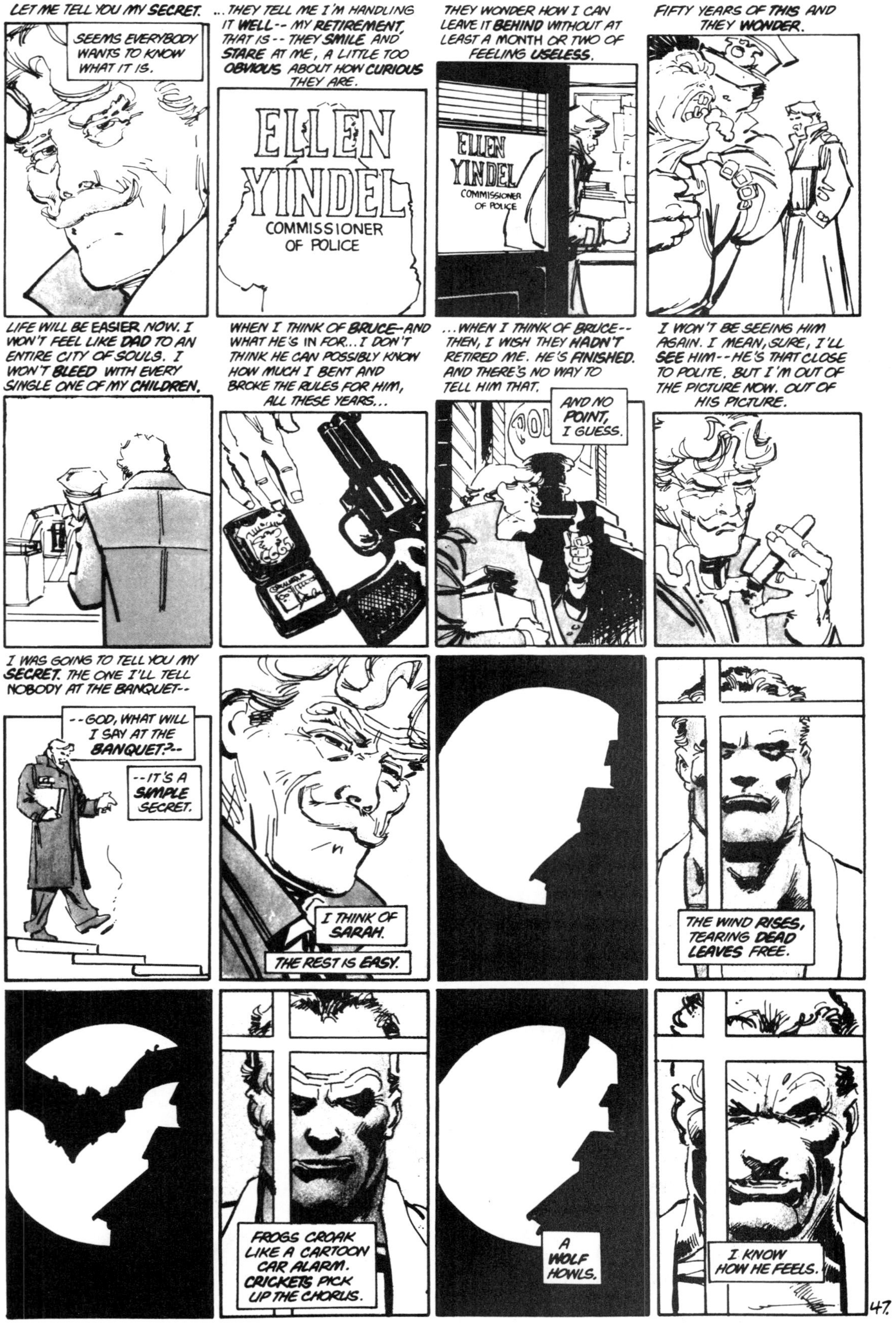

LET ME TELL YOU MY SECRET.
SEEMS EVERYBODY WANTS TO KNOW WHAT IT IS.
...THEY TELL ME I'M HANDLING IT WELL-- MY RETIREMENT, THAT IS-- THEY SMILE AND STARE AT ME, A LITTLE TOO OBVIOUS ABOUT HOW CURIOUS THEY ARE.
ELLEN YINDEL COMMISSIONER OF POLICE
THEY WONDER HOW I CAN LEAVE IT BEHIND WITHOUT AT LEAST A MONTH OR TWO OF FEELING USELESS.
ELLEN YINDEL COMMISSIONER OF POLICE
FIFTY YEARS OF THIS AND THEY WONDER.
LIFE WILL BE EASIER NOW. I WON'T FEEL LIKE DAD TO AN ENTIRE CITY OF SOULS. I WON'T BLEED WITH EVERY SINGLE ONE OF MY CHILDREN.
WHEN I THINK OF BRUCE--AND WHAT HE'S IN FOR... I DON'T THINK HE CAN POSSIBLY KNOW HOW MUCH I BENT AND BROKE THE RULES FOR HIM, ALL THESE YEARS...
...WHEN I THINK OF BRUCE-- THEN, I WISH THEY HADN'T RETIRED ME. HE'S FINISHED. AND THERE'S NO WAY TO TELL HIM THAT.
AND NO POINT, I GUESS.
I WON'T BE SEEING HIM AGAIN. I MEAN, SURE, I'LL SEE HIM--HE'S THAT CLOSE TO POLITE. BUT I'M OUT OF THE PICTURE NOW. OUT OF HIS PICTURE.
I WAS GOING TO TELL YOU MY SECRET. THE ONE I'LL TELL NOBODY AT THE BANQUET--
--GOD, WHAT WILL I SAY AT THE BANQUET?--
--IT'S A SIMPLE SECRET.
I THINK OF SARAH.
THE REST IS EASY.
THE WIND RISES, TEARING DEAD LEAVES FREE.
FROGS CROAK LIKE A CARTOON CAR ALARM. CRICKETS PICK UP THE CHORUS.
A WOLF HOWLS.
I KNOW HOW HE FEELS.
47.

In a hypothetical future Commissioner Gordon looks forward to retirement after fifty years on the force, but Bruce Wayne still hears and heeds the call of the dark night. (The Dark Knight Returns, *Book Two, 1986, "The Dark Knight Triumphant," p. 47.*)

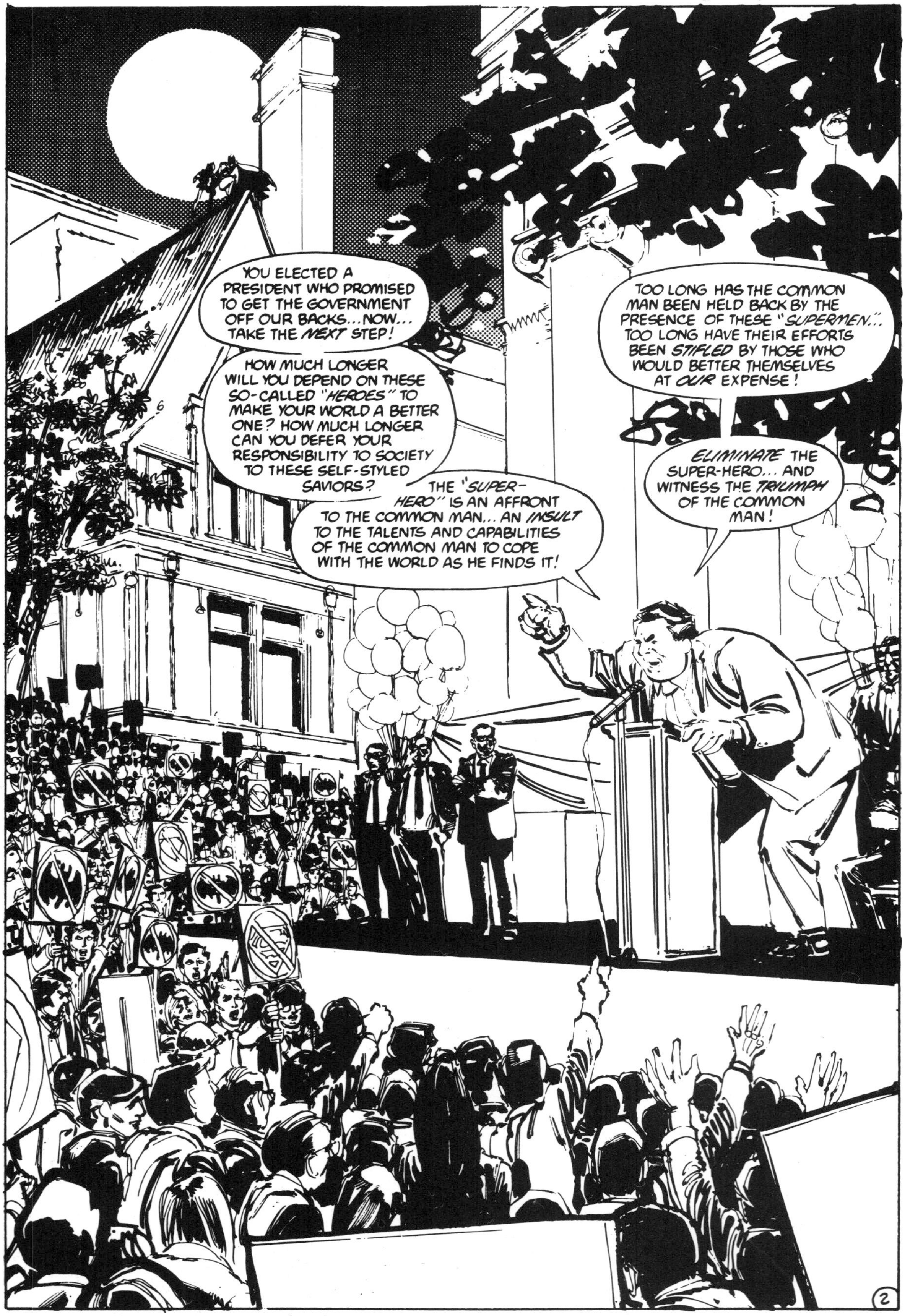
YOU ELECTED A PRESIDENT WHO PROMISED TO GET THE GOVERNMENT OFF OUR BACKS...NOW... TAKE THE NEXT STEP!
HOW MUCH LONGER WILL YOU DEPEND ON THESE SO-CALLED "HEROES" TO MAKE YOUR WORLD A BETTER ONE? HOW MUCH LONGER CAN YOU DEFER YOUR RESPONSIBILITY TO SOCIETY TO THESE SELF-STYLED SAVIORS?
THE "SUPER-HERO" IS AN AFFRONT TO THE COMMON MAN... AN INSULT TO THE TALENTS AND CAPABILITIES OF THE COMMON MAN TO COPE WITH THE WORLD AS HE FINDS IT!
TOO LONG HAS THE COMMON MAN BEEN HELD BACK BY THE PRESENCE OF THESE "SUPERMEN." TOO LONG HAVE THEIR EFFORTS BEEN STIFLED BY THOSE WHO WOULD BETTER THEMSELVES AT OUR EXPENSE!
ELIMINATE THE SUPER-HERO... AND WITNESS THE TRIUMPH OF THE COMMON MAN!
2

In the 1980s the Dark Knight, once valued as the friend and defender of the people of Gotham, became the target of fearmongering politicians. (**Detective** *#568, November 1986, ''Eyrie,'' p. 2.*)

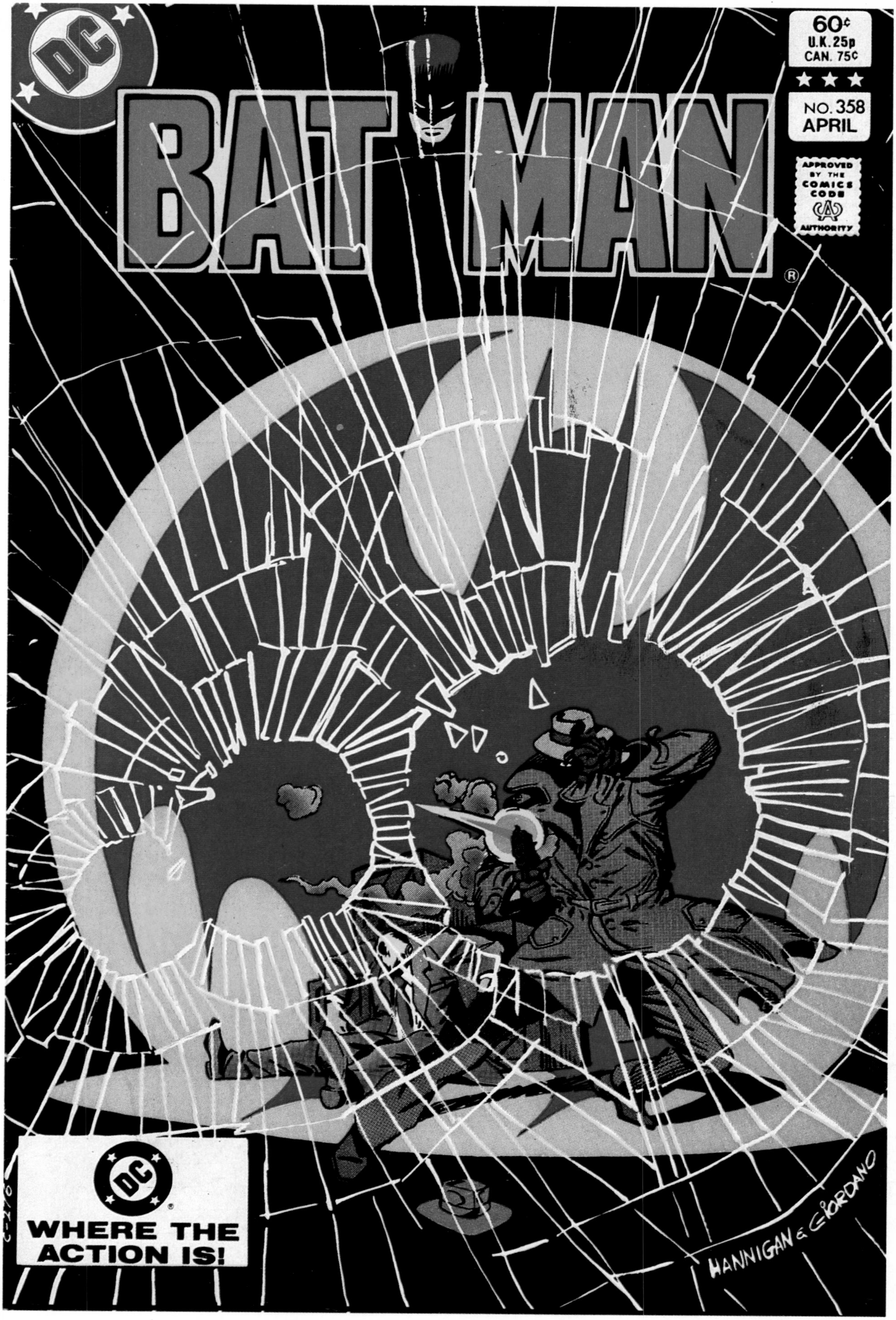
60¢
U.K. 25p
CAN. 75¢
BATMAN
NO. 358
APRIL
APPROVED BY THE COMICS CODE AUTHORITY
WHERE THE ACTION IS!
HANNIGAN & GIORDANO

BATMAN #358, April 1983 (Ed Hannigan, pencils; Dick Giordano, inks)

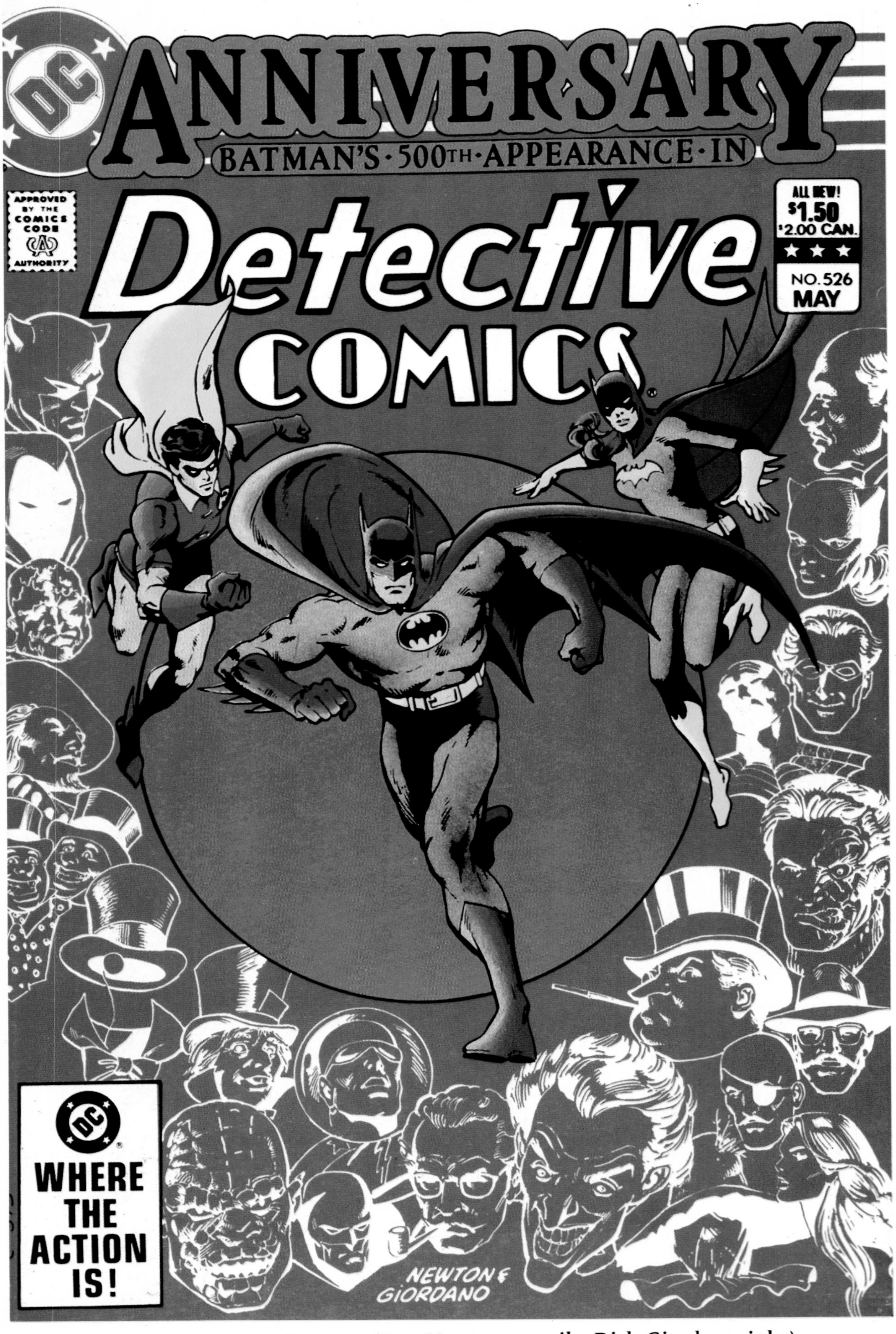
ANNIVERSARY
BATMAN'S·500TH·APPEARANCE·IN
APPROVED BY THE COMICS CODE AUTHORITY
ALL NEW!
$1.50
$2.00 CAN.
NO. 526
MAY
Detective
COMICS
WHERE THE ACTION IS!
NEWTON & GIORDANO

DETECTIVE #526, May 1983 (Don Newton, pencils; Dick Giordano, inks)

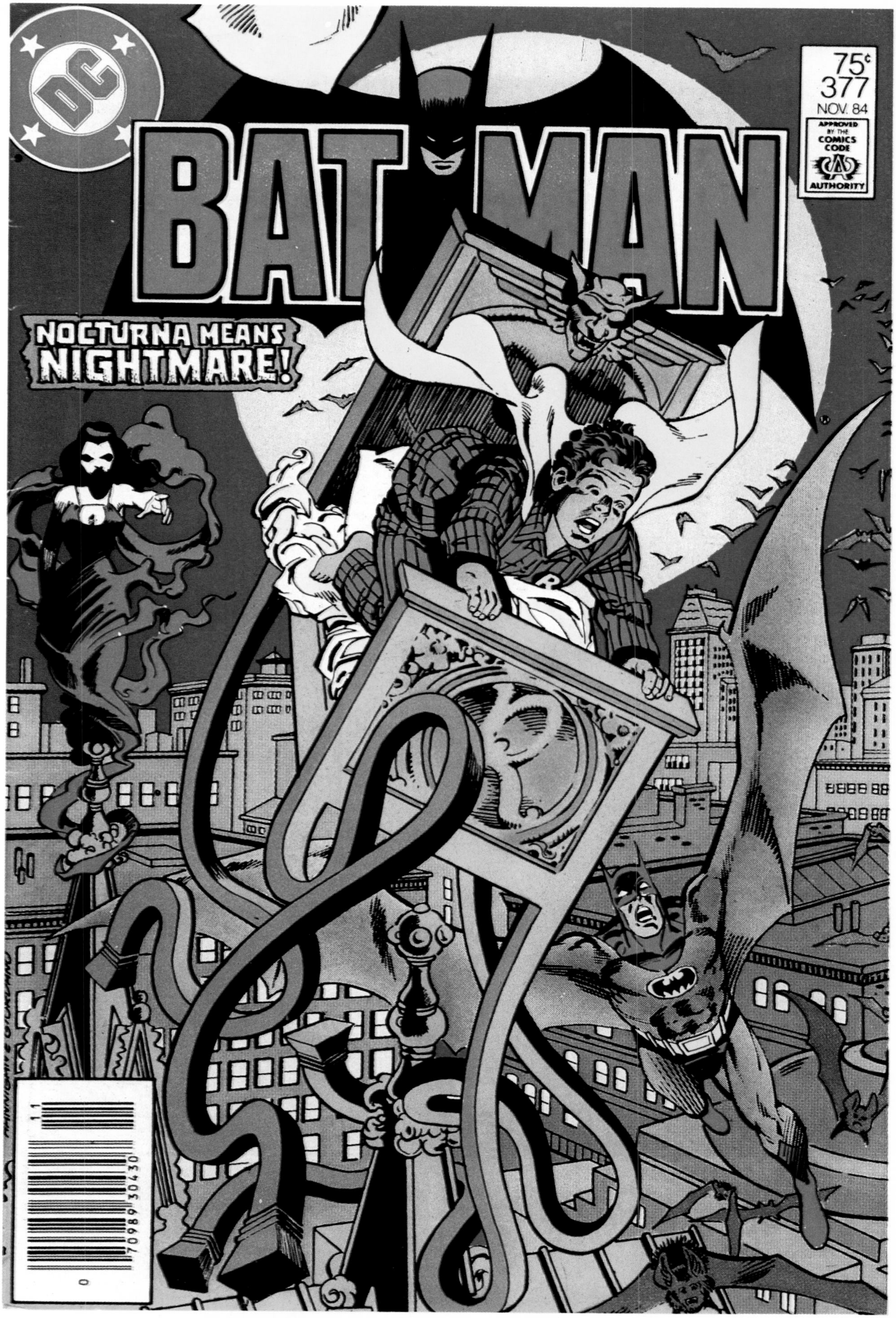
75¢
377
NOV. 84
APPROVED BY THE COMICS CODE AUTHORITY
BATMAN
NOCTURNA MEANS NIGHTMARE!

BATMAN #377, November 1984 (Ed Hannigan, pencils; Dick Giordano, inks)

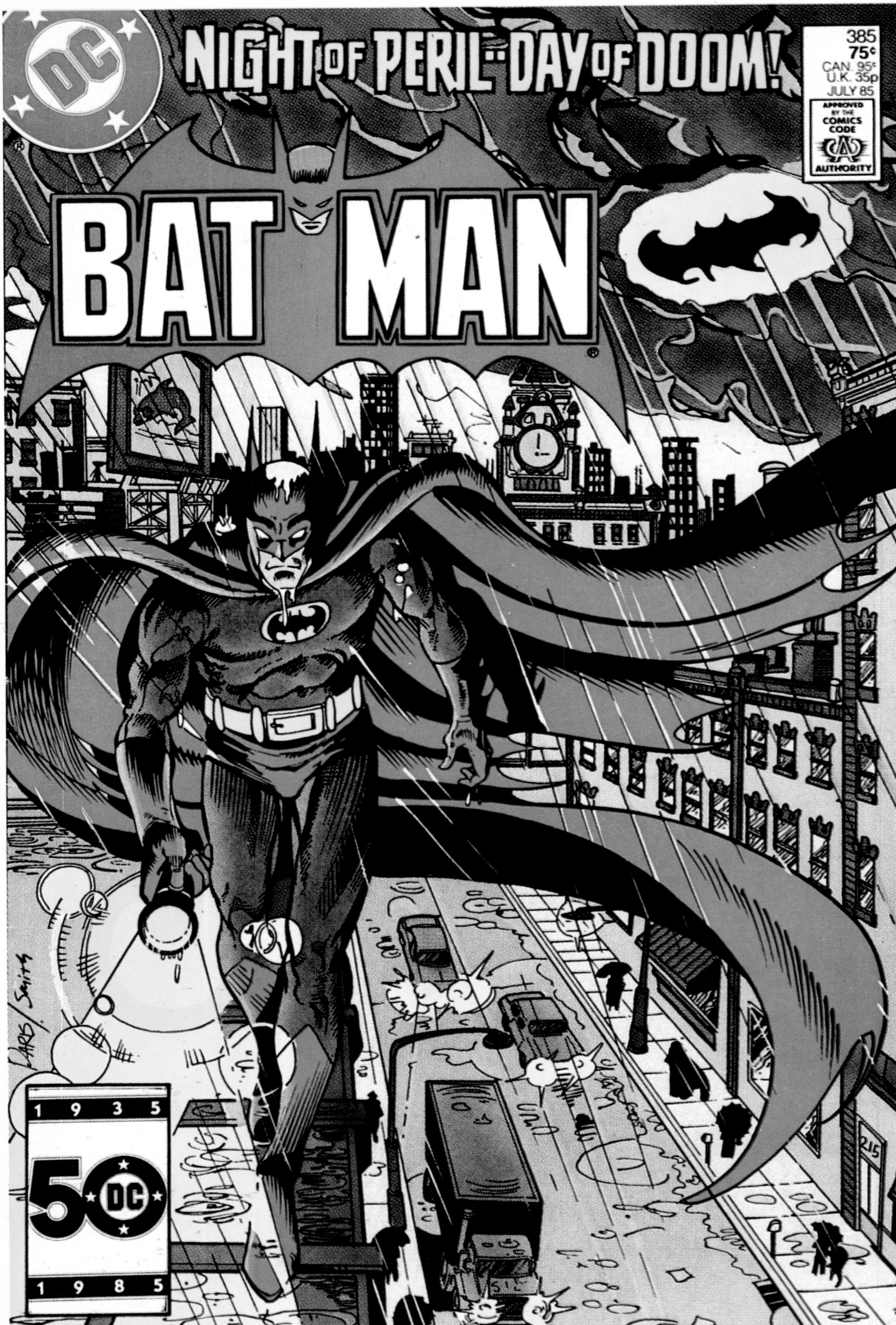

NIGHT OF PERIL-DAY OF DOOM!
385
75¢
CAN. 95¢
U.K. 35p
JULY 85
APPROVED BY THE COMICS CODE AUTHORITY
BATMAN
1935
1985

BATMAN #385, July 1985 (Paris Cullins, pencils; Bob Smith, inks)

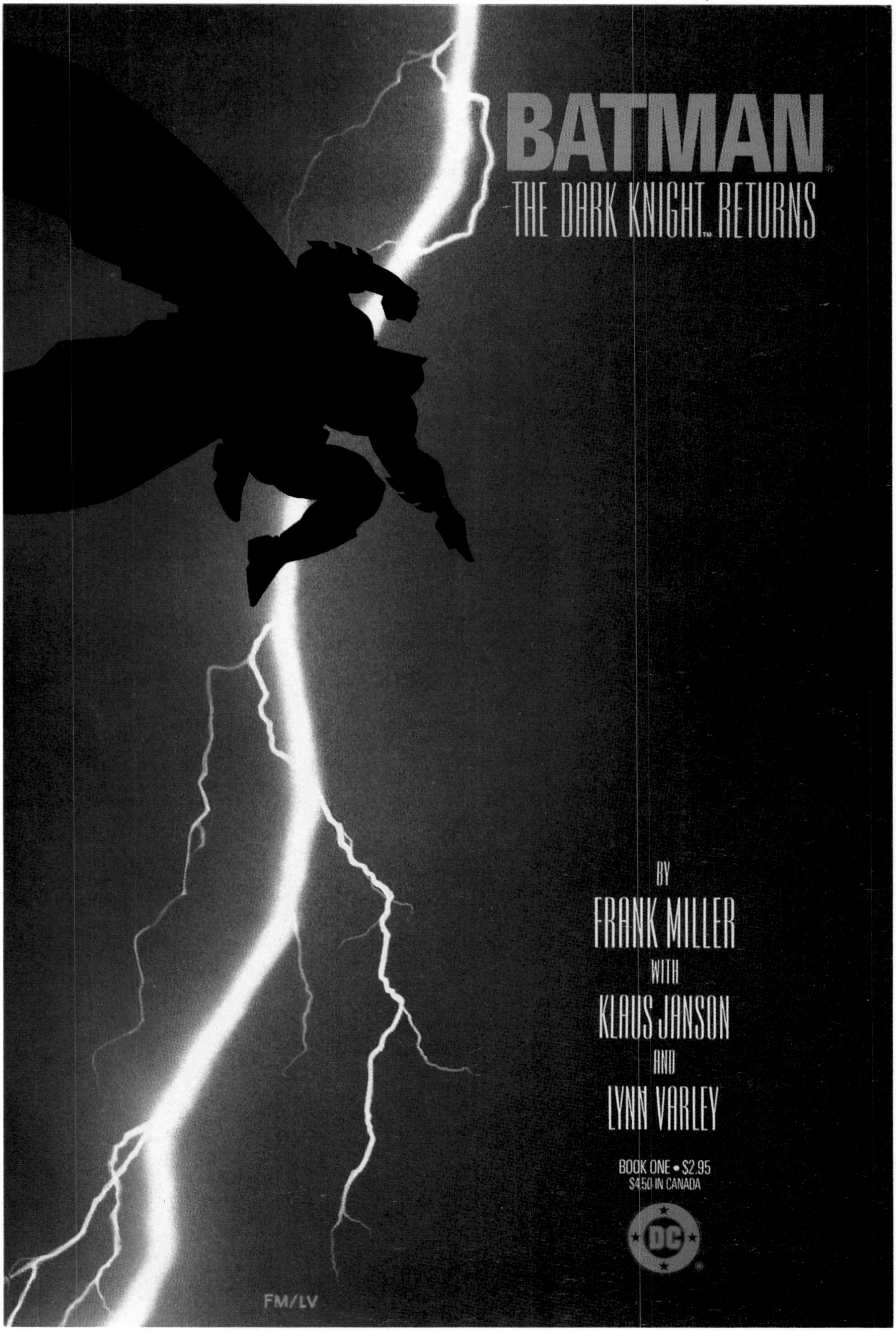
BATMAN
THE DARK KNIGHT RETURNS
BY
FRANK MILLER
WITH
KLAUS JANSON
AND
LYNN VARLEY
BOOK ONE • $2.95
$4.50 IN CANADA
DC
FM/LV

BATMAN: THE DARK KNIGHT RETURNS, Book One, 1986 (Frank Miller and Lynn Varley)

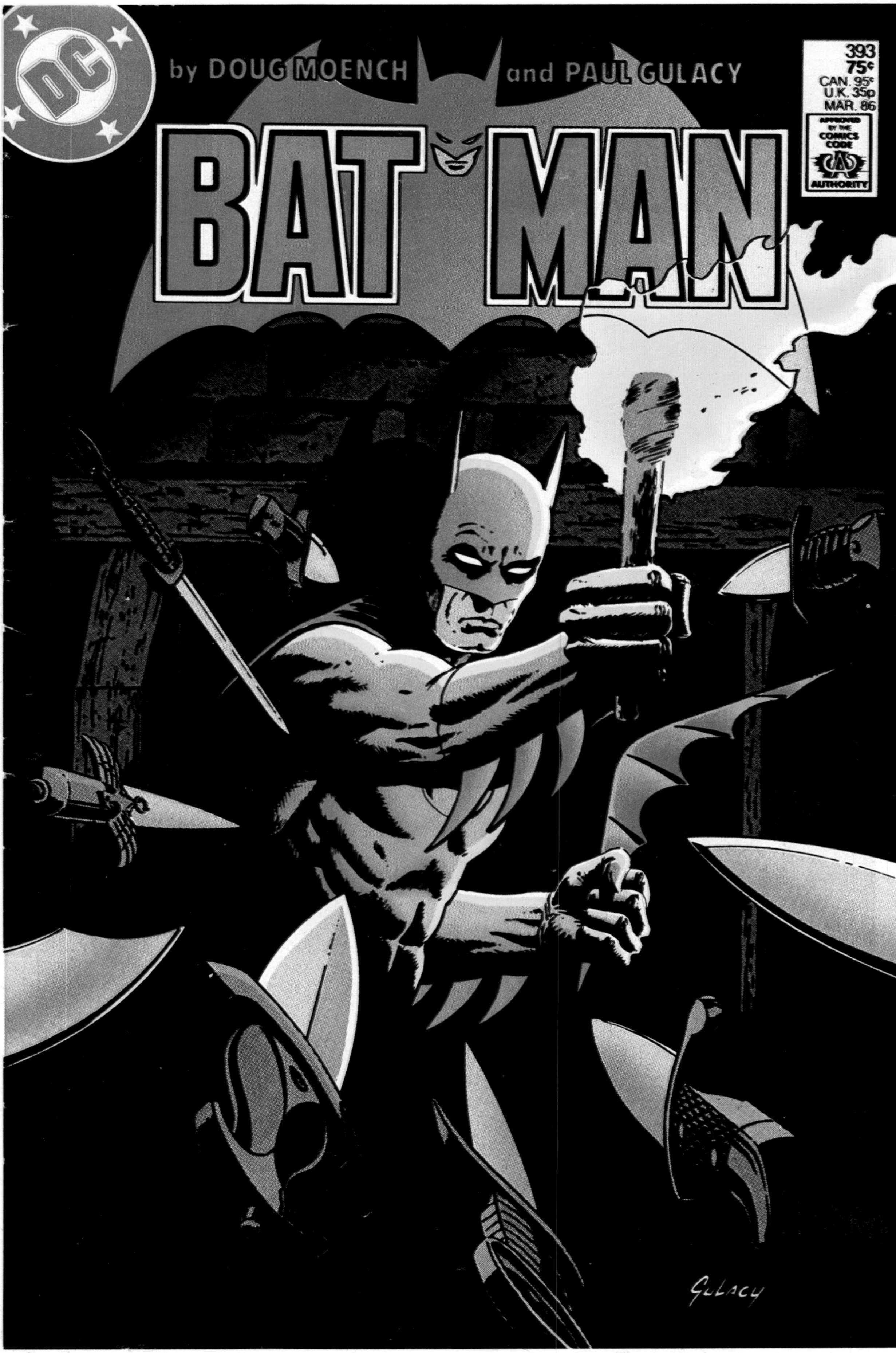
by DOUG MOENCH and PAUL GULACY
393
75¢
CAN. 95¢
U.K. 35p
MAR. 86
APPROVED BY THE COMICS CODE AUTHORITY
BATMAN
GULACY

BATMAN #393, March 1986 (Paul Gulacy)

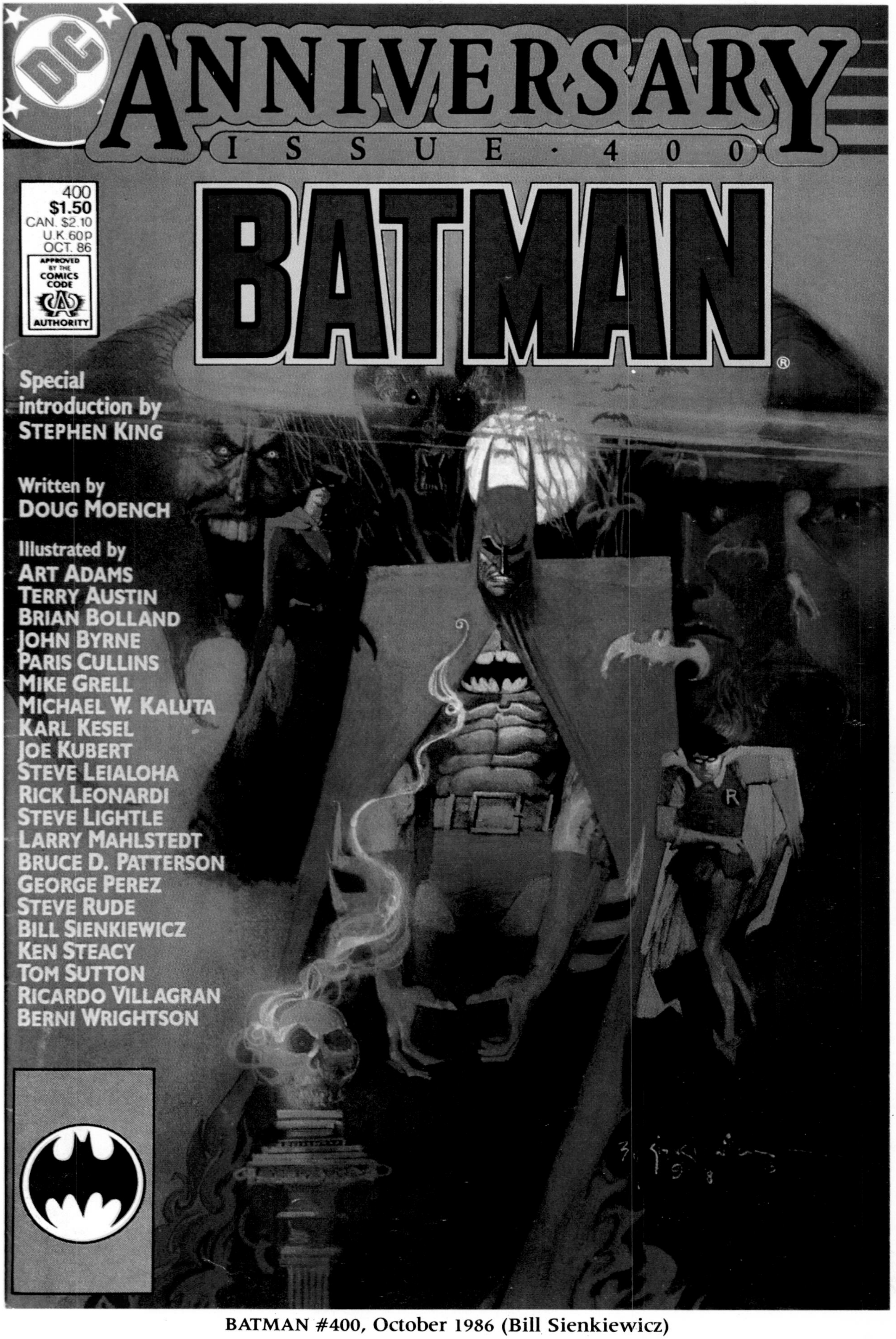
DC
ANNIVERSARY
ISSUE · 400
400
$1.50
CAN. $2.10
U.K 60p
OCT. 86
APPROVED BY THE COMICS CODE AUTHORITY
BATMAN®
Special introduction by STEPHEN KING
Written by DOUG MOENCH
Illustrated by
ART ADAMS
TERRY AUSTIN
BRIAN BOLLAND
JOHN BYRNE
PARIS CULLINS
MIKE GRELL
MICHAEL W. KALUTA
KARL KESEL
JOE KUBERT
STEVE LEIALOHA
RICK LEONARDI
STEVE LIGHTLE
LARRY MAHLSTEDT
BRUCE D. PATTERSON
GEORGE PEREZ
STEVE RUDE
BILL SIENKIEWICZ
KEN STEACY
TOM SUTTON
RICARDO VILLAGRAN
BERNI WRIGHTSON
R

BATMAN #400, October 1986 (Bill Sienkiewicz)

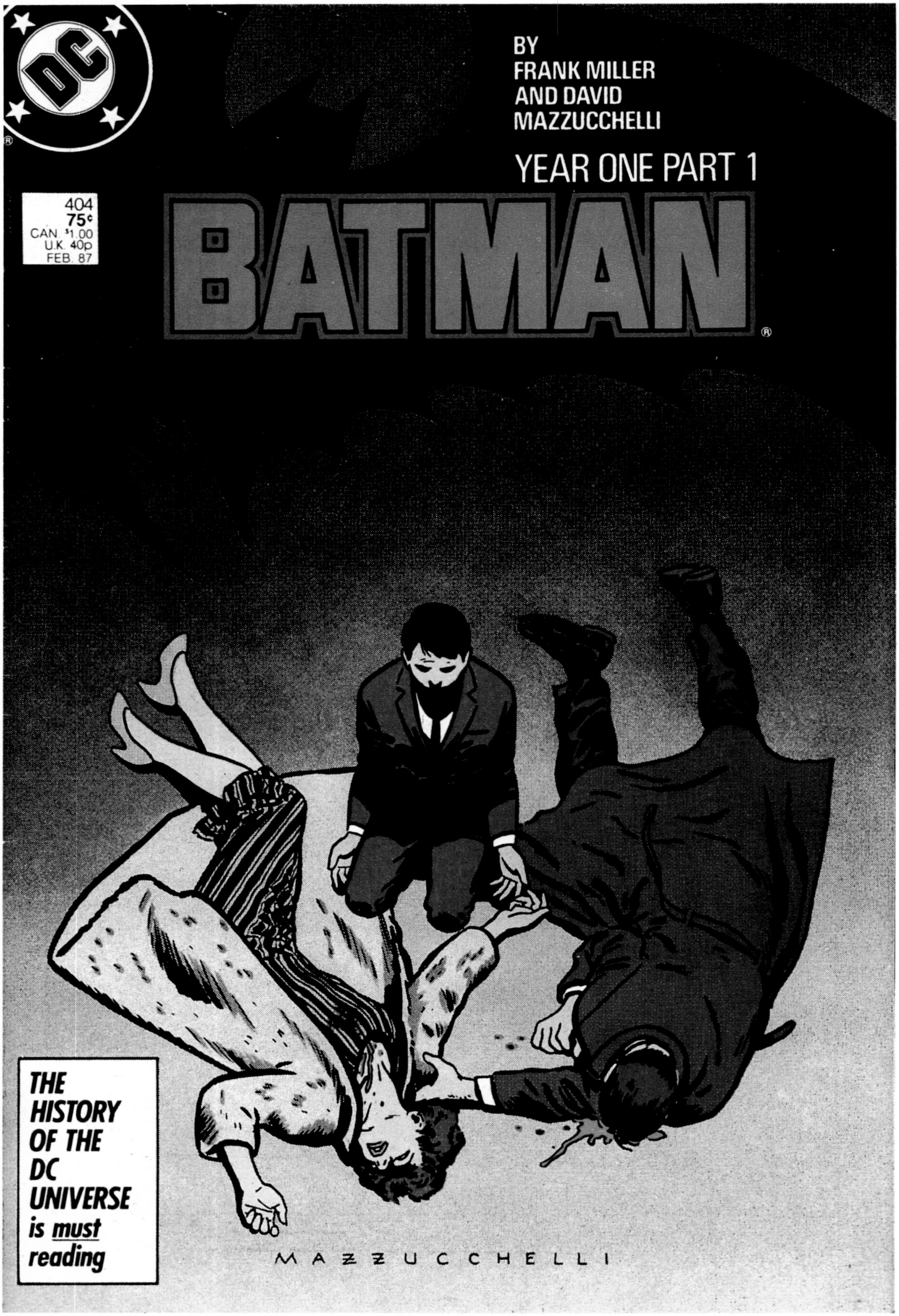
DC
BY
FRANK MILLER
AND DAVID
MAZZUCCHELLI
YEAR ONE PART 1
404
75¢
CAN. $1.00
U.K. 40p
FEB. 87
BATMAN
THE HISTORY OF THE DC UNIVERSE is must reading
MAZZUCCHELLI

BATMAN #404, February 1987 (David Mazzucchelli)

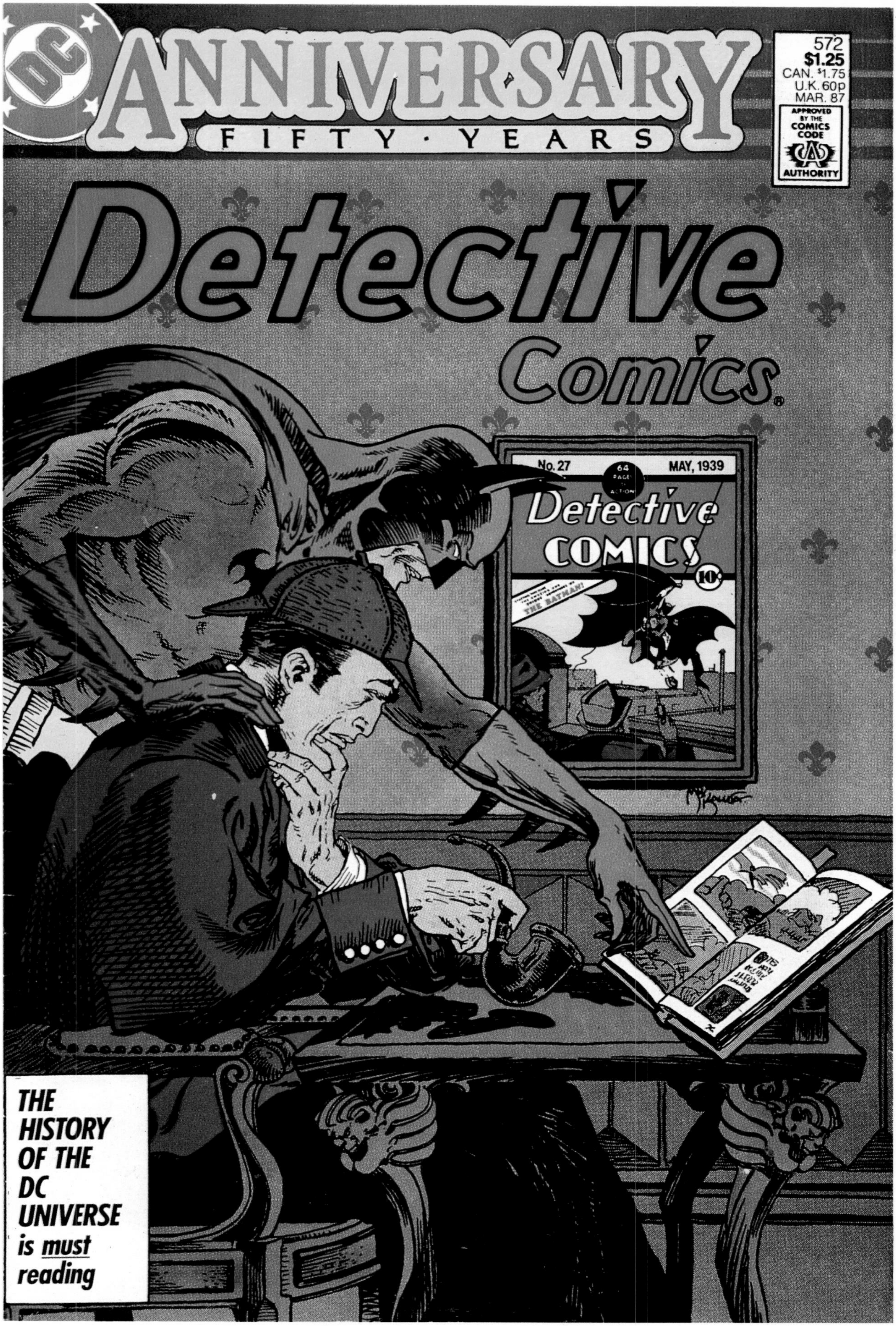
ANNIVERSARY
FIFTY · YEARS
572
$1.25
CAN. $1.75
U.K. 60p
MAR. 87
APPROVED BY THE COMICS CODE
AUTHORITY
Detective Comics
No. 27
MAY, 1939
Detective
COMICS
10¢
THE HISTORY OF THE DC UNIVERSE is must reading

DETECTIVE #572, March 1987 (Mike Kaluta)

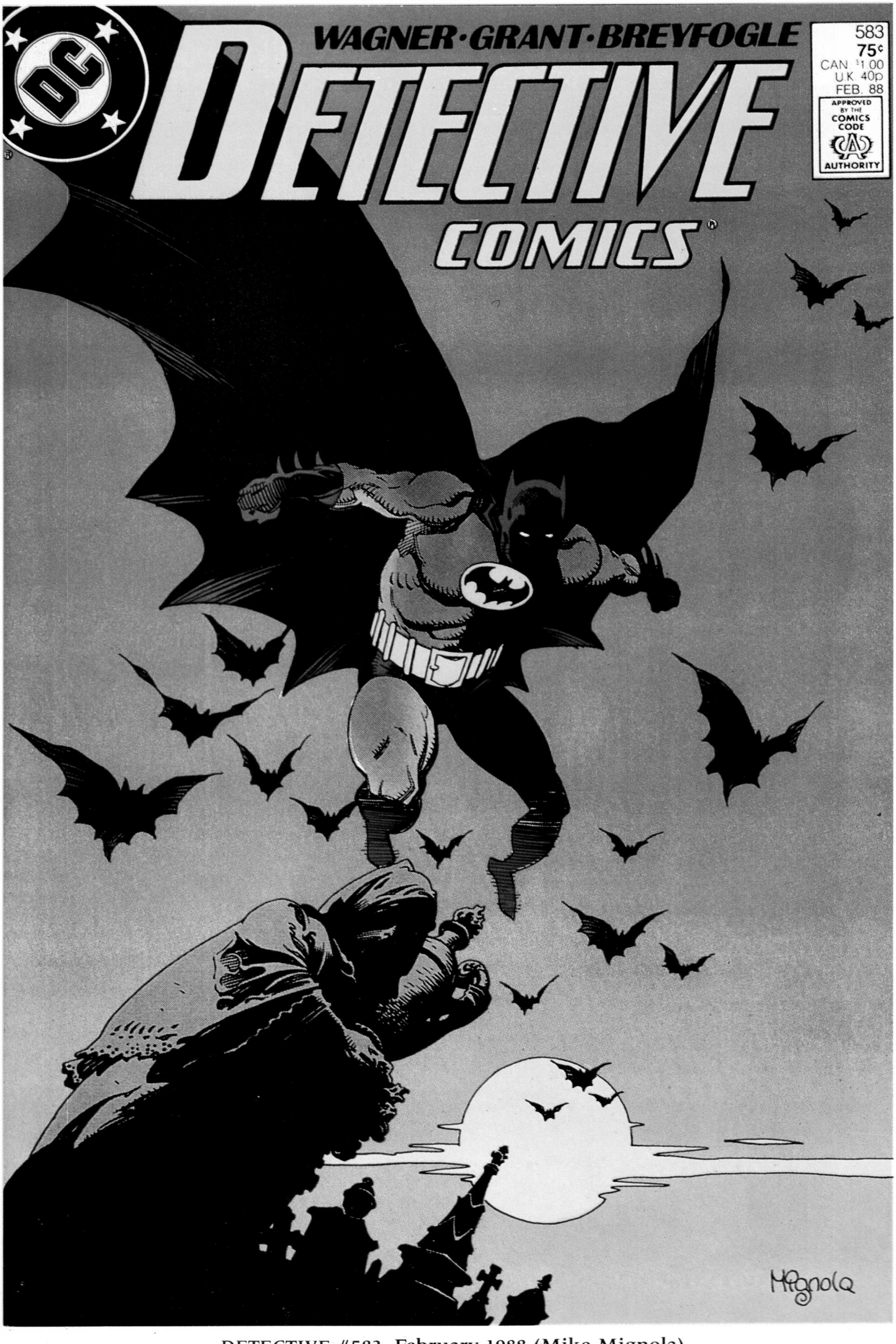
WAGNER·GRANT·BREYFOGLE
DETECTIVE
COMICS
583
75¢
CAN $1.00
U.K. 40p
FEB. 88
APPROVED BY THE COMICS CODE AUTHORITY
MIGNOLA

DETECTIVE #583, February 1988 (Mike Mignola)

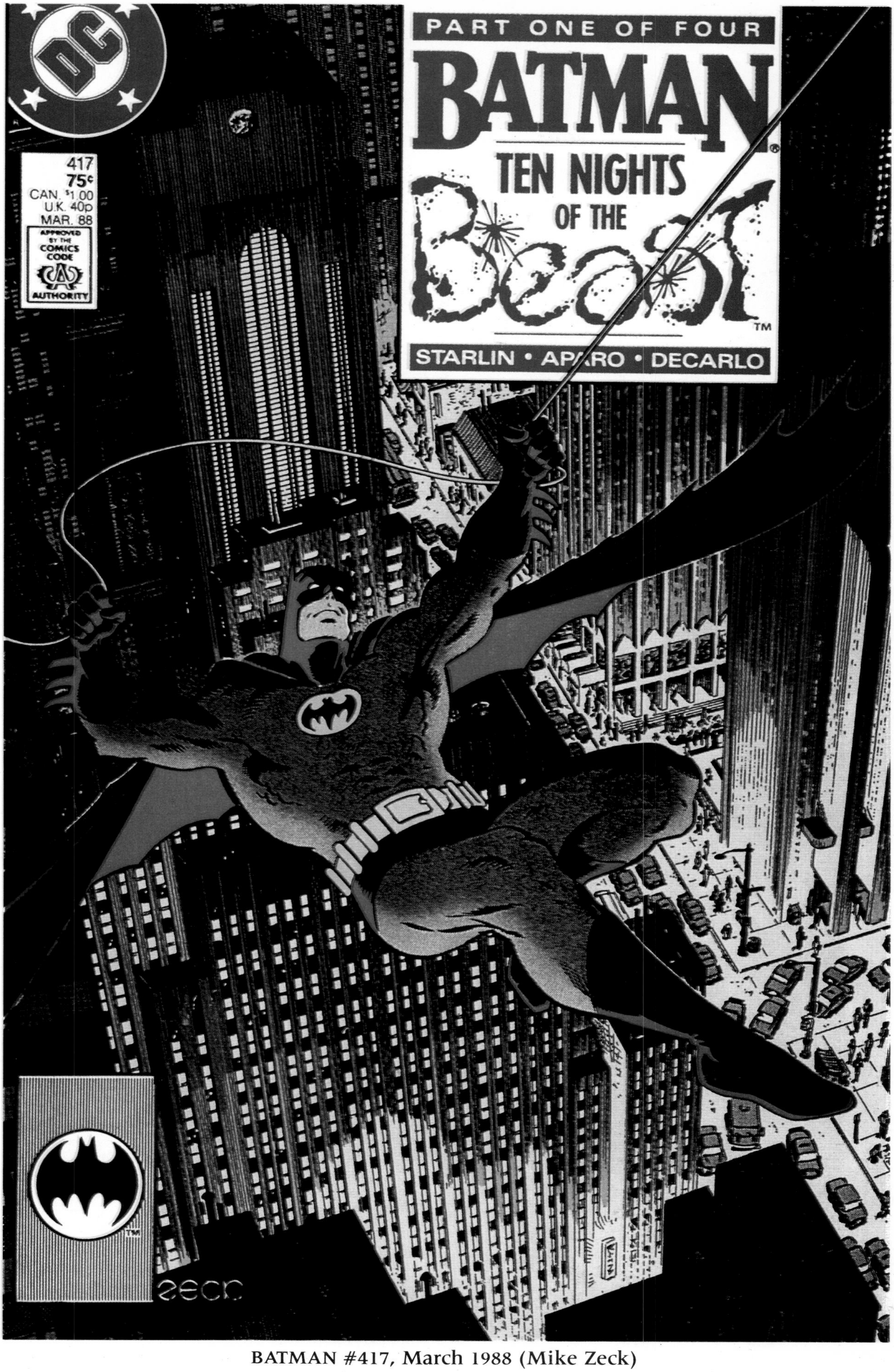
PART ONE OF FOUR
BATMAN
TEN NIGHTS
OF THE
Beast
STARLIN • APARO • DECARLO
417
75¢
CAN. $1.00
U.K. 40p
MAR. 88
APPROVED BY THE COMICS CODE AUTHORITY
ZECK

BATMAN #417, March 1988 (Mike Zeck)

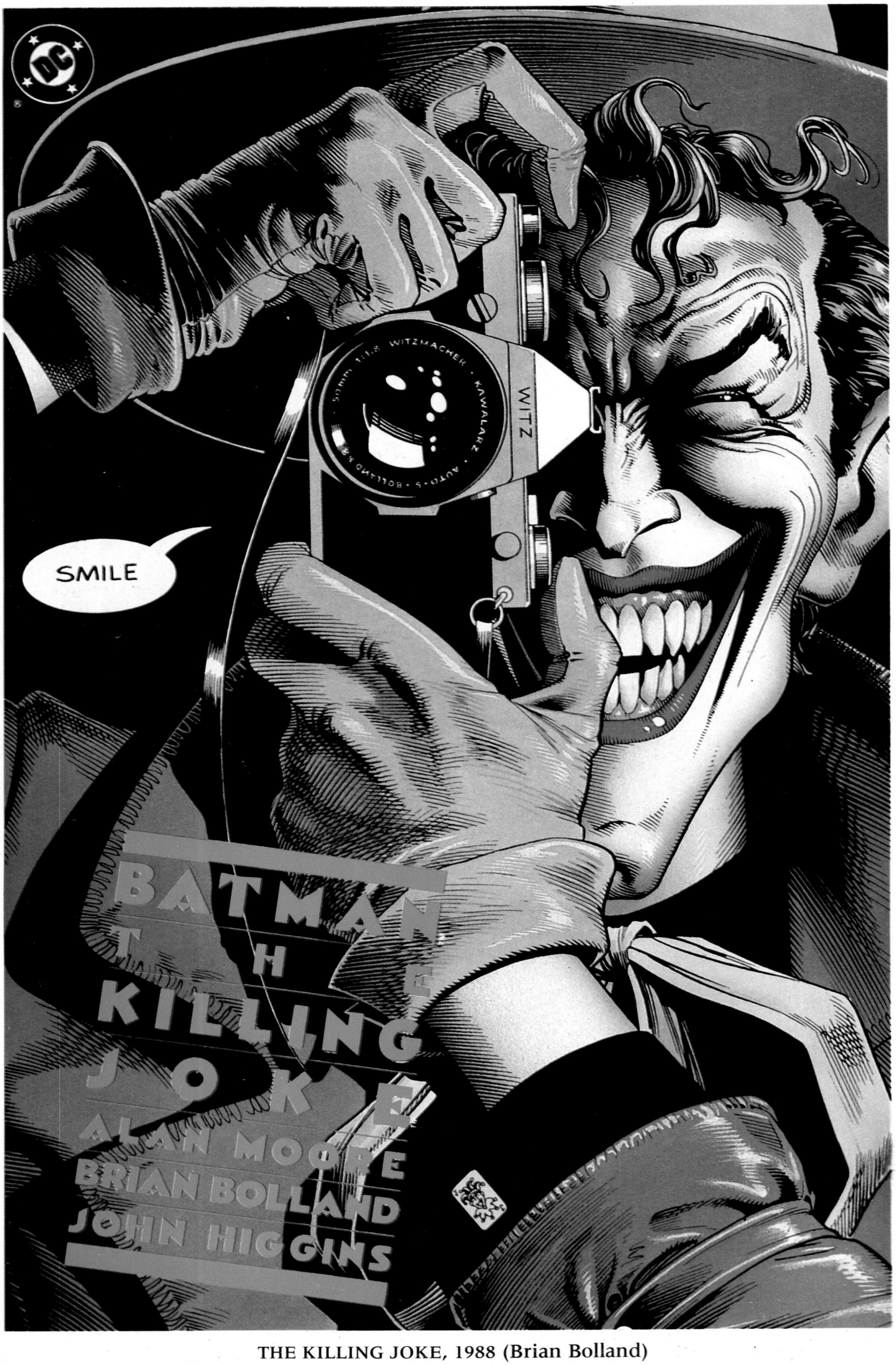
DC
SMILE
WITZ
BATMAN
THE
KILLING
JOKE
ALAN MOORE
BRIAN BOLLAND
JOHN HIGGINS

THE KILLING JOKE, 1988 (Brian Bolland)

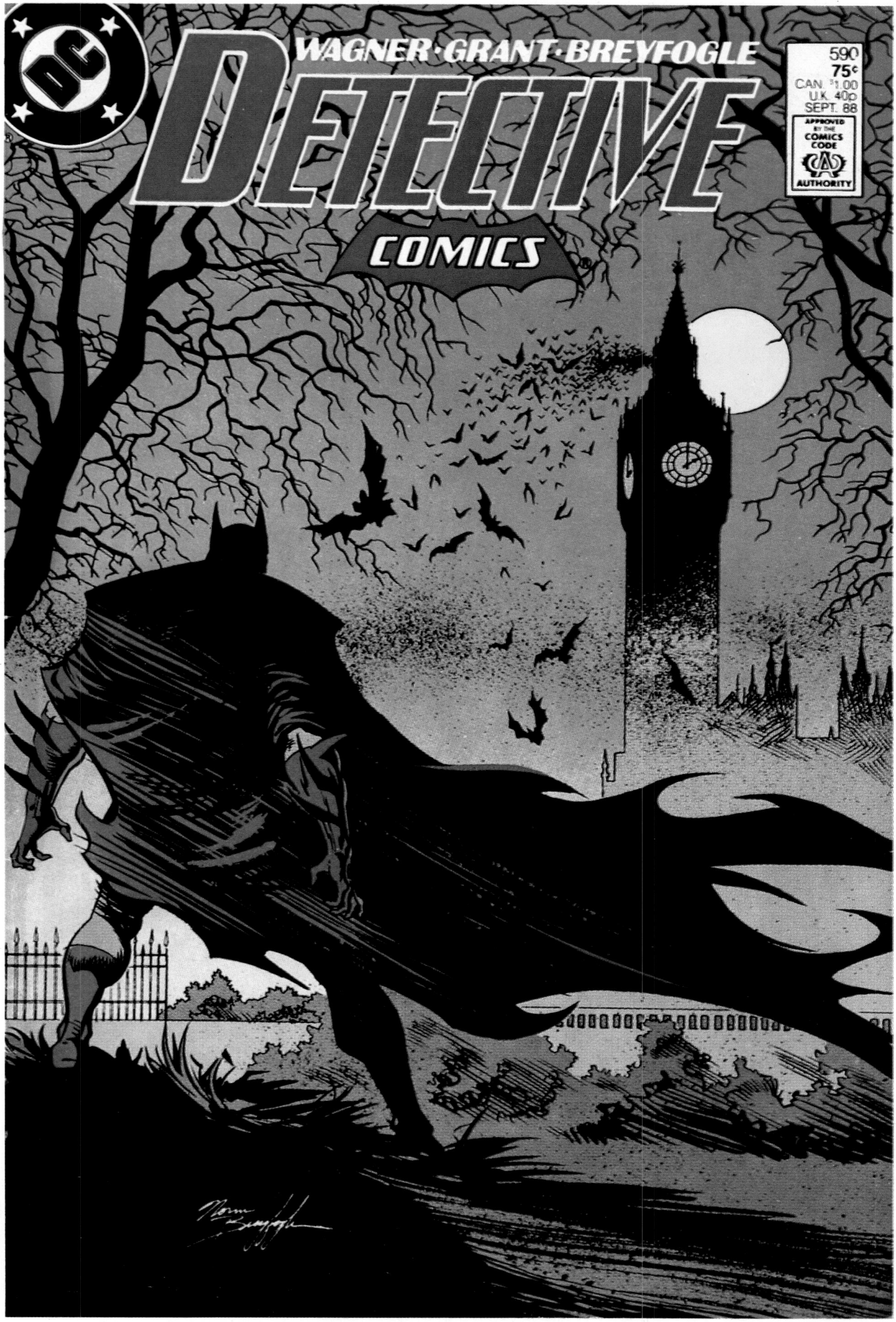
WAGNER·GRANT·BREYFOGLE
DETECTIVE
COMICS
590
75¢
CAN. $1.00
U.K. 40p
SEPT. 88
APPROVED BY THE COMICS CODE AUTHORITY

DETECTIVE #590, September 1988 (Norm Breyfogle)

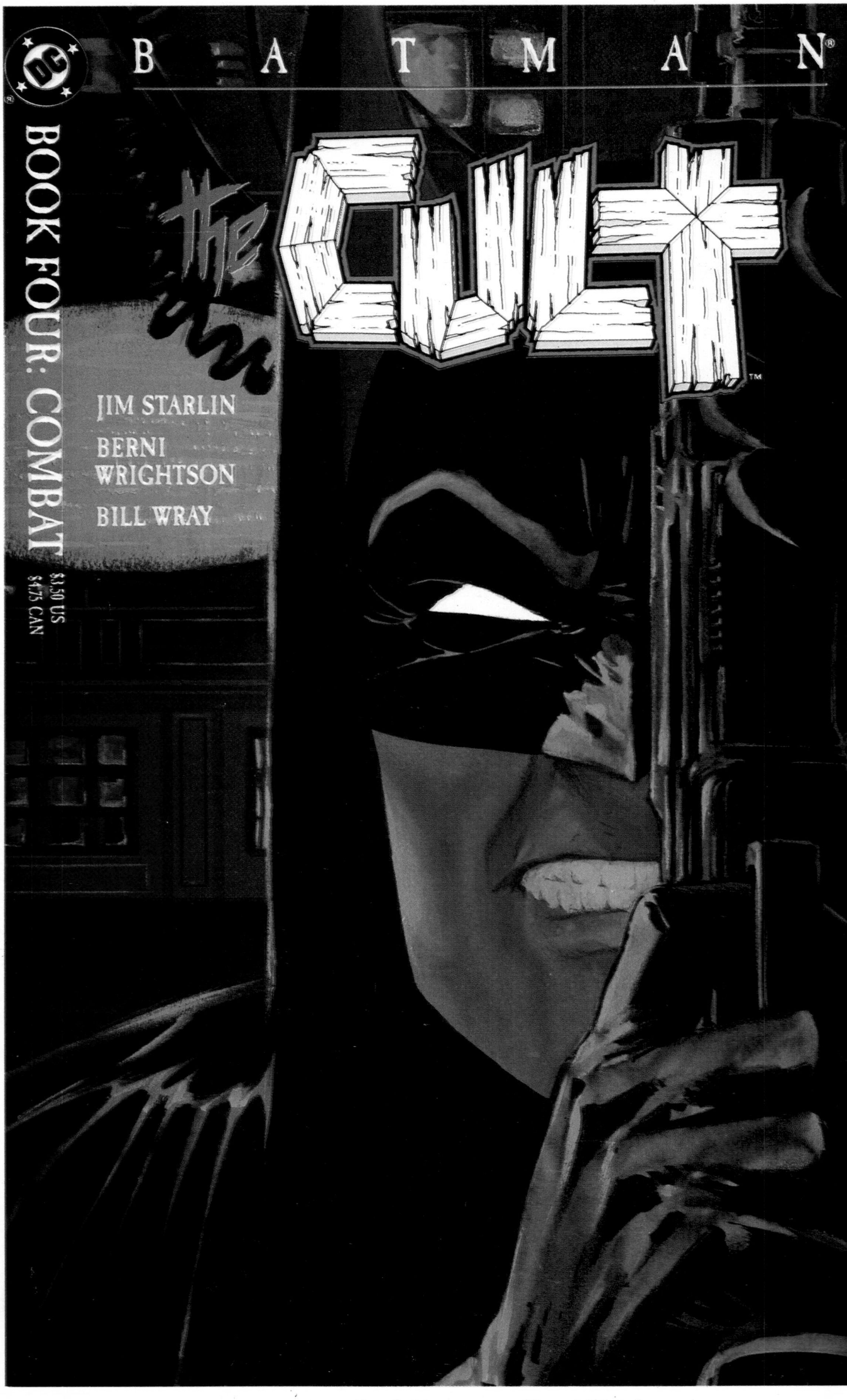
BATMAN®
THE CULT™
BOOK FOUR: COMBAT
JIM STARLIN
BERNI WRIGHTSON
BILL WRAY
$3.50 US
$4.75 CAN

THE CULT, Book Four, 1988 (Berni Wrightson)

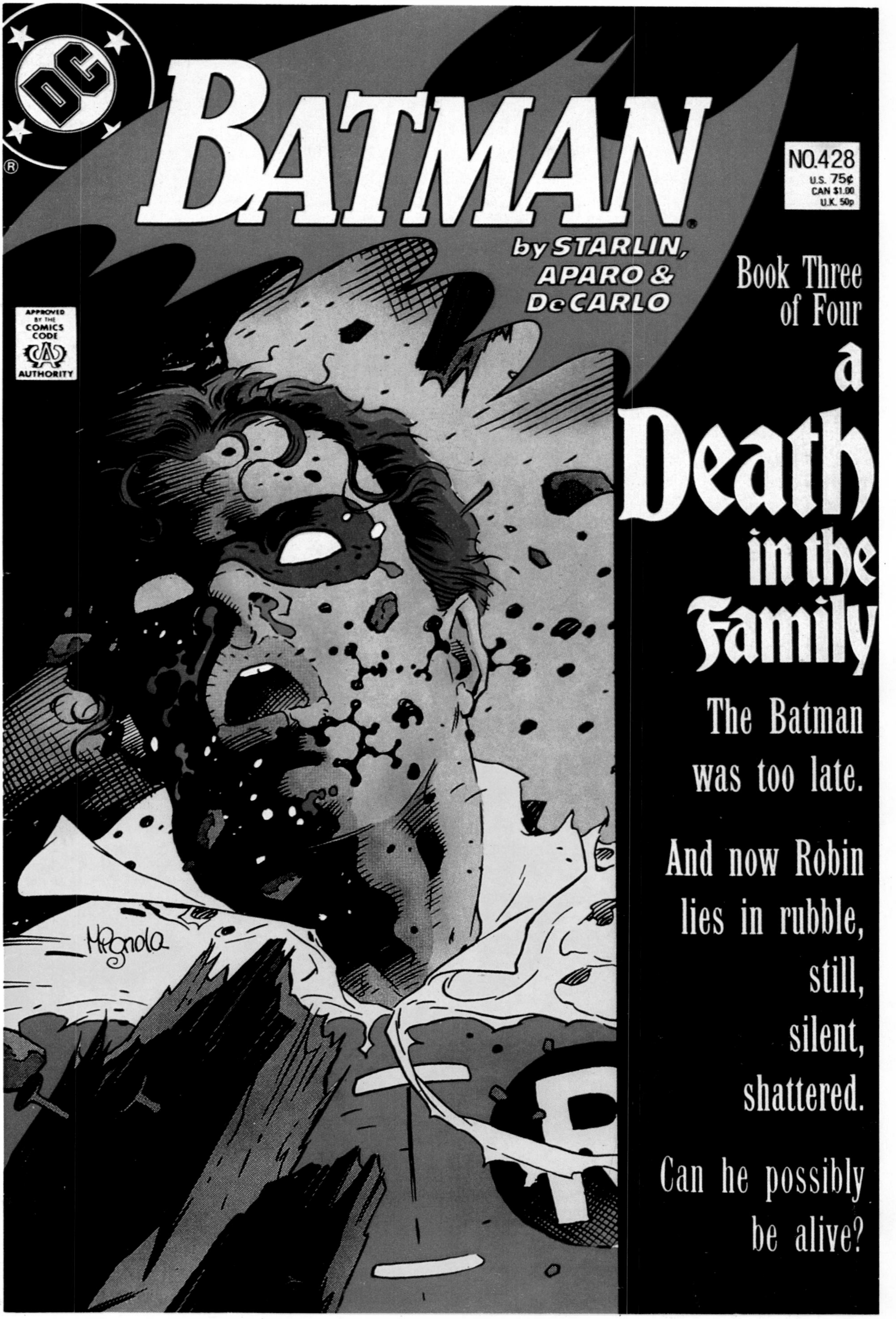
DC
BATMAN
NO.428
U.S. 75¢
CAN $1.00
U.K. 50p
by STARLIN, APARO & DeCARLO
APPROVED BY THE COMICS CODE AUTHORITY
Book Three of Four
a Death in the Family
The Batman was too late.
And now Robin lies in rubble, still, silent, shattered.
Can he possibly be alive?
Mignola

BATMAN #428, 1988 special release (Mike Mignola)

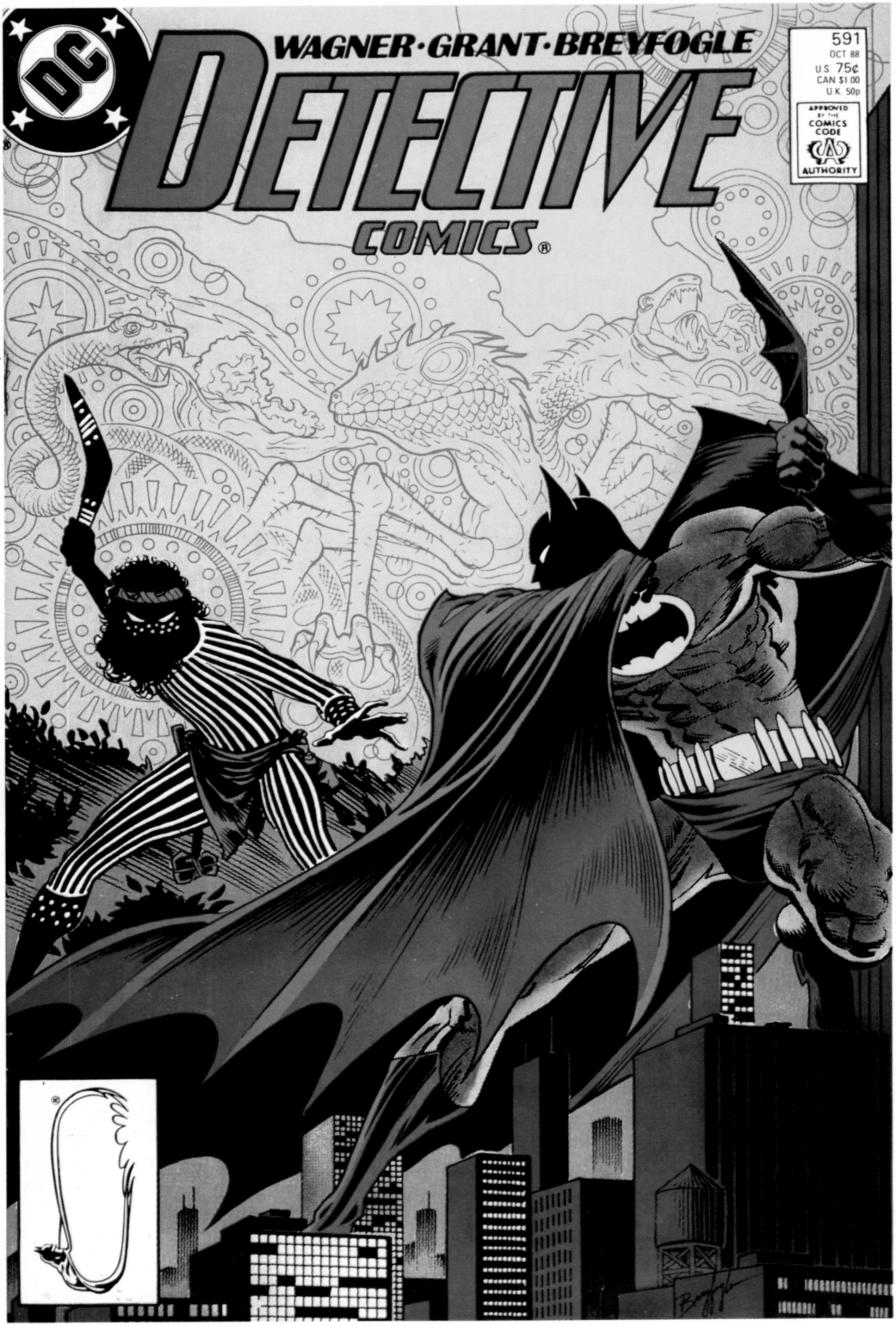
WAGNER·GRANT·BREYFOGLE
DETECTIVE
COMICS
591
OCT 88
U.S. 75¢
CAN $1.00
U.K. 50p
APPROVED BY THE COMICS CODE AUTHORITY

DETECTIVE #591, October 1988 (Norm Breyfogle)

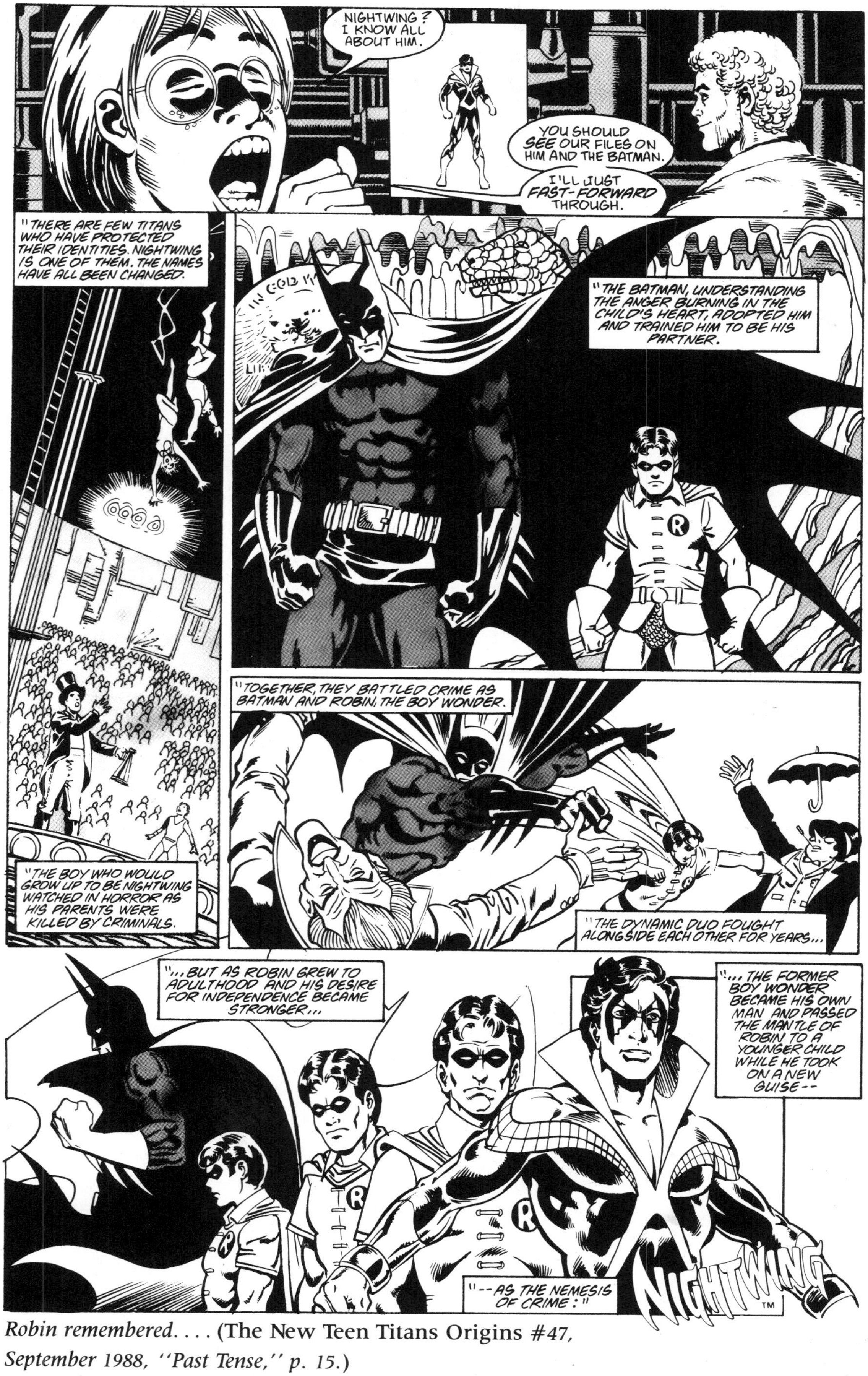
NIGHTWING? I KNOW ALL ABOUT HIM.
YOU SHOULD SEE OUR FILES ON HIM AND THE BATMAN.
I'LL JUST FAST-FORWARD THROUGH.
"THERE ARE FEW TITANS WHO HAVE PROTECTED THEIR IDENTITIES. NIGHTWING IS ONE OF THEM. THE NAMES HAVE ALL BEEN CHANGED.
"THE BOY WHO WOULD GROW UP TO BE NIGHTWING WATCHED IN HORROR AS HIS PARENTS WERE KILLED BY CRIMINALS.
"THE BATMAN, UNDERSTANDING THE ANGER BURNING IN THE CHILD'S HEART, ADOPTED HIM AND TRAINED HIM TO BE HIS PARTNER.
"TOGETHER, THEY BATTLED CRIME AS BATMAN AND ROBIN, THE BOY WONDER.
"THE DYNAMIC DUO FOUGHT ALONGSIDE EACH OTHER FOR YEARS...
"...BUT AS ROBIN GREW TO ADULTHOOD AND HIS DESIRE FOR INDEPENDENCE BECAME STRONGER...
"...THE FORMER BOY WONDER BECAME HIS OWN MAN AND PASSED THE MANTLE OF ROBIN TO A YOUNGER CHILD WHILE HE TOOK ON A NEW GUISE--
"--AS THE NEMESIS OF CRIME:"
NIGHTWING™

Robin remembered. . . . (The New Teen Titans Origins #47, *September 1988, ''Past Tense,'' p. 15.*)

In one form or other, all have helped bring Batman out of the sci-fi, camp, and pop mood that generally characterized the tales from the 1950s through the 1960s, and returned him to the darker themes of his Golden Age beginnings. But in the process Batman has evolved into a more complex and obsessed figure than was ever presented in those classic tales.

Despite his brutal origin and the world of menace he inhabited, the Batman of the forties reflected a resolutely optimistic time—it had to be, considering the nightmare of Fascist domination if the war was lost. But the Dark Knight of the eighties reflects a much more complex and cynical era.

The 1980s Batman also reflects the changing demographics and tastes of the comic book audience.

The adolescent readership that once provided the bulk of sales during the editorial tenures of Schiff and Schwartz is still there, but now includes a larger percentage of readers in their twenties, thirties, and even older. The audience of the eighties is also generally better-educated and more affluent.

In addition, new generations raised on a daily diet of television have become, in Dick Giordano's phrase, "graphic-literate." No longer does it suffice to present the crude drawings or approximations of reality that often passed for superhero art in the forties. Comic book action now has to look, move, and feel real to satisfy discriminating comics fans.

The result has been more realistic art and mature themes for the readers—but a grim time for the characters themselves.

The Gotham City of the eighties has been plagued by so many dangerous psychopaths that a special facility, Arkham Asylum, has been installed in the Gotham environs to handle the

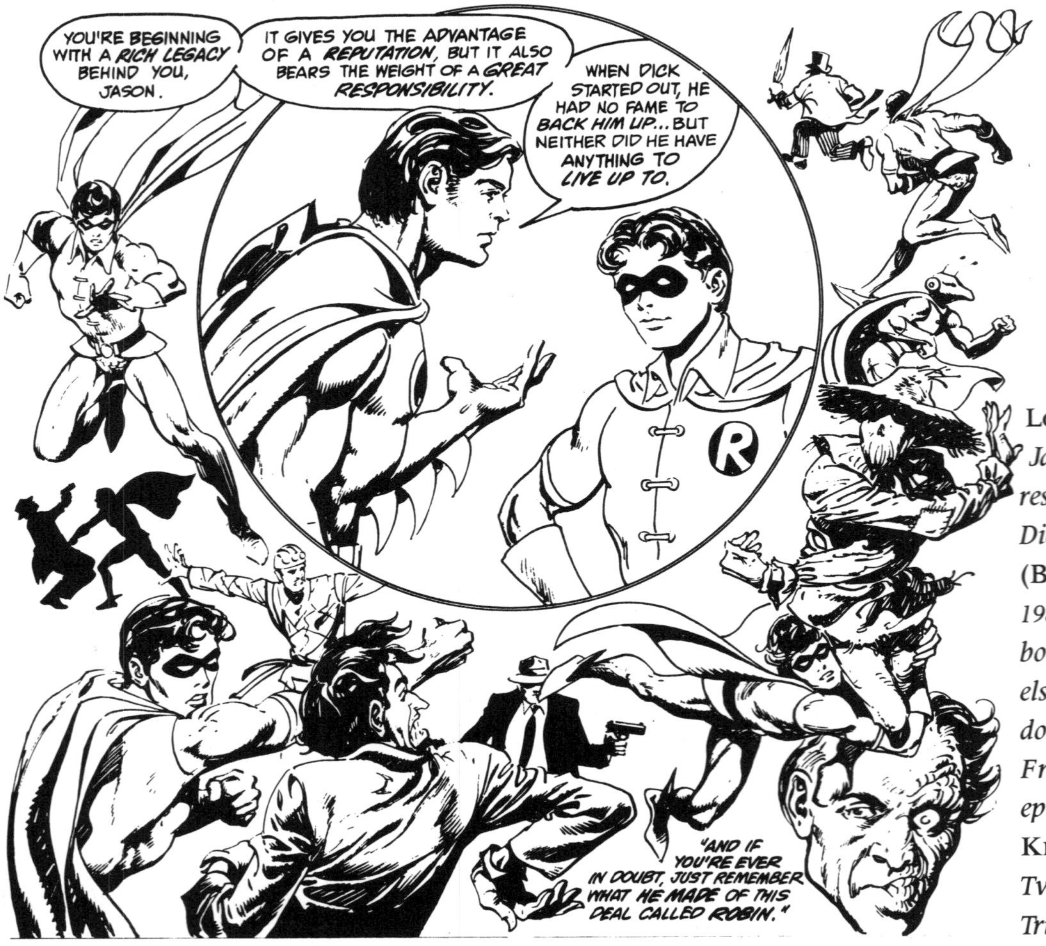
YOU'RE BEGINNING WITH A RICH LEGACY BEHIND YOU, JASON.
IT GIVES YOU THE ADVANTAGE OF A REPUTATION, BUT IT ALSO BEARS THE WEIGHT OF A GREAT RESPONSIBILITY.
WHEN DICK STARTED OUT, HE HAD NO FAME TO BACK HIM UP... BUT NEITHER DID HE HAVE ANYTHING TO LIVE UP TO.
"AND IF YOU'RE EVER IN DOUBT, JUST REMEMBER WHAT HE MADE OF THIS DEAL CALLED ROBIN."

Left: *Batman explains to Jason Todd the awesome responsibility of succeeding Dick Grayson as Robin.* (Batman *#368, February 1984, "A Revenge of Rainbows," p. 10 [select panels].)* Right: *Carrie Kelley dons the Robin uniform in Frank Miller's Batman epic.* (Batman: The Dark Knight Returns, *Book Two, 1986, "Dark Knight Triumphant," p. 4*).

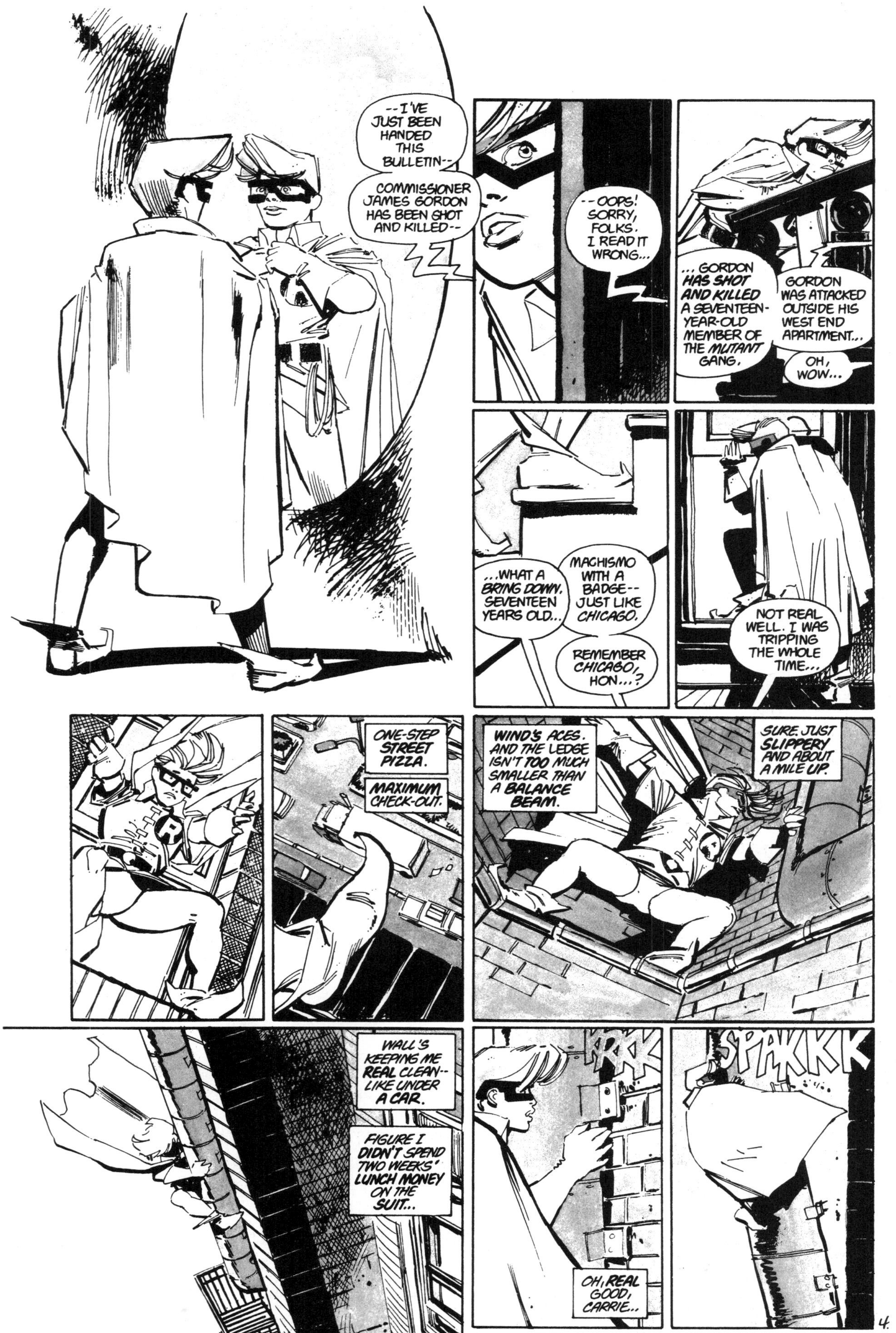
--I'VE JUST BEEN HANDED THIS BULLETIN--
COMMISSIONER JAMES GORDON HAS BEEN SHOT AND KILLED--
--OOPS! SORRY, FOLKS. I READ IT WRONG...
...GORDON HAS SHOT AND KILLED A SEVENTEEN-YEAR-OLD MEMBER OF THE MUTANT GANG.
GORDON WAS ATTACKED OUTSIDE HIS WEST END APARTMENT...
OH, WOW...
...WHAT A BRING DOWN. SEVENTEEN YEARS OLD...
MACHISMO WITH A BADGE--JUST LIKE CHICAGO.
REMEMBER CHICAGO, HON...?
NOT REAL WELL. I WAS TRIPPING THE WHOLE TIME...
ONE-STEP STREET PIZZA.
MAXIMUM CHECK-OUT.
WIND'S ACES. AND THE LEDGE ISN'T TOO MUCH SMALLER THAN A BALANCE BEAM.
SURE. JUST SLIPPERY AND ABOUT A MILE UP.
WALL'S KEEPING ME REAL CLEAN--LIKE UNDER A CAR.
FIGURE I DIDN'T SPEND TWO WEEKS' LUNCH MONEY ON THE SUIT...
KRAK
SPAKKK
OH, REAL GOOD, CARRIE...
4.

most dangerous. Batman fans have seen Commissioner Gordon suffer a serious heart attack; his daughter, Barbara, shot and paralyzed by the Joker; Dick Grayson grow out of his Robin uniform and leave Batman to start his own crime-fighting career as Nightwing; and Alfred hospitalized after a beating administered by a Batman foe (*Batman Special* 1, 1984).

Batman himself has been beset with the pressures of managing the Wayne Foundation, has felt the heat of a growing public animosity against superheroes, and has questioned the very purpose of his long crusade.

There are many compelling images and situations in *The Dark Knight Returns* that capture this angst, but none more gripping than Batman's final encounter with Harvey ''Two-Face'' Dent.

Reconstructive surgery and criminal rehabilitation should have rescued Dent from the grip of his Two-Face identity forever. But we find the former crusading district attorney, his face mysteriously swathed in bandages, threatening to blow up Gotham's Twin Towers unless he's paid a five-million-dollar ransom.

''Harvey—I have to know,'' the aging Dark Knight thinks as he relentlessly tracks Dent down to find out why he still clings to his Two-Face ways.

And when Batman catches up to Dent and sends him reeling with a powerful punch, Dent's bandages unravel, revealing a handsome face, perfectly delivered from the mutilation of the acid that made him Two-Face.

But Dent wears scars that cannot be erased by a surgeon's expertise. He is still Two-Face—in his mind. And the mind has always been the most dangerous terrain in Batman's world.

And then the Dark Knight sees a reflection of what drives himself, the deep scars that compel and propel him. Perhaps it's in that moment that Batman realizes he's lost his war against crime. That his utopian notion of rehabilitating his foes and making them useful members of society had always been doomed.

It was the world, the society, his city, that was mortally sick and beyond the good intentions of a lone crime fighter.

It's a damned vision, this Dark Knight shadow world dreamed of in the 1940s and wedded to the black angst of the eighties.

But what of the future Batman—does salvation or hellfire await the legendary crime fighter?

It's easier to retrace the tracks of what was than to journey pell-mell into what will be. But we have to move ahead, no matter the risks, to see the future face of Batman's world.

You see—we have to know.

I'LL FEEL BETTER IN THE MORNING. AT LEAST, I'LL FEEL IT *LESS*...

IT'S THE *NIGHT*-WHEN THE CITY'S *SMELLS* CALL *OUT* TO HIM, THOUGH I LIE BETWEEN SILK SHEETS IN A MILLION-DOLLAR MANSION MILES AWAY...

...WHEN A POLICE SIREN WAKES ME, AND, FOR A MOMENT, I FORGET THAT IT'S ALL OVER...

BUT *BATMAN* WAS A *YOUNG* MAN. IF IT WAS *REVENGE* HE WAS AFTER, HE'S TAKEN IT. IT'S BEEN *FORTY YEARS* SINCE HE WAS BORN...

Above: *Even in retirement, the Dark Knight persona calls out to a troubled Bruce Wayne.* (Batman: The Dark Knight Returns, *Book One, 1986, ''The Dark Knight Returns,'' p. 5 [select panels].*) Right: Batman: The Dark Knight Returns, *Book One, 1986, ''The Dark Knight Returns,'' p. 47.*

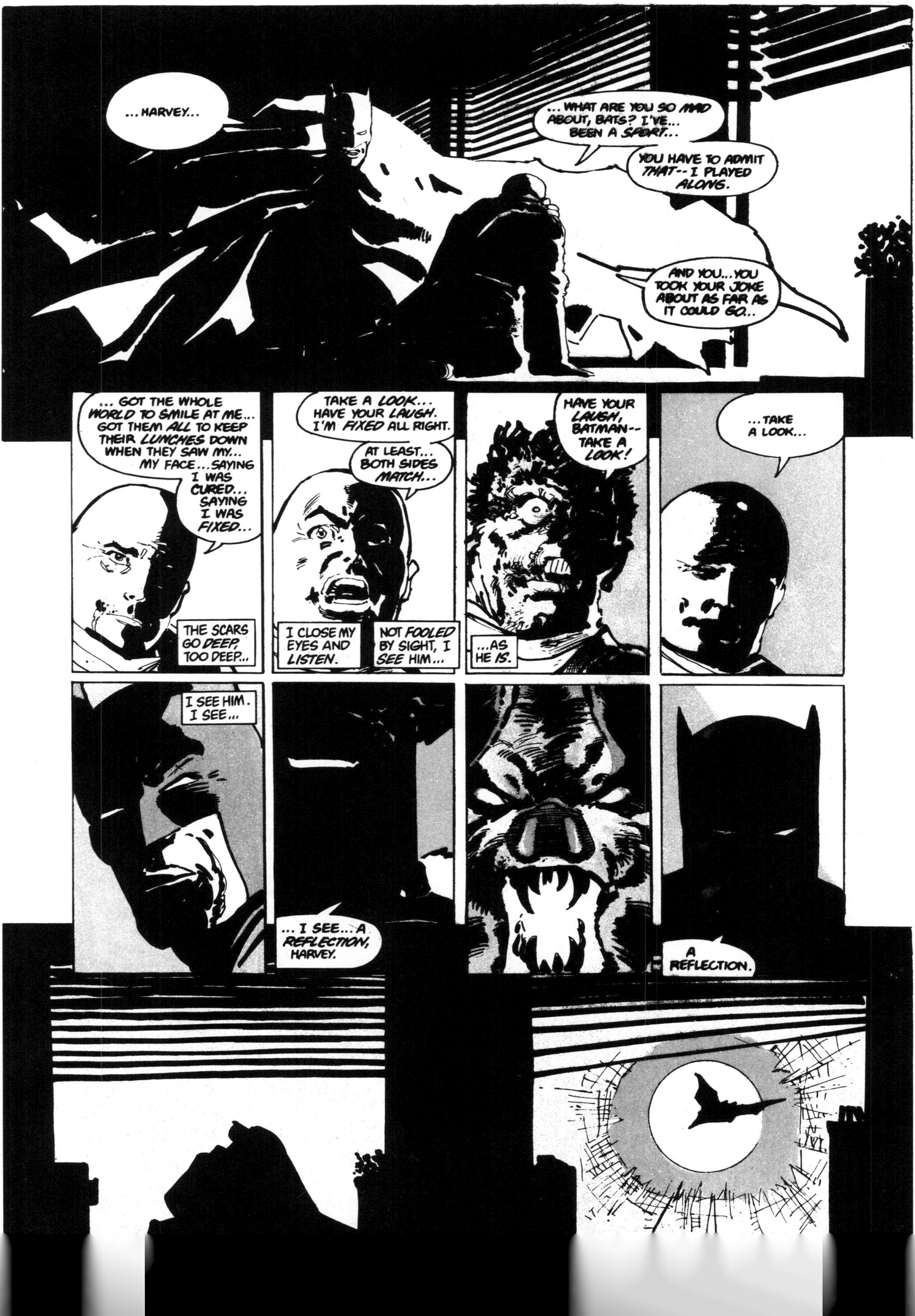
... HARVEY...
... WHAT ARE YOU SO MAD ABOUT, BATS? I'VE... BEEN A SPORT...
YOU HAVE TO ADMIT THAT-- I PLAYED ALONG.
AND YOU... YOU TOOK YOUR JOKE ABOUT AS FAR AS IT COULD GO...
... GOT THE WHOLE WORLD TO SMILE AT ME... GOT THEM ALL TO KEEP THEIR LUNCHES DOWN WHEN THEY SAW MY... MY FACE... SAYING I WAS CURED... SAYING I WAS FIXED...
THE SCARS GO DEEP, TOO DEEP...
TAKE A LOOK... HAVE YOUR LAUGH. I'M FIXED ALL RIGHT.
AT LEAST... BOTH SIDES MATCH...
I CLOSE MY EYES AND LISTEN.
NOT FOOLED BY SIGHT, I SEE HIM...
HAVE YOUR LAUGH, BATMAN-- TAKE A LOOK!
...AS HE IS.
...TAKE A LOOK...
I SEE HIM. I SEE...
... I SEE... A REFLECTION, HARVEY.
A REFLECTION.

CHAPTER 18

GOTHAM GÖTTERDÄMMERUNG

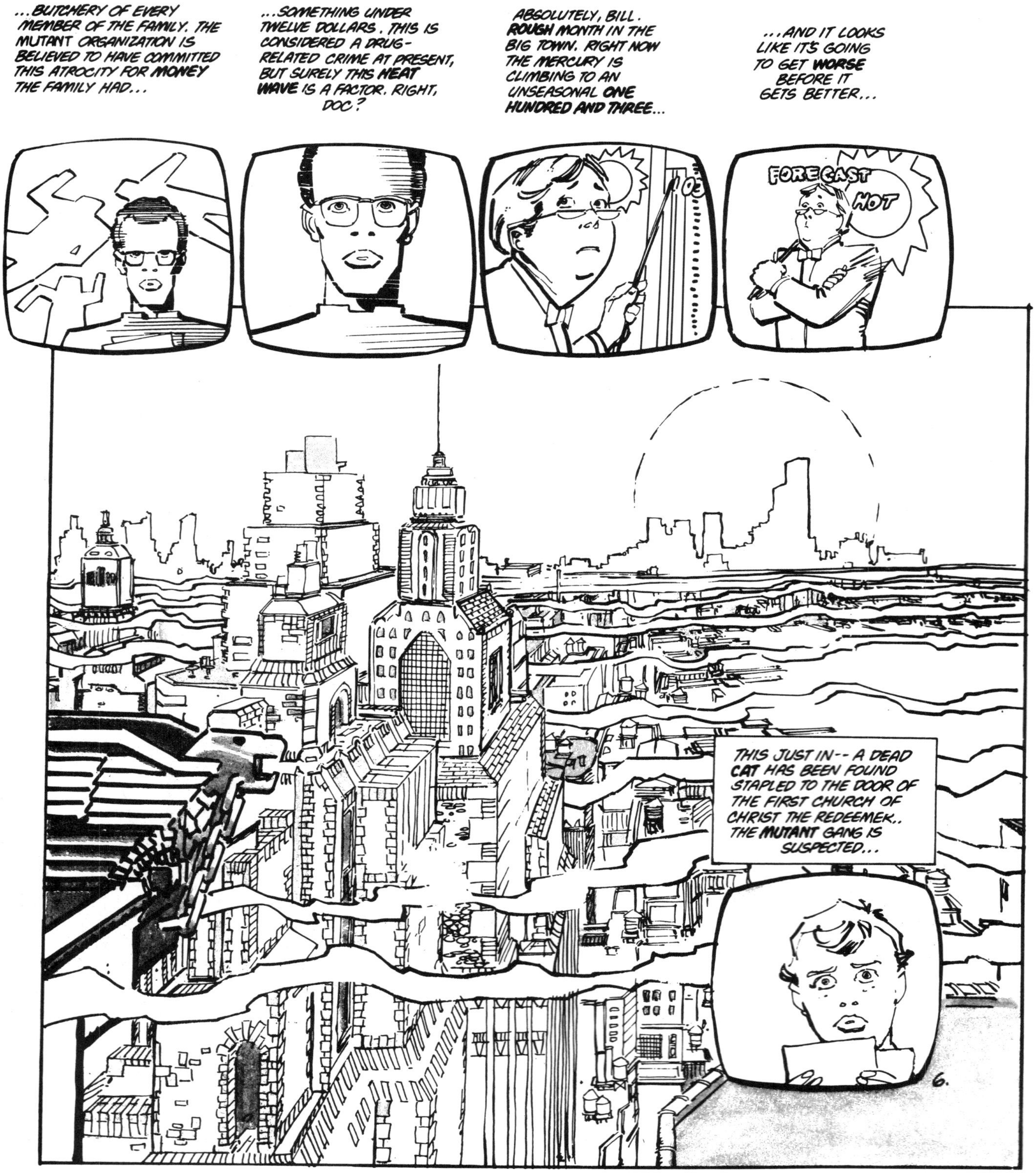
...BUTCHERY OF EVERY MEMBER OF THE FAMILY. THE MUTANT ORGANIZATION IS BELIEVED TO HAVE COMMITTED THIS ATROCITY FOR MONEY THE FAMILY HAD...
...SOMETHING UNDER TWELVE DOLLARS. THIS IS CONSIDERED A DRUG-RELATED CRIME AT PRESENT, BUT SURELY THIS HEAT WAVE IS A FACTOR. RIGHT, DOC?
ABSOLUTELY, BILL. ROUGH MONTH IN THE BIG TOWN. RIGHT NOW THE MERCURY IS CLIMBING TO AN UNSEASONAL ONE HUNDRED AND THREE...
...AND IT LOOKS LIKE IT'S GOING TO GET WORSE BEFORE IT GETS BETTER...
FORECAST
HOT
THIS JUST IN-- A DEAD CAT HAS BEEN FOUND STAPLED TO THE DOOR OF THE FIRST CHURCH OF CHRIST THE REDEEMEK.. THE MUTANT GANG IS SUSPECTED...
6.

Gotham City. The City of Tomorrow: stark angles, creeping shadows, dense, crowded, as if hell had erupted through the sidewalks. A dangling fat moon shines overhead.

—*Opening establishing shot for* Batman *screenplay (Warner Bros., Inc., 1988)*

THE GOTHAM CITY OF THE 1980s IS A VASTLY different city from the days when Batman first began patrolling the streets. Gone are the ethnic neighborhoods, the horse-driven buggies of the milk and ice men, and the squat brick buildings trimmed with candy-striped awnings. The famed Gotham State Building still remains, but it no longer dominates Gotham's skyline.

In Miller's *The Dark Knight Returns,* a hundred skyscrapers as mighty as Gotham's once premier tower choke the sky. Street-level Gotham has been transformed by the superstructures into claustrophobic steel canyons and valleys.

Other Batman artists and writers have taken up Miller's foreboding tone. In this Gotham of doom and decay, an unnamed fear acts like a cancer on the populace, eating away at pride, resolve, and self-respect. Even an older, embittered, more violent Batman has become outdated and irrelevant.

But an even more oppressive, dangerous future awaits the Caped Crusader in the computer-generated work of artist Pepe Moreno.

In Moreno's version, a thousand more Gotham State Buildings crowd the landscape. Everywhere there are concrete and steel superstructures built on the ruins of twentieth-century buildings. The entire city has become so overwhelmingly vast and mazelike that most of the population are born, live, work, and die in their own sprawling neighborhood ghettos, without venturing into the urban mysteries beyond the next stand of skyscrapers.

The wealthy few reap the riches of such Gotham-based technologies as DNA structure transplants, and bio and computer engineering. For the masses, solace and relief from boredom is found in synthetic and genetic drugs.

Law and order are maintained by robotic police enforcers with the authority, and the firepower, to execute any transgressor on the spot.

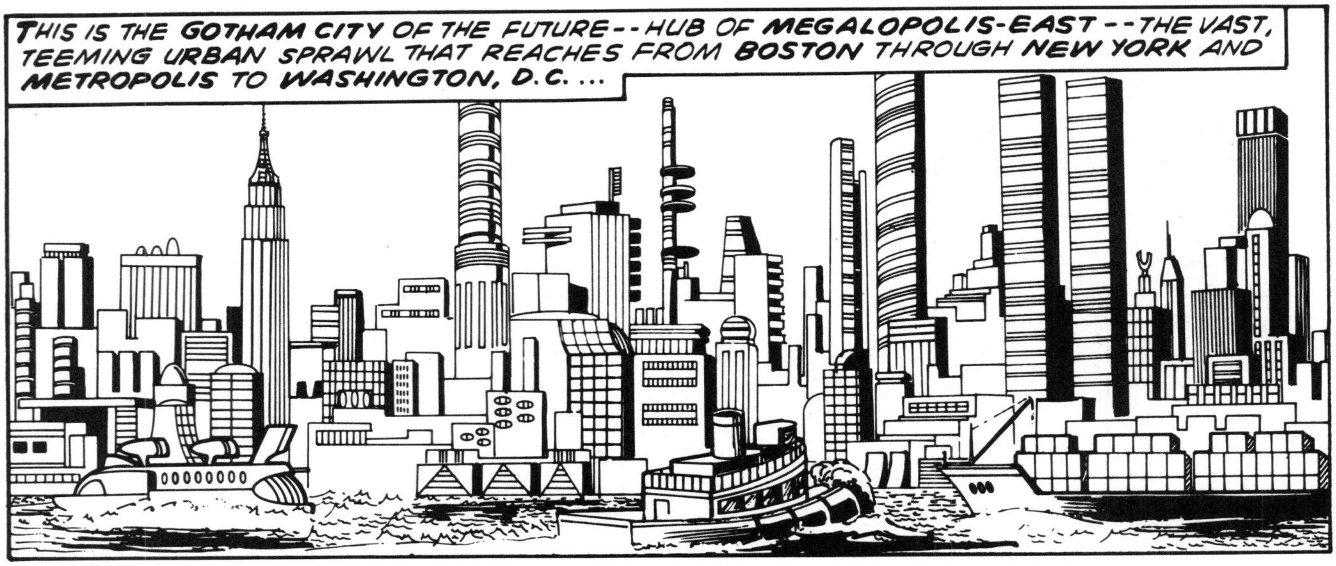
THIS IS THE GOTHAM CITY OF THE FUTURE--HUB OF MEGALOPOLIS-EAST--THE VAST, TEEMING URBAN SPRAWL THAT REACHES FROM BOSTON THROUGH NEW YORK AND METROPOLIS TO WASHINGTON, D.C. ...

Above: *In one possible future a sprawling, but still civilized, Gotham City forms the center of a vast urban megalopolis.* (Batman *#300, June 1978, ''The Last Batman Story . . . ,'' p. 2. [panel.]*) Left: *Frank Miller's Gotham City: A vision of decay and the coming collapse of civilization. . . .* (Batman: The Dark Knight Returns, *Book One, 1986, ''The Dark Knight Returns,'' p. 6 [select panels].*)

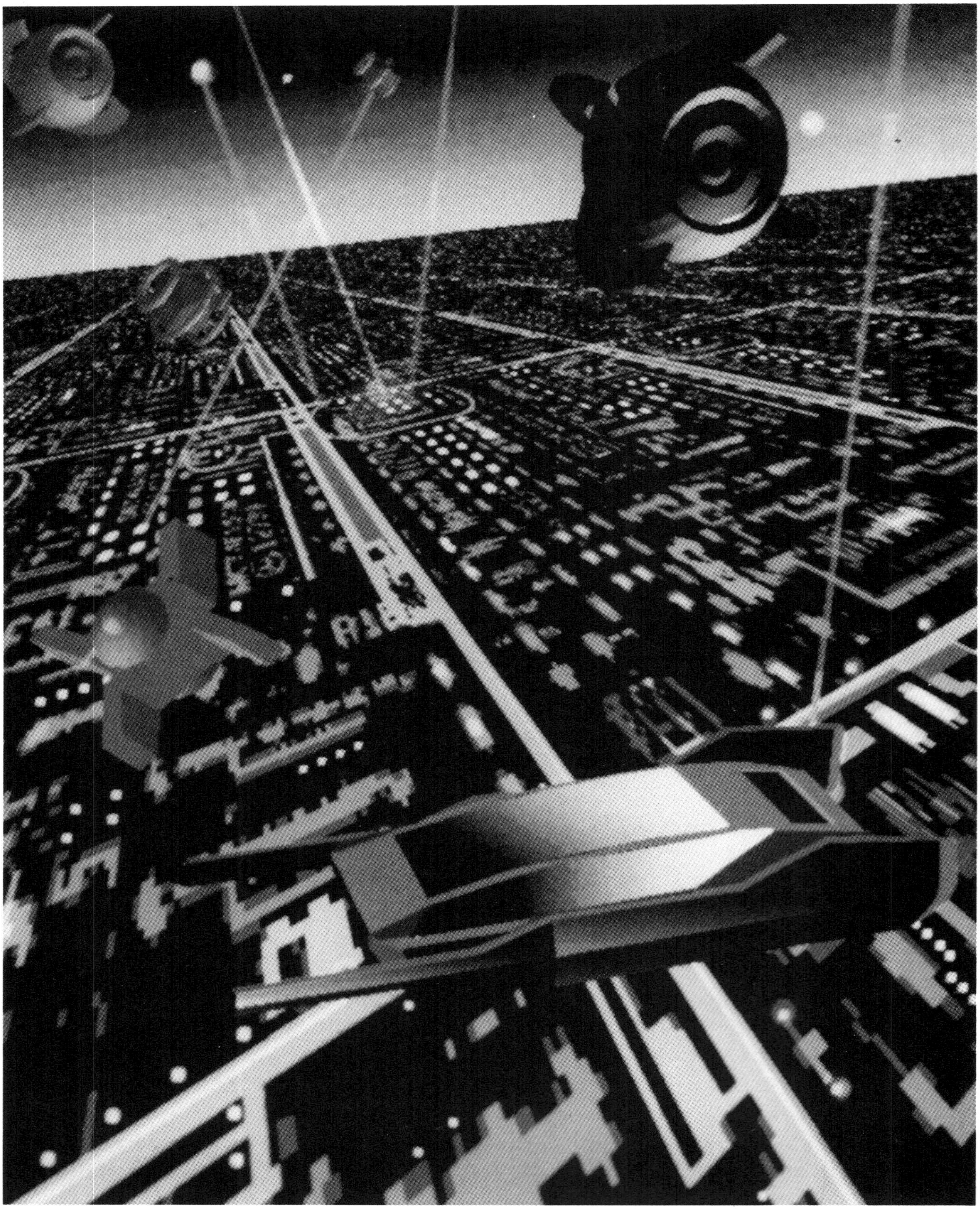

Artist Pepe Moreno's computerized Batman saga depicts the futuristic Gothammegatropolis itself as a vast microcircuitry board. In the sky fly video reporting systems powered by artificial intelligence, while flashing through the foreground is the multipurpose Batman craft equipped to fight crime by land, sea, or sky.

And in the skies above, thousands of remote TV camera satellites buzz, recording the daily grind of violence and decay for millions of video viewers.

And what of Batman? He must long ago have passed away, either from old age or in the line of duty. But given the genetic technologies in this brave, new future, is it possible that Gotham's most honored citizen has been genetically renewed and is still crime-fighting?

To find the answers, we turn to Pepe Moreno's Manhattan studio. An intense young man dressed in black, he is clicking away at the keyboard controls of his computer. On the viewing screen a colorized image of Batman answers his summons. More clicks of the keys and the Batman's eyeless gaze grows to fill the screen. A few clicks more and the view is replaced with the bat-emblem on Batman's chest.

What Moreno has assembled in the row of computer hardware lining one wall is pushing out the frontier boundaries of computer technology. To create his computer Batman story, he's using the most sophisticated innovations, including chips that are smaller and can process more information faster than ever before.

Moreno laughs as he recalls being called a "Bohemian technocrat," but shrugs as if to acknowledge the moniker's perfect fit. His mastery of computer technologies, integrated with his own artistic talent, has allowed him to produce realistic imagery that has never been produced by computer for a comic book before.

"What computers do for you that nothing else does—although at this time it's a lot more work than any other traditional medium—is that once you have data in there, the image control is unlimited in terms of shapes, colors, images— there's just so much you can do to that same information," Moreno explains. "It allows you to become more of an art director because you're able to produce changes in the colors, or in the compositions, without having to do the original again. You can store things—it's a much better medium in terms of distribution of image. That's where it's at. We just have to do it on paper right

now because that's the way the world is working. The idea is to do it through electronic media."

To prove the power at his control, Moreno accesses his files for a futurist Batmobile he's already created, and brings the image to the screen. As he rotates the car, selecting various angles, the model retains a three-dimensional form.

Moreno then closes up the Batmobile picture and brings another piece of data to the screen— an aerial view of the future Gotham. As he adds color and dimension to the drawing, he explains how he created the megatropolis.

"I took one of the boards out of the computer, made a Xerox, and fit it into the scanner and put it into the computer," he says. "So the city is designed like a computer circuit! Why not?! The essence of the structures [of the city] created from the essence of what the technology is all about."

In Moreno's story, Batman has died prior to the development of life-preservation technologies. But before his death, Bruce Wayne saw a way to keep his Batman persona alive and continue his crime-fighting obsession from beyond the grave.

"Bruce Wayne after his retirement embarked on the most ambitious secret project of his career," Moreno writes in his story line notes. "The creation of a super computer that will fight the crime of the future and protect generations long after his time. He dedicated the rest of his days to the programming of this future crimefighter. He fed all the knowledge, experience and accumulated data of a lifetime into the computer by taking advantage of the latest breakthroughs in knowledge engines and artificial intelligence of the fifth generation of computers. Bruce Wayne spent most of his fortune on the project and created the most sophisticated crime fighting machine known to mankind."

In this future Gotham, all business, political, and information centers are networked by computer channels and presided over by artificial intelligence systems (with a few human hangers-on to assist). The main Gothammegatropolis computer is known as "the System." Into this supercomputer circuitry comes the electronic Batman programmed by Wayne to continue the fight for justice—this time against the hackers and viruses (programs designed to destroy a computer's data) that seek to rob bank accounts, scramble data bases, or invade secret government and corporate files. (This is not as far-fetched as it seems. In 1985 a disgruntled former employee of a securities trading firm planted a destructive virus program that wiped out 168,000 records of sales commissions before the program could be disabled. "He could do anything with a computer," marveled a former coworker when asked about the virus maker.[1] And in 1988 a group of embezzlers, reportedly led by a master-

mind known as "the Chairman," nearly robbed the First National Bank of Chicago of $68.7 million by using secret codes to tap into the wire-transfer system, dispatching millions of dollars around the world over computers and phone lines.[2])

In Moreno's story, the System seeks to thwart the crime-fighting intrusion of the electronic Batman by creating personalities to battle it. Detecting the Batman's presence, the System

1. Katherine M. Hafner and correspondents, "Is Your Computer Secure?" *Business Week,* August 1, 1988, p. 64.
2. Gordon Bock, " 'The Chairman' and His Board," *Time,* May 30, 1988, p. 45.

A double-barreled Batman awaits in a computerized future: Commissioner Gordon's grandson will don cape and cowl to fight crime on the physical plane, while an electronic Batman battles a malignant Joker virus code in the wired world of computer circuitry.

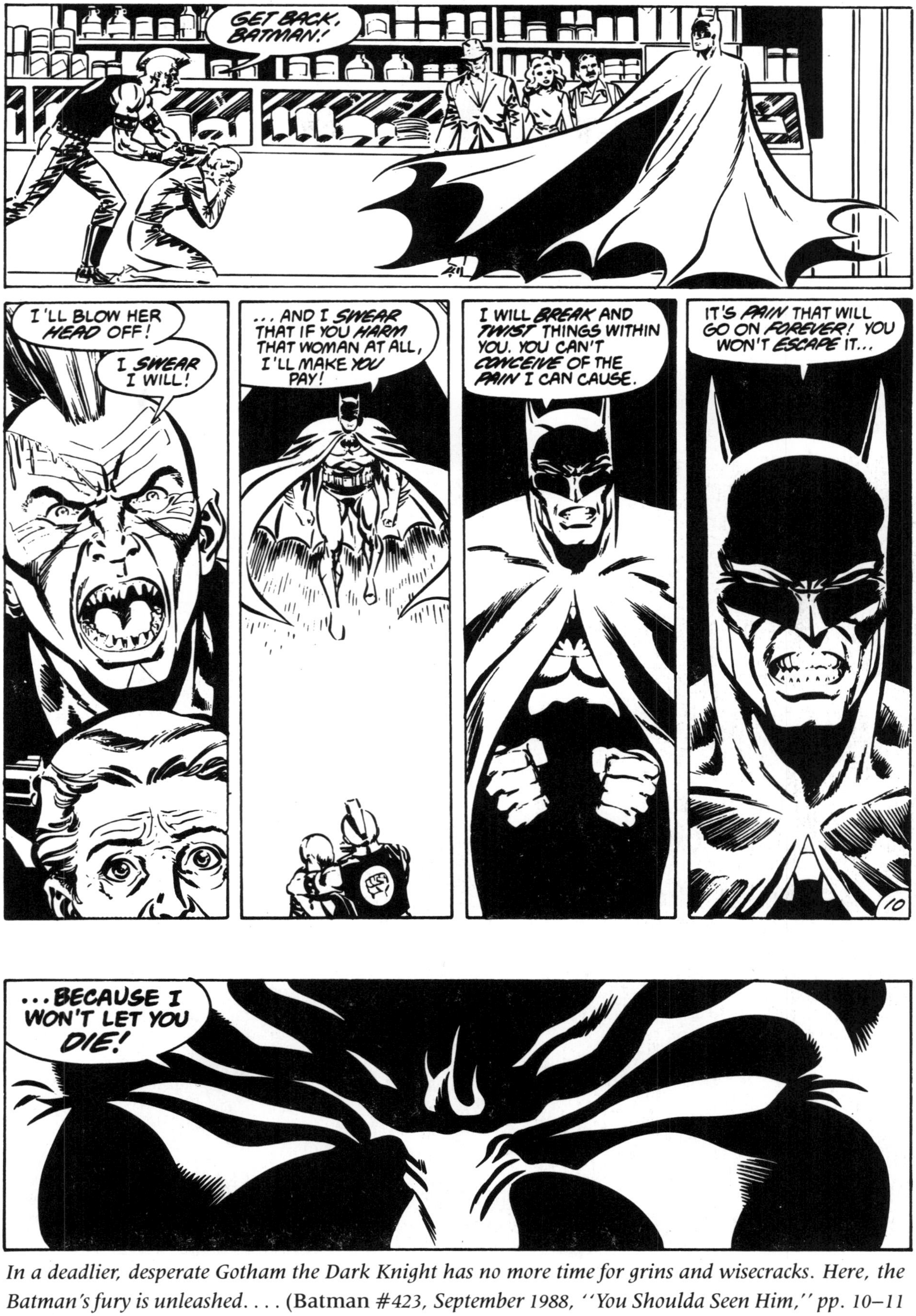
GET BACK, BATMAN!
I'LL BLOW HER HEAD OFF!
I SWEAR I WILL!
...AND I SWEAR THAT IF YOU HARM THAT WOMAN AT ALL, I'LL MAKE YOU PAY!
I WILL BREAK AND TWIST THINGS WITHIN YOU. YOU CAN'T CONCEIVE OF THE PAIN I CAN CAUSE.
IT'S PAIN THAT WILL GO ON FOREVER! YOU WON'T ESCAPE IT...
10
...BECAUSE I WON'T LET YOU DIE!

In a deadlier, desperate Gotham the Dark Knight has no more time for grins and wisecracks. Here, the Batman's fury is unleashed. . . . (Batman *#423, September 1988, ''You Shoulda Seen Him,'' pp. 10–11 [select panels].)*

researches its almost infinite files to create the perfect antagonist—an electronic Joker virus.

"In the end of the Batman story I want Batman to lose," Moreno reveals. "I want to give an image of the world as it is.... Anyone who has a bigger picture is definitely running the show, no two ways about it....

"There will be certain things Batman can do in fighting crime, but [not] in terms of attaining a utopia of justice for all. In other words... after he wins a battle he'll run into the overall picture.

"'I really haven't changed the world,' he'll realize. 'I've just isolated this virus for a time.'"

Perhaps Batman, particularly the brutal crime buster of *The Dark Knight,* has known this all along. The streets of Gotham have grown more dangerous, the villains more ruthless, the people more apathetic. And with Dick Grayson parting to start his own career as Nightwing—and the problems of breaking in a new Robin—Batman has had to bear much of the crime-fighting burden alone.

The Dark Knight of the 1980s is no longer the grinning crime buster who wisecracked while

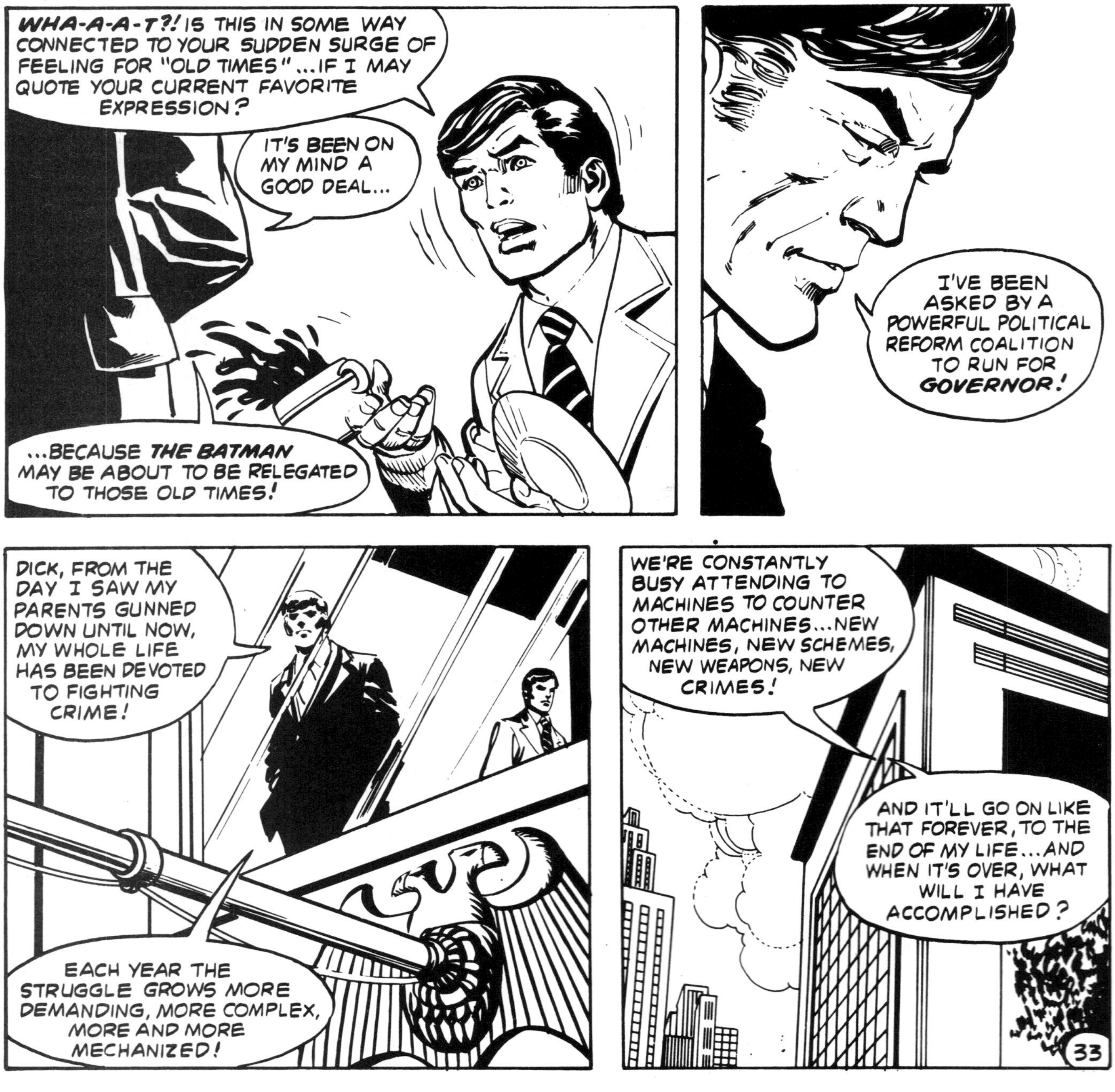
WHA-A-A-T?! IS THIS IN SOME WAY CONNECTED TO YOUR SUDDEN SURGE OF FEELING FOR "OLD TIMES"...IF I MAY QUOTE YOUR CURRENT FAVORITE EXPRESSION?
IT'S BEEN ON MY MIND A GOOD DEAL...
...BECAUSE THE BATMAN MAY BE ABOUT TO BE RELEGATED TO THOSE OLD TIMES!
I'VE BEEN ASKED BY A POWERFUL POLITICAL REFORM COALITION TO RUN FOR GOVERNOR!
DICK, FROM THE DAY I SAW MY PARENTS GUNNED DOWN UNTIL NOW, MY WHOLE LIFE HAS BEEN DEVOTED TO FIGHTING CRIME!
EACH YEAR THE STRUGGLE GROWS MORE DEMANDING, MORE COMPLEX, MORE AND MORE MECHANIZED!
WE'RE CONSTANTLY BUSY ATTENDING TO MACHINES TO COUNTER OTHER MACHINES...NEW MACHINES, NEW SCHEMES, NEW WEAPONS, NEW CRIMES!
AND IT'LL GO ON LIKE THAT FOREVER, TO THE END OF MY LIFE...AND WHEN IT'S OVER, WHAT WILL I HAVE ACCOMPLISHED?
33

landing haymaker punches to the jaws of Gotham's crooks. In the 1980s he wears a frown and, while still keeping true to his vow not to kill, administers enough hurt to sometimes maim a foe.

On the streets of this darker, more brutal Gotham, they're saying these are the last days. There are no more heroes, once-revered institutions are full of corruption, and the city is sinking under the weight of population and pollution. And rising to take command of the streets are Batman's foes—a stronger, smarter, more ruthless lot than the bad guys he used to bag with ease.

For someone like Batman, who has always sought an edge, this is a time of introspection, of asking himself if he's lost it. Of even asking himself if the battle is worth fighting.

In such apocalyptic times, even a Batman can feel his own mortality, and fear the approaching—and familiar—shadow of death.

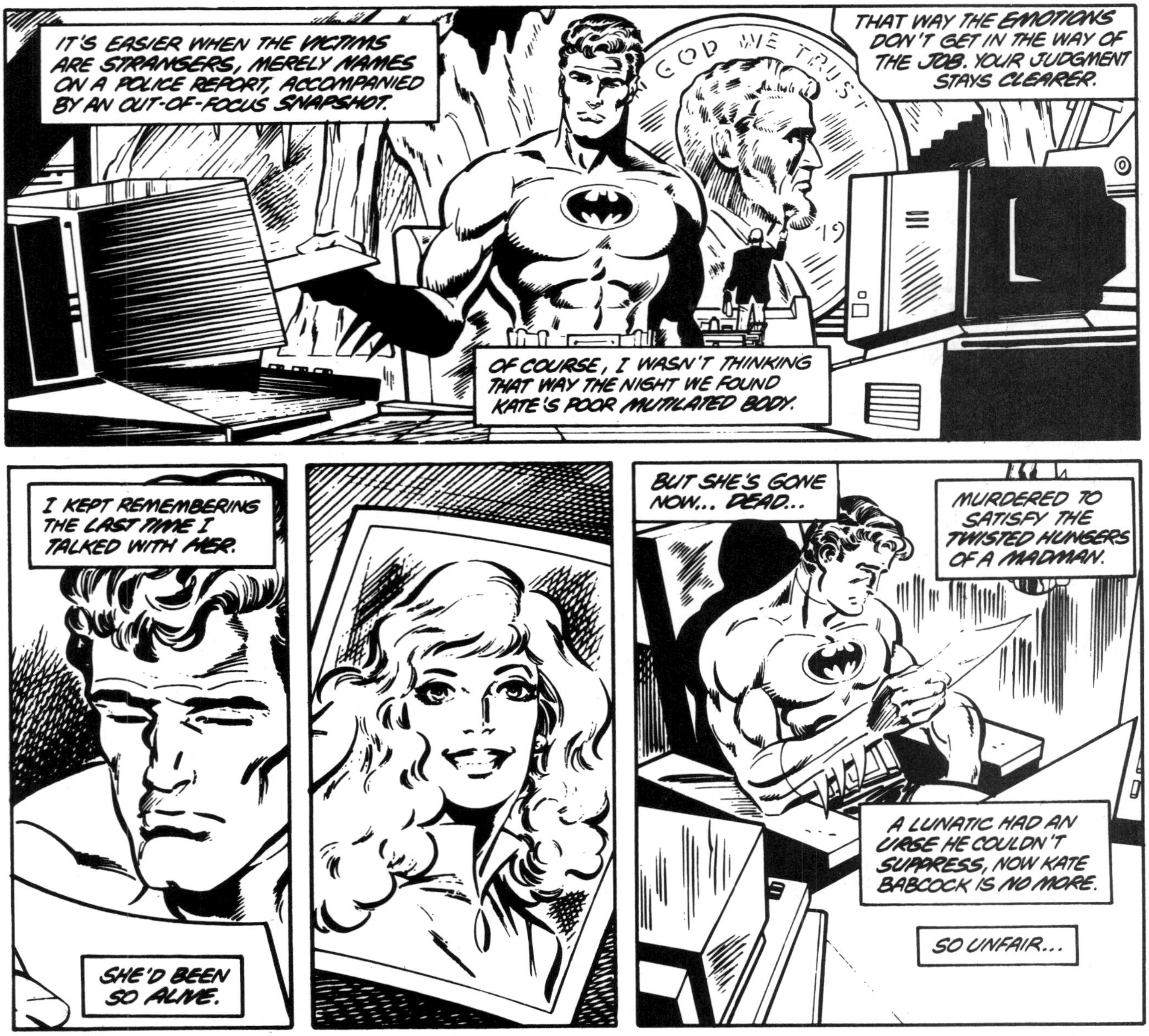
IT'S EASIER WHEN THE VICTIMS ARE STRANGERS, MERELY NAMES ON A POLICE REPORT, ACCOMPANIED BY AN OUT-OF-FOCUS SNAPSHOT.
THAT WAY THE EMOTIONS DON'T GET IN THE WAY OF THE JOB. YOUR JUDGMENT STAYS CLEARER.
OF COURSE, I WASN'T THINKING THAT WAY THE NIGHT WE FOUND KATE'S POOR MUTILATED BODY.
I KEPT REMEMBERING THE LAST TIME I TALKED WITH HER.
SHE'D BEEN SO ALIVE.
BUT SHE'S GONE NOW... DEAD...
MURDERED TO SATISFY THE TWISTED HUNGERS OF A MADMAN.
A LUNATIC HAD AN URGE HE COULDN'T SUPPRESS, NOW KATE BABCOCK IS NO MORE.
SO UNFAIR...

Above: *In the inferno of Gotham, each tragedy is more than a statistic to Batman.* (Batman *#414 December 1987, ''Victims,'' p. 9 [select panels].*) Left: *Commissioner Gordon has retired to Maine, Dick Grayson is an adult, and a brooding Bruce Wayne is still fighting crime and considering a run for Governor.* (Batman *#300, June 1978, ''The Last Batman Story . . . ,'' p. 33 [select panels].*)

CHAPTER 19

THE DEATH OF THE BATMAN

Extra! A NEW ELONGATED MAN STORY!
SUPERMAN DC NATIONAL COMICS
APPROVED BY THE COMICS CODE AUTHORITY
12¢
DETECTIVE
COMICS
AUG. NO. 330
THE STARTLING STORY OF HOW BATMAN BECOMES... "The FALLEN IDOL OF GOTHAM CITY!"
I HATE YOU, BATMAN! GET OUT OF TOWN--AND STAY OUT!
DON'T EVER SHOW UP HERE AGAIN--OR ELSE!
GOTHAM CITY-LIMITS

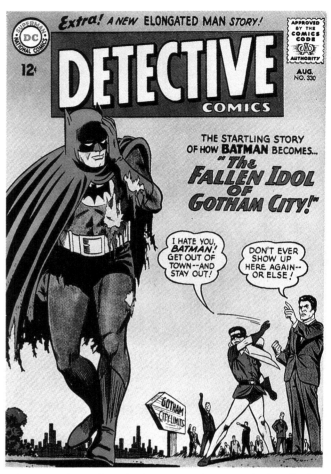

The superhero backlash wasn't just an isolated phenomenon of the 1980s—consider this sad picture from the 1960s. (Detective *#330, August 1964, cover.*)

"BATMAN KILLED," headline, Gotham City Press.

—Detective *347, January 1966.*

Repeating the week's top stories—the spectacular career of the Batman came to a tragic conclusion as the crimefighter suffered a heart attack while battling government troops. He has been identified as fifty-five year old billionaire Bruce Wayne—and his death has proven as mysterious as his life.

—Television news broadcast, Batman: The Dark Knight Returns *Book Four, 1986.*

Batman in his physical form presumably died in the previous century, although there are mysterious circumstances around his disappearance from the public eye. Rumor has it that he went mad, a tormented soul, made numerous secret donations to many crime victim organizations . . . and that afterwards retired to an isolated secret enclave. . . . Others say that after he went mad he simply drifted onto the streets and . . . mixed among the hundreds of poor souls that roam this doomed city and probably ended as an unidentified corpse in one of the city morgues.

The only certainty is that Bruce Wayne consolidated and sold his possessions previous to his mysterious disappearance.

—Pepe Moreno story notes for Batman computer book, 1988.

IT WAS IN 1966 THAT ROBIN WAS PICTURED (on the cover of *Detective* 347) with an EXTRA edition of the *Gotham City Press* clutched in one hand. "Batman Killed," screamed the headline. The front page photo showed the Dark Knight falling backward as a fatal bullet struck.

"I'll bring your killer in, Batman—I swear it!" vowed a weeping Robin.

In the story inside the issue, Batman writer Gardner Fox suddenly appeared. He was leaning back from his typewriter after having finished an ending wherein Batman has won another battle of wits, evaded a deadly trap, and captured his adversary of the moment.

But what if the villain's trap had succeeded and Batman had been killed? Gardner wondered. As his imagination began to drift, a new

DC
NATIONAL COMICS
APPROVED BY THE COMICS CODE AUTHORITY
12¢
BATMAN
ARE YOU SHOCK-PROOF?
DO YOU DARE SEE FOR YOURSELF WHAT'S INSIDE THE MYSTERIOUS ROOM A BATTERED BATMAN IS STAGGERING OUT OF?
THE ASTOUNDING ANSWER IS REVEALED IN... "The DECLINE and FALL of BATMAN!"
LET ME HAVE A CRACK AT HIM!
HOLD IT, ROBIN! DON'T GO IN THAT ROOM! I WAS LUCKY TO GET OUT OF THERE ALIVE!

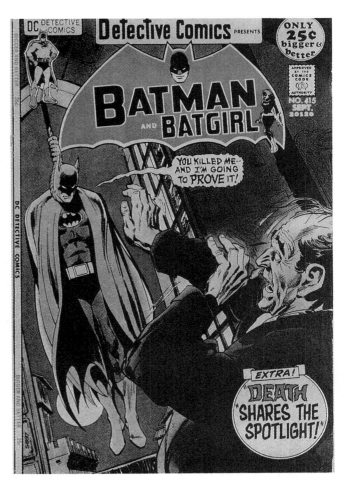

Batman was always experiencing intimations of his own mortality. (Batman *#175, November 1965, cover.*)

DC DETECTIVE COMICS
Detective Comics PRESENTS
ONLY 25¢ bigger & better
BATMAN AND BATGIRL
NO. 415 SEPT.
YOU KILLED ME-- AND I'M GOING TO PROVE IT!
EXTRA!
"DEATH" SHARES THE SPOTLIGHT!"
DC DETECTIVE COMICS
BIGGER AND BETTER

More forebodings of the Dark Knights' death. (Detective *#415, September 1971, cover.*)

ending appeared in the magazine. This time a fatal bullet struck down the Caped Crusader. An assembly of superheroes, led by Superman, arrived in Gotham to pay their final respects. And then Robin single-handedly captured Batman's killer. The tale ended with the Batman of an other-dimensional Earth-Two arriving to take the place of the original Caped Crusader.

For years readers have been teased with such imaginary tales posing the "what if?" situation for many great superheroes. But the game always has had an uncomfortable resonance when applied to the idea of Batman's death.

We've seen Batman beaten, bleeding, and bedridden. Over the decades he's suffered, and survived, innumerable hits to the head, bullet wounds, falls from high places, exposure to the elements, and the travails of hundreds of deadly traps. The Batman comic books themselves have survived times of slumping sales that have swallowed up hundreds of lesser heroes.

Before decades of crime fighting began to take their toll, Batman went about his crusade with boundless energy and enthusiasm. He was constantly in motion, leaping over packs of crooks, diving down on evildoers, and always exiting by vaulting into the sky with the tug of a secured Bat-Rope. As they say, he laughed at death.

But now age has caught up with the Dark Knight. To the physical wounds Batman can add the mental stress of defending a darker, more desperate Gotham than the tough, but good-hearted, metropolis he once knew. These days the Big City burns with portents of decay and destruction. Even Batman is troubled by the times. He's human, after all.

But Batman has shown a tremendous resilience over the years. While others may heed the call of a different drummer, it's an entire spectral symphony that calls Batman to a higher purpose and gives him the inner strength to hold fast to his vision of justice.

The fact, is, Gotham needs its Batman. They've never seen his real face, they don't know why he came to them. All they know is he appeared out of nowhere, ready and willing to dive into the darkness to battle the forces that had always preyed and feasted on them in their innocence.

To the citizenry, Batman not only is their protector (the beleaguered police bureaucracy has enough trouble capturing regular crooks, much less the supercriminals that plague Gotham), but is a symbol. As long as the Bat Signal shines in the night sky and there is a Batman to answer the summons, then will the people of Gotham know that at least one man did not give in to the forces of destruction.

But periodically the Bat Signal has gone unanswered. During times when the Caped Crusader has disappeared from the scene, Gotham is chilled to its heart, wondering if their Dark Knight has finally returned to the darkness of the void from whence he came.

During one such period in the early 1980s, when Batman had not been seen for days, the front-page headlines asked the terrible question:

"IS BATMAN DEAD?" went the banner headline of the *Gotham Courier*.

"WHERE IS BATMAN?" pleaded the *Gotham Gazette*.

And if the good people of Gotham were worried, the underworld was rejoicing. During Batman's disappearance police barricades, set up at the scene of the latest robbery, were sprouting up all over town.

The tension is clear in this exchange between a news reporter and the head of the police forces at the scene of one such heist:

"Night-Owl News Team, here at the scene of the crime," the newsman said, holding his mike out to the police officer. "So tell us, officer Krupke, since this was obviously a more than human robber you were dealing with—why wasn't the Batman around to help out?"

"You tell me, and then we'll both know," the grim officer replied. "Nobody's heard a peep out of that masked man."[1]

But the Dark Knight did return, as always, bringing back with him a sense of order and balance to the streets of Gotham. There is plenty of dread, darkness, and death in the tales of the Dark Knight—but there is also hope for a brighter day and deliverance from the evil that haunts our hearts.

"I don't have any desire to edit a downbeat comic book," admits Batman editor Denny O'Neil. "Because, Dashiell Hammett said, 'life is full of falling beams,' and he's right, but life is also full of falling blossoms—good things happen, too. And I like to get that into the comic books that we work on."

O'Neil has fantasized about a possible end for Batman. In this dream, Batman and Talia survive an earthquake that destroys Ra's al Ghul and a super Sensei.

"And Bruce Wayne and Talia walk off into the sunset, and in my head Batman's finally come to his senses," O'Neil smiles. "He's going to settle down with this terrific woman, he's going to produce three of the most genetically perfect children on earth, and he's going to enjoy life into a fine, mellow old age, and God bless them both!"

Indeed, the old imaginary tales that Alfred wrote as a hobby in the early to mid-sixties often depicted a happily retired Batman usually married to Batwoman. Robin, still a close friend, had long since taken over the family business as Batman II.

It makes for a Currier & Ives portrait: an old Batman, still handsome and fit, in his rocking chair, his crime-fighting family at his feet around a warm hearth. They're all smiles as they remember the grand crime-fighting days of old.

---

1. Situation and dialogue from "While The Bat's Away..." *Batman* 336 (June 1981) pp. 2–3.

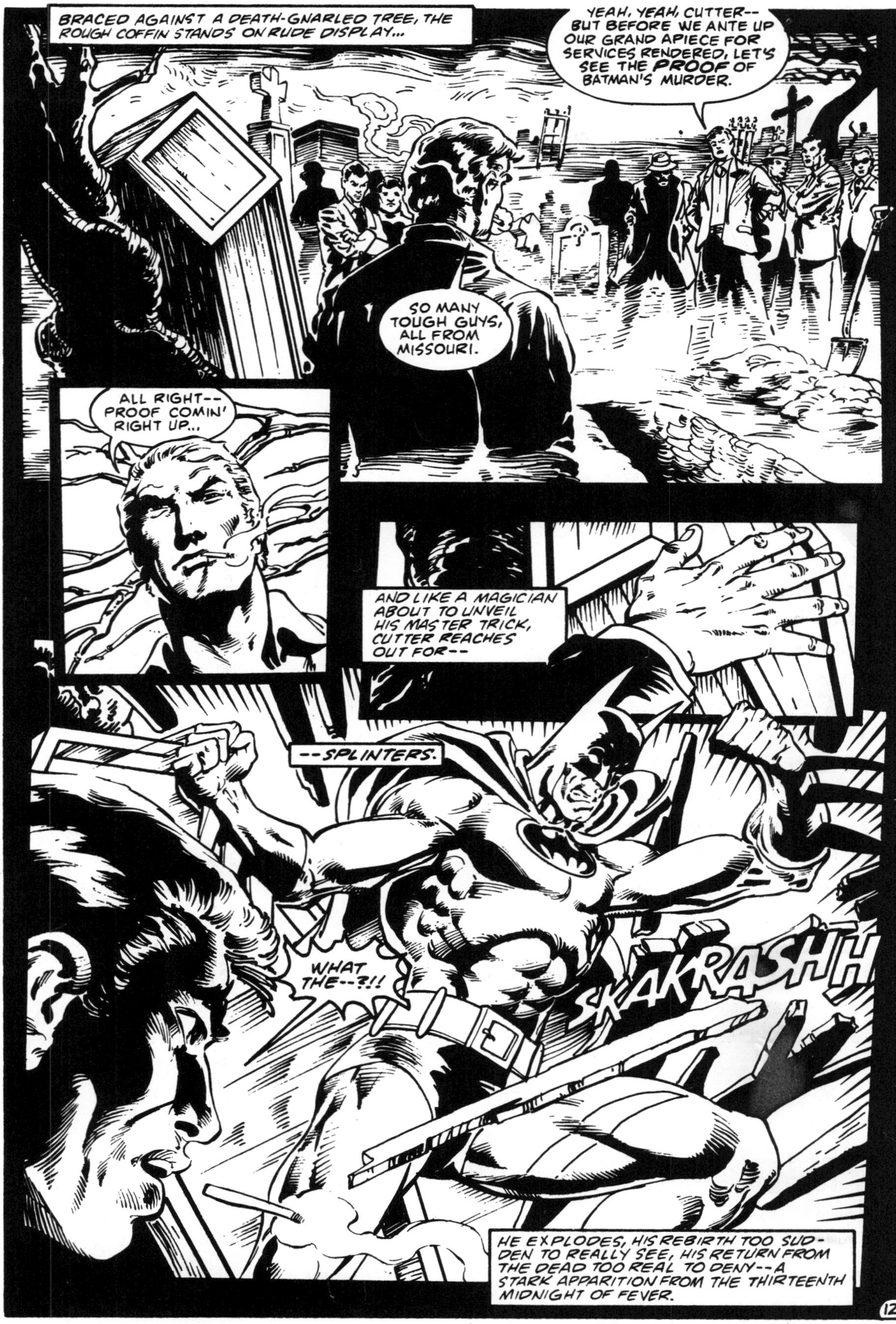
BRACED AGAINST A DEATH-GNARLED TREE, THE ROUGH COFFIN STANDS ON RUDE DISPLAY...
YEAH, YEAH, CUTTER-- BUT BEFORE WE ANTE UP OUR GRAND APIECE FOR SERVICES RENDERED, LET'S SEE THE PROOF OF BATMAN'S MURDER.
SO MANY TOUGH GUYS, ALL FROM MISSOURI.
ALL RIGHT-- PROOF COMIN' RIGHT UP...
AND LIKE A MAGICIAN ABOUT TO UNVEIL HIS MASTER TRICK, CUTTER REACHES OUT FOR--
--SPLINTERS.
WHAT THE--?!!
SKAKRASHH
HE EXPLODES, HIS REBIRTH TOO SUDDEN TO REALLY SEE, HIS RETURN FROM THE DEAD TOO REAL TO DENY--A STARK APPARITION FROM THE THIRTEENTH MIDNIGHT OF FEVER.
12

Batman busts out of a premature burial in this eerie graveyard scene. (Detective #552, *July 1985, "A Stump Grows in Gotham," p. 12.*)

Robin R. I. P.

"Holy Homicide! Robin Buys the Farm," read the *Newsweek* Newsmakers headline on November 7, 1988. That rarest of comic book events—the death of a lead character—had just occurred in the pages of *Batman* 428. But the real news was that Robin's demise had been decreed by Batman fans themselves!

In *Batman* 427, the second installment of the four-part "A Death in the Family" series, Robin had been caught in a warehouse explosion rigged by the Joker.

"Robin will die because the Joker wants revenge," proclaimed the message on the inside cover of that fateful issue, "but you can prevent it with a telephone call." Listed on the page were two 900 numbers that could be called during select hours, one to let Robin live, the other to sentence him to death. A computer at New York Telephone would automatically tabulate the voting.

By a 5,343 to 5,271 vote, Batman fans opted for Robin's death and the Joker's victory.

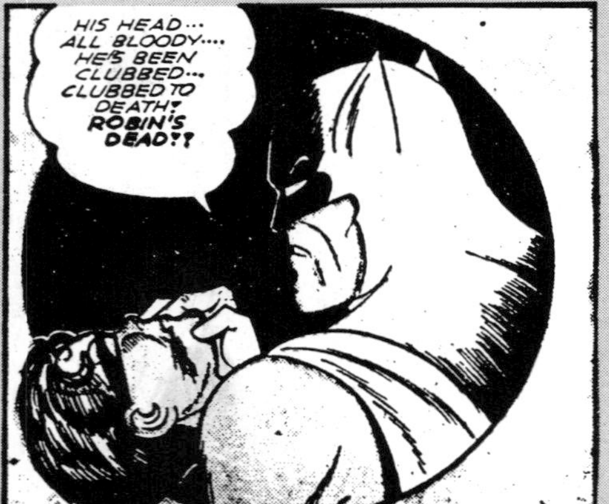
HIS HEAD... ALL BLOODY.... HE'S BEEN CLUBBED... CLUBBED TO DEATH? ROBIN'S DEAD??

Batman's greatest fear was never his own death. For the Dark Knight the worst nightmare was to see Robin killed in the line of duty. Robin will recover from this brutal beating, but the underworld will still pay the penalty of Batman's fury! (Batman *#5, Spring 1941, "The Case of the Honest Crook," p. 4 [panel].*)

Perhaps it never would have happened if Dick Grayson still wore the famed yellow, green, and red garb. But Dick had long since grown up and moved out of the Bat Cave, establishing his own superhero identity as the crime-fighting Nightwing. Jason Todd, a juvenile delinquent rescued from the streets by Batman, had been attempting to fill Dick Grayson's green boots since 1987.

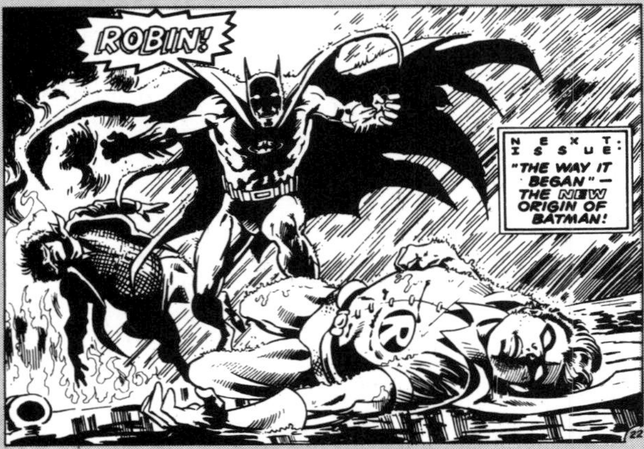
ROBIN!
NEXT ISSUE: "THE WAY IT BEGAN" — THE NEW ORIGIN OF BATMAN!

Batman comes to the aid of a fallen Jason Todd Robin. (Detective *#573, April 1987, "The Mad Hatter Flips His Lids!" p. 22 [panel].*)

As the death sentence directive indicates, Todd, a hotheaded and impetuous character, did not find overwhelming favor with Batman fans. Letters published in the fateful *Batman* 428 exemplified the strong anti-Todd feeling.

"Don't make a big fuss about Robin getting killed," advised reader Daniel Snyder. "Waste him, bury him, and get on to important things.... Life is cheap!"

"Kill him," was Rich Kreiner's succinct directive in the same letters column.

The possibility of Robin dying in the line of duty had always been Batman's greatest nightmare. That his own "fans" had sided with the Joker to kill off the Boy Wonder was more proof of the grim, cynical nature of Batman's world in the 1980's.

"I don't know about you, but I'm disturbed by Robin's . . . demise," wrote California newspaper columnist Ray Orrock. "For one thing, I don't feel any artist should turn his creative instincts over to the public—particularly a bunch as bloodthirsty as these seem to be."[2]

"I'm still reeling from the personal publicity," editor Denny O'Neil admitted a month after Robin's death. What had started out as an exercise in developing a revolutionary interactive comic book event had ended with the death of a character almost as old as the superhero genre itself.

O'Neil, who had cast his vote to save Robin, was inexplicably taking the heat for the final outcome. National news media from the *New York Times* to the *Wall Street Journal* quizzed him about the killing, O'Neil had occasion to endure the obscene taunts of strangers—and even his own dentist gave him no respite, haranguing him about the demise of a beloved childhood hero.

But the topper for O'Neil probably occurred while he was watching the Greenwich Village Halloween parade and the crowd greeted the appearance of a Robin-costumed reveler with the chant of "Robin's dead."

"Comic books are like folklore," O'Neil concludes. "They go more deeply into the psyche than we thought."

But even as the postmortems flooded in, talk turned to the possibility of a new successor to the Boy Wonder role.

"I know a lot of people want Batman solo, but if he stays a brooding avenger forever, he'll crack," lamented Russ Bedell in the "Bat-Signals" letters column of *Batman* 428. "He needs Robin. I'm not sure if that Robin is Jason, but Batman needs someone."

One thing was certain—Jason Todd was dead, and totally beyond the resurrectional powers of even comic book magic. Batman's worst nightmare had been realized, and he, and comics fandom, would have to live with it.

One final postscript. Frank Miller's Dark Knight saga, published in 1986, contains an eerie portent about the death of Jason Todd.

In one sequence, a middle-aged Batman has just told Alfred that he is taking a young girl named Carrie Kelley under his wing as the new Robin.

"Have you forgotten what happened to Jason?" Alfred argues, questioning the decision.

"I will never forget Jason," a grim Batman replies. "He was a good soldier, He honored me. But the war goes on."[3]

2. Ray Orrock, *The Daily Review* (Hayward, California), November 9, 1988.

3. *The Dark Knight Returns*, Book Two, 1986, p. 37.

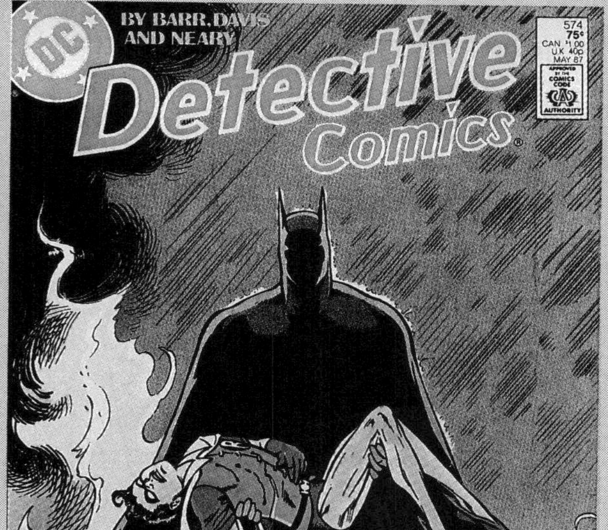
BY BARR, DAVIS AND NEARY
Detective Comics
574 75¢
THE HISTORY OF THE DC UNIVERSE is must reading

Detective *#574, May, 1987, cover.*

The haunting laughter of the Joker echoes in Batman's brain as he delivers death to his evil nemesis. (**Batman The Dark Knight Returns**, *Book Three, 1986, ''Hunt The Dark Knight,'' p.* 47.)

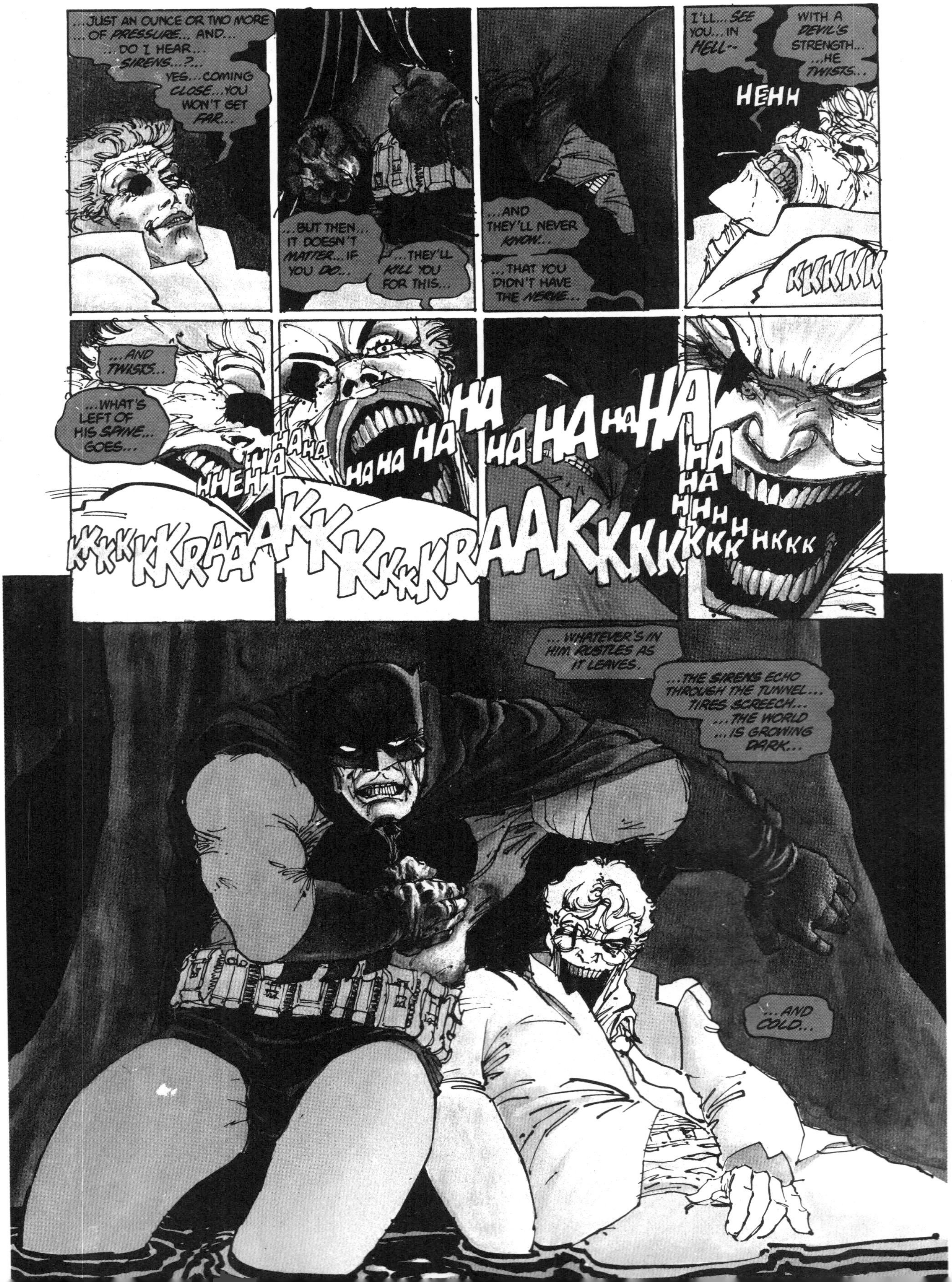
...JUST AN OUNCE OR TWO MORE ...OF PRESSURE... AND...
...DO I HEAR... SIRENS...?...
YES...COMING CLOSE...YOU WON'T GET FAR...
...BUT THEN... IT DOESN'T MATTER...IF YOU DO...
...THEY'LL KILL YOU FOR THIS...
...AND THEY'LL NEVER KNOW...
...THAT YOU DIDN'T HAVE THE NERVE...
I'LL... SEE YOU... IN HELL--
WITH A DEVIL'S STRENGTH... ...HE TWISTS...
HEHH
KKKKK
...AND TWISTS...
...WHAT'S LEFT OF HIS SPINE... GOES...
HHEHH HA HAHA HAHA HA HA HA HA HA HA HA HA HA HA HA HHH HHKKKK
KKKKKRAAAAKKKKKKRAAKKKKKKKK
...WHATEVER'S IN HIM RUSTLES AS IT LEAVES.
...THE SIRENS ECHO THROUGH THE TUNNEL... TIRES SCREECH... ...THE WORLD ...IS GROWING DARK...
...AND COLD...

And what memories! Of a thousand struggles with the likes of the Joker, Penguin, and Two-Face, of journeys to other planets and strange dimensions, of battles with monsters and aliens on earth, of global adventures and impossible time travels, of being feted by presidents and the people of Gotham, of stopping Nazis in World War II, and being a leader among heroes more superpowered than he.

What an ending that would be. One last look at Batman at peace, one last look before he just fades away.

But Batman could also have an ignominious death. Perhaps his personal story will come full circle and it will be a two-bit punk, like the one who shot his parents, who gets in the fatal shot that a thousand foes could not.

After all, what is the longevity of a comic book superhero? Ever since the genre was born in 1938, hundreds of heroes have appeared, fought crime for a time, and then returned to the void, most not even reaching their prime.

Batman is pushing the outside of the envelope (to borrow the jargon of jet pilots) of what is lasting about an American superhero crime fighter.

At the high-water mark of his fiftieth birthday, The Batman has already moved into that rarefied, mythic level inhabited by folklore figures.

Everything else yet to come will be opening up exciting new ground in the Dark Knight's renown.

ALL THE SAME, I WISH YOU HAD LET US KNOW YOU WERE SKIPPING TOWN FOR A WHILE.
ALL THOSE "BATMAN IS DEAD" STORIES--
--WERE SLIGHTLY EXAGGERATED, AS A MAN FROM MISSOURI ONCE SAID.
THESE THINGS DON'T ALWAYS COME OFF AS PLANNED.
BESIDES, THOSE RUMORS BROUGHT MORE RATS OUT OF HIDING THAN A DERAILED CARLOAD OF CHEESE... AND YOU KNOW IT, OLD FRIEND.
AND NOW, IF YOU'LL EXCUSE ME...
...I'VE GOT SOME MUCH-NEEDED SLEEP TO CATCH UP ON!
SURE, BATMAN... SURE.
AS FOR ME, I INTEND TO TAKE A NICE LONG, LEISURELY READ OF THE MORNING PAPERS...
... AGAIN!
Gotham News
BATMAN ALIVE!
25

Batman #336, *June 1981, ''While The Bat's Away . . . ,'' p. 25 (select panels).*

CHAPTER 20
DREAM OF THE DARK KNIGHT

WE'RE IN THE MAGICAL STUDY OF RON Schwartz, a comics collector in San Jose, California. It's magic because the cozy space is filled to the rafters with cartoon stuff: stacks of Big Little Books, files of old Sunday Funnies, movie posters, volumes of reprints recording the adventures of everyone from Dick Tracy to Prince Valiant, original cartoon art, and dozens of cartoon toys and trinkets that peek out from their places of honor. But his most prized possessions are in the boxes he pulls out from a closet—they contain the Golden Age Batman comics he bought for a dime as a kid. Schwartz is one of that unique cadre of fans who first sighted Batman in 1939, was instantly hooked by the Dark Knight's moody, unsettling, thrilling world—and has been on for the ride ever since.

He notes that it's been years since he's opened up the boxes. He sets them down with the care of a diver pulling up chests of buried treasure. He opens one box and takes out *World's Best* 1. On the cover a grinning Batman, Robin, and Superman once again fall out of the sky.

More boxes are opened, and out comes *Detective* 38, marking the debut of Robin, the Boy Wonder. There's a *Batman* 2, with the strange case of the Jekyll/Hyde killer Adam Lamb. Stacks more of ancient *Batman, Detective,* and *World's Finest* issues are laid on a table, to the amazement of all.

Ron Schwartz doesn't have all those early issues, though. Conspicuous by their absence are Batman's debut in *Detective* 27 and *Batman* 1. Back in the forties Schwartz tried to capture those two historic issues by writing directly to DC. One response, dated August 17, 1942 (with "One day closer to Victory" typed on the stationery), regretted that no back issues were available

and returned the fifteen cents—a whopping five cents above the cover price!—the young Schwartz had mailed in.

The value of those early Batman issues has gone up considerably from the original ten-cent cover price. A very fine near-mint copy of *Detective* 27 (no mint conditions are known to exist) can command twenty thousand dollars.[1]

Of course, collectors like Ron Schwartz don't part with treasured Batman issues that have been their property for a lifetime. Wonderful childhood memories can't be bought for any amount of money.

Even the comics creators who sometimes let slip the omnipresent business side of comics publishing when they refer to superhero "properties" get personal when they talk about Batman.

Jenette Kahn says it's a "special thrill and pleasure" to help direct the mythos of the character she loved in youth. To her, a Batman tale is a perfect example of the apocryphal superhero world where young readers learn there is right and wrong, and that evil should be punished, and good rewarded.

"Batman became the reason why I got into comic books, if you come right down to it," reveals Dick Giordano. "... Batman was always important to me, first as a young reader.... It was always my dream to be involved in Batman in some fashion.... I sort of gravitated, without realizing it, towards the kinds of things that were very Batman-like.... When I came to DC, working on my first Batman story was like a dream come true. I feel very, very close to the character. Much closer than any other character in this company."

1. Robert M. Overstreet, *The Official Overstreet Comic Book Price Guide* (New York: House of Collectibles, 1988), p. 114.

Jack Schiff, who last edited Batman in 1964, warmly remembers his Batman days. He recalls going on a vacation trip and being surprised at the large numbers of kids he met who had an affinity for Batman.

Nowadays Schiff is involved in the nuclear freeze movement ("trying to get peace in this world"), and he believes that Batman would support the nuclear freeze as a noble cause.

For Jerry Robinson, his Batman work marked the beginning of a long and continuing cartooning career that has received national and international acclaim.

"Once I got into it [his 1940s Batman work], I found it very exciting," Robinson remembers. "I saw the potential of combining pictures and words."

Dick Sprang still does occasional Batman work for DC, in addition to his ongoing exploration and documentation of the remote canyon country of the Southwest for various historical societies.

"It's consoling that the efforts of the editors, writers, and artists of the Golden Age are continued by their opposite numbers of today," Sprang says. "The longevity of Batman could continue for another fifty years if tomorrow's editors, writers, and artists, operating with a somewhat changed focus, play the game with the dedication we old-timers did.

"As to the decades of fans who made and continue to make their great contribution to the longevity of Batman, I salute you all in humble appreciation of your expertise in identifying my vast body of unsigned work. Your doing so moves this old professional to an awed awareness that work I thought would have nothing more than a thirty-day newsstand life actually lives on."

Batman creator Bob Kane lives on also—in the comfort of a West Hollywood condo. These days Kane, enjoying the renown of a living legend, paints vibrant-colored canvases depicting Batman and Robin (which he sells for big bucks), dabbles in various Batman-related projects, and follows an interest in metaphysics.

"Bob was thinking in terms of the Disney pattern—Walt was the cartoonist that had made it big," remembers Will Eisner, marveling at the success of his childhood chum and colleague. "Bob ultimately achieved it—the Hollywood success, what he had dreamed about . . . Bob is on top of the mountain; he's in Mecca for him. At least that's what he dreamed about when we dreamed together."

And there is Batman himself. The artists and writers come and go with the decades, but the Dark Knight remains, an enduring legend in an ever-changing universe. The Batman has made it not only through World War II, but ten presidents, numerous moon walks and space shots, and into sight of brave new worlds ahead.

The Batman is obviously no ordinary character. He's kept his intensity at a super level for half a century. But he's changed with the times, too.

The Batman of the 1940s War Bonds drives was a cheering quarterback for the home front effort. Even in the fifties he would mingle with kids, telling them how to stay clean and live right.

But nowadays the Dark Knight moves through crowds with a detached air. He saves his energy for his herculean crime-fighting challenges, marshaling his strength like an Olympic athlete prior to a world-class event.

He's got a lot on his mind. For one thing, the Dark Knight realizes he has come full circle and now, with the death of Robin, he is once again a lone crime fighter. And even if he were to find a new Robin to replace the late Jason Todd, it still would not be the same as it was when Dick Grayson was the Boy Wonder. But Dick had long since grown up and left his Robin role behind to embark on his own crime-fighting career—no waiting for a future Batman II slot for him.

Even the Dark Knight's old alliances have changed. Batman is no longer friends with Superman, the hero he disdains as a "boy scout" despite decades of battling crime side by side with the Man of Steel.

Batman has also come to the realization that he is obsessed. In the old days he sometimes dreamed of the time when he would retire, marry, and raise a family—he now knows what an impossible dream that would be. He ended his brief union with Talia because of the crime-fighting calling that owns his heart. (Batman does not, however, know about the child he fathered whom Talia put up for adoption—such knowledge would only increase his sorrow.[2])

Is this the sort of man you approach with happy birthday wishes on his fiftieth birthday?

"I think I might enjoy talking to Bruce Wayne, because at his best Bruce is witty and charming and delightful," Jenette Kahn observes. "I think talking to Batman would be very arduous. I don't think he has time for small talk."

Denny O'Neil gives a bemused smile when he is asked if he would give Batman a fiftieth birthday greeting.

"If he really existed?" O'Neil asks. "I would be real hesitant to do that. What if he took it wrong?"

And do the comic book characters themselves have anything to say about the legendary crime fighter?

As it turns out, Robin has plenty to say. Dick Grayson, outfitted in his dark Nightwing costume, is more aloof, more noble, than the "laughing, fighting, young daredevil" who first burst on the superhero scene with the moniker lifted from the legendary Robin Hood.

"The funny thing is that even more than my parents' death, my most vivid memory from that time was meeting *him*!" Grayson revealed in 1987.

"Batman seemed more than human—like a god or a storybook hero. And when he told me how he'd seen his own parents gunned down before my eyes I knew I wanted to be exactly like him—a sworn avenger in the cause of justice.

"It was years before I realized how different we truly were," he finally says. "Maybe it was okay for him to be a grim, obsessed avenger—full-time and forever—but I was different.

"He couldn't save his parents as a boy—although he'd saved so many others since. I sometimes think he feels responsible for their deaths—as if he were the one who killed them!"

But Dick Grayson's tone softened as he remembered those youthful days racing over rooftops, diving into space to swing on the end of silken cords, dropping down in the midst of gangsters—and sending them flying!—racing through the darkness, feeling the chill, living the thrill.

"Y'know, I wear this Nightwing costume partly as a tribute to The Batman—but I really think the Robin outfit was a lot more my style!" Nightwing concludes. "I was always a swashbuckler at heart—right from the beginning!"[3]

"I don't know what it is that motivates him, except that he hates crime," Police Commissioner Jim Gordon says. "For whatever his reasons he takes criminals and the things they do personally enough to make it his business to stop them, regardless of whom they victimize."[4]

The cops of Gotham City have an opinion of the Dark Knight, too. And if you want to have some good talk, hot food, and good coffee, you go to Willy's Diner, a late night hangout for off-duty police.

In one story, readers got a chance to find a vacant booth and listen to three cops swapping Batman tales over a midnight breakfast. Two of them had seen the Dark Knight himself during their evening patrols.

One of the cops had been called in on a hostage situation. Three punks, hopped-up on crack and loaded with weapons, had attempted to rob a deli. When the police showed up, they settled for four innocent bystanders. With twisted smiles, and cocked guns, the crack-heads demanded one hundred thousand dollars in cash and a Cadillac.

One of the crack-heads had pressed the muzzle of his gun to the forehead of an old woman when Batman appeared out of nowhere.

"Yeah, Bart, you shoulda seen him—he real-

2. *Batman: Son of the Demon* (New York: DC Comics, Inc., 1987), p. 78.
3. Nightwing dialogue taken from "The Secret Origin of Nightwing," *Secret Origins* 13 (April 1987), pp. 6–17.
4. Gordon's dialogue from "Sole Survivor," *Detective* 582 (January 1988), p. 3.

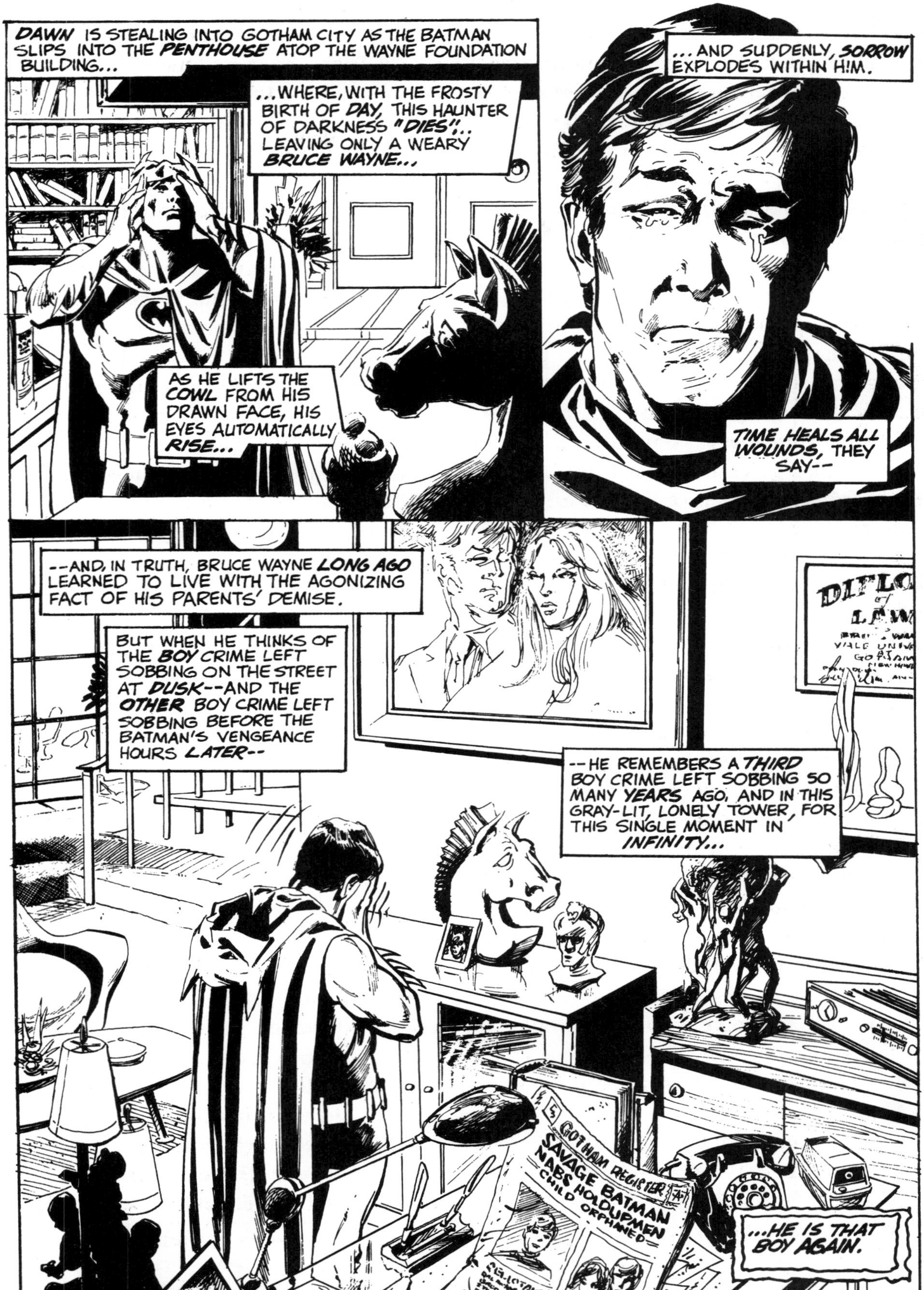
DAWN IS STEALING INTO GOTHAM CITY AS THE BATMAN SLIPS INTO THE PENTHOUSE ATOP THE WAYNE FOUNDATION BUILDING...
...WHERE, WITH THE FROSTY BIRTH OF DAY, THIS HAUNTER OF DARKNESS "DIES"... LEAVING ONLY A WEARY BRUCE WAYNE...
AS HE LIFTS THE COWL FROM HIS DRAWN FACE, HIS EYES AUTOMATICALLY RISE...
...AND SUDDENLY, SORROW EXPLODES WITHIN HIM.
TIME HEALS ALL WOUNDS, THEY SAY--
--AND, IN TRUTH, BRUCE WAYNE LONG AGO LEARNED TO LIVE WITH THE AGONIZING FACT OF HIS PARENTS' DEMISE.
BUT WHEN HE THINKS OF THE BOY CRIME LEFT SOBBING ON THE STREET AT DUSK--AND THE OTHER BOY CRIME LEFT SOBBING BEFORE THE BATMAN'S VENGEANCE HOURS LATER--
--HE REMEMBERS A THIRD BOY CRIME LEFT SOBBING SO MANY YEARS AGO, AND IN THIS GRAY-LIT, LONELY TOWER, FOR THIS SINGLE MOMENT IN INFINITY...
GOTHAM REGISTER
SAVAGE BATMAN NABS HOLDUPMEN
CHILD ORPHANED
...HE IS THAT BOY AGAIN.
14
the END.

Bruce Wayne will never forget. . . . (Detective *#439, March 1974, "Night of the Stalker!" p. 14*).

ly kicked some tail!" the cop exclaimed. "I tell ya, he went through them like a chain saw! That Batman is one tough ol' mother. Mean and cold as ice."

"No, he's not," said another cop at the table. That night he, too, had seen the Batman.

The officer told of spotting two kids, a boy and a girl, out at night in the warehouse district. He gave chase, but they were fast and would have given him the slip—if they hadn't run into Batman. The boy had then grabbed a stick and struck a protective stance over the girl.

"I'd heard all the stories about, you know, how violent he could get," the cop said. "I was kind of afraid for the kids. He knew just what to say, to put them at ease. I figured they were a couple of runaways. Once again, I was wrong. Batman finally convinced them to show him where they lived. Their home was a packing crate under the West Side Highway. I couldn't believe it. They burned garbage at night to stay warm. They lived on what food they could find in dumpsters behind restaurants. They survived in Gotham City for three months without two cents between them."

The kids were brother and sister. As Batman and the cop silently listened, they told how their mother had been killed in a tragic car crash in their home state of Florida. Their father, laid off from his job at a textile plant, had come to Gotham looking for a new life. Instead he was killed from a knife wound during a deadly poker game. The kids had been on the streets ever since.

And their story had brought tears to the Dark Knight's eyes that the shadows could not hide.

And then Batman had hugged the children and had asked the cop if he had any objections to seeing that his friend, millionaire Bruce Wayne, take care of the kids until other relatives could be found.

"What could I say?" the cop asked rhetorically. "We went back to my patrol car, called Commissioner Gordon on the radio to take care of the paperwork needed so Wayne could take custody of the kids."[5]

Two views of the Dark Knight—one a terrible force of vengeance, the other a figure of compassion. But in both cases he came to the aid of the innocents, bringing whatever was needed to achieve a resolution.

But for Batman there will never be a final resolution—that tragic, lost night in Crime Alley prohibits that. It's what haunts him, drives him, makes him the hero he is.

"I made a pact with my fear," Batman has said (*Detective* 593, December 1988). "I ignore it or not, as I choose."

And we have made a pact with Batman. We've followed the obsessions recorded in his strange tales for half a century now—and that's a long, long career for a crime fighter. But nobody has ever done it better.

He is the stuff of dreams. Bob Kane has seen him as a figure of mystery, silhouetted against a full moon. Dick Sprang has seen him as a laughing daredevil, swooping down on crooks with joyous abandon. Neal Adams has seen him in the darkness, a figure of physical power. Frank Miller has seen him riding a black stallion, leading his disciples on a thundering charge through the midnight streets of Gotham. David Mazzucchelli has seen him as a force of supernatural power, calling his beloved bats to descend on Gotham in a black cloud, blotting out the sun.

And there are the hundreds of thousands of readers who have also taken this dream and made it their own.

There are so many dreams, so many images we can conjure up out of these shadows.

This dream of the Dark Knight is full of power and magic—enough to weave a thread through the decades. It is a vision of tragedy and evil, of warped villains and zoot-suited crooks casting long shadows, of deserted streets with a full moon watching the evil that men do. With its tragedies and calamities, it is a world that mirrors our own.

But unlike our own, this dream has a voice

5. Situation and dialogue from "You Shoulda Seen Him..." *Batman* 423 (September 1988): pp. 16–20.

that answers the cries of the innocents, that seeks to rebuild what has been destroyed, that is the bringer of justice.

Like the generations of old, a new wave of fans will pick up the famous comic magazines that chronicle Batman's adventures. The new generation of readers will represent a new link in time, from the Golden Age into the future, continuing an unbroken succession of storytelling. This new generation, like the ones before it, will dream the tales of the Dark Knight.

Happy Birthday, Batman.

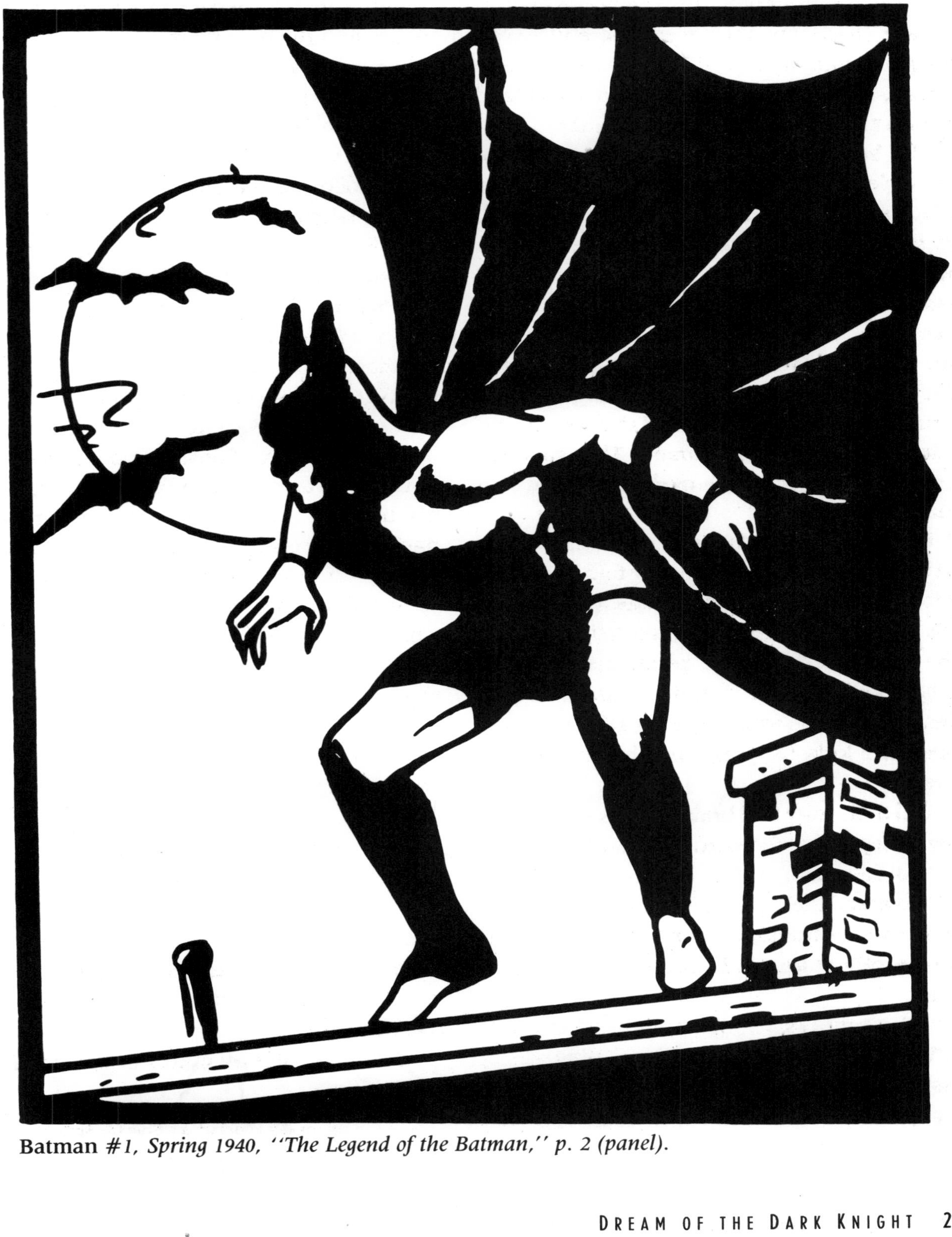

Batman *#1, Spring 1940, "The Legend of the Batman," p. 2 (panel).*

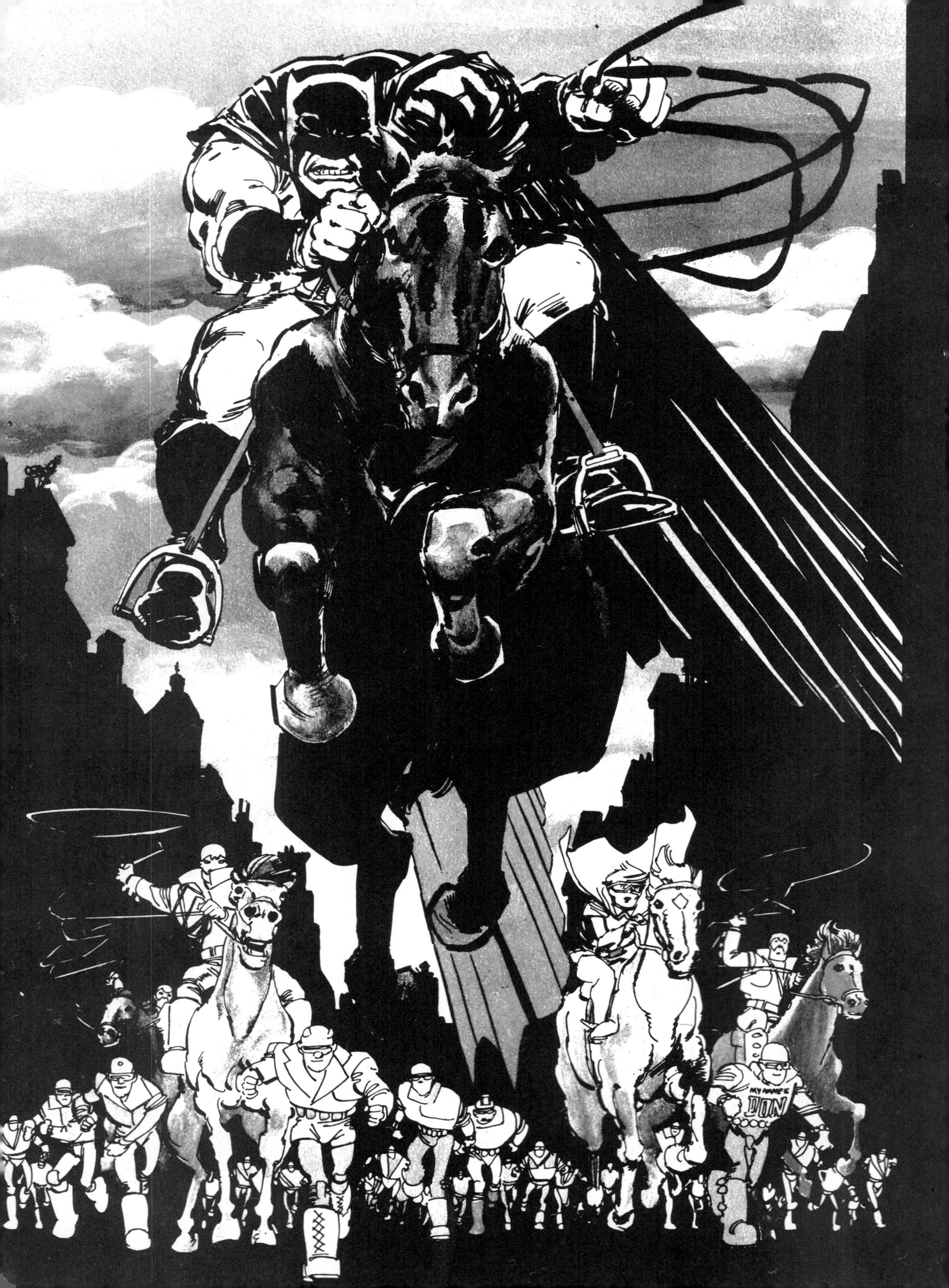
MY NAME IS
DON

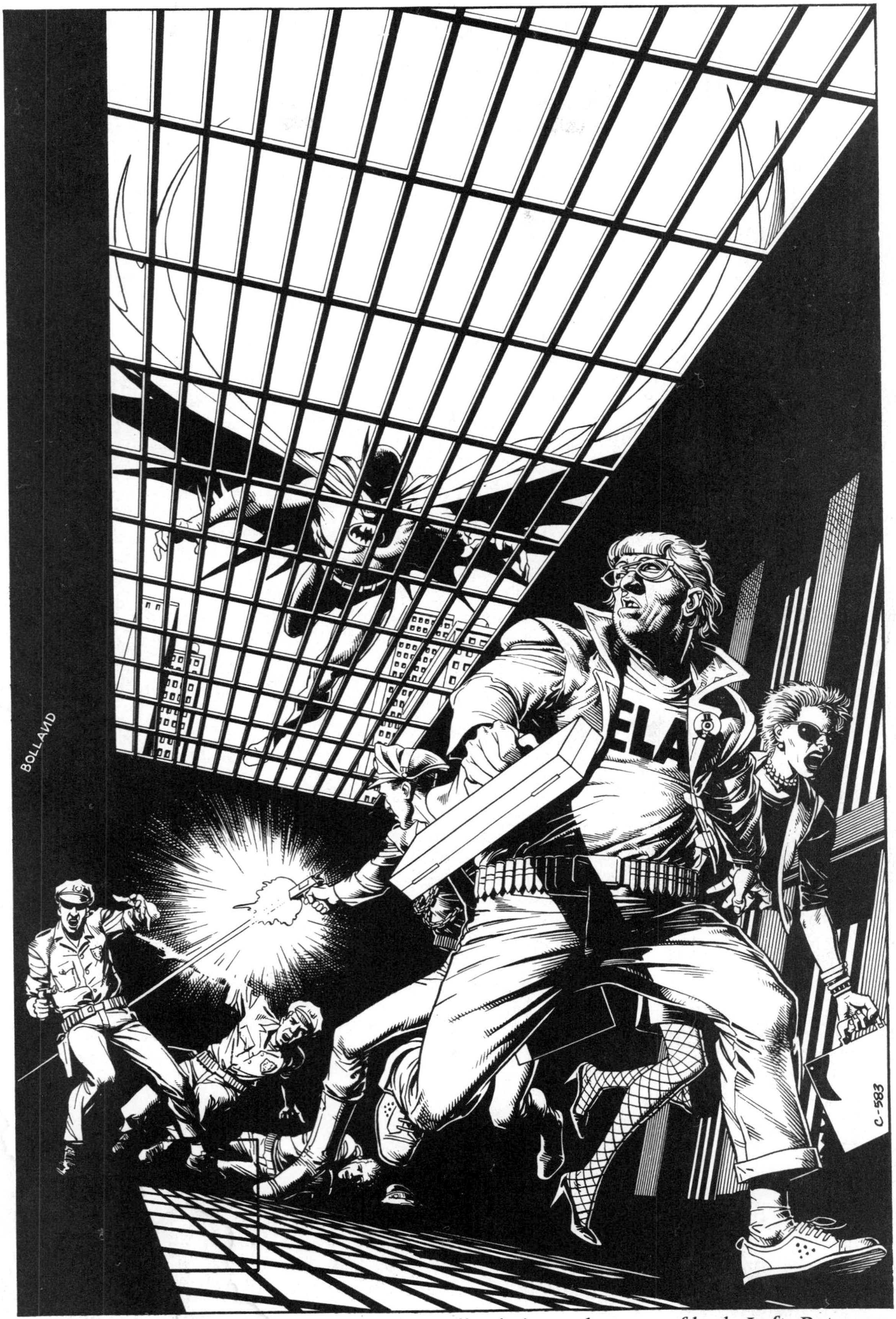
BOLLAND
ELA
C-583

Above: Batman #400, *October 1986, Brian Bolland pin-up, last page of book.* Left: Batman: The Dark Knight Returns, *Book Four, 1986, ''The Dark Knight Falls,'' p. 30 (full page).*

INDEX

About the Author

Mark Cotta Vaz holds a B.A. in political science/ journalism from San Francisco State University. He is active as a board of directors member for the Cartoon Art Museum of California. Vaz is also a martial arts instructor, and has traveled extensively throughout Europe and the Orient. His first book, *Spirit In the Land*, an investigation of mysticism in America, was published in 1988. Vaz lives in San Francisco.

WELL, YOU SEE, SIR--I JUST WANTED TO TRY OUT THIS NEW TYPEWRITER, AND BEFORE I REALIZED IT, I WAS WRITING A STORY OF WHAT POSSIBLY MIGHT HAPPEN TO US ALL IN THE FUTURE!
TOO BAD IT CAN'T BE PUBLISHED BECAUSE IT WOULD GIVE AWAY MY SECRET IDENTITY! NOBODY WILL EVER READ IT!
TRUE--NOBODY WILL EVER READ IT...BUT I HAD SO MUCH FUN WRITING THIS IMAGINARY STORY OF THE FUTURE THAT I THINK I'LL WRITE ANOTHER ONE SOMETIME...
The End

During those rare moments of free time, Alfred, amateur novelist, enjoyed working up a "What if?" tale featuring his famous boss. (Batman *#131, April 1960, "The Second Batman and Robin Team!" p. 9 [select panels].)*

THANKS FOR BEING WITH US AGAIN THIS MONTH! ROBIN AND I LOOK FORWARD TO THESE LITTLE GET-TOGETHERS WITH ALL YOU READERS EVERY MONTH IN DETECTIVE COMICS! LET'S MAKE IT A STANDING DATE!
BOB KANE

Batman often took time out from his busy crimefighting schedule to thank his loyal fans for dropping by to catch the action. (Detective *#46, December 1940, "The Return of Professor Hugo Strange," p. 12 [panel].)*